Handbook of Research on Service-Oriented Systems and Non-Functional Properties:

Future Directions

Stephan Reiff-Marganiec
University of Leicester, UK

Marcel Tilly
European Microsoft Innovation Center, Germany

T0321705

Managing Director:	Lindsay Johnston
Senior Editorial Director:	Heather Probst
Book Production Manager:	Sean Woznicki
Development Manager:	Joel Gamon
Development Editor:	Michael Killian
Acquisitions Editor:	Erika Carter
Typesetters:	Lisandro Gonzalez, Mackenzie Snader
Print Coordinator:	Jamie Snavely
Cover Design:	Nick Newcomer

Published in the United States of America by
Information Science Reference (an imprint of IGI Global)
701 E. Chocolate Avenue
Hershey PA 17033
Tel: 717-533-8845
Fax: 717-533-8661
E-mail: cust@igi-global.com
Web site: http://www.igi-global.com

Library of Congress Cataloging-in-Publication Data

Handbook of research on service-oriented systems and non-functional properties
: future directions / Stephan Reiff-Marganiec and Marcel Tilly, editors.
   p. cm.
  Includes bibliographical references and index.
   ISBN 978-1-61350-432-1 (hardcover) -- ISBN 978-1-61350-433-8 (ebook) --
ISBN 978-1-61350-434-5 (print & perpetual access) 1. Service-oriented
architecture (Computer science)--Handbooks, manuals, etc. 2. Business--Data
processing--Handbooks, manuals, etc. I. Reiff-Marganiec, Stephan. II. Tilly,
Marcel, 1971-
   TK5105.5828.H36 2012
   004.6'54--dc23
                                    2011031924

British Cataloguing in Publication Data
A Cataloguing in Publication record for this book is available from the British Library.

List of Contributors

Table of Contents

Section 1
Perspectives on Non-Functional Properties

Ernest Sithole, University of Ulster at Coleraine, UK
Sally McClean, University of Ulster at Coleraine, UK
Bryan Scotney, University of Ulster at Coleraine, UK
Gerard Parr, University of Ulster at Coleraine, UK
Adrian Moore, University of Ulster at Coleraine, UK
Dave Bustard, University of Ulster at Coleraine, UK
Stephen Dawson, SAP Research Belfast, UK

Section 2
Service Selection

Yudith Cardinale, Universidad Simón Bolívar, Venezuela
Joyce El Haddad, Université Paris-Dauphine, France
Maude Manouvrier, Université Paris-Dauphine, France
Marta Rukoz, Université Paris-Ouest Nanterre La Défense & Université Paris-Dauphine, France

Pierluigi Plebani, Politecnico di Milano, Italy
Filippo Ramoni, Politecnico di Milano, Italy

Stephan Reiff-Marganiec, University of Leicester, UK
Hong Qing Yu, Open University, UK

Yves Vanrompay, Katholieke Universiteit Leuven, Belgium
Manuele Kirsch-Pinheiro, Université Paris 1 Panthéon-Sorbonne, France
Yolande Berbers, Katholieke Universiteit Leuven, Belgium

Kyriakos Kritikos, ICS-FORTH, Greece
Dimitris Plexousakis, ICS-FORTH, Greece

Section 3
Service Contracts

Section 5
Future Directions

Detailed Table of Contents

Section 1
Perspectives on Non-Functional Properties

Chapter 1

   Bryan Stephenson, HP Labs, USA

This chapter provides a good overview from an industrial perspective as to which non-functional properties could be of interest. It highlights how to measure the diverse range of non-functional properties – that is it proposes kinds of metrics that can be used. It also discusses why good values for some properties are harder to achieve than for others. Most crucially, the chapter provides a good insight into the variety (in terms of the properties themselves, but also the values that they can take) of non-functional properties that can be of interest and highlights why non-functional properties are of interest to the industrial practitioner.

Chapter 2

   Agostino Cortesi, Università Ca' Foscari, Italy
   Francesco Logozzo, Microsoft Research, USA

The chapter considers the important question of how guarantees about non-functional properties can be given. The authors lift the concepts to a higher level of abstraction, based on what can be observed of a property, to then reason in a sound way about the properties in the context of not only services but the wider system that they operate in. A semantic framework is defined to make the issues mathematically precise. A number of properties are examined in detail to show how the semantics can be defined for them which is then exemplified with examples for each.

Chapter 3

Laura Bocchi, University of Leicester, UK

José Fiadeiro, University of Leicester, UK

Monika Solanki, University of Leicester, UK

Stephen Gilmore, The University of Edinburgh, UK

João Abreu, Altitude Software, Portugal

Vishnu Vankayala, Lapilluz Software Solutions, India

Many non-functional properties influence service behaviour in a way that can be measured. It is useful for service designers to understand at an early stage what impact certain design decisions have on the behaviour of a service -- often the speed with which it can perform its function in the wider architecture where it is used. This chapter explores, based on a specific modelling notation for services, how stochastic analysis of time related properties can be conducted in an analysis framework.

Chapter 4

Ioan Toma, University of Innsbruck, Austria

Flavio De Paoli, Universita degli studi di Milano – Bicocca, Italy

Dieter Fensel, University of Innsbruck, Austria

A large area of providing models that place concepts in relation is governed by ontologies. Ontologies are heavily used in the semantic web community, and by extension in the semantic web services community – usually centred around languages such as OWL. This chapter provides concrete ontological models for many non-functional properties. In some way it picks up on Chapter 1 which introduced many non-functional properties, but it does now break these into well-structured sub-elements and makes the links between these explicit. As is typical for ontological models, much of the content is conveyed through diagrams.

Chapter 5

Ernest Sithole, University of Ulster at Coleraine, UK

Sally McClean, University of Ulster at Coleraine, UK

Bryan Scotney, University of Ulster at Coleraine, UK

Gerard Parr, University of Ulster at Coleraine, UK

Adrian Moore, University of Ulster at Coleraine, UK

Dave Bustard, University of Ulster at Coleraine, UK

Stephen Dawson, SAP Research Belfast, UK

This chapter starts with the observation that the growth in complexity of data processing needs and infrastructures requires performance quantification to determine capacity planning, service level agreements, QoS determination. The proposed solution uses on chip registers to monitor performance in a largely non-intrusive way. The monitored data provides run-time values for non-functional aspects.

Section 2
Service Selection

Chapter 6

Yudith Cardinale, Universidad Simón Bolívar, Venezuela
Joyce El Haddad, Université Paris-Dauphine, France
Maude Manouvrier, Université Paris-Dauphine, France
Marta Rukoz, Université Paris-Ouest Nanterre La Défense & Université Paris-Dauphine, France

Transactional properties of Web services are an often ignored non-functional property. However, many composition approaches consider how transactional properties of services compose. Considering this from a different angle, one can ask the question of how a specific overall transactional property can be achieved by selecting the right services. This paper presents an overview and classification of existing approaches in the area of service composition and selection based on transactional properties.

Chapter 7

Pierluigi Plebani, Politecnico di Milano, Italy
Filippo Ramoni, Politecnico di Milano, Italy

The chapter introduces a quality of service model that can be used during the selection phase by a service broker. In particular it considers that providers express properties at low levels of abstractions, while users use higher levels of abstraction to express their requirements. The contribution is a mapping between the two levels of abstraction which is followed through with a service selection method.

Chapter 8

Stephan Reiff-Marganiec, University of Leicester, UK
Hong Qing Yu, Open University, UK

The authors present an extensible model for non-functional properties which provides the basis for a generic selection method. The focus is on the model and not on specific properties – these can be added as they emerge without the selection method changing. An additional aspect considered is the "composition context" which allows to capture information of the process context in which the service is executed. This context provides further non-functional information to select the most appropriate service.

Chapter 9

Yves Vanrompay, Katholieke Universiteit Leuven, Belgium
Manuele Kirsch-Pinheiro, Université Paris 1 Panthéon-Sorbonne, France
Yolande Berbers, Katholieke Universiteit Leuven, Belgium

Context-aware services are emerging in the context of ubiquitous and pervasive systems. Descriptions of these services are enriched with context information linked to non-functional properties. The nature of context information is such that it is highly dynamic, unreliable and not always available, thus posing extra challenges for service selection. The paper presents a graph matching based algorithm to allow service selection in the face of uncertain information.

QoS for services is modelled using different models by different entities as there is currently no established standard. The models share sufficient commonality to allow for mapping through meta-models. However, for matchmaking one also needs to compare actual values and these are obtained through various metrics which are much harder to consolidate. This paper presents algorithms to align metrics and to address numerous issues arising through the underlying mismatches.

Chapter 11

Obtaining and measuring QoS levels is a non-trivial task and can be quite intrusive on the system. Quality prediction allows providers to determine QoS levels that they can achieve and guarantee. This paper considers modelling systems and using the Palladio Component Model for analysis and performance prediction. These techniques can be applied before the system is deployed and also apply in event-based SoA.

Chapter 12

Choosing services is non-trivial as the plethora of research contributions in this field shows. One difficult issue is to capture the expectations of a user -- users tend not to be technical staff and hence cannot judge the effect of some decisions which could lead to no service being available. On the other hand they understand the need to compromise and settle for "inferior" services. This paper proposes methods to obtain user requirements using the mid-level splitting technique and to assign weights using the hypothetical equivalents technique.

Section 3
Service Contracts

This chapter considers the plethora of work to describe service contracts – most of which covers similar aspects but presents these in different notations. This presents a syntactic and semantic problem when negotiating contracts. The authors provide an overview of the existing languages and present a solution to reconcile contracts presented in different languages. Their work covers the whole contract lifespan from identification, through negotiation and contract creation to monitoring contracts.

    Mohamed Hamdy, Ain Shams University, Egypt
    Brigitta König-Ries, Friedrich-Schiller-University Jena, Germany

How often a service is invoked is a non-functional property reflecting interest in or need for a specific service. This paper presents a model to describe service popularity and a meassure called 'Gross interest' to capture service propulariry. This specific NFP can be used like any other one, but additionally proves useful when deciding on which services to replicate as shown by the authors' example.

    Assia Ait-Ali-Slimane, Université Paris 1 Panthéon-Sorbonne, France
    Manuele Kirsch-Pinheiro, Université Paris 1 Panthéon-Sorbonne, France
    Carine Souveyet, Université Paris 1 Panthéon-Sorbonne, France

SoA has made big impact on how software solutions are produced at a technical level, and always had the ambition to lift software to the business level. Chapter 15 considers the intentional Service-Oriented Architecture (iSOA), aimed at business people by moving from functional to intention driven service descriptions. Clearly such a move needs to consider Quality of Service aspects and the paper introduces this aspect using quality goals and their quantitative and qualitative evaluation.

    Júlio Cezar Estrella, University of São Paulo, Brazil
    Regina Helena Carlucci Santana, University of São Paulo, Brazil
    Marcos Jose Santana, University of São Paulo, Brazil
    Sarita Mazzini Bruschi, University of São Paulo, Brazil

The authors are concerned with evaluating the performance of Web Services. A platform for monitoring service providers and identifying the most appropriate service is presented. The platform can be used as an analytical vehicle for testing Web Services and understanding their behaviour. The measured data can support creation of service contracts since the measurements focus on performance and a characterization of what to evaluate and how.

    Ulrich Winkler, SAP Research Belfast, UK
    Wasif Gilani, SAP Research Belfast, UK

This chapter considers the topic of Business Continuity Management which is concerned with ensuring that potential threats are identified and resolution strategies are in place to handle IT failures. Specifically the chapter discusses major challenges in this area and presents approaches to map business requirements to service level terms and metrics in the context of SoA.

Section 4
SLA Governance

Chapter 18

Martin Hall-May, IT Innovation Centre, UK

Ajay Chakravarthy, IT Innovation Centre, UK

Thomas Leonard, IT Innovation Centre, UK

Mike Surridge, IT Innovation Centre, UK

This chapter surveys semantic modelling of security and SLAs and the state of the art in SLA-based governance. Based on this survey and observation of the essential aspects a semantic model of resource dependability is defined. This model allows to describe the service commitments made to customers and resource capacity required from suppliers as non-functional properties. An approach to SLA-based system governance allowing for elastic provisioning of resources makes use of the model.

Chapter 19

Peer Hasselmeyer, NEC Laboratories Europe, Germany

Bastian Koller, High Performance Computing Center Stuttgart, Germany

Philipp Wieder, TU Dortmund University, Germany

Service level agreements are usually defined through a negotiation process. Chapter 19 introduces various models, specifications and realizations of service level agreement negotiations. This existing work shares a common core which is identified and exploited to define a coherent framework applicable to different negotiation models and protocols covering all functions of the negotiation phase. Challenges are discussed, predominately the need to increase acceptance of service level agreement negotiation and enhancing interoperability.

Chapter 20

Wolfgang Theilmann, SAP Research, Germany

Sergio Garcia Gomez, Telefonica Investigacion y Desarrollo, Spain

Davide Lorenzoli, CITY University, UK

Christoph Rathfelder, FZI Research Center for Information Technology, Germany

Thomas Roeblitz, Dortmund University of Technology, Germany

Gabriele Zacco, Fondazione Bruno Kessler, Italy

Service-oriented architecture allows for systems to be built from loosely-coupled components with SLAs describing how services are used in conjunction with each other. These SLAs typically describe what a customer can expect from the provider, but there is no agreed understanding of how these high-level contracts can be mapped into operational artefacts in different layers of the IT system. This chapter presents a framework to manage SLAs across the IT stack in an integrated framework.

Chapter 21

Toni Ruokolainen, University of Helsinki, Finland

Lea Kutvonen, University of Helsinki, Finland

The authors present a vision of a future where services form part of an open eco system, where services are provided by independent parties, services evolve and collaborations are dynamically established. For this vision to work it is essential that features of services and their dependencies can be governed effectively. The paper presents a framework and the required underlying conceptual models to enable such governance in open service eco systems.

Chapter 22

The authors present a compliance dashboard. The need for this is motivated by the fact that assessing whether business practices conform to laws and agreements is difficult and hence there is a need for appropriate tools. Developing such tools has to address such as addressing the right level of abstraction in descriptions, visualizing analysis results for different stakeholders and more fundamentally managing and visualizing large amounts of data in a time effective manner.

Section 5
Future Directions

Web Services, the Programmable web and Web 2.0 have appeared, seen much support from IT companies and have seen much hype and also good uptake within business boundaries – however there have been problems hindering a universal uptake. This chapter presents a concise summary of the current state of affairs and then explores persisting problems with data management and data integration as well as capturing and processing non-functional properties (especially in a time efficient manner) which have to be solved across technology boundaries, including traditional SOAP based services as well as Web APIs and RESTful services.

Foreword

The promise of Service Oriented Computing technologies is a world of cooperating services where application components are assembled with little effort into end-to-end services that are loosely coupled to create business processes and flexible Service Oriented Architecture (SOA)-applications that span organizations and computing platforms. As such, Service Oriented Computing improves productivity by enabling enterprises to develop and bring new products and services to the market more rapidly.

An important characteristic of the Service Oriented Computing paradigm is that it enables application developers to dynamically grow application portfolios by creating compound SOA-application solutions that inter-mix internally existing organizational software assets with external services that possibly reside in remote locations. Understanding the nature of service composition is a daunting task. So far, the composition of distributed services is still far from being fully achieved. No effective, easy-to-use, flexible technology support is provided to assist in coping with many of the intricacies of service composition. These include, for instance, configuration of end-to-end service compositions by delivering the expected functionality with guaranteed multi-dimensional Quality of Service (QoS) levels, i.e., at both the application and system or IT-level, the ability to guarantee acceptable QoS levels for a composed service even when the operational conditions and regulations of its constituent services may continuously change.

An important area of services research gathering momentum is QoS-aware service composition. Service composition requires discovering service providers and delivering composed services that satisfy not only functional but also non-functional requirements meeting QoS constraints. For example, knowing that a service adopts a Web services security standard such as one from the stack of WS-Security specifications is not enough information to enable successful composition with other services. The service developer needs to know if the service actually requires WS-Security, what kind of security tokens it is capable of processing, and which one it prefers. Moreover, the developer must determine if the service should communicate using signed messages. If so, s/he must determine what token type must be used for the digital signatures. Finally, the developer must decide when to encrypt the messages, which encryption algorithm to use, and how to exchange a shared key with the service. For example, a purchase order service may indicate that it only accepts username tokens that are based signed messaged using X.509 certificate that is cryptographically endorsed by a third party. Such considerations require understanding and respecting the component service policies, performance levels, security requirements, end-to-end Service Level Agreement (SLA) stipulations, and so forth.

When a developer designs a new SOA-application solution or performs a refactoring of an existing business process, determining the dependability and reliability of the final end-to-end composition of operations and QoS levels that make up the process is of paramount importance. These non-functional (or QoS) requirements may describe essential performance and dependability requirements and apply across different logical layers of the application, from business-related details to system infrastructure; i.e., they are cross-cutting and considered multi-dimensional. Without considering QoS aspects of the business process such as determining inventory levels, delivery constraints, the maximum throughput, or time required to complete the process or its availability, the process will not meet the expectations of an enterprise or its clients. Achieving this effectively is a challenging problem as the service-oriented software is fully decentralized, and typically no single organization is in control of all the services involved in an SOA-application solution. Without a disciplined approach to non-functional properties of Service-oriented Systems, it would be impossible to understand how the software that will eventually run in production meets acceptable QoS levels, let alone automate the composition of business processes and mission critical applications.

This book deals with non-functional properties of Service-oriented Systems, which is a notoriously complex topic in a very sound and intuitive manner. It addresses a multitude of research problems in this field by providing a mixture of theoretical and practical solutions.

The book addresses compelling problems such as service selection on the basis of user specified measurable QoS properties, methods for ranking services and selecting services that are part of larger execution chains, techniques for capturing delays that may occur during service provision and confirming whether required time-related properties are met, quality prediction techniques that support a service provider to determine possible QoS levels that can be guaranteed to a client in a manner that meets SLA expectations, contract reconciliation and SLA negotiation techniques, managing multi-dimensional SLAs, and many more interesting research issues. The book chapters are organized in four logical parts: Perspectives on Non-Functional Properties, Service Selection, Service Contracts, and SLA Governance.

This book covers an impressive number of topics and presents a wealth of research ideas and techniques that will excite any researcher (or practitioner) wishing to understand QoS management for Service-oriented Systems. It is pleasant to see that diverse and complex topics relating to QoS management are explained in an eloquent manner and include extensive references to help the interested reader find out more information about these topics. All in all this is an impressive book and an invaluable source of knowledge for advanced students and researchers working in or wishing to know more about this exciting field.

I commend the editors and the authors of this book on the breadth and depth of their work and for producing a well thought out and eminently readable book on such a complicated topic. Enjoy!

Michael P. Papazoglou
European Institute in Service Science, The Netherlands, July 2011

Michael Papazoglou is Scientific Director of the European Research Institute in Service Science (ERISS) and of the EC's Network of Excellence, S-Cube. He is also an honorary Professor at the University of Trento in Italy, and Professorial Fellow at the Universities Lyon (France), New South Wales (Australia) and Rey Juan Carlos, Madrid (Spain). He has acted as an Adviser to the EC in matters relating to the Internet of Services and as a reviewer of national research programs for numerous countries around the world. His research interests lie in the areas of service oriented computing, web services, large scale data sharing, business and manufacturing processes, and distributed computing systems, where he has published 22 books (including monographs and conference proceedings), and well over 200 journal and conference papers with an H-index factor of 37.

Preface

"A verbal contract isn't worth the paper it is written on." (Samuel Goldwyn)

Last year, at a conference in Paris we decided to go out for dinner. Our little group consisted of four different people with various expectation and requirements of a good dinner. Everybody has their own experience in finding the right place for just two persons – but how difficult does it become to satisfy 4 people's requirements! Thus, we started to collect different wishes: vegetarian food must be served, credit cards should be accepted, the restaurant must be in walking distance, and last but not least, it cannot be too expensive. Finally, we just jumped into one restaurant, which was close by. The menu outside looked quite promising in terms of food offerings (vegetarian and non-vegetarian) and stickers at the door pointed out that credit cards are accepted.

While waiting for the food – quite a long wait already hinting at more surprises in the making on that evening – we started to discuss our selection process. You can easily image that folks with computer science backgrounds try to analyse it using their domain knowledge. Thus, one of us started directly to model restaurant offerings as non-functional properties of services while the second looked into service selection based on these offerings. The third member of our group was more concerned with validating that all offerings are satisfying requirements and finally, the last member wanted to see how feedback can be used to allow for a more agile offering. While discussing all these it turned out that there was no vegetarian food available on that evening, and even settling for other dishes we found out after the meal that credit cards were not accepted after all. Having settled the bill we retired to a nearby bistro to exchange stories about broken service promises …

Why are we telling this story and how is it related to the book? A restaurant is an everyday service, services have characteristics that go beyond their pure functionality (here delivering the needed calories for survival), people have different expectations and agreements are needed and often promised characteristics of a service are not met.

So, we can say we have learned a lot during the diner experience:

1. Service modelling, non-functional properties, quality of service, and service level agreements can be applied easily in daily life and are not limited to Service-oriented Architectures.

2. There is common understanding of the existence of non-functional properties of services, but there is no concrete agreement on how to express them. This problem starts with a lack of agreed syntax extending into understanding the semantics of specific properties.

3. Non-functional properties have a very significant impact on how any service is chosen and how satisfied users are – this impact extends into Service-oriented Computing.

WHY SHOULD THERE BE HANDBOOK IN THIS AREA?

Notions of services and Service-oriented Computing have emerged and matured over the last decade, bringing with them a plethora of available services that are selected by users and developers and composed into larger applications. The general view with services is that they expose business level functionality, and hence, are at an abstraction level previously not typically addressed by IT. However, with a growing number of services available and selected by business organizations to fulfil much of their business operation concerns beyond pure functionality come to the fore.

In general, one can consider the functionality of a service as an essential requirement for selecting it, but if there is a choice of such services other concerns, called non-functional are evaluated in decision-making. As an example from daily life – besides perfect restaurant selection - we can consider car insurance: the service provided by different insurance companies is comparable: they provide insurance that covers theft and third party damage (the functional aspect). However when buying insurance we consider issues such as the reliability of the insurer, the costs of insurance, extra benefits provided, the process of dealing with the insurer, and others: these would be the non-functional properties (NFPs).

The area of non-functional properties for services is quite wide, covering aspects from describing and classifying NFPs, obtaining values for them (either as part of the design or automatically during execution), and using NFPs for discriminating between services. In addition NFPs form an essential component in quality of service (QoS) guarantees – usually referred to as service level agreements (SLAs). Here questions arise regarding describing SLAs, embedding NFPs in them, providing assurance that NFPs are indeed adhered to. As orthogonal dimensions both NFPs and SLAs must be (1) managed and (2) can be general or domain specific. These two dimensions place additional requirements on the aspects described before and have led to much work of their own.

The area of non-functional properties for services is quite diverse and has been evolving very fast, with industrial contributions and standard bodies as well as academic work providing (partial) solutions to certain aspects. Various research domains provided approaches to describe, map, and use NFPs, such as the Semantic Web researchers as well as service-oriented academics. Therefore, there is a huge variety of different approaches and methods to address NFPs. Work in this area has no unique forum in which it is presented; in contrast, publications are distributed in a large number of conferences and workshops (e.g. ECOWS, ICWS, ICSOC, NFPSLA-SOC, NFPSLAM, SCC, ServiceWave).

This handbook brings together results from the different communities and provides a clear overview of the work done and we would hope also a clear direction for future work. It should also bring the diverse communities closer together by highlighting synergies between and complementation of approaches and lead to more focused efforts of making progress rather than duplicating work in one community because of unawareness of that done (or ongoing) in another.

WHO SHOULD READ THIS BOOK?

As we have seen service, their non-functional properties and aspects related to these affect all services – so one could argue that everyone should read this book! However, when selecting chapters for the book and editing the final version we had a narrower focus in mind: we want the book to be a reference and starting point for new researchers and industrial practitioners in the area of non-functional properties and SLAs for services as well as an up-to-date reference for those already active in this field. In particular the mix of industrial and academic perspectives presented in the book which are, as expected, not necessarily married up, in that many academic solutions do not address the industrial problems is invaluable to both communities. With service computing making its way into academic curricula, a need arises for students to be exposed to more advanced topics such as the ones presented in this book, so the book or individual chapters should make suitable advanced reading for final year Undergraduate or Masters students.

SHALL THE BOOK BE READ FRONT TO BACK? OR WHERE DO I FIND CHAPTERS MATCHING MY INTEREST?

There might be books, which you can read from the first sentence up to the end. We believe such books mainly to be non-academic books. Academic books, or in this case a researchers' handbook, are following a different path: the reader is invited to jump from one chapter to another driven by his interest and needs. In this way the book features as a reference text. If you are new to the area you might want to start reading at the beginning and work your way through it: the structure of the book is such that it is open to end-to-end reading.

In any case, getting an overview of the basic roadmap and organizational philosophy of this book will prove useful.

Section 1 (Perspectives on Non-Functional Properties) of the book covers questions around non-functional properties in general, such as how they can be modelled and how to reason about it. The reasoning can be in terms of providing guarantees on their values but also on the behaviour of the services that they characterize. This section sets the scene for many of the uses of non-functional properties discussed in the latter sections, where authors use such fundamental considerations to achieve more specific aims. This section starts with an industrial perspective and highlights how to measure the various set of non-functional properties. It provides also some insights into guarantying NFPs and how to express in a mathematically precise way using a semantic framework. Furthermore, this section investigates how NFPs influences service behaviour in a way that can be measured. Looking on ontologies for NFPs presents a more semantic viewpoint. The final chapter in this section looks at measuring performance data through hardware solutions – providing data to populate non-functional property models. A more detailed description of the chapters follows.

Chapter 1 provides a good overview from an industrial perspective as to which non-functional properties could be of interest. It highlights how to measure the diverse range of non-functional properties – that is, it proposes kinds of metrics that can be used. It also discusses why good values for some properties are harder to achieve than for others. Most crucially, the chapter provides a good insight into the variety (in terms of the properties themselves, but also the values that they can take) of non-functional properties that can be of interest and highlights why non-functional properties are of interest to the industrial practitioner.

Chapter 2 considers the important question of how guarantees about non-functional properties can be given. The authors lift the concepts to a higher level of abstraction, based on what can be observed of a property, to then reason in a sound way about the properties in the context of not only services but also the wider system that they operate in. A semantic framework is defined to make the issues mathematically precise. A number of properties are examined in detail to show how the semantics can be defined for them, which is then exemplified with examples for each.

Chapter 3 talks about how non-functional properties influence service behaviour in a way that can be measured. It is useful for service designers to understand at an early stage what impact certain design decisions have on the behaviour of a service – often the speed with which it can perform its function in the wider architecture where it is used. This chapter explores, based on a specific modelling notation for services, how stochastic analysis of time related properties can be conducted in an analysis framework.

Chapter 4 is finally diving into ontologies. A large area of providing models that place concepts in relation is governed by ontologies. Ontologies are heavily used in the semantic web community, and by extension in the semantic web services community – usually centred on languages such as OWL. This chapter provides concrete ontological models for many non-functional properties. In some way it picks up on *Chapter 1*, which introduced many non-functional properties, but it breaks these into well-structured sub-elements and makes the links between these explicit. As is typical for ontological models, much of the content is conveyed through diagrams.

Chapter 5 starts with the observation that the growth in complexity of data processing needs and infrastructures requires performance quantification to determine capacity planning, service level agreements, and QoS determination. The proposed solution uses on chip registers to monitor performance in a largely non-intrusive way. The monitored data provides run-time values for non-functional aspects.

Section 2 (Service Selection) of the book is looking into how to use NFPs to support service selections which is a key use case for NFPs. In the domain of service and NFPs, there are quite a lot of different approaches around service selections in various contexts – just remember the restaurant in Paris. With the uptake of service computing, the amount of available services has been rapidly increasing, leading to a situation where a user can find many services for a specific requirement. This choice comes with a need to identify the best service for a user's need based on non-functional properties such as cost or performance. The contributions in *Section 2* deal with different approaches for selecting services. Firstly, this part starts with transactional properties for service compositions. Secondly, some work introduces a quality of service model that can be used during the selection phase by a service broker. Other chapters present an extensible model for NFPs as basis for a generic selection model and methods for selecting context-ware services for ubiquitous and pervasive systems. In *Chapter 10* the topic is quality of service modelling. Here, the goal is to identify models, which share sufficient commonality to allow a mapping through meta-models. *Chapter 11* is talking about quality prediction to determine QoS level that can be achieved and guaranteed. The last chapter of this part, *Chapter 12*, is kind of summarizing this part by looking at service selection from a user's perspective. This chapter proposes methods to obtain user requirements using the mid-level splitting technique and to assign weights using hypothetical equivalents technique.

Chapter 6 considers transactional properties. Transactional properties of Web services are an often-ignored non-functional property. However, many composition approaches consider how transactional properties of services compose. Considering this from a different angle; one can ask the question of how a specific overall transactional property can be achieved by selecting the right services. This chapter presents an overview and classification of existing approaches in the area of service composition and selection based on transactional properties.

Chapter 7 introduces a quality of service model that can be used during the selection phase by a service broker. In particular it considers that providers express properties at low levels of abstractions, while users use higher levels of abstraction to express their requirements. The contribution is a mapping between the two levels of abstraction that is followed through with a service selection method.

In *Chapter 8* the authors present an extensible model for non-functional properties, which provides the basis for a generic selection method. The focus is on the model and not on specific properties – these can be added as they emerge without the selection method changing. An additional aspect considered is the "composition context" which allows capturing information of the process context in which the service is executed. This context provides further non-functional information to select the most appropriate service.

In *Chapter 9* the authors consider Context-aware services are emerging in the context of ubiquitous and pervasive systems. Descriptions of these services are enriched with context information linked to non-functional properties. The nature of context information is such that it is highly dynamic, unreliable, and not always available, thus posing extra challenges for service selection. This chapter presents a graph matching based algorithm to allow service selection in the face of uncertain information.

Chapter 10 provides an approach to model QoS for services, modelled using different models by different entities, as there is currently no established standard. The models share sufficient commonality to allow for mapping through meta-models. However, for matchmaking one also needs to compare actual values, and these are obtained through various metrics that are much harder to consolidate. This chapter presents algorithms to align metrics and to address numerous issues arising through the underlying mismatches.

In *Chapter 11* obtaining and measuring QoS levels is a non-trivial task and can be quite intrusive on the system. Quality prediction allows providers to determine QoS levels that they can achieve and guarantee. This chapter considers modelling systems and using the Palladio Component Model for analysis and performance prediction. These techniques can be applied before the system is deployed and also apply in Event-based SOA.

Chapter 12 talks about capturing user requirements. Choosing services is non-trivial, as the plethora of research contributions in this field shows. One difficult issue is to capture the expectations of a user -- users tend not to be technical staff and hence cannot judge the effect of some decisions, which could lead to no service being available. On the other hand they understand the need to compromise and settle for "inferior" services. This chapter proposes methods to obtain user requirements using the mid-level splitting technique and to assign weights using the hypothetical equivalents technique.

Service contracts are the topic of *Section 3 (Service contracts)*. A progressive use of services in business environments, but also a growing use of services for crucial personal affairs lead to and increased dependence on services. Therefore, service contracts between consumer and provider are becoming key issues for service usage in various environments. Thus, this dependence requires, like any business transaction in the real world, a good agreement between the expectations of all parties involved in a transaction. Service contracts attempt to provide this agreement and they are fundamentally dependent on non-functional properties: it is much easier to agree on the functionality than on the quality with which a service should be delivered or can be expected to be delivered. The first chapter provides already a good overview of approaches to express service contracts. The other chapter pick up on more specific aspects to measure service behaviour as input for service contracts by introducing concepts such as service popularity or service goals.

Chapter 13 considers the plethora of work to describe service contracts – most of which covers similar aspects but presents these in different notations. This presents a syntactic and semantic problem when negotiating contracts. The authors provide an overview of the existing languages and present a solution to reconcile contracts presented in different languages. Their work covers the whole contract lifespan from identification, through negotiation and contract creation to monitoring contracts.

How often a service is invoked is a non-functional property reflecting interest in or need for a specific service. *Chapter 14* presents a model to describe service popularity and a measure called 'Gross interest' to capture service popularity. This specific NFP can be used like any other one, but additionally proves useful when deciding on which services to replicate as shown by the authors' example.

SoA has made a big impact on how software solutions are produced at a technical level, and always had the ambition to lift software to the business level. *Chapter 15* considers the intentional Service-Oriented Architecture (iSOA), aimed at business people by moving from functional to intention driven service descriptions. Clearly such a move needs to consider Quality of Service aspects and the chapter introduces this aspect using quality goals and their quantitative and qualitative evaluation.

The authors of *Chapter 16* are concerned with evaluating the performance of Web Services. A platform for monitoring service providers and identifying the most appropriate service is presented. The platform can be used as an analytical vehicle for testing Web Services and understanding their behaviour. The measured data can support creation of service contracts since the measurements focus on performance and a characterization of what to evaluate and how.

Chapter 17 considers the topic of Business Continuity Management, which is concerned with ensuring that potential threats are identified and resolution strategies are in place to handle IT failures. Specifically the chapter discusses major challenges in this area and presents approaches to map business requirements to service level terms and metrics in the context of SoA.

In *Section 4 (SLA Governance),* we are moving the SLA topic further towards SLA governance. While *Section 3* is talking about service contracts and SLAs in general, *Section 4* is more about the interactions with SLA and the necessity of SLAs in terms of contracts and impact on the business. As these interactions are very critical, it is necessary to arrive at good contracts (that is one might need to negotiate on details of an agreement) as well as ensuring that contracts are adhered to. The area of SLA governance is concerned with these aspects. The chapters cover topics focused on negotiation of SLAs including provisioning of resources to fulfil SLAs, which is even more relevant down the entire IT stack. However, the final chapter is covering business aspects and compliance with a focus on the end-user perspective by visualising data. SLA governance could easily fill a book by itself, so this part touches on some key aspects of the area with a high correlation to NFPs.

Chapter 18 surveys semantic modelling of security and SLAs and the state of the art in SLA-based governance. Based on this survey and observation of the essential aspects a semantic model of resource dependability is defined. This model allows describing the service commitments made to customers and resource capacity required from suppliers as non-functional properties. An approach to SLA-based system governance allowing for elastic provisioning of resources makes use of the model.

Service level agreements are usually defined through a negotiation process. *Chapter 19* introduces various models, specifications, and realizations of service level agreement negotiations. This existing work shares a common core which is identified and exploited to define a coherent framework applicable to different negotiation models and protocols covering all functions of the negotiation phase. Challenges are discussed, predominately the need to increase acceptance of service level agreement negotiation and enhancing interoperability.

Service-oriented architecture allows for systems to be built from loosely-coupled components with SLAs describing how services are used in conjunction with each other. These SLAs typically describe what a customer can expect from the provider, but there is no agreed understanding of how these high-level contracts can be mapped into operational artefacts in different layers of the IT system. *Chapter 20* presents a framework to manage SLAs across the IT stack in an integrated framework.

The authors of *Chapter 21* present a vision of a future where services form part of an open eco system, where services are provided by independent parties, services evolve, and collaborations are dynamically established. For this vision to work, it is essential that features of services and their dependencies can be governed effectively. The paper presents a framework and the required underlying conceptual models to enable such governance in open service eco systems.

Chapter 22 presents a compliance dashboard. The need for this is motivated by the fact that assessing whether business practices conform to laws and agreements is difficult, and hence, there is a need for appropriate tools. Developing such tools, such as addressing the right level of abstraction in descriptions, visualizing analysis results for different stakeholders, and more fundamentally, managing and visualizing large amounts of data in a time effective manner is important.

Section 5 (Future Directions) provides a perspective authors view on future directions, how to use NFPs in large data sets or how to handle real-time requirements for NFPs. This section tries to come up with some predictions on what will be required in a wider field of view. The last section contains only one chapter, but if you wish to only read one chapter, make it this one. Each individual chapter in the previous sections provides the respective authors view on future directions of their area of work. The motivation for this part is a bit more ambitious in that it tries to look into a future that is further afield and that tries to make predictions on what will be required in a wider field of view.

Chapter 23 is concerned with Web Services, the Programmable Web, and Web 2.0, which have appeared, seen much support from IT companies, and have seen much hype and also good uptake within business boundaries; however, there have been problems hindering a universal uptake. This chapter presents a concise summary of the current state of affairs and then explores persisting problems with data management and data integration as well as capturing and processing non-functional properties (especially in a time efficient manner) which have to be solved across technology boundaries, including traditional SOAP based services as well as Web APIs and RESTful services.

WHAT HAS BEEN ACHIEVED?

Whether you are new to the field of non-functional properties for services or a seasoned researcher or industrial practitioner, we believe that this book will be a useful resource for you. The book provides structure to existing work, sets clear future directions for the field, and brings together results from different communities.

The book presents a unique mixture of results achieved by both industry and academia, and thus bridges (or at least identifies the gaps) between these results and covers the whole span from defining NFPs through to their use and management in systems.

We hope that you will enjoy the book and that you will pick it up frequently to consider new dimensions or aspects. Most of all we hope that this book will inspire you to contribute your own solutions and ideas into an exciting field of research and industrial practice, and that together with the existing community, you will ultimately help people to be able to enjoy the best services without disappointment, or considering that dinner in Paris, *get the food they like without any disappointments and be able to enjoy every aspect of an evening out!*

Stephan Reiff-Marganiec
University of Leicester, UK

Marcel Tilly
European Microsoft Innovation Center, Germany

Acknowledgment

A research handbook is never an individual effort of the authors or editors. There are several other people involved who spent quite some time on reviewing papers, formatting material, and supporting the authors and editors. Many thanks are due.

We would like to thank Mike Killian from IGI Global in helping and pushing us towards finalizing this project.

The experts of the editorial advisory board provided feedback and led us into the – hopefully – right direction. Thanks to Brian, Flavio, Ioan, Justin, Peer, and Schahram.

Special thanks go to all the authors who contributed chapters to this book. We know that it was sometimes painful to reply to our requests: You all are the real heroes of this book.

Mike, thanks for the honest foreword, we really appreciate it. It also made us see that producing the book is a worthwhile endeavour, something that can easily get lost in dealing with copyright forms and formats of chapters!

The reviewers of all the chapters of this book and their constructive feedback needs to be acknowledged: you allowed the authors to produce contributions that stand up to academic rigour.

Last but not least, a word of gratitude to our families and friends for all their patience while waiting for this endeavour to come to its conclusion.

Stephan Reiff-Marganiec
University of Leicester, UK

Marcel Tilly
European Microsoft Innovation Center, Germany

Section 1
Perspectives on Non-Functional Properties

Chapter 1
A Business Perspective on Non-Functional Properties for Services

Bryan Stephenson
HP Labs, USA

ABSTRACT

This chapter provides an overview from a business perspective of some of the important non-functional properties of services, such as availability, performance, and security. It discusses the typical metrics for these non-functional properties which are used in service level agreements to measure and report how well a service is meeting customer expectations. It briefly discusses cost considerations for service providers and consumers, as some levels of service are expensive to attain. The goal is to provide the reader with an understanding of these non-functional properties, their measures and cost implications, and related interesting research opportunities.

INTRODUCTION

In the context of this chapter, a *service* is defined as a collection of people, processes, and technology which provides some business value. The organization or individual providing the service is the *service provider*. The organizations, individuals, and/or services using the service are the *service consumers*. As shown in Figure 1, the service consumer may also be a service provider, and the service provider (and a service instance) may also be a service consumer. A service must

DOI: 10.4018/978-1-61350-432-1.ch001

have some *service front-end interface* by which the service consumers use the service. This interface can include interfaces for people such as web sites, telephones, email, postal mail, and face-to-face conversations, as well as interfaces for IT systems such as SOAP, REST, EDI, and proprietary APIs or communication channels. All such communication channels are represented in Figure 1 as solid black lines. A service may have a *service back-end interface* by which elements of the service consume other services and/or interact with people. The consumed services may be *internal services* (delivered by the service provider) or *external services* (delivered by other service

Figure 1. Service ecosystem

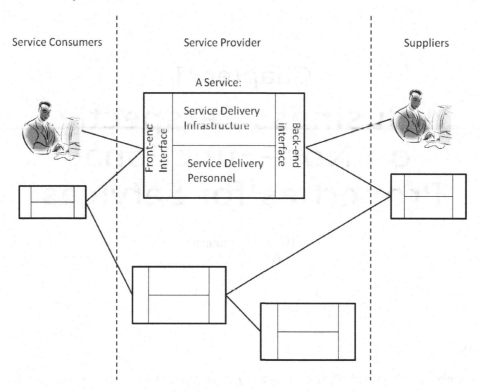

providers). A service must have some *service delivery personnel.* Depending on the nature of the service, these personnel can directly provide the service themselves, and/or they may operate the *service delivery infrastructure.* The service delivery infrastructure helps to provide the service and/or support the service delivery personnel. This chapter focuses mainly on *IT-based services;* that is, services which include some amount of service delivery infrastructure in addition to the service delivery personnel. The service delivery infrastructure for IT-based services typically includes the datacenters, software, servers, storage systems, network equipment, and other IT systems which provide the service in concert with the service delivery personnel. Many of the non-functional properties can be applied to any type of service. These terms will be used throughout the chapter.

The IT industry is undergoing significant changes in the way critical parts of the service delivery infrastructure, such as datacenters, are

evolving. This is similar to changes which happened over 100 years ago during the industrial revolution. When electricity was first used to power manufacturing and other industrial processes, many companies ran their own electricity generation facilities onsite. As the technology matured, some companies specialized in the operation of electricity generation facilities and sent the electricity to a broad base of customers using power transmission lines. Soon very few companies bothered to construct and operate their own electricity generation facilities. Very large datacenters gain significant economies of scale but are very expensive to construct, so a small number of companies are building very large datacenters and selling various services from those datacenters to a broad base of customers. The services range from low-level "Infrastructure as a Service" offerings to various business capabilities provided as a service. As the industry matures, even mission critical business capabilities with very demanding requirements will be able to be consumed as a service provided by remote datacenters and personnel. To enable this requires the explicit specification of customer expectations and service provider responsibilities regarding a variety of non-functional properties. These expectations and responsibilities are documented in a Service Level Agreement (SLA).

This chapter provides an overview of some of the non-functional properties of IT-based services that are important from a business perspective. It discusses the typical metrics for these non-functional properties which are used in SLAs to measure and report how well a service is meeting a customer's expectations. It describes cost considerations for service providers and consumers, as some levels of service are expensive to attain. Interesting research opportunities are identified in sections D and E.

SERVICE LEVEL AGREEMENTS

IT and business services have proliferated to such an extent that today it is possible to operate a startup company almost exclusively using external services for everything from IT infrastructure to employee benefits. Even large companies often outsource their payroll or benefits administration to specialized companies. To do this with proper risk management requires diligence on the part of the service consumer. If a critical business process such as payroll stops working for an extended period of time, the loss can be so devastating that the company cannot recover from the disruption.

A legal contract between a service consumer and a service provider which includes a service level agreement (SLA) is one way to mitigate the risk of using services. The SLA specifies the requirements the service is expected to deliver, and the penalties for not meeting those requirements. There are several questions the consumer should consider when contemplating using a service:

1. Do I believe that the provider can meet the requirements specified in the SLA?
2. If they do, will this service adequately support the way I intend to use it as a part of my business?
3. How will I migrate away from the service if needed (for example if this provider goes out of business)?
4. Should I consider a second source for this service? In some cases, a workload could be split among two or more providers of similar services to reduce risk.
5. How might things evolve? For example, would a price change cause a major problem for my business?

Historically, IT-based services have often been custom-built to provide the precise service and service levels required by the service consumer. This enables the consumer and provider to negotiate the service levels and the associated costs and penalties. The result of this negotiation is typically detailed in a Service Level Agreement document. For a custom-built service, significant portions of the service delivery infrastructure may be dedicated to the customer, such as the IT systems running applications which are part of the service. Some parts of the service delivery infrastructure may be shared with other service consumers to reduce costs, such as the datacenter which houses the IT systems.

Recently, multi-tenant services which attempt to serve the needs of many service consumers using a shared service delivery infrastructure have gained popularity. Significant examples include customer relationship management services from Salesforce.com and IT infrastructure services from Amazon.com. These types of services may also have SLAs, but these SLAs are usually not negotiated on a per-customer basis. With these types of services, a customer may have a choice among a set of service levels which are predefined by the provider and built into the service delivery infrastructure. Sometimes SLAs describe that a service is provided on a "best effort" or similar basis. This means that there are no guarantees for performance, availability, and other important non-functional properties, but this may be acceptable if the track record of the service provider is good and the price is right. For example, if a company needs 99.9% service availability, a service that offers no availability guarantee but has been independently certified to be available 99.99% of the time over the last five years may be a better choice than a service that guarantees and delivers 99.9% uptime, if the services provide similar business value and are similarly priced.

TRADITIONAL NON-FUNCTIONAL PROPERTIES OF SERVICES

The functional properties of the service specify *what* the service does, for example host a corporate website. The non-functional properties of a service specify *how* the service does it, for example at what level of performance or availability. This section will define and discuss some of the useful non-functional properties which are typically defined in SLAs. Many will not be discussed, but a long list of non-functional properties is available in (Rosa, 2001). Section D will discuss non-functional properties which are not typically defined in SLAs today, but may be in the future. Section E will discuss research opportunities relating to the non-functional properties presented in this section.

Accessibility

Accessibility is commonly used to refer to two different concepts. In the EU and US legal systems, accessibility refers to the ability of persons with disabilities to successfully access and use a service without too much hassle. In the context of IT-based services, accessibility also refers to the restrictions placed upon service access by the service provider. These will be discussed separately.

Accessibility for Disabled Persons

Some services include audio alerts for users and thus assume that the user can hear the sounds. An *accessible service* will consider the needs of hearing-challenged users and include alternate means for such an alert to take place, such as a visual alert. Certain accessibility requirements are mandated in the US by the Americans with Disabilities Act (ADA) and in the EU by the European Directive on Equal Treatment in Employment and Occupation. In the US, courts were interpreting the ADA too narrowly so Congress passed the ADA Amendments Act of 2008 to more clearly spell out the intended protections for disabled persons. In the US, these laws protect disabled persons from discrimination in employment and in the use of "public accommodations" which include most products or services offered to the public by companies, including web sites. This means that every service targeted for US consumers is legally obligated to take accessibility into account. In the EU, the protection is limited to discrimination in employment, so only services which are used in employment are legally required to consider accessibility. However, additional protections have been under consideration, and it's only a matter of time until they are adopted in the EU. The "Digital Divide" generally refers to the divide between those with and without the financial means to have access to technology and services and the benefits which this access confers. As we work to remove this divide, we need to ensure we don't unnecessarily create or perpetuate a similar divide which prevents those with disabilities from also gaining these benefits.

In some cases, a service which is delivered using computer technology can take advantage of existing means for disabled persons to use computer technology. For example, a service which is delivered via a web browser can be used by blind people with one of the web browsers for the blind without constructing a special version of the service. However, consideration of accessibility requirements during the design of the service's web interface is still required in certain jurisdictions such as the US where corporations have been sued for not making a web site easy enough for blind people to use. The Web Content Accessibility Guidelines (WCAG) (W3C, 1999) are an international standard useful for this purpose. The New York Institute for Special Education lists many relevant resources on their accessibility page ("New York Institute," 2010). An SLA defines the accessibility standards to which the service is expected to comply, which is frequently the WCAG for web-based services.

Accessibility of the Service

A service provider may place restrictions on service access. These restrictions may be based on context such as geographical location or age of the service consumer. They may be based on technical compatibility issues such as restricting the service to be accessed only from certain hardware devices running certain versions of certain software, the combinations of which have been tested by the service provider. The SLA defines the specifics of the hardware and software which the service provider will support to access the service, and any restrictions on accessing the service.

Availability

Availability is sometimes considered as a subset of security, such as in the Common Body of Knowledge used by the International Information Systems Security Certification Consortium, Inc., an organization which certifies information security professionals. In this chapter availability is considered at the top level of the taxonomy of non-functional properties. Five key availability metrics are defined below, with uptime being the most common metric for availability.

Uptime

Uptime is typically expressed as the percentage of time the service is up and providing the functional and non-functional requirements per the SLA, for example "99.9% uptime". It is common to use uptime as the only metric for availability and instead say "99.9% availability". Often a number of nines is used as shorthand to describe uptime, such as "five nines" which means 99.999% uptime. Five nines of uptime is approximately equal to 5 minutes of downtime per year. Many services don't need this very high level of uptime. A notable exception is land-line telephone service in countries like the United States. The US land-line telephone service was designed to provide six nines of uptime so it could be used during many disaster scenarios. Most people in developed countries have never picked up the phone and not heard a dial tone. It should be noted that there is no such thing as 100% uptime or 100% availability unless a time period is also specified. At some point, every service will experience operational difficulties including unplanned downtime. It may not happen until the sun explodes, but it will likely happen long before then.

Downtime

Downtime can be considered the opposite of uptime. Downtime measures the percentage of time the service is not running and providing the functional and non-functional requirements per the SLA. Some service providers define a third state of service operation which is neither uptime nor downtime, such as a period when the service is working but with impaired performance, functionality, or other properties. Depending on the specific problems which occur and their business impact, the service consumers may consider this third state as uptime if they can still get their work done, but will consider it as downtime if they cannot.

SLAs usually distinguish between planned and unplanned downtime. Planned downtime is periods of time when the service is scheduled to be unavailable. The service provider will inform consumers in advance of planned downtime. In some cases, the dates and times of planned downtime are negotiable. Many services have a weekly maintenance window of a few hours when backups are performed, patches are installed, and other maintenance occurs. Unplanned downtime is periods of time when the service is not available which are not known in advance. In some cases, planned downtime is distinguished from unplanned downtime in the SLA metrics, and planned downtime does not count against the uptime metric. Many service consumers can tolerate planned downtime and it generally makes the service infrastructure less complex and thus makes the service less expensive.

MTBF

Mean Time Between Failures (MTBF), also sometimes called MTTF for Mean Time To Fail (or Failure), measures the expected and actual time intervals between failures of the service. This metric is very common for hardware, but it is useful for services also because it provides additional information beyond the uptime and downtime metrics. Two services might have the same uptime metrics but one service might be experiencing a large number of failures of short duration, while the other service experiences a small number of failures of longer duration. Depending on the nature of the business processes which depend on the service, one of these services might be preferable due to the differing failure patterns.

MTTR and MaxTTR

Mean Time To Repair (MTTR) is another metric which historically was applied to hardware, but is also relevant for services. Service consumers typically can tolerate the absence of the service for only so long before they experience disruptions to their business operations. The MTTR specifies the average length of time the service was unavailable for each downtime event. Since averages can hide some very long times, the MaxTTR (Maximum Time To Repair) experienced by the service should also be examined by prospective consumers. An SLA may place a limit on the MaxTTR and specify the penalties for not restoring service operation within this time.

BUSINESS CONTINUITY

Swanson (2002) states that Business Continuity "focuses on sustaining an organization's *mission/business functions* during and after a disruption" (p. 9). Also called Disaster Recovery or DR, this property defines how the service will respond to severe disruptions such as natural or man-made disasters. In the past, preparations were seldom made for such unexpected events. However, time has taught us to expect such events, plan for them, and test these plans which are called Business Continuity Plans or Disaster Recovery Plans. Depending on the service and the business processes using the service, the business continuity plans could be very simple or very complex. In any case, the plans need to be tested and refined, generally at least once per year. The SLA may specify certain events which fall into the disaster category, and defines the usual availability metrics to exclude such events.

Some services are so critical that they are designed to handle a disaster which causes the complete loss of one or more datacenters with minimal or no impact to the service levels. But this is usually very expensive, and so more often a service is designed to be able to recover from such a disaster within a specified amount of time. As an example, a remote site (called a DR site) may receive a nightly copy of a database and real-time transaction logs which allow the last valid version of a destroyed database to be recreated and the service to be restored within 24 hours. The DR site also needs hardware, software, and personnel to bring up and operate the standby service infrastructure. A critical issue during disaster recovery is that usually many services need to be recovered and there are not enough personnel to work on all services simultaneously. Thus, services are prioritized with the most critical services receiving attention first. This criticality is determined by the service provider, so it will probably be based on the impact to their profit, which should be aligned with the criticality of the service consumer by the SLA. Third parties may also influence these priorities, for example a law or government official may influence these decisions.

The SLA metrics for business continuity define which services will be restored after a disaster, how quickly, and possibly in what order. The order can be important. If a company and their competitor both use the same service provider, the company may wish to pay extra to have the limited staff of the service provider prioritize restoration of their service above that of their competitor. Even with extensive planning and testing, the service restoration time can be hard to predict and meet after a disaster. The SLA may define that some services will operate at a lower level of performance for some time period after a disaster. The SLA may also define how the service provider and customer need to work together to restore the services and the business processes dependent on the services, and test that things are properly recovered. If the disaster is resolved, usually the service provider will want to move the service back to the primary site. This may involve some planned and scheduled downtime, which the SLA may define to not count against the service availability metrics.

Customer Satisfaction

Rating systems have been used for some time now to empower a community of people to reward good behavior and penalize bad behavior within that community. For example, Amazon.com is a broker for many other businesses and individuals to sell goods to consumers. The consumers rate their level of satisfaction with the sellers and the aggregate rating of a seller provides an indication of how trustworthy a seller is. Within a services ecosystem, a rating system can be used to judge customer satisfaction with services and service providers. Organizations like JDPower and BBBOnLine track customer satisfaction and complaints for a variety of services and can instill confidence in an unfamiliar service provider.

In many areas, ratings systems are mature enough that new service providers have difficulty entering the market because they have no or too few ratings from customers. For this reason, new service providers may offer incentives to new customers to use their services and provide ratings. Such incentives can include free trial periods and guarantees of a full refund if not satisfied. For the consumer, the opportunity cost to try a service is often more of a consideration than the monetary cost, so enticements like free goods just for trying the service are popular where this is legal in order to compensate for the time required to try the service.

Performance

Performance is an overloaded term. Many companies define Key Performance Indicators or KPIs which they use to measure how well the business is operating. The web site kpilibrary.com has over 4,600 KPIs. SLA reports may include various KPI metrics, but a discussion of this type of business performance metric is beyond the scope of this book. The focus here is on typical performance metrics for IT-based services. The relevant performance metrics for an IT-based service depend upon the nature of the service, but for many services some common performance metrics can usually be used, so these will be discussed.

Response Time

Response times are often used as part of a service performance metric. Mean response time defines the average amount of time it takes the service to process a request. This is an indicator of the responsiveness of the service, but additional metrics may also be useful because the mean response time metric can mask a significant number of very slow responses. Examples of additional useful metrics are the response time at which a certain percentage of the requests complete, and the number of requests which take longer than a certain time to complete. If the average response time is 2 seconds and only 1 in 1,000 requests takes longer than 5 seconds, this may be acceptable. However, if the average response time is 2 seconds but 25 in 1,000 requests take longer than 5 seconds, this may not be acceptable. At the very least, it shows that response time can vary significantly. The maximum response time

may also be a useful metric. Some services may offer many different operations which take different amounts of time. In this case, response time metrics for each operation type may be useful.

The graph in Figure 2 plots the actual response times for requests to a service against the number of requests which were served within that response time at 1 second granularity. The dashed lines show the mean response time thresholds specified in the SLA. This type of graph makes it easy to see the distribution of response times during the time period, but it can be hard to determine if the SLA is satisfied. A graph showing the CDF or Cumulative Distribution Function of the response times is useful for this purpose because it shows the percentage of requests that complete within various response time thresholds and the maximum response time. Figure 3 shows the same response time data as Figure 2 but plotted as a CDF. The SLA will often state that a CDF of response times should be produced on a periodic basis, and define

Figure 2. Graph of response time vs. number of requests

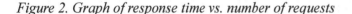

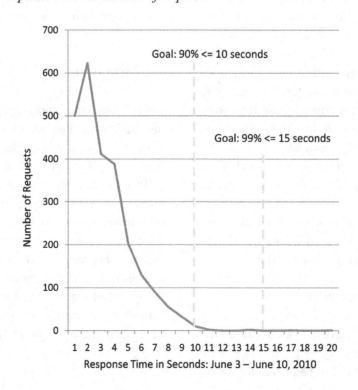

the percentage of requests that must complete within one or more response time thresholds. In this example, the SLA states that 90% of requests complete in less than 10 seconds, and 99% of requests complete in less than 15 seconds. It is easy to see from Figure 3 that the response time SLA is satisfied for this time period for this service.

Throughput

Throughput very generally is how much work can be pushed through the service in a specific amount of time. What that work is depends on the service. A set of cashiers at a retail store can handle, on average, a certain number of items and customers per hour. A web site can handle a certain number of page views and unique customer visits

per hour. A car manufacturing line can produce a certain number of cars per day.

A service may have many operations, and these operations may have very different rates of throughput. As with response time, specific metrics for each operation type may be required to adequately convey the required throughput numbers in an SLA or the actual throughput numbers in a report. Throughput measurements can vary significantly, for example based on how busy a service is and what time of day it is. For this reason, specifying or reporting the average throughput for every service operation every day may not be adequate. Throughput may need to be calculated on an hourly or more frequent basis to ensure that the service meets the needs of the business processes using that service. To get a very granular picture of throughput, the throughput

Figure 3. CDF of response times

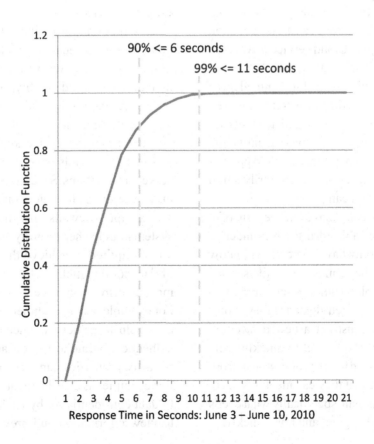

can be calculated for each invocation of a service operation, and the CDF of these results plotted.

Scalability

Scalability defines how large and small something can get, and perhaps more importantly, how quickly it can get that large or small. The lag time from intention to availability for large amounts of infrastructure, including many services, has decreased dramatically. If you wanted access to a significant amount of computer power last millennium, you had to arrange to lease time on the computers, which typically took several days to weeks or longer. In this millennium, IBM and Sun began offering computing on demand services ("Deep Computing," n.d.; "Sun Utility," n.d.) but numbers on how large and how fast these services could scale at their inception are hard to find. In 2005 HP introduced its flexible computing services (HP Flexible Computing Services, 2010) which enabled scaling up to over 1,000 processors in 2 days. In 2006 Amazon introduced the beta version of the Elastic Compute Cloud service ("Amazon Elastic Compute Cloud," 2010) which later allowed scaling to the virtual machine equivalent of several thousand processors in a matter of minutes. Today, services like corporate email accounts are available on demand in whatever quantity the customer is willing to pay for. Google Apps has many services which can scale arbitrarily small or large, assuming you can pay.

Services which don't have the benefit of a shared and highly scalable infrastructure underlying them will generally have some limits to how large and how fast they can scale. While service providers may be able to quickly add more servers to meet an unexpected demand, they won't be able to quickly construct a new datacenter. Service consumers who expect to quickly scale out operations will need to get a commitment from the service provider that they can meet this need. The SLA will need to state specifically what needs to scale out, to what degree, and how quickly.

Security

Security is perhaps the most complex non-functional property of a service, and also one of the most important. Due to this complexity and importance, often many security requirements are collected together into a standard. The Payment Card Industry Data Security Standard known as PCI DSS (PCI Security Standards Council, 2008) is an example of an industry standard which defines a collection of security requirements. The Federal Information Security Management Act (United States Public Law 107-347, 2002) is a US law which defines security standards for federal systems. This enables a provider to offer or a consumer to require that the service conforms to a particular standard like PCI DSS version 1.2 instead of listing pages full of detailed security properties. This section will explain many of the important security properties of services at a high level using an online banking portal as an example service.

It is important to distinguish between security properties and security mechanisms. Security properties are somewhat conceptual in nature and include data confidentiality, data integrity, data or service availability, and user authentication or authorization. Security mechanisms are specific technologies in the service delivery infrastructure and include firewalls, encryption software, and access control systems. Several security mechanisms may be necessary to achieve one security property. For example, firewalls, encryption, access control systems, and other security mechanisms might all be required to achieve the security property of data confidentiality. One security mechanism may contribute to several security properties. For example, using an authentication mechanism may help to achieve the security properties of authentication, authorization, and confidentiality. Security properties can also be interdependent. For example, user authentication may contribute to data confidentiality by enabling certain users to view information and preventing other users from viewing the information. But in a service that doesn't have any data confidentiality requirements, user authentication may be used to provide confidence that the audit logs which detail who did what using the service are correct.

Confidentiality

Confidentiality usually applies to the data used by a service. Preserving the confidentiality of data means that only the people you wish to see the data have seen the data. When an unauthorized person sees data which they shouldn't see, this is called a data leak.

Encryption is an important mechanism to preserve data confidentiality. Browsers have encryption software which encrypts data between the user's computer and the service to provide data confidentiality across the communications links. This is standard for many services, including online banking portals. Data at rest is being encrypted more regularly, especially for backup tapes which may be lost, for example when being delivered by a courier to an offsite location for fulfilling disaster recovery requirements. An SLA should specify when data is encrypted. This brings up the issue of key management for the cryptographic keys which are used to encrypt and decrypt data. An online banking portal targeted at consumers typically doesn't reveal the details of key management, but a banking service targeted at businesses may include such details in an SLA.

Access control systems are another important mechanism to preserve data confidentiality. These systems control who can see and change data within the service. The details such as names of persons are seldom defined in SLAs, because they change too frequently, for example due to personnel turnover. The SLA may define the roles which can see and change data, and leave the mapping of persons to roles to be performed by the operations team.

Confidentiality can also apply to things besides data, such as the fact that a service is being used.

A company may not wish it to be known that it is using a particular service. In this case, the SLA needs to define that even this fact is confidential.

Privacy

Privacy is closely related to confidentiality, but it is worth treating it separately because there are so many regulations governing the details of privacy. Privacy deals with personally-identifiable information (PII) which is protected by laws in many countries and states. PII is information which can uniquely identify a person, such as a name and telephone number together in a data record. Odds are good that you, the reader, has received a letter from some organization which has experienced a privacy breach. These breaches of privacy have been happening for decades, but only recently have most people become aware of them because now companies are required by law in many jurisdictions to notify the person when their PII has been improperly disclosed.

The EU has a strong tradition of protecting the privacy of the citizens of member states. The Directive on Data Protection of 1995 (European Parliament Directive 95/46/EC, 1995) created many protections regarding PII of EU citizens. Each member state follows the directive to provide at least that much protection, and some states, notably Germany, have gone farther and enacted additional protections. In particular, the EU Directive mandated that PII of EU citizens cannot flow across international borders without the consent of the citizen. As a result, the US Commerce Department negotiated with the EU to create the Safe Harbor provisions (United States Department of Commerce, 2010) to enable PII to flow from the EU to US firms which promise compliance with these provisions under penalty of fines or other enforcement actions from the FTC (Federal Trade Commission, a part of the Commerce Department). This has enabled corporations to receive PII on EU citizens, but it leaves a problem for non-profit and educational institutions because they are not regulated by the FTC. Thus, they have a more difficult time receiving PII on EU citizens.

In contrast to the EU, the US federal government does not have strong laws in place to protect the privacy of PII of US citizens. This is because US citizens tend to not trust the federal government to protect their privacy, which likely stems from various privacy-violating actions such as the use of federal census records to intern US citizens of Japanese decent during World War II. Most US states have laws of some form which protect PII, including requiring data owners to be notified when their PII has been improperly disclosed. Even though some US states do not have such laws, best practice is to notify all the data owners of the leak, even those that live in states which do not require such notification. Many Asian countries also have privacy laws, but they vary widely and a proper treatment of them is out of scope.

Services generally conform to the privacy laws of the jurisdictions they serve. Such compliance is often specified in the SLA by stating that the service conforms to the EU Data Protection Directive, Safe Harbor principles, or laws of a specific jurisdiction. Many services also have a privacy policy for the service which the provider intends to follow. It can be difficult for a service consumer to verify that all of the privacy requirements are being delivered. It can also be difficult for a service provider to know this due to the international nature of the Internet. For example, on February 24, 2010, three US-based Google executives were found guilty of violating privacy laws in Italy and sentenced to six months in jail. One was actually arrested when he went to Milan for a conference ("Google executives convicted," 2010).

Integrity

Integrity applies to data sent to and used by the service. Integrity gauges the likelihood that the data has not changed during transmission or storage unless the service intended to change the data. Integrity does not gauge the correctness of data

when it initially is received by a service. Data integrity can be lost when data is maliciously tampered with or incurs errors during transmission or storage. Various algorithms such as checksums, ECC (error correcting codes), and HMAC (hashed message authentication codes) can detect to an arbitrary degree of certainty when data integrity is lost. The online banking portal would likely use data integrity techniques on the systems which store actual account data. The service SLA may specify what protections the service uses to detect and correct loss of data integrity, but this is not common today.

Authentication

Authentication provides confidence that people or services are who they claim to be, and not imposters. There is no such thing as 100% certain authentication of users or services, so the goal is to attain an adequate level of confidence, which varies between services and within a service. When a user checks weather.com to find weather information, the user may trust that DNS (the Domain Name System) is sending the browser session to the real weather.com site and not to an imposter site. This is an adequate level of authentication for this activity. In contrast, when a user accesses an online banking service, this level of authentication is not adequate because there are many ways to break DNS. A security-sensitive service accessible via a web browser, such as an online banking portal, generally has a certificate which the browser uses to cryptographically verify that it is talking to the real service and not an imposter.

A service may also authenticate its users. Requiring users to enter a username and password is the most common method, but passwords can be guessed, stolen, phished, purchased, or read from a Post-It ® note on the user's monitor. Password-based authentication does not provide high confidence that the user is who they claim to be. Two-factor authentication methods use two independent means to identify a user, generally chosen from the set:

1. Something you know (like a password)
2. Something you have (like a USB security token or dongle)
3. Something you are (like your fingerprint, retina pattern, or hand geometry)

This prevents a lost or stolen password from being used to gain access to a service, unless the other authentication factor was also stolen. USB and similar security tokens generally require a password to be input to the device so that the device is not useful if lost. Fingerprint readers may check that the finger has a pulse and is within a certain temperature range to try to thwart attacks using stolen fingers. At the extreme, remote user authentication fails because a person can be coerced to give the attacker access to the service.

An online banking portal typically allows usernames and passwords to identify users for customer convenience, and chalks up the cost of fraud as a cost of doing business. Many banks provide options for stronger authentication on their online portals, including security tokens and passcodes sent to mobile phones. For any service, the SLA typically specifies how strong a method of user authentication is required to perform various operations using the service, and what options the service provides for users (including other services) to authenticate to the service.

Authorization

Authorization defines "who can do what, and when." An online banking service gives you authorization to manipulate your accounts but not the accounts of other customers. It may have a feature that lets you set up accounts for your children, and allow you to give your children authorization to manipulate their accounts, but not your accounts.

The most common form of an authorization is an explicit definition which specifies the actions that a specific user or group is allowed to take using a service. Such an authorization can be applied to individual people, groups of people, individual services, or groups of services. These types of authorizations usually need to be defined by the service provider within the service delivery infrastructure, unless the service provides an interface for the consumer to configure the authorizations which they desire. Changing this form of authorization requires the action of a person with the authority to make such changes, which can take time and be error-prone.

Authorizations can also be an entity in their own right which people or services can transfer to each other without any predetermined process on where or how the authorization gets transferred. In this case, the authorization is some digital data such as a SAML token which, when presented to the service with a request for action, causes the service to allow the actions specified by this authorization to happen. Changing this form of authorization also requires the action of a person with the authority to make such changes, but the important distinguishing characteristic is that anyone who possesses such an authorization also has the authority to pass the authorization on to someone else without involving someone with access to the system. This digital data which is the authorization can be transferred among people and services by any means, such as email, carrier pigeon, or FTP.

Auditability

The goal of an audit is to know "who did what, and when." The use of the service by the consumer's personnel may have certain audit requirements. It may be necessary to record who performed certain actions using the service, for example when and by whom database changes were performed. The SLA may specify the information which should be included in a periodic audit report and where to send such a report. This enables the customer to understand how their personnel are using the service.

In addition, the service consumer may have audit requirements for the service delivery infrastructure and personnel. In the case of an online banking portal, these audits are required by the applicable laws and regulations which govern banks rather than directly from service consumers. There are many non-functional properties which a service provider could deliver, but many of them are difficult for the consumer of the service to verify. Many audit standards specify certain process requirements in the operation of the service and the management and actions of the service delivery personnel. Auditing of the service delivery infrastructure (including IT systems, processes, and personnel) by trusted external companies will become increasingly critical as the number and importance of services used by companies and individuals increase. There are a number of control standards which audits can verify, including COBIT (ISACA, 2010), SAS 70 (American Institute of Certified Public Accountants, Inc., 1993), ISO 27002 (International Organization for Standardization, 2005), and PCI-DSS (PCI Security Standards Council, 2008), but a discussion of them is beyond the scope of this book. Using a service which has passed certain audits can increase confidence that the service will perform as expected. At a minimum, the SLA should state which control standards are being used for auditing and how audit compliance issues will be handled. The SLA may also state the details of how each of the control objectives within the control standard(s) are being applied within the service.

Data Retention

Often there is no need to keep data sitting around, but it happens anyway because there is no pressing need to remove or destroy it. This issue has gained more attention due to incidents such as military secrets being discovered on disk drives purchased at auction sites. Services now offer limits on how long they will retain the data which they collect and guarantees on how they will destroy the data when the time comes to do so.

An SLA for data retention states when data in the service will be destroyed. This depends greatly on the type of data, type of service, and any regulations which govern that data. Medical records in a service designed to preserve them may be stored for years after a patient has died. These same medical records in a computational biology service which is using them for medical research may be destroyed as soon as the experiment completes. Intermediate results generated during the operation of such a service may be destroyed every week.

An SLA for data retention also states how data in the service will be destroyed. Extremely sensitive data generally requires that the media on which it resided be destroyed, for example by soaking the media in acid and/or shredding the media. Data at this level of sensitivity is usually protected by extensive physical security mechanisms which generally preclude it from being sent into any kind of service, so service SLAs which require physical media destruction are rare. An SLA which deals with data retention will usually state that a particular data destruction standard will be used to destroy data. There are many such standards, but two relevant standards are the NIST Guidelines for Media Sanitization (Kissel et. al., 2006) and the NATO Data Destruction Standard. The goal of performing these operations is to destroy the data without destroying the media on which the data resides, usually by writing various patterns of bits over the data many times. This can be extraordinarily difficult if you assume that the adversary is technologically advanced and well-financed. For example, the head of a disk drive doesn't trace exactly the same path over the disk media each time the disk rotates beneath it. Some magnetic traces of data from a write many passes and years ago can remain on the fringes of the track and can sometimes be detected with specialized equipment and used to reconstruct the data. Another concern is that future advances in technology may provide methods to recover data which was erased using these standards.

Usability

Usability measures how easy or difficult it is to use a service. During an iterative service design cycle, qualitative usability testing provides insight into usability issues in order to change the design to improve the usability of the service, but doesn't provide metrics for usability. When a service is ready to be released to the world, quantitative usability testing can provide metrics with which the service can be compared against other services. A common metric in this regard is a rating of user satisfaction with the usability of the service or the service as a whole. If more detailed metrics are desired, a number of users perform certain tasks using the service, and the average time required and number of errors made are calculated for each task. These metrics can provide an objective way to compare service usability for two services which provide such metrics for a task which they both enable. However, in practice the service preferred by users may not be the service with the lowest task time or error rate, as other factors are in play. For example, in some cases the service with the prettiest user interface may be preferred. Usability metrics often are not purchase or SLA criteria because a service can be directly experienced on a trial basis to gain a personal understanding of how usable it is. A service which is a project to develop another service may have specific usability metrics for the developed service.

RESEARCH OPPORTUNITIES IN TRADITIONAL NON-FUNCTIONAL PROPERTIES OF SERVICES

Accessibility

Accessibility for Disabled Persons

The Web Content Accessibility Guidelines are useful and are part of the effort towards enabling disabled persons to more fully participate in society, but much more work is needed. IT-based services have the potential to provide disabled persons with new opportunities. Research opportunities include:

- Creating innovative assistive services for disabled persons and their caregivers
- Improving the tools used by service developers such that the tools help to ensure that the service is accessible to disabled persons
- Better understanding what makes a service (in)accessible in order to further improve accessibility guidelines

Accessibility of the Service

Historically, providing compatibility between different parts of an IT system such as the hardware, operating system, and software applications has been very challenging. As an example, if you were designing a service which included a GUI in the early 1990's you would need to build multiple GUI versions: a version using Motif for some flavors of Unix (TM X/Open Company), another version using OpenLook for other flavors of Unix, another version for Microsoft systems and yet another version for Apple systems. Each version would only work properly with certain versions of the underlying operating system, windowing system, and other dependent software, and only on certain hardware systems. For this reason, most services were accessible from only a small subset of the available hardware platforms. At this time Java (TM Oracle America, Inc.) held the promise of solving this problem with its "write once, run everywhere" potential, but the reality was closer to "write once, debug everywhere" because the JVMs weren't compatible with each other and were buggy. Performance of programs written in Java often compared poorly to the same program written in another language. Now that Java and other languages are mature enough to run the same code on a wide variety of devices with reasonable performance without extensive qualification testing, service accessibility can be thought of differently. It is now possible to create a program which is likely to work on many operating systems and hardware devices, even without testing all combinations. Many have speculated that the dominant deployment model for services of the future is a mobile device connecting to the cloud. An open research question in this context is "What are the limits of the 'write once, run everywhere' paradigm?" For example, is it possible to provide abstraction layers such that the developer doesn't need to know what types of input devices are being used to gather user input?

Business Continuity

An interesting research direction is to push the limits of software, service, and business process design to minimize or eliminate the need for the service to keep state information. Perhaps business processes can be redesigned such that state information can be retained with each service consumer instead of within the service, or even be eliminated entirely. In this way, the bulk of the work a service performs could be handled by stateless processing modules which are easy to move to disaster recovery sites. The necessary state information, if any, could be strategically located to provide adequate service performance and disaster resilience. Assuming state information can be reduced or even eliminated within the service, it will be necessary to judge the tradeoffs

and study the effects of the techniques which accomplish this on both the other desirable service properties and the business processes using the service. Open research questions include:

- Can business processes which currently depend upon state information being retained within a service be redesigned to remove this requirement? What is the impact?
- Are there better ways to manage the state information required by a service?

Scalability

As data continues to grow and billions more people come online, scalability will continue to be a problem for many service providers. Many research challenges exist in this area:

- How to manage servers, software, and networks at scales much larger than today?
- How to better handle "flash crowds" which suddenly increase demand on the service by several thousand times and then disappear as suddenly?
- How to build a relational database at very large scale?
- How to power all the necessary equipment cost-effectively and without too much environmental damage?

Security (Integrity)

An interesting research problem is to create a lightweight framework which can check data integrity as data is moved among services so that unauthorized or accidental changes to data can be spotted quickly and the causes found. The algorithms exist to do this, but they are not yet packaged into tools which are easy enough for service developers to use.

EMERGING NON-FUNCTIONAL PROPERTIES OF SERVICES

This section discusses non-functional properties which typically are not used today to select services, and thus are not included in most SLAs, but are emerging as potentially important for the future. Research opportunities are identified.

Anonymity

The anonymity property guarantees that users of a service cannot be identified. While anonymity can hide illegal or improper activities, there are many legitimate reasons that a service may wish to provide anonymous access. Anonymity is an important property for communication services which serve the needs of people who cannot freely express opinions or access information online, for example due to fear of retribution from an oppressive government. Anonymity can be difficult to achieve, depending on who wants to uncover the information about service consumers. Many technical steps are necessary, but careful screening of the personnel who design and operate the service delivery infrastructure is essential. People are the most serious threat to anonymity, either from mistakes they make or from infiltration of an organization. Anonymity is generally absent from service SLAs today.

Several anonymized data sets have been de-anonymized in the last few years, for example the Netflix Prize data (Narayanan & Shmatikov, 2007). Techniques such as correlating data from an anonymized data set with data from other data sets can enable information to be obtained about the anonymized data. Better anonymization techniques are needed. Open questions include:

- How to determine what other data sets may be available and relevant to assist in de-anonymizing a particular data set, and what threats do they pose to anonymity?

- How to determine and measure the likelihood that a data set will remain anonymized over a certain time period?

Composability

Composability should measure how easy it is to compose a service with other services to create a new service. However, there is no direct metric for this today. At the time of writing, the author is aware of only one service composability metric, SCOMP (Renuka et. al., 2009). SCOMP measures how often a service is composed with other services as a proxy for how easy this composition is to perform. However, as Renuka states, this may instead measure the value of a service as part of a composition, even if the composition process was very difficult.

The promise of SOA is to build more complex services from simple services. To do this, services need to be composable. More work is needed to better understand what makes service composition easy and difficult. In particular, research to find a way to directly measure the ease with which a service can be composed (for example, measuring average development and testing time to reuse the service as part of a composition) would help improve the discipline of service design to make services more easily composable.

Composing services across cultural boundaries will also pose interesting challenges, for example due to different laws, privacy frameworks, expectations, and social norms across those cultures and countries. Ironically, the US was considered a reasonably safe place to store data before the Patriot Act was passed, but now this has reversed as thousands of people in the government can secretly obtain access to any data in the US without involving a judge.

Assuming services become more easily composable, the actual process of composing services also needs improvement. The Web Services Business Process Execution Language (OASIS, 2007) enables developers to compose services, but an

17

opportunity exists to enable non-developers who have business domain expertise to compose services to help run their business. New governance frameworks will be necessary if a line of business manager has the capability to compose services to address a business need without involving the IT department.

Evolvability

Many corporations use IT as part of their everyday business processes. This has enabled the lines of business to move more quickly, and some claim it is the primary reason for the productivity improvements and strong economies of the 1990s. As the pace of change in business has quickened, more pressure has been placed on corporate IT departments to rapidly respond to changes in the environment of the business. But the pace at which IT systems can be changed to meet new requirements is rather slow unless the system has been designed for evolvability from the start. This is rarely done because it takes longer, and the decision-maker for the project is usually under pressure to show a particular value as soon as possible and thus is penalized, not rewarded, for building an evolvable system or service.

"Service evolvability" is nascent. Metrics for evolvability of services don't exist. There are at least two interesting areas for research in this regard. Finding appropriate metrics for evolvability of services is needed. Finding better methods to evolve services is also needed. Since a service is a software system (which also includes people and processes), the related work in evolvability of software is a potential starting point for both areas. For methods to evolve services, a fruitful approach may be to "design for evolvability" which is underexplored, but in the context of SOA some work has been done.

Sustainability

The sustainability property considers the level of environmental responsibility of a process or service. On the process input side, usage of energy and raw materials is a key factor. The notion of sustainability attempts to understand how long a process could continue in its current form before a required consumable input is exhausted. Generally the goal is to find sustainable ways to run that process such that required inputs never run out because they are being consumed at or below the rate at which they can be naturally replenished. As an example, consider how long we can run machines on petroleum before the supply of petroleum is gone, compared to how long we can run machines on sunlight before the supply of sunlight is gone. On the process output side, the effects of undesired outputs such as pollution are also considered. These effects can eventually create enough political pressure to cause the process to be stopped by concerned people, for example by legislation outlawing the process.

Many methods of varying complexity exist to quantify the sustainability of a process or service. These methods look at the impact of the process across the entire lifecycle and thus are called Life Cycle Assessment (LCA) or Life Cycle Impact Assessment (LCIA) methods (Jolliet et. al., 2003). Hertwich provides a comparison of six methods (Hertwich et. al., 1997). The models used by these methods can be very sensitive to the input values, some of which may need to be estimated. Thus, comparison of results even using the same method must be undertaken carefully. The results of these assessments are not regularly used as a basis for selecting one service over another today, because usually a service will not have been through this type of detailed assessment. If sustainability continues to grow in importance, a measure for overall environmental responsibility will become an important purchase criterion for services. It is likely that the complex details will be aggregated into a numerical score so that different services can be easily compared by the person who makes such decisions. How to perform this aggregation in a way that allows for a fair comparison is an open research question today.

Sustainability metrics for services attempt to measure how environmentally responsible the service delivery infrastructure is, but give little detail today compared to the results of LCIA methods. Sustainability metrics which show up in SLAs for IT services are nascent, and may apply to the company as a whole instead of the specific service being provided. These include recycling metrics, sources of electricity used, and in some cases details on certain pollutants generated and/or treated by the service, including carbon dioxide or other greenhouse gasses. Today this may be enough to make the purchasing decision, because there may be only one provider for the desired service which claims that it recycles and uses mostly renewable energy sources. But the entire field of service sustainability is wide open for additional research, from how to create and standardize the necessary models and their input parameters, to how to make sustainability metrics a criterion that service designers and operators can consider when making the many trade-offs during service design and operation.

COST CONSIDERATIONS

Higher levels of service generally require more extensive IT infrastructure and/or staff, and thus are more expensive. Some metrics for non-functional properties, for example throughput, scale linearly and so you might expect to pay only ten times as much for ten times the throughput (less if economies of scale apply). Some metrics for non-functional properties, for example uptime, typically do not scale linearly. For many types of services, each step closer to 100% uptime requires more expenditure than the previous step. Note that some simple services may not follow this rule of thumb. For example, a document storage

service might reach very high levels of uptime simply by keeping multiple copies of documents in datacenters in different geographies and defining the service to be up if at least one of those datacenters is providing document access services to the internet connection point. In this case, the likely factor to cause a customer to not be able to use the service is the customer's internet connection. Services which process transactions or need to retain state information typically require more infrastructure and expense to reach high levels of uptime. This is partly due to the need to remotely replicate transaction logs or some other type of state information in case a disaster destroys the datacenter which handled the transaction moments after the transaction is committed.

Some taxonomies of non-functional properties include the cost of service as a non-functional property. This is certainly valid. Cost is modeled in many different ways, and the proper way to measure cost depends greatly on the specifics of the service. For example, some services will incur a cost per time, while others will incur a cost per resource used. Composite services may compose services that have different cost models. The proper way to model and treat costs during service creation, and in particular during service composition, is an important but unanswered research question. Simple approaches exist, such as using a fixed cost per service invocation, but the real world is more complex than this and thus more research is needed.

CONCLUSION

Looking back over time, two trends are clear and feed off each other in a virtuous cycle. One, service providers are offering ever higher levels of service and better addressing a larger set of desired non-functional properties with their service offerings. Two, businesses are moving more work and more complex work from within their enterprise to external service providers so that they can focus on their core competencies. These trends are enabled by increasing understanding of how to provide and measure challenging non-functional properties within the service, and significant economies of scale attained by very large service providers that even the largest enterprises can't hope to meet with their internal workloads. The economics of outsourcing non-core business functions will continue to drive this cycle of increasing service provider capability and increasing usage of external services, if researchers can continue to find ways to address the challenges, some of which have been identified in this chapter.

REFERENCES

W3C. (1999). *Web content accessibility guidelines*. Retrieved September 24, 2010, from http://www.w3.org/TR/WCAG10/

Amazon. (2010). *Elastic compute cloud* (Amazon EC2). Retrieved September 23, 2010, from http://aws.amazon.com/ec2/

American Institute of Certified Public Accountants, Inc. (1993). *Statements on auditing standards*, No. 70. Retrieved September 24, 2010, from http://www.aicpa.org/Research/Standards/AuditAttest/DownloadableDocuments/AU-00324.pdf

Deep Computing. (n.d.). *Capacity on demand*. Retrieved September 23, 2010, from http://www-03.ibm.com/systems/deepcomputing/solutions/cod/

European Parliament. (1995). *Directive 95/46/EC*. Retrieved September 24, 2010, from http://www.cdt.org/privacy/eudirective/EU_Directive_.html

Google executives convicted in Italy of violating privacy laws over bullying video. (2010). *Daily Telegraph*. Retrieved September 23, 2010, from http://www.telegraph.co.uk/technology/google/7305616/Google-executives-convicted-in-Italy-of-violating-privacy-laws-over-bullying-video.html

Hertwich, E., Pease, W., & Koshland, C. (1997). Evaluating the environmental impact of products and production processes: A comparison of six methods. *The Science of the Total Environment, 196*(1). doi:10.1016/S0048-9697(96)05344-2

HP. (2010). *Flexible computing services*. Retrieved December 9, 2010, from http://wpcfs.corp.hp.com/TSGWW_WPC/outsourcing/solutions/flexible_computing.htm

International Organization for Standardization. (2005). *ISO/IEC 27002*.

ISACA. (2007). *COBIT 4.1 framework for IT governance and control*. Retrieved from http://www.isaca.org/Knowledge-Center/COBIT/Pages/Overview.aspx

Jolliet, O., Margni, M., Charles, R., Humbert, S., Payet, J., Rebitzer, G., & Rosenbaum, R. (2003). IMPACT 2002+: A new life cycle impact assessment methodology. *International Journal of Life Cycle Assessment, 8*(6). doi:10.1007/BF02978505

Kissel, R., Scholl, M., Skolochenko, S., & Li, X. (2006). *Guidelines for media sanitization*. (NIST Special Publication 800-88). Retrieved September 24, 2010, from http://csrc.nist.gov/publications/nistpubs/800-88/NISTSP800-88_rev1.pdf

Narayanan, A., & Shmatikov, V. (2007). *How to break anonymity of the Netflix prize dataset*. Retrieved September 24, 2010, from http://arxiv.org/abs/cs/0610105

New York Institute for Special Education. (2010). *Access to the Internet, Web and Windows*. Retrieved September 24, 2010, from http://www.nyise.org/access.htm

OASIS. (2007). *Web Services business process execution language*. Retrieved September 24, 2010, from http://www.oasis-open.org/committees/tc_home.php?wg_abbrev=wsbpel

PCI Security Standards Council (2008). *Payment card industry data security standard* (version 1.2).

Renuka, S., Sengupta, B., & Ponnalagu, K. (2009). Measuring the quality of service oriented design. In Baresi, L., Chi, C., & Suzuki, J. (Eds.), *Lecture Notes In Computer Science* (*Vol. 5900*, pp. 485–499). Springer.

Rosa, N. (2001). *NFi: An architecture-based approach for treating non-functional properties of dynamic distributed systems.* Retrieved September 24, 2010, from http://www.cin.ufpe.br/~nsr/docs/rosa-thesis-01.pdf

Sun. (n.d.). *Utility computing.* Retrieved September 23, 2010 from http://www.sun.com/service/sungrid/

Swanson, M., Bowen, P., Phillips, A., Gallup, D., & Lynes, D. (2010). *Contingency planning guide for federal information systems* (p. 9). (NIST Special Publication 800-34 Rev. 1).

United States. Public Law 107-347-DEC. 17 2002, 116 STAT. 2899 (2002). *Federal information security management act (FISMA).* Title III of the E-Government Act of 2002. Retrieved September 24, 2010, from http://frwebgate.access.gpo.gov/cgi-bin/getdoc.cgi?dbname=107_cong_public_laws&docid=f:publ347.107.pdf

United States Department of Commerce. (2010). *Safe harbor home page.* Retrieved September 24, 2010, from http://www.export.gov/safeharbor/index.asp

KEY TERMS AND DEFINITIONS

Accessibility: Service accessibility considers how easily disabled persons can use the service.

Availability: Service availability considers how important it is to maintain access to the service in the face of failures.

Composability: Service composability considers how easy it is to use the service as part of a larger service.

Evolvability: Service evolvability considers how quickly the service can be adapted to respond to changes in the business environment.

Scalability: Service scalability considers how quickly the service capacity can change, and the limits on service capacity.

Security: Service security considers how the service ensures the confidentiality, integrity, and privacy of service data, service users, and the service itself.

Sustainability: Service sustainability considers the level of environmental responsibility of the service.

Chapter 2
Verification of Non-Functional Requirements by Abstract Interpretation

Agostino Cortesi
Università Ca' Foscari, Italy

Francesco Logozzo
Microsoft Research, USA

ABSTRACT

This chapter investigates a formal approach to the verification of non-functional software requirements that are crucial in Service-oriented Systems, like portability, time and space efficiency, and dependability/robustness. The key-idea is the notion of observable, i.e., an abstraction of the concrete semantics when focusing on a behavioral property of interest. By applying an abstract interpretation-based static analysis of the source program, and by a suitable choice of abstract domains, it is possible to design formal and effective tools for non-functional requirements validation.

INTRODUCTION

Effective and efficient management of customer and user requirements is one of the most crucial, but unfortunately also least understood issues (Karlsson, 1997), in particular for Service Oriented Systems. In Service Oriented Architectures the non-functional aspects of services and connections should be defined separately from their functional aspects because different applications use the services and connections in different non-functional contexts. The separation between functional and non-functional aspects improves the reusability of services and connections. It also enables the two different aspects to evolve independently, and improves the ease of understanding application architectures. This contributes to increase the maintainability of applications (Wada, Suzuki, & Oba, 2006 and O'Brien, Merson, & Bass, 2007).

Problems in the non-functional requirements are typically not recognized until late in the development process, where negative impacts are substantial and cost for correction has grown large. Even worse, problems in the requirements may

DOI: 10.4018/978-1-61350-432-1.ch002

go undetected through the development process, resulting in software systems not meeting customers and users expectations, especially when the coordination with other components is an issue. Therefore, methods and frameworks helping software developers to better manage software requirements are of great interest for component based software.

Abstract interpretation (Cousot & Cousot, 1977) is a theory of semantics approximation for computing conservative over-approximations of dynamic properties of programs. It has been successfully applied to infer run-time properties useful for debugging (e.g., type inference (Cousot, 1997 and Kozen, Palsberg, & Schwartzbach, 1994)), code optimization (e.g., compile-time garbage collection (Hughes, 1992)), program transformation (e.g., partial evaluation (Jones, 1997), parallelization (Traub, Culler & Schauser, 1992)), and program correctness proofs (e.g., safety (Halbwachs, 1998), termination (Brauburger, 1997), cryptographic protocol analysis (Monniaux, 2003), proof of absence of run-time errors (Blanchet, Cousot, Cousot, et al., 2003), semantic tattooing/watermarking (Cousot & Cousot, 2004)). As pointed out in (Le Métayer, 1996), there is still a large variety of tasks in the software engineering process that could greatly benefit from techniques akin to static program analysis, because of their firm theoretical foundations and mechanical nature.

In this chapter we investigate the impact of Abstract Interpretation theory in the formalization and automatic verification of Non-Functional Software Requirements, as they seem not adequately covered by most requirements engineering methods ((Kotonya, & Sommerville, 1998), pag. 194). Non functional requirements can be defined as restrictions or constraints on the behavior of a system service (Sommerville, 2000). Different classifications have been proposed in the literature (Boehm, 1976, Davis, 1992, and Deutsch & Willis, 1988)), though their specification may give rise to

troubles both in their elicitation and management, and in the validation process.

Let us start from a quite naive question: *"what do we mean when we say that a program is portable on a different architecture?"*. In (Ghezzi, Jazayeri & Mandrioli, 2003) a software is said portable if it can run in different environments. It is clear that it is assumed not only that it runs, but that it runs the same way. And it is also clear that if we require that the behavior is exactly the same, portability to different systems (e.g., from a PC to a PDA, or from an OS to another) can almost never be reached. This means that implicit assumptions are obviously made about the properties to be preserved, and about the ones that might be simply disregarded. In other words, portability needs to be parameterized on some specific properties of interest, i.e. it assumes a suitable abstraction of the software behavior. The same holds also for other product non-functional requirements, like space and time efficiency, dependability, robustness, usability, etc. It is clear that, in this context, the main features of abstract interpretation theory, namely modularity, modulability, and effectiveness may then become very valuable.

The main concepts introduced in this chapter can be summarized as follows:

- We extend the usual abstract interpretation notions to the deal with systems, i.e. programs + architectures.

- We show that a significant set of product qualities (non-functional requirements) can be formally expressed in terms of abstraction of the concrete semantics when focusing on a behavioral property of interest. This yields an unifying view of product non-functional requirements.

- We show how existing tools for automatic verification can be re-used in this setting to support requirements validation; their practicality directly depends on the complexity of the abstract domains.

The advantage of this approach with respect to previous attempts of modelling software requirements, e.g., by using Milner's Calculus of Communicating Systems (Halbwachs, 1995) or formal methods like Z (Spivey, 1992) or B (Abrial, 1996 and Abrial, 2003) is twofold: (1) the soundness of the approach is guaranteed by the general abstract interpretation theory, and (2) the automatic validation process can be easily tuned according to the desired granularity of the abstraction.

Applying the Abstract Interpretation theory to the treatment of non-functional software requirements (Cortesi & Logozzo, 2005) can be seen as a contribution towards the achievement of a more challenging objective: to integrate formal analysis by abstract interpretation in the full software development process, from the initial specifications to the ultimate program development (Cousot, 2001).

Chapter Structure: In Section 2, the concrete semantics of a simple imperative language is introduced to instantiate our framework. In Section 3, the core abstract interpretation theory is extended to deal with program and architecture abstractions. In Section 4 we show how to instantiate our framework on a suite of non-functional product requirements. In Section 5 we discuss its use in the Service Oriented scenario. Section 6 concludes the paper.

OPERATIONAL SEMANTICS OF A CORE IMPERATIVE LANGUAGE WITH EXCEPTIONS

In order to better illustrate the approach, we instantiate our framework with a core imperative language with exceptions and a core architecture. The results can be generalized to more complex languages and architectures. We give the syntax, the transition relations and the trace semantics of systems, composed by architectures and a programs.

Syntax

We let an architecture be a tuple $\langle bits, Op, stdio, stdout \rangle$, where $bits$ is the number of bits used to store integer numbers, Op is a set of functions implementing basic arithmetic operations, $stdio$ is the input stream (e.g., the keyboard) and $stdout$ is the output stream (e.g., the screen). The input stream has a method $next$ that returns immediately the next value in the stream, and the output stream has a method add to put a pair $\langle v,c \rangle$, i.e., a value v with a color c. We assume that if an arithmetic error occurs in the application of an operation $op \in Op$ (e.g., an overflow or a division by zero), then the exception ExcMath is raised.

The syntax of programs is specified by the following grammar:

$$C ::= \quad \text{skip} \mid x=E \mid C_1;C_2 \mid \text{if } (E!=0) \ C_1 \text{ else } C_2 \mid \text{while } (E!=0) \ C$$
$$\text{write(x,col)} \mid \text{throw Exc} \mid \text{try } C_1 \text{ catch(Exc) } C_2$$
$$E ::= \quad k \mid \text{read} \mid E_1 + E_2 \mid E_1 - E_2 \mid E_1 * E_2 \mid E_1 / E_2$$

where x and col belong to a given set Var of variables, Exc belongs to a given set Exceptions of exceptions (including the arithmetic ones) and k is (the *syntactic* representation of) an integer number.

A system is a pair $\langle A,C \rangle$, where A is an architecture and C is a program.

Semantics

The semantics of a system is described in operational style. We assume that the only available type is that of architecture-representable natural numbers: $N_{bits} = \{0, \ldots, 2^{bits} - 1\}$. Given the *syntactic* representation k of a number, $\underline{k}$ is the *semantic* correspondent. For instance, $\underline{0xFFFF} = 65535$ so that $\underline{0xFFFF} \notin N_8$. An environment is a partial map from variables to representable integers: Env= $[\text{Var} \to N_{bits}]$. If a variable x is not defined in a state σ, we denote that by $\sigma(x) = \Omega$. A state is either a command to execute in a given environment, or an environment, or an exception raised within an environment. Formally:

$$\Sigma = C \times \text{Env} \cup \text{Env} \cup \text{Exceptions} \times \text{Env} .$$

The transition relations for expressions and programs are defined by structural induction, and they are depicted in Figure 1. It is worth noting that the transition rules are parameterized by the underlying architecture (e.g., the raising of an overflow exception depends on $\mathbf{N}_{bits}$).

Let Σ^* denote the set of finite traces on Σ, and let $S_0 \subseteq \Sigma$ be a set of initial states. With a slight abuse of notation, we refer to a state as a trace of unitary length. The partial-traces semantics (Cousot & Cousot, 2002) of a system is then

Figure 1. The transition relations for expressions and programs

$$s\langle A,C\rangle(S_0) = \text{lfp}_{\varnothing}^{\subseteq}\lambda X.\ S_0 \cup \{\sigma_0 \ldots \sigma_n \sigma_{n+1} \mid \sigma_0 \ldots \sigma_n \in X,\ \sigma_n \longrightarrow \sigma_{n+1}\}.$$

$$\frac{\underline{k} \in \mathbf{N}_{bits}}{\langle k,\sigma\rangle \xrightarrow{E} k} \qquad \frac{\underline{k} \notin \mathbf{N}_{bits}}{\langle k,\sigma\rangle \xrightarrow{E} \langle \text{ExcMath},\sigma\rangle} \qquad \frac{A.stdio.next = v}{\langle \text{read},\sigma\rangle \xrightarrow{E} \langle v,\sigma\rangle}$$

$$\frac{\langle E_1,\sigma\rangle \xrightarrow{E} \langle v_1,\sigma\rangle\ \langle E_2,\sigma\rangle \xrightarrow{E} \langle v_2,\sigma\rangle\ v_1,v_2 \neq \text{ExcMath}\ A.op(v_1,v_2) = v \neq \text{ExcMath}}{\langle E_1 op E_2,\sigma\rangle \xrightarrow{E} \langle v,\sigma\rangle}$$

$$\frac{\langle E_1,\sigma\rangle \xrightarrow{E} \langle v_1,\sigma\rangle\ \langle E_2,\sigma\rangle \xrightarrow{E} \langle v_2,\sigma\rangle\ v_1,v_2 \neq \text{ExcMath}\ A.op(v_1,v_2) = \text{ExcMath}}{\langle E_1 op E_2,\sigma\rangle \xrightarrow{E} \langle \text{ExcMath},\sigma\rangle}$$

$$\frac{\langle E_1,\sigma\rangle \xrightarrow{E} \langle v_1,\sigma\rangle\ \langle E_2,\sigma\rangle \xrightarrow{E} \langle v_2,\sigma\rangle\ (v_1 = \text{ExcMath})or(v_2 = \text{ExcMath})}{\langle E_1 op E_2,\sigma\rangle \xrightarrow{E} \langle \text{ExcMath},\sigma\rangle}$$

$$\frac{}{\langle \text{skip},\sigma\rangle \longrightarrow \sigma} \qquad \frac{\langle E,\sigma\rangle \xrightarrow{E} \langle v,\sigma\rangle\ v \neq \text{ExcMath}}{\langle x = E,\sigma\rangle \longrightarrow \sigma[x \mapsto v]} \qquad \frac{\langle E,\sigma\rangle \xrightarrow{E} \langle \text{ExcMath},\sigma\rangle}{\langle x = E,\sigma\rangle \longrightarrow \langle \text{ExcMath},\sigma\rangle}$$

$$\frac{\langle C_1,\sigma\rangle \longrightarrow \sigma'}{\langle C_1;C_2,\sigma\rangle \longrightarrow \langle C_2,\sigma'\rangle} \qquad \frac{\langle C_1,\sigma\rangle \longrightarrow \langle \text{Exc},\sigma\rangle}{\langle C_1;C_2,\sigma\rangle \longrightarrow \langle \text{Exc},\sigma\rangle}$$

$$\frac{\langle E,\sigma\rangle \xrightarrow{E} \langle \underline{k},\sigma\rangle\ \underline{k} \neq 0}{\langle \text{if}(E!= 0)C_1\text{ else }C_2,\sigma\rangle \longrightarrow \langle C_1,\sigma\rangle} \qquad \frac{\langle E,\sigma\rangle \xrightarrow{E} \langle 0,\sigma\rangle}{\langle \text{if}(E!= 0)C_1\text{ else }C_2,\sigma\rangle \longrightarrow \langle C_2,\sigma\rangle}$$

$$\frac{\langle E,\sigma\rangle \xrightarrow{E} \langle \text{ExcMath},\sigma\rangle}{\langle \text{if}(E!= 0)C_1\text{ else }C_2,\sigma\rangle \longrightarrow \langle \text{ExcMath},\sigma\rangle}$$

$$\frac{\langle E,\sigma\rangle \xrightarrow{E} \langle \underline{k},\sigma\rangle\ \underline{k} \neq 0}{\langle \text{while}(E!= 0)\ C,\sigma\rangle \longrightarrow \langle C;\text{while}(E!= 0)\ C,\sigma\rangle} \qquad \frac{\langle E,\sigma\rangle \xrightarrow{E} \langle 0,\sigma\rangle}{\langle \text{while}(E!= 0)\ C,\sigma\rangle \longrightarrow \sigma}$$

$$\frac{\langle E,\sigma\rangle \xrightarrow{E} \langle \text{ExcMath},\sigma\rangle}{\langle \text{while}(E!= 0)\ C,\sigma\rangle \longrightarrow \langle \text{ExcMath},\sigma\rangle}$$

$$\frac{A.stdout.add(\sigma(x),\sigma(\text{col}))}{\langle \text{write}(x,\text{col}),\sigma\rangle \longrightarrow \sigma} \qquad \frac{\text{Exc} \in \text{Exceptions}}{\langle \text{throw Exc},\sigma\rangle \longrightarrow \langle \text{Exc},\sigma\rangle}$$

$$\frac{\langle C_1,\sigma\rangle \longrightarrow \sigma'}{\langle \text{try }C_1\text{ catch(Exc)}C_2,\sigma\rangle \longrightarrow \sigma'} \qquad \frac{\langle C_1,\sigma\rangle \longrightarrow \langle \text{Exc},\sigma'\rangle}{\langle \text{try }C_1\text{ catch(Exc)}C_2,\sigma\rangle \longrightarrow \langle C_2,\sigma'\rangle}$$

$$\frac{\langle C_1,\sigma\rangle \longrightarrow \langle \text{Exc}',\sigma'\rangle\ \text{Exc}' \neq \text{Exc}}{\langle \text{try }C_1\text{ catch(Exc)}C_2,\sigma\rangle \longrightarrow \langle \text{Exc}',\sigma'\rangle}$$

expressed as a least fixpoint over the complete boolean lattice $\langle \Sigma^*, \subseteq \rangle$ as follows.

ABSTRACTING SYSTEMS = PROGRAMS + ARCHITECTURES

Abstract interpretation (Cousot & Cousot, 1977) is a general theory of approximation which formalizes the idea that the semantics of a program can be more or less precise depending on the considered observation level. In this section we revise some basic concepts, and we extend them to deal with composed systems.

In the abstract interpretation terminology, $\langle \Sigma^*, \subseteq \rangle$ is the *concrete domain*, its elements are semantic properties, and the order $\subseteq$ stands for the logical implication. As a consequence, the most precise property about the behavior of a system is the semantics s, called the *concrete semantics* (Cousot, 1999). Set of traces are approximated are represented by suitable abstract elements, which capture interesting properties while disregarding other execution properties that are out of the scope of interest. Abstract properties (or elements) belong to an *abstract domain of observables*, $\overline{D}$, and they are ordered according to $\leq$, the abstract counterpart for logical implication. In this work we assume that $\langle \overline{D}, \leq \rangle$ is a complete lattice.

The correspondence between the concrete and the abstract semantic domains is given by a pair of monotonic functions $\langle \alpha, \gamma \rangle$. The function $\alpha \in [P(\Sigma^*) \to \overline{D}]$, called the abstraction function, formalizes the notion of the abstraction ($P(\Sigma^*)$ denotes the powerset of Σ^*), and $\alpha(T)$ represents the *best* approximation in $\overline{D}$ of the set of traces T (with respect to the order in $\overline{D}$). If $\alpha(T) \leq p$ then p is also a correct, although less precise, abstract approximation of T. On the other hand, the function $\gamma \in [\overline{D} \to P(\Sigma^*)]$, called the concretization function, returns the set of traces that are captured by an abstract property p. The ab-

straction and concretization functions must satisfy the following property:

$$\forall T \in P(\Sigma^*).\forall d \in \overline{D}.\ \alpha(T) \leq d \Leftrightarrow T \subseteq \gamma(d),$$

in such a case, we say that $\langle \alpha, \gamma \rangle$ form a Galois connection between the concrete and the abstract domains. We write is as

$$(\langle P(\Sigma^*), \subseteq \rangle, \alpha, \gamma, \langle \overline{D}, \leq \rangle) \qquad (1)$$

The abstract semantics of a system, $\overline{s}$, is defined over an abstract domain that is linked to the concrete domain by a Galois connection. It must satisfy the soundness criterion, (Cousot & Cousot, 1977):

$$\forall S_0 \subseteq \Sigma.\ \alpha(s\langle A,C \rangle(S_0)) \leq \overline{s}\langle A,C \rangle(\alpha(S_0)).$$

The soundness criterion above imposes that, when the properties encoded by a given abstract domain are considered, the abstract semantics s $\langle A,C \rangle$ captures all the behaviors of $\langle A,C \rangle$. As a consequence, given a specification of a system $\langle A,C \rangle$ expressed as an abstract property p, if $\overline{s}\langle A,C \rangle(\alpha(S_0)) \leq p$, by the soundness criterion and by the transitivity of $\leq$, we have that

$$\alpha(s\langle A,C \rangle(S_0)) \leq p.$$

This means that $\langle A,C \rangle$ respects the specification p.

In the following, we instantiate the abstract domain and p in order to reflect non-functional requirements of systems and we show how well-known static analyses can be re-used in this enhanced context for the automatic verification of such properties.

APPLICATION: NON-FUNCTIONAL REQUIREMENT ANALYSIS

Non-functional software requirements are requirements which are not directly concerned with the specific functions delivered by the system (Sommerville, 2000). They may relate to emergent system properties such as reliability, response time and store occupancy. Alternatively, they may define constraints on the system like the data representation used in system interfaces.

The 'IEEE-Std 830 – 1993' (IEEE, 1988) presents a comprehensive list of non-functional requirements. In the following we will focus on a few of such requirements, namely *portability*, *efficiency*, *robustness* and *usability*. The approach can be extended to cope with other non-functional requirements.

In this section, we show (1) how such requirements admit a rigorous formalization, unlike, e.g., what stated in (Kotonya, & Sommerville, 1998, section 8.2), (2) how, by a suitable choice of abstract domains, existing tools can be re-used to verify such requirements, and (3) the effectiveness of the approach on a public-domain static analyzer (Cousot, 1999).

Portability

Informal Definition

According to (Ghezzi, Jazayeri & Mandrioli, 2003), a software *"is portable if it can run on different environments"*. The term *environment* may refer to a hardware platform or a software environment. Analogously, another widespread textbook, (Meyer, 1997), defines portability as *"the ease of transferring software products to various hardware and software environments"*. The first observation is that the two definitions implicitly link the requirement to unspecified software metrics. Furthermore, as any natural-based language specifications, they are intrinsically ambiguous. For instance, the word *"run"* can be read as just

the possibility of recompiling and executing the software on different system, but also as the request that some behavioral properties of the software are preserved in different platforms.

Formal Definition

We specify portability as a property of the execution of a program that is preserved when it is ported on different architectures. This means that up to a certain property of interest, the behavior of a software is the same on a different architecture. [Portability] Let us consider a program C, an architecture A and a Galois connection ($\langle P(\Sigma^*), \subseteq \rangle, \alpha, \gamma, \langle \overline{D}, \leq \rangle$). We say that C, developed on A, is portable on the architecture B w.r.t. the observable domain D, if

$$\forall S_0 \subseteq \Sigma.\ \alpha(s\langle B, C\rangle(S_0)) \leq \alpha(s\langle A, C\rangle(S_0)).$$

Abstraction

A class property one is interested to keep unchanged among different porting of the software is the behavior w.r.t. arithmetic overflow. For instance, the violation of such a property in porting the control software on a different architecture was at the origin of the Arianne V crash (Lacan, Monfort, Ribal, et al, 1998).

Arithmetic overflow can be checked by using numerical abstract domains, e.g., (Cousot & Cousot, 1977, Cousot & Halbwachs, 1978 and Miné, 2001). In such domains the range of the values assumed by a variable can be constrained so that it can be checked against the largest representable number in a given architecture.

Example

Let us consider the program C in Algorithm 1(a), and let us consider an architecture A such that $A.bits = 32$. We can use the Intervals abstract domain (Cousot & Cousot, 1977), and the public-domain static analyzer (Cousot, 1999) to infer that $\overline{s}\langle A,C\rangle(i \mapsto [-\infty, +\infty]) = [1, 2^{16}]$, and as 2^{16} is representable on a 32 bit architecture, then program C does not cause any arithmetic overflow. As a consequence, by the soundness of the static analysis (guaranteed by abstract interpretation theory), we can safely infer that the program is portable to any architecture in which 2^{16} is representable (this is not the case in a 16 bits architecture).

Oberve that what is described above is a "low level" portability, assuming implicitly the same interface with the rest of the world (graphical interface, for instance). But we can also define portability as reproducing the same user experience, and that may require different behaviors (for example, to cater for temporary loss of connectivity in mobile systems – of course, this is another example of restriction of domain).

Efficiency

Informal Definition

In the existing literature, efficiency "*refers to how economically the software utilizes the resources of the computer*" (Ghezzi, Jazayeri & Mandrioli,

Algorithm 1. Four programs on which we verify non-functional requirements

```
i=1;
while (2¹⁶-i != 0)
i =i*4;
(a)                                                    C
      , a program non portable on 16 bits architectures
try
  i=?;
  if (i!=0) c = i/0
  else throw Err
catch (Err)
  c=0;
write(c,255)
(b)                                                    D
      , a robust program.
i=1;
while (2¹⁶-i != 0)
i =i+2;
(c)                                                    C
      ', a   non efficient program
x=?; r=?; g=?; b=?;
if (r+g-1 != 0)
  col = 2ʳ + 2ᵍ + 2ᵇ
else col=0;
write(x,col)
(d)                                                    E
      , a program usable by daltonians
```

28

2003), or it is *"the ability of a software system to place as few demands as possible on hardware resources, such as processor time or space occupied"* (Meyer, 1997). Once again, such definitions suffer from the ambiguity of the natural language, e.g., it is not clear if when verifying efficiency requirements the underlying architecture must be considered or not, or if space and time requirements must be considered independently or not.

Formal Definitions

Efficiency can be formally defined as an abstraction of the execution traces of a program. As such behavior depends on the underlying architecture, our definition explicitly mentions the architecture in which the program is executed. Efficiency requirements can be specified by natural numbers, standing, for instance, for the number of processor cycles or the size of the heap. As a consequence our abstract domain will be set of natural numbers with the usual total order, $\langle \mathsf{N}, \leq \rangle$.

We distinguish between efficiency in time and space. The first one corresponds to the length of a trace, i.e. the number of transitions for executing the system, and the second one to the size of the environment, i.e. the maximum quantity of memory allocated during program execution. It is worth noting that the following definitions are well-formed as we consider partial execution traces, i.e., (possible infinite) sets of finite traces. Recall that Ω denotes an uninitialized variable.

For Time Efficiency, let C be a program, A an architecture, $\mathrm{length} \in [\mathsf{P}(\Sigma^*) \to \mathsf{N}]$ be the length of a trace, and $(\langle \mathsf{P}(\Sigma^*), \subseteq \rangle, \alpha_t, \gamma_t, \langle \mathsf{N}, \leq \rangle)$ be a Galois connection where

$$\alpha_t = \lambda T.\, \sup(\{\mathrm{length}(\tau) \mid \tau \in T\})$$
$$\gamma_t = \lambda n.\, \{\tau \in \mathsf{P}(\Sigma^*) \mid \mathrm{length}(\tau) \leq n\}.$$

We say that the system $\langle A, C \rangle$ respects the time requirement k if

$$\forall S_0 \subseteq \Sigma.\, \alpha_t(s\langle \mathrm{A,C}\rangle(S_0)) \leq k.$$

For Space Efficiency, let C be a program, A an architecture, $\mathrm{size} \in [\mathsf{P}(\Sigma) \to \mathsf{N}]$ be the function defined as

$$\mathrm{size} = \lambda \sigma.\, \#\{x \in \mathrm{Vars} \mid \sigma(x) \neq \Omega\},$$

and $(\langle \mathsf{P}(\Sigma^*), \subseteq \rangle, \alpha_s, \gamma_s, \langle \mathsf{N}, \leq \rangle)$ be a Galois connection where

$$\alpha_s = \lambda T.\, \max_{\tau \in T}\{\mathrm{size}(\sigma) \mid \sigma \in \tau\}$$
$$\gamma_s = \lambda n.\, \{\tau \in \mathsf{P}(\Sigma^*) \mid \forall \sigma \in \tau.\, \mathrm{size}(\sigma) \leq n\} \cdot$$

We say that the system $\langle A, C \rangle$ respects the space requirement k if

$$\forall S_0 \subseteq \Sigma.\, \alpha_s(s\langle \mathrm{A,C}\rangle(S_0)) \leq k.$$

Abstractions

In order to automatically verify time requirements, we must find an upper bound to the number of transitions performed during the execution of a system. Once again, we can do it by using a numerical abstract domain. In fact, we can endow a concrete state σ with a (hidden) variable time, to be incremented at each transition (Halbwachs, 1979). Then, the values taken by time will be upper-approximated in the numerical domain, say by $\overline{\mathrm{time}}$, so that the verification boils to check that $\overline{\mathrm{time}} \leq k$. In the same way, the verification of space requirements can be obtained by abstracting a state with the number of variables different from Ω it contains. The approach can be generalized to more complex languages, e.g., a language with recursive functions. In this case, the stack will be approximated by its height.

In our approach, verification of time and space efficiency requirements can be easily combined by considering the reduced product of the two abstract domains (Cousot & Cousot, 1977).

Example

Let us consider the programs C and C' in Algorithm 1, an architecture A , where the multiplication is a primitive operation, and an architecture A' where the multiplication is implemented as a sequence of additions, e.g., i=i*4 becomes i=i + i;i=i + i . Using the analyzer described in (Cousot, 1999), we can infer:

$$\overline{s}\langle A,C\rangle(\langle i \mapsto [-\infty,+\infty], time \mapsto \underline{0}\rangle) = \langle i \mapsto [1,2^{16}], time \mapsto [0,9]\rangle$$
$$\overline{s}\langle A',C\rangle(\langle i \mapsto [-\infty,+\infty], time \mapsto \underline{0}\rangle) = \langle i \mapsto [1,2^{16}], time \mapsto [0,25]\rangle,$$
$$\overline{s}\langle A,C'\rangle(\langle i \mapsto [-\infty,+\infty], time \mapsto \underline{0}\rangle) = \langle i \mapsto [0,2^{16}], time \mapsto [0,32769]\rangle.$$

Observe that the results above can be used for comparing different programs on different architectures.

Robustness

Informal Definition

Robustness, or dependability, for (Ghezzi, Jazayeri & Mandrioli, 2003) is *"the ability of a program to behave reasonably, even in circumstances that were not anticipated in the specifications"*, for (Meyer, 1997) is *"the ability of software systems to react appropriately to abnormal conditions"*, and for (Kotonya, & Sommerville, 1998) is *"the time to restart after failure"*. Once again, the three definitions are not rigorous enough: the first definition does not specify what is a reasonable behavior, the second one does not specify what is an abnormal condition, and the latter has implicit the strong assumption that all possible failures are considered.

Formal Definition

A software is robust, if any exception raised during its execution, in any architecture and with any initial state, is caught by some exception handler. We recall that exceptions can be raised either by the architecture, e.g., division-by-zero, or by the software itself. As a consequence, a robust program never terminates in an exceptional state.

Let C be a program, and let

$$(\langle P(\Sigma^*),\subseteq\rangle, \alpha_d, \gamma_d, \langle P(\Sigma),\subseteq\rangle)$$

be a Galois connection where

$$\alpha_d = \lambda T. \{\sigma_n \mid \sigma_0...\sigma_n \in T\}$$
$$\gamma_d = \lambda S. \{\sigma_0...\sigma_{n-1}\sigma_n \mid \forall i \in [0, n-1].\sigma \in \Sigma \wedge \sigma_n \in S\}.$$

We say that a system is robust if for all the architectures A ,

$$\forall S_0 \in P(\Sigma). \ \alpha_d(s\langle A,C\rangle(S_0))$$
$$\cap Exceptions \times Env = \varnothing.$$

Abstraction

Robustness can be checked either by considering an abstract domain for inferring the uncaught exceptions (Pessaux & Leroy, 2000), or by considering an abstract domain for reachability analysis (Cousot, 1999). In the first case, a program is robust if the analysis reports that no exception can be raised; in the latter, a program is robust if the analysis reports that the lines of code that may raise an exception (e.g., with a throw statement) are never reached.

Example

Let us consider the program D of Algorithm 1(b). An interval analysis determines that when the true-branch of the if statement is taken, i is different from zero, so that the MathErr exception cannot be raised. In the other case, the exception Err is raised and then it is also caught. As a consequence, D is robust with respct to the chosen abstraction.

Of course, this is just one possible formalization of Robustness. For instance, the system also might know what to do in case any of the possible exceptions happens, and do so while continuing in an operational state. This can be formalized by abstracting properties of the subtraces that originate from a catch statement.

Usability/Accessibility

Informal Definition

The definition of usability (or accessibility) is probably the most contrived one. The definition in (Ghezzi, Jazayeri & Mandrioli, 2003) says that "*software system is usable [...] if its human users find it easy to use*", whereas (Meyer, 1997) talks about ease of use as "*the ease with which people of various backgrounds [...] can learn to use software*" and (Kotonya, & Sommerville, 1998) defines it in function of other, undefined, basic concepts as "*learnability, satisfaction, memorability*".

Formal Definition

In our setting, usability is a abstraction of the output stream that is preserved when a given property, depending on the particular user, is considered. For instance, an abstraction that considers the colors of the output characters can be used to verify if a system is usable for daltonians. We need some auxiliary definitions. Output streams belong to the set Stdout. Given a state $\sigma \in \Sigma$, the function $\text{out} \in [\Sigma \to \text{Stdout}]$ is such that $\text{out}(\sigma)$ is the output stream in the state σ.

Let C be a program, A an architecture, $(\langle \mathsf{P}(\Sigma^*), \subseteq \rangle, \alpha_\Sigma, \gamma_\Sigma, \langle \mathsf{P}(\text{Stdout}), \subseteq \rangle)$ be a Galois connection where

$$\alpha_\Sigma = \lambda T. \{\text{out}(\sigma) \in \Sigma \mid \exists \tau \in T. \sigma \in T\}$$
$$\gamma_\Sigma = \lambda O. \{\tau \in \Sigma^* \mid \forall \sigma \in \tau. \exists o \in O. \text{out}(\sigma) = o\},$$

let $(\langle \mathsf{P}(\text{Stdout}), \subseteq \rangle, \alpha, \gamma, \langle \bar{\mathrm{D}}, \leq \rangle)$ be a Galois connection, and let $\mathrm{p} \in \bar{\mathrm{D}}$. We say that the system $\langle \mathrm{A}, \mathrm{C} \rangle$ is usable w.r.t. the observable p if

$$\forall S_0. \ \alpha(\alpha_\Sigma(s\langle \mathrm{A}, \mathrm{C} \rangle)(S_0)) \leq \mathrm{p}.$$

Abstraction

The definition above can be instantiated to consider the usability of a system for daltonians, i.e., people afflicted by red/green color blindness. In fact, the colors of the output stream can be abstracted in order to collapse together colors indistinguishable by daltonians. As colors are represented by integers in the RGB color system, numerical abstract domains can be used to automatically check properties on colors.

Example

Let us consider the program E in Algorithm 1(d), an architecture where the input stream is a sequence of 0/1 digits, and colors are represented as in RGB schema using 3 bits, i.e. colors range between 0 (black) and 7 (white). Using the static analyzer of (Cousot, 1999) instantiated with the Intervals abstract domain, and refined with trace partitioning (Handjieva & Tzolovski, 1998), one infers that

$$\bar{s}\langle \mathrm{A}, \mathrm{E} \rangle(\ \langle \mathrm{x} \mapsto [0,1], \mathrm{r,g,b} \mapsto [0,1] \rangle)$$
$$= (\langle \mathrm{x} \mapsto [0,1], \mathrm{r,g,b} \mapsto [0,1], \mathrm{col} \mapsto [0,1] \cup [6,7] \rangle),$$

so that as col is always in the set of the colors distinguishable by daltonians (i.e. { black, blue, yellow, white}), E respects the usability specification.

Other Non-Functional Requirements

We showed how four typical non-functional requirements can be encapsulated in our framework. This approach based on preservation of a property up to a given observation, can be easily generalized to other product non-functional requirements. For instance, *upgrade* means that when a new program N, replaces a program O on a given architecture A, then the observed behavior is preserved: $\alpha(s\langle A,N\rangle) \leq \alpha(s\langle A,O\rangle)$. Similarly, if *compatibility* is a property specified by an abstract element c, then we say that two programs P and P′ are compatible w.r.t. c if $\alpha(s\langle A,P\rangle) \leq c$ and $\alpha(s\langle A,P'\rangle) \leq c$.

Non Functional Requirements in Service Oriented Scenarios

In the previous sections, we discussed how Abstract Interpretation theory can be used as a provably sound way to model non functional software requirements and to support their automatic validation. One may argue that the we dealt mainly with a one computer-one program view with statically decidable semantics, which in today's world of dynamic, complex and distributed systems seems a limited domain. In Service Oriented Scenarios, systems interact by asking/providing services, that are expressed in terms of functional and non functional requirements that should satisfy suitable Service Levels Agreements. The adeguacy of the functionalities with respect to the client requirements can be formally verified through type matching techniques.

On the other hand, the approach we advocate in this chapter can be used to verify the adeguacy of non-functional properties of Service Oriented Applications. In fact, one can think of expression non-functional properties in a suitable specification language, and use abstract interpretation-based static analysis tools to verify the conformance of the implementation or of the model with the specification. This is for instance the key idea behind the design and the development of a language agnostic abstract interpretation-based static contract analyzer and checker for .NET, whose static checker can be downloaded as part of the Code Contracts in DevLabs (http://msdn.microsoft.com/en-us/devlabs/dd491992.aspx).

CONCLUSION

Recent very encouraging experiences show that abstract interpretation-based static program analysis can be made efficient and precise enough to formally verify a class of properties for a family of large programs with few or no false alarms, also in case of critical embedded systems (Blanchet, Cousot, Cousot, et al., 2003). We strongly believe that also the treatment of non functional requirements can well fit in this picture. For instance, recent works on Security analysis through Abstract Interpretation (Zanioli & Cortesi, 2011), focussing on information leakage detection, may be seen as another instance of the framework presented in this chapter.

As already mentioned, the key issue (which deserves to be investigated end experimentally validated) is finding appropriate formalizations of the properties to be "observed", by re-using or designing new numerical domains (e.g., this would be the case when approaching requirements like Effectiveness, Availability, Response time, etc.) or logical domains keeping track of dependencies (e.g., for Modifiability of Privacy), or categorical symbolic domains (e.g., for Testability or Supportability).

REFERENCES

Abrial, J.-R. (1996). *The B-Book: Assigning programs to meanings.* Cambridge University Press. doi:10.1017/CBO9780511624162

Abrial, J.-R. (2003). B#: Toward a synthesis between Z and B. In Bert, D., Bowen, J. P., King, S., & Waldén, M. (Eds.), *ZB'2003 - Formal Specification and Development in Z and B, Lecture Notes in Computer Science* (pp. 168–177). Turku, Finland: Springer. doi:10.1007/3-540-44880-2_12

Blanchet, B., Cousot, P., Cousot, R., Feret, J., Mauborgne, M., & Miné, A..... Rival, X. (2003). A static analyzer for large safety-critical software. *Proceedings of the 2003 ACM Conference on Programming Language Design and Implementation (PLDI'03),* (pp. 196-207). ACM Press.

Boehm, B. W. (1976). Software engineering. *IEEE Transactions on Computers*, 1266–41.

Brauburger, J. (1997). Automatic termination analysis for partial functions using polynomial orderings. In P. Van Hentenryck (Ed.), *Proc. 4 th Int. Symp. SAS '97, Paris, Lecture Notes in Computer Science: Vol. 1302,* (pp. 330--344).

Cortesi, A., & Logozzo, F. (2005). Abstract interpretation-based verification of non functional requirements. *Proceedings of the 7th International Conference on Coordination Models and Languages, LNCS 3654, (COORD'05),* (pp. 49-62). Berlin, Germany: Springer-Verlag.

Cousot, P. (1997). Types as abstract interpretations, invited paper. *24th ACM Symposium on Principles of Programming Languages (POPL '97),* (pp. 316-331). ACM Press.

Cousot, P. (1999). The calculational design of a generic abstract interpreter. In Broy, M., & Steinbrüggen, R. (Eds.), *Calculational system design. NATO ASI, Series F.* Amsterdam, The Netherlands: IOS Press.

Cousot, P. (2001). Abstract interpretation based formal methods and future challenges, invited paper. In Wilhelm, R. (Ed.), *Informatics - 10 years back, 10 years ahead, Lecture Notes in Computer Science* (pp. 138–156). Springer-Verlag.

Cousot, P., & Cousot, R. (1977). Abstract interpretation: A unified lattice model for static analysis of programs by construction or approximation of fixpoints. *4th ACM Symposium on Principles of Programming Languages (POPL '77),* (pp. 238-252). ACM Press.

Cousot, P., & Cousot, R. (2002). Systematic design of program transformation frameworks by abstract interpretation. *29th ACM SIGPLAN-SIGACT Symposium on Principles of Programming Languages (POPL '02),* (pp. 178-190). New York, NY: ACM Press.

Cousot, P., & Cousot, R. (2004). An abstract interpretation-based framework for software watermarking. *Conference Record of the Thirtyfirst Annual ACM SIGPLAN-SIGACT Symposium on Principles of Programming Languages*, Venice, Italy, (pp. 173--185). New York, NY: ACM Press.

Cousot, P., & Halbwachs, N. (1978). Automatic discovery of linear restraints among variables of a program. *5th ACM SIGPLAN-SIGACT Symposium on Principles of Programming Languages (POPL '78),* (pp. 84-97). ACM Press.

Davis, A. (1992). *Software Requirements: Objects, functions and states.* Prentice Hall.

Deutsch, M. S., & Willis, R. R. (1988). *Software quality engineering.* Prentice-Hall.

Ghezzi, C., Jazayeri, M., & Mandrioli, D. (2003). *Foundamentals of software engineering* (2nd ed.). Prentice Hall.

Halbwachs, N. (1979). Determination Automatique de Relations Lineaires Verifees par les Variables d'un Programme. *These de 3eme cycle d'informatique, Universite scientifique et medicale de Grenoble.*

Halbwachs, N. (1995). Non-functional requirements in the software development process. *Software Quality, 5*(4), 285–294.

Halbwachs, N. (1998). About synchronous programming and abstract interpretation. *Science of Computer Programming, 31*(1), 75–89. doi:10.1016/S0167-6423(96)00041-X

Handjieva, M., & Tzolovski, S. (1998). Refining static analyses by trace-based partitioning using control flow. *Proceedings of the Static Analysis Symposium (SAS '98), Lectures Notes in Computer Science,* (pp. 200-215). Springer-Verlag.

Hughes, S. (1992). Compile-time garbage collection for higher-order functional languages. *Journal of Logic and Computation, 2*(4), 483–509. doi:10.1093/logcom/2.4.483

IEEE. (1988). *Recommended practice for software requirement specification.* IEEE Press.

Jones, N. D. (1997). Combining abstract interpretation and partial evaluation. In P. Van Hentenryck, (Ed.), *Static analysis, Proc. 4th Int. Symp SAS '97, Paris, Lecture Notes in Computer Science,* (pp. 396-405). Springer-Verlag.

Karlsson, J. (1997). Managing software requirements using quality function deployment. *Software Quality Control, 6*(4), 311–326. doi:10.1023/A:1018580522999

Kotonya, G., & Sommerville, I. (1998). *Requirements engineering - Processes and techniques.* Wiley.

Kozen, D., Palsberg, J., & Schwartzbach, M. I. (1994). Efficient inference of partial types. *Journal of Computer and System Sciences, 49*(2), 306–324. doi:10.1016/S0022-0000(05)80051-0

Lacan, P., Monfort, J. N., Ribal, L. V. Q., Deutsch, A., & Gonthier, A. (1998). The software reliability verification process: The Ariane 5 example. *Proceedings DASIA 98 – Data Systems In Aerospace,* Athens, GR. ESA Publications.

Le Métayer, D. (1996). Program analysis for software engineering: New applications, new requirements, new tools. *ACM Computing Surveys, 28*(4es), 167. doi:10.1145/242224.242435

Meyer, B. (1997). *Object-oriented software construction. Professional technical reference* (2nd ed.). Prentice Hall.

Miné, A. (2001). *The octagon abstract domain. AST 2001 in WCRE 2001* (pp. 310–319). IEEE CS Press.

Monniaux, D. (2003). Abstracting cryptographic protocols with tree automata. *Science of Computer Programming, 47*(2-3), 177–202. doi:10.1016/S0167-6423(02)00132-6

O'Brien, L., Merson, P., & Bass, L. (2007). Quality attributes for service-oriented architectures. *Proceedings of the International Workshop on Systems Development in SOA Environments (May 20 - 26, 2007),* Washington, DC: IEEE Computer Society.

Pessaux, F., & Leroy, X. (2000). Type-based analysis of uncaught exceptions. *TOPLAS, 22*(2), 340–377. doi:10.1145/349214.349230

Sommerville, I. (2000). *Software engineering* (6th ed.). Addison Wesley.

Spivey, J. M. (1992). *The Z notation.* Prentice Hall.

Springer Verlag.

Traub, K. R., Culler, D. E., & Schauser, K. E. (1992). Global analysis for partitioning non-strict programs into sequential threads. *ACM LISP Pointers, 5*(1), 324–334. doi:10.1145/141478.141568

Wada, H., Suzuki, J., & Oba, K. (2006). Modeling non-functional aspects in service oriented architecture. *SCC '06: Proceedings of the IEEE International Conference on Services Computing,* (pp. 222-229). Washington, DC: IEEE Computer Society.

Zanioli, M., & Cortesi, A. (2011). Information leakage analysis by abstract interpretation. Proceedings of the 37th International Conference on Current Trends in Theory and Practice of Computer Science. *Lecture Notes in Computer Science, 6543,* 545–557. doi:10.1007/978-3-642-18381-2_45

KEY TERMS AND DEFINITIONS

Abstract Interpretation: A theory of semantics approximation for computing conservative over-approximations of dynamic properties of programs.

Abstract System: An abstraction of an architecture and of programs running on it.

Portability: Set of properties of the execution of a program that are preserved when it is ported on different architectures.

Space Efficiency: Maximum quantity of memory allocated during program execution.

Software Robustness: A software is robust, if any exception raised during its execution, in any architecture and with any initial state, is caught by some exception handler.

Software Usability: Set of properties of the program's user interface that are preserved during program execution.

ENDNOTE

This chapter is an extended and revised version of (Cortesi & Logozzo, 2005).

Chapter 3
Analysing Time–Related Properties of Service–Oriented Systems

Laura Bocchi
University of Leicester, UK

José Fiadeiro
University of Leicester, UK

Monika Solanki
University of Leicester, UK

Stephen Gilmore
The University of Edinburgh, UK

João Abreu
Altitude Software, Portugal

Vishnu Vankayala
Lapilluz Software Solutions, India

ABSTRACT

We present a formal approach for expressing and analysing time-related properties of service-oriented systems. Our aim is to make it possible for analysts to determine, based on models of services developed at early stages of design, what quality-of-service properties can be expected from, or offered by, the providers of those services. Our approach is based on an extension of SRML, a high-level modelling language developed in the SENSORIA project for architectural and behavioural specification of dynamically reconfigurable service-oriented systems. The proposed language extension offers primitives that capture several kinds of delays that may occur during service provision. Quantitative analysis is supported by mapping SRML models to PEPA, a Markovian process algebra supported by a range of efficient software tools that can either confirm that required properties are met or provide feedback that can be used to improve the SRML model.

DOI: 10.4018/978-1-61350-432-1.ch003

INTRODUCTION

One of the foundational characteristics of service-oriented applications is that they are composed "on the fly" out of services externally procured from potentially different providers. Service requesters select and bind to a required service based on how candidate services meet required functional requirements and maximise expected levels of quality of service, at the time they are needed. For this process to work, it is essential that providers can certify that the published services satisfy the service level agreements (SLAs) that they advertise and, therefore, guarantee the fulfilment of their contractual obligations. For example, one may want to certify that a mortgage-brokerage service satisfies an SLA of the form *"In at least 80% of the cases, a reply to a request for a mortgage proposal will be sent within 7 seconds"* before signing off a contract with a customer. In this chapter, we propose a formal approach to the modelling and analysis of such time-related properties of service-oriented systems.

A number of approaches – see (Balsamo, 2004) for a survey – feature quantitative analysis in the early stages of design in order to prevent design choices from affecting the deployment of systems in a negative way. However, to the best of our knowledge, we are still lacking: (1) a formal model of how such quantitative aspects arise in service-oriented architectures (SOAs), and (2) methods, languages and tools that can be used by designers to develop services that can be certified to meet given timing constraints. One of the challenges raised by such scenarios to the usage of existing quantitative analysis techniques in the context of service-oriented applications is that the full extent of the system through which a service will be provided is not known at design time: designers can only rely on a model of a part of that system plus a number of requirements on the properties of the services to be discovered at run time.

The approach that we propose in this chapter is based on an extension of the SENSORIA Reference Modelling Language – SRML (Fiadeiro, 2010). SRML is a high-level modelling language that supports both the architectural and behavioural specification of service-oriented artefacts. SRML offers a technology-agnostic framework in which models are independent of the languages in which components are implemented and the network protocols through which they communicate. The architectural definition of SRML has been inspired by the Service Component Architecture (SCA) a middleware-independent framework for service deployment proposed by an industrial consortium (SCA Consortium, 2005). SCA makes available a general assembly model and binding mechanisms for service components and clients that may have been programmed in possibly many different languages, e.g., Java, C++, BPEL, or PHP. However, where SCA supports bottom-up low-level design, our aim for SRML is, instead, to address top-down high-level design. More specifically, SRML provides a language for the high-level behavioural description of each element of the architecture and mechanisms that support the design of complex services from business requirements. The analysis techniques that we have been defining for SRML aim at allowing designers to verify or validate properties of composite services that can then be put together from (heterogeneous) service components using assembly and binding techniques such as the ones provided by SCA.

The proposed extension of SRML includes semantic primitives for capturing different kinds of delays that can occur during service provision. Delays are considered at a high level of modelling, i.e., independently of the choice of implementation language or infrastructure, but on the basis of explicit assumptions on how decisions taken at lower levels of design may affect and interfere with timing properties. More precisely, the kind of delays that we model concern the internal structure/behaviour of the service (the time that internal components take to process events and perform computations on their local states), the SOA middleware (the delays that arise due to discovery and selection of external services), and the communication with the services to which they bind.

From a methodological point of view, the proposed extension allows designers to validate a model against a number of time-related requirements (e.g., upper bounds on the delays between interactions) and, from the feedback received by using an analysis tool, improve the overall structure (e.g., by adding or substituting components in the original SRML model) and the individual components themselves to meet such requirements. The delays in a model provide a measure of the upper bounds that should not be exceeded by the implementation of each part of the model. In order to analyse such extended SRML models, we encode them in PEPA (Hillston, 1996), a Markovian process algebra adopted in SENSORIA for quantitative analysis. PEPA has a well-defined semantics and is supported by a range of efficient software tools that can perform the analysis needed for service-level agreements. Our experience showed that PEPA is indeed well suited to give a timed account of behaviour as specified in SRML and evaluate the service-level agreements that are of interest to us in this context.

We illustrate our approach by using a simplified version of a case study on mortgage-brokerage services that we have developed within SENSORIA. The paper proceeds as follows. In Section 2 we present an overview of SRML and PEPA. In Section 3 we present the proposed extension of SRML with delays. In Section 4 we present the encoding of SRML models as PEPA configurations. In Section 5 we discuss the quantitative analysis of such encoded models. Finally, we discuss related work and present our conclusions in Section 6.

BACKGROUND

Assumptions

Services vs. Components

The term 'service' is being widely used in software engineering with a variety of meanings, which suggests that we make clear from the very beginning what precise aspects we are considering in this chapter. Starting from a universe of software components as structural entities, Component-Based Development (CBD), in the sense of (Broy, 2007), views a service as a way of orchestrating interactions among a subset of components in order to obtain some required functionality. (Broy, 2007) sees services as "*crosscutting elements of the system under consideration*", describing "*partial views on the set of components in the system under consideration*". SOC differs in that there is no system conceived a priori that services crosscut, and that services do not compute within a fixed configuration of a universe. Indeed, a very basic difference between SOC and CBD, which we share with (Elfatatry, 2007), is in the fact that SOC deals with run-time, not design-time complexity.

SOC provides a means of obtaining functionalities by orchestrating interactions among components that are procured at run time according to given functional types and service-level constraints. The processes of discovery and selection do not need to be programmed as they are provided by the underlying middleware (SOA) from a dynamically changing repository of services. This means that, when designing a system, we abstract from both the identity of the components that will provide the outsourced functionalities and the process of discovery: we focus instead on the description of the functional and non-functional properties of the required outsourced functionalities. In this context, we use the word *policy* to characterise, in general terms, the elements of a model that concern the dynamic aspects associated with a system – when a required service should be discovered, which SLA requirements the discovered service should satisfy, how it should be initialized, and so on).

The added flexibility provided through SOC comes at a price – dynamic interactions have the overhead of selecting the co-party at each invocation – which means that the choice between invoking a service and calling a component needs to be carefully justified. This is why we consider, in our high-level models, both tight (e.g., between local components) and loose (e.g., with remotely procured services) connections between architectural elements.

We analyse the time properties of a single instance of a model; we abstract from performance issues deriving from the concurrent execution of multiple instances of the model. For example, we model the simultaneous usage of a resource from different entities of the model under consideration, but we do not consider the simultaneous usage of the resource from entities belonging to different instances of the model. Resource contention is modelled as a delay affecting each resource usage. This delay, representing the average time to use a resource, can implicitly reflect the usage of the resource by different instances of the modelled application.

Our approach is concerned with machine-to-machine interactions. The involvement of humans in the process has not been investigated at this stage.

Delays and Their Exponential Distribution

One of the techniques used in this chapter is to annotate individual parts of a model with expressions denoting the delays caused by the usage of those parts in the context of a business protocol, which are then used to analyse time-related properties of the overall module. We associate delays with connectors, resources (e.g., the synchronization delay with a database system), the computations performed by components, the response-time ex-

pected from an external party, and the process of run-time discovery and composition of services. We assume that delays follow an *exponential distribution* of the form $F_{Delay(a,b)}(t) = 1 - e^{-rt}$. The annotations are expressed as *rates* –the coefficients r of the exponential distributions. Intuitively, the exponential distribution defines the probability that a certain event has already happened at time t.

The justification for using exponential distributions derives from the fact that, in practical applications, it is rarely the case that a complete response-time distribution can be obtained for all services in the problem under study. It is far more likely that one will only know the average response time. In this setting, the best possible course of action is to capture the inherent stochasticity in the system through an exponential distribution. The exponential distribution requires only a single parameter – the average response time. Notice that other distributions would require knowledge of higher moments and other parameters, which we do not necessarily have. We take care not to require too many parameters because determining each of them accurately would require careful measurement or estimation. We apply our modelling only in settings where the average response time is a meaningful quantity to use. For example, we do not model systems that have a substantial component requiring a response from a single human participant because the great variance in human response time makes knowledge of the average response time alone insignificant for analysis purposes. This setting connects us to the rich theory of stochastic process including Continuous-Time Markov Chains (CTMC), and a wealth of efficient numerical procedures for their analysis.

A Short Introduction to PEPA

PEPA (Hillston, 1996) is a timed process algebra in which processes perform activities with exponentially-distributed rates. PEPA models consist of a parallel composition of sequential components and thus are finite-state by construction. Activities may be performed in isolation or in cooperation with other components. The term $(\alpha, r).P$ denotes a component that performs activity α with rate r and evolves to P. This can be performed in cooperation with a component $(\alpha, \top).Q$ which allows the other partner in the cooperation to determine the rate of the shared activity (the symbol $\top$ denotes this permission). In the term $P \bowtie_L Q$ components P and Q cooperate on the activities in the set L, but are free to proceed with other activities independently. Finally, a choice such as $(\alpha, p\lambda).P_1 + (\alpha, (1-p)\lambda).P_2$ performs activity α with rate λ and evolves to P_1 with probability p and P_2 with probability $1-p$.

We perform quantitative analysis of SRML models by mapping them to PEPA and using the PEPA analysis tools (Canevet, 2003; Tribastone, 2007).

The Structure of SRML Models

SRML (Fiadeiro, 2010) provides primitives for modelling composite service-oriented applications by orchestrating interactions among local components and services provided by external parties. The SRML unit of design is called a "module".

Figure *1* illustrates the structure of the SRML module *GetMortgage*, which models a service able to find the best mortgage according to per-sonal data and preferences obtained from the client application. *GetMortgage* includes:

1. A provides-interface **CR**, which describes the interface of the service that is offered by the module
2. Three requires-interfaces, **LE**, **BA**, and **IN**, specifying the interfaces to the services that may need to be procured on-the-fly from external parties (the lender, the bank account and the insurance, respectively)
3. A uses-interface **RE** that describes the interface to a persistent resource (in this case a registry of trusted lenders that is consulted when selecting the lender)
4. A component-interface **MA** that specifies the orchestration of the parties involved in the delivery of the service
5. A number of wire-interfaces that specify interaction protocols between different parties

The difference between uses- and requires-interfaces is that, upon instantiation of the module, the former are bound to existing components offering some degree of persistency whereas the latter are instantiated and bound, on the fly, when they are needed by the business process executed by the module. Each requires-interfaces has a trigger event (e.g. *trigger(LE)* for **LE**) that launches the

*Figure 1. Structure of the SRML module G*ET*M*ORTGAGE

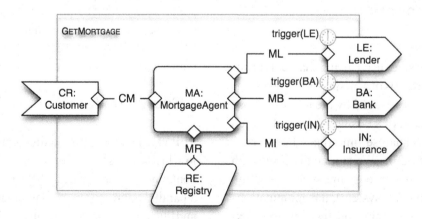

run-time discovery of a service that matches the requires-interface.

Definition 1 (Module)

A *module M* consists of

- A set *nodes(M)* which is the union of the following four disjoint sets:
  - *provides(M)* consisting of a single "provides-interface",
  - *uses(M)* consisting of "uses-interfaces",
  - *requires(M)* consisting of "requires-interfaces",
  - *components(M)* consisting of "component-interfaces" (or components for short).
- A set *edges(M)* of edges ("wire-interfaces") where each edge *w* is a set of two nodes *w:m↔n*.
- An internal configuration policy *trigger(n)* for every *n∈requires(M)*, which defines the event that triggers the discovery of *n*. Every *trigger(n)* is a pair *(m,e)* where *m∈nodes(M)* and *e* is an event published by *m* as part of an interaction between the components that bind to *n* and *m*.
- A labelling function *label$_M$* that associates a behavioural specification with every node.
- An external configuration policy *cs(M)* that describes the SLA properties of *M*.

For every node *n*, the behavioural specification associated with it consists of a signature *sign(label$_M$(n))* — the set of interactions that the entity *n* can engage in — and a definition of the behavioural protocol that is required of those interactions. Different formalisms are used for defining the behavioural protocol depending on the nature of the node as described in Sections 2.4, 2.5 and 2.6.

All behavioural specifications are based on the same computational model (Abreu, 2008).

SRML supports a number of interaction types to reflect both the interactions occurring within an enterprise and the typical business conversations that arise in (Benatallah, 2004). More specifically, interactions can be synchronous (i.e., the party waits for the co-party to reply), or asynchronous (i.e., the party does not block). Typically, synchronous interactions occur in communications with persistent components, namely through uses-interfaces, reflecting interconnections based on the exchange of *products* (clientship as in OO). Asynchronous interactions are non-blocking. We distinguish the following types of interactions, each described from the point of view of the party in which it is declared:

- **snd** and **rcv** are one-way asynchronous (send or receive) interactions.
- **s&r** and **r&s** are conversational asynchronous interactions. The interaction **s&r** is initiated by the party, and the interaction **r&s** is initiated by the co-party.
- **ask** and **tll** (resp. **prf** and **rsp**) are synchronous interactions initiated by the party/co-party to obtain data (resp. to ask to perform an operation).

Asynchronous interactions are associated with one or more *interaction events*. One-way interactions (i.e., **snd** and **rcv**) are associated only with event *interaction⏁*, which is the initiation event for *interaction*. Conversational interactions (i.e., **s&r** and **r&s**) involve a number of events exchanged between the two parties:

- interaction⏁: The event of initiating *interaction*.
- interaction⊠: The reply-event of *interaction*.
- interaction✓: The commit-event of *interaction*.
- interaction✗: The cancel-event of *interaction*.

- interaction ⚕: The revoke-event of *interaction*.

The meaning of these events should be self-explanatory: once the initiation event $e\boxtimes$ is issued by a party, a reply-event $e\boxtimes$ is sent by the co-party. Then, the party that initiated the conversation may either commit to the deal (issuing $e\checkmark$) or cancel the interaction (issuing $e\boldsymbol{\times}$); after committing, the party can still revoke the deal (issuing $e⚕$), triggering a compensation mechanism. We abstract here from the parameters exchanged in the interactions, as they are not involved in the performance analysis.

The textual specification of GETMORTGAGE – defining nodes, triggers and wires – is given below. The trigger *trigger(LE)* of **LE** is the event *getProposal*⌂ occurring in **MA**. When the trigger is set to default, the service is discovered at the first attempt to interact with it. Each node is associated with a specification. For instance, **CR** is associated with *Customer,* **LE** to *Lender*, and so on. The wire *ML:MA↔LE* is defined as a set of pairs *<a,b>* where *a* is an interaction of *MA* and *b* is the corresponding interaction of *LE*. We omit the other wires as they are defined in a similar way. In the rest of this section we present in more detail the specifications for each type of node.

```
MODULE GetMortgages is
PROVIDES
   CR: Customer
REQUIRES
   LE: Lender          trigger(LE):
MA.getproposal⌂?
   BA: Bank            trigger(BA): de-
fault
   IN: Insurance           trigger(IN):
default
COMPONENTS
   MA: MortgageAgent
USES
   RE: Registry
WIRES
```

```
ML:{<askProposal,askProposal>,<si
gnOut,getSignature>,
      <confirmation,confirm>}
```

Business Roles

The behavioural description of each SRML node *n∈components(M)* is given as a "business role".

Definition 2 (Business Role)

The business role of a node *n∈components(M)* consists of:

- A signature *sign(label_M(n))*
- An orchestration consisting of a set of transitions *trans(label_M (n))* defined on the events associated with the interactions in *sign(label_M(n))*.

The set of transitions can be modelled as a UML statechart diagram involving two types of nodes – state-nodes and transition-nodes. Each *SRML transition* (i.e., each element of *trans(label_M(n))*) is represented in the statechart by a transition-node. According to our computational model, the execution of a transition involves two steps. The first step (from a state-node) consists in the processing of the event that triggers the transition, which leads to an intermediate state (a transition-node). In the second step, depending on the values of the parameters attached to the triggering event, the SRML transition may branch to a number of exit states (state-nodes).

Figure 2 illustrates a fragment of the statechart diagram that defines the orchestration of the business role *MortgageAgent* that labels the component-interface *MA*. The signature of this business role includes *getProposal*—a conversational interaction that *CR* initiates with *MA*—and *askProposal*, which is used by *MA* to initiate a conversation with *LE*. The diagram defines two transitions *GetClientRequest* and *GetProposal*:

Figure 2. Fragment of the orchestration of **MortgageAgent**

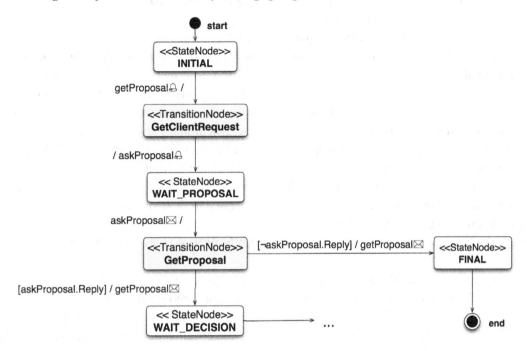

- *GetClientRequest* is triggered by *getProposal*◬ (i.e., the customer initiates a conversation asking for a mortgage proposal) and is guarded by the fact that the process is in the state *INITIAL*. The execution of transition *GetClientRequest* publishes the event *askProposal*◬ (i.e., the mortgage agent initiates a conversation with the lender to ask for a proposal) and moves the process to the state WAIT_PROPOSAL.
- *GetProposal* is triggered by *askProposal*⊠ (i.e., the mortgage agent receives the reply from the lender) and forwards the reply to the customer through *getProposal*⊠. Depending on the value of the Boolean parameter *Reply*, the business process either proceeds (i.e., goes to state *WAIT_DECISION*, waiting for the decision of the customer on whether to accept the proposal) or terminates (i.e., goes to state *FINAL*).

Business Protocols

The specifications used for SRML provides- and requires-interfaces are called "business protocols".

Definition 3 (Business Protocol)

The business protocol of $n \in requires(M) \cup provides(M)$ consists of:

- A signature $sign(label_M(n))$
- A behaviour specification consisting of a set of statements *statements(n)* defined on the events associated with the interactions in $sign(label_M(n))$.

Each statement in *statements(n)* captures typical patterns of conversational behaviour that arise in service provision. The semantics of such statements is expressed as sentences of the temporal logic UCTL (Beek 2008), which facilitates the use of model-checking techniques for analysing functional properties (Abreu, 2009). Statements are defined on events using the connectives below. Hereafter we use *e!* to refer to the publication (i.e., sending/issuing) of event *e* by the sender, and *e?* for the processing of *e* by the receiver. If we want to refer generically to either of them we use *e**.

- *initiallyEnablede?* — the event *e* is never discarded until it is executed.
- e_1*enablese$_2$?untile$_3$** — after e_1* happens, and while e_3* does not happen, e_2? will not be discarded. Also, e_2? cannot be executed either before e_1* or after e_3*.
- e_1*ensurese$_2$!* — e_2 will be published after, but not before, e_1* happens.

As an example, consider the business protocol *Lender* — the specification of the requires-interface *LE*:

```
sign(label_GETMORTGAGE(LE))
= {r&saskProposal,
rcvsignOut,sndconfirm}
statements(LE) = {initiallyEnabledask
Proposal🔔?,
    askProposal✔?enablesaskProposal🛡
?untilgetSignature🔔?,
    getSignature🔔?ensuresconfirm🔔
! }
```

The statement *initiallyEnabledaskProposal🔔?* is used to express that the lender should be ready to accept a request for a proposal from the moment it is bound to the mortgage agent. The statement *askProposal✔?enablesaskProposal🛡?untilgetSignature🔔?* is used to express that if the lender receives a confirmation then it allows the co-party to revoke the loan contract but only until the contract is signed. The statement *getSignature🔔?ensuresconfirm✉!* is used to express that the lender will send a confirmation to *MA* once a signature is received.

Layer Protocols

Uses-interfaces specify synchronous interactions with persistent components, for instance to obtain or store information in database systems. Their specifications are called "layer protocols". Typically, the interactions involved in layer protocols are synchronous and specified through pre/post conditions. For simplicity, we omit their specifications and restrict ourselves to layer protocols that merely expose the synchronous interactions declared in their signatures.

Definition 4 (Layer Protocol)

The layer protocol of a node $n \in uses(M)$ consists of a signature $sign(label_M(n))$.

As an example, the layer protocol *Registry* — the specification of the uses-interface *RE*— consists of the signature:

```
sign(label_GETMORTGAGE(RE)) = {tll-
getLenders}
```

External Configuration Policies (SLA Constraints)

In SRML, we express SLAs using the algebraic approach developed in (Bistarelli, 1997) for constraint satisfaction and optimization based on c-semirings. A precise account on SLA in SRML can be found in (Fiadeiro, 2010).

Every SRML module includes an external configuration policy consisting of a constraint system defined on a fixed fuzzy c-semiring, i.e., the degree of satisfaction lies in the range [0, 1]. More specifically, an external configuration policy $cs(M)$ consists of

- A set of SLA variables $var_{SLA}(M)$,
- A set of constraints $SLA(M)$.

The variables and constraints determine the quality profile to which the provided service and each discovered service need to adhere. Below we show *cs(GETMORTGAGE)*.

```
EXTERNAL POLICY
    SLA VARIABLES
        CR.AVAILABILITY, LE.AVAILABILITY,
BA.AVAILABILITY, IN.AVAILABILITY,
        LE.ServiceId,
        CR.COST, LE.COST, CR.RESPONSE-
TIME, LE.RESPONSETIME
    CONSTRAINTS
    C₁:          {CR.AVAILABILITY, LE.
AVAILABILITY, BA.AVAILABILITY, IN.AVAILABILITY}
```

$$def(c,t,u,v) = \begin{cases} 1 & \text{if } c \leq \min(10,t,u,v) \\ 0 & \text{otherwise} \end{cases}$$

C_2:   {LE.ServiceId}

$$def(s) = \begin{cases} 1 & \text{if } s \in RE.askLenders \\ 0 & \text{otherwise} \end{cases}$$

C_3:   {CR.COST, LE.COST}

$$def(c,t) = \begin{cases} 0 & \text{if } t > c \\ c - t & \text{otherwise} \end{cases}$$

The set $var_{SLA}(GETMORTGAGE)$ includes the following SLA variables:

- *CR.AVAILABILITY* represents the availability provided by *GETMORTGAGE* through the interface *CR*.
- *LE.AVAILABILITY*, *BA.AVAILABILITY* and *IN.AVAILABILITY* represent the availabilities required by the module for interfaces *LE*, *BA*, and *IN*, respectively.
- *LE.ServiceId* represents the service identifier (e.g., URI) of *LE*. It represents a specific service implementation/identity/provider[1].
- *CR.COST* and *LE.COST* are the cost for a transaction asked to the customer and by the lender.
- *CR.RESPONSETIME*, *LE.RESPONSETIME* are the response times promised to the customer and by the lender.

We consider three constraints in *SLA(GETMORTGAGE)*:

- C_1 states that the availability provided by the service is not higher than each of the availabilities of the external services. Here 10 represents a lower bound that can be ensured by the internal components of the module itself.
- C_2 states that, during the discovery of the service matching *Lender*, the considered services will be only those among the trusted set of lenders,
- C_3 states that there will be a positive charge for the customer. This constraint also aims at optimizing the income of the module (i.e., the difference between the charge asked to the customer and the charge asked by the lender).

Defining a property through the constraint system ensures that we find a solution (if there exists any) that respects the requirements and constraints of each party, namely the parties reach a SLA that expresses all the mutual requirements. In this way, a requester will select only those external services that promise to meet the requirements the requester desires, and a provider will not sign a contract that promises more than the provider wanted to advertise.

Nevertheless, the constraint system does not ensure that the properties expressed by a party can in fact be met by the provided service implementation. The violation of an agreed QoS property is undesirable to the provider as he could be subject to a fine. On the other hand, the provider may accept a reasonably small degree of risk, considering that a too pessimistic advertisement would fail to attract customers. In this paper we present an approach for analysing the probability that a time-related SLA can be met by a model. As an example, consider the following SLA constraint for *GETMORTGAGE*:

$C_4:$ $\{CR.\textsc{ResponseTime}, LE.\textsc{ResponseTime}\}$

$$def(c,t) = \begin{cases} 1 \text{ if } c \geq 7 \text{ and } t \leq 0.79 \\ 0 \text{ otherwise} \end{cases}$$

C_4 promises that the provider of *GetMortgage* will deliver a response within 7 seconds and requires *LE* a response time of at most 0.79 seconds. In the next sections, we will use the proposed approach to certify that the property expressed above is met in at least 80% of the cases.

TIMING IN SRML MODELS

In this section we extend SRML in order to model the delays involved in the business process through which a service is provided. We analyse properties such as the one discussed in Section 1, e.g., properties that certify that *GetMortgage* can guarantee, with a certain probability, that the reply to a mortgage proposal requested by a customer remains within a given bound. This approach draws from the work developed in (Vankayala, 2008) and builds on the computational and coordination model that was presented in (Abreu, 2008).

Given two events *a* and *b*, we denote by *Delay(a,b)* the time that separates their occurrences, e.g., *Delay(getProposal⏏,getProposal⊠)* in the example above. As explained in Section 2, we assume that such delays follow an exponential distribution of the form $F_{Delay(a,b)}(t)=1-e^{-rt}$. The rate *r* is associated with the entity that processes and publishes the events, and used as a modelling primitive in the proposed extension of SRML.

Event-based selection of continuations in SRML is modelled through probabilistic choice in PEPA. We estimate the probability of the relative outcomes and use the resulting probabilities to weigh the rates in the PEPA model to ensure the correct distribution across the continuations. In this way, all number distributions remain exponential and thus we can achieve probabilistic branching while remaining in the continuous-time Markovian realm.

We list below the kinds of delay that, according to the computation and coordination model of SRML, can affect service execution. The rates can be negotiated as SLAs with service providers in the constraint systems mentioned in Section 2.7.

- **Delays in components:** because they may be busy, components store the events they receive in a buffer where they wait until they are processed, at which point they are either executed or discarded. Two kinds of rates are involved in this process:
  - **processingRate:** this rate represents the time taken by the component to remove an event from the buffer. Different components may have different processing rates but all events are treated equally by the same component.
  - **executionRate:** this represents the time taken by the component to perform the transition triggered by the event, i.e. making changes to the state and publishing events. We assume that discarding an event does not take time. Each transition declared in a business role has its own execution rate, which should be chosen taking into account the specific effects of that transition.
- **Delays in requires-interfaces:** as already mentioned, requires-interfaces represent parties that have to be discovered at run time when the corresponding trigger becomes true. Two kinds of rates are involved in this process:
  - **compositionRate:** this rate applies to the run-time discovery, selection and binding processes as performed by the middleware, i.e. (1) the time to connect to a broker, (2) the time for matchmaking, ranking and selection, and (3) the time to bind the selected service. We chose to let differ-

ent requires-interfaces have different composition rates in order to reflect the fact that different brokers may be involved, depending on the nature of the required external services.

◦ **responseRate:** these are rates that apply to the responses that the business protocol requires of the external service through statements of the form e_1 *ensurese*$_2$!. More specifically, we consider a rate *responseRate(e$_1$,e$_2$)* for each such pair of events, which include *responseRate(a⌂,a⌧)* for every interaction *a* of type **r&s** declared in the business protocol.

- **Delays in wires:** each wire of a module has an associated transfer rate.
- **Delays in synchronous communication and resource contention:** the interface of a resource consists of a number of synchronous interactions. We define a synchronisation rate for each such interaction and associate it with the events that resolve synchronisation requests by replying to a query or executing an operation.

In summary, we extend every module *M* with a time annotation *A(M)* that consists of several collections of rates. Each rate is a term of type $R^+ \cup \{T\}$, where T is the passive rate — an event with a passive rate occurs only in collaboration with another event, when this second event is ready.

Definition 5 (Time Annotation)

A time annotation *A(M)* for a module *M* consists of the following rates:

- For every requires-interface *n∈requires(M)*
  ◦ *compositionRate(n)*
  ◦ *responseRate(n)(e$_1$,e$_2$)* for every statement of the type e_1 *ensurese*$_2$!
- For every *w∈edges(M)*
  ◦ *transferRate(w).*

- For every *n∈components(M)*
  ◦ *processingRate(n)*
  ◦ *executionRate(n,P)* for every transition *P∈trans(label$_M$(n))*
- For every *n∈components(M)∪uses(M)* and interaction *a* of type *rpl/prf*
  ◦ *synchronisationRate(n)(a).*

The sequence diagram in Figure 3 illustrates how the response time associated with *getProposal⌂* in *CR* depends on the delays associated with the rates discussed in this section.

REPRESENTING SRML MODULES AS PEPA CONFIGURATIONS

In this section, we explain how a SRML module can be coded as a stochastic process so that the timing properties that derive from the timing annotation of the module can be analysed using PEPA.

This encoding involves several steps. First, the structure of the SRML module is decomposed into a PEPA configuration consisting of a number of PEPA terms. Each PEPA term corresponds to either a node or a wire of the original SRML model. In this way, we can easily map the results of the quantitative analysis back to the original SRML specification. Second, the behavioural interface of each entity of the SRML model is encoded into a PEPA term, making it possible to analyse the delays due to each single component. We use $\langle\langle m \rangle\rangle = t$ to express that the encoding of the SRML element *m* is the PEPA term *t*.

Encoding the Modules

In SRML, the signatures (sets of interactions) associated with specifications of different entities involved in a module are not assumed to be mutually disjoint. This is because we want to promote reuse, which is also why interconnections are established explicitly through wires. Therefore, because in PEPA interconnections are based on

Figure 3. Cascade of delays in a fragment of GETMORTGAGE

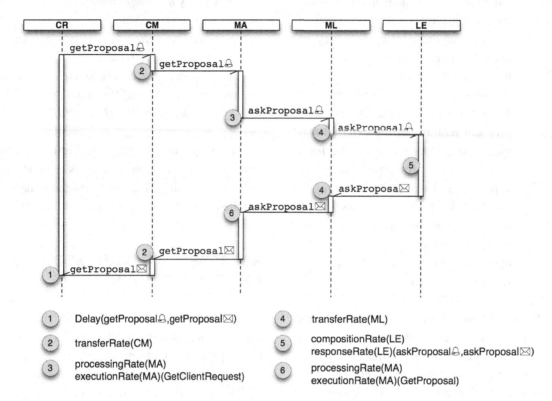

shared names, the first step of our encoding consists of renaming all the interactions to guarantee that the interconnections of the SRML model are properly represented by the scopes of action names in PEPA. We do so by defining, for every node n, its encoding signature $esign_M(n)$ obtained by prefixing each interaction name in $sign(label_M(n))$ with n. That is, given an asynchronous interaction a, $\langle\langle a\triangle\rangle\rangle=n.a\triangle$, $\langle\langle a\boxtimes\rangle\rangle=n.a\boxtimes$, $\langle\langle a\checkmark\rangle\rangle=n.$ $a\checkmark$, $\langle\langle a\boldsymbol{x}\rangle\rangle=n.a\boldsymbol{x}$, $\langle\langle a\dagger\rangle\rangle=n.a\dagger$, and for every synchronous interaction i, $\langle\langle i\rangle\rangle=n.i$.

The overall encoding $\langle\langle M\rangle\rangle$ of a module M is a cooperation process that includes one sequential component for each node of M, one sequential component for each edge of M, and one additional sequential component for each requires-interface:

$$\langle\langle M\rangle\rangle = \prod_{n\in nodes(M)} \langle\langle n\rangle\rangle \bowtie_L \prod_{w\in edges(M)} \langle\langle w\rangle\rangle$$
$$\bowtie_Q \prod_{n\in requires(M)} \langle\langle trigger_n\rangle\rangle$$

The cooperation set L includes all the interaction events associated with all the interaction names of all the nodes (note that the synchronisation event associated with synchronous interaction types has the same name as the interaction):

$$L=\cup_{n\in nodes(M)}\cup_{i\in esignM(n)} \{i\triangle, i\boxtimes, i\checkmark, i\boldsymbol{x}, i\dagger, i\}$$

The cooperation set Q includes all the interaction events that act as triggers for requires-interfaces and, for each requires interface n, an event *discovery$_n$* that controls the discovery process associated with n:

$$Q=\{m.e: trigger(n)=(m,e), n\in requires(M)\}\cup\{discovery_n:n\in requires(M)\}$$

For every requires-interface n with $trigger(n)=(m,e)$, the process $\langle\langle trigger(n)\rangle\rangle$ is defined by the equation:

$\langle\langle trigger(n)\rangle\rangle = P$ where $P=(m.e, \top).(discover\ y_n, compositionRate(n)).P$

This term models the delay due to the discovery process that occurs when the trigger becomes true. As shown later, a wire connecting a node to a requires-interface n must wait for the activity $discover_n$ to complete before enacting any interaction with n.

Example 1 (Encoding a Module)

The encoding of the module structure of GET-MORTGAGE is:

$\langle\langle$ GETMORTGAGE $\rangle\rangle =$

 $\langle\langle$ CR $\rangle\rangle$ | $\langle\langle$ MA $\rangle\rangle$ | $\langle\langle$ LE $\rangle\rangle$ | $\langle\langle$ BA $\rangle\rangle$ | $\langle\langle$ IN $\rangle\rangle$ | $\langle\langle$ RE $\rangle\rangle$

 $\bowtie_L$ $\langle\langle$ CM $\rangle\rangle$ | $\langle\langle$ MR $\rangle\rangle$ | $\langle\langle$ ML $\rangle\rangle$ | $\langle\langle$ MB $\rangle\rangle$ | $\langle\langle$ MI $\rangle\rangle$

 $\bowtie_Q$ $\langle\langle$ trigger(LE) $\rangle\rangle$ | $\langle\langle$ trigger(BA) $\rangle\rangle$ | $\langle\langle$ trigger(IN) $\rangle\rangle$

The set L includes all the interaction events associated with the signatures of the nodes *CR, MA, LE, BA, IN, RE*. The set Q includes the triggering events and the special discovery event for each requires-interface:

- $L=\{CR.getProposal\ominus, CR.getProposal\boxtimes, CR.getProposal\checkmark, CR.getProposal\times, CR.getProposal\maltese, LE.askProposal\ominus, LE.askProposal\boxtimes,... \}$
- $Q = \{ MA.getProposal\ominus, discovery_{LE}, BA.openAccount\ominus, discovery_{BA}, IN.getInsurance\ominus, discovery_{IN}\}$

We discuss later how the encodings of nodes and edges are obtained.

We show below the equations that define the encoding of the triggers of *LE* and *BA* (the trigger of *IN* is similar). Recall that *trigger(LE) = (getProposal⊖,MA)* and *trigger(BA) = (getProposal⊖,BA)*.

$\langle\langle trigger(LE)\rangle\rangle =(MA.getProposal\ominus, \top).(discovery_{LE}, compositionRate(LE)). \langle\langle trigger(LE)\rangle\rangle$

$\langle\langle trigger(BA)\rangle\rangle =(BA.getProposal\ominus, \top).(discovery_{BA}, compositionRate(BA)). \langle\langle trigger(BA)\rangle\rangle$

The following propositions show that the architectural information (i.e., of the structure) of a SRML module is preserved by the encoding into PEPA. In other words, the graph-like structure of a SRML module is still described by the 'flattened' PEPA configuration expressed as the parallel composition of processes. Hereafter we assume that the set of node names is disjoint from the set of interactions names, and that each node does not have an interaction name connected with more than one wire.

Proposition 1 (Uniqueness of Names in Nodes)

The encoding signatures of all the nodes of a SRML module are pairwise disjoint.

Proof

Since (1) all the names of the nodes in a module are pairwise distinct, (2) all the interaction names in a node are pairwise distinct and (3) the interaction names for the encoding of each node are obtained by appending interaction names to the names of the node, there is no pair of nodes whose encoding signatures contain the same interaction name.

Proposition 2 (Uniqueness of Names in Wires)

The encoding signatures of the wires of a module are pairwise disjoint.

Proof

Since (1) the encoding signature of an edge is a subset of elements from two encoding signatures of nodes, (2) for Proposition 1 the encoding signatures of nodes are pairwise disjoint and (3) any interaction name of a node is assumed to be connected to at most one edge, there is no pair of edges whose encoding signatures contain the same interaction name.

Proposition 3 (Structure Preservation)

The cooperating terms in $\langle\langle M \rangle\rangle$ correspond to a node and a wire that in M are contiguous.

Proof

Straightforward from Proposition 1 and Proposition 2, observing that the cooperation activities of $\langle\langle M \rangle\rangle$ are always between exactly one term representing a node and exactly one term representing an edge.

Encoding Components

The PEPA term corresponding to a component-interface n is obtained in two steps: first, we refine the statechart that defines the business role associated with n, and then we apply the translation provided by the PEPA toolset (Canevet, 2003) to obtain the corresponding PEPA term.

The refinement of the statechart is performed in three sub-steps. Firstly, the events that occur in the SRML statechart are translated using $esign_M(n)$ as defined previously. Secondly, we assign a probability to the branches of the statechart that are associated with each SRML transition. More precisely, given a transition P with n branches P_{ci}, we associate a probability p_{ci} with each branch such that $\sum_{i=1..n} p_{ci} = 1$. Designers can assign these probabilities taking into account specific knowledge of the application domain, or decide for an equal probability $1/n$, or otherwise experiment with different values to analyse different possible behaviours. Thirdly, we assign the rates: for every SRML transition P of a component n, the incoming arrow is assigned the rate *processingRate(n)* and each branch

P_{ci} is assigned the rate $p_{ci} \times executionRate(n,P)$. Figure 4 illustrates the statechart diagram for the orchestration of *MA*, annotated with information on *executionRate* for each transition. Whenever there are synchronous interactions involved in the statechart diagram, we assign the passive rate to *ask* and *prf* interactions and the synchronization rate to *tll* and *rsp* interactions.

Wires and Interaction Protocols

In order to encode a SRML edge $w{:}m\leftrightarrow n$, we consider first the case when none of the nodes involved is a requires-interface. In this case, all we have to do is model the transfer of the events from one component to the other. As discussed in Section 2, every wire w defines a set of pairs of interactions *pairs(w)*. We define:

$$\langle\langle w \rangle\rangle = \prod_{<a,b>\in pairs(w)} \langle\langle <a,b> \rangle\rangle$$

The encoding of the pairs of interactions depends on their types. In the case of a pair of type $<s\&r,r\&s>$, the wire forwards the initiation, commit, cancel and revoke events from n to m and the reply back from m to n. We assign the delay $r=transferRate(w)$ to the second leg (delivery to the target). The encoding is defined by the equations

$$\langle\langle <a,b> \rangle\rangle = Q$$

$Q = (n.a\triangle,T).(m.b\triangle,r).Q + (m.b\boxtimes,T).$
$(n.a\boxtimes,r).Q + (n.a\checkmark,T).(m.b\checkmark,r).Q +$

$+ (n.a\boldsymbol{\times},T).(m.b\boldsymbol{\times},r).Q + (n.a\text{⇪},T).(m.b\text{⇪},r).Q$

The encoding that applies to the other types of interactions is defined in a similar way. In the case of a one-way asynchronous protocol $<snd,rcv>$ the encoding only includes event $\triangle$.

In the case of a synchronous interaction $<ask,rpl>$ (the case of $<tll,prf>$ being identical) the encoding is defined by the equation:

Figure 4. Statechart for MA with the notation for performance analysis

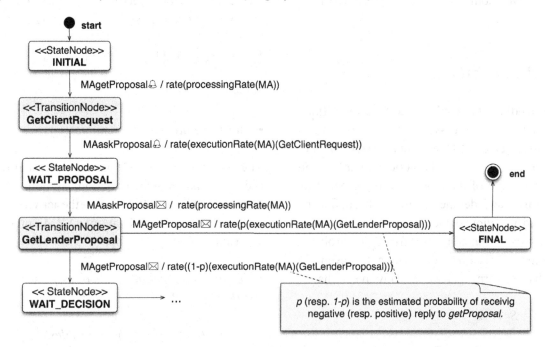

$\langle\langle <a,b> \rangle\rangle = (n.a, \top).(m.b\triangle, synchronisationRat$
$e(m,b)).\ \langle\langle <a,b> \rangle\rangle$

In the case of an edge connecting a requires-interface *n*, the encoding is:

$\langle\langle\ w\ \rangle\rangle = (discovery_n, \top).\prod_{<a,b> \in pairs(w)} \langle\langle <a,b> \rangle\rangle$

Example 2 (Encoding a Wire)

The encoding of the wire *ML* of *GETMORTGAGE* is given through the equations below, where *pairs(ML)* = {*<askProposal,askProposal>*, *<signOut,getSignature>*, *<conformation,confirm>*}. Note that the first pair is of type *<s&r,r&s>*, the second of type *<snd,rcv>* and the third of type *<rcv,snd>*.

$\langle\langle ML \rangle\rangle = P_{ML}$

$P_{ML} = (discovery_{LE}, \top).(MA.askProposal\triangle, \top).$
$P_{MLB} + (LE.askProposal\boxtimes, \top).P_{MLE} +$

$+ (MA.askProposal\checkmark, \top).P_{MLV} + (MA.$
$askProposal\times, \top).P_{MLF} +$

$+ (MA.askProposal\dagger, \top).P_{MLR} + (MA.$
$signOut\triangle, \top).P'_{MLB} + (LE.confirm\triangle, \top).P''_{MLB}$

$P_{MLB} = (LE.askProposal\triangle, transferRate(ML)).$
P_{ML}

$P_{MLE} = (LE.askProposal\boxtimes, transferRate(ML)).$
P_{ML}

$P_{MLC} = (LE.askProposal\checkmark, transferRate(ML)).$
P_{ML}

$P_{MLF} = (LE.askProposal\times, transferRate(ML)).P_{ML}$

$P_{MLR} = (LE.askProposal\dagger, transferRate(ML)).$
P_{ML}

$P'_{MLB} = (LE.getSigature\triangle, transferRate(ML)).$
P_{ML}

$P''_{MLB} = (MA.confirmation \ominus, transferRate(ML)).$
P_{ML}

Requires-Interfaces

The encoding of a requires-interface n is defined in terms of two processes that cooperate over a set L that includes all the events in $esign_M(n)$ and, for each $e \in esign_M(n)$, the actions $enables_e$ and $disables_e$. One of the processes (represented by the term S_n) encodes the statements that define the required behaviour of the external party. The other process (represented by the term E_n) controls the enabling and disabling of the interaction events in which the external party can be involved. That is,

$$\langle\langle\, n \,\rangle\rangle = S_n \bowtie_L E_n$$

Let us consider each process in turn, starting with E_n. We need to control the incoming events, i.e. those received by the external party, all of which have a passive rate. The outgoing events are controlled by the components that receive them through the use of guards as discussed before.

$E_n = \prod_{type(i)=rcv} E(n.i \ominus) \prod_{type(i)=s\&r} E(n.i \boxtimes) \prod_{type(i)=r\&s} E(n.i \ominus) \mid E(n.i\checkmark) \mid E(n.i\times) \mid E(n.i \dagger)$

$E(e) = (enables_e, \top).$
$(e, \top).E(e)+(disables_e, \top).E(e)$

That is, $E(e)$ synchronises with the enabling of the event, after which it either executes it or disables it again.

Consider now the term S_n. We have seen in Section 2.5 that the business protocol associated with a requires-interface n defines a set of statements $statements_M(n)$. We distinguish three kinds of statements: those that use the connective *initiallyEnabled*, the set of which we denote by IE; those that use *enablesUntil*, the set of which we denote by EU; and those of the form *ensures*,

the set of which we denote by ES. Each kind of statement is encoded separately, leading to:

$$S_n = \prod_{s \in IE} \langle\langle s \rangle\rangle \prod_{s \in EU} \langle\langle s \rangle\rangle \prod_{s \in ES} \langle\langle s \rangle\rangle$$

Where

- $\langle\langle initiallyEnabled\, e? \rangle\rangle = enables\langle\langle_e \rangle\rangle$

The enabling action for e has no associated rate (i.e., it is an immediate action, as defined in (Argent-Katwala, 2008) because the activity does not involve any of the delays of a SRML module we want to analyse.

- $\langle\langle e_1 *enables\, e_2? until_3 * \rangle\rangle = (\langle\langle e_1 \rangle\rangle, \top).$
$P_1 + (\langle\langle e_3 \rangle\rangle, \top).P_2$

$P_1 = enables\langle\langle_{e2} \rangle\rangle.(\langle\langle e_3 \rangle\rangle, \top).disables\langle\langle_{e2} \rangle\rangle.$
$\langle\langle e_1 * enables\, e_2? until_3 * \rangle\rangle$

$P_2 = disables\langle\langle_{e2} \rangle\rangle.\langle\langle e_1 * enables\, e_2? until_3 * \rangle\rangle$

We distinguish between the situation in which e_3 occurs first, disabling e_2, or e_1 occurs first, enabling e_2 until e_3 occurs. The enabling/disabling actions are immediate.

- $\langle\langle e_1 *ensures\, e_2! \rangle\rangle = (\langle\langle e_1 \rangle\rangle, \top).$
$(\langle\langle e_2 \rangle\rangle, responseRate(n)(e_1, e_2)).\langle\langle e_1 *ensures\, e_2! \rangle\rangle$

That is, the execution of e_1 is followed by that of e_2 with a delay whose rate is given by an SLA variable as discussed in Section 3.

Example 3 (Encoding a Requires-Interface)

We consider the requires-interface LE:

$$\langle\langle\, LE \,\rangle\rangle = S_n \bowtie_L E_n$$

• E_n is the parallel composition of *E(e)* for the following events: *askProposal⌂, askProposal✓, askProposal✗, askProposal✝, signOut⌂*. We only show the case of *askProposal⌂*:

$E(askProposal⌂) = (enables_{askProposal}⌂, \top).E'(askProposal⌂)$

$E'(askProposal⌂) = (askProposal⌂, \top).E(askProposal⌂)$

$+(disables_{askProposal}⌂, \top).E(askProposal⌂)$

• S_n is defined as the parallel composition of the encoding of each statement in *statements(LE)*:

$\langle\langle initiallyEnabledaskProposal⌂?\rangle\rangle = enables\langle\langle_{askProposal}⌂_?\rangle\rangle = enables_{LE.askProposal}⌂$

$\langle\langle askProposal✓?enablesaskProposal✝?untilgetSignature⌂?\rangle\rangle = P$

$P = (L.EaskProposal✓, \top).P_1 + (LE.getSignature⌂, \top).P_2$

$P_1 = enables_{LE.askProposal}✝.(LE.getSignature⌂, v).disables_{LE.askProposal}✝.P$

$P_2 = disables_{LE.askProposal}✝.P$

$\langle\langle getSignature⌂?ensuresconfirm⌂!\rangle\rangle = P'$

$P' = (LE.getSignature⌂, \top).(confirm⌂!, responseRate(LE)(getSignature⌂, confirm⌂)).P'$

Uses-Interfaces

As explained in Section 2.6, uses-interfaces provide synchronous interactions with components that offer a certain degree of persistence. For the nodes *n∈uses(M)* (notice that synchronous interactions can occur more than once during one module instance):

$\langle\langle n\rangle\rangle = \sum_{\forall i\in sign(labelM(n))} P_{ni}$

where $P_{ni} = (n.i, synchronisationRate(i)).P_{ni}$

Example 4 (Encoding a Uses-Interface)

We consider the case of the uses-interface **RE**:

$\langle\langle RE\rangle\rangle = (RE.getLenders, synchronisationRate(getLenders))$

QUANTITATIVE ANALYSIS OF TIME PROPERTIES

At the time this chapter is being written, the encoding is semi-automated: only the encoding of business roles is fully automated, the remaining parts (e.g., module structure, business protocols) requiring the assistance of a person. The encoding is modular in the sense that each SRML node can be encoded independently from the other nodes. The encoding of each node can then be plugged into the PEPA term representing the skeleton of the SRML module structure defined in Section 4. Modularity simplifies the non-automated encoding by dividing it in independent sub-tasks and allowing the automatically derived sub-terms to be combined with those encoded by a person.

As shown in the example below, it is easy to use the results of the performance analysis to track back the feedback obtained on the performance of a SRML module. This is due to the modularity of the encoding: for example, the structure of the derived PEPA term keeps the information about the original structure of the module. Moreover, the name of each PEPA activity contains information on the node (or wire) of the SRML module in which the corresponding event occurs and of the specific interaction event that it represents.

Quantitative analysis is performed by using the PEPA Eclipse Plug-in (Tribastone, 2007) and IPC (Canevet, 2003), formal analysis components of the SENSORIA Development Environment (Wirsing, 2010). We now discuss the proposed method, using the results obtained on the specific case study for illustrative purposes. Figure 5 presents a screenshot of the PEPA Eclipse Plugin with a fragment of the service corresponding to the sequence diagram given in Figure 3.

Recall that the rates annotating the SRML module (i.e., Time Annotation in Definition 5) have been included in the PEPA term that represents the original SRML module, as defined in Section 4. Therefore, the rates specified in Figure 5 are the rates that have been defined for GET-MORTGAGE, although the tool uses a slightly different syntax (e.g., *cmTransferRate* in Figure 5 is in fact *TransferRate(CM)* which is the transfer rate of wire *CM*). The input of the tool required only the addition of one rate *startRate* to associate to the event "start the experiment".

First, we use the PEPA Eclipse Plug-in tool to generate the statespace of the derived PEPA

configuration. We used the static analyser and qualitative analysis capabilities of this tool. We determined that the configuration is deadlock free and has no unreachable local states in any component (no "dead code" in the model).

The analysis of a PEPA term encoding a SRML module is inexpensive because the statespace of the model is relatively small — the number of states of a module grows linearly with respect to the number of nodes. The reason is that the nodes of a SRML module do not execute independently but they wait for one another (i.e., typically, not more than one at a time is active).

We performed the passage time analysis of the example illustrated in Figure 3 to investigate the probability of each possible delay between *CRgetProposal*⊖ and *CRgetProposal*⊠. We conducted a series of experiments on our PEPA model to determine the answers to the following question:

Figure 5. Screenshot of the PEPA Eclipse plugin

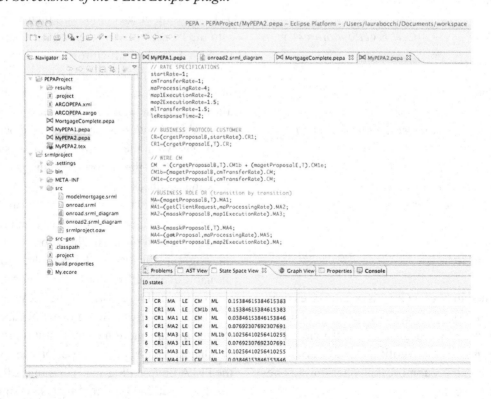

- Is the advertised *"80% of requests receive a response within 7 seconds"* satisfied by the system at present?

The question is answered by computing the cumulative distribution function (CDF) for the passage from request to response and determining the value at time $t=10$.[2] Figure 6(a) shows that the property is not guaranteed by the given model and time policy. In order to tune the model with the advertised SLA one could

1. Change the SLA constraints by weakening the guaranteed properties, e.g., the constraint C_4 in Section 2.7 could be substituted to

C_4: $\{CR.RESPONSETIME, LE.RESPONSETIME\}$

$$def(c,t)=\begin{cases}1 \text{ if } c \geq 8 \text{ and } t \leq 0.79\\0 \text{ otherwise}\end{cases}$$

where the service guarantees to the customer that a response will be sent within 8 seconds (and not 7).

2. Use *sensitivity analysis* to determine the most convenient way of refining the model to guarantee the property. Sensitivity analysis allows us to answered the following question: *"What is the bottleneck activity in the system at present, i.e., where is it best to invest effort in making one of the activities more efficient?"*

Figure 6. Sensitivity analysis of response time distributions (a) coSingleTransferRate (b) cmTransferRate (c) leResponseTime (d) orp1ExecutionRate

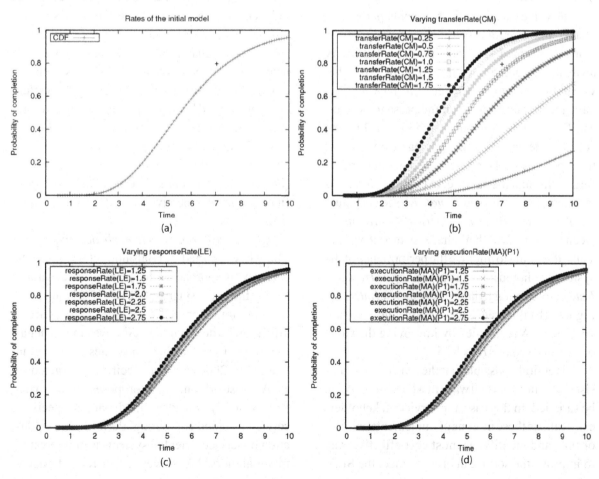

In the rest of this section we focus on (2). That is, we vary each of the rates used in the model (both up from the true value, and down from it) and evaluate the CDF repeatedly over this range of values. The resulting graphs are shown in Figure 6 (the plus denotes the coordinate for 7 seconds and 80%).

Each of the graphs is a CDF that plots the probability of having completed the passage of interest by a given time bound. To determine whether the stated SLA is satisfied we need only inspect the value of this probability at the time bound. For the given values of the rates we find that it is the case that this SLA is not satisfied (Figure 6(a)).

In performing sensitivity analysis we vary each rate through a fixed number of possible values to see if we can identify an improvement that satisfies the SLA. We have begun by considering seven possible values here. Three of these are above the true value (i.e. the activity is being performed faster) and three are below (i.e. the activity is being performed slower). From the sensitivity analysis we determine (from Figure 6(b)) that variations in rate parameter *transferRate(CM)* have the greatest impact on the passage of interest. Due to the structure of the model this rate controls the entry into the passage from request to response so delays here have a greater impact further through the passage. In contrast variations in rate parameter *responseRate(LE)* (seen in Figure 6 (c)) and *executionRate(MA)(getClientRequest)* (seen in Figure 6(d)) have the least impact overall. Thus, if seeking to improve the performance of the system we should invest in improving *coTransferRate* before trying to improve *responseRate(LE)*. Figure 6(b) illustrates, for example, how the advertised SLA is satisfied by improving the value of *transferRate(CM)* to 1.25.

It is entirely possible that the sensitivity analysis will identify several ways in which the SLA can be satisfied. In this case, the service stakeholders can evaluate these in terms of implementation cost or time and identify the most cost-effective way to improve the service in order to meet the SLA.

It is also possible for the designer to address the presence of a bottleneck by changing the structure of the model, for example adding components or wires. In this case the method described in this chapter must be applied again to the refined SRML model.

RELATED WORK

Modelling languages. In other work, process calculi models are generated from formalisms such as BPMN (Prandi, 2008), WS-CDL (Bravetti, 2008; Gorrieri, 2005) or BPEL (Guidi, 2006). The advantage of using a modelling language like SRML is that the analysis can be performed over models that are more abstract than the representations used by these other languages. In particular, analysis can be performed over SRML modules independently of the fact that the orchestration will have been designed in BPMN, BPEL, or any other language, or even as an assembly of heterogeneous components. SRML also allows to capture the difference between tight-coupled components and loose-coupled components (e.g., abstract references to outsourced functionalities). This allows us, for example, to consider the delay of service discovery only where appropriate (i.e., the SRML requires-interfaces) and to have a finer grained perspective of the delays in internal components.

Quantitative analysis in early design phases. The work reported in (Balsamo, 2004) presents a survey of approaches for performance evaluation at the early stages of design. Early analysis has the aim of preventing design choices from affecting the deployment of the system in a negative way. However, the approaches described in (Balsamo, 2004) are not specifically targeted to SOAs. Instead, our work proposes an approach that explicitly considers the dynamic aspects of service-oriented computing. Performance evaluation of service-oriented systems is of interest to many authors. We survey a few related papers here. In (Grundy, 2006) the authors focus on tools for business process composition, performance engineering and dynamic system architectures. In this approach the authors may describe systems in Business Process Modelling Notation (BPMN) (White, 2008), their own high-level modelling notation or at a lower level of abstraction in a performance modelling formalism. The authors' tool suite generates code to implement this performance evaluation as a Java application, an Apache JMeter script, or in other formats. Stub code is generated for services with either delays according to a stochastic model or according to historical measurement data. Other approaches work directly over terms of process calculi directly (untimed calculi are used in (Borelae, 2008; Bravetti, 2007), timed calculi are used in (De Nicola, 2009; Prandi, 2007). (Iacob, 2006) proposes a layered analysis approach covering technical infrastructures, software applications, business processes and products. Our approach considers two layers – architectural and behavioural – and focuses on properties that arise from the dynamic aspects of service-oriented systems, namely discovery and loose coupling, which are key for flexible architectures.

Monitoring. Run-time monitoring for the performance evaluation of service-oriented systems is addressed by several authors, e.g., (Baresi, 2007; Sammapun, 2005). Our approach involves models at the early phases of design, whereas the approach suggested in (Baresi, 2007; Sammapun, 2005) uses run-time monitoring on existing implementations. The two aspects are orthogonal and could possibly be combined. Run-time monitoring and validation of an implementation against a model are out of the scope of this paper.

CONCLUSION

We presented an encoding from SRML, a language for high-level modelling of structural and behavioural aspects of service-oriented applica-

tions (Fiadeiro, 2010), into the stochastic process algebra PEPA (Hillston, 1996), which enables quantitative analysis of timing properties. The aim of this work is to certify SLAs of complex services modelled in SRML, defining an upper bound, up to a certain probability, for the delay between pairs of events. Through sensitivity analysis of response time distributions, the tools offered by PEPA allow us to vary rates for efficiency to improve overall performance. We tested the proposed approach on a financial case study. A formal proof of correctness of the encoding based on the semantics of both languages is under way.

We also plan to further investigate the implications of delays in expressing SLA constraints in SRML. We are currently working on a more accurate representation of interaction parameters, namely when they influence the choice of a branch in an orchestration. The aim is to represent them as probabilities, specifically the probability of receiving such a value through an interaction, and to associate them with the rates in a way that does not alter the analysis by introducing unwanted delays.

REFERENCES

Abreu, J., & Fiadeiro, J. L. (2008). A coordination model for service-oriented interactions. In *Coordination Languages and Models*. In *LNCS* (*Vol. 5052*, pp. 1–16). Springer.

Abreu, J., Mazzanti, F., Fiadeiro, J. L., & Gnesi, S. (2009). A model-checking approach for service component architectures. In *Formal Methods for Open Object-Based Distributed Systems*. In *LNCS* (*Vol. 5522*, pp. 219–224). Springer.

Argent-Katwala, A., Bradley, J., Clark, A., & Gilmore, S. (2008). Location-aware quality of service measurements for service-level agreements. In *Trustworthy Global Computing (TGC'07), Vol. 4912 of LNCS,* (pp. 222–239). Springer

Balsamo, S., Di Marco, A., Inverardi, P., & Simeoni, M. (2004). Model-based performance prediction in software development: A survey. *IEEE Transactions on Software Engineering*, *30*(5), 295–310. doi:10.1109/TSE.2004.9

Baresi, L., Bianculli, D., Ghezzi, C., Guinea, S., & Spoletini, P. (2007). A timed extension of wscol. In *Web Services (ICWS'07)*, (pp. 663–670). IEEE.

Beek, M., Fantechi, A., Gnesi, S., & Mazzanti, F. (2008). An action/state-based model-checking approach for the analysis of communication protocols for service-oriented applications. In *Formal Methods for Industrial Critical Systems*. In *LNCS* (*Vol. 4916*, pp. 133–148). Springer.

Benatallah, B., Casati, F., & Toumani, F. (2004). Web services conversation modeling: A cornerstone for e-business automation. *IEEE Internet Computing*, *8*(1), 46–54. doi:10.1109/MIC.2004.1260703

Bistarelli, S., Montanari, U., & Rossi, F. (1997). Semiring-based constraint satisfaction and optimization. *Journal of the ACM*, *44*(2), 201–236. doi:10.1145/256303.256306

Boreale, M., Bruni, R., De Nicola, R., & Loreti, M. (2008). Sessions and pipelines for structured service programming. In *Formal Methods for Open Object-Based Distributed Systems*. In *LNCS* (*Vol. 5051*, pp. 19–38). Springer.

Bravetti, M., Lanese, I., & Zavattaro, G. (2008). Contract-driven implementation of choreographies. *In Trustworthy Global Computing (TGC'08): Vol. 5474 of LNCS*, (pp. 1–18). Springer.

Bravetti, M., & Zavattaro, G. (2007). Service oriented computing from a process algebraic perspective. *Journal of Logic and Algebraic Programming*, *70*(1), 3–14. doi:10.1016/j.jlap.2006.05.002

Broy, M., Krüger, I., & Meisinger, M. (2007). A formal model of services. *ACM TOSEM*, *16*(1), 1–40. doi:10.1145/1189748.1189753

Canevet, C., Gilmore, S., Hillston, J., Prowse, M., & Stevens, P. (2003). Performance modelling with the unified modelling language and stochastic process algebras. In *Computers and Digital Techniques, IEE Proceedings, Vol. 150*, (pp. 107–120). IEEE.

Clark, A. (2007). The ipclib PEPA library. In M. Harchol-Balter, M. Kwiatkowska, & M. Telek, (Eds.), *Proceedings of the 4th International Conference on the Quantitative Evaluation of SysTems (QEST)*: (pp. 55–56). IEEE.

Consortium, S. C. A. (2005). *Building systems using a service oriented architecture*. Whitepaper.

De Nicola, N., Latella, D., Loreti, M., & Massink, M. (2009). MarCaSPiS: A Markovian extension of a calculus for services. In *Proceedings of the Workshop on Structural Operational Semantics, Satellite Workshop of ICALP*. Elsevier.

Elfatatry, A. (2007). Dealing with change: components versus services. *Communications of the ACM*, *50*(8), 35–39. doi:10.1145/1278201.1278203

Fiadeiro, J. L., Lopes, A., Bocchi, L., & Abreu, J. (2010to appear). The SENSORIA reference modelling language. In Wirsing, M., & Hölzl, M. (Eds.), *Rigorous software engineering for service-oriented systems, LNCS*. Springer.

Gorrieri, R., Guidi, C., & Lucchi, R. (2005). Reasoning about interaction patterns in choreography. In M.Bravetti, L. Kloul, & G. Zavattaro (Eds.), *EPEW/WS-FM, Vol. 3670 of LNCS*, (pp. 333–348). Springer.

Grundy, J., Hosking, J., Li, L., & Liu, N. (2006). Performance engineering of service compositions. In *Service-Oriented Software Engineering* (pp. 26–32). ACM.

Guidi, C., Lucchi, R., Busi, N., Gorrieri, R., & Zavattaro, G. (2006). SOCK: A calculus for service oriented computing. In *Proceedings of International Conference on Service Oriented Computing (ICSOC'06), Vol. 4294 of LNCS*, (pp. 327–338). Springer.

Hillston, J. (1996). *A compositional approach to performance modelling*. Cambridge University Press. doi:10.1017/CBO9780511569951

Iacob, M., & Jonkers, H. (2006). Quantitative analysis of enterprise architectures. In *Interoperability of Enterprise Software and Applications* (pp. 239–252). Springer. doi:10.1007/1-84628-152-0_22

Prandi, D., & Quaglia, P. (2007). Stochastic COWS. In *Proceedings of International Conference on Service Oriented Computing (ICSOC'07), Vol 4749 of LNCS*, (pp. 245–256). Springer.

Prandi, D., Quaglia, P., & Zannone, N. (2008). Formal analysis of BPMN via a translation into COWS. *In Coordination, Vol. 5052 of LNCS*, (pp. 249–263). Springer.

Sammapun, U., Lee, I., & Sokolsky, O. (2005). RT-MaC: Runtime monitoring and checking of quantitative and probabilistic properties. In *Real-Time Computing Systems and Applications* (RTCSA'05), (pp. 147-153), IEEE.

Tribastone, M. (2007). The PEPA Plug-in project. In *Quantitative Evaluation of SysTems* (pp. 53–54). IEEE.

Vankayala, V. (2008). *Business process modelling using SRML*. MSc Project Dissertation, University of Leicester, Leicester, UK.

White, S. A., & Miers, D. (2008). *BPMN modeling and reference guide*. Perfect Paperback, 2008.

Wirsing, M., Hölzl, M., Koch, N., & Mayer, P. (2010 to appear). Sensoria – Software engineering for service-oriented overlay computers. In Wirsing, M., & Hölzl, M. (Eds.), *Rigorous software engineering for service-oriented systems, LNCS*. Springer.

KEY TERMS AND DEFINITIONS

Component: A software package that encapsulates a sub-functionality of a system and that is statically bound to the system, in the sense that it is included in the architecture of the system at design time. In SRML a component is a sub-functionality of a service and its lifetime spans only the execution of a single service instance.

Component-Interface: The supported set of interactions and behavioural properties of a component.

External-Interface: The supported set of interactions and behavioural properties of a (provided or required) service. The behavioural description is more abstract than the one of component-interfaces (e.g., it does not include information on the local state).

Rate: A probabilistic measure of the delay incurred in an action of the system. Rates are drawn from the exponential distribution (i.e., rate r is the parameter of $F(t)=1-e^{-rt}$). More specifically, if action is associated to rate r then that action will be executed within time t with probability $1-e^{-rt}$.

Resource: A component that is persistent with respect to the life cycle of the single service instances and is possibly shared by many service instances (e.g., a database).

Service: *"an abstract resource that represents a capability of performing tasks that form a coherent functionality from the point of view of providers entities and requesters entities." (from W3C Glossary* http://www.w3.org/TR/ws-gloss/). The functionality is typically provided externally to the system that uses it and it is procured at runtime. A service publshes a service description and is invokable according to a set of access policies.

Uses-Interface: The supported set of interactions and behavioural properties of a resource.

ENDNOTES

1. Although typically in SOC we specify only abstract references for the required services, abstracting from the identity of the provider or from the specific implementation, in some cases it is useful to specify constraints on such information. For example, in C_2 we ensure that the lender is in the list of trusted lenders provided by *RE* through interaction *getLenders*.

2. By the SLA constraint C_4 we assume the response time of *LE* to be at least 0.79 seconds in the 80% of the cases, thus *responseRate(LE)=2*, i.e., $1-e^{-2*0.8}=0.798...$ (this being an assumption, we have been slightly pessimistic).

Chapter 4
On Modelling Non-Functional Properties of Semantic Web Services

Ioan Toma
University of Innsbruck, Austria

Flavio De Paoli
Universita degli studi di Milano – Bicocca, Italy

Dieter Fensel
University of Innsbruck, Austria

ABSTRACT

Service-Oriented Architectures (SOAs) are a widespread solution for realizing distributed applications. Empowered by semantic technologies these architectures will evolve in what is known as Semantically Enabled Service Oriented Architectures (SESAs) providing automatic support for various service related tasks such as discovery, ranking, composition, etc. Services are the core building blocks of both SOA- and SESA- based systems and therefore modelling various aspects of services becomes a fundamental challenge to any enterprise building SOA solutions. Among these aspects, non-functional properties of a service need to be addressed given the high dynamism of any SOA-based system. Non-functional properties descriptions are highly relevant for many of the service related tasks such as discovery, ranking, selection, and negotiation. This chapter investigates several research problems which arise in the area of Semantic Web services, namely how to describe non-functional properties of services, what models are required, and what is the proper language support for describing Non-functional Properties. Our solution was developed, and is part of the Web Service Modelling Ontology, one of the major initiatives in Semantic Web services area. We present a comprehensive set of ontological models for non-functional properties, our approach to attach non-functional properties descriptions to services, and the language support needed to formalize non-functional properties descriptions.

DOI: 10.4018/978-1-61350-432-1.ch004

INTRODUCTION

Built on current Web services technologies, such as WSDL (Christensen et al., 2001), SOAP (W3C, 2003) and UDDI (Bellwood et al., 2002), Semantic Web services provide a new level of automation for service related tasks such as: discovery, ranking, composition, selection, negotiation or invocation. Both technologies, Web services as well as their extension into semantics, consider services as fundamental, core entities. The way services are described is crucial for the successful realization of all previous mentioned service related tasks.

Three different aspects must be considered when talking about services: (1) *functional*, (2) *behavioural* and (3) *non-functional* aspects. The *functional* description contains the formal specification of what exactly a service can do. The *behavioural* description is about how the functionality of the service can be achieved in terms of the interaction with the service and in terms of the functionality required from other Web services. Finally, the *non-functional* descriptions capture constraints over the previous two (Chung, 1991). For example, in case the case of a train booking service, invoking its functionality (booking a train ticket) might be constrained by using a secure connection (security as non-functional property) or by actually performing the invocation of the services at certain point in time (*temporal availability* as non-functional property).

Among the three aspects of a service description, the *functional* and *behavioural* aspects are the most investigated aspects so far ((Keller et al., 2006), (Ye & Chen, 2006), (Preist, 2004)). Although the third aspect, *non-functional properties*, has not captured a comparatively very broad attention from the Web service research community its importance is wildly acknowledged ((Paoli et al., 2008), (Rosenberg et al., 2008), (Menasce´, 2002)). This is due to their high relevance for all service related tasks. It is easy to imagine a scenario in which services that can fulfil a user request and that provide basically the same functionality are selected based on some non-functional properties like price or performance.

The lack of support in terms of languages, methodologies and tools for non-functional properties might be due to various factors ((Eenoo et al., 2005), (Rosa et al., 2002)):

- In most of the cases there is no clear delimitation between the functional and non-functional aspects of a service.
- Often non-functional properties are considered to be represented after the functional and behavioural have been described. Most service description frameworks focus on the first two aspects (i.e. functional and behavioural) given less attention to the description of non-functional properties of services.
- Non-functional properties are often contradictory, thus being difficult to represent and engineer. A typical example is the relation between performance and security. More advanced security features require more computational power that results into a decrease of performance.
- It is difficult to formalize non-functional properties due to their complex models.
- Non-functional properties are more dynamic and dependent on many factors such context/environment.

The problem that we address in this book chapter is how to model such properties of Semantic Web services and how to attach them to service descriptions. We aim to provide language support to semantically describe these properties, which will enable reasoning over them.

This chapter proposes a solution towards a better support for Non-functional Properties descriptions of Semantic Web services in general and WSMO/WSML service in particular. The rest of this chapter is organized as follows. Section 2 provides a short introduction to Semantic Web services in general, and Web Service Modelling

Ontology in particular, setting up the context of the work described in the rest of the paper. Section 3 presents the related work in the areas of modelling and languages support for non-functional properties. Section 4 identifies the Semantic Web services tasks for which non-functional properties are likely to be relevant. Section 5 describes the types of non-functional properties. The modelling of these properties, by means of ontologies is discussed in Section 6. Finally, Section 7 proposes how to attach non-functional properties descriptions to elements such as services and goals. Finally, Section 8 concludes the chapter.

BACKGROUND

Our work is addressing the modelling of non-functional properties of Semantic Web services. This section provides an overview of the Web Service Modelling Ontology (Roman et al., 2005) and its associated representation language Web Service Modelling Language (Bruijn et al., 2005).

The Web Service Modelling Ontology is one of the major initiatives in Semantic Web services area. WSMO provides an overall framework for Semantic Web services that aims at supporting automated Web service discovery, selection, composition, mediation, execution, monitoring, etc. WSMO inherits a set of design principles from the Web Service Modelling Framework (WSMF, (Fensel & Bussler, 2002)) among which we mention: (1) the *principle of maximal de-coupling*: all WSMO components are specified autonomously, independent of connection or interoperability with other components and (2) the *principle of strong mediation*: the connection and interplay between different components is realized by mediators that resolve possible occurring heterogeneities between the connected components. Additionally every WSMO component description may include an extensible set of non-functional properties, based on the Dublin Core Metadata Set (Weibel, Kunze, Lagoze, & Wolf, 1998).

WSMO defines four top-level notions related to Semantic Web services:

- **Ontologies:** are formal explicit specifications of shared conceptualizations. They define a common agreed upon terminology in terms of concepts and relationships among concept instances. Ontologies are then used within all other WSMO elements.
- **Goals:** are descriptions of the objectives a requestor may have when consulting a service in terms of functionality, behaviour or non-functional properties.
- **Web Services:** are descriptions of services that are requested by service requesters, provided by service providers, and agreed between service providers and requestors.
- **Mediators:** address the heterogeneity problem that occurs between descriptions at different levels including data, protocol and process level. WSMO defines four types of mediators: *OO Mediators*, *GG Mediators*, *WG Mediators* and *WW Mediators*. The *OO Mediators* address the mismatch that might occur at the data level. They connect and mediate heterogeneous terminologies expressed as ontologies. The *GG Mediators* are the WSMO elements that link two goals. The link represents the refinement of the source goal into the target goal or state equivalence if both goals are substitutable. The *WG Mediators* link Web services to goals. A link between a Web service and a goal represented using a *WG Mediator* indicates that the Web service fulfils the goal totally or partially. Finally, the *WW Mediators* connect Web services resolving mismatches between them.

The Web Service Modelling Language (Bruijn et al., 2005) is a formal language for describing ontologies, goals, Web services and mediators. WSML follows the WSMO conceptual model. It is based on a set of well-known logical formalisms including Description Logics (Baader et al., 2003), Logic Programming (Lloyd, 1987), F-Logic (Kifer et al., 1995) and First Order Logic. These formalisms are taken as starting points for the development of a number of WSML language variants: WSML-Core, WSML-Flight, WSML-Rule, WSML-DL and WSML-Full. WSML-Core it is based at the intersection of Description Logics and Logic Programming, more precisely on Datalog programs. It has the least expressive power but provides a low formal complexity and is decidable. By extending WSML-Core in the direction of Logic Programming with default negation, cardinality constraints, n-ary relations with arbitrary parameters and meta- modelling features, a new language called WSML-Flight was defined. A further extension in the same direction with function symbols results into WSML-Rule. WSML-Rule no longer requires the safety of rules. The only differences between WSML-Rule and WSML-Flight are in the logical expression syntax (Bruijn et al., 2005). WSML-Core was extended into a full-fledged Description Logic based language called WSML-DL. WSML-Full is based on First Order Logic and acts as umbrella language, unifying all the above variants.

RELATED WORK

Modelling of non-functional properties is a popular research topic that has been ad- dressed in different areas, including Web services or software components. This section gives an overview of some of the existing approaches for modelling of non-functional properties focusing on the particular aspects of conceptualization and formal representation for each approach.

In the Web services area, all major initiatives provides to a leaser or greater ex- tend support for non-functional properties. UDDI (Bellwood et al., 2002) considers non-functional properties for business entities and implicitly for the services provided by this entity: *the address, the*

phone numbers, and *the email addresses* of the service provider. Non-functional properties can be accessed using the UDDI APIs. In Web Service Level Agreement (WSLA) (Ludwig et al., 2003), providers and requesters can specify service level agreements by defining metrics and SLA parameters in terms of non-functional properties. The set of non-functional properties supported by WSLA is not predefined. The metrics, SLA parameters and non-functional properties of interest are agreed between the parties. WS-Policy (Bajaj et al., 2006) is generic framework for policies specification. Policies apply to services and express requirements and preferences in terms of non-functional properties. Typical policies refer to non-functional aspects such as *reliability, transaction,* or *security*.

Semantic Web service approaches give as well a great importance to non-functional properties. OWL-S (The OWL Services Coalition, 2004) considers the following non-functional properties: *service name, text description, quality rating*. The model can be extended with other properties that are attached to the ServiceProfile and described as OWL ontologies. In the case of SWSF (SWSL, 2005) the following non-functional properties: *service name, service author, service contact information, service contributor, service description, service URL, service identifier, service version, service release date, service language, service trust, service subject, service reliability* and *service cost*.

No model is enforced for any of these non-functional properties. O'Sullivan (O'Sullivan et al., 2005) identifies a set of non-functional properties that are considered the most relevant properties for services, both for conventional and electronic services. The models are defined using Object Role Modelling and include models for: service provider, temporal model, locative model, service availability, obligations, price, payment, discounts, penalties, rights, language, trust, quality and security. The approach presented in (Paoli et al., 2008) focuses on defining a meta-model for non-functional properties. Key characteristics of the meta-model are the aggregation of non-functional properties into a concept called policy and the definition of conditions over such policies. The approach provides support for defining requests in terms of non-functional properties using the constrain operators.

Modelling of non-functional properties has been intensively investigated also in the software components area. Some of the approaches dealing with this topic are: Process^{NFL} (Rosa et al., 2002), CQML (Ro¨ttger & Zschaler, 2003), QML (Frølund & Koistinen, 1998) or QuO (Zinky, Bakken, & Schantz, 1997). Process^{NFL} is a general purpose non-functional properties specification language that provides support for describing correlations, conflicts and composition for non-functional properties. CQML is a QoS specification language which provides means to specify QoS characteristics and QoS measurements at different level of abstraction. It allows QoS characteristics to be refined and also to be aggregated. QML is a general purpose QoS specification language. The language allows QoS specification to be defined as refinements of previously defined QoS properties. QuO proposes a framework for QoS specification which includes three languages. QuO follows a contract-based approach for QoS specification. Besides QoS modelling, QuO offers constructs that can be used to define actions to be taken if QoS requirements are not satisfied.

NON-FUNCTIONAL PROPERTY TASKS

Three different types of properties must be considered when talking about services: (1) *functional*, (2) *behavioural* and (3) *non-functional*. In this section we discuss the latter. More precisely, we investigate what are the tasks in the services usage lifecycle for which non-functional properties might be relevant. The set of tasks relevant for annotations are:

1. **Discovery:** Discovery based on *annotations* might not be relevant from the end user perspective, in the sense that it is unlikely that a user will ask for service descriptions that were created at a specific date. Nevertheless, this approach plays a role in the preparatory steps of the discovery process. For example, a discovery engine could first collect the latest version of the service descriptions available online.

2. **Selection:** *Annotations* might be relevant as well in the selection process. For example if multiple versions of the same service description are being consider during the selection process, a selection engine might choose always the latest version of the service that by default should be the most relevant one.

3. **Versioning:** The version property of a service description, or any of its parts should be used to keep track of different versions of the description.

The set of tasks relevant for "real" non-functional properties of a service are:

1. **Discovery:** The discovery task depends on how services are modelled and, implicitly, on their descriptions (Keller et al., 2004). As discussed before, a service description covers three distinct aspects: functional, behavioural and non-functional. All these aspects might be considered when a user request is matched against the available services. For example, on a set of discovered services that offer online television, an additional new matching step can be performed by considering constraints on non-functional properties specified by the requestor (e.g., the delay should be lower than a specified value)

2. **Negotiation and Agreement:** Very often the execution of a service is preceded by a negotiation and agreement step. Different alternatives for non-functional properties

values can be negotiated between service provider and consumer, which both try to enforce their preferences. Non-functional properties such as price, payment method, security, trust, and, most notably quality of service, are often the basis of such negotiation.

3. **Ranking and Selection:** Ranking and selection are tasks that depend heavily on the discovery task. These tasks consider as input the set of discovered services which can fulfil the requested functionality. Ranking and selection can be based on some non-functional proper- ties such as availability or price. For instance from a set of services that offer online television, the requester will select one service which is available in that moment in time and which has the lowest delays.

4. **Monitoring:** Once an agreement is reached the parties involved need to know if the other partners comply with the agreement or not. As mentioned above, such an agreement is usually constructed by negotiating on the non-functional properties of the service. The monitoring of the agreement will be based on these agreed non-functional proper- ties.

Semantic Web services aim at automating most of the tasks mentioned above. This vision can only be realized if semantic formalizations of the Web services descriptions, including then non-functional properties, are available. The benefits of using and pro- cessing semantic descriptions as part of the solutions for the previous listed tasks in general, and ranking in particular, is illustrated by the following situation. A requestor searches for a currency exchange service available during the working days of the week. In an informal way, he might express his request for service availability as I want all currency exchange services available from Monday till Friday. On the other hand, the service providers might advertise their services as follows: currency exchange service available

during working days or currency exchange service available during the whole week. The informal descriptions of the availability requested by the user, respectively provided by the service providers have to be semantically described in order to enable a meaningful ranking in such situations. Background information captured through ontologies and rules (e.g. the interval Monday to Friday is equivalent to the interval working days) would improve the ranking of services. We call the ranking process which uses semantic information and reasoning semantic ranking.

NON-FUNCTIONAL PROPERTY TYPES

In this section we discuss two types of non-functional properties and investigate what are the properties that belong to each of these two categories.

A closer look at non-functional properties shows that there are two categories in which these properties can be divided: (1) *annotations* – which provide metadata about any type of element description (service, goal, ontology, etc.) and (2) *non-functional properties* – which are properties that strictly belong to a service, properties other than functional and behavioural.

1. *Annotations* apply to all WSMO elements descriptions, such as services, goals, mediators, ontologies. They provide metadata about these elements, such as *contributor*, *coverage*, *creator*, *date*, *format*, *identifier*, *language*, *owner*, *publisher*, *rights*, *source*, and *version*. Properties such as *subject*, *title*, *type*, and *description* can be used to provide additional information about the service description, and about the service itself. They can also give hints about the functionality of the service (e.g., the service category).

2. The second category of non-functional properties are those properties which strictly be-

long to a service and which are not functional and behavioural. We call these properties "*non-functional properties*". They cover the following aspects of a service: *locative, temporal, availability, obligation, price, payment, discounts, rights, trust, quality of service, security, intellectual property, rewards, provider, reliability, robustness, scalability, performance,* and *transactional*.

It is important to mention that the set of non-functional properties from both categories is extensible.

NON-FUNCTIONAL PROPERTY ONTOLOGIES

A crucial challenge towards a better support for non-functional properties in WSMO and WSML is the modelling of this information. A first important step in this respect is the definition of ontologies capturing non-functional properties. These ontologies provide the terminology for specifying non-functional properties of services. Ontologies, which describe the non-functional properties domain, can be imported and concepts referring to non-functional properties can be instantiated and used in service descriptions. We created a set of non-functional properties ontologies (Toma & Foxvog, 2006) in WSML based on the models provided in (O'Sullivan et al., 2005). These ontologies provide formal conceptualization for Web service non-functional properties such as availability or security. A WSML formalization of these ontologies is available at http://www.wsmo.org/ontologies/nfp/. The set of non-functional properties includes models for: locative, temporal, availability, obligation, price, payment, discounts, rights, trust, quality of service, security, intellectual property, rewards, provider, measures and currency aspects. In the remainder of the section we shortly describe the purpose and the important concepts of these ontologies. For a

detailed description of the non-functional properties models we refer the reader to (O'Sullivan et al., 2005).

Locative Ontology

The *Locative Ontology* provides the concepts that are needed for locative descriptions of a service. Using the terminology provided in these ontology aspects such where a service can be requested from, where it can be provided, and so on, can be modelled. Main concepts include: *LocativeEntity, GeoLocation, Address, RouteSpecification,* etc. Figure 1 illustrates a fragment of the Locative Ontology.

Temporal Ontology

The *Temporal Ontology* provides the concepts that are needed to formalize time related descriptions of a service. Different temporal granularities are considered. Using the terminology provided in this ontology restrictions such as when the service can be requested, provided or queried for further information, can be expressed. Main concepts include: *TemporalEntity, TimeInterval, TimePoint, TimeZone, TemporalDate,* etc. Figure 2 illustrates the ontology.

Availability Ontology

The *Availability Ontology* provides the terminology needed to specify when, where, and to whom a service is available. Examples of concepts in this ontology are: *Availability* and *RequestAvailability*. Figure 3 illustrates the ontology.

Obligation Ontology

The *Obligation Ontology* describes the various obligations which may be connected to the request and provision of a service. This includes, for example, pricing and payment obligations. Pricing obligations refer to service providers and

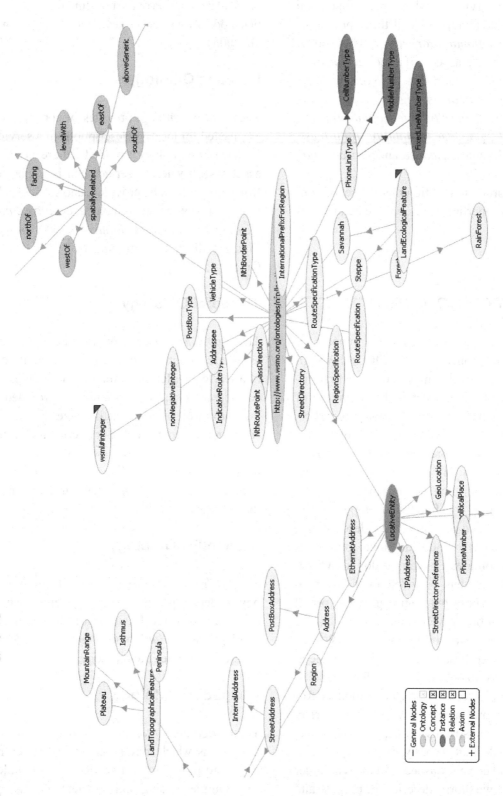

Figure 1. Locative ontology - fragment

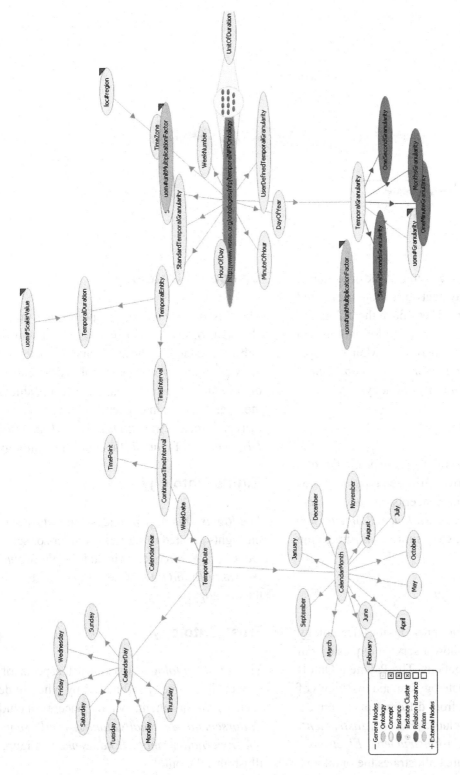

Figure 2. Temporal ontology

Figure 3. Availability ontology

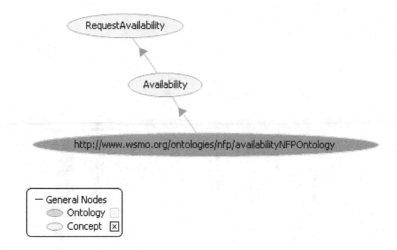

include information regarding refund procedures, negotiability, etc. Payment obligations are related to service requestors. These have the obligation to pay the service and provide information such as payment discounts, charge, etc. Main concepts include: *PaymentObligation, PricingObligation,* etc. Figure 4 illustrates the ontology.

Price Ontology

The *Price Ontology* is about those properties of a service related to price. Different types of prices are modelled. Main concepts include: *Price, AbsoutePrice, ProportionalPrice, RangedPrice, MechanismAuction,* etc. Figure 5 illustrates the ontology.

Payment Ontology

The *Payment Ontology* provides the terminology needed to describe how a service requestor can fulfil payment obligations. The Payment Ontology and the Price Ontology contain two views of the same thing but from different perspectives. Main concepts include: *PaymentInstrument, PaymentScheme, CashInstrument, Electronic-CashType,* etc. Figure 6 illustrates the ontology.

Discounts Ontology

The *Discounts Ontology* captures information about various types of discounts. Dis- counts are either dependent of how a requestor pays (e.g., early payment, type of payment instrument) and of who the requestor is (e.g., age group, student, membership). Main concepts include: *Discount, PayeeDiscount, StudentDiscount, Membership-Discount,* etc. Figure 7 illustrates the ontology.

Rights Ontology

The *Rights Ontology* provides concepts describing rights granted to service providers or service requestors. Main concepts include: *Right, RightOf-Warranty, RightOfAccess,* etc. Figure 8 illustrates the ontology.

Trust Ontology

The *Trust Ontology* covers trust aspects of a service. It is directly influenced by other models such as endorsement. Main concepts include: *Endorsement, InternallyManagedEndorsement and ExternallyManagedEndorsement.* Figure 9 illustrates the ontology.

Figure 4. Obligation ontology

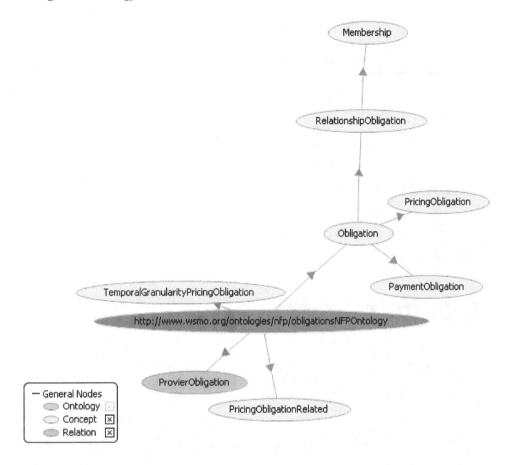

Quality of Service Ontology

The *Quality of Service Ontology* captures information about various standards, bench- marks and rating schemes that the service attempts to comply with or compares itself with. Main concepts include: *Standard, Rating, Rated, Ranking*, etc. Figure 10 illustrates the ontology.

Security Ontology

The *Security Ontology* contains concepts such as *IdentificationRequirement, Confidentiality, EncryptionTechnique, IdentificationType*, etc. Two aspects are modelled: identification and confidentiality. Figure 11 illustrates the ontology.

Intellectual Property Ontology

The *Intellectual Property Ontology* provides the concepts that are needed to describe IPR aspects. Examples of concepts are: *IPRight, Trademark, Patent, Design*, etc. Figure 12 illustrates the ontology.

Rewards Ontology

The *Rewards Ontology* includes concepts such as *AccumulatedReward, AccumulatedPriceReward, RedeemableReward*, etc. Figure 13 illustrates the ontology.

Figure 5. Price ontology

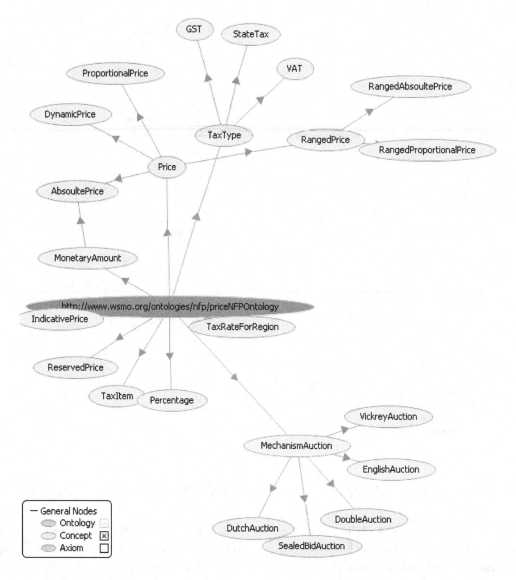

Provider Ontology

The *Provider Ontology* provides the basic terminology that is required when talking about service providers. Main concepts include: *Provider, ProviderMembership, Compliance, PartnerType*, etc. Figure 14 illustrates the ontology.

Measures Ontology

The *Measures Ontology* provides a general measures terminology. Main concepts include: *UnitOfMeasure, MeasurableQuantity, Distance*, etc. Figure 15 illustrates the ontology.

Figure 6. Payment ontology

Figure 7. Discounts ontology

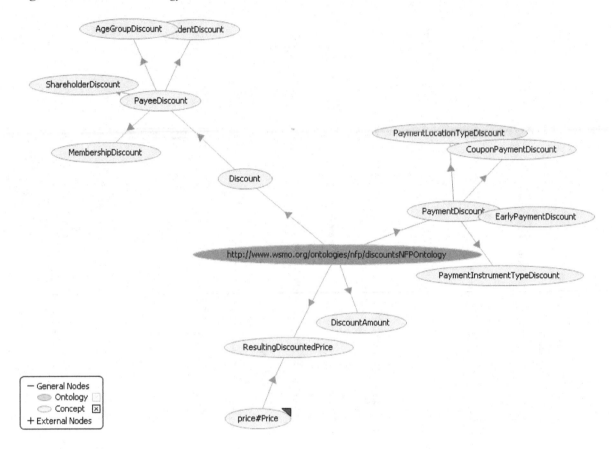

Currency Ontology

The *Currency Ontology* is a simple ontology that contains the most used currencies. Figure 16 illustrates the ontology.

ATTACHING NON-FUNCTIONAL PROPERTIES TO SERVICES AND GOALS

Once a model is available for non-functional properties a second challenge that has to be addressed is how to attach non-functional properties descriptions to services, goals or any other WSMO element. This section provides a concrete solution for this problem.

The solution consists in modelling non-functional descriptions of services or goals just as capabilities are modelled in WSMO/WSML. A service is an entity which provides a functionality (e.g. given a date, a start location, a destination and information about a client a service can book a ticket for the desired trip); in the same time a service can be seen as an entity which provides one or more non-functional properties (e.g., given a particular type of client, a service charges a particular price). A simplified model of a WSMO service following this approach is:

```
webService
    capability idCapability
            precondition definedBy
axiom1
            postcondition definedBy
```

Figure 8. Rights ontology

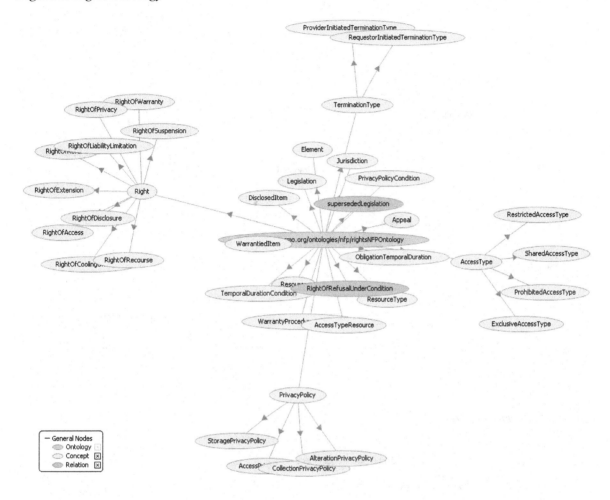

Figure 9. Trust ontology

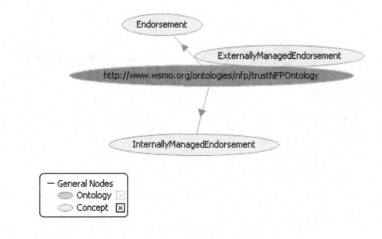

Figure 10. Quality of service ontology

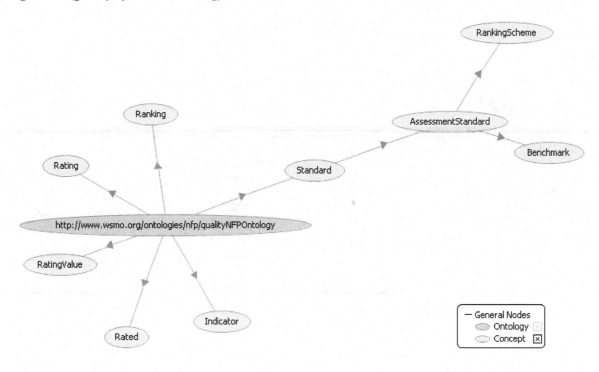

Figure 11. Security ontology

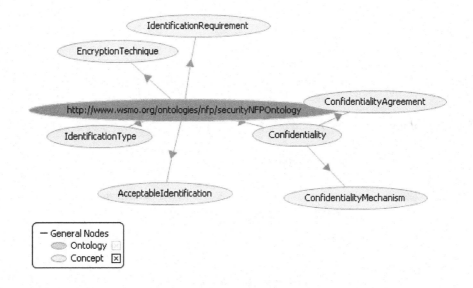

Figure 12. Intellectual property ontology

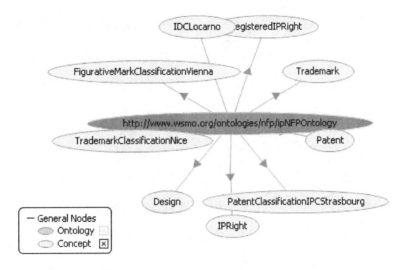

Figure 13. Rewards ontology

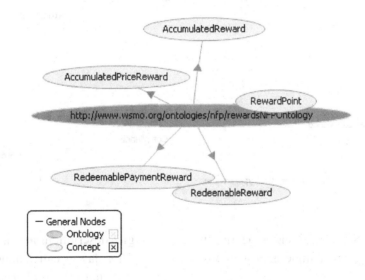

```
axiom2
        assumption definedBy axiom3
        effect definedBy axiom4
nonFunctionalProperty idNFP
    definition definedBy axiom5
```

This approach has the following advantages:

- The set of non-functional properties is not an explicit, finite set. Users of WS- MO/ WSML can define and attach an open set of non-functional properties to a goal or a service.

- Non-functional property models are attached to services in the same way as capabilities are.

The rest of this section elaborates on the approach in terms of the changes to WSMO conceptual model in Section 7.1, changes to the WSML

Figure 14. Provider ontology

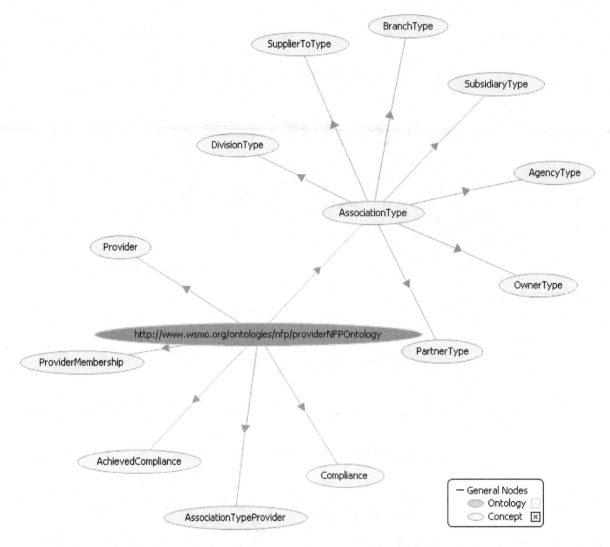

language syntax in Section 7.2 and semantics in Section 7.3. Finally, an example is provided in Section 7.4.

Model

The WSMO conceptual model is modified as illustrated in Exhibit 1.

The modified WSMO model contains two classes for non-functional properties:

- A class which covers the annotations aspects of service, goal, mediators, ontologies descriptions and any of their elements. This class is called annotations and can be used not only for service descriptions but for any elements of WSMO model. Non-functional properties that are represented by this class are for example author and subject. The set of annotation properties is not restricted to the proper- ties contained in Exhibit 1.

- A class which covers strictly the service related non-functional properties. This class is called simply nonFunctionalProperty

Figure 15. Measures ontology

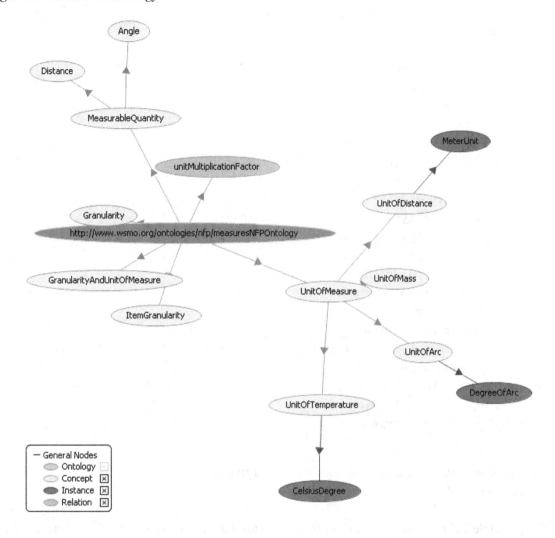

Figure 16. Currency ontology

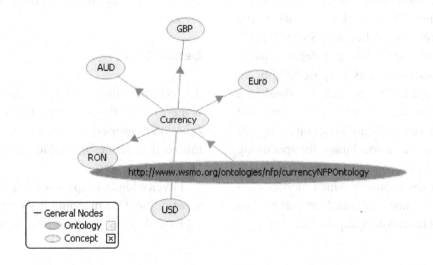

Exhibit 1. WSMO conceptual model extensions

```
Class annotations
        hasContributor type dc:contributor
        hasCoverage type dc:coverage
        hasCreator type dc:creator
        hasDate type dc:date
        hasDescription type dc:description
        hasFormat type dc:format
        hasIdentifier type dc:identifier
        hasLanguage type dc:language
        hasOwner type owner
        hasPublisher type dc:publisher
        hasRelation type dc:relation
        hasRights type dc:rights
        hasSource type dc:source
        hasSubject type dc:subject
        hasTitle  type dc:title
        hasType type dc:type
        hasTypeOfMatch type typeOfMatch
        hasVersion type version
Class nonFunctionalProperty
        hasAnnotations type annotations
        hasDefinition  type axiom
```

and is used to describe properties such as price and availability.

The principle behind this extension is that functional and non-functional aspects of services could be modelled in a similar way. Thus, we model the nonFunctionalProperty class similarly to the way a capability is modelled in WSMO/WSML. Non- functional properties are defined using logical expressions same as pre/post-conditions, assumptions and effects are being defined in a capability. Modelling non-functional properties of a service or goal using the nonFunctionalProperty construct re- quires a vocabulary for specifying non-functional properties (c.f. (Toma & Foxvog, 2006)). A similar approach which models conditions over the non-functional properties was proposed in (Hauswirth et al., 2005).

Syntax

Extending the WSMO conceptual model generates a set of changes to WSML syntax. Exhibit 2 provides the WSML syntax extensions based on the conceptual model ex- tensions previously presented.

Semantics

The central notion for a non-functional property is the *value* of the respective property. The non-functional properties semantics described in this section defines the values of a specific non-functional property.

Given a logical expression logExp, a variable substitution θ is a mapping from free variables in logExp, denoted *var*(logExp), to identifiers: θ:

Exhibit 2. WSML syntax extensions

```
annotations = 'annotations' attributevalue* 'endAnnotations'
nfp = 'nfp' attributevaluenfp |
      'nonFunctionalProperty'  attributevaluenfp
attributevaluenfp = id 'hasValue' valuelistnfp annotations?
              log definition?
```

var(logExp) → *Id*. With logExpθ we denote the application of θ to logExp, i.e. the replacement of every free variable *x* in logExp with $\theta(x)$.

Let $\langle \ldots, \text{ontID}, \ldots, \{\ldots, \text{nf p}, \ldots\}, \ldots \rangle_x$ be a WSML Web service, goal, capability, interface or mediator, where *ontID* is the set of imported ontologies and nf p = $\langle$name, val, logExp$\rangle_{nfp}$ is a non-functional property. Let O be an ontology map such that *dom*(O) = *ontID*, and Θ the set of variable substitutions such that for every $\theta \in \Theta$ it holds that for all logExp $\in$ *logExp*, O $\models$ logExpθ. Then, an identifier $i \in Id$ is a value of name if there is a $\theta \in \Theta$ such that $i = \theta(\text{val})$.

Note that in case val is an identifier, the logical expressions act as a filter: if all of the logical expressions are entailed by the ontologies *ontID*, val is a value of the property. This means that the logical expressions of a non-functional property can be seen as queries over the ontologies *ontID*, and the query answers are projected onto the value val.

Example

In Exhibit 3, we present a concrete example on how to model non-functional properties of a service based on the proposed extensions to WSMO conceptual model and WSML syntax. For exemplification, we consider a service from the shipping domain. The service can deliver a package to a given destination for a certain price and offers discounts if certain conditions are fulfilled. The basic price for delivery depends on the weight of the package being 30 USD cents per kilogram. This price is modelled, in Exhibit 3, using the

computeDeliveryPrice predicate. The service offers a 5% discount if the client pays cash and the basic delivery is not less than 100 dollars. This is modelled using the *computeDeliveryReduced-PriceCash* predicate. All conditions are modelled as logical expressions. The final price charged to ship the package is the minimum between the reduced price and the basic price, and is modelled using the *computePriceAndDiscounts* predicate. Please note that *nonFunctionalProperty*, *capability* and *interface* are all constructs at the same level. To model the price and discounts we use the terminology from three of the non-functional properties we developed, i.e., price, payment, discounts and currency ontologies. The base price charged by the service is modelled using the *AbsoultePrice* concept from price ontology. To model the discounts offered by the service we use the *ResultingDiscountedPrice* concept from the discounts ontology. From the payment ontology the concept *CashInstrument* is used in the specification of the condition when discounts apply. The price information of the service is expressed in US dollars therefore we use the corresponding instance from the currency ontology.

CONCLUSION

In this chapter a service ranking approach based on semantic descriptions of services non-functional properties was proposed. We briefly introduce our approach for modelling and attaching non-functional properties descriptions to services and goals. The pro- posed ranking mechanism makes use of logical rules describing non-functional

Exhibit 3. Example of NFPs descriptions based on the proposed extensions

```
wsmlVariant    "http://www.wsmo.org/wsml/wsml-syntax/wsml-rule"namespace {
"http://sws-ranking/WSRacer.wsml#",
        so "http://sws-ranking/Shipment.wsml#",
        list    "http://sws-ranking/ListOntology.wsml#",
        po    "http://www.wsmo.org/ontologies/nfp/priceNFPOntology#",
        pay    "http://www.wsmo.org/ontologies/nfp/paymentNFPOntology#",
        cur    "http://www.wsmo.org/ontologies/nfp/currencyNFPOntology#",
        dis    "http://www.wsmo.org/ontologies/nfp/discountsNFPOntology#",
        dc    "http://purl.org/dc/elements/1.1#",
        wsml    "http://www.wsmo.org/wsml/wsml-syntax/"}webService    "http://
example.org/ws"
                    annotations
                        dc#creator hasValue {"Ioan Toma"}
                    endAnnotations
nonFunctionalProperty
                    priceAndDiscounts hasValue ?priceAndDiscounts
                        definedBy
                    computePriceAndDiscounts(?order,?priceAndDiscounts):-
                        computeDeliveryPrice(?order,?price1) and
                        computeDeliveryReducedPriceCash(?order,?price2) and
                        list#min(?price1Value,?price2Value,?priceAndDiscountsValue).
                    computeDeliveryPrice(?order, ?deliveryPrice):-
                        ?order[so#paymentMethod hasValue ?paymentMethod,
                            so#package  hasValue ?package]
                        memberOf so#ShipmentOrderRequest and
                        ?package[so#declaredValue hasValue ?value,
                            so#weight  hasValue ?weight] and
                        ?deliveryPrice[hasAmount hasValue ?amount,
                            hasCurrency hasValue cur#USD]
                        memberOf po#AbsoultePrice and ?amount= (?weight * 0.3).
                    computeDeliveryReducedPriceCash(?order, ?reducedPrice):-
                        computeDeliveryPrice(?order, ?price) and
                            ?order[so#paymentMethod hasValue ?paymentMethod]
                        memberOf so#ShipmentOrderRequest and
                        ?paymentMethod = pay#CashInstrument and
                        ?price[hasAmount hasValue ?amount, hasCurrency hasValue
cur#USD]
                        memberOf po#AbsoultePrice and ?amount >= 100 and
                        ?reducedPrice[hasAmount hasValue ?reducedAmount,
                            hasCurrency hasValue cur#USD]
                        memberOf dis#ResultingDiscountedPrice and
                        ?amountReduced = (?amount * 0.95).
```

continued on following page

Exhibit 3. Continued

```
            computeDeliveryReducedPriceCash(?order, ?reducedPrice):-
            computeDeliveryPrice(?order, ?price) and
?order[so#paymentMethod
            hasValue ?paymentMethod]
            memberOf so#ShipmentOrderRequest and
            ?price[hasAmount hasValue ?amount, hasCurrency hasValue
cur#USD]
            memberOf po#AbsoultePrice and
            (?paymentMethod != pay#CashInstrument or ?amount < 100) and
            ?reducedPrice[hasAmount hasValue ?reducedAmount,
            hasCurrency hasValue cur#USD]
            memberOf dis#ResultingDiscountedPrice and
            ?reducedAmount = ?amount.
capability wsCapability
interface wsInterface
```

properties of services and evaluates them using a reasoning engine. As a last step it builds an ordered list of services considering the values computed during the rules evaluation step.

As future work we plan to specify and implement other types of ranking approaches namely social and context-aware ranking. Further on, a set of open issues and improvements need to be addressed and integrated with the current ranking solution. These include but are not limited to: how to integrate non-functional properties values collected by monitoring tools with the service ranking, how to predict non-functional values of services, which are the best solutions to collect and incorporate user feedback and last but not least to consider trust and reputation issues.

REFERENCES

W3C. (2003). *SOAP version 1.2, part 0: Primer.*

Baader, F., Calvanese, D., McGuinness, D. L., Nardi, D., & Patel-Schneider, P. F. (Eds.). (2003). *The description logic handbook.* Cambridge University Press.

Bajaj, S., Box, D., Chappell, D., Curbera, F., Daniels, G., Hallam-Baker, P., et al. (2006, April). *Web services policy 1.2 - Framework* (WS-Policy) (Tech. Rep.). Retrieved from http://www.w3.org/Submission/2006/SUBM-WS-Policy-20060425/

Bellwood, T., Cle´ment, L., Ehnebuske, D., Hately, A., Hondo, M., Husband, Y., et al. (2002). *UDDI version 3.0.*

Christensen, E., Curbera, F., Meredith, G., & Weerawarana, S. (2001). *Web services description language (WSDL) 1.1.* Retrieved from http://www.w3.org/TR/wsdl.

Chung, L. (1991). Representation and utilization of non-functional requirements for information system design. In *CAiSE '91: Proceedings of the Third International Conference on Advanced Information Systems Engineering* (pp. 5–30). New York, NY: Springer-Verlag, Inc.

de Bruijn, J., Lausen, H., Krummenacher, R., Polleres, A., Predoiu, L., Kifer, M., et al. (2005). *The Web service modeling language WSML* (Tech. Rep.). WSML Final Draft D16.1v0.21. Retrieved from http://www.wsmo.org/TR/d16/d16.1/v0.21/

Eenoo, C. V., Hylooz, O., & Khan, K. M. (2005). Addressing non-functional properties in software architecture using ADL. In *Proceedings of the 6th Australian Workshop on Software and Systems Architectures - AWSA'05*, March 29, 2005, Brisbane, Australia (pp. 6–13).

Fensel, D., & Bussler, C. (2002). The web service modeling framework WSMF. *Electronic Commerce Research and Applications, 1*(2), 113–137. doi:10.1016/S1567-4223(02)00015-7

Frølund, S., & Koistinen, J. (1998, 02). *QML: A language for* quality of service specification (Technical Report). Hewlett Packard. Retrieved from http://www.hpl.hp.com/techreports/98/HPL-98-10.html

Hauswirth, M., Porto, F., & Vu, L.-H. (2005). *QoS-enabled service discovery specification (Working Draft No. D4.17)* (p. 2P). DIP.

Keller, U., Lara, R., Polleres, A., Toma, I., Kiffer, M., & Fensel, D. (2004, October). *Web service modeling ontology – Discovery* (Working Draft). Digital Enterprise Research Insitute (DERI). Retrieved from http://www.wsmo.org/2004/d5.1/v0.1

Keller, U., Lausen, H., & Stollberg, M. (2006, June). On the semantics of functional descriptions of web services. In *Proceedings of 3rd European Semantic Web Conference* (ESWC) (pp. 54–59).

Kifer, M., Lausen, G., & Wu, J. (1995). Logical foundations of object-oriented and frame-based languages. *Journal of the ACM, 42*(4), 741–843. doi:10.1145/210332.210335

Lloyd, J. W. (1987). *Foundations of logic programming* (2nd ed.). Springer-Verlag.

Ludwig, H., Keller, A., Dan, A., King, R. P., & Franck, R. (2003, July). *Web service level agreement (WSLA) language specification* (Tech. Rep.). Retrieved from http://www.research.ibm.com/wsla/WSLASpecV1-20030128.pdf

Menasce', D. A. (2002). QoS issues in web services. *IEEE Internet Computing, 6*(6), 72–75. doi:10.1109/MIC.2002.1067740

O'Sullivan, J., Edmond, D., & ter Hofstede, A. H. (2005). *Formal description of non-functional service properties* (Technical Report). Brisbane, Australia: Queensland University of Technology. Retrieved from http://www.service-description.com/

Paoli, F. D., Palmonari, M., Comerio, M., & Maurino, A. (2008). A meta-model for non-functional property descriptions of web services. In *ICWS'08: Proceedings of the 2008 IEEE international conference on web services* (pp. 393–400). Washington, DC: IEEE Computer Society.

Preist, C. (2004). A conceptual architecture for semantic Web services. In *International Semantic Web Conference* (pp. 395-409).

Roettger, S., & Zschaler, S. (2003, 06). *CQML+: Enhancements to CQML*. In QoS in CBSE Workshop 2003. Toulouse, France.

Roman, D., Lausen, H., & Keller, U. (Eds.). (2005). *Web service modeling ontology* (WSMO) (Working Draft No. D2v1.2). WSMO. Retrieved from http://www.wsmo.org/TR/d2/v1.2/

Rosa, N. S., Cunha, P. R., Freire, L., & Justo, G. R. (2002). Process NFL: A language for describing non-functional properties. In *Proceedings of the 35th annual Hawaii International Conference* (HICSS), March 29, 2005, Hawaii, USA (pp. 3676–3685).

Rosenberg, F., Michlmayr, A., & Dustdar, S. (2008). Top-down business process development and execution using quality of service aspects. *Enterp. Inf. Syst., 2*(4), 459–475. doi:10.1080/17517570802395626

SWSL. (2005). *Semantic Web service framework*. Retrieved from http://www.daml.org/services/swsf/1.1/overview/

The OWL Services Coalition. (2004). *OWL-S 1.1 release*. Retrieved from http://www.daml.org/services/owl-s/1.1/

Toma, I., & Foxvog, D. (2006, August). *Non-functional properties in Web services* (Working Draft). Digital Enterprise Research Insitute (DERI). Retrieved from http://www.wsmo.org/TR/d28/d28.4/v0.1/

Weibel, S., Kunze, J., Lagoze, C., & Wolf, M. (1998). *RFC 2413 - Dublin core metadata for resource discovery* (Tech. Rep.). Internet Engineering Task Force (IETF). Retrieved from http://www.ietf.org/rfc/rfc2413.txt

Ye, L., & Chen, J. (2006). Formal functional description of semantic web services: The logic description method. In *SOSE'06: Proceedings of the 2006 International Workshop on service-Oriented Software Engineering* (pp. 54–59). New York, NY: ACM.

Zinky, J. A., Bakken, D. E., & Schantz, R. E. (1997). Architectural support for quality of service for CORBA objects. *Theory and Practice of Object Systems, 3*(1). Retrieved from citeseer.ist.psu.edu/zinky97architectural.html

KEY TERMS AND DEFINITIONS

Goals: Are descriptions of the objectives a requestor may have when consulting a service in terms of functionality, behaviour or non-functional properties.

Mediators: Address the heterogeneity problem that occurs between descriptions at different levels including data, protocol and process level.

Ontologies: Formal explicit specifications of shared conceptualizations. They define a common agreed upon terminology in terms of concepts and relationships among concept instances.

Web Service Modelling Language: A formal language for describing ontologies, goals, Web services and mediators.

Web Service Modelling Ontology: WSMO provides an overall framework for Semantic Web services that aims at supporting automated Web service discovery, selection, composition, mediation, execution, monitoring, etc.

Web services: are descriptions of services that are requested by service requesters, provided by service providers, and agreed between service providers and requestors.

Chapter 5
Quality of Service Monitoring Strategies in Service Oriented Architecture Environments using Processor Hardware Performance Metrics

Ernest Sithole
University of Ulster at Coleraine, UK

Sally McClean
University of Ulster at Coleraine, UK

Bryan Scotney
University of Ulster at Coleraine, UK

Gerard Parr
University of Ulster at Coleraine, UK

Adrian Moore
University of Ulster at Coleraine, UK

Dave Bustard
University of Ulster at Coleraine, UK

Stephen Dawson
SAP Research Belfast, UK

ABSTRACT

The sharp growth in data-intensive applications such as social, professional networking and online commerce services, multimedia applications, as well as the convergence of mobile, wireless, and internet technologies, is greatly influencing the shape and makeup of on-demand enterprise computing environments.

In response to the global needs for on-demand computing services, a number of trends have emerged, one of which is the growth of computing infrastructures in terms of the number of computing node entities and the widening in geophysical distributions of deployed node elements. Another development has been the increased complexity in the technical composition of the business computing space due to the diversity of technologies that are employed in IT implementations. Given the huge scales in infrastructure sizes

DOI: 10.4018/978-1-61350-432-1.ch005

and data handling requirements, as well as the dispersion of compute nodes and technology disparities that are associated with emerging computing infrastructures, the task of quantifying performance for capacity planning, Service Level Agreement (SLA) enforcements, and Quality of Service (QoS) guarantees becomes very challenging to fulfil. In order to come up with a viable strategy for evaluating operational performance on computing nodes, we propose the use of on-chip registers called Performance Monitoring Counters (PMCs), which form part of the processor hardware. The use of PMC measurements is largely non-intrusive and highlights performance issues associated with runtime execution on the CPU hardware architecture. Our proposed strategy of employing PMC data thus overcomes major shortcomings of existing benchmarking approaches such as overheads in the software functionality and the inability to offer detailed insight into the various stages of CPU and memory hardware operation.

MAJOR DEVELOPMENTS AND CHALLENGES IN ON-DEMAND COMPUTING

Given the current developments in eEnterprise implementations, the infrastructure planning tasks of accurately determining performance that can be delivered by on-demand computing resources and in turn, obtaining accurate estimates of the appropriate infrastructure hardware performance capabilities required for business computing solutions are becoming an increasingly challenging exercise to undertake. One major cause that has led to the difficulty in quantifying performance in business computing systems has been the huge amounts of user-generated data as a result of the exponential adoption of on-demand hosted computing services and applications such as social networking, e-commerce, and multi-media content sharing services. Yet another development that has caused a huge increase in consumer-generated data is the convergence of mobile, wireless and web technologies into a ubiquitous computing platform. In response to the challenges arising from these major trends, there has been a phenomenal growth in the size of deployed computing infrastructures, with the magnitude of the infrastructure expansion being characterised by three main dimensions of growth: (a) the increases in the number of computing machines brought together to form server domains, (b) the

wide geographic locations, over which participant server nodes are physically deployed and (c) the different types of technologies that are used to produce computing solutions.

Challenges for Performance Evaluation

Arising from the physical distribution of compute nodes due to the dispersion of resources in the infrastructures, are the performance-related challenges pertaining to the need to quantify network delays. The delays emanate from the communications of status and coordination messages as well as the actual data transfers between host machines. The calculation of overall performance metrics in distributed systems, which are dependent on network delays, is not straightforward to perform given that application routines running inside server nodes generate data in quantities that can vary dynamically. As a result of the changing loads, traffic levels introduced on network links usually follow irregular patterns leading to congestion and bandwidth delays that cannot be easily established. It is important to emphasize that while network delays do not feature in the proposed performance evaluation strategy considered in the latter sections of this chapter, they nevertheless make a key aspect which is captured in the Service Taxonomy presented in Figure 4.

In most business computing solutions, the server nodes that are networked together usually come from multiple vendors, which mean that the resulting infrastructure is a broad collection of non-uniform components with considerable disparities in their functional design. The resultant heterogeneity of the assembled hardware architectures means that a uniform approach cannot be applied in calibrating performance on each of the individual machines and, in turn, the calculations of overall performance for compute service implementations that run on heterogeneous resources will be challenging to perform.

The adoption of various middleware technologies in crafting IT solutions is a further obstacle to the tasks of quantifying performance levels in business computing infrastructures and of estimating infrastructure capacity to match projected future workload levels from user environments. Some of the popular middleware-driven strategies that are employed in developing applications and business processes use SOA-based approaches such as Representational State Transfer (REST), Simple Object Access Protocol (SOAP) and Common Object Request Broker Architecture (CORBA) as well as database packages. On the infrastructure resource fabric, middleware-based approaches for enabling service provision usually take the form of Grid or Cloud computing strategies. From the execution of the basic protocol and other support services provided in the middleware functionality, software-based overheads are introduced to program operations, thus subjecting the output performance metrics of the middleware-supported solutions to additional latencies. The impact of middleware overheads on the overall performance depends on the combination of technology packages that are employed in developing the user applications and the resource infrastructure solutions. As in the case of network delays, this section highlights the impact of middleware overheads on performance given their relevance to the Service Taxonomy as shown by the classifications for Interfacing Definitions, Service and Other Properties in Figure 4.

KEY STRATEGIES FOR PERFORMANCE EVALUATIONS IN E-ENTERPRISE

In order to quantify the performance levels that can be achieved by server hardware with respect to enterprise application solutions, benchmarking methods are generally employed, with the output metrics associated with specific implementations being established through direct measurements conducted on the server machine in use. Some benchmarks approaches specifically target the performance of application routines leading to the output metrics being presented as user-level performance indicators. Example benchmarks which are application-related include the Transaction Processing Performance Council (TPC) metrics for transaction processing and database operations on server hardware[1], and the SAP benchmarks for workloads associated with various enterprise application routines such as Sales Distribution (SD), Assemble-to-Order (ATO), Cross Assemble Time Sheet (CATS), Material Management (MM), Production Planning (PP), Financial Accounting (FI) and Human Resources Payroll (HR) services[2]. One major drawback with application benchmarks is the software-based overheads emanating from the use of utility programs that are set up to calculate the output performance metrics derived from measurements. Furthermore, the output metrics are essentially compound performance indicators i.e. they combine many stages of application execution with the result that they reflect only the overall application response as perceived at end user level. Thus, the application benchmarks provide very little information about the response patterns of individual low-level operations that are associated with applied user loads.

Beside application-centric benchmarks, hardware-specific benchmarks such as the Standard

Performance Evaluation Corporation (SPEC) CPU measurements can be conducted to provide metrics for the calibrations of performance of processor and memory hardware[3]. Essentially, the SPEC CPU metrics are calculated as ratios of the CPUs' (floating point and integer) operational performance. The performance ratios are obtained from the respective comparisons of throughput rates and response times as measured on the CPU and memory hardware of various server hardware kits. The normalisation of SPEC CPU benchmark results is achieved through comparisons with corresponding metrics obtained on the hardware of the Sun SPARC Ultra Enterprise 2 reference machine that uses a 296 MHz UltraSPARC II processor[4,5]. In other approaches that employ server hardware benchmarks, the performance of CPU and memory architectures are considered in the context of parallel processing implementations as in (Terpstra, D., 2010; D. Levinthal; Azimi, R., Stumm, M. & Wisniewski, R. W., 2005), while hardware performance benchmarks for disk drive systems are considered in (PassMark Software, 2010). While it is possible to gain deeper understanding of the operational capabilities of various server devices using hardware-related benchmarks, the output metrics provided are still not detailed enough given that they are obtained as compound measurements that group multiple operational stages inside the server hardware into a single metric. As an example, the SPEC CPU benchmarks are based on combining the processor, caching and system memory functions into a single measured operation. The result is that the SPEC CPU data provide very little insight as to the inner workings of the various components of server processor architecture and it is therefore not possible to conduct in-depth analysis of the resource utilisation patterns such as duration distributions that are associated with each of the key operational stages in the processor and memory hardware.

Performance Evaluation Based on Performance Monitoring Counters

In this paper we propose a performance monitoring and evaluation strategy that uses data gathered by the on-chip registers called Performance Monitoring Counters (PMCs). Performance Monitoring Counters are increasingly becoming a standard feature on the processor architectures of most the current server hardware (Drongowski, P.J., 2008; D. Gove, 2007a; D. Gove, 2007b; IBM alphaWorks, 2009). Unlike the SPEC CPU benchmarks, which provide high-level data in a format that reveals little about the internal performance and resource utilisation trends occurring within the subcomponents of CPU and memory architecture, PMCs provide rich sets of information. The information can highlight performance issues associated with almost all the main components of operation in the memory and processor hardware. Thus, by targeting appropriate PMC events for collection during performance monitoring, it is possible to obtain performance data that is pertinent to hardware functional stages such as processor cores, thread instances, multilevel cache and system memory elements as well as information relating to hardware activities such as address translations for both data and instruction fetch operations (Advanced Micro Devices Inc., 2010; Levinthal, D.; Dongarra J., Moore, S., Mucci P., Seymour, K. & You, H., 2004; Drongowski, P. J., 2010). Another advantage of using PMCs is that the process of invoking monitoring registers is largely non-intrusive since the data that is obtained through this strategy comes from on-chip counters whose operations are ordinarily separate from that of CPU cores. Therefore, apart from the interrupt operations that track specified events of interest, no significant workload is added to processor and memory operations through the invocation of PMC measurements.

It is worth emphasising that while our proposal acknowledges the impact of disk hardware operational performance and its contribution towards

Figure 1. Operational elements of the CPU hardware

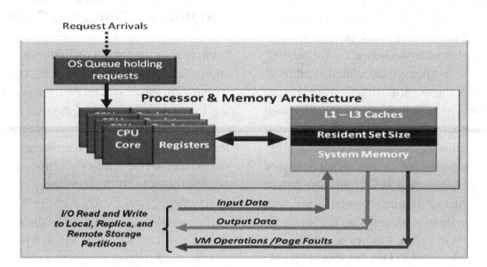

supporting SLA and QoS guarantees in enterprise computing infrastructures, it is only the hardware events pertinent to CPU and memory functions that will be featured in this discussion. The principal reason for the focus of our proposal on the performance of processor and memory architecture is that in many enterprise IT implementations there is a rising trend in the adoption of the in-memory database strategies (Oracle Corporation, 2009; IBM, 2009 and [6,7]) in order to speed up application response times. The in-memory database configurations ensure that once the user data has been transferred from the backend database into the system-memory buffer, it is kept there for almost the entire duration of the computational operations. Hence, with most of the operational activities for servicing database functions being largely confined to CPU and memory stages due to increased use of the in-memory computing techniques, we consider the objective of coming up with detailed considerations of CPU and memory hardware events as a highly valuable approach for providing accurate evaluations and characterisations of obtainable performance trends on server hardware. The principal CPU and memory hardware operational components

that will be the focus of PMC measurements are shown in Figure 1.

While the proposal to use hardware counters for performance monitoring offers greater insight into the trends associated with the internals of CPU and memory elements, the role we that envisage for our approach is one of providing a complementary rather than an alternative set of metrics to the data obtained from application-specific benchmarks that have been discussed in this section.

Figure 2 shows the proposed framework for monitoring performance on CPU and memory hardware. A typical example of the complementarity between the two sets of measurements is shown in the case study presented in Section 6, where the application metrics of the SAP Sell-from-Stock benchmarked routine are translated into hardware operational metrics that are obtained through use of the CodeAnalyst monitoring tool running on the AMD Opteron hardware. Additionally, Figure 2 also shows the Enterprise Resource Planning middleware tools, which run on top of the operating system services as an enabling facility for developing and customising specific application solutions for business user needs.

Figure 2. Proposed framework for monitoring CPU hardware metrics

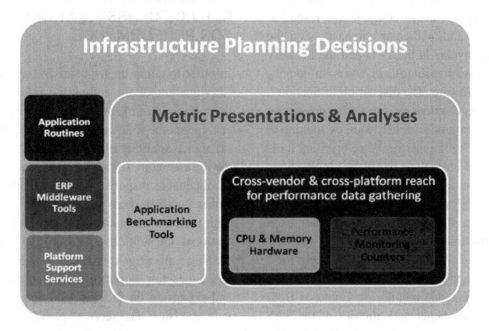

Thus, we consider the strategy of obtaining the data from Performance Monitoring Counters to be potentially useful as a follow-up strategy, particularly in scenarios where the initial output metrics obtained from top-level application measurements may point to the need to address the infrastructure resource provisioning and configuration arrangements so that SLA and QoS parameters can be protected. Through the capabilities offered by performance APIs of the CPU profiling tools, the PMC hardware data associated with the runtime execution of enterprise applications deployed on various operating system platforms and middleware technologies that are based on such paradigms as SOA, Grid or Cloud can be gathered for performance analysis. The PMC-based methods can therefore be employed to determine the specific operational elements in the hardware resource fabric where reconfigurations are required and, also the type of resource management remedies that are effective based on the observed resource consumption patterns. Section 6 also

discusses how PMC data can be used to support interventions at application and system management levels so that operational performance can either be maintained or improved.

Roadmap for Discussion

Given that the proposed use of PMCs is intended to provide support for performance evaluation with particular focus on hosted application services in IT infrastructures, it is considered fitting to highlight the key functional components in computing infrastructures that have a bearing upon the delivery of output performance in the service oriented systems. Hence, in Sections 3 and 4 we present the descriptions of the principal components that influence performance in SOA-based IT systems. The descriptions provided are based on the taxonomy made up of a set of sub-classifications, which were also featured in our previous contribution of (Sithole, E., McClean, S. I., Scotney, B. W., et al., 2008). From the taxonomy of service properties we isolate for detailed consideration the category of physical deployment of compute node resources in Section 5 and, particular emphasis is on the operational events in the CPU and the memory components such caching levels and main memory in server hardware. The discussion in Section 5 also considers various performance monitoring techniques on processor hardware by looking at some of the leading performance profiling tools that are used on various hardware architectures and operating system platforms. The strategies for capturing PMC data using generic tools that have both cross-platform and cross-vendor reach are also discussed in Section 5.

In Section 6 we consider a case study for a SOA-based application that can benefit from the use of performance monitoring counters. Both the application benchmark metrics of the SAP Sell-from-Stock application and CPU/Memory hardware events that have important bearing on performance are featured. To guarantee that the strategies of employing performance registers can be an aid in fulfilling performance goals, Section 6 also highlights specific PMC events that can be used to answer important questions such as (a) which trends in the processor hardware utilisation that can be discerned from the foundation and derived metrics obtained from the PMCs (b) which management policies are appropriate to enforce so that any observed degradation(s) in performance or disproportionate workload distributions are addressed, thereby preventing any SLA and QoS violations (c) and what infrastructure sizes and configurations are necessary for initial deployment and capacity upgrades so as to cope with rising levels in user workloads. The concluding section looks at areas for further research work in CPU operational performance in order to achieve seamless integration between hardware performance monitoring utilities and enterprise application tools.

TAXONOMY OF KEY SERVICE CLASSIFICATIONS FOR PERFORMANCE

In order to come up with satisfactory QoS and SLA guarantees for computing infrastructures, the full scope of planning considerations should encompass the following principal requirements (a) high availability of resources and services on the infrastructure (b) high performance in terms of obtainable response times, throughput rates and scalability trends (c) resilience in terms of fault-tolerant mechanisms for recovery from operational interruptions (d) security to protect the running applications and (e) appropriate physical topologies for supporting resource distribution and expansion for in-house and outsourced service provision. The service taxonomy takes into account these considerations and also builds on other related research contributions on the subject. The discussion in (Biske, T., 2006) highlights the need for first taking into account the technical objectives that are common to most SOA implementations, and then applying those aims in developing service classifications.

A common objective in most SOA solutions is the need for infrastructure designers to obtain a clear appreciation of the architecture in the service landscape. Thus, for the service taxonomy to be useful in this regard, it should structure service properties in such a way that architecturally significant aspects of the SOA environment are easily conveyed. We consider architectural aspects to be the collection of definitions and properties, which describe the *composition, organisation, coordination* and *interactions* of constituent service elements that are brought together to accomplish SOA-based IT solutions.

Another guiding objective which is becoming increasingly important to take into account when developing SOA-based IT systems is the need to design infrastructure deployments that meet specific performance targets. Therefore, the consideration of how service categories can

Figure 3. Elements of the SOA performance framework

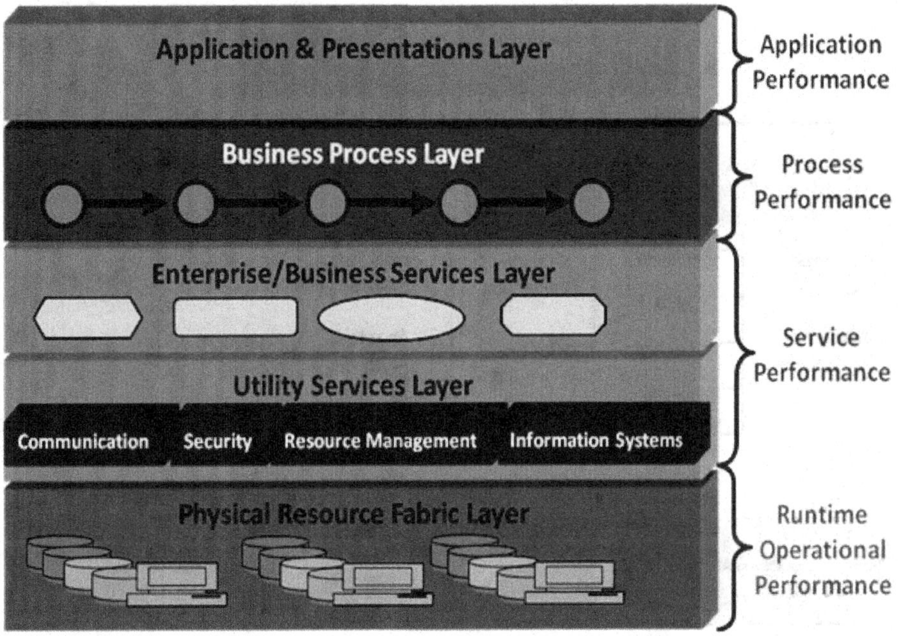

present information for supporting evaluation and planning of performance delivery over the IT infrastructure is another important aspect that forms part of the choices of service classifications which we adopt. Figure 3 shows the principal components of performance on the SOA stack, which need to be captured by the service taxonomy.

Principal Categories for Taxonomy

In order to come up with service characteristics that are relevant to performance delivery, the following categories are adopted as the main classifications of the taxonomy: (a) Service Functionality, (b) Relationships, (c) Interfacing and Runtime Properties, (d) Deployment and (e) Execution Strategies. As has been acknowledged, some of the categories presented in the taxonomy are derived from already existing classifications (Biske, T., 2006; Cohen, S., 2007; Forster, I., Kishimoto, H., Savva, A., et al., 2006). Figure 4 presents a comprehensive service taxonomy,

which contains the key principal dimensions of service characteristics and also shows how they impact on performance.

Classifying Service Functionality

Classifications of service functionality provide clear boundaries on the capabilities that individual services can and cannot offer. Such classification enables solution architects to determine the appropriate combinations of service components that can be brought together in order to meet the specific needs of SOA-enabled applications. The discussion by Cohen in (Cohen, S., 2007) provides two major sub-categories that services can be further classified into on the basis of functional capability; Business and Infrastructure Services. Business services are specific to the particular enterprise domain while Infrastructure services are common to all SOA-driven IT implementations. The Business functionality is subdivided into 3 levels of service integration. The scope of integra-

Figure 4. Identifying performance components from service taxonomy

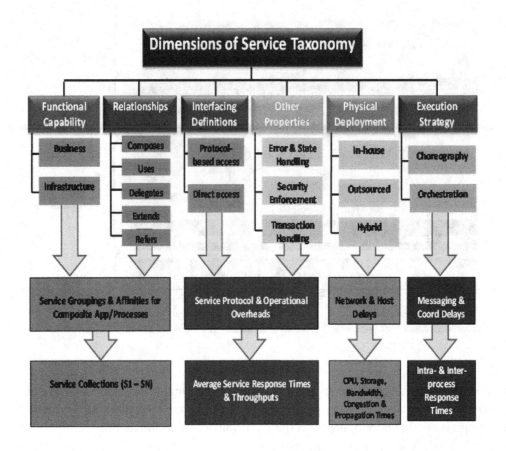

tions can be at Entity, Capability or Activity level. In Figure 4 our taxonomy only presents functional category at Business and Infrastructure levels of operation since we consider those subdivisions to be sufficient in conveying important information about functional capabilities of SOA solutions.

Classifying Service Deployments and Execution Strategies

The approaches followed in the deployment and execution of services make up further categories that we consider important to include in the taxonomy. As Figure 4 shows, Service Deployment determines the physical location within the resource infrastructure where services are installed to run (i.e. whether the intra- or extra-organizational arrangements can be made for accessing required

services, with hybrid approaches encompassing the sue of both internal and outsourced IT services). The Service Execution choices determine the approaches taken in the invocation of individual services that make up compound applications such as business processes. The choice of marshalling strategy depends on the number of dependencies between constituent services that are assembled into a SOA solution. Choreography-based techniques direct the execution of service routines through the operational logic residing inside the service components themselves. Orchestration approaches use external logic to fix the order and coordination of constituent service operations.

Classifying Service Relationships

As shown in Figure 4, the interactions between services form an important dimension that the service taxonomy captures. The description of the interactions through service relationships summarises the respective roles that constituent services play in accomplishing SOA solutions, particularly in scenarios where composite services are used. Based on the set of relationships described in the OGSA document (Forster, I., Kishimoto, H., Savva, A., et al., 2006), the primary behaviours we adopt for our taxonomy are summarised as follows: (a) *Composes Relationship* encompassing situations where a complex service such as business process integrates a collection of underlying service capabilities in order to achieve a requested functionality, (b) *Extends Relationship* characterised by service entities that inherit and supplement the features of parent services, (c) *Uses Relationship* for service interactions whereby one service directs requests to other target services to handle, (d) *Delegates Relationship* for service responses that may optionally redirect requests to other services for execution and (e) *Refers Relationship* that describes responses involving prior consultations between associated services to establish or validate particular status attributes before the execution of received requests can proceed.

Classifying Service Runtime Properties

Each service component has attributes according to which its principal behaviours are characterised. The taxonomy according to (Cohen, S., 2007) presents seven attributes for capturing key service behaviours. From that list our taxonomy adopts five service properties we consider as having strong bearing on performance at runtime: Interfacing Definitions, State Management, Transaction Handling, Error Handling, and Security Enforcement. Reference can be made to Figure 5 to determine the runtime and interfacing properties of services.

The *Interfacing* definitions provide protocol-based descriptions for exposing functions in a service. The *State Management* definitions deter-

Figure 5. Performance components from interfacing definitions and properties

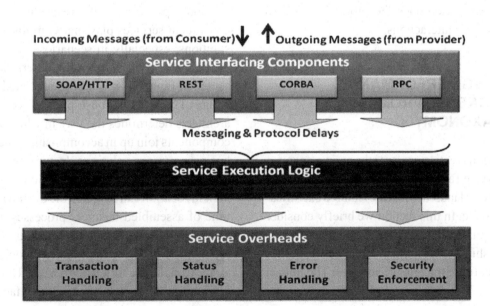

Figure 6. Model for service performance based on taxonomy descriptions

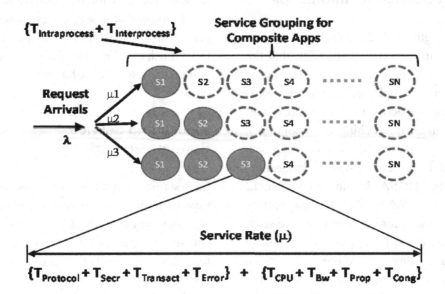

mine how a service responds to messages having a bearing on the status of a running application. The *Transaction Handling* characteristic provide the service's capability to receive, process, generate and transmit data in collaboration with other service objects that it has dependencies with. The *Error Handling* functions specify the corrective ability in a service to deal with operational inconsistencies of SOA-enabled applications. *Security Enforcement* determines the protection offered during service interactions.

DERIVING PERFORMANCE COMPONENTS FROM THE TAXONOMY

The previous section presents the main categories of the Service Taxonomy and the architectural view of the service landscape that the featured classifications provide. In this section we briefly consider the performance implications of the Functionality, Relationships, Deployment, Runtime Properties and Execution Strategies of services. The impact

on performance of the service categories are summarised in Figure 6.

Service and Process Performance from Functionality and Relationships

As discussed in Section 3, the taxonomy summarises the interactions of services through the service relationship category. The service relationships describe the respective roles that constituent services play in accomplishing SOA solutions, especially in scenarios involving use of multiple services. From the descriptions presented in Figure 4, it can be appreciated that the nature of service relationships employed by SOA architects determines the way in which services components join up in accomplishing end-to-end business process solutions. In turn, the integration of services as well as conditions governing their invocation can lengthen the overall response time of assembled business processes. In order to formally describe the phenomenon of service relationship in SOA performance models, Rud et al. in (Rud, D., Schmietendorf, A. & Dumke, R., 2007) propose the use of correlation factors that denote the affinities between service parameters based on previous behavioural patterns.

Service Performance from Interfacing Definitions and Runtime Properties

Interfacing descriptions are a key component of Service Properties as presented in the taxonomy (Cohen, S., 2007). The descriptions specify the formatting of messages, protocol-based exchanges and validations so that users can access and use service capabilities. In terms of the actual sequence of service execution, interfacing determines how the procedures of service discovery, allocation and invocation are performed. Figure 5 shows service interfacing features, which can be SOAP/ HTTP, REST/HTTP, CORBA, or RPC-based. Since service functionalities cannot be invoked without the initial exchange of protocol messages, overheads in terms of time delays are inevitable for SOA-based IT implementations. These overheads directly impact on overall service response times, and also on throughput levels for workloads associated with high rates of service requests. Besides the delays occurring prior to service execution, properties of state management, transaction handling, security enforcement and error correction contribute to additional overheads during runtime as Figure 6 also shows.

Process Performance from Service Location and Execution Strategy

We have highlighted that physical deployments of individual services determine how readily they can be accessed from user environments due to network delays arising from geophysical separation. For local deployments of services, performance evaluation would consider host system settings such as CPU speed, Caching Techniques, Page Fault levels and Disk access mechanisms. In most end-to-end process integrations, significant increase in overall process

response times is experienced when component services are scattered over a wide geographic area. For distributed SOA systems, additional overheads due to network latencies made up of bandwidth, congestion and propagation-related delays need to be considered. Network latencies are especially significant in distributed infrastructures where the SLA guarantees of the SOA implementation are in part dependent on the end-to-end data transfer and communication times. However, considering that network performance is a well researched issue, while CPU and Memory hardware is still an emerging area for investigation, the discussion in the next section focuses on operational performance but only with respect to CPU and Memory hardware activity.

SERVER HARDWARE OPERATIONAL PERFORMANCE AND CPU PERFORMANCE MONITORING COUNTERS

Sections 3 and 4 considered the Service Taxonomy and presented aspects of the service classifications that can impact on the performance service-based computing solutions. In this section we focus on in-house physical deployment of services and consider how detailed operational performance in such a configuration can be obtained from the CPU hardware, which is the physical resource entity upon which the burden to service or execute the received application request is ultimately passed. While processor hardware performance forms only part of the overall performance in service implementations involving multiple machines, it is worth emphasising that detailed study of CPU and memory hardware performance warrants focused attention given it has largely been an unexplored area while network performance has been considered extensively.

We have highlighted earlier that accurate performance evaluation in computing infrastructures requires the ability to gather detailed performance data on the low-level CPU operations of executing processes in a non-intrusive manner. Within operating system functions, standard features are provided such as the GPROF utilities in Unix and Linux environments, and these features can be invoked to produce performance profiles of process executions at runtime (Neville-Neil, G., 2009; Biske, T., 2006). However, the kernel-based functionalities suffer from inherent probe effects due to overheads that are associated with the software-based measurements. Depending on the runtime processes being monitored, the accuracy of results can be severely compromised. Furthermore, and as in the case of the SPEC benchmarks[8,9,10], only narrow sets of metrics on the performance of the CPU and memory operations are provided by the basic operating system-based monitoring functions.

The Advent of CPU Performance Profiling Tools

While the kernel-based utilities have limitations on performance measurements, significant improvements in CPU hardware features have been and continue to be made towards the provision of information-rich and accurate metrics. In most of the emerging families of processor hardware kits delivered by leading manufacturers in the IT market, additional hardware is incorporated that is made up of special registers called Performance Monitoring Counters (PMCs) (Advanced Micro Devices Inc., 2010; Terpstra, D. & Jakonde, H., 2009; Terpstra, D., 2010; Drongowski, P. J., 2010). The PMCs provide a low-level access to the CPU operational elements and thus have the capability to present detailed information on the processor hardware events as they execute at all the important stages of runtime operation. Another noteworthy aspect associated with the PMC-enabled capacity to drill down to the lowest level of hardware operation, is the fact that the tracking of runtime performance is implemented as a separate function from the standard CPU and memory operations

that service scheduled user requests. Hence, with the PMCs existing on the CPU architectures essentially as a standalone functional entity, the operational performance data that is gathered from the monitoring registers is accurate and essentially free from significant overhead.

CPU Profiling Tools and Basic Makeup

A variety of software packages called Profiling Tools have been developed for providing sets of libraries and kernel driver utilities that perform the following main functions in accessing PMC-derived metrics: (a) interfacing to the operating system kernel (b) plugging into the specific hardware architecture and ensuring that the software configurations achieve compatibility with machine-dependent features of the monitored hardware and (c) API support for user-level control, presentation options that enable specific application routines to be selected for performance monitoring, options for choosing specific operational events of interest to be monitored and recorded, optional features for tuning the counting/sampling modes of the performance monitoring functions so that metrics can be captured at the appropriate resolution and, interactive aids for initiating and termination of measurement runs. Figure 7 shows the main functional components that are brought together in coming up with the functional implementations of performance profiling. We briefly consider some of the well known CPU hardware performance profiling tools below.

In order to accommodate the diversity of OS platforms and hardware architectures used in most IT implementations, a number of performance profiling tools provide extensive sets of libraries and driver components. The provision of the interfacing features ensures that both multi-platform and multi-vendor compatibilities are in place whenever CPU performance monitoring functions are invoked. Most prominent among the performance monitoring software packages with diverse

Figure 7. Basic configuration for performance monitoring counters

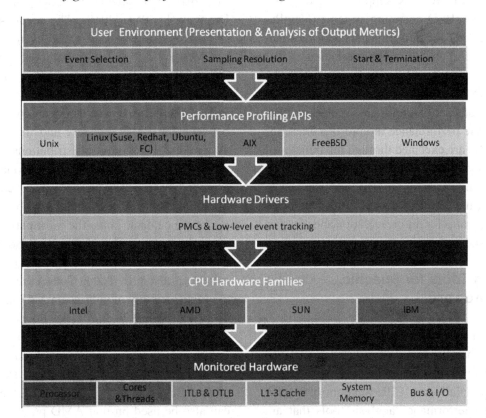

reach across CPU hardware architectures and operating system environments are the Performance Application Programming Interface (PAPI), PERFORMANCE COUNTER (PERFCTR) [11], OPROFILE and Hardware Performance Monitoring Counter (HWPMC) tools (Drongowski, P.J., 2008; Advanced Micro Devices Inc., 2010; IBM alphaWorks, 2009; Terpstra, D., 2010).

The PAPI software libraries provide interfacing capabilities that enable user environments to access and use the performance monitoring registers on the CPU hardware in a consistent manner (Terpstra, D. & Jakonde, H., 2009; Terpstra, D., 2010). Provisions in the PAPI software layers enable generic or platform neutral events as well as platform-dependent native events to be referenced for performance monitoring and collection. The latest releases of PAPI can be deployed on many of current CPU architectures and Operating Systems

used in high-end computing implementations such as IBM POWER (versions 4, 5, 5+, 6) with AIX or Linux, PowerPC (versions 32, 64, 970) with Linux, the Intel Pentium hardware (II, III, etc) with Linux, Intel and AMD (Athlon, Opteron) with Linux. The PERFCTR utility is used as a software patch for adding support in Linux kernels for accessing PMCs on modern processors. Some of the modern CPU architectures that are supported by the PERFCTR drivers are the Intel Pentium family, Celeron and Xeon version, AMD K7 and K8 processor families and PowerPC 604, 7xx, and 74xx processors. The OPROFILE utility is similar to PERFCTR in that it has system-wide capability for supporting performance profiling of processes running in most Linux environments. OPROFILE can work across a range of processor architectures that include AMD Athlon, AMD64, Intel families and ARM CPUs (Levon, J.). The

HWPMC tool provides support for accessing PMCs in FreeBSD operating systems (Neville-Neil, G., 2009) and performance profiling functions are achieved through interfacing driver programs, which enable performance data to be obtained from all modern Intel and AMD CPUs as well as other modern processor chipsets. Essentially, the performance monitoring functions in HWPMC are executed through the transfer of collected event data from performance counters into the main memory buffer by drivers. From the buffer, the captured data is further exported to user programs for the presentation and analysis of processed metrics.

Profiling Tools for Specific CPU Hardware

Apart from the performance profiling packages with the capability to deploy over wide varieties of processor hardware architectures and operating system platforms, CPU vendors have also developed performance analysis tools that are specially designed to plug into their own hardware and thus access more intimate performance data pertaining to the machine-dependent events as they are tracked by PMCs on processor chipsets.

The Intel VTune Performance Analyser[12,13] is a commercial profiling package that captures and presents performance metrics for C, C++, Java and Fortran-based application code as it executes on modern Intel server processors that include the Xeon, IA 32, Intel 64 and Itanium-based hardware. Apart from Windows-based platforms, the VTune tool can deploy most of the Linux distributions such a SLES versions 9-11, Ubuntu, Fedora Core, Debian and Red Hat Enterprise versions 4 and 5.

For detailed performance monitoring on AMD processors, the CodeAnalyst tool has been developed. The CodeAnalyst utility can be used for performance measurements on the K7 and K8 hardware families and these include Athlon 64, AMD Opteron and AMD Phenom processors (Drongowski, P.J., 2008; Advanced Micro Devices

Inc., 2010; Advanced Micro Devices Inc., 2009; Drongowski, P. J., 2010). The special-purpose drivers capturing AMD hardware events recorded by PMCs are able to work in Linux environments through the interfacing functionality provided by libraries. Instead of using OPROFILE, CodeAnalyst has internal drivers for achieving compatibility between the PMC registers and the operating system kernel in Windows distributions. The level of penetration into hardware operational events provided by CodeAnalyst permits several levels of granularity in the presentation of the collected performance data. Thus, the information can be viewed at Process, Thread, Function, Source Line and Instruction levels. Various modes of performance are also provided in CodeAnalyst in order to obtain a variety of metrics on AMD hardware. The Timer-Based Profile (TBP) shows the system components and applications on which most of the CPU time is spent during runtime execution. Since the TBP mode provides performance summaries of non-architecture-specific metrics, the feature can also be used on non-AMD processors. The Event-based Profile (EBP) feature interacts with PMCs to track and record specific events (such as cache accesses and cache misses) that impact on performance inside code regions of running programs. The Instruction Based Sampling (IBS) setting also works with performance monitoring registers in the same way as the EBP, but at a much lower level of granularity since it enables output metrics to be linked to the specific source-program lines and instructions that will have generated the hardware operational events. Given that both the EBP and IBS modes have hardware dependencies, they can therefore only work on AMD processors.

The IBM Counter Analyser is used to capture processor performance data from IBM enterprise server hardware. The Counter Analyser tool is compatible with the AIX and Linux operating systems. Running internally as a component of the Visual Performance Analyser toolkit, Counter Analyser invocations for hardware performance monitoring are achieved through AIX features

Table 1. Dialog steps of the sell-from-stock routine and their runtime functions

Transaction	Dialog Step	Summary Description of Step
		Operation
VA01	D 0101	Create Customer Order
Create order with 5 line items	D 4001	Enter Order Info
	D 4001	Enter Details for 5 items
	D 0101	Save
VL01N	D 4001	Create a Delivery
Create Delivery for this order	D 1000	Enter Delivery Info
	D 4001	Save
VA03	D 0102	Display Customer Order
Display the customer order	D 4001	Choose Customer Order
VL02N	D 4004	Change Delivery Order Info
Change the delivery & post goods	D 4004	Post Goods (schedule delivery)
VA05	D 0100	List Orders
List 40 orders for one sold-to party	D 0500	Choose Set of Orders
VF01	D 0102	Create Invoice
Create an invoice	D 0102	Save

and data-base support facilities for storing PMC data (IBM alphaWorks, 2009). Some of the IBM hardware on which monitoring registers can be accessed by Counter Analyser for detailed performance measurements includes the POWER4, POWER4-II, POWER5, POWER5-II, POWER6, PowerPC970 and PowerPC970MP families of processors.

PERFORMANCE EVALUATION OF ENTERPRISE APPLICATIONS

We now consider how the functionality that is offered by CPU hardware counters can be used to obtain detailed understanding of the top-level metrics associated with SOA-based enterprise applications. The example SOA-based enterprise application that is featured in our consideration is the SAP Sell-from-Stock routine, whose performance evaluation is initially determined according to high-level benchmark metrics at each of the six main service stages of application execution.

Table 1 presents the list of Dialog Steps and the respective functionality provided by each step toward the realisation of Sell-from-Stock operation.

The component steps of the Sell-from-Stock scenario, on which we base the composition of the enterprise application routine in our experiments, are structurally similar to the SAP Sales and Distribution (SD) Benchmark execution sequence[14] (Forster, I., Kishimoto, H., Savva, A., et al., 2006). The Sell-from-Stock is a component module that forms part of the application suite provided by the SAP Enterprise Resource Planning (ERP) Software package[14]. While the monitored application routine bears compositional similarity to the SD Benchmark, the actual resource consumption patterns that are involved in the runtime events as measured in both the application benchmarks and on the CPU hardware are only applicable to the implementation described here. Figure 8 presents the principal components that are brought together for the execution of the Sell-from-Stock benchmark routine.

Figure 8. Basic configuration for sell-from-stock application benchmark

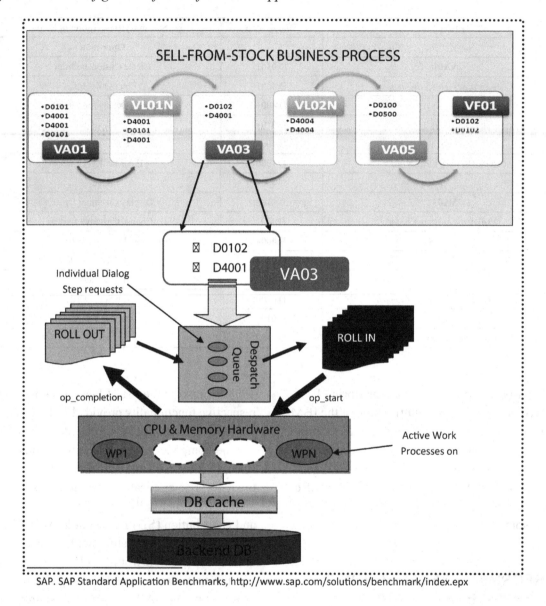

SAP. SAP Standard Application Benchmarks, http://www.sap.com/solutions/benchmark/index.epx

The Sell-from-Stock routine is configured as a business process that is made up of six transactions, with each transaction element functioning as a process component. Inside each process are a number of service operations involving interactions with the CPU, memory and storage hardware and the operations are executed in terms of user-initiated dialog steps. Principal definitions for the execution and benchmarking of the Sell-from-Stock's process components are as follows:

- **VA01**: Create an order with five line items.
- **VL01N**: Create a delivery for this order.
- **VA03**: Display the customer order.
- **VL02N**: Change the delivery and post goods issue.
- **VA05**: List of orders for one sold-to party.
- **VF01**: Create an invoice.

The user-generated requests associated with each transaction stage are held in a despatch queue pending assignment to the processor for execution. The pending requests remain in the scheduler queue until a free Work Process (WP) is available at the CPU. The WP is an active runtime process that has been defined to respond to the Sell-from-Stock user requests and executes directly on the CPU hardware. A set number of active WP instances for the Sell-from-Stock benchmark routine can be invoked by the scheduler in the SAP server. Hence, the definitions of server processing capability should take into account the total WPs provided, not solely the number of processor core units that are allocated on the hardware.

The ROLL_IN mechanism loads onto a free WP all the program runtime data that is related to the received request. Upon completion of the WP execution, the ROLL_OUT routine switches out the completed request from the CPU core, cache and main memory and, finally, the database entries associated with a request are deleted. The WP is then freed and the timer settings for the application performance are reset and stay ready to capture the metrics of the next received request.

The server hardware used for SOA implementation is made up of the AMD Opteron 8354 Quad core Processor, which has three levels of caching. Each CPU core has dedicated L1 (Data) and L1 (Instruction) caches which are 64 KB in size and a 512 KB unified L2 cache. The Level 3 cache is 2MB in size and is shared by 4 cores on a single CPU, while the Main memory with 68 GB is shared across all the 4 CPUs on the processor hardware.

Components of the SAP Sell-from-Stock Business Process Response Time

The key benchmark metrics for Sell-from-Stock routine's main operational events, which are also shown in Figure 9, are briefly described as follows:

- *Generation and Load Time,* which encompasses the times that are spent loading all the relevant functional objects such as the source code, Central User Admin interfaces, screen information from the database in

Figure 9. Component metrics for application benchmarks

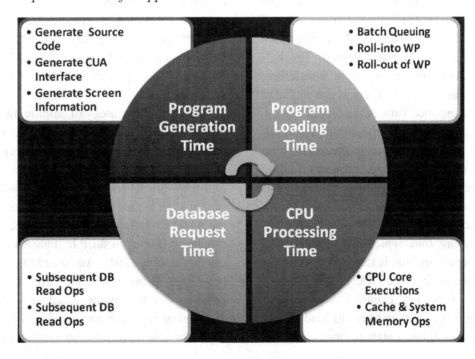

the memory buffer and generating the executable objects into active runnable programs, if necessary.

- *Queuing Time for Work Process,* which is the time that the dispatcher spends waiting for a WP to be free before a received dialog step request is forwarded for runtime execution.
- *Roll-in Time,* which is the amount of time that is taken for user-specific operational data to be loaded onto the runtime work process area from the roll buffer area of the shared memory in preparation for the execution of the dialog step request.
- *Roll-out Time,* which is the amount of time taken for user-specific operational data to be moved out of the runtime work process area to the roll buffer area in the shared memory for eventual deletion upon completion of the execution of the dialog step request.
- *Dispatched or Response Time of the Dialog Step,* which is the time duration from the instant that a user request is sent through by the dispatcher onto an available work process up to the instant that the runtime processing of the dialog step request and transfer of output data to the presentation facilities have been completed. The network delay time involved in transferring responses to remote users is not included in the Response Time at the server.
- *CPU Time,* which is the duration that encompasses times spent in the performing these operational steps: program loading and generation, runtime processing of DB requests and CPU execution of the program code.
- *Processing Time,* which is a component of Response Time that is spent processing the program code at the CPU cores. The processing time thus, excludes other component metrics such as program loading and generation times, database operations, the

roll-in and roll-out and work process waiting times.

- *Frontend GUI Time,* which is the time spend executing the communication steps that are associated with the interactions between the user front-end machine and the application server whenever the dialog step advances through its sequence of operations. The accumulated GUI time includes time spent on the GUI and in the network, but excludes time spent on the application server.

As stated in the introduction, application benchmark measurements provide broad metrics associated with the performance of application execution and, the benchmarking approaches are useful largely in the situations where output metrics can serve as a quick pointer to the loading and operational scenarios that can result in violations of QoS thresholds. Through the use of performance monitoring counters, it is possible to quantify the running program's low-level operations on CPU hardware and establish the respective contributions of hardware activities to the overall performance of the applications. The next section considers how the data provided by the CPU performance monitoring registers can be used as a supporting tool for evaluating the Processor and Memory QoS that is offered by server hardware.

The example strategy of employing the PMC utility featured in our discussion is based on accessing performance monitoring registers on the AMD Opteron 8354 hardware, on which the Sell-from-Stock benchmark routine was deployed run. In order to gain detailed event data, the use of the AMD CodeAnalyst tool is considered in our discussion (Drongowski, P.J., 2008; Advanced Micro Devices Inc., 2010; Advanced Micro Devices Inc., 2009; Drongowski, P. J., 2010). It is worth pointing out that while example performance monitoring approach presented here is based on AMD tools, the overall strategy we propose is as shown by Figure 7 in Section 5, which is generic enough to be applied across various combinations of hardware monitoring and presentation tools. As has been stated, the use of PMC measurements is intended to serve as a complementary or follow up approach to the application benchmark measurements. The output data from PMCs provides insight into the hardware operational bottlenecks, thereby supporting the tuning of running processes so that optimal performance can be achieved. For an insight into the use of PMC-based strategy in evaluating application workload performance on CPU and memory hardware, reference can be made to the studies presented in (Sithole, E., McClean, S. I ., Scotney, B. W., et al., 2011), which were conducted using the CodeAnalyst profiler on the AMD Athlon dual core hardware to monitor a multithreaded C++ application workload based on SAP characteristics.

Translating SD Benchmark Metrics into CPU Hardware Events

In order to understand the Sell-from-Stock measurements in terms of hardware activities executing in the CPU and memory architecture, it is important to provide an approximate mapping between the Sell-from-Stock's component metrics to the low-level CPU operational events. The CPU performance metrics in CodeAnalyst are categorised into five main sets of measurements. The summary CPU and memory functionalities for the Sell-from-Stock application as shown in Figure 10 are also presented in terms of monitored hardware operations in Figure 11.

The impact of Program Loading and Generation functions can roughly be taken to correspond to the enterprise application's resultant Instruction Cache Fetch patterns and the Instruction Cache Hit trends in the Translation Look-aside Buffer tables (I-TLBs) as the program code executes on

Figure 10. Runtime events monitored by Application Benchmark Measurements

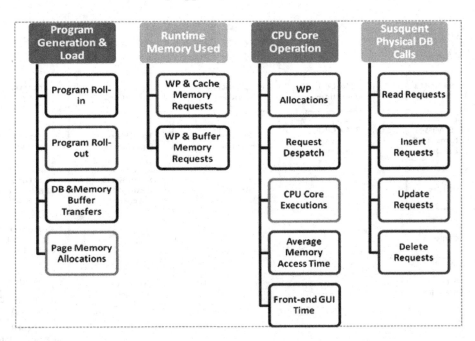

the processor hardware. The Instruction Fetch Events provide the record of the following key metrics during program execution: Completed and Aborted Fetch operations, Translation Lookaside Buffer Hits, Translation Lookaside Buffer Misses in L1 and L2 cache page tables, Instruction Cache Hits and Misses at L1 stage, and Instruction fetch latencies in CPU cycles. The overall performance of executed instructions can be quickly summarised in terms of the Total Retired Instructions which are tracked by the PMCs from sampling to completion and, the CPU cycles consumed during the monitoring period. The derived metric for instruction completion rate is expressed as the number of processor cycles per instruction (CPI) or the inverse, IPC.

In addition to Instruction Fetch patterns, the code shape of the loaded and generated executable program has an influence on the CPU branching operations that are captured by performance counters. As shown in Figure 11, detailed hard-

ware measurements capture the number of retired branch operations, mispredicted branches and returns from subroutine calls. The Application benchmark's Memory Usage metrics are basically related to the CPU Load and Store Operations at processor and memory hardware. The load operations involve transfer of data parameters from memory (both cache and system buffer stages) into the CPU registers while store operations feature transfer of data in the opposite direction.

Apart from the Store operations, the PMC data provides a detailed breakdown of Load operations in terms of Data Fetch and Data Access events.

Data Fetch operations are made up cache hits and misses in the Translation Lookaside Buffers (D-TLBs) of the address page tables provided in the L1 and L2 cache memories. The sub-events that make up the monitored Data Access operations are the Total Data Misses and Hits for all the cache levels, the access operations that were associated with Write Combining (WC) and Uncacheable

Figure 11. Summary of operational events monitored by PMCs

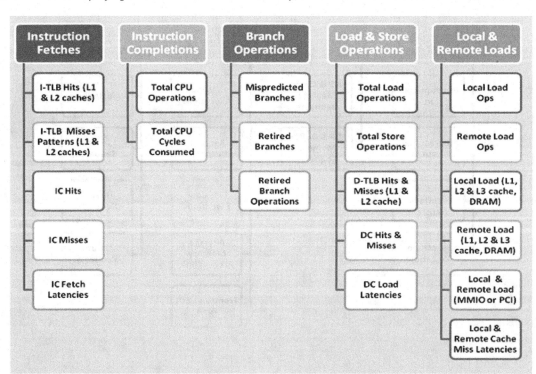

(UC) memory and the latencies in CPU cycles that are incurred in loading data from memory.

Obtaining Detailed Operational Metrics

From the combination of Work Process-initiated data requests at the processor cores that result in access operations in the Cache units, the Memory Buffer and the DB Calls, we can infer the monitored low-level events that will be involved in Northbridge data transfers within the hardware architecture as shown in Figure 12.

The breakdown of the Local Northbridge events monitored by PMCs is as follows (Advanced Micro Devices Inc., 2010; Advanced Micro Devices Inc., 2009):

(a) Total Load operations (for L1, L2, and L3) data access events that are handled by the Local CPU, (b) Load events handled in L1 and L2 caches of the local CPU, (c) Loads handled by the Local L3 cache, (d) Load operations that were serviced at the local system memory (local DRAM via the memory controller), (e) Load operations handled by a local memory partitions via the memory controller interface, (f) Load operations serviced from the local Memory Mapped Input Output (MMIO) devices or PCI space, or from the local APIC, and (g) Data Cache miss latency (in processor cycles) for load operations serviced by the local CPU.

The breakdown of the Remote Northbridge events monitored by PMCs is as follows:

(a) The total load operations handled by a remote processor, (b) number of load operations handled by L1, L2 or L3 cache levels of a remote CPU, (c) load operations serviced by remote system memory, (d) load operations serviced from remote MMIO, configuration or PCI space and (e) total data cache miss latency (in processor cycles) for load operations handled at a remote processor.

Support for Optimisation, Resource Allocation, and Infrastructure Sizing

The collections of PMC data sets described above enable detailed analysis of and optimisation considerations for the performance at the following stages of operation in the CPU and memory hardware to be carried out:

(a) Trends in the distribution of user request levels over the CPU cores. The PMC data sets permit the breakdown of scheduled workloads according to active runtime processes and threads. From the records of Retired Instructions and

Figure 12. Derivation of performance indicators of processor hardware

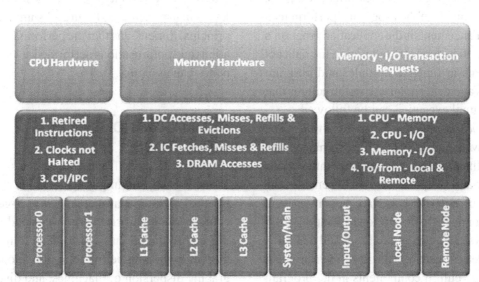

Consumed CPU Cycles, the calculated IPC/CPI trends can be presented according to the respective loads that are applied on the CPUs and processor cores. Should the study of output metrics reveal any load imbalances across the processor and core elements on the server hardware, modifications can be performed in the OS scheduler by changing values of thread and process affinities. Processor and thread affinities determine preference weights according to which runtime processes and threads are mapped onto CPUs and processor core elements for execution. Such corrections to uneven workload distributions through tweaks to thread and process affinities can improve operational efficiencies over multi-processor and multi-core systems, and the approach can be particularly effective for scenarios with uniform CPU architectures running similar workloads.

(b) Trends in cache hits, misses and latencies for TLBs, L1, L2, and L3 cache events. From the performance data associated with multiple cache levels, it is possible to drill down to the specific functional modules and statements in the program code as well as the assembly-language instructions, so that cache hits and misses that are attributed to each of the levels of program execution can be established. With great such penetration into the program structure, it is possible to identify data-locality inefficiencies that can lead to cache misses. Thus, the analysis of the program's performance enables enhancements in the application program's code shape to be made by redefining the data access patterns in function modules and program statements and data organisational structures that permit optimal execution can be followed.

(c) Trends in remote data access events. The CPU hardware registers provide performance data related to the processor and memory interactions with Input and Output devices. This enables the incidence of external hardware operations and latencies connected with data load operations from backend systems such as databases and disk storage to be determined from the PMC measurement reports. Any culprit components in the program

structure that are exposed by the PMC data can be modified so that performance enhancement is achieved through adoption of in-memory buffer techniques.

(d) Wide distribution of service requests. Beyond enabling decisions for optimising the internal program structure of running applications as well as supporting system interventions for redistributing disproportionate load allocations across the processor cores inside the server node, PMC data can also be used to quantify operational performance that server devices can sustain at full capacity i.e. before SLA thresholds are violated. In turn, the information on server peak operational capacity can serve as an aid in high-level planning decisions affecting the size of infrastructure deployments that can successfully deal with projected levels in user demands.

Additionally, the information from PMCs can enable short and medium term strategies for migrating or redirecting flow of requests to alternative server nodes of suitable operational capacity in the event of transient rises in demand or when interruptions occur at regular server machines. Should increases in user demands permanently go beyond service provision capability of existing infrastructure, performance calibrations based on PMC measurements can also be used to determine the size of the capacity upgrades to deal with new levels in user demand. Figure 13 summarises the principal dimensions that the performance evaluations and optimisations performed at local server nodes can assume.

SUMMARY AND FURTHER DIRECTIONS

We started by highlighting how the emerging trend of phenomenal increase in user-generated content in e-enterprise and on-demand computing environments has led to such dynamics as growth in the number of computing nodes, geographic dispersion of machines, and diversity of

Figure 13. Dimensions for considering SLA and QoS evaluations

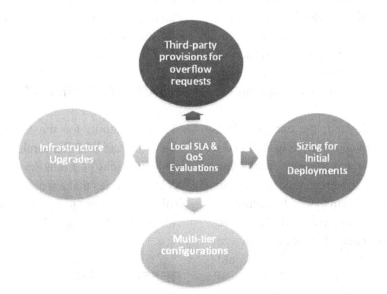

implementation technologies. We also discussed that these developments have led to challenges in coming up with effective strategies for evaluating the performance of enterprise applications, particularly for SOA-based implementations. Limitations associated with current approaches such as benchmarking techniques for both application packages and server hardware were highlighted. As an alternative approach, we proposed the use of PMC utilities, which have the capacity to perform detailed measurements on the low-level functions of the processor hardware in order to establish CPU and Memory QoS. Since performance monitoring registers exist as a separate functional feature on the CPU hardware, the rich data sets associated with low-level events that are captured by PMCs with very low overhead thus permit the monitored application's operational performance to be quantified with greater technical certainty.

By putting emphasis on hardware operational performance (which is a subcategory under main classification relating to resource physical deployment considered in the service taxonomy), the discussion went on to consider the monitoring of CPU operational performance on most server

hardware architectures. Various packages for accessing, processing and presenting CPU performance data were considered in this discussion and, a generic performance monitoring framework based on such packages as OPROFILE or PAPI with broad interfacing capabilities to diverse CPU hardware and operating system environments was proposed. The role which we envisage for PMC-based evaluation of CPU and Memory QoS in enterprise applications is a complementary one to the existing application benchmarks. An example strategy for performance evaluation, which is based on the SAP's SOA-based Sell-from-Stock application using PMC measurements, carried out in the AMD CodeAnalyst tool on the Opteron hardware was featured in Section 6.

Starting with the component metrics obtained from conducting benchmark measurements of the Sell-from-Stock application routine, corresponding metrics of low-level performance data that can be collected from PMCs were considered. The PMC data can be used to show how the hardware operations at each of the main stages of application's runtime execution contribute to the observed results in the output performance of the benchmarked application. The performance data captured from PMCs can also lead to internal program optimisations, system-based enhancements to achieve greater efficiency on the server operation, and external decisions on reallocation of load to other servers and recommendations for capacity upgrades.

As has been highlighted, the two principal merits for the proposed approach of using PMCs are (a) the accuracy of measurements results due to low overhead and (b) greater detail on the low-level operational events, which illuminate performance issues associated with hardware components and the internal program structure of the monitored application. Both aspects would otherwise go unnoticed if standard OS-based monitoring tools or application benchmarks were used in performance evaluations. We thus consider PMC-based approaches to be a very promising frontier in exploring viable strategies for performance evaluations and optimisation of eEnterprise systems. However, the PMCs are a relatively recent feature that has been built into the chipset composition on modern CPU hardware, and the software packages for capturing PMC data from the various processor architectures are still in early stages of development.

Therefore, some of the potentially valuable directions that can result in greater usefulness of PMCs are (a) Provision of interfacing capabilities for seamless integration of hardware performance monitoring tools into Business Application Suites so that automated access into PMC utilities is achieved (b) Resolution of the various information formats of performance data obtained from diverse hardware architecture by filtering out the architecture-specific aspects in some of the low-level measurements in order to standardise output metrics (c) Provision of interfacing support in the PMC and profiling facilities so that interaction with grid and virtualisations technologies can be achieved to support dynamic migration of running processes across nodes in order to alleviate load imbalances and (d) Provision of interfacing support between profiling tools and network management tools so that end-to-end performance can be established and complete SLA guarantees in distributed computing infrastructures achieved.

ACKNOWLEDGMENT

We are grateful for the valuable inputs from researchers at SAP Research Belfast with whom we had insightful discussions regarding some of technical issues that are considered in this paper. This research was jointly supported by INVEST Northern Ireland and SAP.

REFERENCES

Advanced Micro Devices Inc. (2009). *BIOS and Kernel developer's guide for AMD NPT family 0Fh processors*. Retrieved November 4, 2009, from http://developer.amd.com/documentation/guides/pages/default.aspx

Advanced Micro Devices Inc. (2010). *CodeAnalyst user manual*. Retrieved March 4, 2010, from http://developer.amd.com/cpu/CodeAnalyst/codeanalystlinux/assets/

Azimi, R., Stumm, M., & Wisniewski, R. W. (2005). *Online performance analysis by statistical sampling of microprocessor performance counters*. 19th International Conference on Supercomputing (ICS05), Boston, USA, June 2005.

Biske, T. (2006). *Outside the box: SOA, BPM, and other strategic IT initiatives - Service taxonomy*. Retrieved from http://www.biske.com.

Cohen, S. (2007). Ontology and taxonomy of services in SOA. *Microsoft Architect Journal, 11*.

Dongarra, J., Moore, S., Mucci, P., Seymour, K., & You, H. (2004). Accurate cache and TLB characterization using hardware counters. *Computational Science - ICCS. Lecture Notes in Computer Science, 3038*, 432–439. doi:10.1007/978-3-540-24688-6_57

Drongowski, P. J. (2008). *Basic performance measurements for AMD Athlon 64, AMD Opteron and AMD Phenom processors.* Advanced Micro Devices, Inc. Boston Design Center, 25 September 2008.

Drongowski, P. (2010). *Instruction-based sampling and AMD CodeAnalyst,* IEEE International Symposium on Performance Analysis of Systems and Software (ISPASS), White Plains, 29 March 2010.

Finkelstein, S., Brendle, R., Jacobs, D., Hirsch, M., & Marquard, U. (2008). *The SAP transaction model: Know your applications.* ACM. SIGMOD. Conference., June 2008.

Forster, I., Kishimoto, H., Savva, A., Berry, D., Djaoui, A., Grimshaw, A., … Von Reich, J. (2006). *Open Grid services architecture.*

Gove, D. (2007a). *Calculating processor utilisation from the UltraSPARC T1 and UltraSPARC T2 performance counters.* Sun Developer Network (SDN) Technical Article, September 2007.

Gove, D. (2007b). Using performance counters on UltraSPARC T1 and T2 Processors - Finding core load as a means to improving performance. *System News, 116*(1). October 2007.

IBM. (2009). *IBM solidDB v6.5.* IBM Data Management Solutions. Retrieved October 2009, from http://www-01.ibm.com/software/data/soliddb/

IBM AlphaWorks. (2009, September 10). Emerging Technologies: *Pmcount for Linux on power architecture - A hardware performance counter tool for the IBM POWER4, POWER4+, POWER5, POWER5+, POWER6, and PowerPC 970 processors.*

Levon, J. (n.d.). *OProfile manual.* Retrieved from http://oprofile.sourceforge.net/doc/index.html

Levinthal, D. (n.d.). *Performance analysis guide for Intel Core i7 processor and Intel Xeon 5500 processors.* Retrieved from http://software.intel.com/sites/products/collateral/hpc/vtune/

Neville-Neil, G. (2009). *Understanding performance with HWPMC.* BSD Conference (DCBS-DCon), Washington DC, USA, February 2009.

Oracle Corporation. (2009). *Using Oracle in-memory database cache to accelerate the Oracle database.* Oracle Technology Network.

PassMark Software. (2010). *Hardware drive benchmark.* Retrieved August 9, 2010, from http://www.harddrivebenchmark.net/

Rud, D., Schmietendorf, A., & Dumke, R. (2007). Resource metrics for service-oriented infrastructures. In *Proc. Workshop on Software Engineering Methods for Service Oriented Architecture (SEMSOA),* Hanover, Germany.

Sithole, E., McClean, S. I., Scotney, B. W., Parr, G. P., Moore, A. A., Bustard, D. W., & Dawson, S. (2008). *A taxonomy-driven approach for performance measurement and modelling in service oriented architectures.* 2nd Non Functional Properties and Service Level Agreements in Service Oriented Computing Workshop, NFPSLA-SOC'08. November 12, 2008.

Sithole, E., McClean, S. I., Scotney, B. W., Parr, G. P., Moore, A. A., Bustard, D. W., & Dawson, S. (2011). *Characterization, monitoring and evaluation of operational performance trends on server processor hardware.* 2nd ACM/SPEC Internal Conference on Performance Engineering ICPE 2011. Karlsruhe, 14th-16 March 2011.

Terpstra, D., & Jakonde, H. (2009). *Introduction to PAPI, the performance application programming interface.* Retrieved February 2009, from http://www.cs.utk.edu/ terpstra/

Terpstra, D. (2010). *PAPI-C: What can performance components do for you?* Retrieved August 2010, from http://www.cs.utk.edu/ terpstra/

ADDITIONAL READING

Browne, S., Deane, C., Ho, G., & Mucci, P. (1999). PAPI: A Portable Interface to Hardware Performance Counters. *IEEE Proceedings Department of Defense High Performance Computer Modernisation Program Users Group Conference.*

Dongarra, J., London, K., Moore, S., Mucci, P., Terpstra, D., You, H., & Zhou, M. (2003) Experiences and Lessons Learned with a Portable Interface to Hardware Performance Counters. *International Parallel and Distributed Processing Symposium.*

Wolf, F., & Mohr, B. Hardware-Counter Based Automatic Performance Analysis of Parallel Programs. (2003). *Elsevier Proc. of the Minisymposium 'Performance Analysis', Conference on Parallel Computing (PARCO).*

Moore, S., Cronk, D., Wolf, F., Purkayastha, A., Teller, P., Araiza, R., et al. (2005). "Performance Profiling and Analysis of DoD Applications using PAPI and TAU. *IEEE Proceedings Department of Defense High Performance Computer Modernisation Program Users Group Conference.* Andersson, U., Mucci, P. (2005). Analysis and Optimization of Yee_Bench using Hardware Performance Counters," *Proceedings of Parallel Computing.*

Terpstra, D., Jagode, H., You, H., Dongarra, J. (2009). Collecting Performance Data with PAPI-C. *Tools for High Performance Computing* 157-173.

Weaver, V., & Dongarra, J. (2010). Can Hardware Performance Counters Produce Expected, Deterministic Results? *Proceedings of Workshop on Functionality of Hardware Performance Monitoring.*

Drongowski, P. J. AMD CodeAnalyst Team, Advanced Micro Devices, Inc., Boston Design Center. (2007). Improving program performance with AMD CodeAnalyst for Linux. Retrieved December 16, 2010, from AMD Developer Central - Articles and Whitepapers web site: http://developer.amd. com/documentation/articles/Pages/default.aspx.

Drongowski, P. J. AMD CodeAnalyst Team, Advanced Micro Devices, Inc., Boston Design Center. (2007). Instruction-Based Sampling: A New Performance Analysis Technique for AMD Family 10h Processors. Retrieved December 16, 2010, from AMD Developer Central - Articles and Whitepapers web site: http://developer.amd. com/documentation/articles/Pages/default.aspx.

Drongowski, P. J. AMD CodeAnalyst Team, Advanced Micro Devices, Inc., Boston Design Center. (2008). An introduction to Analysis and Optimization with AMD CodeAnalyst Performance Analyzer. Retrieved December 16, 2010, from AMD Developer Central - Articles and Whitepapers web site: http://developer.amd.com/ documentation/articles/Pages/default.aspx.

Advanced Micro Devices. (2009). AMD64 Technology AMD64 Architecture Programmer's Manual Volume 1: Application Programming. Publication No. 24592 - Publication No. 3.15. Retrieved December 16, 2010, from AMD Support Search – Technical Documents web site: http://support.amd.com/us/Pages/AMDSupportHub.aspx.

Drongowski, P. J., Yu, L., Swehosky, F., Suthikulpanit, S., & Richter, R. (2010). Incorporating Instruction-Based Sampling into AMD CodeAnalyst. *Proceedings of International Symposium on Performance Analysis of Systems and Software.*

Drongowski, P. J. (2010). Instruction-Based Sampling and AMD CodeAnalyst. *International Symposium on Performance Analysis of Systems and Software Poster Session.*

Intel Software Development Tools. (2010). Product Brief – Intel VTune Amplifier XE Performance Profiler. Retrieved December 16, 2010, from Intel Software Network web site: http://software.intel. com/sites/products/

Intel Software Development Tools. (2010). Intel VTune Amplifier XE 2011 Release Notes for Linux". Retrieved December 16, 2010, from Intel Software Network web site: http://software.intel. com/sites/products/documentation/.

Intel Software Development Tools. (2010). Intel VTune Amplifier XE 2011 Release Notes for Windows. Retrieved December 16, 2010, from Intel Software Network web site: http://software.intel.com/sites/products/documentation/

Intel Software Development Tools. (2010). Intel VTune Amplifier XE 2011 - Getting Started Tutorials for Linux OS. Retrieved December 16, 2010, from Intel Software Network web site: http://software.intel.com/sites/products/documentation/

Intel Software Development Tools. (2010). Intel VTune Amplifier XE 2011 - Getting Started Tutorials for Windows OS. Retrieved December 16, 2010, from Intel Software Network web site: http://software.intel.com/sites/products/documentation/.

Mericas, A. IBM Corporation. (2005). Performance Monitor – PowerPC Perspective. *Proceedings of International Symposium on High-Performance Computer Architecture (HPCA-11)*.

Siewert, S. (2005). Big iron lessons, Part 3: Performance monitoring and tuning - Considerations for the system architect. Retrieved 16 December 2010, from IBM Technical Library – Multicore Acceleration website: http://www.ibm.com/developerworks/power/library/pa-bigiron3/

IBM Software Group STG Systems Performance Team Development. (2006). CPI analysis on POWER5, Part 1: Tools for measuring performance - An introduction to software resources. Retrieved 16 December 2010, from IBM Technical Library – Multicore Acceleration website: https://www.ibm.com/developerworks/power/library/pa-cpipower1/

IBM Software Group STG Systems Performance Team Development. (2006). CPI analysis on POWER5, Part 2: Tools for measuring performance - An introduction to software resources. Retrieved 16 December 2010, from IBM Technical Library – Multicore Acceleration website:https://www.ibm.com/developerworks/power/library/pa-cpipower2/

Weaver, D. L. Sun Microsystem Inc. (2008). APPENDIX C - Overview of OpenSPARC T2 Design. C.11 Performance Monitor Unit (PMU). *OpenSparc Internals – OpenSparc T1/T2 Chip Multithreaded Throughput Computing*.

Sun System News. (2009). Sun SPARC Enterprise M9000/32 SPARC64 VII Results on SAP-SD 2-Tier App Benchmark. - Achieves 24,650 Users on this 2-Tier ERP Business Test. *Volume 131, Issue 4 on Performance.* http://sun.systemnews.com/articles/131/4/Performance/.

Itzkowitz, M., & Maruyama, Y. (2009). HPC Profiling with the Sun Studio Performance Tools. *Third Parallel Tools Workshop*.

Sun Microsystems, Inc. (2010). *Chip and platform specific performance counters*. UltraSPARC Virtual Machine Specification.

KEY TERMS AND DEFINITIONS

Operational Performance: The quantitative measure of a computing implementation's capabilities with particular focus being on the functionality that is provided by the physical low-level activities executing in the resource fabric's CPU, memory, disk and network hardware elements. Operational performance does not take into account the impact of software-related functions at platform, middleware and application levels.

Performance Monitoring Counters: The set of special registers incorporated in modern CPU chipsets that serve the purpose of tracking the performance of low-level operational events as they execute at processor cores, cache memory, main memory and Input/Output stages of server hardware.

Performance: The quantitative measure of a computing implementation's capabilities to deliver specific functions, which it has been designed and set up to serve. Key performance measures are quoted in terms of throughput rates, response/completion times of received work items and scalability trends. The scalability trends describe the sensitivity of the captured metrics to operational changes such as increases in workload levels and changes to physical configurations of the computing implementations.

Profiling Tools: The middleware packages that provide interfacing capability to performance monitoring counters so that the performance associated with low-level hardware events being tracked by monitoring counters can be conveyed to the user environment for processing, presentation and interpretation.

Quality of Service: The range or agreed boundaries within which the overall output performance that is delivered to the end user has to remain in order that minimum requirements for satisfactory service are maintained in the consumer environment.

Service Level Agreement: The range or agreed boundaries within which the performance in the computing infrastructure has to be maintained by service providers in order to meet the minimum requirements for satisfactory service that is to be ultimately delivered to the consumer environment.

Service-oriented Architecture Taxonomy: The set of classifications that are intended to convey key architectural, functional and performance attributes of the service oriented-based computing implementations.

ENDNOTES

[1] Transaction Processing Performance Council. TPC Results Listing, http://www.tpc.org/information/bencmarks.asp

[2] SAP. SAP Standard Application Benchmarks, http://www.sap.com/solutions/benchmark/index.epx

[3] Standard Performance Evaluation Corporation. SPEC CPU 2006 Results, http://www.spec.org/cpu2006/results/

[4] Standard Performance Evaluation Corporation. SPEC CPU 2006: Readme First, http://www.spec.org/cpu2006/Docs/readme1st.html

[5] Standard Performance Evaluation Corporation. SPEC CPU2006 Benchmark Descriptions, http://www.spec.org/cpu2006/publications/CPU2006benchmarks.pdf

[6] SAP. SAP MaxDB Components, SAP Community Network: SAP NetWeaver Releases. http://www.sdn.sap.com/irj/sdn;

[7] StreamBase Systems. StreamSQL Overview. http://www.streambase.com/developers-docs.htm;

[8] Standard Performance Evaluation Corporation. SPEC CPU 2006 Results, http://www.spec.org/cpu2006/results/

[9] Standard Performance Evaluation Corporation. SPEC CPU 2006: Readme First, http://www.spec.org/cpu2006/Docs/readme1st.html

[10] Standard Performance Evaluation Corporation. SPEC CPU2006 Benchmark Descriptions,
http://www.spec.org/cpu2006/publications/CPU2006benchmarks.pdf

[11] http://www.intel.com/software/products/documentation/

[12] http://www.intel.com/software/products/documentation/

[13] Intel Software Network. Using Intel VTune Performance Analyzer to Optimize Software on Intel Core i7 Processors, http://software.intel.com/enus/intel-vtune/

[14] SAP. SAP Standard Application Benchmarks, http://www.sap.com/solutions/benchmark/index.epx

Section 2
Service Selection

Chapter 6
Transactional–Aware Web Service Composition:
A Survey

Yudith Cardinale
Universidad Simón Bolívar, Venezuela

Joyce El Haddad
Université Paris-Dauphine, France

Maude Manouvrier
Université Paris-Dauphine, France

Marta Rukoz
Université Paris-Ouest Nanterre La Défense & Université Paris-Dauphine, France

ABSTRACT

Web Service (WS) composition consists in combining several WSs into a Composite WS (CWS), which becomes a value-added process. In order to provide reliable and fault-tolerant CWSs, several transactional-aware composition approaches have been proposed. However, as far as we know, no real classification survey of such approaches exists. This is the contribution of this chapter. Our classification distinguishes the more relevant and recent propositions in two groups: approaches based on WS transactional properties and the ones also integrating QoS criteria to the composition process. All these studied approaches are compared according to several criteria: the transactional model used or proposed, the control flow model used or automatically generated, the mechanism proposed to verify the transactional property of the composition, the step(s) of the composition process involved in, and the protocols or the standard languages used or extended. This classification allows underlining the lacks and the future directions which should be studied.

DOI: 10.4018/978-1-61350-432-1.ch006

INTRODUCTION

Web Services (WSs) are quickly raising as a standard for publishing data and operations for weakly loose, heterogeneous systems, by handling simple request and response messages from/to users to satisfy their requirements. WSs are the most famous implementation of Service-Oriented Architectures (SOA) (Erl, 2005) allowing the construction and the sharing of independent and autonomous software. Flexible SOA connections between services, as well as, software components that pass simple data among other services or that coordinate simple activities, are seen as services which can be combined with other services to achieve specific goals. Thus, SOA provides a scalable and robust framework to integrate heterogeneous software agents and enhance reliability of isolated software components (Papazoglou et al., 2007).

As WSs proliferate, it becomes more difficult to find a specific service that can perform a given task, and combinations of several services may be required to satisfy the more complex user queries, which claim for functional and non-functional requirements. SOA technology trend proposes that applications should not be manually developed but integrated from an adequate set of already existing and available WSs. Successive compositions of WSs usually create a complex structure of interactions among a large number of Composite WSs (CWSs) distributed over the Internet. In this sense, automatic service composition has a great potential to facilitate the integration of WSs deployed in distributed platforms (Rao & Su, 2004). In this context, Web Service Composition (WS Composition) consists in aggregating pre-existing WSs, developed by different organizations and offering diverse functional (e.g. ticket purchase, information search), Quality of Service (e.g. execution time, price), and transactional (e.g. compensable or not) properties, to produce a CWS. It allows building, what is called by Ben

Lakhal et al. (2009), value-added services or more powerful and feature-rich processes.

Web Service Selection corresponds to the step of the WS Composition process where the most appropriate service is selected for each operation from a set of candidates which are differentiated by their non-functional properties (Li et al., 2009). The selection task can be static or dynamic. As explained by Egambaram et al. (2010), the differentiation between both selection techniques deals with the moment at which a concrete WS is integrated into the CWS. With static selection the concrete services are determined and integrated into the CWS at design time. With dynamic selection on the other hand, at design-time there is only a specification of the type of required service and the concrete WS is then integrated at run-time. The order in which WSs should be executed is called the control flow structure of the CWS. This control structure can be generated automatically in the selection step (Shin et al., 2009) or can be generated "by hand" by the designer/user by specifying an abstract representation of processes (e.g., a workflow, a Petri Net) (Huang et al., 2009).

After the selection step, the CWS should be executed over the distributed environment; however the interoperation of distributed software-systems is always affected by failures, dynamic changes, availability of resources, user errors, or interference of concurrently executing actions. In this context, Liu et al. (2010) consider that delivering reliable CWS over unreliable services is a challenging problem. A service that does not provide a proper transaction management support that prevents the system from entering undesired states might be as useless as a service not providing the desired functional results (Cardinale et al., 2010). If the composition is based on WSs by only considering functional requirements and QoS properties, then it is possible that during the execution, the whole system becomes inconsistent in presence of failures. Thus, considering transactional properties in WS Composition allows the system to guarantee reliable composition execution. Indeed, the execution of Transactional CWSs (TCWSs) will leave the system in a consistent state even in presence of failures. As explained by Badr et al. (2010), "today's WS applications require advanced transactional models to guarantee integrity and continuity of business processes" (p.30).

Besides considering the matching of WSs functionalities with thoses required by user queries, some WS Composition approaches are QoS-driven, others are transactional-driven, and some others are based on both non-functional (i.e., QoS and transactional) properties. While functional requirements and QoS properties are mainly considered at the selection process in order to select appropriated WSs to produce a CWS, transactional properties have to be also considered during the execution of the CWS in order to coordinate and manage the transactional activity. During the execution of a CWS, concurrent execution and failures of transactions have to be controlled in order to keep the state consistence of the whole system. This transactions control is normally expressed as transaction coordination protocols, many of them combine the well-known Two-Phase Commit (2PC) protocol with compensation techniques.

Recently, there have been proposed many transactional-driven WS composition mechanisms, but there does not exist any work for classification or comparative analysis for better understand them; meanwhile, QoS-aware approaches have been deeply studied, analyzed, and classified - see for example recent works of Eid et al. (2008), Huang et al. (2009), Sivasubramanian et al. (2009), Yu & Reiff-Marganiec (2008), and Zhang et al. (2007). We are rather interested in analyzing and classifying those approaches which consider transactional properties to select appropriated WS in order to produce Transactional CWS (TCWS).

In this chapter, we present the definitions needed to resolve the transactional WS composition problem by classifying the transactional properties and the coordination protocols. We also propose a classification of the more recent existing approaches, organized in two categories: transactional-driven approaches and transactional-QoS-driven approaches. The former approaches only consider WS transactional properties to produce TCWS, while the later ones also try to optimize the TCWS aggregated QoS.

BACKGROUND AND DEFINITIONS

Before selection approaches, based on WS transactional properties, can be classified, this section first presents the definitions we have taken into account to propose our classification.

WS Composition Process

The WS Composition is a highly complex task, and it is already beyond the human capability to deal with the whole process manually. The complexity, in general, comes from the following sources. First, the number of services available over the Web increases dramatically during the recent years; in consequence it is necessary to have a huge WS repository to be searched. A universal registry, called UDDI (Maximilien & Singh, 2004), is normally used. UDDI allows for the creation of registries that are accessible over the Web. Second, WSs can be created and updated on the fly, thus the composition system needs to detect the updating at run-time and the decision should be made based on the up to date information. Third, WSs can be developed by different organizations, which use different concept models to describe the services, then a standard language to define and evaluate the WSs in an identical means is needed (Rao & Su, 2004). Semantic WSs technology (McIlraith et al., 2001) aims to provide for rich semantic specifications of WSs through several specification languages such as OWL for Services (OWL-S) (Martin et al., 2004), the Web Services Modeling Ontology (WSMO) (Lausen et al., 2005), WSDL-S (Akkiraju et al., 2005), and Semantic Annotations for WSDL and XML Schema (SAWSDL) (Farrell & Lausen, 2007).

The complex WS Composition problem can be view as a three-steps process (El Haddad et al., 2010b), as it is graphically shown in Figure *1*:

1. User query specification or Composite Web Service (CWS) specification. At this step (see Step 1 in Figure *1*), a user submits the goal he/she wants the CWS achieves, possibly along with some pre-conditions, effects, constraints, and preferences that need to be satisfied (Yu et al., 2008). These specifications can be defined in terms of the set of input attributes that will be bound in the query and the set of attributes that will be returned as the output by the CWS (Blanco et al., 2011; Brogi & Corfini, 2007; Shin et al., 2009); or represented by a predefined control structure, such as workflows (Bhiri et al., 2006; El Haddad et al., 2010b; Liu et al., 2010), Advanced Transactional Models (ATMs) (Ben Lakhal et al., 2009; El Haddad et al., 2007; Vidyasankar & Vossen, 2004), and Petri Net (Zhang et al., 2008).

2. Selection of the component WSs. During the second step (see Step 2 in Figure *1*), component WSs fulfilling the user's goal are selected among a set of available services. If the control structure is not provided by the user in the first step, all services and their control flow (i.e., the control structure) are automatically discovered in this step. Otherwise, if the control structure is defined by the user at the first step, the selection step becomes in identifying services that best match each abstract process specified in the control structure. In both scenarios, the purpose of WS selection is to select optimal WS for a particular task, based on criteria such as functional requirements, QoS parameters, transactional properties, etc. Other tasks that can be included in this step are regarding to the CWS analysis and

validation. A CWS may be analyzed and verified at design time by checking that it ensures certain relevant properties, related to, for example, its composite semantic, its transactional properties, or the correct construction of the control flow.

3. Execution of the CWS. When component WSs are selected at design time (Step 2), the third step of the composition process (see Step 3 in Figure *1*) consists in immediately executing each component WS of the provided CWS and the selection step is called *Static Selection*. If the selection of WS is made at run-time, selection and execution steps are integrated and the selection

Figure 1. The three-steps WS composition process

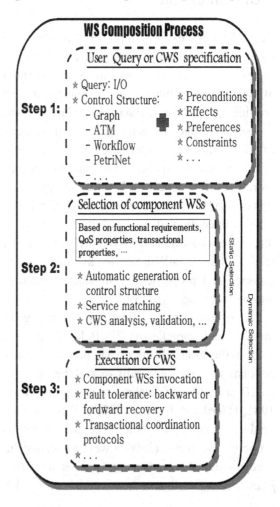

process is described as *Dynamic Selection*. During the execution step, other issues besides WS invocation should be taken into consideration. For example, fault tolerance mechanisms for error recovery or transactions management protocols to control transaction activities. Regarding fault tolerance mechanisms, there are two main classes of recovery: backward (based on rolling system components back to the previous correct state and normally implemented with transactions compensation mechanisms) and forward error recovery (which involves transforming the system components into any correct state and normally based on exception handling).

WS Transactional Properties: A Classification

Recently, the role of WSs has been extended from a support of information interaction to a middleware of process integrations. Nowadays, the idea of dynamically combining individual services to provide new value-added services and make them accessible via the Web is a main interest in scientific institutions and enterprises. To achieve this goal, transaction support has become a more and more important aspect for WS technology, since it is critical to ensure a correct integration and a reliable execution of the integrated services. In this sense, a transactional WS is defined by Bhiri et al. (2005) as "a Web Service that emphasizes transactional properties for its characterization and correct usage" (p. 139).

There are many classifications concerning the transactional properties of a WS. Below we present some of these classifications. The proposed transactional properties generally extend the classical ACID properties of database transactions (Gray, 1981; Häerder & Reuter, 1983) to WSs, by particularly relaxing the atomicity (i.e., all or nothing) property. As Liu et al. (2006b), we consider that the lifecycle of a WS contains two phases: an *active phase* corresponding to the execution of the WS

and a *completed phase* beginning after the end of WS execution. A failure of the WS can occur during the active phase. However a WS could be required to recover independently of the phase it is in. Depending which lifecycle phase the WS is in, different recovery techniques can be applied to preserve the relax atomicity:

- **Backward recovery**: After a failure has occurred during a WS execution, a backward recovery consists in restoring the state that the system had at the beginning of the WS execution or in reaching a state semantically closed to the state that the system had at the beginning of the WS execution. A WS supports backward recovery if, in case of failure during its execution, all the effects produced by the WS before the failure can be undone.

- **Forward recovery**: After a failure has occurred during a WS execution, a forward recovery consists in repairing the failure and to allow the failed WS to continue its execution.

- **Semantic recovery**: After the end of a WS execution, a semantic recovery consists in reaching a state, which is semantically closed to the state the system had before the WS execution.

The two WS lifecycle phases and the different recovery techniques are represented on Figure 2.

To compare the different definitions of WS transactional properties, in terms of termination conditions, we consider two additional criteria:

- **Successfully termination guarantee**: A WS supports a successfully termination guarantee if it provides mechanisms to guarantee that its complete execution will always be reached.

- **Supporting 2PC**: A WS, which participates into a composition, supports the 2PC protocols (Gray 1978; Lampson & Sturgis,

Figure 2. Lifecycle of a WS and the different possible recovery techniques

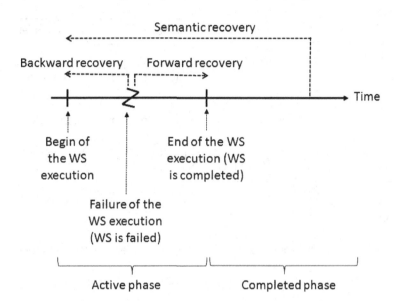

1976) if it is not allowed to complete (commit) unless the entire component WSs participating in the 2PC protocol are able to complete.

Considering the previous criteria, we propose a classification of the different WS transactional properties proposed in the literature.

Many authors, for example Bhiri et al. (2005), Cardinale et al. (2010, 2011), El Haddad et al. (2010a, 2010b), Gaaloul et al. (2010), Li et al. (2007a), Maamar et al. (2007), Montagut et al. (2008), and Zhao et al. (2008), use the same properties (i.e., *pivot, compensatable,* and *retriable*) to define transactional WSs:

- A WS is said to be *pivot* (*p*) if once it successfully completes, its effects remains forever and cannot be semantically undone. If it fails, then it has no effect at all. Therefore a *pivot* service supports backward recovery. A completed *pivot* WS cannot be rolled back and cannot be semantically undone.

- A WS is said to be *retriable* (*r*) if it guarantees a successfully termination after a finite number of invocations. Therefore a *retriable* service supports forward recovery.

- A WS *s* is said to be *compensatable* (*c*) if it exists another WS, *s'*, or compensation policies, which can semantically undo the execution of *s*. WS *s* supports backward recovery and can be semantically undone while WS *s'* has to guarantee a successfully termination.

- The *retriable* property is never used alone by the authors but is combined with properties *p* and *c* defining *pivot retriable* (*pr*) WS (equivalent to *retriable*) and *compensatable retriable* (*cr*) WS (supporting both forward recovery and semantic recovery).

Figure 3 presents the state diagrams of these WS transactional properties. Final states of the diagrams are represented by dotted lines.

These properties are adapted from the transactional properties identified by Mehrotra et al. (1992) for MultiDataBase Systems (MDBS), due to the autonomy and heterogeneity of both WSs

Figure 3. WS transactional properties

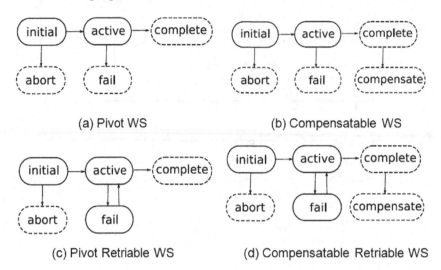

(a) Pivot WS (b) Compensatable WS

(c) Pivot Retriable WS (d) Compensatable Retriable WS

and local DBMSs in the MDBS (Liu et al., 2010). As explained by Bhiri et al. (2005) or Montagut et al. (2008) these transactional properties can be integrated to the WSDL interface or the OWL-S profile of a WS.

These properties are the main used ones. Therefore, in the following of the chapter, we use them as reference, unless otherwise stated.

These properties have been extended to CWSs by El Haddad et al. (2010b), defining *atomic, compensatable, retriable,* and *transactional* CWS:

- A CWS is said to be *atomic* (*a*) if once its entire component WSs complete successfully, their effect remains forever and cannot be semantically undone. On the other hand, if one component WS does not complete successfully, then all previously successful component WSs have to be compensated. A similar definition is used by (Liu et al., 2009a). Therefore, an *atomic* CWS supports the same criteria than a *pivot* WS, except that the backward recovery of an atomic CWS allows to reach a state of the system semantically closed to the state that the system had at the beginning of the WS execution.

- A CWS is said to be *compensatable* (*c*) if its entire component WSs are *compensatable* and it is said to be *retriable* (*r*) if its entire component WSs are *retriable*.

- The *retriable* property is combined with properties *a* and *c* defining *atomic retriable* (*ar*) CWS (supporting the same criteria than a *pivot retriable* WS) and *compensatable retriable* (*cr*) CWS (supporting the same criteria than a *compensatable retriable* WS).

Thus, according these definitions a CWS is said to be *transactional* if its transactional property is in {*a, ar, c, cr*}.

Pires et al. (2003) also use the transactional properties: *compensatable, pivot,* and *retriable* defined above. They also define a *virtual-compensable* property. As explained by the authors, a WS is *virtual-compensatable*, if its effects are not compensated by the execution of another WS but whose underlying system supports the standard 2PC protocol.

Ben Lakhal et al. (2009) introduce the notion of vitality degree associate to the *compensatable* property to define four transactional properties: *vital-compensatable* (equivalent to the *compen-*

satable retriable property defined above except that it can fail after a finite number of invocations and then supports backward recovery), *non-vital compensatable* (equivalent to the *compensatable* property defined above), *vital non-compensatable* (equivalent to the *pivot retriable* property defined above except that it supports also backward recovery), and *non-vital non-compensatable* (equivalent to the *pivot* property defined above). Another exception with the previous definitions is that the failure of a *non-vital* WS *s* does not have any impact on the successful execution of a CWS having *s* as WS component (i.e., it does not produce the CWS failure).

Portilla et al. (2007) use their own taxonomy of transactional WS properties. In this approach, all WSs support backward recovery. The authors define a WS as *non vital* if when it has to be undone, it does not need to be compensated (e.g., commercial information sending), as *critical* if it cannot be compensated, as *undoable* if its effects can be undone without side-effects, and as *compensatable* if its effects can be undone with side-effects. The transactional properties of a CWS depend on the transactional properties of its components. Therefore, a CWS is *non-vital* if all its components are *non-vital*; a CWS is *critical* if it contains at least one *critical* component; a CWS is *undoable* if all its components are *undoable* or *non-vital* and is *compensatable* if all its component are *non vital, undoable,* or *compensatable*.

Liu et al. (2006a) adopted and adapted terms *atomic, quasi-atomic,* and *non-atomic* to label transactional properties of WSs. They define an *atomic* service as a service that has no effect when it aborts. Therefore a backward recovery is useless for such service. A *quasi-atomic* service is a service that needs compensation to undo its effect when it aborts. Therefore, it supports a backward recovery, while a *non-atomic* service is a service whose effects cannot be eliminated once is completed, i.e., a service which does not support semantic recovery. As Portilla et al. (2007), Liu et al. (2006a) consider that the transactional

properties of a CWS depend on the transactional properties of its components: They consider that an *atomic* CWS contains only *atomic* components; a *quasi-atomic* CWS contains at least one *quasi-atomic* and no *non-atomic* ones and a *non-atomic* CWS contains at least a *non-atomic* CWS.

Based on the two phases (active and complete) of the service lifecycle, Liu et al. (2006b) classified transactional properties of WSs into *atomic, semantic-atomic, weak-atomic,* and *pivot* services. An *atomic* service is a service that supports 2PC in its active phase and compensation when completed. A *semantic-atomic* service is a service that only provides compensation when completed, and then does not supports 2PC. A *weak-atomic* service is a service that only supports 2PC in its active phase. Finally, a *pivot* service is a service that is not *atomic*, neither *semantic-atomic*, nor *weak-atomic*.

Recently, Liu et al. (2010) use the same terms to define their own taxonomy of transactional WS properties, considering *compensatable* and *cancellable* (i.e., the possibility for the user to cancel a WS during its execution) properties as two dimensions. They define a *pivot* service as a service which is neither *cancellable* nor *compensatable*, while an *atomic* one is defined to be both *cancellable* and *compensatable*. They also define a *weak-atomic* WS to be *cancellable* but no *compensatable* one and a *semantic-atomic* WS to be a *compensatable* but no *cancellable* WS. The forward recovery and the successfully termination guarantee are not considered by the authors. Indeed, they consider that because a service can disappear, it cancels its eventually *retriable* property: it can disappear after several invocations but before its completion.

Table 1 summaries our WS transactional properties comparison according to the five criteria defined at the beginning of the section. A *Yes* value (resp. *No*) in a column means that the WS with the corresponding transactional property supports (resp. does not support) the criterion. When a criterion has no sense for this transac-

Table 1. Classification of the WS transactional properties

Transactional property	Backward recovery	Forward recovery	Semantic recovery	Successfully termination guarantee	Supporting 2PC
pivot (Bhiri et al., 2005;Cardinale et al., 2010; Cardinale et al., 2011; El Haddad et al., 2010a; El Haddad et al.; 2010b; Gaaloul et al., 2010; Li et al., 2007a; Maamar et al., 2007; Montagut et al., 2008;Pires et al., 2003; and Zhao et al., 2008; Liu et al., 2010[*]) **atomic** (El Haddad et al., 2010b) **non-vital non-compensatable** (Ben Lakhal et al., 2009) **weak-atomic** (Liu et al., 2010) (*) the backward recovery can be fired by the user	Yes	No	No	No	No
Transactional property	**Backward recovery**	**Forward recovery**	**Semantic recovery**	**Successfully termination guarantee**	**Supporting 2PC**
compensatable (Bhiri et al., 2005, Cardinale et al., 2010; Cardinale et al., 2011; El Haddad et al., 2010a; El Haddad et al., 2010b; Gaaloul et al., 2010; Li et al., 2007a; Maamar et al., 2007; Montagut et al., 2008; Pires et al., 2003;and Zhao et al., 2008) **non-vital compensatable** (Ben Lakhal et al., 2009) **atomic** **semantic-atomic**[*] (Liu et al., 2010) (*) the backward recovery can be fired by the user	Yes	No	Yes	No	No
retriable **pivot retriable** (Bhiri et al., 2005, Cardinale et al., 2010; Cardinale et al., 2011; El Haddad et al., 2010a; El Haddad et al., 2010b; Gaaloul et al., 2010; Li et al., 2007a; Maamar et al., 2007; Montagut et al., 2008; Pires et al., 2003;and Zhao et al., 2008) **atomic retriable** (El Haddad et al.; 2010b)	No	Yes	No	Yes	No
compensatable retriable (Bhiri et al., 2005, Cardinale et al., 2010; Cardinale et al., 2011; El Haddad et al., 2010a; El Haddad et al., 2010b; Gaaloul et al., 2010; Li et al., 2007a; Maamar et al., 2007; Montagut et al., 2008; and Zhao et al., 2008)	No	Yes	Yes	Yes	No
virtual compensatable (Pires et al., 2003)	Yes	Yes/No	No	Yes/No	Yes
vital non-compensatable (Ben Lakhal et al., 2009)	Yes	Yes	No	No	No
vital compensatable (Ben Lakhal et al., 2009)	Yes	Yes	Yes	Yes	No

continued on following page

Table 1. Continued

Transactional property	Backward recovery	Forward recovery	Semantic recovery	Successfully termination guarantee	Supporting 2PC
non-vital (Portilla et al., 2007)	Yes	Yes/No	Useless	Yes/No	No
critical (Portilla et al., 2007)	Yes	Yes/No	No	Yes/No	No
Undoable[a] **Compensatable**[b] (Portilla et al., 2007) *(a) semantic recovery without causing side-effects* *(b) semantic recovery causing side-effects*	Yes	Yes/No	Yes	Yes/No	No
atomic (Liu et al., 2006a)	Useless	Yes/No	Yes/No	Yes/No	No
quasi-atomic (Liu et al., 2006a)	Yes	Yes/No	Yes/No	Yes/No	No
non-atomic (Liu et al., 2006a)	Yes/No	Yes/No	No	Yes/No	No
atomic (Liu et al., 2006b)	Yes	Yes/No	Yes	Yes/No	Yes
semantic-atomic (Liu et al., 2006b)	Yes	Yes/No	Yes	Yes/No	No
weak-atomic (Liu et al., 2006b)	Yes	Yes/No	No	Yes/No	Yes
pivot (Liu et al., 2006b)	Yes	Yes/No	No	Yes/No	No

tional property, we use value *Useless*. Finally, a *Yes/No* value means that the criterion can or not be supported by the WS with the corresponding transactional property. This value is generally put when the definition given by the authors does not allow us to know how the criterion can be exactly supported.

Transactional Coordination Protocols for CWS

Functional requirements and transactional and QoS properties are mainly considered at the CWS specification and selection steps in order to identify appropriated WSs that fulfill user query requirements. Meanwhile, transactional properties have to be also considered during the execution step in order to coordinate and manage the transactional

activity. In this context, the transactional coordination models focus on relaxing the isolation property of the well-known transaction ACID properties (Gray, 1981; Häerder & Reuter, 1983) and rely on compensation mechanisms to ensure the atomicity of transactions in presence of failures. Isolation usually enforces locking the resources used by each WS until the entire component WSs reach a unanimous outcome. Because the resources accessed by WSs belong to different organizations, locking resources for a long time can be unfeasible. Therefore, isolation has to be relaxed allowing transactions to commit independently. In case of failure of one WS component, the concept of compensation seems suitable to model CWS scenarios and plays an important role in semantic recovery. The mechanism of compensation was originally proposed by Gray, (1981), applied in

Sagas (Garcia-Molina & Salem, 1987) for long running transaction processing, and then widely used in both ATMs (Elmagarmid, 1992) and transactional workflows (Grefen, 2002) to maintain atomicity when the isolation property has to be relaxed. When compensation is necessary, the transactional managing protocols have to take into account the transactional dependencies produced by the CWS to avoid inconsistency problems. When compensation is not always possible for all WS components, a transaction protocol, like 2PC (Gray 1978; Lampson & Sturgis, 1976), has to be used associated with compensation techniques for transactional coordination.

Transactional coordination protocols can be classified as centralized, distributed, or hybrid. When a protocol is centralized, a coordinator manages both the process flow and its transactional scopes (Alves et al., 2007). In totally distributed transactional coordination, all participant WSs come to an agreement obtaining a transactional outcome. Hybrid protocols combine centralized and decentralized features by interposing coordinators defining for example a hierarchy of transaction coordinators.

The most popular centralized protocol, the Business Transaction Protocol (BTP) (Furniss et al., 2004) proposes a two-phase orchestration of composite WSs. It coordinates the transactions by exchanging messages among the transaction parties. This involves a two-phase protocol that ensures that either the entire attempted transaction is abandoned or a consistent set of participants is confirmed.

To overcome the bottleneck associated with a centralized controller, several approaches (Choi et al., 2005, Fauvet et al., 2005; Türker et al. 2005) propose a distributed orchestration of composite Web services. Fauvet et al. (2005) use an extension of the two-phase coordination protocol. In addition, their approach allows the user to express maximal and minimal constraints over the set of services expected to the validation phase. However, this model is limited to a sequential

execution of transactions. Choi et al. (2005) and Türker et al. (2005) propose protocols based on the recoverability criterion, serialization graph testing and partial semantic recovery. Particularly, Türker et al. (2005) propose a peer-to-peer transaction processing framework that deals with grid-specific requirements. This approach is based on serialization graph testing and is limited to a sequential execution of transactions.

The standard protocols Web Service Composite Application Framework (WS-CAF) (Bunting et al., 2003) and the Web Service Transactions Framework (WS-Tx) (Robinson et al., 2009) are hybrid. WS-CAF supports multiple coordination protocols such as the classic 2PC protocol, long running actions with compensation, and complex business process and orchestration flows. WS-Tx consists in WS-Coordination (WS-C) (Feingold & Jeyaraman, 2009), WS-Atomic Transaction (WS-AT) (Little & Wilkinson, 2009), and WS-Business Activity (WS-BA) (Freund & Little, 2009) from the OASIS project. The WS-C specification provides an extensible framework for the definition of protocols that coordinate distributed activities. The framework can be used to support different coordination types, including classic atomic transactions and long-running business transactions. WS-C enables the creation of coordination contexts for propagation among coordination participants, and the registration of participants for particular coordination protocols of a given coordination type. WS-AT and WS-BA define agreement coordination protocols, such as a durable 2PC protocol (WS-AT) or a participant-driven completion protocol for business transactions (WS-BA). Among the approaches based on a hierarchy of transaction coordinators we can mention the work of Vidyasankar & Vossen (2004) and of El Haddad et al. (2007). Vidyasankar & Vossen (2004) present a multi-level model for service composition that does not support users' constraints. El Haddad et al. (2007) present a transactional execution model of composite Web services exploiting the transactional properties

Table 2. Comparison of the transactional coordination protocols

Protocol	Type	Supporting 2PC or an extension of 2PC	Compensation
Furniss et al. (2004) - BTP	Centralized	Yes	Yes/No (depending on the participant)
Choi et al. (2005) Türker et al. (2005)	Distributed	No	Yes
Fauvet et al. (2005)	Distributed	Yes	No
El Haddad et al. (2007) Vidyasankar & Vossen (2004)	Hybrid	No	Yes
Feingold & Jeyaraman (2009)– WS-C Little & Wilkinson (2009)– WS-AT	Hybrid	Yes	No
Freund & Little (2009)– WS-BA	Hybrid	Yes	Yes

of their component Web services. The proposed concurrency control is ensured by a decentralized serialization graph based on an optimistic protocol and on the hierarchical structure of the composition.

Table 2 presents a comparison of these protocols and specifies, for each protocol, if it supports 2PC or an extension of 2PC and/or provides compensation mechanisms. A concise survey and analyze of the evolution of transaction models focused on coordination transaction protocols is presented in (Wang et al., 2008). Recently, the aforementioned protocols have been extended by (Alrifai et al., 2009; Liu & Zhao 2008; Schäfer et al. 2008; Wang et al., 2009) to improve their performance and reliability by relaxing the ACID properties but still ensuring the system state consistency in presence of failures.

TRANSACTIONAL WS COMPOSITION: A CLASSIFICATION

We classify the transactional WSs approaches based on WS composition process steps (see Figure 1). We consider two categories: transactional-aware and transactional-QoS-aware approaches. The former only consider WS transactional properties to produce TCWS, while the later also try to optimize the TCWS aggregated QoS.

Some approaches claim the user participation to define the WSs control structure in the CWS; meanwhile others automatically produce the WS control flow in the CWS. On the other hand, some of these approaches, besides the proposition or implementation of a selection mechanism, also propose coordination protocols to control the transactions activity during the execution of the CWS. Additionally, there exist some works proposing frameworks to support users in the whole process of WS Composition.

The studied transactional-aware approaches are summarized in Table 3 and the transactional-QoS-aware ones in Table 5. They are compared in Table 4 and in Table 5 respectively, according to the transactional and the control flow models used, the mechanism to relax atomicity, the step of the WS composition process they concern, and if they use or extend standard languages or protocols for transactions management. Finally, Figure 4 presents a classification of these approaches grouping together each category depending on the WS composition process step and if the control flow model is provided by the user or not.

Transactional-Aware Approaches

Transactional-aware WS selection consists in selecting WSs to build a transactional CWS, i.e.,

Figure 4. Classification of the transactional WSs composition approaches

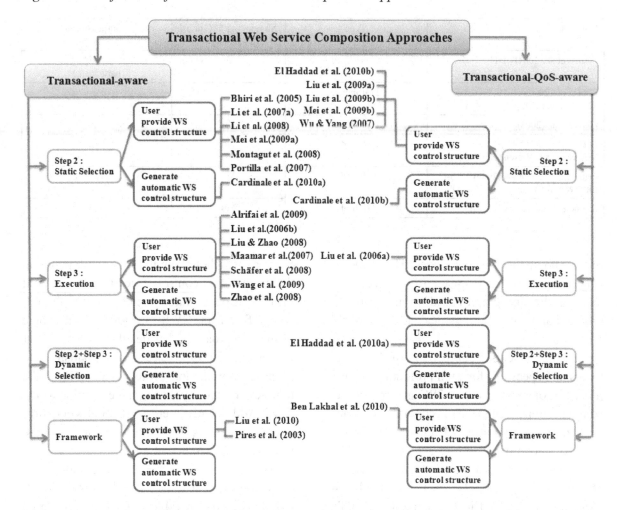

combining component WSs such that the aggregation of their transactional property corresponds to a transactional property of the CWS. Zhao et al. (2008) defines a CWS as transactionally correct if it verifies a "relax atomicity criteria", i.e., if all component WSs reach a unanimous outcome or a completed accepted state, relaxing the "all-or-nothing" well-known principle of atomicity database transaction. As defined by Bhiri et al. (2005), "an accepted state of a composite service *cs* is a state for which designers accept the termination of *cs*" (p. 142). Correctness criterion can be defined by Acceptable Termination States (ATSs) (Rusinkiewicz & Sheth, 1995), by transactional rules defining the possible combinations of com-

ponent WSs to obtain a TCWS (El Haddad et al. 2010b), by transactional coordination protocols (Pire et al., 2003), or by specifying the fault handling logic of the CWS (Liu et al., 2006b).

For static selection, Bhiri et al. (2005) propose an algorithm to verify the validity according to all the ATSs of a CWS. The main contribution of this work is the CWS validation approach according to WS transactional properties. If the CWS is not valid, designers are assisted to select new component WSs respecting the defined ATSs. Montagut et al. (2008) also use ATS and propose a WS selection process. Both propositions are based on workflows provided by users, and use

Table 3. Summary of transactional-aware approaches for WS composition

Approach	Objective
Alrifai et al.(2009)	Extend the WS-TX protocol by introducing a WS-Scheduler to implement service-level concurrency control using an optimistic protocol and handling global waiting cycles
Bhiri et al. (2005)	Validate CWS with regards users' requirements and assist designers to compose a transactional CWS. The user provides a workflow with additional dependencies and the required ATS, and the algorithm indicates if the CWS is transactionally valid (i.e., if it verifies the ATS) or not.
Cardinale et al. (2010)	Propose an automatic generation of a CWS control structure based on the aggregated transactional property, where the user provides inputs, outputs, and a risk level (i.e., compensatable or not).
Li et al. (2007a)	Define the transactional property of a CWS depending on its components WSs and on the workflow constructs.
Li et al. (2008)	Specify and verify CWS based on compensation features.
Liu et al. (2006b)	Ensure fault-tolerant orchestration of transactional WSs via relaxed atomic execution and exception handling.
Liu et al. (2010)	Propose a framework for fault-tolerant composition of transactional WSs.
Liu & Zhao (2008)	Associate a set of compensation operations to each WS components in order to propose a flexible compensation mechanism.
Maamar et al. (2007)	Propose an approach to execute context-driven transactional WSs and to manage exception handling.
Mei et al. (2009a)	Build the compensation process of a CWS only composed by compensatable WS components.
Montagut et al. (2008)	Select component WSs of a TCWS, where the user provide a workflow (without any service assigned) and the ATS. The algorithm returns a TCWS (with services assigned for each task of the workflow) verifying the ATS.
Pires et al. (2003)	Propose a framework for building reliable WS composition.
Portilla et al. (2007)	Propose a transactional behavior model for specifying transactional properties to WS coordination.
Schäfer et al. (2008)	Extend a transactional WS protocol by proposing an environment for flexible compensations of CWS.
Wang et al. (2009)	Extend the WS-BA protocol by proposing a distributed agreement algorithm to relax isolation and verify consistence in case of compensation
Zhao et al. (2008)	Manage the concurrency among concurrent transactional CWSs execution by defining concurrency control policy to refuse or delay the execution of the component WSs of concurrent transactional CWSs.

the skeleton as a functional requirement to be satisfied in addition to the ATSs.

Defining all ATS is neither simple nor scalable (i.e., the bigger the workflow, the bigger the number of ATS). Additionally, ATSs may be "valid from business viewpoint but invalid from control flow perspective" (Liu et al., 2010, p. 53). Therefore, other approaches use transactional rules as correctness criterion. For example, Li et al. (2007a) propose that a *pivot* service can only be composed sequentially with a *retriable* service and in parallel with only a *compensatable retriable* one. Authors show that depending on the workflow structure and on the transactional property of the components,

the transactional property of a CWS is decidable. The transactional rules (proposed in El Haddad et al., 2010b) have also been used by the selection algorithm of Cardinale et al. (2010) which automatically generates the control structure of the CWS, guided by aggregated transactional property of the TCWS. The proposed algorithm satisfies functional conditions, expressed by input and output attributes, and transactional properties, expressed by a risk level, which indicates if the resulting CWS should be *compensatable* or not.

Some approaches like Portilla et al. (2007) add transactional behavior to WSs coordination. In Portilla et al. (2007) approach, a CWS is divided

Table 4. Comparison of the transactional-aware approaches for WS composition

Approach	Main goal	Transactional model	Control flow model (Step1)	Mechanism to relax atomicity	WS Composition Process Step	Protocol or standard language
Alrifai et al. (2009)	Extension of protocol	Compensatable only	Worflow, provided by users	Compensation	Step 3	WS-TX
Bhiri et al. (2005)	CWS validation	Pivot Compensatable Retriable	Worklfow, provided by users	ATS	Step 2 (only validation)	No apply
Cardinale et al. (2010)	Static WSs Selection according to aggregated transactional property	Pivot Compensatable Retriable	Petri-Net, automatically generated	Transactional rules of (El Haddad et al., 2010b)	Step 2	No apply
Li et al. (2007a)	Definition of transactional CWS rules	Pivot Compensatable Retriable	Workflow, provided by users	Transactional rules	Step 2 (only validation)	No apply
Li et al. (2008)	Specification and verification of CWS	Compensatable only	Transactional language, t-calculs, of (Li et al., 2007b)	Compensation	Step 2 (only validation)	No apply
Liu et al. (2006b)	Fault-tolerant execution transactional WS	Pivot Atomic Weak-atomic Semantic-atomic	Workflow, provided by users	Scalable Commit Protocol (2PC + Compensation)	Step 3	No apply
Liu et al. (2010)	Framework for fault tolerance management of CWS	Pivot Atomic Weak atomic Semantic-atomic	Event-Condition –Action rules	Compensation and transfer service	Step 2 (only validation) and after Step 3	WS-BPEL
Liu & Zhao (2008)	Extension of protocol	Compensatable only	Unspecified but provided by users	Compensation	Step 3	WS-BA
Maamar et al. (2007)	Execution and exception handling management of CWS	Pivot Compensatable Retriable	State chart diagram	Context policies	Step 3	No apply
Mei et al. (2009a)	Analysis of a CWS	Compensatable only	Petri Net, provided by users, but compensation part is automatically generated	Compensation	Step 2 (only validation)	No apply
Montagut et al. (2008)	Static WSs Selection	Pivot Compensatable Retriable	Worklfow, provided by users	ATS	Step 2	OWL-S
Pires et al. (2003)	Framework for building reliable WS composition.	Pivot Compensatable Retriable Virtual-compensatable	Transactional XML-based language, WSTL	Mediator services	Step 2 (only validation) and after step 3	No apply
Portilla et al. (2007)	CWS coordination	NonVital Critical Undoable Compensatable	Petri Net, provided by users	Contracts	Step 2 (only validation)	No apply
Schäfer et al. (2008)	Extension of protocol	Compensatable only	Workflow, provided by users	Compensation	Step 3	WS-BA

continued on following page

Table 4. Continued

Approach	Main goal	Transactional model	Control flow model (Step1)	Mechanism to relax atomicity	WS Composition Process Step	Protocol or standard language
Wang et al. (2009)	Extension of protocol	Compensatable only	Worflow, provided by users	Compensation	Step 3	WS-BA
Zhao et al. (2008)	Concurrency control of CWSs	Pivot Compensatable Retriable	Unspecified but provided by users	ATS	Step 3	No apply

Table 5. Summary of transactional and QoS-aware approaches for WS composition

Approach	Objective
Ben Lakhal et al. (2009)	Propose a framework for specifying and executing WS composition, associated with a QoS evaluation.
Cardinale et al. (2011)	Propose a QoS and transactional driven algorithm, for WS composition, where the user's functional conditions are expressed as input and output attributes, its QoS properties are represented by weights over QoS criteria and its transactional requirements are expressed by a risk level.
El Haddad et al. (2010a)	Propose a selection approach of WSs for composition based on Context, QoS, and Transaction properties. In this dynamic selection algorithm, decisions are made task by task of the workflow based on the current local and global composition context.
El Haddad et al. (2010b)	Propose a QoS and transactional driven algorithm, for WS composition, where the user's control flow is expressed as workflow, its QoS properties are represented by weights over QoS criteria, and its transactional requirements are expressed by a risk level.
Liu et al. (2006a)	Evaluate the QoS of a composite service with various transactional requirements.
Liu et al. (2009a)	Schedule a CWS, provided by the user and containing only compensatable components, to minimize the compensation cost.
Liu et al. (2009b)	Propose a risk-driven selection algorithm based on the execution time, compensation time, and reliability.
Mei et al. (2009b)	Evaluate the QoS of a CWS based on the compensation cost and on the control flow structure.
Wu & Yang (2007)	Predict the CWS aggregated QoS by considering the compensation costs.

into groups of WSs, called atomicity contract, in such way the approach guarantees that all WSs of a group will be executed with success or all of them will fail. They also propose recovery strategies depending on the contract transactional behavior, deduced from the transactional behavior of its components.

Generally, transactional protocols are based on a strong assumption that each WS is *compensatable* for recovery purpose. Therefore, several approaches deal with the management of CWS only composed by *compensatable* WSs. Li et al. (2008) propose an approach to specify and analyze a CWS. The specification is done by using a transactional language, called t-calculus (defined in Li et al. 2007b). The verification is done by using ATS or temporal constraints. Mei et al. (2009a) propose an approach for automatically building the compensation part of a CWS represented by a Petri Net. Liu & Zhao (2008) extend the WS-BA protocols in order to propose a flexible compensation mechanism, which consists in associating several compensation operations to each WS component and selecting the appropriate compensation operation based on some pre-fixed conditions.

None of these transactional-aware approaches consider the execution of transactional composite

WSs. Zhao et al. (2008) propose some concurrent control policies for relax *atomic* composite WSs, based on the ATS. Others, like Liu et al. (2006b) and Maamar et al. (2007) also consider the failure management of transactional CWS execution. Liu et al. (2006b) ensure fault-tolerant transactional WSs execution by using relaxed atomic execution and exception handling. To achieve backward error recovery via relaxed atomic execution, Liu et al. (2006b) propose a Scalable Commit Protocol (SCP) inspired from the 2PC protocol. To achieve forward error recovery, they propose an algorithm which ensures a reliable orchestration of services in the presence of failure through exception handling. Maamar et al. (2007) propose an execution of TCWS based on a forward strategy for exception handling and on context policies which integrate the transactional behavior of WSs. Schäfer et al. (2008) extend the WS coordination protocol by proposing an environment for flexible compensations of CWS. Authors used the term compensation to put together activities like WS replacement and additional WS invocation to adopt a forward recovery strategy. Alrifai et al. (2009) and Wang et al. (2009) propose hybrid agreement protocols, based on the WS-BA model, with distributed coordinators and participants. Their protocols allow relax isolation and verify consistence in case of compensation. Alrifai et al. (2009) introduce a WS-Scheduler to implement service-level concurrency control using an optimistic protocol and handling global waiting cycles. Wang et al. (2009) present algorithms which implement the coordination protocol and a classical circular waiting (deadlock) detection protocol.

If a fault occurs during the execution of a CWS, a framework, like FACTS proposed by Liu et al. (2010) can be used. This framework assists the designer to specify the fault handling logic of a CWS, by using Event/Condition/Action rules. It verifies if the component WSs have proper transactional properties, verifying for example that a *pivot* component WS (which cannot be

compensated) is *transferable*, i.e., its result can be used by other ones in case of the other component WS fail. Then, FACTS provides a service transfer based termination protocol, which allows CWSs to terminate in a consistent state in case of an unrepairable fault occurs. Pires et al.(2003) provided another framework, called WebTransact, where WSs are statically integrated by the designer. This framework is based on a multilayered architecture and uses a set of mediators to gather functionally but transactionally different WSs. They also proposed an XML-based language, Web Service Transaction Language (WSTL), for coordinating WSs without enforcing all WS components to support the same transactional protocol.

Transactional and QoS-Aware Approaches

As mentioned before, to guarantee the correctness and the reliability of CWSs, transactional support needs to be added. This is done by selecting transactional WSs. However, transaction usage in the WS composition may affect the QoS of the composition. For example, a *compensatable* service may cost more than a non-transactional service or a *pivot* service; improper usage of transaction may degrade the QoS of the composition. Therefore, it is not sufficient to only consider transactional properties, QoS, should also be taken into account. In this section, we present the most relevant and recent works that have been done in the selection of component WSs based on their transactional properties and QoS criteria.

On design-time static selection, El Haddad et al. (2010b) propose a selection algorithm, based on an extension of the transactional rules proposed by Li et al. (2007a), which receives as input the user functional requirements and control structure, represented with a workflow, weights over QoS criteria and transactional requirements expressed by a risk level. Two levels of risk are considered: Risk 0, meaning that if the execution is successful, the obtained outcomes can be compensated by the user and Risk 1 where the outcomes cannot be semantically recovered by the user. The same transactional rules and requirements are used in Cardinal et al. (2010b) to propose a selection algorithm where the user's functional requirements are expressed as input and output and the control structure is automatically generated.

How transaction will influence the QoS of a CWS is discussed in Mei et al. (2009b), Wu & Yang (2007), Liu et al. (2009a) and Liu et al. (2009b). Mei et al. (2009b) propose a method to evaluate the QoS of CWS taking into account the compensation cost, allowing to detect the dominant QoS metrics that affect the whole TCWS, depending on the execution pattern used. They use a paired Petri-Net to model the normal control flow and the reverse flow in case of compensation. Wu & Yang (2007) propose a model to predict the CWS aggregated QoS by considering the compensation costs. The cost of compensation operations are calculated based in the probability of occurrence of exceptions and are incorporated into the aggregated QoS of the resulting CWS. Authors model with workflows, both the normal flow and the compensation flow which is executed according to exception handling policies. During the composition, the algorithm predicts the average of the QoS, considering all services and their respective compensation actions. Also considering the compensation cost, Liu et al. (2009a) propose several algorithms to schedule transactional CWS only composed by *compensatable* WSs. The input of their algorithms is a CWS and the output is a schedule of the CWS generated by taking into account the compensation constraints. Independently from any transactional protocol, the authors propose two types of algorithms: time-aware scheduling, guaranteeing the atomicity of the CWS when compensation operations have temporal constraints, and cost-aware scheduling generating an optimal schedule in which the overall compensation cost is minimum based on the compensation duration. Liu et al. (2009b) propose a risk-driven (reliability-

driven) selection approach in which services are selected according to their failure impact in the aggregated QoS. The algorithm builds a failure causing tree for each task (i.e., an instance of a WS) in the workflow, provided by users. That tree describes the consequences of a failure of each task in terms of failure causing dependency (i.e., which tasks should be canceled or compensated because of the failure of this task) and compensation causing dependency (i.e., which tasks should be compensated because of the compensation of tasks with failure causing dependency). Thus, the failure causing tree allows calculating the total loss of failure in terms of execution time and compensation time, and the reliability (risk) of each task according to its impact in the execution plan. Then in the selection process, this reliability is considered as a QoS parameter and is compared with the desired reliability of the user.

Liu et al. (2006a) also propose a model to evaluate the impact of transaction on CWS but at execution step. Indeed, they evaluate the execution cost and response time of a CWS taking into account the penalty when aborting a service. In this work, two algorithms are proposed based on the transactional composition operator to determine the QoS of the composition. The first algorithm evaluates the QoS of a service. The second algorithm evaluates the penalty when aborting a service.

On the run-time dynamic selection, El Haddad et al. (2010a) propose a context-aware QoS and transaction-based selection algorithm where the control flow is a workflow provided by the user. The proposed algorithm, in which decisions are made task by task, is based on the current local and global composition context. More precisely, this work proposes a method to select the most appropriate service for a task of a workflow optimizing the interplay of local and global QoS and transactional properties dynamically while the workflow executes.

As far as we know, only Ben Lakhal et al. (2009) propose a framework, FENECIA, which allows the specification, the execution, the failure recovery, and the QoS evaluation of WS composition. The authors propose a new transaction model, WS-SAGAS, based on SAGAS nested transactions (García-Molina & Salem, 1987), to specify the WS composition. They propose a failure handling execution architecture. However, this architecture only currently considers *compensatable* WSs (the authors indicate that the integration of *non-compensatable* WSs will be addressed in their future work). Finally, they propose a QoS model, based on the estimation of the QoS properties on the basis of CWS execution observations. According to the authors, this model allows to facilitate the selection of the more reliable WSs rather than the selection of WSs which often fail.

CONCLUSION AND OPEN ISSUES

The contribution of this chapter is triple. Firstly, a classification of the WS transactional properties has been proposed. This classification allows grouping the different WS transactional properties proposed in the literature according to the recovery techniques they allow and in terms of termination conditions. Secondly, a comparison of WS coordination protocols has been presented, based on type of coordination and on the techniques used to relax isolation. Thirdly, we propose a classification of transactional WS Composition approaches. This classification underlines that a big effort has been done for static WS selection in both directions transactional-aware and transactional-QoS-aware, but highlights that several issues still remain open:

- **Static Selection (Step 2):** Even when many efforts have been focused in static selection, we note a lack of works interested in static selection when the control flow should be generated automatically. Only two works (Cardinale et al., 2010; Cardinale et al., 2011) have extended the results reached in (non-transactional) QoS-

driven approaches by incorporating transactional support.

- **Execution (Step 3):** The biggest effort has been done for the execution of transactional WS composition. Only Liu et al. (2006a) consider both transactional properties and QoS criteria by evaluating the cost of the transactional behavior on the QoS of the CWS. In all these approaches, the control structure is provided by the user. An open issue remains in execution approaches where the control structure is generated automatically.

- **Dynamic Selection (Step 2 + Step 3):** As far as we know, the only work that has been done in dynamic selection is a seminal work proposed by El Haddad et al. (2010a) presenting a context-based QoS and transactional-driven WS selection algorithm, where the user provide the control structure. Open challenges remain in this domain and in the domain of execution of TCWS. A lot of work has been done for context-aware approaches and dynamic execution; they are not mentioned here since they do not consider transactional aspects (i.e., they are out of the scope of this chapter).

- **Framework:** Three frameworks have been proposed, only two of them (Liu et al. 2010; Pires et al. 2003) are based on transactional WS properties and one of them (Ben Lakhal et al., 2009) uses QoS and transactional properties. Among these frameworks, only WebTransact (Pires et al. 2003) is based on the main used transactional model (i.e., *pivot/compensatable/retriable*); while the authors of the other frameworks propose their own transactional model. In all these frameworks, the control structure is provided by the user. An open issue remains in developing frameworks where the control structure is generated automatically.

Table 6. Comparison of the transactional and QoS-aware approaches for WS composition

Approach	Main goal	Transactional model	Control flow model (Step1)	Mechanism to relax atomicity	WS Composition Process Step	Protocol or standard language
Ben Lakhal et al. (2009)	Framework for CWS specification, execution and QoS assessment	Vital- compensatable Non-vital-compensatable Vital- non-compensatable Non-vital-non-compensatable	WS-SAGAS transaction model	Nested transactions	Step 2 and after Step 3	No apply
Cardinale et al. (2011)	Static selection according to aggregated transactional and QoS properties	Pivot Compensatable Retriable	Petri Net automatically generated	Transactional rules of (El Haddad et al., 2010b)	Step 2	No apply
El Haddad et al. (2010a)	Dynamic selection according to Context, QoS and transactional properties	Pivot Compensatable Retriable	Worklfow provided by users	Transactional rules of (El Haddad et al., 2010b)	Step2 and Step3 (dynamic selection)	No apply
El Haddad et al. (2010b)	Static selection according to aggregated transactional and QoS properties	Pivot CompensatableRetriable	Worklfow provided by users	Transactional rules	Step 2	No apply
Liu et al. (2006a)	Evaluation of the QoS of a CWS taking into account aborting cost	Atomic Quasi-atomic Non-atomic	Workflow provided by users	Transactional dependencies	Step 3	No apply
Liu et al. (2009a)	Scheduling of CWS	Compensatable only	Workflow, provided by users	Compensation	Step 2 (only scheduling)	No apply
Liu et al. (2009b)	Risk-driven static selection algorithm	Compensatable only	Workflow, provided by users, whose failure causing tree is automatically generated	Compensation	Step 2	No apply
Mei et al. (2009b)	Evaluation of the QoS of a CWS taking into account compensation cost	Compensatable only	Paired Petri Net, provided by users, whose compensation part is automatically generated	Compensation	Step 2 (only validation)	No apply
Wu & Yang (2007)	Static selection with QoS prediction	Compensatable only	Workflow, provided by users, whose compensation part is automatically generated	Compensation	Step 2	No apply

Most of the transactional-aware propositions do not consider QoS, even there has been a lot of work done for (non-transactional) QoS-aware approaches (they are not mentioned here since they are out of the scope of this chapter). We think that an interesting work to do in the WS Composition process is to extend the existing approaches by considering WS transactional properties. In this way, it will be possible to obtain efficient and reliable CWSs.

ACKNOWLEDGMENT

This work was supported by the Franco-Venezuelan CNRS-FONACIT project N°22782 and the ANR PERSO project N°JC07_186508. The authors would like to thank the referees of this article for their helpful comments and suggestions.

REFERENCES

Akkiraju, R., Farrell, J., Miller, J., Nagarajan, M., Schmidt, M. T., Sheth, A., & Verma, K. (2005). *Web service semantics - WSDL-S*. Technical report, W3C Member Submission 7 November 2005. Retrieved July 25, 2010, from http://lsdis.cs.uga.edu/projects/METEOR-S/WSDL-S

Alrifai, M., Dolog, P., Balke, W., & Nejdl, W. (2009). Distributed management of concurrent Web service transactions. *IEEE Transactions on Services Computing, 2*(4), 289–302. doi:10.1109/TSC.2009.29

Alves, A., Arkin, A., Askary, S., Barreto, C., Bloch, B., & Curbera, F. … Yiu, A. (2007). *OASIS Web services business process execution language, version 2.0*. Retrieved July 27, 2010, from http://docs.oasis-open.org/wsbpel/2.0/OS/wsbpel-v2.0-OS.pdf

Badr, Y., Benslimane, D., Maamar, Z., & Liu, L. (2010). Guest editorial: Special section on transactional Web services. *IEEE Transactions on Services Computing, 3*(1), 30–31. doi:10.1109/TSC.2010.13

Ben Lakhal, N., Kobayashi, T., & Yokota, H. (2009). FENECIA: Failure endurable nested-transaction based execution of composite Web services with incorporated state analysis. [Berlin, Germany: Springer.]. *The VLDB Journal, 18*(1), 1–56. doi:10.1007/s00778-007-0076-8

Bhiri, S., Perrin, O., & Godart, C. (2005). Ensuring required failure atomicity of composite Web services. In *International Conference on World Wide Web* (pp. 138-147). ACM.

Bhiri, S., Perrin, O., & Godart, C. (2006). Extending workflow patterns with transactional dependencies to define reliable composite Web services. In t*he Advanced International Conference on Telecommunications and International Conference on Internet and Web Applications and Services* (pp. 145-150).

Blanco, E., Cardinale, Y., & Vidal, M.-E. (2011). Aggregating functional and non-functional properties to identify service compositions. In Milanovic, N. (Ed.), *Engineering reliable service oriented architecture: Managing complexity and service level agreements*. Hershey, PA: IGI Global. doi:10.4018/978-1-60960-493-6.ch008

Brogi, A., & Corfini, S. (2007). SAM: A Semantic Web service discovery system. In *International Conference on Knowledge-Based Intelligent Information and Engineering Systems* [Berlin, Germany: Springer-Verlag.]. *Lecture Notes in Computer Science, 4694*, 703–710. doi:10.1007/978-3-540-74829-8_86

Bunting, D., Chapman, M., & Hurley, O. (2003). *OASIS Web services composite application framework (WS-CAF) ver 1.0*. Retrieved July 28, 2010, from http://xml.coverpages.org/WS-CAF-Primer200310.pdf

Cardinale, Y., El Haddad, J., Manouvrier, M., & Rukoz, M. (2010). Web service selection for transactional composition. *Procedia Computer Science: Vol. 1. Issue 1. International Conference on Computational Science* (pp. 2683-2692). Elsevier.

Cardinale, Y., El Haddad, J., Manouvrier, M., & Rukoz, M. (2011). CPN-TWS: A colored Petri-Net approach for transactional-QoS driven Web service composition. *International Journal of Web and Grid Services*, 7(1). doi:10.1504/IJWGS.2011.038389

Choi, S., Jang, H., Kim, H., Kim, J., Kim, S., Song, J., & Lee, Y. (2005). Maintaining consistency under isolation relaxation of Web services transactions. In *International Conference in Web Information Systems and Engineering, Lecture Notes in Computer Science*. Berlin, Germany: Springer-Verlag.

Egambaram, I., Vadivelou, G., & Sivasubramanian, S. P. (2010). *Dynamic selection of Web services*. In International Conference on Computing, Communications and Information Technology Applications.

Eid, M., Alamri, A., & Saddik, A. E. (2008). A reference model for dynamic web service composition systems. [Inderscience.]. *International Journal in Web and Grid Services*, 4(2), 149–168. doi:10.1504/IJWGS.2008.018885

El Haddad, J., Manouvrier, M., Reiff-Marganiec, S., & Rukoz, M. (2010a). *Context-based transactional service selection approach for service composition. Technical report N°49*. LAMSADE, Université Paris-Dauphine.

El Haddad, J., Manouvrier, M., & Rukoz, M. (2007). A hierarchical model for transactional Web service composition in P2P networks. In *IEEE International Conference on Web Service* (pp. 346–353).

El Haddad, J., Manouvrier, M., & Rukoz, M. (2010b). TQoS: Transactional and QoS-aware selection algorithm for automatic Web service composition. *IEEE Transactions on Services Computing*, 3(1), 73–85. doi:10.1109/TSC.2010.5

Elmagarmid, A. (Ed.). (1992). *Database transaction models for advanced applications*. San Francisco, CA: Morgan Kaufmann.

Erl, T. (2005). *Service-oriented architecture: Concepts, technology, and design*. Prentice Hall PTR.

Farrell, J., & Lausen, H. (Eds.). (2007). *Semantic annotations for WSDL and XML schema*. W3C Candidate Recommendation 26 January 2007. Retrieved July 25, 2010, from http://www.w3.org/TR/sawsdl/

Fauvet, M., Duarte, H., Dumas, M., & Benatallah, B. (2005). Handling transactional properties in web service composition. In *International Conference on Web Information Systems Engineering* (pp. 273–289). Berlin, Germany: Springer-Verlag.

Feingold, M., & Jeyaraman, R. (Eds.). (2009). *OASIS Web services coordination (WS-Coordination) version 1.2*. Retrieved July 28, 2010, from http://docs.oasis-open.org/ws-tx/wscoor/2006/06

Freund, T., & Little, M. (2009). *OASIS Web services business activity (WS-Business Activity) version 1.2*. Retrieved July 30, 2010, from http://docs.oasis-open.org/ws-tx/wstx-wsba-1.2-spec-os.pdf

Furniss, P. (Ed.). Dalal, S., Fletcher, T., Green, A., Haugen, B., Ceponkus, A., & Pope, B. (2004). *OASIS business transactional protocol (BTP 1.1)*. Retrieved July 30, 2010, from http://docs.oasis-open.org/business-transaction/business_transaction-btp-1.1-spec-cd-01.pdf

Gaaloul, W., Bhiri, S., & Rouached, M. (2010). Event-based design and runtime verification of composite service transactional behavior. *IEEE Transactions on Services Computing*, 3(1), 32–45. doi:10.1109/TSC.2010.1

Garcia-Molina, H., & Salem, K. (1987). Sagas. *SIGMOD Record, 16*(3), 249–259. doi:10.1145/38714.38742

Gray, J. (1978). Notes on data base operating systems. In M. J. Flynn, J. Gray, A. K. Jones, K. Lagally, H. Opderbeck, G. J. Popek, ... H.-R. Wiehle (Eds.), *Operating systems: An advanced course* (pp. 393-481). Berlin, Germany: Springer-Verlag

Gray, J. (1981). The transaction concept: Virtues and limitations. In *International Conference on Very Large Data Bases* (pp. 144-154).

Grefen, P. (2002). Transactional workflows or workflow transactions? In *International Conference on Database and Expert Systems Applications* (pp. 60-69).

Häerder, T., & Reuter, A. (1983). Principles of transaction-oriented database recovery. *ACM Computing Surveys, 15*(4), 289–291. doi:10.1145/289.291

Huang, A. F. M., Lan, C.-W., & Yang, S. J. H. (2009). An optimal QoS-based Web service selection scheme. *Information Sciences, 179*(19), 3309–3322. doi:10.1016/j.ins.2009.05.018

Lampson, B. W., & Sturgis, H. E. (1976). *Crash recovery in a distributed data storage system. Technical report.* Xerox Palo Alto Research Center.

Lausen, H., Polleres, A., & Roman, D. (2005). *Web service modeling ontology (WSMO).* Retrieved July 25, 2010, from http://www.w3.org/Submission/WSMO/

Li, J., Zhu, H., & He, J. (2008). Specifying and verifying Web transactions. In *International Conference on Formal Techniques For Networked and Distributed Systems* [Berlin, Germany: Springer-Verlag.]. *Lecture Notes in Computer Science, 5048,* 149–168. doi:10.1007/978-3-540-68855-6_10

Li, J., Zhu, H., Pu, G., & He, J. (2007b). Looking into compensable transactions. In *IEEE Software Engineering Workshop* (pp. 154-166). IEEE Computer Society.

Li, L., Liu, C., & Wang, J. (2007a). Deriving transactional properties of composite Web services. In *IEEE International Conference on Web Services* (pp. 631-638). IEEE Computer Society.

Li, Q., Liu, A., Liu, H., Lin, B., Huang, L., & Gu, N. (2009). Web services provision: Solutions, challenges and opportunities (invited paper). In *International Conference on Ubiquitous information Management and Communication* (pp. 80-87).

Little, M., & Wilkinson, A. (Eds.). (2009). *OASIS Web services atomic transaction (WS-AtomicTransaction) version 1.2.* Retrieved July 26, 2010, from http://docs.oasis-open.org/ws-tx/wsat/2006/06

Liu, A., Huang, L., & Li, Q. (2006a). Qos-aware Web services composition using transactional composition operator. In *International Conference Advances in Web-Age Information Management (WAIM), Lecture Notes in Computer Science 4016.* Berlin, Germany: Springer-Verlag.

Liu, A., Huang, L., Li, Q., & Xiao, M. (2006b). Fault-tolerant orchestration of transactional Web services. In *International Conference on Web Information Systems Engineering,* (pp. 90-101).

Liu, A., Li, Q., Huang, L., & Xiao, M. (2010). FACTS: A framework for fault-tolerant composition of transactional Web services. *IEEE Transactions on Services Computing, 3*(1), 46–59. doi:10.1109/TSC.2009.28

Liu, A., Liu, H., Li, Q., Huang, L., & Xiao, M. (2009a). Constraints-aware scheduling for transactional services composition. [Berlin, Germany: Springer-Verlag.]. *Journal of Computer Science and Technology, 24*(4), 638–651. doi:10.1007/s11390-009-9264-x

Liu, C., & Zhao, X. (2008). Towards flexible compensation for business transactions in Web service environment. [Berlin, Germany: Springer-Verlag.]. *Service Oriented Computing and Applications, 2*(2), 79–91. doi:10.1007/s11761-008-0024-5

Lui, H., Zhang, W., Ren, K., Liu, C., & Zhang, Z. (2009b). A risk-driven selection approach for transactional Web service composition. In *International Conference on Grid and Cooperative Computing*, (pp. 391-397).

Maamar, Z., Narendra, N. C., Benslimane, D., & Subramanian, S. (2007). Policies for context-driven transactional web services. In *International Conference on Advanced information Systems Engineering, Lecture Notes in Computer Science* (pp. 249-263). Berlin, Germany: Springer-Verlag.

Martin, D., Burstein, M., Hobbs, J., Lassila, O., McDermott, D., & McIlraith, S. ... Sycara, K. (2004). OWL-S: Semantic markup for Web services. Retrieved July 25, 2010, from http://www.w3.org/Submission/2004/SUBM-OWL-S-20041122/

Maximilien, E., & Singh, M. (2004). Towards autonomic Web services, trust and selection. In *International Conference on Service Oriented Computing* (pp. 212–221).

McIlraith, S., Son, T. C., & Zeng, H. (2001). Semantic Web services. *IEEE Intelligent Systems, 16*(2), 46–53. doi:10.1109/5254.920599

Mehrotra, S., Rastogi, R., Korth, H. F., & Silberschatz, A. (1992). A transaction model for multidatabase systems. In *International Conference on Distributed Computing Systems* (pp. 56-63). IEEE Computer Society Press.

Mei, X., Jiang, A., Zheng, F., & Li, S. (2009a). Execution semantics analysis based composition compensation mechanism in Web Services composition. In *CSIE, vol. 7: WRI World Congress on Computer Science and Information Engineering* (pp. 820-824). Washington, DC: IEEE Computer Society

Mei, X., Jiang, A., Zheng, F., & Li, S. (2009b). Reliable transactional Web service composition using refinement method. In *WASE International Conference on Information Engineering: Vol. 1* (pp. 422-426). Washington, DC: IEEE Computer Society.

Montagut, F., Molva, R., & Tecumseh Golega, S. (2008). Automating the composition of transactional Web services. [Hershey, PA: IGI Global.]. *International Journal of Web Services Research, 5*(1), 24–41. doi:10.4018/jwsr.2008010102

Papazoglou, M. P., Traverso, P., Dustdar, S., & Leymann, F. (2007). Service-oriented computing: State of the art and research challenges. *IEEE Computer, 40*(11), 38–45.

Pires, P. F., Benevides, M. R., & Mattoso, M. (2003). Building reliable Web services compositions. In *Web and Database-Related Workshops on Web, Web-Services, and Database Systems* [Berlin, Germany: Springer-Verlag.]. *Lecture Notes in Computer Science, 2593*, 59–72. doi:10.1007/3-540-36560-5_5

Portilla, A., Vargas-Solar, G., Collet, C., Zechinelli-Martini, J.-L., & García-Bañuelos, L. (2007). Contract based behavior model for services coordination. In *International Conference on Web Information Systems and Technologies, Lecture Notes in Computer Science* (pp. 109-123). Berlin, Germany: Springer-Verlag.

Rao, J., & Su, X. (2004). A survey of automated Web service composition methods. In *International Workshop on Semantic Web Services and Web Process Composition* [Berlin, Germany: Springer-Verlag.]. *Lecture Notes in Computer Science, 3387*, 43–54. doi:10.1007/978-3-540-30581-1_5

Robinson, I., Knight, P., & McRae, M. (2009). *OASIS Web services transaction* (WS-TX). Retrieved July 12, 2010, from http://www.oasis-open.org/committees/tc_home.php?wg_abbrev=ws-tx

Rusinkiewicz, M., & Sheth, A. (1995). Specification and execution of transactional workflows. In Kim, W. (Ed.), *Modern database systems: The object model, interoperability, and beyond* (pp. 592–620). New York, NY: ACM Press/Addison-Wesley Publishing Co.

Schäfer, M., Dolog, P., & Nejdl, W. (2008). An environment for flexible advanced compensations of Web service transactions. *ACM Transactions on the Web*, *2*(2), 1–36. doi:10.1145/1346337.1346242

Shin, D.-H., Lee, K.-H., & Suda, T. (2009). Automated generation of composite web services based on functional semantics. *Web Semantic*, *7*(4), 332–343. doi:10.1016/j.websem.2009.05.001

Sivasubramanian, S. P., Ilavarasan, E., & Vadivelou, G. (2009). Dynamic Web service composition: Challenges and techniques. In *International Conference on Intelligent Agent & Multi-Agent Systems* (pp. 1-8).

Türker, C., Haller, K., Schuler, C., & Schek, H.-J. (2005). How can we support Grid transactions? Towards Peer-to-Peer transaction processing. In *Biennial Conference Innovative Data System Research* (pp.174-185).

Vidyasankar, K., & Vossen, G. (2004). A multi-level model for Web service composition. In *the IEEE International Conference on Web Services* (pp. 462–469).

Wang, T., Vonk, J., Kratz, B., & Grefen, P. (2008). A survey on the history of transaction management: From flat to grid transactions. [Berlin, Germany: Springer.]. *Distributed and Parallel Databases*, *23*(3), 235–270. doi:10.1007/s10619-008-7028-1

Wang, X., Li, Y., Wu, X., & Min, L. (2009). Ensuring consistency of Web services transaction. *Journal of China Universities of Posts and Telecommunications*, *16*(4), 59–66. doi:10.1016/S1005-8885(08)60249-6

Wu, J., & Yang, F. (2007). QoS prediction for composite Web services with transactions. In *International Conference on Service-Oriented Computing* [Berlin, Germany: Springer-Verlag.]. *Lecture Notes in Computer Science*, *4652*, 86–94. doi:10.1007/978-3-540-75492-3_8

Yu, H. Q., & Reiff-Marganiec, S. (2008). *Non-functional property-based service selection: A survey and classification of approaches*. In Non-Functional Properties and Service Level Agreements in Service Oriented Computing Workshop co-located with the IEEE European Conference on Web Services.

Yu, Q., Liu, X., Bouguettaya, A., & Medjahed, B. (2008). Deploying and managing Web services: Issues, solutions, and directions. [Berlin, Germany: Springer.]. *The VLDB Journal*, *17*(3), 537–572. doi:10.1007/s00778-006-0020-3

Zhang, W., Yang, Y., Tang, S., & Fang, L. (2007). QoS-driven service selection optimization model and algorithms for composite Web services. In *Annual International Computer Software and Applications Conference* (vol. 2, pp.425-431).

Zhang, Z.-L., Hong, F., & Xiao, H.-J. (2008). A colored petri net-based model for web service composition. [English Edition]. *Journal of Shanghai University*, *12*(4), 323–329. doi:10.1007/s11741-008-0409-2

Zhao, Z., Wei, J., Lin, L., & Ding, X. (2008). A concurrency control mechanism for composite service supporting user-defined relaxed atomicity. In *IEEE International Computer Software and Applications Conference* (pp. 275-278).

KEY TERMS AND DEFINITIONS

Automatic Control Flow: Control structure generated automatically in the selection step.

Dynamic Selection: At design-time there is only a specification of the type of required services and concrete services are integrated at run-time.

No Automatic Control Flow: Control structure provided "by hand" by the users by specifying an abstract representation of process.

QoS and Transactional-Aware Selection: Selection process based on the transactional properties where QoS criteria are embedded in.

Static Selection: Concrete services are determined and integrated into the composite service at design time.

Transactional Web Service: A service that supports transactional properties for its correct usage.

Transactional-Aware Selection: Selection based on transactional properties of component Web services.

Web Service Composition: Combination of several existing services to create a value-added composite service.

Chapter 7
A Quality Driven Web Service Selection Model

Pierluigi Plebani
Politecnico di Milano, Italy

Filippo Ramoni
Politecnico di Milano, Italy

ABSTRACT

The chapter introduces a quality of Web service model which can be exploited by a Web service broker during the Web service selection phase. The model considers both user and provider standpoints. On the one hand, providers express their capabilities with respect to measurable dimensions (e.g., response time, latency). On the other hand, users can define the requirements with a higher level of abstraction (e.g. performance). Since the quality is subjective by definition, the presented quality model also maps the user preferences, i.e., how much a quality dimension is more important than another one in evaluating the overall quality. The Analytic Hierarchy Approach (AHP) has been adopted as a technique for expressing user preferences. The chapter also describes how the model can be exploited in the Web service selection process. Starting from a set of functionally equivalent Web services, the selection process identifies which are the Web services able to satisfy the user requirements. Moreover, according to a cost-benefit analysis, the list of selected Web services is sorted and, as a consequence, the best Web service is identified.

INTRODUCTION

Service Oriented Computing aims at providing a set of methods and tools to support the design and the execution of applications based on Web services. According to this paradigm, at the design-time, the programmer identifies which

DOI: 10.4018/978-1-61350-432-1.ch007

is the activity to be performed and tries to find and to select the Web services closer to such requirements. In some cases, the requirements can be figured out only at run-time and specific modules are involved to perform the discovery and selection activities. This is the typical scenario where automatic composition techniques work. Finally, a third situation occurs when a user needs to find a Web service for a specific goal. In this case, the final user manually browses dedicated Web sites to find the Web services able to fulfill the needs. As discussed in (Garofalakis, Panagis, Sakkopoulos, & Tsakalidis, 2006), several tools have been developed to support all of these actors in finding the best Web service according to a set of requirements. Although plenty of proposals aim at finding a solution for the non-functional matchmaking, very few of them are really adopted in practice. The same does not occur in case of functional matchmaking. This situation is probably caused by the different maturity of the models for describing the functional aspects from the model describing the quality of a Web service. In fact, nowadays, WSDL can be considered the standard de-facto for describing how a Web service can be invoked. In the same way, languages as OWL-S or WSMO represent the most well-known approaches for describing the semantics underlying a Web service. On the opposite, the Web service community does not provide the same level of agreement about the description of the quality of Web service. Actually, efforts like WS-Policy (Vedamuthu, Orchard, Hondo, Boubez, & Yendluri, 2007) or the model proposed by the OASIS Consortium (Kim & Lee, 2005) start to offer an attempt of organizing all the aspects concerning the description of the quality of Web services. Nevertheless such models, as well as all other approaches, suffer of two main limitations. Firstly, existing approaches are mainly focused on the technical aspects of Web services (e.g., reliability, security) without any considerations about aspects closer to the business. Secondly, the quality description is usually too technical (e.g., 3DES or AES encryption algorithms) and the final user cannot easily figure out what is the real quality offered by a Web service.

Goal of this chapter is to introduce a quality of service model (1) able to express both technical and business quality aspects, and (2) which considers both programmer and final user perspectives. In a Service Oriented Architecture, our quality model can be adopted by the Web service broker

to identify which is the best Web service among a set of functionally equivalent Web services. Such a selection considers the quality of Web service along with the user preferences combining two decision making models: cost-benefit analysis and Analytic Hierarchy Process (AHP). For the sake of simplicity, we assume that our quality-driven selection process commences when a set of functionally equivalent Web services has been previously identified. So, in this work, we skip this preliminary step.

To make the model presentation clearer, we rely on a reference example where we assume that a programmer adopts our model during the implementation of a touristic Web portal. In particular, the programmer, after discovering a set of *flight reservation Web services*, wants to propose them to the user taking into account the user preferences. Indeed, final users express both functional (e.g., departure date, arrival date) and non-functional (e.g., business vs. economy class, meal offers) requirements and the Web portal has to rank them from the most suitable Web service able to fulfill such requirements, to the less suitable one.

The chapter is structured as follows. First of all we introduce the quality model in terms of who and in which way the quality is defined, and how the user can define the preferences. Exploiting this quality model the following section discusses the approach we propose for a quality-aware Web service selection. A complete example will summarize the whole approach. Finally, after a discussion on related work, we present our standpoint about the future development that could be done in this area.

QUALITY MODEL

Web service selection process involves two main actors: the Web service provider, who advertises the capabilities of its Web services, and the user, who expresses its requirements. Capabilities and requirements reflect, namely, the offered quality of service and required quality of service; thus a Web service, for being selected, must at least offer what a user requires. Both offered and required quality can be organized as a set of dimensions (a.k.a. attributes or parameters) each of them stating a particular quality aspect.

Some of these dimensions represent the technical quality: all the quality aspects related to the infrastructure used to provide a Web service. Some work (Mani & Nagarajan, 2002; Ran, 2003) identify a set of quality dimensions most relevant in a Web service environment: availability, accessibility, integrity, performance, reliability, regulatory, scalability, security, supporting standards, and more. Another class of quality dimensions is tied to the business logic of the Web service and, as a consequence, is directly related to a given application domain. Considering the flight booking Web service, its quality can be defined by dimensions such as: business class available, movies available, on-line check-in, and more.

Even if quality is subjective by definition, everyone may agree on this list of quality dimensions. We formalize such an agreement introducing a new actor called *community*. Such an actor is not involved in the Web service selection process, but only during the Web service quality description phase. As defined in (Marchetti, Pernici, & Plebani, 2004), a community could be a group of people, a standardization body, or even an implicit agreement that aims at proposing a specification for a group of objects with some relevant common characteristics. It is worth noting that an example of community has been presented above when we have mentioned the set of technical quality dimensions (e.g., availability, accessibility). In fact, such a set has been defined by what we usually call the "Web service community". In a federated environment, community can be explicitly identified by a group of people that represents all the members of the federation. Indeed, the federation reflects the set of companies that operates on the same domain and shares the same goals. Thus, we can assume that these companies agree on the same set

of quality dimensions. More generally, given an application domain, we suppose that a community exists and produces the set of relevant quality dimensions. Sometimes, the community can be easily identified since it is explicitly constituted (e.g., the Web service community). Most of the times the community associated to an application domain does not explicitly exist and cannot be easily detectable. In this case, the community results in an implicit agreement. For instance, considering our reference example, even it is hard to find a "flight booking service community", we can say that lot of people agree on the set of quality dimensions listed above (i.e., class and so on). For this reason, we assume that an implicit community exists and the list of quality dimensions it defines reflects the common experience about flight booking services. As discussed in the following, given an application domain, the related community is in charge to explicitly or implicitly define the set of relevant quality dimensions. Moreover, for each of those dimensions, the community also identifies which are the admissible values.

According to the characteristics of the Service Oriented Computing, providers and users might not know each other in advance. Due to the subjectiveness of quality, we must be sure that providers and users not only rely on the same language for expressing capabilities and requirements, but also use the same set of quality dimensions for expressing them. About the former constraints, as several languages are now available on the state of the art to express the quality of a Web service, we assume that mediators or ontologies can help in this agreement. About the former constraint, the definition of a commonly accepted set of quality dimensions is exactly one of the goals of the community. According to this hypothesis, Figure 1 shows the main elements and actors involved in our quality model. The Quality Tree (QT) collects all the quality dimensions relevant for a given application domain along with the technical quality dimensions identified by the Web service community. In case the community

Figure 1. Overall view of quality of service model

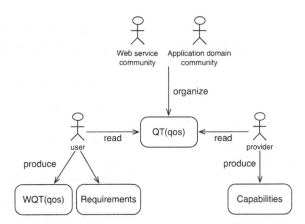

really exists, the set of quality dimensions will be more accurate and complete. On the opposite, in case of implicit community, we cannot be sure that everyone agrees on the defined set of dimensions: e.g., someone might add a new quality dimension to the list. Considerations about the definition and management of a community and the list of quality dimensions is out of the scope of this chapter, but they must be included in the future research agenda. Both users and providers rely on the QT for expressing the requirements and the capabilities, namely. In addition, the user also revises the QT and produces a Weighted QT (WQT) reflecting the user preferences.

We assume that the involved communities are able to create the set *QD* of relevant quality dimensions *qd* that is formally defined as:

$$QD=\{qd_i\} = \{PQD|DQD\}=\{\{pqd_l|dqd_m\}\}$$
$$i=1,...,I \ l=1,...,L \ m=1,...,M \ I=L+M.$$

QD can be split between two subsets: PQD and DQD. PQD collects the set of L primitive quality dimensions pqd_p whereas DQD includes the set of M derived quality dimensions dqd_m.

A $pqd_l \in$ PQD is a directly measurable quality dimension defined as:

$$pqd_l= <name, V, ef(V), PC> \ l=1,...,L$$

where:

- *name* uniquely identifies the quality dimension.
- *V* corresponds to either categorical or interval admissible values:
  - In case of categorical admissible values, they will be included in a specific vector $V=\{v_h\}$ *(h=1,...,H)* where *H* is the number of admissible values;
  - In case of interval admissible values, V will be defined by its extremes, i.e., $V=[v_{min}; v_{max}]$.
- The function *ef: $V \rightarrow [0..1]$* represents the *quality evaluation function*, i.e., how the quality increases or decreases with respect to the admissible values: the function returns the quality evaluation e_{qd} with *0* as lowest quality, and *1* as highest quality. The trend of *ef* is usually defined by a utility function, e.g., linear, logarithmic, exponential, sigmoidal.
- The admissible value set *V* is organized in disjoint primitive service classes

$PC=\{pc_k\}$ *(k=1,...,K)* and are obtained as follows:

- In case of categorical values, the primitive service classes coincide with the values that the dimension may assume: i.e, $qd_i.PC \equiv qd_i.V, i=1,..,H=K.$
- In case of interval values, primitive service classes are obtained by splitting $V=[v_{min}, v_{max}]$ into *K* intervals, so $PC=\{pc_k = [pc_{kmin}; pc_{kmax}]\}$ where

$pc_{kmax} = pc_{(k+1)min}, pc_{1min}=v_{min}, pc_{Kmax}=v_{max}, pc_k$ ranges are obtained as follows: let divide $qd_i.ef(V)$ in *K* ranges $\{[e_{kmin}; e_{kmax}]\}$, then $p_{kmin}=qd_i.ef^{-1}(e_{kmin})$ and $pd_{kmax}=qd_i.ef^{-1}(e_{kmax})$.

A $dqd_m \in DQD$ is a quality dimension not directly measurable, but it depends on other quality dimensions; it is defined as:

$dqd_m = $<name, values, $\{qd_j\}$> m=1,...,M j=1,...,J

where:

- *name* uniquely identifies the quality dimension.
- *values* $\subseteq [0..1]$: defines the admissible values set for the dimension.
- $\{qd_j\} \in QD$: is the set of the *J* quality dimensions - both primitive and derived - affecting dqd_m.

Relationships among quality dimensions in QD are identified by the involved communities and they are represented as a tree called Quality Tree (QT). In particular, giving a qd_i its quality tree, i.e., QT (qd_i) is defined as follows:

$QT(qd_i)=$ <pqd_h | < dqd_k, {QT ($dqd_k.qd_j$)}>>

We assume that, given an application domain, a *qd* named "QoS" always exists in QD, and the related *QT(QoS)* describes the organization of all the dimensions in QD; the *qd* "QoS" is the root of the tree that collects all the dimensions.

Figure 2 shows the quality tree related to the flight reservation service sample. Considering such an example, *PQD = {availability, response time, latency, destination, entertainment, delay, class}*.

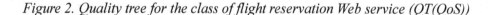

Figure 2. Quality tree for the class of flight reservation Web service (QT(QoS))

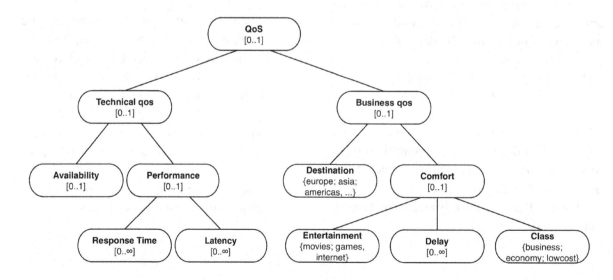

PQD can regards on the quality of the Web service or the quality of offering product or service.

For each of them, the community states how to measure such dimensions and defines the admissible values regardless of a specific service implementation. For example, *availability* can be defined as *uptime/(uptime+downtime)*, and its values will be included in a continuous range, i.e., [0..1]. On the contrary, the *class* quality dimension collects all the possible variants and the range of values will be discrete, i.e., *class.values = {business; economy; lowcost}*. The ranges of values might be unbounded as well. For example, the *delay* can assume any positive value: *delay. values = [0..∞]* that represents the average delay occurred to the airline flights.

In addition to the primitive quality dimensions, the community also defines the derived quality dimensions DQD. A $dqd_m \in DQD$ describes a higher level aspect of quality of service which depends on other - either primitive or derived - quality dimensions. For example, the *performance* depends on *latency* and *response time*. In our main example, *DQD = {QoS, technicalqos, businessqos, performance, comfort}*. Regardless of the nature of a dqd_m, we assume that dqd_m. *values* is always subset in the [0..1] range. Such a value is obtained by evaluating, composing, and normalizing the values of the quality dimensions qd_j affecting dqd_m.

Due to the definition of *QT*, it is worth noting that the division of quality of service dimensions between technical and business dimensions is not mandatory. Anyway, we think that such a structure is able to separate the quality dimensions closer to providers from the dimensions closer to users. We decide to model the quality of service according to a tree for two main reasons. Firstly, such a structure enables an explicit representation of the influence among quality dimensions. It is worth noting that we only state that such a relationship exists and not how it occurs. In some sense, we state a qualitative dependency: the higher the quality of a child, the higher the quality of the father node.

It might happen that a quality dimension affects several other quality dimensions. For instance, if along with the *availability* we want to consider the *instantaneous availability*, the *response time* could affect both of them. For the sake of clarity, even if in this situation a graph results more suitable, we still represent the dependencies among quality dimensions with a tree. Here, the affecting node will be appended several times as a child of the quality dimensions that it affects.

Secondly, the tree-based structure also reflects the different abstraction levels according to which the quality can be described. At highest level we have a generic *QoS* dimension which is affected by all the quality dimensions that the community considers relevant. Going down to the tree, at lowest level the leaves of a QT identify the primitive dimensions which really determine the quality. According to the values that such dimensions assume, the quality will increase or decrease. In this way, service providers always work at the bottom level since they need to describe how much is really the quality: they need to state which will be the values for a given quality dimension they are able to offer. On the contrary, final users can work towards the entire tree. If a user knows the exact meaning of a primitive quality dimension, the requirements can be described by a subset of the admissible range (e.g., *entertaiment.values = {movies; internet}*). Otherwise, the user can rely on the derived quality dimensions (e.g., *technicalqos. values ∈ [0.7..1]*) and, in this way, the user can be agnostic with respect to the influencing primitive quality dimensions. Obviously, working at lower level implies a more accurate quality description.

The community, by means of the QT, gives a general picture about the quality description of a given application domain. Here, the relationships among several quality dimensions are only sketched, since the QT does not state how much a $dqd_m.qd_j$ influences the related dqd_m.

In our quality model, we assume that a user is able to customize a QT producing a Weighted

Quality Tree WQT. So, given a quality dimension $qd_i \in DQD$:

$$WQT(qd_i) = \ < pqd_l, e_{pqdl}(value)| \ dqd_m, WQT(dqd_m), \{w_{m,j}\} >$$

where e_{pqdl} is the evaluation function of the quality dimension pqd_l and the structures of $QT(qd_l)$ and $WQT(qd_l)$ are the same.

Given a dqd_m, the weights $w_{k,j}$ represent how much the related quality dimensions $dqd_m.qd_j$ influence the dqd_m. Such values can be obtained manually or even suggested by a recommendation system. It might happen that during the definition of a QT, especially when technical dimensions are involved, the community also performs the weights assignment process, defining a set of weights able to drive the user during the final customization. We can also suppose that the user exploits a suitable software during each step of the weight assignment process as described in the following.

The weight assignment is a quite critical activity since it has to map what are the user preferences with only one constraint: given a tree node, the sum of weights on the edges connecting to the direct children must be *1*. Thus, the main problem is to realize how to distribute these weights. For instance, considering our running example, it is hard to quantify with a number in *[0..1]* range, how much each sub-dimension influences the *businessQoS* dimension. Due to this difficulty, we propose to drive the weight assignment by the *AHP (Analytic Hierarchy Process)* approach: a decision making technique developed by T.L. Saaty (Saaty, 1980). This is a qualitative approach where the user only states if a sub-dimension is more influent than another one on the overall quality. AHP is a decision-making technique that assigns to each sub-dimension a score that represents the overall performance with respect to the different parameters. AHP is suitable for hierarchical structures as *QT* and proposes to user pairwise comparisons between sub-dimensions. In this way, the weight assignment process is divided into several steps, each of them focused on a sub-tree, starting from the lower levels to the higher ones.

According to this approach, given a dqd_m the user should fill tables similar to what shown in Table 1. The first column and the first row are populated with the names of the $dqd_m.qd_j$, i.e. the qd that influence the dqd_m. For each table cell, the user assigns a number in the *[1/9..9]* range according to the meaning defined in Table 3 which is the usually adopted one in AHP. This can help the user because it is simpler to state how much (in a five-level scale) a dimension is more or less important that another one, instead of think about an absolute evaluation independently from other dimensions.

For example, in Table 2 we state that *delay* has strong importance than *entertainment* in defining the *comfort* (value 5). At the same time, the *entertainment* has a moderated importance with respect to the *class* (value 3). According to the AHP method, the table must be mutual, so *entertainment* with respect to *delay* has an importance of *1/5*, and *class* with respect to *entertainment* has an importance of *1/3*.

Starting from the table expressing the users' comparisons, the AHP method use an averaging technique based on eigenvalue/eigenvector to

Table 1. Comparison matrix for dqd comfort

comfort	entertainment	delay	class
entertainment			
delay			
class			

Table 2. Comparison matrix for dqd comfort and computed weights

comfort	entertainment	delay	class	$w_{i,j}$
entertainment	1	1/5	3	0.202
delay	5	1	5	0.700
class	1/3	1/5	1	0.098

Table 3. The Saaty pairwise combination scale

$a_{i,j}$	Definition
1	Equal importance
3	Moderate importance
5	Essential or strong importance
7	Demonstrated importance
9	Extreme importance
2,4,6,8	Intermediate values (compromise)

compute a set of weights that better represents users' preferences. Following the AHP approach, the principal eigenvector of the comparison matrix collects the weights we need. About our example, the eigenvector of the matrix in Table 2 is *{0.202; 0.700; 0.098}*. This motivates the values reported in *WQT* of Figure 3 which shows the *WQT(QoS)* of the flight reservation service example.

Expressing evaluations by comparisons can determine a set of preferences that is not consistency: in an ideal users the pairwise comparisons should respects the transitive property. For example, if the dimension *a* is preferred 3 with respect to dimension *b* and *b* is preferred 2 with respect to dimension *c*, then dimension *a* should be preferred *3*2=6* with respect to *c*, but the user can

Figure 3. Weighted quality tree (WQT(QoS))

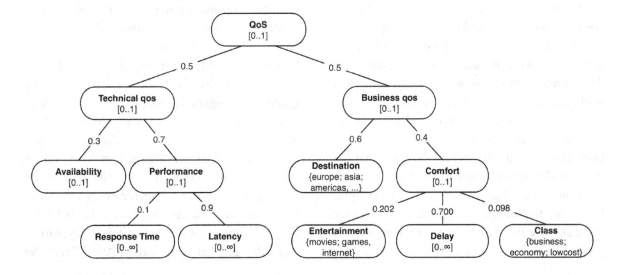

Table 4. Incomplete comparison matrix for the dqd Comfort and computed weights

Comfort	entertainment	delay	class	$w_{i,j}$
entertainment	2	(0)	3	0,333
delay	(0)	2	5	0,556
class	1/3	1/5	1	0,111

choose for example 5 or 7. If the majority of the values in the matrix does not satisfies the pairwise transitive relation the obtained weights vector is not significant.

For this reason in the AHP approach the Consistency Index (CI) is also calculated (Saaty, 1980) as the parameter able to identify unbalancing in weights assignment. According to the adopted technique the consistency index should be less than 0.1 (in our example, *CI =0.07*). Building the comparison matrix is a time consuming activity since it requires, for each *dqd$_m$* in *WQT*, *n*(n-1)/2* comparisons where *n* is the number of sub-dimensions.

The large number of required pairwise comparisons could be an obstacle in the adoption of our approach, due to the difficult and the time required to choose evaluations for each couple of dimensions.

There are some extensions of the AHP method, like the Harker variant (Harker, 1987), which increase usability, performance, and consistency by skipping some pairwise comparisons. In this approach the user can skip some comparisons: the value 0 is assigned for the evaluation of the skipped pairwise. Harker has demonstrated that through mathematical passages a vector of weights is obtainable from a matrix that contains some 0 values. Obviously the choice of the number of comparisons to be made involves a tradeoff between time and reliability of the result that the user is willing to spend for express its preferences.

Applying the Harker variant to our example, let assume that in *dqd Comfort* definition, a user chooses only two values: *class* with respect to

entertainment and *class* with respect to *delay*, as shown in Table 4.

In this case, the required eigenvector (last column) is computed for a matrix that sets to zero the missing values. Moreover, values in the dominant matrix diagonal must be replaced with the number of zeros present in each row increased by one. In this particular case, the diagonal values of the first two rows are set to two, since one zero exists in each of the first two rows.

Along with the weights, *WQT* also includes in its leaves the quality evaluation $e_{pqdl}(value)$ functions. Here, given $pqd_i \in PQD$ the user specifies which is the best and the worst values and how the quality varies with respect to pqd_i *values*. Regarding of the kind of admissible values, continuous range vs. discrete range, the evaluation function is defined in different ways.

In case of continuous range of values, the best and worst values can be easily identified considering the lowest and highest values in pqd_i *values*, and the semantic of the quality parameter. For example, considering the *availability* the lowest value corresponds to the worst quality and, as a consequence, the highest value corresponds to the best quality. On the opposite, if we consider the *responsetime*, the higher the value the lower the quality (see Figure 4) and vice versa. The trend of the evaluation function is usually defined by a utility function: e.g., linear, logarithmic, exponential, sigmoidal. We assume that the output of a e_{pqdl} is normalized and always included in [0..1].

If pqd_i *values* is discrete, the evaluation function associates to every element a value in [0..1]: the higher the value, the better the quality. Moreover, the gap between two values reflects the

Figure 4. Quality evaluation functions $e_{availability}$ and $e_{responsetime}$

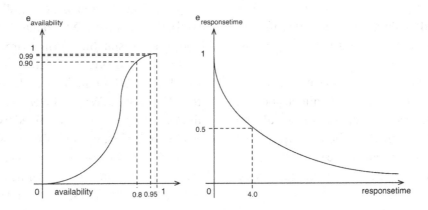

quality variation in case the quality dimension changes its value. Even in this case, the AHP technique can support the user during the evaluation function definition. Considering the *entertainment* dimension, as shown in Table 5, the values in the *entertainment.values* are compared through a pairwise matrix and, in this case, according to the same scale (see Table 3) adopted for the weights assignment. The eigenvector of such a comparison matrix will define the evaluation function.

Quality Offering

From a provider perspective, the quality model defined above allows to define the quality offering. In detail, for each service that the provider is going to make available, a capability document is defined and attached to the functional description of the service.

According to our quality model, a capability $c(pqd_l)$ is an instance of a $pqd_l \in PQD$ where:

$$c(pqd_l).name = pqd_l.name$$

$$c(pqd_l).values \subseteq pqd_l.values$$

So, a capability expresses, for a given primitive quality dimension, the real values that the provider is able to support during the Web service execution. Such a range of values will always be a restriction on the values defined in pqd_l, since, by definition, the latter has been defined by the community and collects all the possible values regardless of a specific service. Moreover, a capability can refer only to primitive quality dimensions because they are the only ones able to be measured.

A service provider, for each $pqd_l \in QT$ declares throughout the $c(pqd_l)$ which will be the quality really supported. The collection of all of these capabilities are organized in a Service Level (*SL*):

$$SL(QT)= <\{c(pqd_l)\}, price> \forall\ pqd_l \in PQD$$

Table 5. Comparison matrix for entertainment and corresponding quality evaluation function ($e_{entertainment}$)

entertainment values	Movies	Games	Internet	$e_{entertainment}$ (eigenvector)
Movies	1	5	3	0.636
Games	1/5	1	1/3	0.104
Internet	1/3	3	1	0.260

In detail, an *SL* includes both the definition of benefit and cost for the service provider. The cost corresponds to the set of capabilities offered, whereas the benefit coincides with the price of the service.

An SL determines one possible configuration of values of the primitive quality dimensions. In this way, an SL can be monitored since all the elements are measurable by definition. A provider, for each Web service, can define several of these configurations and collects them in the Service Levels Document (*SLD*).

$$SLD(QT) = \{SL_s(QT)\}$$

SLD describes the quality aspects of a Web service and it is used along with WSDL or BPEL which instead describe the functional aspects. All of these documents are stored in suitable registry, e.g., UDDI, available to the final user during the discovery phase. In this work we do not deal with the formalization able to express a *SLD*. Actu-ally, languages such as WS-Policy (Vedamuthu, Orchard, Hondo, Boubez, & Yendluri, 2003), as well as WSOL (Tosic, Ma, Pagurek, & Esfandiari, 2004) can be suitable for this purpose.

Figure 5 shows two Service Levels Documents (*SLD*$_A$ and *SLD*$_B$) associated to the flight reservation Web services WS$_A$ and WS$_B$, respectively. For the WS$_A$ the provider has defined two alternative quality offerings, whereas for the WS$_B$ only one. As occurred for the other primitive quality dimensions, even the price is defined by a range of values. Since the Web service is not yet invoked, a precise flight price is not available but the provider can calculate which will be a possible range of prices starting from the constraints expressed by the other primitive quality parameters.

Quality Request

From a user perspective a requirement document expresses the set of quality dimensions, taken from both primitive and derived quality dimensions

Figure 5. Service and requirements levels document samples

SLD$_A$

SL$_{A,1}$

c(availability).values = [0.80..0.99]
c(response time).values = [0..4ms]
c(latency).values = [0..1ms]
c(entert).values = {movies, internet}
c(delay).values = [0..30m]
c(class).values = {business, economy}
c(destination).values = {europe, asia}
price = [100..200$]

SL$_{A,2}$

c(availability).values = [0.80..0.99]
c(response time).values = [0..3ms]
c(latency).values = [0..1ms]
c(entert).values = {movies, games, internet}
c(delay).values = [0..1h]
c(class).values = {business}
c(destination).values = {europe, asia}
price = [150..300$]

SLD$_B$

SL$_{B,1}$

c(availability).values = [0.90..0.99]
c(response time).values = [0..2ms]
c(latency).values = [0..1ms]
c(entert).values = {movies, games,internet}
c(delay).values = [0..1h]
c(class).values = {economy}
c(destination).values = {europe, asia}
price = [300..400$]

RLD

RL$_1$

r(technicalqos).values = [0.4..0.7]
r(entertainment).values = {movies, internet}
r(delay).values = [0..2h]
r(comfort).values = [0.3..1.0]
r(destination).values = {europe}
cost = [0..200$]

sets that define the quality that a service should support. Users follow a process similar to the one followed by the providers to formalize their quality requirements. Once a user has identified the *QT* collecting all the relevant quality dimensions a customization process produces the related *WQT*. User requirements *r(qd)* are defined starting from *WQT(qos)*:

$$r(qd_i).name = qd_i.name$$

$$r(qd_i).values \subseteq qd_i.values$$

Differently from a constraint *c*, a requirement *r* can operate a restriction on both primitive and derived quality dimensions. This allows the user to express its requirements at different levels of abstraction as mentioned before. If a requirement predicates on a primitive quality dimension, then the user is aware about the meaning of the dimension and its possible values. On the opposite, if a requirement predicates on a derived quality dimension, then the user does not care about the real values of the measurable quality parameter. In this way, users only know that a value close to *1* means higher quality and vice versa.

As occurred for the capabilities, even the requirements are collected in a Requirement Level (*RL*), which expresses a configuration of requirements along with the amount of money that the user is willing to pay for exploiting the service. In this case, as discussed in (Hung & Haifei, 2003), the requirements reflect the benefit for the user and the price corresponds to the user cost. As we present in the next section, the selection process aims at mediating between the two contrasting perspectives of user and provider.

Finally, the set of alternative *RLs* are grouped in the Requirement Levels Document (*RLD*).

$$RL(WQT)= <\{r(pqd_{lr})\}, \{r(dqd_{mr})\}, cost>$$

where $pqd_{lr} \in PQD$, $dqd_{mr} \in DQD$, $LR \leq H$, $MR \leq K$

$$RLD(WQT)= \{RL_r(WQT)\}$$

It is worth noting that in a *RL* a user can include a dqd_m and even qd_j influencing the dqd$_m$ itself. As shown in Figure 5, the user asks for a service with a specific range of *comfort* quality, i.e., *[0.3..1.0]*. At the same time, the user also specifies admissible values for one of the dimensions influencing the *comfort*, i.e., *entertainment*. This means that the required customization must be obtained also satisfying the constraints at lower levels.

We assume that the requirements entirely cover the quality tree. This means that it is clear, for each quality dimensions what are the requirements. This means that for each $pqd_i \in QT$ either a direct requirement is expressed $r(pdq_i)$, or a indirect requirement is expressed by a $r(dqd_m)$ where dqd_m is affected by the pdq_i.

QUALITY AWARE MATCHMAKING

Web service selection refers to the activity able to identify which is the best Web service among a set of available ones. As discussed in the introduction of this chapter, such an activity only considers the functional aspects and, usually, the quality aspects are not really took into account. In our opinion, the lack of a common, shared, and flexible quality model implies the lack of a quality driven selection process. With the quality model presented in the previous section we aim at filling the gap and, in the following, we propose an approach for selecting Web services according to such a quality model. Here, we suppose that a set of functionally equivalent Web services has been already identified. Thus, the selection process described in this section only refers to the quality aspects. At this stage, our approach clearly separates the functional and non-functional matchmakings. In this way, the non-functional analysis is performed only for the Web services that already satisfy the functional requirements. Future work will aim at performing these two analyses at the same time.

Thus, it will be possible for the user to also consider the possibility to select a service that does not fully offer the required functionalities but it has a higher quality than the compliant functional services.

As shown in Figure 6 our selection process is composed by two main activities. First of all, for every functionally equivalent available Web service, a *quality matchmaking* step is performed to state if the user requirements are met; if so, the Web service is included in the Selected Web Service set (SWS). This set represents the input of the second activity, i.e., *Ranking*, which performs a cost-benefit analysis and returns a sorted list of Web services in SWS.

Quality matchmaking receives as inputs the user requirements, $RLD(WQT) = \{RL_r(WQT)\}$, along with the user preferences expressed by the

Figure 6. Web service selection process

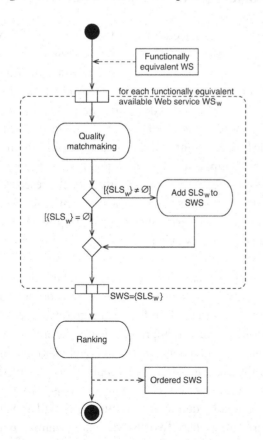

customized quality tree WQT, and the service capabilities for each Web service, $SLD_w(QT) = \{SL_{w,s}(QT)\}$. The matchmaking process, shown in Figure 7, is composed by two main steps: *low-level evaluation* and *high-level evaluation*. Both of these steps are performed comparing an $RL_r(WQT) \in RLD(WQT)$ with every $SL_{w,s}(QT) \in SLD(QT)$. The documents shown in Figure 5 reflect this scenario and they will be used as a reference example in the following. In particular, SLD_A and SLD_B are the service level documents for the Web services A and B, namely. A user specifies its requirements by the document *RLD* composed by only one requirement level RL_1.

Roughly speaking, the low-level evaluation activity identifies which are the $SL_{w,s}(QT)$ able to fulfill all the requirements about primitive quality dimensions in $RL_r(WQT)$. Then, exploiting the WQT, the high-level evaluation performs the same verification on derived quality dimensions included in $RL_r(WQT)$.

Result of this two-steps evaluation process will be, for each Web service, the list of Service Levels Selected $SLS_w = \{SL_{w,a}(QT)\} \subseteq SLD_w(QT)$ passing both evaluation steps. If $SLS_w \neq \varnothing$ then at least one service level provider offering is able to satisfy one of the alternative user requirements $RL_r(WQT)$ and the related Web service *w* can be selected.

Low-Level Evaluation

A $RL_r(WQT)$ might contain, by definition, requirements on both primitive and derived quality dimensions. In the former case, the user strictly identifies which are the measurable aspects that the provider must support. This usually happens about quality dimension more related to the use of Web service: e.g., *destination = {Europe, Asia}*. So, given a user requirements $RL_r(WQT) \in RLD(WQT))$ and a provider offering $SL_{w,s}(QT) \in SLD_w(QT)$, the low-level evaluation aims at stating if $SL_{w,s}(QT)$ satisfies $RL_r(WQT)$ where:

Figure 7. Quality matchmaking process

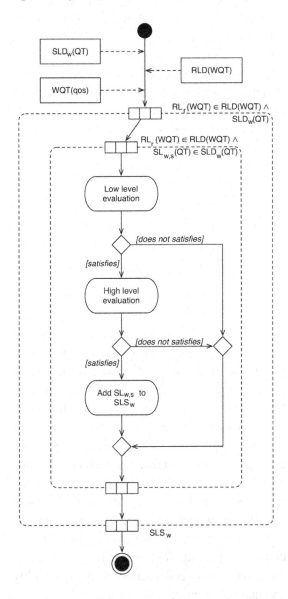

SL$_{w,s}$(QT) satisfies RL$_r$(WQT) $\Rightarrow$ ($\forall$r(pqd$_{lr}$) $\in$ RL$_r$(WQT), $\exists$ c(pqd$_c$) $\in$ SL$_{w,s}$(QT) |

pqd$_{lr}$.name = pqd$_c$.name $\wedge$ c(pqd$_c$).value $\supseteq$ r(pdq$_{lr}$).value) $\wedge$

max(SL$_{w,s}$(QT).price) $\leq$ max (RL$_r$(WQT).cost)

Generally speaking, the low-level evaluation verifies that the offering is able to provide a

wider range of values than the user requires. In this phase, cost and price are compared as well: the highest offering price must be less or equal to the maximum amount of money that the user is willing to pay.

For example, the *c(delay).values* is satisfied by SL$_{A,2}$ and SL$_{B,1}$. This means that both services are able to support such a requirement. If we consider the *price*, we can easily state that WS_B asks for a higher price (see *SL$_{B,1}$*). For this reason the Web service WS$_B$ cannot be further analyzed and it will not be included in the SWS.

High-Level Evaluation

The second step of the quality matchmaking process considers the derived quality dimensions in *RL$_r$(WQT)*. According to our quality model, the range of values of a *dqd$_m$* is always *[0..1]*, and the *r(dqd$_m$)* $\subseteq$ *[0..1]*. In this way, the user indicatively defines the quality required for a high level parameter which actually cannot be measured, but depends on other quality dimensions. Similarly to the low-level evaluation, given a *SL$_{w,s}$(QT)* $\in$ *SLD$_w$(QT)*, the high-level evaluation aims at stating if *SL$_{w,s}$(QT)* satisfies *RL$_r$(WQT)*, where:

SL$_{w,s}$(QT) satisfies RL$_r$(WQT) $\Rightarrow$ $\forall$ r(dqd$_{mr}$) $\in$ RL$_r$(WQT)

q(dqd$_{mr}$, SL$_{w,s}$(QT), WQT) $\in$ r(dqd$_{mr}$).values

In this case, a SL$_{w,s}$(QT) - which only includes primitive quality dimensions - satisfies a requirement on a derived quality dimensions *r(dqd$_{mr}$)*, if the required range of values about such a quality dimension (*r(dqd$_{mr}$).values*) includes the result of the quality function *q* defined as follows:

$$q(dq_i, SL(QT), WQT) = \begin{cases} \sum_{j=1}^{l+m} [q(qd_i.qd_j, SL(QT), WQT) \cdot w_{i,j})] & qd_i \in DQD \\ \min(e_{qd}(c(qd_i).values)) & qd_i \in PQD \end{cases}$$

155

where $c(qd_j) \in SL(QT)$, $e_{qdi} \in$ WQT. This function quantifies the quality of a primitive or derived dimension qd_i calculated by the capabilities in *SL(QT)*, with respect to the user preferences *WQT*. In detail, if the quality dimension is derived, the quality function is the weighted sum of the quality of the influencing dimensions qd_i, qd_j. On the contrary, in case of a primitive quality dimension, we consider the quality evaluation function defined in *WQT* and associated to such a dimension. In particular, we consider the worst quality associated to the values offered by the provider, which corresponds to the minimum values obtained invoking e_{pqdi} for each values in the $c(qd_i).values$.

Considering our example, in the user requirements we have $r(technicalqos).values = [0.4..0.7]$. Starting from the capabilities expressed in $SL_{A,1}$:

$q(\text{technicalqos}, SL_{A,1}, WQT) =$

$\min (e_{\text{availability}}(c(\text{availability}).values)) * 0.3 +$
$q(\text{performance}, SL_{A,1}, WQT) * 0.7 =$

$\min (e_{\text{availability}}(c(\text{availability}).values)) * 0.3 + [m$
$in(e_{\text{responsetime}}(c(\text{responsetime}).values) * 0.1 +$

$\min(e_{\text{latency}}(c(\text{latency}).values) * 0.9] * 0.7 =$
0.489

In this way, we can state that $SL_{A,1}$ offers, in the worst case, a quality about the technical aspects (*0.489*) included in the range required by the user (*[0.4..0.7]*). Skipping the further computations, in our example both $SL_{A,1}$ and $SL_{A,2}$ satisfy all the requirements on derived quality dimensions, so WS_A belongs to *SWS*.

Ranking

So far, we have realized which are the Web services able to satisfy the user quality requirements. Every member of *SWS* can be used for the user purpose and, if the provider really supports what is promised in the *SL*, no problems will occur. Actually, since the capabilities are different for every Web services, one of them should be better than the other ones. Goal of the last step of the selection process is to rank the service levels about the Web service included in the *SWS*. The order relationship ($\prec q$) is obtained performing a Cost-Benefit Comparison (*CBC*). In detail, regardless of the Web service to which the service levels SL_a is considered better then SL_b iif:

$$SL_a \prec_q SL_b \Leftrightarrow CBC(SL_a) > CBC(SL_b)$$

where:

$$CBC(SL_i) \equiv w_{cost} * \left(1 - \frac{SL_i(price)}{\max(price)}\right) + w_{ben} * q(QoS, SL_i, WQT))$$

In the CBC function the result depends on the weights given to the cost (w_{cost}) and the benefit (w_{ben}) where $w_{cost} + w_{ben} = 1$. In particular, the cost for the service depends on the price declared by the provider, where *max(price)* is the maximum price among the prices exposed by the candidate services. On the other side, the benefit depends on the overall quality obtained by the function $q(dq_i, SL(QT), WQT)$ considering the overall quality tree identified by the derived quality dimension *QoS*.

In this way, during the ranking activity we can realize how much the money saving is more important than the quality for the user. For example, for users that really need a service with high quality and that do not mind about money, $w_{cost} < w_{ben}$.

Considering the running example, let assume the worst case: maximum price and the minimum quality. About the latter, we have:

$q(QoS, SL_{A,1}, WQT) = 0.5 * q(\text{TechnicalQos}, SL_{A,1}, WQT) +$
$0.5 * q(\text{BusinessQos}, SL_{A,1}, WQT) = 0.57$
$q(QoS, SL_{A,2}, WQT) = 0.5 * q(\text{TechnicalQos}, SL_{A,2}, WQT) +$
$0.5 * q(\text{BusinessQos}, SL_{A,2}, WQT) = 0.55$

As a consequence, assuming that the user assigns the same importance to cost and benefit, i.e. $w_{cost} = w_{ben} = 0.5$, then:

$$CBC(SL_{A,1}) = 0.5 * \left(1 - \frac{180}{200}\right) + 0.5 * 0.57 = 0.835$$

$$CBC(SL_{A,2}) = 0.5 * \left(1 - \frac{200}{200}\right) + 0.5 * 0.55 = 0.775$$

$$\Rightarrow SL_{A,1} \prec SL_{A,2}$$

So, with respect to the user requirements, the Web Service WS_A provided with the service level $SL_{A,1}$ has a better quality then the same Web service with the service level $SL_{A,2}$.

A QUANTITATIVE EXAMPLE

In this section we show how our approach works in a more complete scenario. We based the scenario on the same example previously proposed, related to a flight booking service. The WQT(QoS) that describes the service quality is the same of the one showed in Figure 3 and also the user requirements RLD are the same as the ones shown in Figure 5.

On the contrary, we consider a new set of three functionally equivalent Web service WS_R, WS_S, and WS_T as listed in Table 6. For each service, service level offerings are detailed.

As a first step of process, i.e., the low-level evaluation, we check if a Service Level fully meets user requirements. Here $SL_{S,1}$ and $SL_{T,2}$ does not satisfy the RLD, in fact $SL_{S,1}$ does not offer *Europe* as destination, and $SL_{T,2}$ offers a price higher than the maximum accepted by user. Consequently, these two Service Levels does not pass the low evaluation step, and only three SLs constitute input for the next process step, i.e. the high level evaluation.

In order to obtain an evaluation of the offered quality, the high level evaluation needs the evaluation functions, that associate a [0..1] value to each primitive quality dimension *pqd*. Assuming that the community chooses the functions detailed in Table 7, for each *pqd* the normalized values are the ones represented in Table 8.

Starting from the evaluation of the *pqd*, the *dqd* are computed following the description of the WQT as defined in the high level evaluation (see Table 9). Starting from the leaves to the root, i.e., the QoS.

It is worth noting that the computation of QoS does not include the price and the importance that user gives to it. Indeed, this element is relevant for the very last step of the matchmaking: the ranking. Supposing that user has chosen weight 0.5 for QoS and 0.5 for price, the Cost-Benefit Comparison CBC computes an overall evaluation as shown in Table 10.

Table 6. Set of Web service

Id	Availability	Response Time (ms)	Latency (ms)	Destination	Entertainment	Delay	Class	Price
$SL_{R,1}$	95%	0.2	0.4	Europe Asia Americas	Internet	2	Business LowCost	70
$SL_{R,2}$	95%	1	0.4	Europe Asia Americas	Movies	3	Economy Business LowCost	17
$SL_{S,1}$	83%	1.5	1.1	Asia Americas	Movies Internet	4	Economy LowCost	123
$SL_{T,1}$	95%	0.1	3	Europe Asia Americas	Movies Games Internet	2	Economy Business LowCost	260
$SL_{T,2}$	99%	1	1.1	Europe Asia Americas	Internet	1	Economy LowCost	310

Table 7. Evaluation functions for pqd in the example scenario

pqd	Evaluation function type	Evaluation function
Availability	Linear function	$ef(v) = v$
Response Time	Exponential function	$ef(v) = exp(-v/2)$
Latency	Exponential function	$ef(v) = exp(-v)$
Delay	Exponential function	$ef(v) = exp(-v/2)$
Entertainment	Punctual function	$e(movie) = 0.3$ $e(internet) = 0.6$ $e(games) = 0.1$
Class	Punctual function	$e(business) = 0.3$ $e(economy) = 0.3$ $e(lowcost) = 0.4$
Destination	Punctual function	$e(Europe) = 0.5$ $e(Asia) = 0.2$ $e(Americas) = 0.3$

Table 8. Evaluation of offered pqd

	Availability	Response Time	Latency	Destination	Entertainment	Delay	Class
$SL_{R,1}$	0,95	0,90	0,67	1,00	0,60	0,37	0,70
$SL_{R,2}$	0,95	0,61	0,67	0,00	0,30	0,08	1,00
$SL_{T,1}$	0,95	0,95	0,05	1,00	1,00	0,37	1,00

Table 9. Evaluation of offered dqd

	Comfort	Performance	Technical qos	Business qos	QoS
$SL_{R,1}$	0,45	0,69	0,77	0,78	0,77
$SL_{R,2}$	0,22	0,66	0,75	0,09	0,42
$SL_{T,1}$	0,56	0,14	0,38	0,82	0,60

In this case, the Service Level that better satisfies user requirements is $SL_{R,1}$, that has a $CBC(SL_{R,1})=0.75$.

Assuming that the user prefers to save money by setting weight about price at 0.7, the Ranking step computes a different CBC as shown in Table 11; in this case the best choice is $SL_{R,2}$, that has a lower quality but also a lower price.

RELATED WORK

A complete service description is an important requirement for users who aim at searching the most suitable Web services. Besides the functional description, where WSDL represents the most adopted specification, even non-functional specifications are considered. In (Ruckert & Paech, 2006) a complete comparison of the current quality models is presented. In this area, WSOL (Tosic et al., 2004), WSLA (Keller & Ludwig,

Table 10. Computation of CBC in case of wPrice=wQos=0.5

	QoS	wPrice	wQoS	CBC
SL$_{R,1}$	0,77	0,5	0,5	**0,75**
SL$_{R,2}$	0,42	0,5	0,5	0,68
SL$_{T,1}$	0,60	0,5	0,5	0,30

Table 11. Computation of CBC in case of wPrice=0.7 and wQos=0.3

	QoS	wPrice	wQoS	CBC
SL$_{R,1}$	0,77	0,7	0,3	0,74
SL$_{R,2}$	0,42	0,7	0,3	**0,78**
SL$_{T,1}$	0,60	0,7	0,3	0,18

2002), and WS-Agreement (GRID Forum, 2003) (Lock, Dobson, & Sommerville, 2005) provide some description models that our work can exploit to express primitive quality dimensions. Even in the area of semantic web some proposals are available. In this case, different ontologies had been proposed to model the quality of service: QoSOnt (Lock et al. 2005), OWL-Q (Kritikos & Plexousakis, 2006), QoSOnto (Tran, 2008), and onQoS-QL (Giallonardo & Zimeo, 2007).

In this work the quality designer is inspired by the community's role in the QoS defining process as it is developed in (Marchetti, Pernici, & Plebani, 2004). A sort of community effort is the ISO/IEC 9126 specification which might be used to organize the set of technical quality dimensions (ISO/IEC, 2001). Here, six main characteristics and 27 sub-characteristics are identified; each of them stating a class of quality dimensions specifically related to the software quality domain. Due to its generality, every technical quality dimension can be associated to one of the six characteristics defined in the ISO 9126. About the dimension on the business aspects, (Zhang & Prybutok, 2005) presents a model of service quality definition according to a consumer perspective. More recently, (Yu, Rege, Bouguettaya, Medjahed, & Ouzzani, 2010) proposes a quality–aware selection for

planning composite service based applications. Here, to overcome the difficulty of dealing among different kinds of service, the concept of community is adopted as a space of Web services within a given application domain.

Individual differences, e-Service convenience, web site quality, risk, e-satisfaction, and intention are the set of considered dimensions. This work also demonstrates that the service convenience, Web site service quality, and risk are significant factors affecting consumers' satisfaction level, which in turn affects intention. Organization among several quality dimension is also discussed in (O'Sullivan, Edmond, & ter Hofstede, 2005) and the tree-based structure has been inspired by (Sabata, Chatterjee, Davis, Sydir, & Lawrence, 1997) and (Chung, Nixon, Yu, & Mylopoulos, 2000). Finally, WS-Policy (Vedamuthu et al., 2003) can be adopted as a language for exchanging quality documents.

Focusing on the selection process, (Yu & Reiff-Marganiec, 2008) proposes a survey of the current quality-aware discovery mechanisms and compares some of the existing approaches. According to this classification our approach is considered as policy-based. About other significant approaches (Makripoulias et al., 2006) proposes a complete framework for considering the QoS but they are mainly related to the technical aspects. In addition, in (Maximilien & Singh, 2004) the dynamical selection of the services is discussed proposing a solution based on agents, using the Web Services Agent Framework (WSAF), that includes an ontology for the QoS and a ad-hoc language to specify quality. The proposed approach only evaluates services with feedback assigned from the user that have already used the service, and does not consider the actual users' needs. In (Lamparter & Agarwal, 2005), considering Web Service as highly configurable objects and that the simple attribute-value pairs are insufficient to describe offers and requests, two requirements are identified for the automatic selection and the negotiation of services: the preferences information and the cardinal preferences. The proposed utility theory uses utility functions to estimate every parameter. Moreover, the authors do not focus on the dynamic creation of the dimensions and do not suggest how users could personalize quality dimensions. In (Fugini, Plebani, & Ramoni, 2006) a similar approach is discussed without considering the community as a way to mediate between the providers and the users. In addition, a cost benefit comparison is also considered in this work during the ranking phase. Finally, (Palmonari, Comerio, & De Paoli, 2009) presents a web service selection approach based on a semantic technologies. The matchmaking algorithm is based on a common ontology for expressing non-functional requirements to mediat between the user requests and the provider offerings. In (Godse, Sonar, & Mulik, 2008) the AHP method is used to solve the quantitative problem of assign an evaluation to a Web Service, focusing on non-functional parameters. Authors study literature to collect the most important non-functional Web Service features, and group them into a tree-structure. Authors do not use evaluation functions to compute the evaluation of parameters and do not consider the cost of each service in the final ranking.

In (Casola, Fasolino, Mazzocca & Tramontana, 2009) the authors focus on the importance of security in the definition of the quality of a web service. They describe Service Level Agreement (SLA) with a meta model, and use AHP to determine the importance of security-related aspects. This work does not consider the price of the service and propose a fixed model to describe the service quality.

In (Sun, He & Leu, 2007) authors motivate the use of AHP in the service selection problem and proposed the use of the Brown Gibson variant (BG) to alleviate the problem of time consuming pairwise comparisons. This work does not propose a community or a way to define and share tree quality structures and weights. This work take into account the cost of each service by using the BG variant.

CONCLUSION AND FUTURE RESEARCH DIRECTIONS

This chapter presented a model for describing the quality of Web services according to both user and provider perspectives. To mediate between these two standpoints, we introduce the community as the actor able to provide a shared knowledge about the quality of a service in a specific application domain. Relying on a tree-based structure, the proposed quality model is able to define the relationships among high-level and low-level quality dimensions. The work also exploits the introduced quality model to define a quality-driven Web service selection process. Here, the Web service capabilities and the user requirements are compared. A verification step states if at least one capability is able to fulfill the user requirements. Yet, a ranking activity sorts the provider offerings with respect to the user preferences and balancing benefits and costs.

At this stage, an application has been developed. The application assists providers, users, and communities during the quality definition activities. In the meanwhile, we are also developing a Web application able to support the selection process. Such an application results in a dashboard where all the user preferences are included. According to a set of cursors, users can express their preferences and the list of selected Web services dynamically changes. The software has been developed with Java and it can be downloaded at http://home.dei.polimi.it/plebani/download/qos/QoSModel.zip.

As remarked in the introduction, Web service selection driven by non-functional properties has captured a lot of attention but very few work had been really adopted in practice. Currently there are plenty of quality models and meta-models available to express these non-functional properties. Some of them are purely syntactic; some others also adopt semantic description to make possible more effective reasoning. Often, the same authors of a quality model adopted it only in their own work. More generic solutions exist but usually the quality dimensions related to the Web service performances and security are the ones really used. For this reason, future work need to focus on solutions that consider non-functional properties at meta-model level. Considering concept as *quality dimension* or *quality dimension dependencies* instead of focusing on a specific subset of quality dimensions could be, in our opinion, the best way to achieve the definition of a framework that can be widely applied. It is worth noting that working at meta level also allows to achieve another goal: i.e., the interoperability among the different non-functional models. Having a common meta-model, indeed, could make possible the translation from a quality model to another one. Obviously, it will be hard to have a single meta-model but, exploiting the common elements among the existing model a set of them could be identified.

In addition to this possible developments, further future work could take into account the Cloud Computing (Zhang, Cheng, & Boutaba, 2010). Indeed, with the introduction, in the recent year, of the Cloud Computing as a new paradigm for delivering application and, thus, service also the research in this area is affected. In particular, in the

Cloud Computing, the loosely coupling assumption, that usually characterizes the service-based applications, is now much more strong. From the provider side, the number of application instances to be considered becomes higher and higher, so the complexity to manage the service provisioning. From the user standpoint, the number of Cloud providers will increase and the need for identifying the right partner is more stringent.

From a research perspective, a more dynamic management of the community is required. The goal is to support the dynamic changes of the quality tree. In this way, both users and providers may rely on different versions of a quality tree related to a given application domain. According to this goal, semantic techniques can play a fundamental role in the quality tree definition to manage a sort of quality dimensions ontology and to map additional relationships among the included dimensions. In this way, ontology is able to reflect the mediator role that is implied in the community.

In addition, also the negotiation process, that represents the step to be taken after the selection process took place, needs to be considered. Actually, in this area several work are now available, but we think that the new scenarios proposed in the Cloud Computing make the situation more challenging. Indeed, users and providers to make the negotiation possible need to share the same negotiation protocol. Thus, to increase its market share, a service provider must support as many protocols as possible. The same if we play the user role: to be able to talk with all possible providers the user needs to support as much negotiation protocols as possible. To overcome to the consequent complexity, where all the possible actors support all the protocols, the usual situation is to introduce the role of the negotiation broker (Comuzzi & Pernici, 2009). Alternatively, we can consider the negotiation by delegation: when a negotiation protocol supported by all the participant does not exist, then we assume that a participant can fully or partially delegate the negotiation to someone else that supports other negotiation protocols that make possible to find a common protocol. About this issue a first approach has been proposed in (Comuzzi, Kritikos, & Plebani, 2009).

REFERENCES

Casola, V., Fasolino, A. T., Mazzocca, N., & Tramontana, P. (2009). An AHP-based framework for quality and security evaluation. In *International Conference on Computational Science and Engineering, CSE '09* (pp. 405 – 411).

Chung, L., Nixon, B., Yu, E., & Mylopoulos, J. (2000). *Non-functional requirements in software engineering*. Kluwer Academic.

Comuzzi, M., Kritikos, K., & Plebani, P. (2009). A semantic based framework for supporting negotiation in service oriented architectures. In *Proceedings IEEE Conference on Commerce and Enterprise Computing, CEC '09* (pp. 137-145). Vienna, Austria.

Comuzzi, M., & Pernici, B. (2009). A framework for QoS-based Web service contracting. *ACM Transaction on the Web, 3*(3).

Forum, G. R. I. D. (2003). *WS-agreement framework*. Retrieved from https://forge.gridforum.org/projects/graap- wg

Fugini, M. G., Plebani, P., & Ramoni, F. (2006). A user driven policy selection model. In *Proceedings Intl. Conference on Service Oriented Computing, ICSOC '06, LNCS 4294* (pp. 427-433). Chicago, IL: Springer.

Garofalakis, J., Panagis, Y., Sakkopoulos, E., & Tsakalidis, A. (2006). Contemporary Web service discovery mechanisms. *Journal of Web Engineering, 5*(3), 265–290.

Giallonardo, E., & Zimeo, E. (2007). More semantics in QoS matching. In *International Conference on Service-Oriented Computing and Applications, SOCA '07* (pp. 163-171). Newport Beach, CA, USA.

Godse, M., Sonar, R., & Mulik, S. (2008). The analytical hierarchy process approach for prioritizing features in the selection of Web service. In *European Conference on Web Services* (pp. 41-50).

Harker, P. T. (1987). Incomplete pairwise comparisons in the analytic hierarchy process. *Mathematical Modelling, 9*(11). doi:10.1016/0270-0255(87)90503-3

Hung, P., & Haifei, L. (2003). Web services discovery based on the trade-off between quality and cost of service: A token-based approach. *SIGecom Exch., 4*(2), 21–31. doi:10.1145/1120709.1120714

ISO/IEC. (2001). ISO/IEC 9126-1 Software engineering product quality, Part 1: Quality model.

Keller, A., & Ludwig, H. (2002, May). *The WSLA framework: Specifying and monitoring service level agreements for Web services*. Technical Report RC22456(W0205-171). IBM Research Division, T.J. Watson Research Center.

Kim, E., & Lee, Y. (2005). *Quality model for web service. Technical report*. OASIS Open Consortium.

Kritikos, K., & Plexousakis, D. (2006). Semantic QoS metric matching. In *Proceedings 4th European Conference on Web Services, ECOWS '06* (pp. 265-274). Zurich, Switzerland.

Lamparter, S., & Agarwal, S. (2005). *Specification of policies for Web service negotiations*. In Semantic Web and Policy Workshop. Galway.

Lock, R., Dobson, G., & Sommerville, I. (2005). QoSOnt: A QoS ontology for service-centric systems. *Proceedings 31st EUROMICRO Conference on Software Engineering and Advanced Applications* (pp. 80-87). Porto, Portugal.

Makripoulias, Y., Makris, C., Panagis, Y., Sakkopoulos, E., Adamopoulou, P., & Tsakalidis, A. (2006). Web service discovery based on quality of service. In *IEEE International Conference on Computer Systems and Applications* (pp. 196-199).

Mani, A., & Nagarajan, A. (2002). *Understanding quality of service for Web services*. Retrieved from http://www.ibm.com/developerworks/library/ws-quality.html

Marchetti, C., Pernici, B., & Plebani, P. (2004). A quality model for multichannel adaptive information. In *WWW Alt. '04: Proceedings of the 13th International World Wide Web Conference on Alternate Track Papers & Posters* (pp. 48-54). New York, NY: ACM Press.

Maximilien, E. M., & Singh, M. P. (2004). A framework and ontology for dynamic web services selection. *IEEE Internet Computing, 8*(5), 84–93. doi:10.1109/MIC.2004.27

O'Sullivan, J., Edmond, D., & ter Hofstede, A. H. M. (2005). *Formal description of non-functional service properties. Technical report.* Queensland University of Technology.

Palmonari, M., Comerio, M., & De Paoli, F. (2009). Effective and flexible NFP-based ranking of Web services. In *Proceedings 7th International Joint Conference on Service-Oriented Computing (ICSOC-ServiceWave 2009)* (pp. 546-560). Stockholm, Sweden: Springer-Verlag.

Ran, S. (2003). A model for web services discovery with QoS. *SIGecom Exch., 4*(1), 1–10. doi:10.1145/844357.844360

Ruckert, J., & Paech, B. (2006). Web service quality descriptions for Web service consumers. In *Proceedings CONQUEST2006.*

Saaty, T. L. (1980). *The analytic hierarchy process.* New York, NY: McGraw Hill.

Sabata, B., Chatterjee, S., Davis, M., Sydir, J. J., & Lawrence, T. F. (1997). Taxonomy for QoS specifications. In *Proceedings of the Third International Workshop on Object-Oriented Real-Time Dependable Systems* (pp. 100-107).

Sun, Y., He, S., & Leu, J. Y. (2007). Syndicating Web services: A QoS and user-driven approach. [Elsevier.]. *Decision Support Systems, 43*(1), 243–255. doi:10.1016/j.dss.2006.09.011

Tosic, V., Ma, W., Pagurek, B., & Esfandiari, B. (2004). Web service offerings infrastructure (WSOI) - A management infrastructure for XML Web services. In *Network Operations and Management Symposium, NOMS 2004* (vol. 1, pp. 817-830).

Tran, V. X. (2008). WS-QoSOnto: A QoS ontology for Web services. In *Proceedings IEEE International Symposium on Service-Oriented Systems Engineering, SOSE 2008* (pp. 233-238). Jhongli, Taiwan: IEEE Computer Society.

Vedamuthu, A., Orchard, D., Hirsch, F., Hondo, M., Yendluri, P., Boubez, T., & Yalçinalp, Ü. (2003). *Web services policy 1.5 - Primer.* W3C Working Group Note. Retrieved from http://www.w3.org/TR/ws-policy-primer/

Yu, H. Q., & Reiff-Marganiec, S. (2008). Non-functional property based service selection: A survey and classification of approaches. In *Proceedings Non Functional Properties and Service Level Agreements in Service Oriented Computing Workshop co-located with The 6th IEEE European Conference on Web Services, ECOWS 2008.* Dublin, Ireland.

Yu, Q., Rege, M., Bouguettaya, A., Medjahed, B., & Ouzzani, M. (2010). A tw-phase framwork for quality-aware Web service selection. [Springer.]. *Journal on Service Oriented Computing and Applications, 4*(2), 63–79. doi:10.1007/s11761-010-0055-6

Zhang, Q., Cheng, L., & Boutaba, R. (2010). Cloud computing: State-of-the-art and research challenges. [London, UK: Springer.]. *Journal of Internet Services and Applications, 1*(1), 7–18. doi:10.1007/s13174-010-0007-6

Zhang, X., & Prybutok, V. R. (2005). A consumer perspective of E-service quality. *IEEE Transactions on Engineering Management, 52*(4), 461–477. doi:10.1109/TEM.2005.856568

KEY TERMS AND DEFINITIONS

Community: Group of people, a standardization body, or even an implicit agreement that aims at proposing a specification for a group of objects with some relevant common characteristics.

Derived Quality Dimension: A quality dimension which value depends on other quality dimensions.

Primitive Quality Dimension: A direct measurable quality dimension (e.g. response time).

Quality Tree: All the quality dimensions defined relevant for a given application domain.

Service Selection: Process that aims at identifying a set of services able to satisfy a given set of functional and non-functional constraints.

Chapter 8

An Integrated Approach for Service Selection Using Non–Functional Properties and Composition Context

Stephan Reiff-Marganiec
University of Leicester, UK

Hong Qing Yu
Open University, UK

ABSTRACT

In the maturing world of service oriented computing and Web services, we find ourselves in a position where numerous services are available, all of which address a specific need. Selecting the best such service based on the service context and a user's current need becomes an important aspect. Services can be evaluated based on functional and non-functional criteria: the former represent the operation that the service provides, the latter criteria that differentiate functionally equal services. This chapter presents three closely related items addressing the problem of differentiating functionally equal services to find the most appropriate one in any given situation: (1) a generic and extensible model for non-functional properties, (2) a method for ranking services, and (3) an algorithm for selecting services that are part of larger execution chains. The method is evaluated, and the needs are exemplified with some motivating examples.

INTRODUCTION

Service-oriented computing (and its predominant incarnation as web services) is reaching a certain maturity, which is reflected in the number of services that are becoming available. Well established technologies for Service-oriented computing allow providers to describe and deploy services while allowing clients to bind to and invoke these over the internet on demand. Much of the matchmaking task involved in finding an appropriate service is a manual task. Selecting the service is often a question of retrieving

DOI: 10.4018/978-1-61350-432-1.ch008

functional descriptions from service repositories and then ensuring that the described and required interfaces match a technical level. However, with the rapidly growing number of available services, clients are presented with a choice of functionally similar (or even identical) services. This choice gives clients the opportunity to select services that match other criteria: these are referred to as non-functional properties.

From the single service selection point of view, the non-functional properties are related to local constraints. The local constraints reflect the user preferences and context of the demanded service. From the a service composition point of view, the selection problem becomes more challenging, because the composition context needs to be considered in addition to capture the larger context of the service invocation. For example, assume that service s2 has a better coordination record with service s1 than service s3. Now, if service s1 is selected in the composition, then service s2 is a better choice according to this particular composition constraint. In this chapter we will present more case studies with composite service scenarios. We use a scenario driven approach to identify a non-functional properties model, which allows to capture the properties of relevance for single and composite service selection. We present a service selection method which considers all relevant constraints both for single service selection and composed scenarios – the development of which presents an additional challenge in aggregating the different constraints to get comparable scores for the competing services.

In this chapter, we will address web service selection based on non-functional properties and bring together a complete overview of techniques and approaches developed over a number of years. The main contributions are:

- A generic and extensible model for non-functional properties,

- A method for ranking services, based on the LSP (logic scoring for preference) method, and
- A stepwise backwards algorithm for selecting services in composition scenarios.

The chapter is structured as follows: Case studies from real world scenarios presented in the next section aid in understanding the non-functional properties and composition context and add further motivation for the work. We then present the non-functional properties model for single service properties and the composition context model. Next we introduce our service selection method which is based on Logic Scoring Preference aggregation functions and type-based evaluation functions. Following that, we illustrate the Backward Composition Context based Service Selection approach for service composition focusing on the general operation and use of the concepts illustrated in this chapter. The chapter is completed with an evaluation of the approach and comparison to related work.

MOTIVATING CASE STUDIES

In this section, we describe two typical service composition cases of organising a meeting and planning a trip. Each example includes different composition scenarios which highlight a set of different types of non-functional properties – both properties of the services in question as well as properties of the composition context.

Case Study 1: Organizing a Meeting

A meeting is required to be settled for discussing the detailed plan of a particular event. Organizing a meeting involves a series of activities (or tasks). The tasks include searching for suitable attendees, finding a suitable date, booking a meeting room and sending notifications to the invited people. The meeting organiser integrates these tasks as a

Figure 1. Workflow of organising a meeting

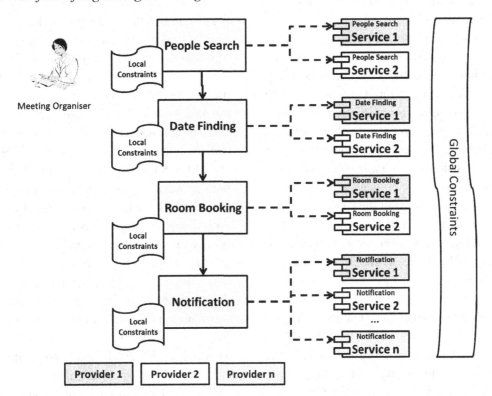

workflow template shown in Figure 1. For simplicity we assume that each task can be performed by a service (that is we can find services in our repository that provide the required functionality for each task).

We will now look at the tasks and the concretely available services in some more detail:

• *The task of searching for participants can be performed by a people lookup service.* There are two available people lookup services. Both services have the same functionality of providing a list of people that match an input list of requirements containing attributes such as skills, experiences and position in the company. However, these two services have different non-functional properties. One service can find the people who are in this organization and provides highly accurate information

about them. The other service can search for people inside and outside the organization, but it is less accurate. Moreover, the first service's response speed is slower than the second one. The two services are provided by two different providers.

• *The task of finding a meeting date can be completed by a meeting scheduler service.* There are two scheduler services which use people's calendar URLs as input and return the most suitable date for all involved people as output. One scheduler service only has ability to check Google and MSN online calendar systems and provides a date with 90% suitability (that is 9 people out of 10 are available on the scheduled date). The other service has ability to check all kinds of currently existing online calendar systems and finds dates with 70% suitability. Again, the two services are offered by different providers.

- *The room booking task can be executed by a meeting-room booking services.* The booking service takes the date and facility requirements as input and provides the place address and room information as output. There are two room booking services available. One service supports to book rooms inside the organization, the other service supports to book all available business meeting rooms in the whole city.
- *The task of sending notifications is performed by notification services.* There are many such services available, e.g. email or SMS services.

The meeting planner (user) starts to invoke the composition workflow. For the first task, a people search service is required and two services are discovered. In this scenario, the target people should be in the organization – hence there is a hard requirement on choosing the service in that it must be able to find people inside the organization. The user also has preferences on accuracy with a weight of 0.7 and response speed with a weight of 0.3. We should say here that the higher the weight, the more important the factor is for the user and also that weights always add up to 1. Both services introduced earlier satisfy the hard requirement, so the selection problem becomes one of finding a best match on the weighted score of the other two properties.

Supposing Provider 1's service is selected based on the accuracy and speed wishes. However, its invocation fails with a permanent error – the system should fall back on the second best option and invoke the service from Provider 2. It is very useful to store this failure information, so that it can be used when consider using the service in a future service composition. Clearly this can help in the future to increase the composition reliability and reduce composition time.

As discussed Provider 2's service was used for the people search. For the task of date finding, we find that all people are using Google calendars. The information as to which calendar is used by a user is encoded in the user's context – to be more precise it is part of the user profile which forms the more static part of the user's context. A more detailed definition of the user context ontologies can be found in (Truong, Dustdar, Baggio, et al., 2008). So, as all users use Google calendars, both services for date finding are suitable as they can search the required calendars. The factor for optimizing the selection is the suitability rate. It is easy to see that the second service is the best one, if only local constrains are considered. However, we have some historical data which shows that the selected people search service has more coordination failures with the scheduling service from Provider 1 than its own scheduling service. Therefore, it is now difficult and complex to decide which service is better. The difficulty is to balance the local constraints and constraints from the invocation context. On the one side, the local constraints ensure the service satisfying the user's preferences to the best extent. On the other hand, the global constraints can reduce chances of the composition failure which is clearly also desirable.

Supposing the scheduler chosen is also from Provider 2, we see that all selected services are provided by the same provider. For the third task of booking a room there is a wish to book a room inside the organization's building which again both services can do. There are no other user preferences, so either service would be fine. However, we might have more historical information that shows that services from the same provider work better together; in which case the second service may be the better choice because it comes from the provider we have chosen for the previous steps.

Case Study 2: Planning a Trip

The second case study is one of planning a trip. The activity requires three tasks of booking

Figure 2. Planning a trip

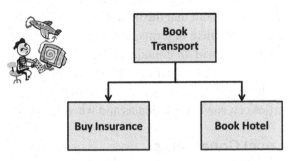

transport, buying travel insurance and booking a hotel as shown in Figure 2. Moreover, once the transport has been booked the dates are fixed and the insurance purchase and hotel booking tasks are independent and can be conducted in parallel.

Rather than considering specific service here we can observe the following:

- There are many different transport services available. The relevant non-functional properties are speed (how fast is the service) and cost (how expensive is it).
- There are many insurance services available; the properties of relevance are cost and reputation of the provider.
- There are many hotel services available; the properties are the location, the quality (star rating), the cost and the reputation.

For each task we can make a local decision based on a weighted evaluation of the relevant properties, in such a way that cost should be kept low, speed and reputation should be high and the star rating should be as high as possible. However, the star rating has the extra constraint of having to be at least "3 stars" and the hotel location should of course be at the destination intended for the trip.

Now, we find that services from different providers might come with special relations e.g. the airline provider chosen has a business cooperation policy with a hotel provider: it would probably be useful to make selections dependent on previous

selections to benefit from these co-operations. Of course there might be others expressed as policies:

- It is not allowed to a call a service s1 more than 2 times per minute.
- It is not allowed for services from provider B to be invoked more than 10 times a day.
- Provider A does not allow for its services to be used in conjunction with services from provider B.

Allowance policies represent the corporation constraints existent in a competitive business context. The overall value of properties is crucial – we might wish to find the cheapest or most reliable composite service. However, for example the cheapest composite service is usually not obtained by selecting the cheapest service in each place because of the coordination between different providers.

There are clearly many more scenarios in the real world – both for properties of specific services or service groups as well as for relations in compositions. However, the presented scenarios provide a good insight into the general requirements for non-functional property models for services and compositions.

NON-FUNCTIONAL PROPERTIES AND COMPOSITION CONTEXT

As shown in the case studies, it is important to consider both local constraints and composition context for service selection and composition. In this section we will discuss non-functional properties and introduce our model for them; we will also make the concept of composition context ore precise.

Non-Functional Properties

To enable understanding the concept of non-functional properties, we need to define what functional properties are. Functional properties are normally described as IOPE properties (Input, Output, Precondition and Effect). Functional properties specify the requirements of service invocation and promised results from successful service execution from a purely functional sense: a printing service "prints" things or a hairdresser "cuts hair".

In contrast non-functional properties refer to the attributes which describe the QoS (Quality of Service, e.g. security and speed) and other metadata about the service (e.g. provider and cost): the printing service might print 40 pages per minute at 1200dpi resolution, the hairdresser might have been trained by a famous school and charge 50GBP for a haircut. There are many other ways to distinguish different non-functional properties.

Non-functional properties can be separated as *annotations* attributes and non-functional *behavioural* attributes (Toma, 2007). The annotations attributes are the properties which can apply to all elements descriptions, e.g. services, goals, mediators, ontology, etc. They are simply providing a way to provide metadata about any type of element description. The non-functional behavioral attributes are specific to a service element.

Non-functional properties also can be distinguished by *generic quality* criteria and *domain specific* criteria (Liu, Ngu, & Zeng, 2004). The generic criteria are applicable to all services, e.g. price and execution duration. The domain specific criteria refer to the specific aspects of services from different service selection domains. For example a printing service may have non-functional properties of speed, color options and quality while a weather service may consider accuracy and range.

In this chapter, we consider non-functional properties separated into *local* constraints and *composition context* constraints. The former are properties of a single service, while the latter are properties of the execution context in which the service used.

When developing this model we followed a scenario driven approach based on the case studies

taking into account existing work where relevant. We do not claim that the model as it is presented here is complete in terms of being able to cover all properties of all domains; in fact it was never intended to be this. The model was developed in such a way that it is extensible, so that new properties can easily be added as and when required.

Local Constraints

Usually services are categorised by their functional properties, e.g. in the categorisation system used in UDDI (OASIS, 2004). This kind of service categorisation is insufficient for automatic service selection processes because it does not specify NPFs that are essential to differentiate functionally similar services in different situations. We propose to extend the functional properties based categorisation with details of NFPs, following a well-structured data model.

From one angle we can consider the source of the data, providing a top level model as that shown in Figure 3. The differentiation of the categories is based on the sources for the values of these properties. The general properties are provided by the services' provider to describe the provider's information such as name of the provider, the location and price of the service and other "easily verifiable" properties of the service. The trust properties are provided by the third parties who can monitor the services behaviors and give feedback about the services, e.g. the reputation, trust and satisfaction of the service. QoS includes all aspects about the service's quality. QoS attributes are widely summarized by International Organization for Standardization (ISO/IEC, 2001).

Rather than reinventing detailed attributes for QoS models, we have reused and slightly modified the QoS model from (Olsina & Rossi, 2002) designed for measuring Web application. The model provides the four main elements of usability, reliability, efficiency and security. Their model is quite detailed and many QoS criteria apply directly; with the different elements, of

Figure 3. Hierarchy model of the local constraints

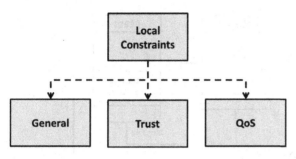

course, having different types of sub-elements according to different service domain and context. We defined some basic sub-elements which may be included in these QoS main elements. For example:

- Reliability may include details on error rates and stability. Error rates shows chances of getting unsuccessful results from the service. The stability represents the long term stability of the service performance.
- Efficiency may include the execution duration, accessibility and accuracy. The execution duration describes the speed of the service for completing successfully. The accessibility shows the states of being accessible or not. For example, the service is not accessible from wireless. The accuracy indicates the correctness and freshness level of the data or information produced by the service.

However, any model for QoS properties could be substituted instead of the Olsina and Rossi one used, as we are only using the model to inform the generic model presented next in terms of suitable Meta information for services.

We have defined a category model that allows for metadata to be assigned to services and this data to be stored in the repository[1]; the stored data can then be retrieved to evaluate services. Different service categories have different sets of relevant metadata. For example, printing services

can consider colour options, while communication services might consider the transmission mode (e.g. synchronous).

The service registration process (see Figure 4) builds a link between the service and the category. Meanwhile, the OWL-S description of the service should specify the metadata which is required for the category. In the following we provide more details about the category, metadata (Meta) and service. Each category has a name, which identifies the category (there is also an identifier for computer rather than human use). This is useful for service developers who wish to register a new service, however for searches and finer grained understanding of what the category represents a number of keywords describing the functional properties of services (or more accurately operations) in the category are provided. A detailed description adds further detail for human use. Each category has a set of metadata associated to it, which captures the non-functional properties typical for that category. Note that this meta data does (of course) not contain concrete values (as these need to stem from concrete services), but rather states which information one would typically expect for services of that category – there might be additional elements for specific services and not all elements typically expected might be available for all services. So for example, a typical notification service might have a cost and a coverage area associated to it (hence the category would have cost and coverage), while a specific service, e.g. an SMS service, might show its cost, but no coverage information. It could also have an additional metadata item relating to encryption provided.

Each metadata element has an AbstractType, which is used to identify the correct evaluation function for this type of data. The associated WeightSet reflects the importance of this particular non-functional property in the category, from a service provider point of view. However, different situations require a shift in importance, as do individual users. So weights are more flexible

Figure 4. The conceptual model of category, service and service registration

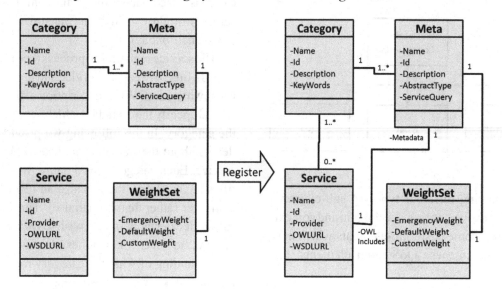

in that they provide the default weight as specified by the provider, they allow for an emergency weight (usually defined for the application domain) and custom weights (usually defined by the end user). In order to indicate that a small value is desirable, weights take on negative values in the range of [0,-1], if a larger value is desirable values come from the [0,1] interval (this is just a mechanism to express the evaluation inside a unified framework; for user's it would be possible to express these requirements in any way which then can be mapped into the mathematical constraint mentioned here). In addition, an absolute value of 1 means that the criteria is a hard constraint (that is it must be satisfied, or we are not interested in the service).

Examples for these cases are cost (the smaller the better), speed (the faster the better) and availability in a certain country (e.g. a retail service not shipping to the UK would be of no interest to a UK customer).

While some metadata values are fairly static and can be found in the service profile (for example the speed of a printer, or whether it prints in colour), there are some criteria that depend on the service context (they are dynamic) and need to be

more up to date (e.g. the length of a print queue). To obtain such data the ServiceQuery attribute specifies a SPARQL (Prud'hommeaux, Seaborne, 2008) query statement which can be used to locate this kind of information from the service context. Service queries effectively specify where the framework can obtain up-to-date information on a services context; this could be a query directly against the service (maybe a service offers an additional interface for such information) or it could be a query against a database to which services periodically publish their status information. The former is something that we find implemented in most current network printers; the latter will require further enhancements and an approach based on complex event processing is described in (Tilly, Reiff-Marganiec, 2011).

A service is described by typical elements, such as information about its provider. The service OWLURL is a link to the location of the OWL-S description file of the service, which should contain the required data for the non-functional attributes. WSDLURL provides a link to the services WSDL file, as is required for using the service in current web service technologies.

Table 1. Composition context elements

Composition Context	Explanation	Expression Type
1. Execution context		
1.1 Execution error	The workflow execution engine detected an exception, when the service is invoked.	Numerical type
1.2 Connection error	Two services worked fine independently. However, an error appeared during their coordination.	Numerical type
2. Coordination context		
2.1 Provider distance	Do services belong to the same provider?	Boolean type
2.2 Coordination time	The coordination time for communications between services.	Numerical type
2.3 Physical distance	How far apart are the services in terms of physical location?	Numerical type
3. Service Relation Policies		
3.1 Special Cost	This captures special deals between services.	Numerical type
3.2 Allowance	This captures which services can and which cannot be used together, or "Is composition allowed?"	Boolean type
3.3 Time limitation	This specifies the times of continuous invoking	Numerical type

Registering a service involves linking this to the service category model, which is assigning one or more categories for each service (or operation). This has the side effect of linking the service to typical non-functional criteria for which users might require values and this data is populated from the services OWL-S file. In case that the service provides additional non-functional criteria they can be easily added into the model.

Composition Context

In the last section we introduced our extensible non-functional properties model and discussed how individual criteria for services can be stored. The kind of criteria that we considered there were local criteria, that is measurements for each individual service. In the introduction we discussed at length the need to also correlate how services interact when used inside larger execution chains or workflows.

In order to categorise and store the information of the interrelation of services in a way accessible to our evaluation methodology we have introduced the novel concept of Composition context. Compo-

sition context focuses on the context information which will affect service composition.

Based on the presented case studies, we define eight composition context constraints in three categories: execution context, coordination context and service relation policies (see Table 1).

We believe that the three top-level categories are complete, as information either is related to events occurring during service execution, is given by the static relation between two services or can be influenced by business decisions. We do not claim the elements defined inside the categories are complete, but they have shown sufficient for the case studies encountered in our work. Further elements can be added if needed and they should not affect the feasibility of our selection mechanism.

Analysing the 3 groups of context, we find that composition context can also be separated into dynamic context and static context. The dynamic context (e.g. coordination time, execution context of execution error rate and connecting error rate) means the context changes very frequently. Thus, dynamic context needs to be detected, calculated and stored at runtime. Static context refers to the composition information which does not change frequently (e.g. provider distance and special cost).

We will briefly explain the composition context ideas introduced in table 1 in some more detail. Execution errors are detected when the workflow engine tries to invoke a service and finds that the service does not respond or reports a service failure. Connection errors occur when services were attempted to be used in conjunction and the composition did not execute, however, neither of the services has failed individually. In both cases a crude but effective measure is the ratio of attempted executions over failed executions. Clearly more sophisticated mechanisms can be introduced that give more weight to more recent failures, or reset remote history after a certain amount of time has lapsed.

Provider Distance is self-explanatory as per the description in the table. Coordination time measures how long it takes for the services to communicate with each other (that is how long does it take for messages produced by one service to be received by the other. Physical distance considers the distance of the services and is more relevant for real services rather than virtual services. However, if larger amounts of data need to be transferred the physical distance of two virtual services could also be relevant as the data transfer involves significant need of time (e.g. if a genome set needs to be sent from a storage service to an evaluation service in a different part of the world a significant bandwidth need will arise).

Special cost is expressed in terms of policies (such as discount policies saying e.g. that using services of provider A will allow you to gain a 20% discount on using services of provider B). Clearly such policies are in general use in many domains, and here we cater for such that can be expressed in terms of some numerical advantage (especially a discount value); however one should consider more expressive mechanisms in the future. Allowance and time limitations are much simpler; the former specifies whether the use of one service together with another service is al-

lowed (e.g. the printing service cannot be used together with the fax service) and the latter states how often a service can be invoked in a certain time span (e.g. the flight quote service can only be used 10 times in any 24 hour period).

THE SERVICE SELECTION METHOD

The Requirements for the Service Selection Method

Service selection is the problem of allowing a prospective user to choose the services which are best suited to his/her functional and non-functional requirements, the non-functional attributes provide the opportunity to differentiate between the competing services (Dan, Ludwig, & Pacffici, 2005). With the rapidly growing number of available services, users are presented with a choice of functionally similar (or even identical) competing services. Making a decision is strongly depended on the non-functional attributes. Service selection can be performed by two types of methodologies:

1. **Manual Service Selection:** The service(s) discovery and selection are manually made through the service discovery protocols (e.g. UDDI) and human readable non-functional property descriptions. Once the service is selected, it will usually not be changed in the future.

2. **Automatic Service Selection:** The service(s) are dynamically discovered and selected based on machine understandable representations (e.g. OWL-S or WSMO) and service requirement gathered at run-time. The selected service is used, and when a future requirement is encountered a new evaluation of the best service will be made.

The second methodology is one of the important goals of the SOA, and is absolutely essential when context aware systems are considered – that is situations where the requirements change dynamically and are usually not the same for several needs of services with the same functionality. An example would be a communication service: whether a phone, SMS or IM service is appropriate depends entirely on what the user is currently doing and how urgently she needs to be contacted. However, the automatic service selection is a very complex task because different types of non-functional properties need to be evaluated. The major requirements for a non-functional properties based service selection method are:

- **Model Based:** The ranking method needs to be based on flexible and extensible models of non-functional properties (such as the one presented in the last section). Due to the versatility of non-functional properties (and the fact that new ones might be required at any time) it is unlikely that a complete standard set covering all domains can be identified and the ranking method needs to allow for that in that it will derive ranking scores for services based on the available information.

- **User Preferences:** Service requesters usually have various preferences for the non-functional criteria depending on situation they find themselves in (their context), and of course different requesters will usually have different preferences. A good mechanism should not only allow expressing values for each property, but preferably also represent the relations among the preferences. For example, a user may consider the security property as more important than privacy when requesting a financial service. Hence, the selection approach needs to provide for mechanisms for users to express which properties they feel more strongly about and also relations between these properties.

- **Evaluation Functions:** As we discussed earlier, it is difficult to predict how many

non-functional properties will be available, as well as the type of these properties. For example, the evaluation function to compute the speed criteria will be very different from the function to calculate the location criteria. It is very difficult to define a universal evaluation function for all kinds of non-functional properties. Hence, the evaluation framework must not only adapt to various numbers of criteria, but also automatically identify the measurement methods that should be used to evaluate each criterion.

- **Dynamic Aggregation:** When all desired non-functional criteria have been evaluated, individual scores need to be aggregated to gain a final score for the service. In this step a suitable aggregation method needs to be selected. Intuitively, arithmetic or geometric means based on weighted sums or products might appear to be an efficient and understandable choice. Unfortunately, they are not the best choice for complex situations with tens or even hundreds of criteria as extremely high values measured for criteria with a low weight can overshadow values of other factors with higher weights (and hence higher importance). Furthermore there are dependencies between properties that need to be considered: some criteria might be mutually replaceable (that is a high score of one criterion should indeed replace a low score of another) or criteria might be simultaneously required and independent of their values should always be seen as important (think of safety and speed of a car: no matter how fast it goes you still would want it to be safe!)

- **Automation:** While a service designer would still specify data for the service when making it available and a user would still be able to specify requirements (unless these are gathered through some context aware system), the selection should be performed without human intervention. Such automatic selection methods are essential when for example considering context aware service provisioning (where requirements are automatically generated, and change rapidly) or selection of services within workflow contexts (essentially allowing for the execution of "abstract" processes where specific service endpoints are not predefined). One aspect demanding automation is the selection of evaluation functions for specific criteria; the other is the selection of aggregation functions.

- **Scalability and Accuracy:** Scalability here does not only mean that the approach can consider large numbers of properties, but also that many ranking processes are taking place simultaneously. Of course there is also a question as to how accurate the result is. While one would aim for perfect accuracy (that is one has provably chosen the best service), it is often sufficient to choose a good enough service if the decision can be made quickly.

We will next present a method that addresses these concerns. The method uses the model for non-functional properties presented earlier and is applicable to both local and composition context based selections (in fact it integrates both). The method is based on LSP – which provides good aggregation options but was meant for human use and hence has been extended in several ways for automatic selection. We refer to the method as type-based LSP extension (TLE for short) and it has been introduced in (Yu, Reiff-Marganiec, 2009a).

The Extended LSP and Type-Based Service Selection Method

Logic Scoring Preference (LSP) method introduced in (Dujmovic, 1973 and Dujmovic, 1975) is a professional evaluation and aggregating method initially designed for solving hardware selection problems (Dujmovic, 1996). LSP aims to evaluate quantitative features for the comparison of different entities. Since then LSP has been used to deal with data management systems (Su, Dujmovic, Batory, S.B., & Elnicki, 1987) and web site evaluation and selection problems (Olsina & Rossi, 2002). The four main steps of LSP evaluation method are: (1) specifying evaluation variables, (2) defining elementary criteria, (3) analyzing degree decision and (4) analyzing cost/preference. Note that these are steps involving much human decision making. The LSP method certainly has lots of power to evaluate the quantitative aspects of competitive Web services and support selection decision making, but there are some enhancements to be made as we will show.

First we will provide more insight into LSP. LSP modifies the traditional weighted sum scoring techniques (Miller III, 1970) (see formula 1).

$$L = (\omega_1 E_1 + \omega_2 E_2 + ... + \omega_n E_n) \qquad (1)$$

The traditional weighted sum scoring techniques only consider the weight of factors in the aggregation, but ignore the relation between criteria such as replaceability, simultaneity and mandatory-ness. These relations normally are observable properties of human reasoning (Dujmovic, Larsen, 2004) and we have discussed this problem when considering the dynamic aggregation requirement. To capture these relations, Conjunction/Disjunction (GCD) operators were introduced in LSP to represent the relation of requirements. The LSP aggregation function is represented as formula 2.

$$L = (\omega_1 E_1^r + \omega_2 E_2^r + ... + \omega_n E_n^r)^{1/r}, \qquad (2)$$

where

$$0 \le E_i^r \le 1, \sum_{i=1}^{n} \omega_i = 1,$$

ω_i is the weight of each criterion. E is the defined evaluation function for providing the scores of the service for each criterion. The r presents the logic relation between different criteria. The complete table of GCD operators with accepted symbols, degrees and values for parameter r are given in Table 2 (based on (Dujmovic, 1996)). The definition of the GCD operators is the disjunction/conjunction degree d (also known as *orness degree*) of combining simultaneity and replaceability. The idea here is that at the ends of the spectrum we have conjunction (and) and disjunction (or) respectively. Values in the range are closer to or, and hence have a higher degree of 'orness' – that is they behave more like or (we could provide a similar definition for 'andness'). We will use these defined operators without adding more new operators. We will use the closest values of d when a calculated degree value result is not found in Table 2. Moreover, $r2$ is the r value for a 2 criteria situation, $r3$ for 3 criteria situation and so on. The d indicates the orness degree as explained above.

However, here is a small issue for non-functional properties evaluation: some non-functional properties should get higher scores for lower values, e.g. price or execution durations while for some other non-functional properties high values are preferable. In order to work with this, we use

absolute values for weights in the LSP aggregation function (see formula 3) but assume that weights $\omega_i < 0$ are used if a lower value should lead to a better evaluation result and weights $\omega_i > 0$ if a higher value is preferable.

$$L = (|\omega_1| E_1^r + |\omega_2| E_2^r + ... + |\omega_n| E_n^r)^{1/r} \qquad (3)$$

Furthermore, the method can be applied hierarchically. That is E_i can be a score for a specific attribute or the result of a previous aggregation for a group of results (subject to some normalization). Taking non-functional properties as example, E_1 can be the LSP aggregation result of local non-functional constraints and E_2 can be the other LSP aggregation result of composition context which are then combined at a higher level. In this case, ω_1 and ω_2 are the weighted importance relation between local constraints and composition context. As this is useful for our approach we define formula 4 to be the higher level aggregation function to consolidate local and composition context scores, where each of L_1 and L_2 is itself an aggregation obtained by formula 3.

$$L = (\omega_1 L_1^r + \omega_2 L_2^r)^{1/r} \qquad (4)$$

Table 2. GCD operators, orness degree and parameter r

Operation	Symbol	d	r2	r3	r3	r5
Disjunction	D	1.0000	+infinity	+infinity	+infinity	+infinity
Strong Quasi Disjunction	D+	0.8750	9.521	11.095	12.270	13.235
Medium Quasi Disjunction	DA	0.7500	3.929	4.450	4.825	5.111
Weak Quasi Disjunction	D-	0.6250	2.018	2.187	2.302	2.384
Square Mean	SQU	0.6232	2.000			
Arithmetic Mean	A	0.5000	1.000	1.000	1.000	1.000
Weak Quasi Conjunction	C-	0.3750	0.261	0.192	0.153	0.129
Medium Quasi Conjunction	CA	0.2500	-0.720	-0.732	-0.721	-0.707
Strong Quasi Conjunction	C+	0.1250	-3.510	-3.114	-2.823	-2.606
Conjunction	C	0.0000	-infinity	-infinity	-infinity	-infinity

In order to judge the orness degree, (Fodor & Roubens, 1994) and (Marichal, 1998) independently proposed the formula 5 to measure the orness of any mean operator M by studying Dujmovic's degree of conjunction and disjunction:

$$OrnessD(M(x)) = \frac{\int_0^n M(x)dx - \int_0^n Min(x)dx}{\int_0^n Max(x)dx - \int_0^n Min(x)dx}$$

(5)

where $M(x)$ is a GCD operator, $Max(x)$ is the pure conjunction (C) and $Min(x)$ is the pure disjunction (D). However, this definition does not solve the problem of dynamically calculating the orness degree without knowing the selected GCD operator. The function provides a suitable replacement for the lookup table (Table 2).

While LSP provides many useful features for our purpose (calculations are relatively simple, the lookup table can be replaced, LSP allows us to work with large numbers of criteria and perform hierarchical aggregation while reflecting dependencies and weights of criteria) it has some shortcomings. These are mostly related to the fact that LSP is quite human oriented and hence does not immediately support fully automatic service selection. The first problem is that the orness degree changes when the preferences (weights and criteria) are changed in the unpredictable environment. Therefore, we cannot predefine the orness in the evaluation formula. The second major problem is identifying the criteria evaluation methods dynamically. In the static environment, the evaluation methods can be predefined for the specified criteria and the mapping relations are also static for the finite criteria. However, if we have a large set of criteria, then the evaluation methods are very difficult to design and to be mapped. Our extensions to LSP are twofold to address the two mentioned shortcomings: We propose a method for automatically determining the orness value by using ordered weighted averaging operators and

expand the LSP method to make use of types of criteria to automatically determine the appropriate evaluation function.

We discuss the solution to the first issue (the orness value calculation) in the next section and the solution to the second issue (identification of evaluation functions) afterwards.

Before turning our attention to these details, we comment on the issue of not all services offering the same criteria for evaluation: we might find that different service candidates provide data for different criteria. Essentially, each service will be evaluated on the criteria that it provides, so if a criterion is not present then the service will be evaluated out of the other criteria. If the criterion is one the user feels strongly about, the service will be scored lower as the worst case is assumed (essentially a "not met" score will be given), while for criteria that the user is indifferent about no score will be included in the calculation.

Ordered Weighted Averaging Operators as Orness Measure for the LSP Method

This section is quite mathematical and might seem quite removed from the relatively user oriented idea of non-functional properties and even from the mathematical evaluation methods explained in the last section. What is important to understand here is that this methods is being used to compute the degree of relation between a number of criteria to derive a key value required in the aggregation. User's and service providers will never be confronted with these ideas as they are embedded in the evaluation mechanism.

Ordered Weighted Averaging operators were introduced in the area of fuzzy logic (Yager, 1988), and have been shown to allow to determine the orness degree on the fly. The Ordered Weighted Averaging (OWA) operators are defined as follows:

Definition: OWA Operator

Let W=(w_1, w_2, ..., w_n) with $\sum_{i=0}^{n} w_i = 1$. Let A=(a_1, a_2, ...,a_n) and B=(b_1, b_2, ...,b_n) be bags, where b_i is the i-th largest element of A. An OWA operator of dimension n is a mapping $F : \mathbb{R}^n \to \mathbb{R}$ such that

$$F(a_1, a_2, ..., a_n) = \sum_{i=1}^{n} w_i b_i$$

For example, if W = (0.4, 0.3, 0.2, 0.1), then F = (0.7, 1, 0.3, 0.6) = (0.4)(1)+(0.3)(0.7)+(0.2)(0.6)+(0.1)(0.3) = 0.76.

A fundamental aspect of this operator is the re-ordering step. An aggregate a_i is not associated with a particular weight w_i but rather a weight is associated with a particular ordered position of the aggregate (Carlsson & Fuller, 1997). In (Yager, 1988), the orness measure of any kind of OWA operator is defined as follows:

$$Orness(OWA) = \frac{1}{n-1} \sum_{j=1}^{n} (n-j) w_j \qquad (6)$$

Also, a link between orness as defined for Fuzzy Logic (OWA) and orness as defined by formula 5 has been shown in (Fenandez Salido & Murakami, 2003):

Theorem:

If the problem can be expressed as and OWA problem, then:

OrnessD(M(x)) = Orness(OWA)

This theorem gives a tool for linking the LSP method and OWA operators, by bridging the gap between the discrete orness definition of formula 5 and the contributions of formula 6.

On the one hand, we argued that the original LSP method does not support an automatic mechanism to select a suitable value for *r* for the aggregation function. On the other hand, it has been proved that if the ranking problem *can be* transformed into an OWA problem, then we can use the OWA orness definition to automatically calculate the LSP orness degree. Therefore, we need to show that the ranking problem can be transformed into an OWA problem, which we will do now.

In general an OWA problem is characterized by being expressible by two bags: one with weights and one with evaluation values. The latter comes in two forms: *A* and *B*, where A is ordered in the same order as the weights and B in order of the value of the elements.

Considering the services ranking problem we naturally have a bag of weights, but we have multiple bags of values as we have one set of criteria evaluation values. From this we can conclude that we can computer an orness degree per service, which is of course not what we want as we are looking for an overall aggregator which should differentiate the services.

The solution is to compute a bag of values that contains the average score for each criterion across all services evaluated.

Assume that we are considering m services and n evaluation criteria. Furthermore, $W=\{w_1, w_2, ..., w_n\}$ is a bag of weights and $V1=\{v_{11}, v_{21}, ..., v_{n1}\}$ ... $V1=\{v_{n1}, v_{n1}, ..., v_{nm}\}$ are the evaluation results of each mapped criteria for the different services, with each vector presenting results for the *n* criteria of one service. Then

$$V = \left\{ \frac{\sum_{i=1}^{m} v_{1i}}{m}, \frac{\sum_{i=1}^{m} v_{2i}}{m}, ..., \frac{\sum_{i=1}^{m} v_{ni}}{m} \right\}$$

$$(7)$$

is the set of average evaluation scores for our *n* criteria.

Table 3. Example 1

Criterion	C1	C2	C3
Weight	0.7	0.2	0.1
Service1	0.3	0.2	0.1
Service2	0.1	0.7	0.9

Using W and V as the respective sets, we have recast the service selection problem into an OWA problem, and hence can use Orness (OWA) to compute our orness degree, which in turn allows us to extract the value r to be used in the global aggregation function 4.

We will now show some very small examples that show the computed orness degree and provide insight about the operator expected for correct aggregation.

Recall that when calculating overall scores, we do not want the evaluation results of less import criteria to outweigh the important ones; we referred to this as simultaneity earlier on. In (Table 3) Example 1 we can see that both services have low evaluation values for the most important criterion C1 – which means that to ensure simultaneity we require a conjunction LSP operator. By using formula (4) and (3), we calculate the orness degree as 0.2, which maps to the strong quasi conjunction operator (the operator has a value 0f 0.25 and that is the closest presented).

Example 2 (Table 4) shows a typical case of replacebility, where a good match on an important criterion is making a service preferable. In the example, we can see that both services have higher evaluation results for the most import criterion. Recall that for replacebility we would expect a disjunction operator. Again, by applying

our formulae we can compute the orness degree (this time as 0.75) and we find that this maps to medium quasi disjunction.

Type-Based Evaluation Mapping Methods

Most of the traditional criteria selection methods strongly rely on human intervention. For example, criteria used for selection are typical tightly bound to a priori defined evaluation mapping; changing criteria require manually retuning the evaluation mapping. Meanwhile, changes of criteria and preferences are unavoidable in the dynamic environment encountered in web service selection. Thus, predefining the service selection criteria and preferences cannot reflect the evaluation requirements of the system at run-time. We propose a type-based evaluation mapping method which is related to the types of the criteria, rather than being dependent on the criteria themselves. We define three types of criteria and each type has a related evaluation method. The three types are "Numerical type", "Boolean type" and "Set overlap type". Further types could of course be defined if required, but we have not encountered a need for them so far.

The Numerical type is used for criteria which take numerical input to the evaluation method

Table 4. Example 2

Criterion	C1	C2	C3
Weight	0.7	0.2	0.1
Service1	0.9	0.2	0.1
Service2	0.7	0.7	0.9

such as cost, time and measurement values. The mapped evaluation method is given by formula 8, where w is the weight of the criterion. When the criterion is of numerical type, the weight can be in the range [-1...0]. Using negative weights provides a very simple way to express the fact that a smaller numerical value is desired (as e.g. for price properties) – they are only a mathematical trick.

v_{max} is the maximum value of all competitive services for the criterion, v is the value for the service under evaluation. v_{min} is the minimum value of all competitive services.

$$E = \begin{cases} 1 - \left(\dfrac{v_{max} - v}{v_{max} - v_{min}} \right) & \text{iff } w \geq 0 \\ \left(\dfrac{v_{max} - v}{v_{max} - v_{min}} \right) & \text{otherwise} \end{cases} \quad (8)$$

Note that the numerical type is not used to express value ranges (such as "the price should be between 0.2 and 0.7") – clearly these ranges stem from the requirements of the user whereas the expression presented here provides the value of service level provided. In that case, we would expect that the measured value falls inside the interval given by the user requirement.

The Boolean type is used for criteria which have a value that is evaluated to 1 or 0. The method is:

$$E = \begin{cases} 1 & \text{if the criteria is met} \\ 0 & \text{otherwise} \end{cases} \quad (9)$$

The Set overlap type is to define criteria which are measured by the size of the evaluation objects' satisfaction subset:

$$E = \left(e_1 + e_2 + ... + e_n \right) / n \quad (10)$$

with e_i being a score for each element of the set.

Now, whenever the criteria are changing or values are being updating at runtime, the system is able to automatically apply the correct evaluation functions based on the detected criteria's type.

STEPWISE BACKWARDS SELECTION OF SERVICES IN COMPOSITE SCENARIOS

In the last section we discussed the selection method with a view of how different criteria are evaluated and the scores are aggregated. In particularly, it solved the problem of using both local constraints and composition context and automatically deciding on the appropriate service. However, for a workflow there are many services to be decided upon and hence the method needs to be applied repeatedly for each task. As the process executes, the composition knowledge will increase and become more and more complex (each step will add information about which service has been selected and whether this was successful). Therefore, we need a well defined composition approach for helping the selection method gathering the related and correct selection constraints.

As composition context builds up with continuing execution of the process while at the same time the environment might change and impose new requirements on services to be selected it is sensible to select services as close to their actual execution time as possible rather than selecting them ahead for the whole process. Hence the selection approach should perform the selection step by step. The step by step strategy means that at each step there are a maximum of n services to be compared. n is the number of competing services for the task. The process needs to build up the composition context as it is committing to services.

A nice side aspect of an approach that makes decisions quite close to execution time is that it is inherently fault tolerant. When selected service can not perform correctly in a certain step, the approach will select the next best service in order to complete the task. Based on the required characters of the composition approach, we developed a backwards composition context based service selection approach. The approach has been described in more detail in (Yu, Reiff-Marganiec, 2009b) and here we will only present an overview.

The basic idea is to select (but not execute) a service for a task, then move to the next task and also select a service. At this stage we return to the previous task and evaluate the previous choice again (the composition context now contains a glance at a possible future, in terms of holding data of the next service candidate). We might keep our choice or select a different service but we will then invoke this service. Finally we move to the next task and repeat the process. The pattern of moving one step ahead to get a glance of the future and then returning to finalize the decision will also be apparent in the approach presented in this paper and its working will be explained in more detail later.

- *Step 1:* Search for and return all candidate services from the registry that fulfil the required functionality for the current task in the workflow.
- *Step 2:* Invoke the TLE method to obtain an evaluation value for each candidate service by considering the user constraints, current context information and composition context criteria of the selected services for previous tasks and the next task. The ranking function will use only the available information, so if there is no previous selected service or no next selected service the composition context might not contain any values. Log the information on the best candidate in the composition context.
- *Step 3:* If the service for the previous task has not been executed (if there is a previous task), then return to the previous task and repeat steps 1 and 2; note that now more information is available in the composition context as a candidate for the next step has been identified. Execute the service for the

previous step – try next best alternatives in case the best fails until we succeed. Log the information of the actually executed service in the composition context, together with any information on failures. Then return to the current task.
- *Step 4:* Re-evaluate the current choice (the actually executed service for the previous task might have been different to what was assumed before). Log the information on the best candidate in the composition context.
- *Step 5:* If the next control flow operator in the workflow is a "split" operation or we have reached the last task, execute the current service (again trying alternatives until one succeeds). Log the information of the actually executed service in the composition context, together with any information on failures.
- *Step 6:* If there is a next task, move to it and repeat from step 1 otherwise finish.

This algorithm fulfills the requirements set out earlier and the brief description highlights how the selection based on relevant properties is conducted at each step, while at the same time the information for decision making grows through additions to the composition context.

EVALUATION AND DISCUSSION

In terms of evaluation we will consider two aspects: the ranking approach in isolation and evaluation of the ranking approach as part of the stepwise backwards selection method.

While the ranking approach is implemented in terms of the relevance engine in the inContext platform (Reiff-Marganiec et al., 2008), the engine itself is developed as a Web service so allows for easy embedding in different environments. For more detailed analysis we have developed a test-bed that also considers the generation of the criteria as described earlier. The test-bed includes

Figure 5. Evaluation results for increasing numbers of services with a fixed number of criteria

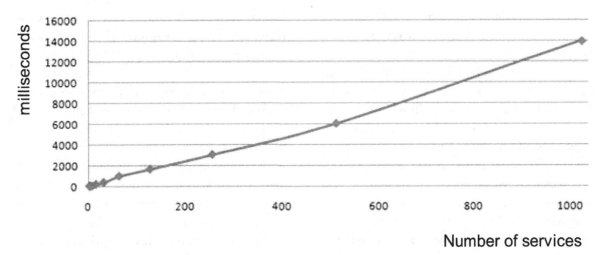

an OWL/RDF context store, a repository that is organised by service category enhanced with the metadata model and the relevance engine performing the TLE selection process.

The evaluation reported here considers scalability and was conducted through 2 evaluation cases for notification service selection scenarios (essentially a question of selecting the most appropriate service notify a user, similar to the last step in the meeting scheduling scenario presented earlier) and we will discuss these in detail. Within the inContext project the ranking method has been evaluated further on real case studies, focusing on functional correctness rather than scalability. The inContext project developed its PCSA (Pervasive Collaborative Service Architecture), which is a platform for supporting collaborative work through a service oriented, context aware platform. Context is used to evaluate what a user needs and then the most appropriate services are selected to support the user in their activity. Service selection is conducted within the Services subsystem, which amongst others consists of a service repository, a service lookup mechanism and the ranking engine. The ranking engine implements the selection algorithms presented here and has been successfully recommending suitable services

for the meeting scheduling and public-fair support case studies of inContext.

The first series of tests focuses on measuring the selection time when the number of services increases. There was a fixed number of criteria that was used to evaluate the services here (there were 6 criteria). We considered up to 1000 services. The graph in Figure 5 shows clearly that the approach is linear with respect to a growing number of service candidates.

The second evaluation case was to evaluate the selection time in the light of increasing the number of criteria. We fixed the number of ser-

Figure 6. Shows that the approach is essential linear with respect to the number of criteria

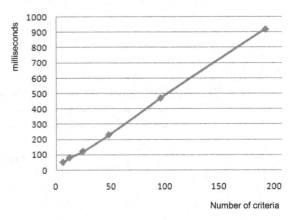

vices to 4, but tested up to 192 criteria. The test results are shown in Figure 6. We can again see that the approach is linear with respect to the number of criteria.

We can see that both factors in increase linearly, which is good news. Of course a large number of criteria combined with a large number of service candidates could lead to rather long actual execution times. This merits some more general discussion: in the real world service selection scenarios, we do not expect there to be vast numbers of criteria, so around 100 seems a good pragmatic upper bound. Also, in terms of competing services, while we expect these to increase with more services becoming available, it seems safe to claim that a choice of 20 services fulfilling our functional requirements and hence been drawn into the comparison should be already a significant number.

Additionally, we should see that the services are chosen in a matter of seconds based on the prototype implementation (which has not been designed with performance in mind, but rather with functional correctness). When considering real service selection scenarios, the runtime of services usually exceed this time by far, and being presented with the best possible service will be 'worth the wait', even more so if we consider this selection to form part of a longer running business process possibly containing human tasks.

It may be more helpful to evaluate the selection correctness from a user point of view. However, correctness is difficult to be defined in general because it depends on different views and concerns. It is often easy to see which decision is wrong, but it is very hard to say which one is marginally better than others and hence we will not present an evaluation on the correctness from the user side here.

Turning our attention to evaluating the performance of the selection method, we evaluated the process by analysing a number of test scenarios. We have added values to all 8 identified aspects of the composition context. Notably increasing the number of service candidates and increasing the number of steps in the workflow each led to a linear increase.

In the first scenario we combine the 8 composition context criteria and increasing numbers of services from 2^1 to 2^8 for a workflow with 3 steps. Figure 7 shows that the method is quite efficient to deal with up to 250 services in this situation.

The second scenario is designed to test the scalability with regard to composition steps. There are again 8 composition context criteria and there are 4 services for each step. The test results in Figure 8 show that the method works efficiently with up to 40 steps. Again, we have a linear increase in run-time when the workflow length increases. In some sense this is not surprising, as the process of looking backward before commit-

Figure 7. Evaluation results for composition selection test case 2

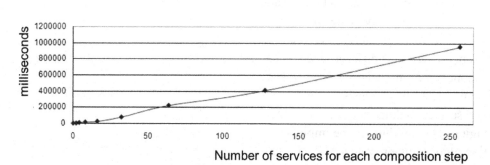

Number of services for each composition step

Figure 8. Evaluation results for composition selection test case 3

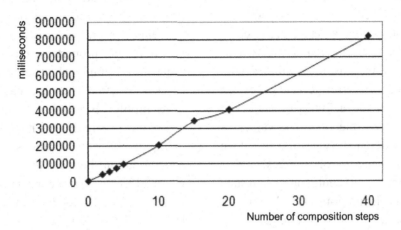

ting is always looking at the same amount of service selection needs with the only difference being the amount of history that has been build up in the composition context. However, only the context relevant to the services under consideration needs to be taken into account, and hence the overhead of querying for the context information stays fairly static.

There are again several observations that should be made here: (1) it is unusual that workflows are much longer than 40 steps (2) the execution of the actual services will also be time consuming and some might be long-running services where it is more crucial that the right service is selected than that it is selected more quickly and (3) the method does interleave execution and selection, so a user does not have to wait until the selection mechanism has completed before the execution of the workflow can start.

From the conducted experimentation, we can conclude that both the selection method on its own as well as the method integrated into a system for selecting services as part of a longer chain is quite efficient as run-time increases are linear with respect to any individual factor such as number of services, number of criteria or length of the workflow.

RELATED WORK

Related work falls into predominantly two areas, (1) non-functional service selection for individual services and the required descriptions of properties and (2) service selection for workflows.

Selecting Individual Services

Policy based service selection approaches allow to specify the non-functional requirements by coding them in a QoS (Quality of Service) policy model or policy language. (Liu, Ngu, & Zeng, 2004) and (Janicke & Solanki, 2007) are typical examples of policy based selection approaches. The QoS policy model in (Liu, Ngu, & Zeng, 2004) offers two types of non-functional properties (generic and domain specific). The content encodes the service requester's constraints and preferences which are evaluated using universal evaluation functions (one for lower values being preferential and one for higher values being more desirable). There are a number of drawbacks, including the fact that no consideration is made to the storage of property values and the aggregation is through a rather complicated matrix approach that is not linked to the user's preferences. Also, final scores are not normalized, making comparison impossible. (Janicke & Solanki, 2007) formalizes NFPs using a conditional policy language, focusing on detecting service properties dynamically by hardware sensors that monitor whether the selected service breaks the requester's requirements. This technique could be very useful combined with a selection strategy that uses service execution history. (Wang & Vassileva, 2007) uses trust and reputation for service selection. The values of the criteria for different services are based on feedback from communities or agencies. Classification uses a centralized reputation system such as PageRank (Page, Brin, Motwani, & Winograd, 1998) or can use decentralized systems. All of these approaches do not explicitly defining NFP models, and neither do they consider that a variety of evaluation functions might be required and that aggregation of scores is a complicated matter as we discussed earlier.

UDDI and Semantic Web technologies have been used for modeling service's properties. (Seo, Jeong, & Song, 2005) adds an extra component into the SOA called Quality broker, which sits between the service requester and UDDI repository. The Quality broker randomly invokes the services which are registered in the UDDI repository in an effort to monitors the performance (response time and throughout), safety (availability and reliability) and cost. Clearly this approach only considers these three properties and does not offer a generic property model. While the method provides independent quality data, it can only be sued for a small number of criteria as monitoring is expensive and impractical (what if service invocations come at a cost?). (Wang, Vitvar, Kerrigan, & Toma, 2006) introduced a WSMO (Web service Modeling Ontology) based approach. The non-functional properties are organized as QoS ontology and vocabulary in WSMO. (Manikrao & Prabhakar, 2005) enhances on this by introducing a DAML-S based service selection approach where the matching algorithm uses the semantics of the vocabulary by introducing concepts such as *Exact match*, *Subsumption* or *PartOf*.

The approaches discussed so far address the provider's perspective they pay little attention to the requester's needs. It is important to express non-functional properties from both provider and requester. A graphical preference modeling and service selection approach has been discussed in (Schropfer, Binshtok, Shimony et al., 2007), where the preferences are modeled as a network graph. These network graphs model the dependency relations between the properties. While it is useful to be able to express the relations, the graphs become quickly very complex and difficult to understand for an average user. Moreover, the selection algorithm is based on simple textual matching without making use of a model for NFPs and hence is less extensible and cannot deal with hierarchically structured properties.

(Maximilien & Singh, 2004) and (Lamparter, Ankolekar, Studer, & Grimm, 2007) are approaches which model both the requester's requirements and service properties using ontologies. (Maximilien & Singh, 2004) proposes a simple selecting method based on full matches to the requirements, while (Lamparter, Ankolekar, Studer, & Grimm, 2007) uses a price based evaluation method. These approaches do not model the aggregation properties.

Selecting Services as Part of Composite Execution Chains

Many projects have studied the QoS driven Web service composition problem. Currently, two kinds of service selection strategies are developed. One focuses on local optimal selection, the other on global optimal selection.

Local optimization refers to selection methods which only take certain selection constrains related to the current activity in the workflow without specifying and considering the constraints implied by the workflow context and the consequences that the choice will have on later activities. For example, a policy based BPEL workflow Web service selection method is presented in (Karastoyanova,

Houspanossian, Cilia, Leymann, & Buchmann, 2005). It extends BPEL for run-time adaptation of Web services by adding the policy reference to each node. The policy documents provide the local optimization rules which are independent from each other. The service selection process is applied at each node separately. A similar approach was also presented in the earlier e-Flow project (Shan, Casati, Ilnicki, Jin, & Krishnamoorthy, 2000). The biggest advantage of the local optimization methods is efficiency in selection time – the worst case can be solved in polynomial time. However, the local optimization strategy has a big drawback: it does not necessarily select the optimal or even close to optimal service in the global composition context.

Global optimization contrasts to local optimization strategy by taking the global selection constraint to select a group of Web services rather than one Web service for a node in the composition workflow. The key assumption of this strategy is that all suitable Web services for each node have already been discovered and are inside the global optimization search space. (G. Canfora, 2005) (Zeng, Benatallah, Ngu, Dumas, Kalagnanam, & Chang, 2005) are approaches of this kind. By studying these approaches, we find they surely narrow the disadvantages pointed out for local optimization. However, they introduce problems of their own: In general, multi-QoS constrained Web Services selection with optimization is an NP-complete problem (Yu & Lin, 2005), reducing scalability of the methods.

Global optimization methods for Web service selection return a set of combined services as the final solution package. However, when one service is not available or creates an exception at run-time, then the whole solution package has failed. As a result, a new solution has to be generated.

Some selection constrains are only known when certain data is produced at run-time. For example, consider a conditional choice in a composition. Only after the condition is evaluated can we know the complete global constraints.

The local constraints are defined by users and are very important. However, global optimization approaches do not take into account local criteria.

FUTURE WORK

Future work includes pursuing a number of questions. On the one hand the selection approach assumes that the data for decision making is available from the non-functional property model (or its instantiation in a registry). We had already indicated that some of the data is dynamic and presented our current approach as one that queries services. Clearly an approach of querying a large number of services to gain insight into their dynamic properties becomes too time consuming. However, this aspect is orthogonal to the work presented here, as there are possible solutions of aggregating properties, using push mechanisms or parallelizing the gathering. In fact in (Tilly & Reiff-Marganiec, 2011) an approach is presented that uses a combined pull-push architecture to aid with this issue. This requires further refinement.

One other aspect of future work is capturing user preferences – that is methods that actually allow users to describe in more abstract ways what is important for them and that are practical in that they do not overburden the user but ensure that the user's wishes are reflected in the choices. This also presents the question as to how can user preferences be expressed and then questions as to how these requirements are linked to the service descriptions. These issues are partly addressed by ongoing work in service matchmaking.

More information on services is required, which comes with two aspects to investigate: who provides the descriptions and how reliable are they. In many ways it can be argued that the service providers should provide the data when registering services (which is what we used). However, future work should investigate the automatic collection of this data through e.g. runtime monitoring of services. This would also aid with the certification of the quality of this data as the measuring agencies could be independent in the same way that we are using certification authorities for security certificates.

Finally, some more infrastructure is required (notably the relevance engine implementing the ranking mechanism). This could be run independently or could exist as part of service repositories. This very practical issue requires further investigation and more crucially agreement within the community to agree on standards for expressing properties.

CONCLUSION

We have presented an extensible model for describing non-functional properties for web services, which provides a structure for storing relevant properties for services in addition to the currently common descriptions of functional properties. Based on this model, we presented a service selection method that allows for identifying the right service automatically. The description and selection methods have been presented to derive decisions on a single service. However, we expanded on that by presenting composition context as a mechanism to gather information on service executions and to model relations between services. The structure of the data in the composition context is such that it fits neatly into the same evaluation and description framework.

The selection methodology automatically determines the appropriate functions to evaluate the non-functional properties required and allows aggregation of the criteria in very fine grained ways, especially linking criteria in logical ways (notably replacability and simultaneity).

We completed the presentation with the introduction of a selection methodology (a stepwise backwards selection of services in composite scenarios approach) which essentially while deciding on the choices for a service does not immediately execute the chosen service, but attempts to decide

on the next service to gain an insight into the future before committing to a choice. This algorithm is pragmatic; it will not guarantee the best global choice and will neither ensure the best local choice but rather will attempt to find a solution that is good locally and goes towards a global optimum based on a local decision. However, its runtime complexity is quite low (it is essentially linear).

One of the biggest drawbacks at using the presented methods currently would be the lack of standardized repositories that allow to store data on non-functional properties. The web services community needs to integrate non-functional descriptions into repositories. Many different approaches to describe non-functional properties have emerged and before integration into repositories some consolidation is required.

REFERENCES

Canfora, G., Penta Raffaele, M., Esposito, R., & Villani, M. (2005). An approach for QoS-aware service composition based on genetic algorithms. *Proceedings of the 2005 Conference on Genetic and Evolutionary Computation*, (pp. 1069-1075).

Carlsson, C., & Fuller, R. (1997). OWA operators for decision support. In *Proceedings of EUFIT'97 Conference, vol. II*, (pp. 1539-1544).

Dan, A., Ludwig, H., & Pacffici, G. (2005). *Web service differentiation with service level agreements*. IBM Corporation.

Dujmovic, J. (1973). Mixed averaging by levels (MAL) –A system and computer evaluation method. *In Proceedings of the Informatica Conference*, Bled, Yugoslavia.

Dujmovic, J. (1975). Extended continuous logic and the theory of complex criteria. *Journal of the University of Belgrade, 537*, 97–216.

Dujmovic, J. (1996). A method for evaluation and selection of complex hardware and software systems. *In Proceedings of 22nd International Conference for the Resource Management and Performance Evaluation of Enterprise Computer Systems.* New Jersey.

Dujmovic, J., & Larsen, H. (2004). Properties and modelling of partial conjunction/disjunction. *Proceedings of Eurofuse Workshop on Data and Knowledge Engineering* (pp. 215-224). Warsaw, Poland.

Fenandez Salido, J., & Murakami, S. (2003). Extending Yager's orness concept for the OWA aggregators to other mean operators. [Elsevier B.V.]. *Fuzzy Sets and Systems, 139*, 515–542. doi:10.1016/S0165-0114(02)00369-X

Fodor, J., & Roubens, M. (1994). *Modelling and multicriteria decision support.* Dordrecht, The Netherlands: Kluwer.

ISO/IEC. (2001). *9126-1:2001, Software engineering - Product quality - Part 1: Quality model.* Geneva, Switzerland: International Organization for Standardization.

Janicke, H., & Solanki, M. (2007). Policy-driven service discovery. *2nd European Young Researchers Workshop on Service Oriented Computing* (pp. 56-62). University of Leicester, Department of Computer Science.

Karastoyanova, D., Houspanossian, A., Cilia, M., Leymann, F., & Buchmann, A. (2005). Extending BPEL for run time adaptability. *Proceedings of the Ninth IEEE International EDOC Enterprise Computing Conference*, (pp. 15-26).

Lamparter, S., Ankolekar, A., Studer, R., & Grimm, S. (2007). Preference-based selection of highly configurable web services. *WWW '07: Proceedings of the 16th International Conference on World Wide Web*, (pp. 1013-1022). ACM.

Liu, Y., Ngu, A. H., & Zeng, L. Z. (2004). QoS computation and policing in dynamic web service selection. *Proceedings of the 13th International World Wide Web Conference on Alternate Track Papers & Posters* (pp. 66--73). New York, NY: ACM.

Manikrao, U. S., & Prabhakar, T. V. (2005). Dynamic selection of web services with recommendation system. *International Conference on Next Generation Web Services Practices (NWESP '05)*, (p. 117). IEEE Computer Society.

Marichal, J. (1998). *Aggregation operations for multicriteria decision aid.* PhD. Thesis, Institute of Mathematics, University of Liege, Belgium.

Maximilien, E. M., & Singh, M. P. (2004). A framework and ontology for dynamic web services selection. *IEEE Internet Computing, 8*(5), 84–93. doi:10.1109/MIC.2004.27

Miller, J. III. (1970). *Professional decision-making.* Praeger Publishers.

OASIS. (2004). *UDDI version 3 specification.* OASIS Standard.

Olsina, L., & Rossi, G. (2002). Measuring Web application quality with WebQEM. *IEEE MultiMedia, 9*(4), 20–29. doi:10.1109/MMUL.2002.1041945

Olsina, L., & Rossi, G. (2002). Measuring Web application quality with WebQEM. *IEEE MultiMedia*, 20–29. doi:10.1109/MMUL.2002.1041945

Page, L., Brin, S., Motwani, R., & Winograd, T. (1998). *The pagerank citation ranking: Bringing order to the web.* Retrieved from http://citeseer.ist.psu.edu/page98pagerank.html

Prud'hommeaux, E., & Seaborne, A. (2008). *SPARQL query language for RDF.* Retrieved from http://www.w3.org/TR/rdf-sparql-query

Reiff-Marganiec, S., Truong, H.-L., Casella, G., Dorn, C., Dustdar, S., & Moretzki, S. (2008). *The inContext pervasive collaboration services architecture. ServiceWave 2008, LNCS vol: 5377* (pp. 134–146). Springer.

Schropfer, C., Binshtok, M., Shimony, S. E., Dayan, A., Brafman, R., Opfermann, P., & Holschke, O. (2007). Introducing preferences over NFPs into service selection in SoA. *Non-Functional Properties and Service Level Agreements in Service Oriented Computing Workshop*, (pp. 68-79). Springer.

Seo, Y. J., Jeong, H. Y., & Song, Y. J. (2005). A study on web services selection method based on the negotiation through quality broker: A maut-based approach. *Embedded Software and Systems*, 65-73.

Shan, F., Casati, S., Ilnicki, L., Jin, V., & Krishnamoorthy, M. C. (2000). *Adptive and dynamic service compostion in eFlow.* HP Laboratories Technical Report.

Su, S. Y. W., Dujmovic, J., Batory, D. S., Navathe, S. B., & Elnicki, R. A. (1987). A cost-benefit decision model: Analysis, comparison, and selection of data management systems. *ACM Transactions on Database Systems, 12*(3), 472–520. doi:10.1145/27629.33403

Tilly, M., & Reiff-Marganiec, S. (2011). *Matching customer requests to service offerings in real-time. ACM SAC 2011 – MESC Track* (pp. 456–461). ACM.

Toma, I. R. (2007). On describing and ranking services based on non-functional properties. *Proceedings of the Third International Conference on Next Generation Web Services Practices* (pp. 61-66). Seoul, Republic of Korea: IEEE Computer Society.

Truong, H.-L., Dustdar, S., Baggio, D., Corlosquet, S., Dorn, C., & Giuliani, G. … Yu, H. Q. (2008). inContext: A pervasive and collaborative working environment for emerging team forms. *2008 International Symposium on Applications and the Internet (SAINT 2008)*, (pp. 118-125). IEEE.

Wang, X., Vitvar, T., Kerrigan, M., & Toma, I. (2006). A QoS-aware selection model for semantic web services. [Springer.]. *Service-Oriented Computing ICSOC, 2006*, 390–401. doi:10.1007/11948148_32

Wang, Y., & Vassileva, J. (2007). *Toward trust and reputation based web service selection: A survey.* Retrieved from http://bistrica.usask.ca/madmuc/papers/yao-julita-ws-mas-survey.pdf

Yager, R. (1988). On ordered weighted averaging aggregation operators in multi-criteria decision making. *IEEE Transactions on Systems, Man, and Cybernetics, 18*, 183–190. doi:10.1109/21.87068

Yu, H. Q., & Reiff-Marganiec, S. (2009a). *Automated context-aware service selection for collaborative systems. Advanced Information Systems Engineering CAiSE 2009, LNCS, vol: 5565* (pp. 261–274). Springer.

Yu, H. Q., & Reiff-Marganiec, S. (2009b). A backwards composition context based service selection approach for service composition. H.Q. Yu & S. Reiff-Marganiec (Eds.), *SCC 2009.* IEEE Computer Society.

Yu, T., & Lin, K. (2005). *Service selection algorithms for composing complex services with multiple QoS constrains. ICSOC2005, LNCS, vol: 3826* (pp. 130–143). Springer.

Zeng, L., Benatallah, B., Ngu, A., Dumas, M., Kalagnanam, J., & Chang, H. (2005). QoS-aware middleware for web services composition. *IEEE Transactions on Software Engineering, 30*(5), 311–327. doi:10.1109/TSE.2004.11

KEY TERMS AND DEFINITIONS

Context: Factors from the environment in which users and services are placed that influence the needs of a user or the provision of a service.

Global Constraints: Constraints for choosing a service as part of a workflow that are based on the required service's execution context.

Local Constraints: Constraints for choosing a service that are based on a single service's current context and the current user's demands.

Replacability: The requirement of a user specifying that either of two criteria, if strong enough, will satisfy the need.

Service Selection: The operation of deciding which of a number of available services to use for addressing a current need.

Simultanenuity: The requirement of a user specifying that independent of the score for a criterion, other criteria must still be considered as equally important.

ENDNOTE

[1] For the purpose of this paper the detailed architecture supporting the framework is not required, and hence not discussed. However, it is assumed that services are registered – as is common – in a repository (e.g. a UDDI repository); the additional descriptions are included in the repository, too (so an enhanced UDDI repository would be required).

Chapter 9
Service Selection with Uncertain Context Information

Yves Vanrompay
Katholieke Universiteit Leuven, Belgium

Manuele Kirsch-Pinheiro
Université Paris 1 Panthéon-Sorbonne, France

Yolande Berbers
Katholieke Universiteit Leuven, Belgium

ABSTRACT

The current evolution of Service-Oriented Computing in ubiquitous systems is leading to the development of context-aware services. Context-aware services are services of which the description is enriched with context information related to non-functional requirements, describing the service execution environment or its adaptation capabilities. This information is often used for discovery and adaptation purposes. However, in real-life systems, context information is naturally dynamic, uncertain, and incomplete, which represents an important issue when comparing the service description with user requirements. Uncertainty of context information may lead to an inexact match between provided and required service capabilities, and consequently to the non-selection of services. In this chapter, we focus on how to handle uncertain and incomplete context information for service selection. We consider this issue by presenting a service ranking and selection algorithm, inspired by graph-based matching algorithms. This graph-based service selection algorithm compares contextual service descriptions using similarity measures that allow inexact matching. The service description and non-functional requirements are compared using two kinds of similarity measures: local measures, which compare individually required and provided properties, and global measures, which take into account the context description as a whole.

DOI: 10.4018/978-1-61350-432-1.ch009

INTRODUCTION

The term Ubiquitous Computing, introduced by Weiser (Weiser, 1991), refers to the seamless integration of devices into users' everyday life (Baldauf, Dustdar, & Rosenberg, 2007). This term represents an emerging trend towards environments composed by numerous computing devices that are frequently mobile or embedded and that are connected to a network infrastructure composed of a wired core and wireless edges (Moran & Dourish, 2001). In pervasive scenarios foreseen by Ubiquitous Computing, context awareness plays a central role. Context can be defined as *any information that can be used to characterize the situation of an entity* (a person, place, or object considered as relevant to the interaction between a user and an application) (Dey, 2001). Context-aware systems are able to adapt their operations to the current context, aiming at increasing usability and effectiveness by taking environmental context into account (Baldauf, Dustdar, & Rosenberg, 2007).

The dynamic nature of pervasive environments encourages the adoption of a Service Oriented Architecture (SOA). Service-Oriented Computing (SOC) is the computing paradigm that utilizes services as fundamental elements for developing applications (Papazoglou & Georgakopoulos, 2003). The key feature of SOA is that services are independent entities, with well-defined interfaces, that can be invoked in a standard way, without requiring the client to have knowledge about how the service actually performs its tasks (Issarny, Caporuscio, & Georgantas, 2007). Such loose coupling fits the requirements of highly dynamic pervasive environments, in which entities are often mobile, entering and leaving the environment at any moment.

The adoption of SOA in pervasive environments is leading to the development of "context-aware" services. Context-awareness becomes a key feature necessary to provide adaptable services, for instance when selecting the best-suited service according to the relevant context

information or when adapting the service during its execution according to context changes (Eikerling, Mazzoleni, Plaza, Yankelevich, & Wallet, 2007). As pointed out by Maamar *et al.* (2006), multiple aspects related to the users (level of expertise, location, etc.) and to the computing resources (on fixed and mobile devices), among others aspects, can be considered in the development of context-aware services. Thus, *context-aware services* can be defined as services of which the description is associated with contextual (notably non-functional) properties, *i.e.*, services whose description is enriched with context information indicating the situations to which the service is adapted to.

According to Suraci *et al.* (2007), in order to provide context-aware services, one has to consider *context inputs and outputs, besides functional ones*. Several authors, such as (Suraci, Mignanti, & Aiuto, 2007), (Toninelli, Corradi, & Montanari, 2008) and (Mokhtar, Kaul, Georgantas, & Issarny, 2006), propose to increase the service description with context information. This information is normally used for adaptation purposes: for indicating service adaptation capabilities, for adapting service composition, execution and output. This context information needs to be compared to the real user's or execution context before starting to use the service.

However, in ubiquitous environments, context information is naturally dynamic and incomplete. Explicitly representing and taking into account the quality of the provided context information is key in being able to select the right service in the right circumstances. Dynamic context changes and incomplete context information may prevent perfect matches between required and provided properties, which may lead to an inappropriate service ranking or even to the non-selection of one (or all) service(s). Service selection mechanisms have to cope with these issues: if some needed context information is missing, service selection still has to proceed and choose a corresponding service that best matches the current situation, even if context information is incomplete. In other words, when executing in pervasive environments, service matching mechanisms have to deal with the question: how to reduce problems related to mismatching between contextual conditions related to the execution of a service and current context information?

In order to overcome this challenge, we propose in this chapter a graph-based algorithm for matching context-aware services. The proposed service selection mechanism assumes that suitable services exist. This means our approach is employed only after the question whether suitable services are available has been answered positively. The proposed algorithm matches contextual non-functional descriptions of context-aware services using similarity measures, allowing inexact matches. The service description and the current context are interpreted as graphs, in which properties correspond to graph nodes and the edges represent the relations between these properties. Through this graph representation, service description and requirements are compared using two kinds of similarity measures: local measures, which compare individually required and provided properties (represented as graph nodes), and global measures, which take into account the context description as a whole, by comparing two graphs corresponding to two context descriptions. Moreover, we consider here only non-functional and context-related aspects of context-aware services. Even if functional aspects are the most relevant, once all services whose capabilities match functional requirements have been discovered, one has to select what service, among all the possible services, is the most suitable one, considering non-functional properties related to each service. Our graph-based service selection algorithm aims at selecting among available compatible services the most appropriate one considering the current context and taking into account the incompleteness of context information.

This chapter is organized as follow: Section 2 presents an overview on related work. Section 3

presents the context modeling approach. Section 4 presents the matching algorithm and similarity measures. Section 5 illustrates the graph-based matching and proposed uncertainty measure with a case study. Finally we discuss future work and conclusions.

BACKGROUND

A growing interest in context-aware services can be observed in the literature. Several European projects (2008IST-DAIDALOS, AMIGO Project, IST-MUSIC and others (Patouni, Alonistioti, & Polychronopoulos, 2008!)) and international conferences (ICSOC, IEEE ICWS, Mobiquitous) are focusing on Service-Oriented Computing (Patouni, Alonistioti, & Polychronopoulos, 2008). In all these works context-awareness appears as a crosscutting issue. On one hand, multiple aspects related to both users and computer resources can be considered in the development of context-aware services (Maamar, Benslimane, & Narendra, 2006). On the other hand, in pervasive scenarios, users require context-aware services that are tailored to their needs, current position, execution environments, etc. (Toninelli, Corradi, & Montanari, 2008). According to Suraci *et al.* (2007), user and service entities have requirements on context information they need in order to work properly. A user may have requirements on context of the service he is looking for (availability, location…) and on the context provided by the environment (wireless connection…). A service can require the user to provide specific context information (location, terminal capabilities…) and the environment to provide context information too (network QoS…).

The support for context-aware services depends on an improved semantic modeling of services by using ontologies that support formal description and reasoning (Issarny, Caporuscio, & Georgantas, 2007). Such a semantic modeling may contribute not only to handle problems related to service interoperability, but also in order to take into account different aspects of the environment in which the service is executed. Actually, such semantic modeling can serve different purposes: adapting service composition; indicating an execution environment (device capabilities, user's location, etc.) to which the service is designed for; indicating adaptation capabilities (mainly content adaptation) of the service, etc. Indeed, authors, such as Zarras *et al.* (2006), advocate that semantic matching is essential for pervasive systems.

In the literature, several works, such as Ben Mokhtar *et al* (2006), propose the semantic modeling and matching of services based on ontologies often expressed in OWL-based languages for enriching service description. These authors (Mokhtar, Kaul, Georgantas, & Issarny, 2006) propose the use of ontologies (in OWL-S) for the semantic description of functional and non-functional features of services in order to automatically and unambiguously discover such services. Klusch *et al.* (2006) propose a service matching algorithm which combines reasoning based on subsumption and similarity measures for comparing inputs and outputs of service description and user request. Reiff-Marganic *et al.* (2007) propose a method for automatic selection of services based on non-functional properties and context. However, inexact matching caused by incomplete or uncertain context information is not taken into account.

Other authors such as Suraci *et al.* (2007) and Yau and Liu (2006) propose to improve service modeling with context information. Suraci *et al.* (2007) propose a semantic modeling of services in which service profile description in OWL-S is enriched with a "context" element pointing to this required context information. Yau and Liu (2006) propose to enrich service description with specific external pre- and post-conditions expressed in the OWL-S service description denoting contextual conditions for using a given service.

Tonielli *et al.* (2008) also adopt semantic languages to model properties of entities and environment in a SOA approach. These authors propose a framework for personalized semantic-based service discovery. This framework aims at integrating semantic data representation and match-making support with context management and context-based service filtering. In such framework, services, users and devices are modeled through a set of profiles, describing capabilities and requirements of the corresponding service. The integration is then performed in a middleware using a matching algorithm based mainly on subsumption reasoning.

Similarly, Sutterer *et al.* (2008) also propose using profiles for matching purposes. They propose a user profile ontology in which they represent information about the user's profile, situation-dependent user's preferences, as well as his location and his activity. The user's profile is decomposed on profile subsets according to the user's context and dedicated to a specific (set of) service(s). For this, Sutterer *et al.* (2008) use a matching process that matches the user's profile with these conditional profile subsets.

Outside the Web Service domain, other authors have been investigating matching problems for context-aware services. Bottaro *et al.* (2007), for instance, propose ranking services according to context models evaluating the interests of a service in a composition. These authors extend the OSGi Declarative Service specification in order to consider context information for service ranking.

It is worth noting that several works cited above belong to larger initiatives, like the AMIGO (AMIGO Project, 2010), SPICE (IST-SPICE, 2010 ;Sutterer, Droegehorn & David, 2010) and DAIDALOS (IST-DAIDALOS, 2010; Suraci, Mignanti, & Aiuto, 2010) projects. For instance, the AMIGO project (*Ambient intelligence for the networked home environment*) aims at developing middleware that dynamically integrates heterogeneous systems to achieve interoperability between services and devices. It adopts an user-centric focus, which leads to the specification of a service description formalism, based on OWL-S, for supporting context constraints (*i.e.* elements provided by client applications and used to describe additional conditions on the context of the requested service) and context profiles (*i.e.* profiles specified by service providers together with service description and containing context parameters).

Another example is the MUSIC Project (IST-MUSIC, 2010), which aims at the development of context-aware self-adapting applications. MUSIC adopts a service-oriented approach in which modeling languages allow the specification of context dependencies and adaptation capabilities. Such adaptation capabilities are based on the specification, at design time, of multiple variations (implementations) for each component. The selection of the most appropriate variant is performed at runtime by the MUSIC middleware based on the context dependencies associated with each variant and based on the current execution context.

The majority of research cited above concentrates the semantic matching on solving ambiguity problems related to service inputs and outputs. Such works focus mainly on functional aspects, using semantic descriptions to enrich input and output description of services. Most works related to context-aware services, as those cited above, do not consider the natural uncertainty of context information. Context information is naturally dynamic and uncertain: it may contain errors, be out-of-date or even incomplete. Uncertainty in context information is traditionally handled by appropriate models, such as Chalmers *et al.* (2004), who represent context values by intervals or sets of symbolic values. In these models, incompleteness of context information is seldom considered. However, semantic matching of context-aware services should take this into account. When considering context-aware services, matching algorithms have to consider the fact that some context information can be simply missing. Such incomplete information may lead to an inexact match between service description and requirements related to the user's current context.

Uncertainty of context information is a central issue for future context-aware services and for any system based on these services. Pervasive scenarios involving smart services are growing and becoming a reality (Tavangarian, 2010; IBM, 2010): intelligent cars that adapt themselves to the road conditions, houses equipped with domotics that help their habitants in everyday tasks, etc. With the development of such scenarios, the availability of different kinds of sensors integrated in the physical environment, varying from embedded GPS sensors up to movement, temperature or humidity sensors, is becoming more common. The more these sensors will be available, the more context-aware services will be able to explore them. However, sensors can fail and become temporally unavailable. The quality of the information they supply can also vary according to several different (and maybe unpredictable) factors (an external interference, for instance). All these have an impact on collecting and exploring context information. Context information that was available at a given moment can simply disappear and become unavailable when needed by a given service. These failure situations tend to grow with the availability of sensors. Any context-aware service, middleware or application using it has to cope with this possibility. The more these services or applications grow and integrate our current lives, the more the consequences of such failures can be disastrous. Thus, it becomes urgent to consider questions such as: "how to proceed if context information is unavailable?"; "how to handle uncertain context information?". Context-aware services should tackle these issues in order to guarantee a minimal reliable service in any circumstance. Otherwise they risk to be deserted by the users.

In this chapter, we focus particularly on this issue: how to deal with incompleteness of context information when selecting context-aware services. We propose a graph-based approach, in which service descriptions and requests are interpreted as graphs whose nodes and overall structure are compared by using similarity measures. The use of similarity measures in Computer Science is not new, as testifies the work of Liao *et al.* (1998). However, unlike Liao *et al.* (1998), our work does not focus on proposing such measures. Our focus is to handle incompleteness of context information on service selection by using similarity measures. Such measures, in our case and unlike those proposed by Klush *et al.* (2006), focus on non-functional and context-related aspects of context-aware services, and not on functional input and output of such services. In this sense, our approach is similar to the one proposed by Bottaro *et al.* (2007), who also propose to rank services according to context information. However, contrary to these authors, we are not particularly focusing on service composition, but on service selection in general.

Our graph-based approach can also be compared with the ranking approach proposed by Palmonari *et al.* (2009), which suggest using non-functional properties, represented on a policy-centered metamodel, for ranking Web services. Even if these authors do not focus particularly on context information, their approach has common principles with ours, notably the presence of a local and a global evaluation. However, due to its general focus, these authors' proposal does neither consider dynamicity of context information (frequent updates on policies are not considered), nor the use of metadata related to this information as part of local and global evaluations. The same can be said about Lamparter *et al.* (2007). These authors propose a framework for Web service selection and configuration based on declarative logic-based matching and on utility function policies for describing Web service offers and requests. Such framework focuses mainly on pricing issues, relegating context information to a secondary plan. Indeed, context information is only used for determining when policies are used. By consequence, updates on context information

are not consided by the framework. Moreover, even if incompleteness could be handled with utility functions, the matching process which is essentially based on subsumption, does not seem to consider this issue.

CONTEXT MODELING

Before introducing context-aware service selection, we need to state what we mean by context and how context is represented. Context information corresponds to a very wide notion. According to Coutaz *et al.* (2005), context entails both recognition and mapping by providing a structured, unified view of the world in which the system operates. It can be defined as any information that can be used to characterize the situation of an entity (a person, place, or object considered as relevant to the interaction between a user and an application) (Dey, 2001). This notion is central to context-aware systems, which use it mainly for adaptation purposes. The way context information is used in these systems depends on what information is observed and how it is represented. In other terms, the adaptation capabilities of a context-aware system depend on the context model it uses (Najar *et al.*, 2009)

A well designed context model is the cornerstone of a context-aware system (Strang & Linnhoff-Popien, 2004). The evolution of context-aware systems in the last decade has been followed by an important evolution on context models, varying from simple key-value structures to ontology-based models (Najar *et al.*, 2009). From pioneering works, such as Schilit and Theimer (1994), which consider context as "the location, identity of nearby people and objects, and changes to those objects", until nowadays works like those presented previously (cf. Section 2), different kinds of formalism have been exploited. Strang and Linnhoff-Popien (2004) pointed out several data structures used to maintain and to exchange contextual information in a given system. However, when observing current works on context-aware computing, an important tendency to ontology modeling can be observed, as pointed out by Najar *et al.* (2009). Among the reasons motivating the use of ontologies, we can underline their capability of enabling knowledge sharing in open dynamic environments and enabling service interoperability in a non ambiguous manner (Suraci, V., Mignanti, S. & Aiuto, 2007).

However, even if ontologies allow the definition of a common vocabulary, they did not prevent by their own all representation issues. When considering context modeling, we should keep in mind that one single concept, such as location, may have multiple representations (GPS coordinates, postal address, etc.). Such representations may vary according to device and software capabilities, and may compromise interoperability offered by ontologies: two applications may understand the same concept, but if its representation differs, they will have difficulties to share and to exploit this knowledge.

Context models focus, in their majority, on information about the physical environment and device capabilities. Nevertheless, we can observe a tendency in some works to widen the notion of the concept context. Works such as (Kirsch-Pinheiro, Gensel & Martin, 2004; Rosemann, Recker & Flender, 2007; Saidani & Nurcan, 2007) have been considering this notion in the business domain, enlarging it to concepts such as the user role and activities in a business process. These works bring closer the notion of context to the notion of business services. In this sense, having a context model that allows the representation of a larger variety of concepts can guarantee the evolution of context-aware systems.

In addition to the context modeling itself, including reasoning capabilities, it is worth noting that such information is normally acquired by dedicated infrastructures (*e.g.* Villalonga *et al.*, 2010; Paspallis, 2009; CoDAMoS, 2010). Such infrastructures, usually middleware, handle not only context acquisition at the physical level, but

also its interpretation or transformation of the obtained raw data into higher abstraction levels (for example, to correlate a set of GPS coordinates with a given postal address, or to deduce the presence of a user in a room based on noisy level). The context middleware detects and manages context information and to observe that context information is missing. The modeling approach adopted by the context middleware must be able to partially handle uncertainty, e.g. through metadata. Nevertheless, this initial handling should be coupled with appropriate algorithms and mechanisms that will allow considering uncertainty inside context-aware systems and their adaptation mechanism. The service selection mechanism we propose in this chapter belongs to this join effort for taking into account uncertainty on context information.

In this chapter, we adopt the context modeling approach proposed by the MUSIC project (IST-MUSIC, 2010), which in our opinion is one of the most promising proposals nowadays. The MUSIC context modeling approach (Reichle *et al.* 2008) adheres to a multi-layer approach, similar to (Najar *et al.* 2009; Villalonga *et al.* 2010), which represents an important tendency for context modeling. MUSIC context modeling approach identifies three basic layers of abstraction that correspond to the three main phases of context management: the conceptual layer, the exchange layer and the functional layer. The *conceptual layer* enables the representation of context information in terms of *context elements*. These provide context information about *context entities* (the concrete subjects the context data refers to: a user, a device, etc.) belonging to specific context scopes. Such *context scopes* are intended as semantic concepts belonging to a specific ontology described in OWL. Moreover, the ontology is used to describe relationships between entities, e.g. a user has a brother. It defines and organizes the concepts that are handled and explored by the other layers. The *exchange layer* focuses on the interoperability between devices. Context data in this layer is represented in XML and is used for

Figure 1. MUSIC context meta-model (Reichle et al. 2008)

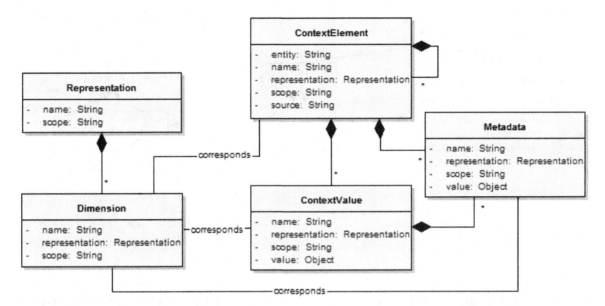

communication between nodes. The *functional layer* refers to the implementation of the context model internally in the different nodes.

The MUSIC ontology describes concepts and entities observed by the MUSIC middleware. It supplies a semantic interpretation for observed context information. This context ontology is coupled with a context meta-model, represented in Figure 1, which establishes, for the exchange and the functional layers, the elements defined by the ontology. This meta-model introduces in the MUSIC context modeling approach the notion of metadata, allowing the representation of non-functional properties related to context information, such as timeout, source identification and any other indicator concerning the quality of collected data. As such, quality of context values can be naturally included in the representation of the context elements.

The adoption of the MUSIC context model is motivated by several reasons. First of all, the MUSIC context model adopts an ontology-based approach, which makes easier interoperability and knowledge sharing, without giving in on performance concerns, through the exchange and

functional layers. Also, the MUSIC context model explicitly introduces the notion of representation, which is not clearly represented in models such as (Villalonga *et al.*, 2010; Najar *et al.* 2009): all context *scopes* are associated with one or more *Representations*, which are also specified in the ontology and which describes the format used to represent context data. By explicitly defining this notion, MUSIC context model allow context middleware to handle different representations and eventually to transform data from one representation to another (as discussed in Section 5.2.1). The presence of metadata on context meta-model allows the representation of non-functional properties related to context data measures, such as an uncertainty degree or the expected error rate, which can be explored for reasoning or for selection purposes. Figure 2 shows this three-part structure (context element, scope and representation) proposed by the MUSIC context model.

Additionally, the MUSIC project proposes a flexible way for collecting context information. The MUSIC middleware collects context information from a set of context plug-ins (Paspallis,

Figure 2. The overall structure of the MUSIC context ontology (Reichle et al. 2008)

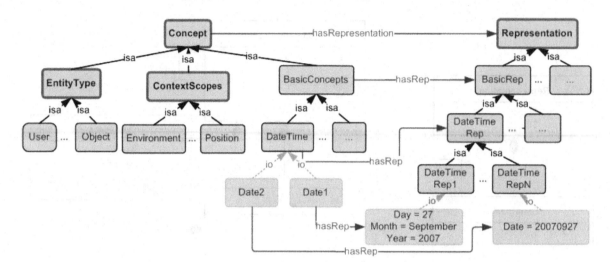

2009). Each plug-in handles a given pair of context entity and scope, periodically updating the corresponding context element. In addition to context values, context plug-ins are responsible for associating different *metadata* with context elements they observe. These metadata include timeout and other indicators concerning the quality of collected data.

GRAPH-BASED SERVICE SELECTION

Proposal Overview

In this chapter, we consider that services can be published by different suppliers, which propose different non-functional properties, including context-related ones, for their services. In other words, several service implementations can supply the same functional capabilities (with a similar syntax), but with different non-functional context-related properties.

The graph-based service selection approach proposed here contributes to the service selection mechanism by selecting the most suitable service among discovered and compatible services. Using this approach, we compare context-aware service descriptions and current execution context in order to select the most suitable service, given the current situation. The proposed service selection mechanism assumes that suitable services exist. It is intended to be integrated as part of the service selection mechanism used on a service directory structure or into a middleware, such as the MUSIC middleware (IST-MUSIC, 2010). Similar to (Palmonari, Comerio & Paoli, 2009), we consider service selection as a two-step process, considering that, first it selects all services whose functional properties match the functional requirements that are needed, then it identifies the services among the selected ones that better fulfill non-functional properties. In this sense, our approach is part of this two-step process. The second step, which deals with non-functional requirements, is employed only after suitable services are discovered. Thus the proposal assumption is the following: if there are several discovered services able to satisfy a request formulated by a user, one has to select the service that suits best the current execution context. Such service selection should take into account the fact that context information is naturally dynamic and incomplete.

As a consequence of this, we focus our approach on non-functional context-related aspects of service description. Indeed, we do not investigate functional aspects (inputs and outputs) of a service, but only non-functional contextual conditions related to the execution environment of a service. Functional aspects of a service have the priority, since mismatching on service input or output may have negative (even disastrous) effects on the running application. Incompleteness on service input or output entries (missing input or output) can lead to severe exceptions (or errors), which may affect correctness and execution flow on both service and calling application. Thus, we decide to focus on non-functional aspects of context-aware services, assuming a selection process for meeting functional requirements already took place.

Each context-aware service describes a set of "contextual" conditions (non-functional properties) describing context elements needed for using it appropriately (in the best conditions). For instance, considering a content sharing service (*e.g.* a photo sharing), several variations of this service can be proposed using different implementations (*e.g.* implementations focusing a given user profile, a particular location, etc.). These contextual conditions refer potentially to any observed context element and they can be expressed using the MUSIC context model (Reichle *et al*., 2008) mentioned previously (cf. Section 3).

In order to perform service selection based on a "contextual" matching, service descriptions are enriched with non-functional context-aware properties related to the execution environment most suited for the service. Such requirements are included in the service profile description, using OWL-S. Such contextual description is analyzed as a graph, in which objects represent concepts and properties and edges represent the relations connecting such concepts. The same analysis is performed on the description of the current execution context, which is represented based on an OWL-ontology, and which acts like a "request" (requested execution environment) for the service. This allows us to compare both based on similarity measures between graphs. The proposed service selection algorithm then ranks the available services, indicating to the middleware (or to the user himself) the services that best match the current context.

In order to compare the graphs built using service description and current context description, we propose local and global similarity measures. Local measures compare two nodes individually, considering only the concept it represents and its properties. Global measures take into account the graph as a whole, evaluating, for instance, the proportion of similar elements in both graphs. By using such measures, our approach allows dealing with incomplete context information and inexact matching between conditions expressed in the service description and current context description, since missing information on the latter will not block the analysis and the ranking of the former. This means that the selection looks for the service that matches the best the contextual conditions, but is not necessarily a perfect match. Figure 3 illustrates these measures. It shows a local measure comparing two individual concepts labeled *conceptA*, and a global measure comparing the graphs formed by these concepts (highlighted in Figure 3). Moreover, this approach assumes that several measures can be considered in order to evaluate local values. These local measures are associated to particular context scopes defined in the MUSIC ontology, taking into account the semantic aspects represented in the ontology.

As one can observe, similarity measures are central to our graph-based approach. Such measures can handle appropriately incompleteness on context information, as well as uncertainty, mainly thanks to its own construction and to the use of context metadata on these measures. Indeed, we consider that similarity measures represent an interesting mechanism for handling non-functional properties, since such measures can deal quite well with inexact matching among properties.

Figure 3. Local and global measures comparing two graphs

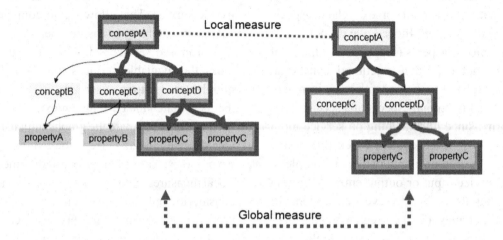

Nevertheless, when considering functional properties, the use of similarity measures should be moderate, since such properties may represent strict requirements for which incompleteness and inexact matching might be avoided.

Describing Context-Aware Services

Service descriptions are expressed in OWL-S. According to Suraci *et al.* (2007), "for describing the semantics of services, the latest research in service-oriented computing recommends the use of the Web Ontology Language for Services (OWL-S)." These authors consider that, even if OWL-S is tailored for Web Services, it is rich and general enough to describe any service. We consider to enrich this description with context information describing the execution context for which the service is best suited. For instance, let us consider a mobile content sharing platform that enables users to browse, search for, and share multimedia content scattered on such devices in different situations, such as conferences, shopping malls, football stadiums, etc. This scenario explores cooperating multi-user applications hosted on mobile devices carried by users. In this scenario, several content sharing services can be available on the platform. Each service can indicate con-

textual conditions in which it runs appropriately. For example, a given photo sharing service can be particularly designed considering client devices with high screen resolution and memory capacities, a second implementation of the same service can be designed considering a particular location (a conference hall or a stadium), or a particular user profile (*e.g.* adult users).

Such contextual information can be considered as part of the service description, since it indicates situations to which the service is better suited. A service description in OWL-S includes three main parts (Martin, 2004): (1) service profile; (2) service model; and (3) service grounding. The service profile corresponds roughly to the service description. The service model specifies the process executed by the service. The service grounding indicates how the service can be accessed (like an API).

Thus, similarly to Suraci *et al.* (2007), we propose to enrich the service profile with a "*context*" element pointing to context description related to the service. This description should be included in an external file (indicated in the "*context*" element) and not directly in the OWL-S description. Context information is dynamic and cannot be statically stored on the service profile. On the one hand, context properties related to the

Figure 4. Example of service profile including the property "context"

```
1    <profile:Profile rdf:ID="CONTEXT_SHARING_MAP_PROFILE">
2      <service:isPresentedBy rdf:resource="#CONTEXT_SHARING_MAP_SERVICE"/>
3      <profile:serviceName xml:lang="en">
4          ContextMapPhotoSharingService
5      </profile:serviceName>
6      <profile:textDescription xml:lang="en">
7          This service provides a facility to find shared photos available
8          in a location.
9      </profile:textDescription>
10     <eprofile:context
11     rdf:resource="http://127.0.0.1/services/contextdescriptionV2.xml"/>
12     <profile:hasInput  rdf:resource="#_REQUEST"/>
13     <profile:hasOutput  rdf:resource="#_LIST"/>
14     <profile:hasOutput rdf:resource="#_MAP"/>
15     <profile:has_process rdf:resource="CONTEXT_SHARING_MAP_PROCESS" />
16   </profile:Profile>
```

execution of a service can evolve and vary according to the service execution environment itself. For instance, the load of the device executing a service may affect the service and consequently the context properties related to it. On the other hand, the service profile is supposed to be a static description of the service in the sense that it is not supposed to change in short intervals of time (as context information does). An external file describing contextual non-functional requirements and properties related to a service allows the service supplier to easily update such context information related to the service without modifying the service description itself. Figure 4 presents an example of service profile including the "*context*" element. This example illustrates the extended profile of a photo sharing service. This service returns, for a given request on input, a list of interesting photos and a map locating them (lines 12 up to 14 on Figure 4). As stated before, such a service may have different implementations, considering particular contexts, indicated on an external file (lines 10-11 on Figure 4). The one related to this particular implementation is given in Figure 5.

Figure 5 presents an example of a context description related to the service in Figure 4. This description follows the MUSIC Context Model described in Reichle *et al* (2008). The MUSIC context modeling approach identifies three basic layers of abstraction that correspond to the three main phases of context management: the conceptual layer, the exchange layer and the functional layer.

The conceptual layer enables the representation of context information in terms of *context elements*. The *context elements* provide context information about *context entities* (the concrete subjects the context data refers to: a user, a device, etc.) belonging to specific *context scopes*. Such context scopes are intended as semantic concepts belonging to a specific ontology described in OWL. Moreover, the ontology is used to describe relationships between entities, *e.g.* a user has a brother. The exchange layer focuses on the interoperability between devices. Context data in this layer is represented in XML and is used for communication between nodes. The functional layer refers to the implementation of the context model internally to the different nodes.

The description illustrated in Figure 5 belongs to the exchange level, since it is used for information exchange among different nodes. Thus, context information in Figure 5 is described in XML by context elements (lines 5-21 and 23-39 on Figure 5), which refer to a given entity (*e.g.* lines 6-7) and scope (*e.g.* location on lines 8-9), and a set of context values, which also refer to a given scope (lines 13-19 and 31-37). It is worth noting that Figure 5 supplies two separate context descriptions: (1) a first description (under

Figure 5. Example of context description associated to a service

```
1    <ctx:context xmlns:ctx="http://www.ist-music.org/ContextSchema"
2                 xsi:schemaLocation=
3                 "http://www.ist-music.org/ContextSchema ContextSchema.xsd ">
4      <ctx:condition>
5        <ctx:contextElement>
6          <ctx:hasEntity resource="http://www.ist-music.org/Ontology
7          /ContextModel.owl#concept.entityType.user"/>
8          <ctx:hasScope resource="http://www.ist-music.org/Ontology
9          /ContextModel.owl#concept.contextScope.location"/>
10         <ctx:hasRepresentation resource="http://www.ist-music.org/Ontology
11         /ContextModel.owl#concept.representation.locationDefaultRepresentation"/>
12         <ctx:contextValueSet>
13           <ctx:contextValue>
14             <ctx:hasScope resource="http://www.ist-music.org/Ontology
15             /ContextModel.owl#concept.contextScope.location.city"></ctx:hasScope>
16             <ctx:hasRepresentation resource="http://www.ist-music.org/Ontology
17             /ContextModel.owl#concept.representation.locationDefaultRepresentation"/>
18             <ctx:value>Paris</ctx:value>
19           </ctx:contextValue>
20         </ctx:contextValueSet>
21       </ctx:contextElement>
22
23       <ctx:contextElement>
24         <ctx:hasEntity resource="http://www.ist-music.org/Ontology
25         /ContextModel.owl#concept.entityType.user"/>
26         <ctx:hasScope resource="http://www.ist-music.org/Ontology
27         /ContextModel.owl#concept.contextScope.userprofile"/>
28         <ctx:hasRepresentation resource="http://www.ist-music.org/Ontology
29         /ContextModel.owl#concept.representation.profileDefaultRepresentation"/>
30         <ctx:contextValueSet>
31           <ctx:contextValue>
32             <ctx:hasScope resource="http://www.ist-music.org/Ontology
33             /ContextModel.owl#concept.contextScope.profile.category"></ctx:hasScope>
34             <ctx:hasRepresentation resource="http://www.ist-music.org/Ontology
35             /ContextModel.owl#concept.representation.profileDefaultRepresentation"/>
36             <ctx:value>Tourist</ctx:value>
37           </ctx:contextValue>
38         </ctx:contextValueSet>
39       </ctx:contextElement>
40     </ctx:condition>
41     <ctx:state>
42       . . .
43     </ctx:state>
44   </ctx:context>
```

the element "*condition*" at line 4) supplying the conditions under which this service adapts the best (*i.e.* the contextual situation in which it is most appropriate to call this service); and (2) a second description referring to the current state of the service execution context (under which conditions this service is running on the service supplier). Thus, through the condition element in Figure 5, the service supplier indicates that the content supplied by this service implementation (whose profile is represented in Figure 4) is proper to tourist users (context element "user profile" at line 23-39), who are familiar with the city they are visiting, and that this service disposes of a detailed

database for the city of Paris, which makes it better adapted to being used when in this location (context element "location" at line 5-21). The next section describes how the proposed graph-based matching algorithm considers and handles these descriptions.

GRAPH-BASED MATCHING

From Description to Graphs

The first step for performing the graph-based matching is to analyze the context description associated with the available service. Based on the context description presented above, we propose a graph-based approach for ranking and selecting services. In this approach, non-functional context-related properties of the services represented in the context description file described previously are interpreted as a graph. In this graph, nodes represent the context elements indicated in this description, and the edges represent the relations that can exist between these elements. The same interpretation is used when analyzing the current execution context. A middleware is responsible for service selection and for collecting and managing context information related to the user. It keeps this information in context elements expressing their current values. These context elements are seen as graph nodes, whereas relations between such elements are seen as graph edges. Thus, a graph G is defined as follow:

- $G = < N, E >$ where:
  - $N = \{ C_{Ei} \}_{i > 0}$: set of context elements C_{Ei};
  - $E = \{ < C_{Ei}, C_{Ej} > \}$: set of relations between context elements C_{Ei} and C_{Ej}.

Thus, comparing two graphs representing two different context descriptions corresponds, with regard to the MUSIC Context Model, to comparing two sets of context elements and their relations.

Matching Algorithm

Once all available services have been analyzed and their corresponding graphs are created, the matching based algorithm may proceed. The goal of this matching algorithm is to rank the available services based on their contextual non-functional properties. It compares the graph generated by each proposed service to the graph created based on the current execution context information. Current context information is detected by the context middleware, which identifies context scopes and representations. The MUSIC context middleware

uses a set of dynamically registered plug-ins (see Paspallis (2009) for details), which identify the scope, representation and uncertainty of acquired context information as context metadata. Thus, as a preprocessing step, we make sure that all nodes in the graphs corresponding to the same concept have the same representation. Then we compare nodes from both graphs (from the context description of the service and from the current context) individually, using local similarity measures. Based on the results of these measures, the matching algorithm compares the graphs globally, using global similarity measures that also consider the edges connecting the nodes. The results of such global measures are used to rank the services corresponding to the compared graphs. Next sections present the representation transformations, and the local and global similarity measures.

Inter-representation Operations

An important issue to consider is how to be able to compare nodes locally which represent the same concept, but use different representations. For instance, location information can be represented using geographical coordinates like latitude and longitude (*e.g. 48°49'38"N, 2°21'02"E*), as well as using a representative name (*e.g. Paris, France*). As a preprocessing step prior to the application of the appropriate local similarity measure, the middleware invokes the *performIROTransformation* method to make sure that both nodes have the same representation. The method uses a library of inter-representation operations (IROPs) to do the correct transformation. The location of this transformation and the way to invoke it are specified in the ontology itself. The following figure specifies a location representation transformation in OWL from address to coordinates. The input and output representation are specified, together with the semantic concept (*LocationDescription*) this operation works on. The listing below (Figure 6) describes the internals of the service to invoke for the transformation (for instance, input

Figure 6. OWL description for an IROP invocation

```
1    <owl:Class rdf:about="#LocationInfoAddressToWGS84">
2        <rdfs:subClassOf rdf:resource="#LocationRepIRO"/>
3        <rdfs:subClassOf>
4            <owl:Restriction>
5                <owl:onProperty rdf:resource="&BasicInformationConcept;hasInput"/>
6                <owl:allValuesFrom rdf:resource="&InformationConcept;AddressRep"/>
7            </owl:Restriction>
8        </rdfs:subClassOf>
9        <rdfs:subClassOf>
10           <owl:Restriction>
11               <owl:onProperty rdf:resource="&BasicInformationConcept;hasOutput"/>
12               <owl:allValuesFrom rdf:resource="&InformationConcept;LocationWGS84"/>
13           </owl:Restriction>
14       </rdfs:subClassOf>
15       <rdfs:subClassOf>
16           <owl:Restriction>
17               <owl:onProperty rdf:resource="&BasicInformationConcept;worksOn"/>
18               <owl:allValuesFrom rdf:resource="&InformationConcept;LocationDescription"/>
19           </owl:Restriction>
20       </rdfs:subClassOf>
21       <rdfs:subClassOf>
22           <owl:Restriction>
23               <owl:onProperty rdf:resource="&BasicInformationConcept;hasDependency"/>
24               <owl:maxCardinality rdf:datatype="&xsd;nonNegativeInteger">
25                   0</owl:maxCardinality>
26           </owl:Restriction>
27       </rdfs:subClassOf>
28   </owl:Class>
```

information indicated on line 5). The address and the type of the service; the serialization scheme and the protocol to be used are specified. All this information is specified in the ontology itself (as illustrated by Figure 7 and Figure 8), and the middleware is able to access this ontology at run-time by using the OWLAPI (2010) library to access the correct transformation operation. Hereby we keep following the philosophy of using external ontology (*i.e.* OWL) files to dynamically access contextual information.

Comparing Graph Nodes: Local Similarity Measures

When comparing two nodes from two graphs defined in Section 5.1, we are comparing two *context elements* representing context information about a given entity and referring a given scope. By considering these elements individually, we focus on how similar their context values are. In order to perform this comparison, we consider local similarity measures $Sim_l(C_{Ei}, C_{Ej})$ that compare two

Figure 7. Grounding information for calling an IROP implementation

```
1    <BasicInformationConcept:IROGrounding
2        rdf:about="#IROGroundingLocationAddressToWGS84_WebService">
3        <BasicInformationConcept:serviceAddress>
4            http://141.51.122.194:8080/ServiceLocationToWGS84?wsdl
5        </BasicInformationConcept:serviceAddress>
6        <BasicInformationConcept:serviceType>
7            WebService</BasicInformationConcept:serviceType>
8        <BasicInformationConcept:serializationScheme>
9            SOAP/XML</BasicInformationConcept:serializationScheme>
10       <BasicInformationConcept:protocol>
11           SOAP</BasicInformationConcept:protocol>
12   </BasicInformationConcept:IROGrounding>
```

Figure 8. Detail on an IROP location indication

```
1    <LocationInfoAddressToWGS84 rdf:about="#IROLocationAddressToWGS84">
2        <BasicInformationConcept:hasGrounding
3        rdf:resource="#IROGroundingLocationAddressToWGS84_WebService"/>
4    </LocationInfoAddressToWGS84>
```

context elements C_{Ei} and C_{Ej} locally (i.e. without considering their position in the corresponding graphs). This measure can be defined as follows:

- $Sim_l (C_{Ei}, C_{Ej}) = x$, where $x \in R$, $x \in [0, 1]$

Ideally, the similarity measure $Sim_l (C_{Ei}, C_{Ej})$ depends on the *context scope*. If the context elements being compared do not belong to compatible context scopes, their similarity is by definition zero. For example, we cannot compare context elements referring to the user's age or preferences with context elements referring to the user's location because both elements belong to context scopes that are incompatible. Similarity measure $Sim_l (C_{Ei}, C_{Ej})$ has to consider the *representation* associated with the context elements. Each measure $Sim_l (C_{Ei}, C_{Ej})$ is proposed considering a given set of possible representations, which it may handle. Only context elements that correspond to the context scope and representation supported by the giving measure can be compared using it. The preprocessing phase described earlier (cf. section 5.2.1) proposes to transform compatible representations, using inter-representation operations. Such transformation allows comparing concepts referring to the same scope but using a different representation. Without such preprocessing phase, this knowledge represented using different formats risk to be ignored or to remain unexplored, which can negatively impact the selection process. Besides, it is worth noting that, similarly to the inter-representation operations, all known similarity measures $Sim_l (C_{Ei}, C_{Ej})$ are kept, by the middleware or directory performing the service selection, in a library. Before comparing two nodes, it looks for the appropriate measure

in its library. This library can be indexed using context scope and representation associated with each local similarity measure. Such indexing allows the context middleware to quickly identify the appropriate similarity measure based on context metadata declared by compared context elements.

Once the appropriate similarity measure $Sim_l (C_{Ei}, C_{Ej})$ is chosen, the matching starts by taking each node in the graph corresponding to the context description of the service and comparing it to the nodes with a compatible scope and representation from the graph corresponding to the current execution context. For each node, it keeps tracks of the best-ranked node, in order to use this value in the global similarity measures (Section 5.2.3). Thus, being $G_{Sk} = < N_{Sk}, E_{Sk} >$ the graph corresponding to the service S_k and

$G_C = < N_C, E_C >$ the graph corresponding to the current context, we compare each node C_{Ei} from G_{Sk} to all nodes C'_{Ei} in G_C for which $C_{Ei}.scope$ and $C'_{Ei}.scope$ and $C_{Ei}.representation$ and $C'_{Ei}.representation$ are compatible, keeping in memory the best-ranked C'_{Ei}. For example, considering the graph generated by the context description in Figure 4, the node referring to the user's profile is compared to all nodes having the same scope (*user profile*) in the graph corresponding to current user's context.

Comparing Graphs: Global Measures

The main goal of global similarity measures is to compare overall composition of two graphs, taking into account both nodes and edges composing each graph. We define such measures as follow:

- $Sim_g (G_{Sk}, G_C) = x$, $x \in R$, where

○ G_{Sk} corresponds to the graph determined by the context description of the service;

○ G_C corresponds to the graph determined based on the current execution context.

Several global measures $Sim_g(G_{Sk}, G_C)$ are possible for comparing two graphs. These measures can be based on different well-know algorithms such as subgraph matching or graph isomorphism. The most important aspect for us is that the global similarity measure $Sim_g(G_{Sk}, G_C)$ must support incompleteness of context information represented in these graphs. This means that the $Sim_g(G_{Sk}, G_C)$ should not stop processing if some context information is missing. For instance, if the context description of a service refers to a given context element for which there is no corresponding element with a compatible context scope in the current context description, the similarity measure $Sim_g(G_{Sk}, G_C)$ should continue the processing, arriving at a valuable result that takes into account this fact.

We propose a single yet powerful similarity measure $Sim_g(G_{Sk}, G_C)$ defined based on the proportion of nodes and edges belonging to the context description of the service that have a similar correspondence in the current context description. For this, the similarity measure considers the results obtained by the local similarity measures. For each pair $<C_{Ei}, C'_{Ei}>$, with $C'_{Ei} \in G_{Sk}$ and $C'_{Ei} \in G_C$ and C'_{Ei} being the node of G_C with the greatest value for $d(C_{Ei}, C'_{Ei})$, the proposed measure $Sim_g(G_{Sk}, G_C)$ analyses the similarity among the edges connecting these nodes to their neighbors. The similarity between two edges is calculated based on the similarity of their corresponding labels (or weights), if the edges are labeled, and the similarity between the objects forming the edges. Similarly to the local measures, we consider in the global measure only the greatest value obtained when comparing each edge connecting a node C_{Ei}. Then, we sum up both nodes and edges best similarities measures and make the proportion

taking into account the total number of nodes and edges in graph defined by the context description of the service. Figure 5 shows the definition of the measure $Sim_g(G_{Sk}, G_C)$.

It is worth noting that, since the maximum value for $Sim_l(a,b)$ is *1* (cf. Section 5.2.2), if the graph G_{Sk} is a subgraph of G_C, for each node and edge, we will have a corresponding node or edge for which the local similarity measure is 1. Thus, by considering the proportion of the greatest values obtained for all individual nodes and edges in the total size of the graph, this measure considers implicitly that some nodes or edges may have no similar element ($max(Sim_l(a,b))=0$). This eventuality leads to a reduction in the value of the global similarity measure $Sim_g(G_{Sk}, G_C)$, but it does not prevent a valuable result. Even if the compared graphs have no element in common ($max(Sim_l(a,b))=0$ for all $a \in G_{Sk}$ and $b \in G_C$), the measure $Sim_g(G_{Sk}, G_C)$ still returns a value that can be used to rank the service. For instance, when considering the photo sharing service represented Figure 4 the measure $Sim_g(G_{Sk}, G_C)$ gives a valuable result ($x \geq 0$) even if the current user's context does not possess any context element referring to the location scope (user's device has no GPS or any location sensor available). This resulting value is then used to rank this particular implementation of photo sharing service. Incompleteness of context information is dealt with in this way.

Matching With Uncertainty

Handling Uncertainty Metada

The goal of the matching algorithm is to rank the available services based on their contextual non-functional properties. It compares the context description related to available services with the current execution context. This matching starts with comparing individual context elements from both descriptions (from the context description of the service and from the current context) individually, using local similarity measures. Then

Figure 9. Definition of the global similarity measure Sim$_g$

Considering that:

$$\text{if } G_{S_k} = \langle N, E \rangle, \text{ where } \begin{array}{l} N = \{C_{E_i}\}_{1 \leq i \leq n} \text{ and} \\ E = \{\langle C_{E_i}, C_{E_j} \rangle_k\}_{0 \leq k \leq m} \end{array} \text{ then } |G_{S_k}| = n + m$$

And considering two edges E_i and E_j that:

$$Sim_l(E_i, E_j) = \frac{Sim_l(l_i, l_j) + \sum_1^p Sim_l\left(C_{E_i}, C_{E_j}\right)}{(p + 1)}, \text{where} \begin{array}{l} l_i \text{ and } l_j \text{ are the edges labels, and} \\ C_{E_i} \text{ and } C_{E_j} \text{ are edges extremeties} \end{array}$$

Thus, $Sim_g(G_{S_k}, G_C)$ can be defined as:

$$Sim_g(G_{S_k}, G_C) = \frac{\sum max\left(Sim_l(C_{E_i}, C'_{E_i})\right) + \sum max\left(Sim_l(E_j, E'_j)\right)}{|G_{S_k}|}$$

the global similarity measure is calculated based on the values obtained from the local measures. The results of such global measures are used to rank the services for their suitability in the current context.

First we compare the current context values with the service requirements using *local similarity measures*. For the node-to-node (*i.e.* context element to context element) comparison, we use measures such as those proposed by *SimPack* (Sim-Pack Project, 2010), depending on the scope of the corresponding context element. For example, for numerical values the measure represents how close the numbers are lying together, relative to their range. The result of one node-to-node comparison is a *mean* (between 0 and 1) with an uncertainty degree. The *uncertainty* of a context value is given as a *metadatum* of that element between 0 and 1. Such kind of *metadatum* concerning uncertainty degree can be estimated when collecting/calculating a given context element. Actually, the context plug-in or widget in charge of the data capture is the only one that can perform such estimation, since the context middleware is not directly aware of how data is collected. Thus, when looking at the similarity, we also take into account uncertainty by combining the uncertainty of a current context value with the uncertainty resulting from

the prediction of the QoS properties of a service. *Incompleteness* of context information can then be dealt with by taking the average value as mean and the *uncertainty* degree as maximal, *i.e.* 1, and not by just ignoring unknown values on global measures.

Thus, the local similarity of the service context requirements with the current context is expressed by the *mean*. A low mean expresses a low similarity and vice versa. In case the uncertainty degree is 0 and the current context value and service context requirement are equal (exact match), the similarity measure is 1. By combining the mean and the resulting uncertainty degree, we can improve local and global measures used for service matching purposes.

When local measures have been calculated, we have to combine them. In other words, based on these partial results, we calculate a *global similarity measure* and use a ranking scheme to select the service with the highest similarity. Such global measure can be "weighted" by uncertainty values associated with local measures. Thus best ranked service is not necessarily the one with the highest means for local values because of the uncertainty of the context information: a given measure with a mean that is only a little bit higher than another, but that has much greater uncertainty degree is

Figure 10. Non-functional properties determining GPS service variants

```
Criteria for GPS service variants:
    •    route quality requested by application varies between 0 and 1
    •    time requested by application varies between 4 and 20
 •    context.routequality and context.response are user preferences
```

worse as a result. We prefer to minimize the "risk", which is defined as the probability that an event will occur times the consequences (impact) if it does occur. A higher uncertainty degree expresses more risk that the actual mean value will be different. For example, when looking at the uncertainty degrees expressing the current available memory, we will prefer a lower amount of memory if we are more certain that the amount of memory will actually be available than risking a memory shortage. If the means are equal then of course less uncertainty degree is better. If the uncertainty degrees are equal then higher mean is preferable. In the borderline case, we use *thresholds* for both mean and uncertainty values. For example, let us consider thresholds of 0.1 for mean values and 0.2 for uncertainty values: if two measures differ less than 0.1 in their mean values, then the one with the highest mean is the best only if its uncertainty degree is maximum 0.2 higher than the uncertainty degree of the measure with lower mean. If mean difference between the overall measures is more than 0.1 than the highest is in each case the best one, whatever the uncertainty degree is.

The following section presents an example of a route planner service ("GPS service") with several variants. We explain how local and global measures are calculated. We also give examples of how uncertainty can be given as *metadatum* of a context element.

Case Study

In this section, we illustrate our approach through a case study. For this, let us consider a route planner service ("GPS service") that calculates the route for a user based on GPS information. This service has several implementations (*i.e.* several different services implementation that supply the same functionality), which vary according to two main criteria (*non-functional properties*): *route quality* and *response time,* as indicated by Figure 10. Such non-functional properties correspond to user preferences represented, according to the MUSIC context modeling approach, as part of the user context, and more precisely, as part of the user profile (i.e. context elements with scopes route quality and response).

Additionally, we have the following observed context scopes: available memory resources, GPS signal strength (0-100), and light conditions (0 or 1). For each context scope observed, a very simple local similarity measure is proposed in order to compare locally context elements corresponding to this scope. Examples of such measures are proposed in Figure 11.

In order to rank available services, the service selection mechanism considers mean values obtained with previous local measures in a global measure. Thus, considering the route planner service, let us suppose that the following context elements are currently available: *context.availablememory*, *context.routequality*, *context.response* and *context.light*. *Service.neededmemory*, *service.routequality*, *service.response* and *service.light* are non-functional requirements of this service, obtained from the XML context description file associate with service variants. It is worth noting that we indicate observed context values by *context.scope* and service values by *service.scope*.

Supposing that service implementations vary considering light, memory needed and offered route quality, attending up to 18 service vari-

Figure 11. Local measures evaluating memory, route quality, response time and light

```
Local similarity measures (mean;uncertainty):
  memory-utility = if (context.availablememory > service.neededmemory) 1
                   else 0
  routequality-utility = if (context.routequality) > service.routequality) 1
                   else 1 - (service.routequality - context.routequality)
  response-utility = if (context.response > service.response) 1
                   else 1 - (service.response - context.response)
  light-utility = if (context.light and service.light) or (!context.light and
                       !service.light) 1
      else 0
```

ants. We need to select the service variant with the highest global measure. However, *service.response* element is uncertain because *context.signalstrength* measured value is uncertain (*e.g.* since signal strength fluctuates and measurement is done by imprecise software). This means that *context.signalstrength* is a context value with a *mean* value and an *uncertainty* as *metadatum*.

The *response-utility* function uses the mean value of the previous step to compute the *response-utility* and transforms the uncertainty value into an uncertainty degree. As a result, the output of the *response-utility* is a *mean* and an *uncertainty degree*, which is used as an extra input for the global measure, as presented in Figure 12.

FUTURE DIRECTIONS

Flexible context-aware service selection taking into account the uncertainty and incompleteness

of context information is a key requirement for incorporating services in context-aware and adaptive applications.

In finding a suitable service with regard to required non-functional properties, we can not only take into account the current context as such. The application running on top of the middleware will typically also specify some context quality requirements associated with the context values. For example, an application that needs a location service can specify a required precision and format for the location information. This quality of information can be dealt with using the same similarity measures as for matching with the current context, also allowing an imperfect match between requirements from the application and (information) quality requirements. Important to notice is that quality properties related to information provided by the service can be regarded as being part both of the quality of service and the quality of context. Both being non-functional

Figure 12. Example of global measure considering uncertainty and mean

```
Global measure:
  global(mean) = if (memory-utility(mean) = 0) 0
         else (0,25 * light-utility(mean) + 0,50 * response-utility(mean)
  + 0,25 * routequality - utility(mean))
  global (uncertainty-degree) = if (memory-utility(mean) = 0)
  memory-utility(uncertainty-degree)
         else (0,25 * light-utility(uncertainty-degree)

  + 0,50 * response-utility(uncertainty-degree)

  + 0,25 * routequality - utility(uncertainty-degree))
```

properties, they can be treated also by our graph-based approach.

An additional mechanism to compare graphs for similarity as a whole is the use of subsumption. In order to efficiently compare graphs globally, as a first step common points can be identified which are in a subsumption relation with each other in the graphs. If a pair of nodes in the different graphs are in a subtype-supertype relation, this can be taken as a starting point for comparing graphs globally. Second, these nodes are compared using local similarity measures. The subsumption relation between the nodes can be used to choose the suitable corresponding measure in the library of similarity measures.

CONCLUSION

In this chapter, we present a graph-based approach for service selecting in ubiquitous computing. The main goal of this approach is to select the most appropriate service for the current situation. We compare contextual non-functional properties of context-aware services to the current execution context in which they are called. Our approach considers in particular the natural incompleteness of context information when selecting a context-aware service among all available services. For this, our approach is based on a graph-based analysis of both the current context situation and the context description associated with the service. This analysis is the basis for a set of similarity measures that compare graphs representing these descriptions. Such measures allow us to compare graphs that represent context information by considering scope and incompleteness of such information. An uncertainty measure is proposed which allows a ranking of available services explicitly dealing with uncertain and incomplete information. Finally, the approach is illustrated with a case study.

ACKNOWLEDGMENT

The authors would like to thank their partners in the MUSIC-IST project and acknowledge the partial financial support given to this research by the European Union (6th Framework Programme, contract number 35166).

REFERENCES

AMIGO Project. (2010). *EU Projects: AMIGO.* Retrieved December 2010, from http://www. hitech-projects.com/euprojects/amigo/index.htm

Baldauf, M., Dustdar, S., & Rosenberg, F. (2007). A survey on context-aware systems. *International Journal of Ad Hoc and Ubiquitous Computing, 2*(4). doi:10.1504/IJAHUC.2007.014070

Bottaro, A., Gerodolle, A., & Lalanda, P. (2007). *Pervasive service composition in the home network.* In 21st International IEEE Conference on Advanced Information Networking and Applications (AINDA'2007).

Chalmers, D., Dulay, N., & Sloman, M. (2004). Towards reasoning about context in the presence of uncertainty. In *1st International Workshop on Advanced Context Modelling, Reasoning and Management,* Nottingham, UK, September 2004.

CoDAMoS. (2010). Retrieved December 2010 from http://distrinet.cs.kuleuven.be/projects/ CoDAMoS/

Coutaz, J., Crowley, J. L., Dobson, S., & Garlan, D. (2005). Context is key. *Communications of the ACM, 48*(3). doi:10.1145/1047671.1047703

Dey, A. (2001). Understanding and using context. *Personal and Ubiquitous Computing, 5*(1), 4–7. doi:10.1007/s007790170019

Eikerling, H.-J., Mazzoleni, P., Plaza, P., Yankelevich, D., & Wallet, T. (2007). *Services and mobility: The PLASTIC answer to the Beyond 3G challenge.* PLASTIC Project. Retrieved December, 2010 from http://www-c.inria.fr/plastic/dissemination/plastic/dissemination

Fraga, L., Hallsteinsen, S., & Scholz, U. (2008). InstantSocial -- Implementing a distributed mobile multi-user application with adaptation middleware. *Communications of the EASST, 11.*

IBM. (2010). *A smarter planet starts with smarter products: Innovation for a smarter planet.* Retrieved December 2010, from http://www-01.ibm.com/software/rational/announce/smartproducts/

ICSOC. (2010). Retrieved December 2010 from http://www.icsoc.org/

ICWS. (2010). Retrieved December 2010 from http://conferences.computer.org/icws/

Issarny, V., Caporuscio, M., & Georgantas, N. (2007). A perspective on the future of middleware-based software engineering. In L. Briand, & A. Wolf (Eds.), *Future of Software Engineering 2007 (FOSE), ICSE (International Conference on Software Engineering).* IEEE CS Press.

IST-DAIDALOS. (2010). Retrieved December 2010 from http://www.ist-daidalos.org/

IST-MUSIC. (2010). *Self-adapting applications for mobile users in ubiquitous computing environments (MUSIC).* Retrieved December 2010 from http://www.ist-music.eu/

IST-SPICE. (2010). Retrieved December, 2010 from http://www.ist-spice.org/

Kirsch-Pinheiro, M., Gensel, J., & Martin, H. (2004). Representing context for an adaptative awareness mechanism. In G. d. Vreede, L. Guerrero, & G. Ravento (Eds.), *X Int. Workshop on Groupware (CRIWG 2004), Lecture Notes in Computer Science, vol. 3198* (pp. 339-348). Springer.

Klusch, M., Fries, B., & Sycara, K. (2006). Automated semantic web service discovery with OWLS-MX. In *Proceedings of the 5th International Joint Conference on Autonomous Agents and Multiagent Systems (AAMAS '06)* (pp. 915-922). ACM.

Lamparter, S., Ankolekar, A., & Studer, R. (2007) Preference-based selection of highly configurable web services. In *16th Int. World Wide Web Conference (WWW '07)* (pp. 1013-1022), ACM.

Liao, T., Zhang, Z., & Mount, C. (1998). Similarity measures for retrieval in case-based reasoning systems. *Applied Artificial Intelligence, 12*(4), 267–288. doi:10.1080/088395198117730

Maamar, Z., Benslimane, D., & Narendra, N. (2006). What can context do for web services? *Communications of the ACM, 49*(12), 98–103. doi:10.1145/1183236.1183238

Martin, D. (2004). *OWL-S: Semantic markup for Web services.* W3C Member Submission 22. W3C.

Mobiquitous. (2010). Retrieved from http://www.mobiquitous.org/

Mokhtar, S. B., Kaul, A., Georgantas, N., & Issarny, V. (2006). Efficient semantic service discovery in pervasive computing environments. In *Proceedings of the ACM/IFIP/USENIX 7th International Middleware Conference (Middleware '06).*

Moran, T., & Dourish, P. (2001). Introduction to this special issue on context-aware computing. *Human-Computer Interaction, 16*(2-3), 87–95. doi:10.1207/S15327051HCI16234_01

Najar, S., Saidani, O., Kirsch-Pinheiro, M., Souveyet, C., & Nurcan, S. (2009). Semantic representation of context models: A framework for analyzing and understanding. In J. M. Gomez-Perez, P. Haase, M. Tilly, & P. Warren (Eds.), *Proceedings of the 1st Workshop on Context, information and ontologies (CIAO 09), European Semantic Web Conference (ESWC '2009).* ACM Press.

OWL-API. (2010). Retrieved from http://owlapi. sourceforge.net/

Palmonari, M., Comerio, M., & Paoli, F. (2009). Effective and flexible NFP-based ranking of Web services. In *7th International Joint Conference on Service-Oriented Computing (ICSOC-Service-Wave '09)* [Springer.]. *Lecture Notes in Computer Science, 5900,* 546–560. doi:10.1007/978-3-642-10383-4_40

Papazoglou, M. P., & Georgakopoulos, D. (2003). Service-oriented computing. *Communications of the ACM, 46*(10), 24–28. doi:10.1145/944217.944233

Paspallis, N. (2009). *Middleware-based development of context-aware applications with reusable components.* Ph.D. Thesis, University of Cyprus.

Patouni, E., Alonistioti, N., & Polychronopoulos, C. (2008). *Service adaptation over heterogeneous infrastructures.* Retrieved from http://www.opuce. tid.es/Publications.htm

Reichle, R., Wagner, M., Khan, M., Geihs, K., Lorenzo, L., Valla, M., et al. (2008). A comprehensive context modeling framework for pervasive computing systems. In *8th IFIP International Conference on Distributed Applications and Interoperable Systems (DAIS).* Springer.

Reiff-Marganiec, S., Yu, H. Q., & Tilly, M. (2007). Service selection based on non-functional properties. In *NFPSLA-SOC07 Workshop at The 5th International Conference on Service Oriented Computing (ICSOC2007).*

Rosemann, M., Recker, J., & Flender, C. (2007). Contextualization of business processes. *Int. J. Business Process Integration and Management, 1*(1/2/3).

Saidani, O., & Nurcan, S. (2007). *Towards context aware business process modeling.* In 8th Workshop on Business Process Modeling, Development, and Support (BPMDS'07), CAiSE'07.

Schilit, B. N., & Theimer, M. M. (1994). Disseminating active map information to mobile hosts. *IEEE Network, 8*(5), 22–32. doi:10.1109/65.313011

SimPack Project. (2010). *SimPack project page.* Retrieved December 2010 from http://www.ifi. uzh.ch/ddis/research/semweb/simpack/

Strang, T., & Linnhoff-Popien, C. (2004). *A context modeling survey.* In Workshop on Advanced Context Modeling, Reasoning and Management as part of UbiComp 2004 - The 6th Int. Conference on Ubiquitous Computing.

Suraci, V., Mignanti, S., & Aiuto, A. (2007). *Context-aware semantic service discovery. In 16th* (pp. 1–5). IST Mobile and Wireless Communications Summit.

Sutterer, M., Droegehorn, O., & David, K. (2008). UPOS: User profile ontology with situation-dependent preferences support. In *First International Conference on Advances in Computer-Human Interaction - ACHI 2008* (pp. 230-235).

Tavangarian, D. (2010) Pervasive computing: What next? In *IEEE International Conference on Pervasive Computing and Communications (PerCom)* (pp. 152-152).

Toninelli, A., Corradi, A., & Montanari, R. (2008). Semantic-based discovery to support mobile context-aware service access. *Computer Communications, 31*(5), 935–949. doi:10.1016/j. comcom.2007.12.026

Villalonga, C., Bauer, M., Huang, V., Bernat, J., & Barnaghi, P. (2010). Modeling of sensor data and context for the real world Internet. In *PerCom'10 Workshops Proceedings.* IEEE Computer Society.

Weiser, M. (1991). The computer for the 21st century. *Scientific American, 66.*

Yau, S., & Liu, J. (2006). Incorporating situation awareness in service specifications. In S. Lee, U. Brinkschulte, B. Thuraisingham, & R. Pettit (Eds.), *9th IEEE International Symposium on Object and Component-Oriented Real-Time Distributed Computing (ISORC 2006)* (pp. 287-294).

Zarras, A., Fredj, M., Georgantas, N., & Issarny, V. (2006). Engineering reconfigurable distributed software systems: Issues arising for pervasive computing. In Butler, M., Jones, C., Romanovsky, A., & Troubitsyna, E. (Eds.), *Rigorous development of complex fault-tolerant systems* (pp. 364–386). Springer. doi:10.1007/11916246_19

KEY TERMS AND DEFINITIONS

Context Models: Informational models representing context information in a well-defined structure.

Context: Sny information that can be used to characterize the situation of an entity (a person, place, or object considered as relevant to the interaction between a user and an application).

Context-Aware Services: Services of which description is enriched with context information related to non-functional requirements, describing the service execution environment or its adaptation capabilities.

Context-Aware Systems: Systems that are able to adapt their operations to the current context, aiming at increasing usability and effectiveness by taking into account environmental context.

Service Selection: The process allowing the identification of all services, among the available ones, that match functional and non-functional requirements.

Services: Independent entities, with well-defined interfaces, that can be invoked in a standard way, without requiring the client to have knowledge about how the service actually performs its tasks.

Similarity Measures: Measures used to compare the degree of similarity (or dissimilarity) between two concepts on a domain.

Chapter 10
Towards Aligning and Matchmaking QoS-Based Web Service Specifications

Kyriakos Kritikos
ICS-FORTH, Greece

Dimitris Plexousakis
ICS-FORTH, Greece

ABSTRACT

QoS plays an important role in all service life-cycle activities, and consequently, has grabbed the researchers' attention. Concerning QoS-based service description, the various approaches proposed adopt different meta-models and propose different QoS models mostly covering domain-independent NFPs and metrics. This lack of a common QoS meta-model and model causes serious accuracy problems in QoS-based service matchmaking. While mapping between QSDs is not difficult as they rely on similar meta-models, mapping between equivalent metrics specified even with the same meta-model is challenging. For this reason, a novel QoS metric matching algorithm has been proposed for metrics specified in the OWL-Q language. In this chapter, this algorithm is exploited for aligning OWL-Q specifications. Moreover, two novel QSM algorithms are proposed that advance the state-of-the-art by solving the problems of non-coverage of QoS demand metrics by QoS offers, erroneous matchmaking metrics, limited service categorization, and non-useful result production for over-constrained QoS demands.

INTRODUCTION

Service-orientation (Georgakopoulos & Papazoglou, 2008; Allen, 2006) is a new design paradigm that promises to change the way software applications are built and business is conducted.

This paradigm relies on exploiting services as application or business process building blocks. Services are modular and self-describing software or business entities exposing a particular functionality that can be discovered and invoked via the Internet. One key advantage of services is that they can be combined into new services offering an integrated functionality. As such, a

DOI: 10.4018/978-1-61350-432-1.ch010

whole application can be built from scratch or existing intra- or inter-organizational processes can be seamlessly integrated together in a loosely-coupled way.

Before services are combined and used, they first have to be discovered. To this end, the service-oriented paradigm relies on a particular architecture (Booth et al., 2002) in which three main entities play particular roles. The service provider offers the service and advertizes it to a service broker. The latter is responsible of storing the service advertisements and answering service queries issued by service requesters for a particular offered-as-a-service functionality. Finally, the list of advertisements fulfilling the requested functionality is returned to the service requester, who selects the best service and binds to it to invoke it. As can be seen, the service broker is the central role in this architecture and many research approaches have been proposed realizing it, thus being able to perform the process of service discovery.

Initially, most service discovery approaches (Stroulia & Wang, 2005) focused on answering user queries concerning only the service functionality. In particular, they used techniques from Information Retrieval (Baeza-Yates & Ribeiro-Neto, 1999) and Software Engineering (Zaremski & Wing, 1997) to match service advertisements and offers focusing on the structure and textual content of these service specifications. However, the accuracy of the service results returned was low as the service description terms semantics was not captured. To this end, the next series of approaches solved this problem first by either annotating the service terms with concepts from domain ontologies (Plebani & Pernici, 2009) or using purely ontological service descriptions (Klusch, Fries, & Sycara, 2009; Cliffe & Andreou, 2009) and then by exploiting Semantic Web (SW) (Berners-Lee, Hendler, & Lassila, 2001) techniques in order to reason about the similarity of the compared semantically-enhanced service specifications.

However, no matter how well the functional service discovery is solved, it is just one aspect of the service discovery problem. In particular, many functionally-equivalent services may exist in various domains and there should be a way to further filter them. Moreover, service requesters should be assisted in selecting the best service from those discovered. The solution to these problems comes with the description of the Quality-of-Service (QoS) of services, the service advertisements filtering (i.e. QoS-based service matchmaking (QSM)) based on the advertized QoS capabilities (i.e. QoS offers) and the requester's QoS requirements (i.e. QoS demand), and the best service selection according to the requester's preferences.

Inspired by the solution adopted in service discovery, the current trend (Kritikos et al., 2010) in QoS-based Service Description (QSD) is to use ontologies to provide rich, extensible, and formal service QoS models so as to increase the accuracy of QoS-based service discovery. To this end, many service QoS models have been proposed using different ontology languages and presenting different coverage of the various QoS aspects. However, the lack of a standard service QoS model increases the probability that different QoS specifications (i.e. QoS offers and QoS demands) may be described through different QoS models. Moreover, this probability is further increased as users may have a different conceptualization of the same QoS concept and measurements of equivalent QoS metrics may be produced by readings of a different abstraction level (high vs. low) in different service instrumentation systems (Kritikos & Plexousakis, 2006). Thus, aligning (Bach et al., 2004) QoS specifications is required.

In this chapter, we claim that QoS attribute models (QoS model parts) are more-or-less standardized as researchers tend to agree on their content so we focus on aligning QoS specifications based on their QoS metrics. To this end, we shortly analyze a metric matching algorithm (Kritikos & Plexousakis, 2006) used to infer the equivalence between QoS metrics of the same or different QoS models. Then we present a novel QSD alignment algorithm (Kritikos, 2008) that exploits the metric matching algorithm. This algorithm relies on metric derivation trees, which describe the way composite QoS metrics are composed from other QoS metrics, and the metric store that stores the discovered QoS metric matches. Moreover, this algorithm is performed in such a way that the QoS metric-to-metric comparisons are minimal.

The alignment of QoS specifications is a serious step towards increasing the accuracy of QSM algorithms (Zhou, Chia, & Lee, 2004; Kritikos & Plexousakis, 2009a). These algorithms are able to match QSDs using two different and alternative techniques: subsumption reasoning and constraint solving. We argue that the second technique is better but requires an additional transformation step while its accuracy depends on two main factors: (a) the matchmaking metric adopted, and (b) the exploitation of QoS metric relationships especially in the case where QoS demand metrics are not contained in the QoS offers.

The second chapter contribution takes into account the above factors in order to improve the service results accuracy. In particular, apart from QoS metric equivalence, other metric relation types are exploited by QoS offer enrichment strategies (Kritikos, 2008), which can be executed solely or jointly so as to enrich the QoS offers with the missing metrics or with constraints connecting missing metrics with existing ones. Moreover, a new matchmaking metric is introduced that takes an open-world perspective, where QoS offers are not hardly penalized if they do not contain particular QoS metrics or attributes, and considers that the user's QoS requirements can be separated into obligatory and optional in order to provide meaningful results even when the overall user requirements are over-constrained. Two different matchmaking algorithms are proposed realizing this matchmaking metric, where the second one can also produce an advanced service results categorization but takes more time to execute than the first one.

Finally, the last chapter contribution involves exploring the Constraint Programming (CP) area (Rossi, Beek, & Walsh, 2006) and proposing a specific technique called explanation constraint programming (eCP) (Verfaillie & Jussien, July 2005) so as to effectively realize the proposed matchmaking metric. Moreover, an empirical randomized evaluation is presented that shows this technique effectiveness with respect to the normal CP techniques for equivalent realizations of the proposed metric.

BACKGROUND

QoS Definition

QoS of a service is a set of non-functional attributes of the entities used in the path from the service to the service requester that bear on the service ability to satisfy stated or implied needs in an end-to-end fashion (Kritikos & Plexousakis, 2009b). The QoS attribute values can vary without affecting the core service functionality, which remains usually constant during the service lifetime. In this way, the QoS of different but functionally-equivalent services can vary and thus can be used as a discriminating factor for filtering and choosing among these services. In fact, QoS can play a critical role during the whole service life-cycle, having a significant impact on the various life-cycle activities, and thus has grabbed the researchers' attention in the latest years.

QoS attributes can be domain-dependent or independent. For instance, *response time* is a domain-independent QoS attribute, while *routes set* is specific for the Vehicle Traffic Monitoring application domain. In addition, they can be measurable (e.g. *response time*) or unmeasurable (e.g. *routes set*). Unmeasurable QoS attributes represent static information which is qualitative in nature. They have a specific value type (e.g. {*inter-state, highways, local*} for *routes set*) and their values are not associated to a specific unit, i.e. they are unit-less. Measurable QoS attributes are described through the abstraction of *QoS metrics*, which describe all measurement details and the measurement procedure for a particular attribute. QoS metrics take values from a specific value type (e.g. positive integer) and these values are associated to a specific unit (e.g. seconds). They can be separated into *resource* and *composite* metrics. Resource metrics (e.g. *uptime*) are computed directly from the instrumentation of the service management system, while composite metrics (e.g. *availability*) are computed from other metrics through applying functions or formulas on the other metrics values.

A QoS specification is a collection (usually a conjunction) of linear and possibly non-linear constraints on variables representing QoS metrics and unmeasurable QoS attributes restricting the values that these variables can take. In most of the cases, QoS specifications contain unary linear QoS constraints involving only one quality term. For instance, the QoS specification

$$rt \leq 5 \wedge r\_set = \{highways, local\}$$

specifies that the *service response time* (represented by the *rt* variable) should be less than 5 (seconds) and that both highways and local routes should be supported (i.e. the *routes set* attribute represented by the *r_set* variable is restricted to contain the two desired values). However, n-ary and possibly non-linear constraints may appear in cases where dependencies between quality terms or cost models are expressed.

There are two QoS specification types: QoS offers and QoS requests. A QoS request is separated into a QoS demand and a QoS selection model. Both QoS offers and demands have similar content, where QoS offers describe the QoS capabilities of particular services, while QoS demands describe the service requester's QoS requirements. A QoS selection model is usually a tree-based representation of QoS attributes and metrics along with their accompanying weight denoting their significance

to the user. These models express user preferences and are used for performing service selection. As the latter models are not exploited and further investigated in this chapter, from now on the term QoS specification will be used to denote QoS offers and demands.

Apart from QoS specifications, another type of QSD is the QoS model (Kritikos et al., 2010). A QoS model comprises QoS categories, attributes, and metrics containing also the relations between these QoS entities. QoS models usually follow a specific structure. They contain a hierarchy or flat list of QoS categories. Each QoS category may contain QoS attributes and other QoS categories. Finally, in some QoS models some QoS attributes are associated with QoS metrics that measure them. As an example of a QoS model part, the *Reliability* QoS category may contain the QoS attributes of *availability* and *reliability*, where the latter attribute may be measured by QoS metrics such as *MTBF* (Mean-Time Between Failures). QoS models are referenced by QSDs or SLAs for populating QoS constraints with the corresponding quality term, i.e. QoS metric or attribute. In this way, they provide the concrete semantics of the quality terms used in QSDs and SLAs.

Various QoS models have been proposed in the literature (Sabata, Chatterjee, Davis, Sydir, & Lawrence, 1997; Anbazhagan & Nagarajan, 2002; Sumra & Arulazi, 2003; K. Lee, Jeon, Lee, Jeong, & Park, 2003; Ran, 2003; Liu et al., 2004; Cappiello, 2006; Cappiello et al., 2008; Kritikos & Plexousakis, 2009b; Mabrouk, Georgantas, & Issarny, 2009) that differ in their extensiveness, richness, and formality. However, none of these models satisfies the previous three criteria in a satisfactory way (Kritikos et al., 2010). Most QoS models describe domain-independent QoS attributes and metrics, which are mainly situated on the service layer, while both the infrastructure and business process management layers are scarcely captured. Very few QoS models define domain-dependent QoS attributes and metrics.

Finally, data quality issues are not taken into account (Kritikos et al., 2010).

As can be seen, there is no QoS model that is better than the others. On the contrary, it seems that QoS models are designed and used only for accompanying a specific research proposal. Thus, there is no commonly accepted QoS model that is widely used for populating QoS specifications and SLAs.

Languages and Meta-Models for QoS-Based Service Description

Both QoS specifications and models are defined by QoS meta-models or languages. The latter specify which quality concepts can be used in QSDs, what are their relationships, how they should be described and in which order or structure. Many QoS meta-models and languages (Frølund & Koistinen, 1998; Maximilien & Singh, 2002; Jin, Machiraju, & Sahai, 2002; Keller & Ludwig, 2003; Tian et al., 2003; Tosic, Pagurek, & Patel, 2003; Zhou, Chia, & Lee, 2004; Cortés, Martín-Díaz, Toro, & Toro, 2005; Oldham, Verma, Sheth, & Hakimpour, 2006; Kritikos & Plexousakis, 2006; Giallonardo & Zimeo, 2007) have been proposed by researchers that differ in their formality, richness, complexity, their ability to specify classes of service (i.e. different service levels), and other criteria (Kritikos et al., 2010).

By reviewing the work, a shift towards semantic/ontology-based meta-models and languages can be deduced. This is justified by the ability of these meta-models and languages to provide a formal meaning to quality-related concepts, so that they are human-understandable and machine-interpretable, while they also enable interoperability. Moreover, they are extensible and enable the use of SW techniques, which are used for performing reasoning on quality concepts and mapping between ontologies. Thus, they can be used by semantic frameworks for performing complex tasks such as service discovery and negotiation.

Among the semantic meta-models and languages, OWL-Q (Kritikos & Plexousakis, 2006) can be distinguished as the one that fulfils most of the previously referenced criteria, especially in terms of the richness of the modeling concepts and relationships used to define QoS specifications or models. OWL-Q is an upper ontology that provides a means for rich, semantic, and extensible QoS-based WS description. It has been carefully designed based on a set of QoS-based service description requirements (Kritikos & Plexousakis, 2006). OWL-Q complements OWL-S and comprises many sub-ontologies/facets. Each facet concentrates on a particular QoS modeling aspect and can be extended independently of the others.

The *QoSDimension* is OWL-Q's main element that can be attached to any service element (*ServiceElement*) to express its capabilities. A dimension has a *Name* attribute and can assume a set of values of a specific *ValueType*. Dimensions can be classified as *Categorical* or *Ordinal*. *Coverage* is a *Categorical* dimension example, where its value set is the list of mobile phone operators supported by the service, e.g., {Orange, Verizon}. An *Ordinal* dimension's value type is a range of values in which this dimension varies. For instance, *availability* can vary from [0%...100%]. Dimensions can be also classified as *Domain Independent*, so they can be used regardless of the considered service type (e.g., *response time* and *availability*), or *Domain Dependent* (e.g., *coverage*), which are related to an *Application domain*.

The OWL-Q Metric Facet defines the *Party* in charge of measuring a QoS dimension and the way the measurement takes place. A *Party* might be a *Provider*, a *Requester*, or a *Third-party*. Metrics encapsulate all the appropriate details for measuring a particular dimension. They can be classified as *SimpleMetric*s *measuredBy* a *Measurement-Directive* or *ComplexMetric*s derived from other metrics with the help of a *MetricFunction*. Metrics can be positively or negatively monotonic. In this way, it can be assessed if one metric's value is better than another value.

QoS Metric Matching

Equivalent QoS metrics may be specified in different ways and with different languages. This is justified as follows. First, people tend to have a different perception for the same concept. For example, they may use a different scale and value type for the same metric. Second, different system readings types may be available for the same metric in different service management systems. For instance, the *Downtime* QoS metric, measuring the percentage of time a service is unavailable, may be a resource metric derived from high-level readings in a system with advanced instrumentation, or it may be derived from the *Status* resource metric, denoting if a service is up or down, obtained from another system's low-level readings. Third, different but equivalent mathematical expressions can be used to define a composite metric. For example, assume that the derivation formulas for the composite metrics A_1 and A_2 are $\dfrac{B_2}{B_1 + B_2}$ and $1 - \dfrac{B_1}{B_1 + B_2}$, respectively. As these two formulas are equivalent, the two metrics should be equivalent. So, there is a need to map QoS metrics specified differently even with the same QoS language.

Our work (Kritikos & Plexousakis, 2006) covers this need by proposing a novel semantic QoS metric matching algorithm able to match two QoS metrics descriptions defined with OWL-Q. This algorithm comprises three main rules, where the first one is the logical disjunction of the remaining rules and is used to infer if the metrics are equivalent. The second rule is used to compare resource with either resource or composite metrics. It checks if the two metrics have compatible scales and value types, they concern the same service object (e.g. the service or its operation) and they measure the same QoS attribute.

The compatibility between scales and value types is computed as follows. If the scales are compatible (this can be deduced from facts fed into the system by domain experts), then the value type of the first metric is transformed into that of the second. Then it is checked if the percentage of common values between the transformed and the second value type with respect to the smallest value type is greater than a user-defined threshold. If this is true, then there is value-type compatibility, so it can be finally inferred that the two compared metrics have compatible scales and value-types.

It should be noted that the common values between value types are those belonging to the values types by definition, i.e. they represent all possible common values that the metrics can take. So these common values are not the actual measurement values that particular metrics take when they are applied on specific services, as these values may differ from service to service and represent a subset of the value set of the metrics value types.

The last rule is used to match two composite metrics. It is similar to the second one as it first performs the same checking, but it differs in the remaining two points. First, it executes a procedure that matches one-by-one the derivation metrics of the two compared metrics and whenever it encounters a match, it updates the derivation formula of one of the two metrics. Second, it checks the equivalence of the metrics' derivation formulas in two different ways: (a) using symbolic computation techniques to simplify the difference of the two derivation formulas and check if it equals to zero, and (b) solving a CSP constructed from the metrics' derivation formulas, where the same metrics are mapped to the same CSP variable. This CSP contains the constraint that the absolute difference between the metrics' derivation formulas is above a certain threshold (e.g. 10^{-6}). If this CSP does not have a solution then the metric derivation formulas are close enough, so we can infer that the compared metrics are more or less equivalent.

The two above techniques for inferring the equivalence between two metric derivation formulas can be used either alternatively, if we know which technique is better in which situation in terms of computation time, or in parallel so that the result of the quickest one can be exploited.

As the above algorithm is used as a component of the QoS-based WS specification alignment algorithm proposed in this chapter, an example of its application is provided. Suppose that there are two composite QoS metrics A_1 and A_2, both measuring the QoS attribute of *Availability*. The first metric is derived from the resource metrics D_1 and U_1, measuring the service *downtime* and *uptime* respectively, by using the derivation formula: $1 - \dfrac{D_1}{D_1 + U_1}$. The second metric is derived from the composite metrics D_2 and U_2, measuring again the service *downtime* and *uptime* respectively and obtained from the *status* resource metric, by using the derivation formula: $\dfrac{U_2}{D_2 + U_2}$. Further, suppose that all metrics have the same value type, i.e. the interval [0.0,1.0] of real numbers, and the same unit (thus also the same scale). Finally, suppose that by comparing the derivation metrics of the two compared metrics, it is inferred that D_1 and U_1 are equivalent to D_2 and U_2, respectively. In this way, the derivation formula of A_1 is transformed into: $1 - \dfrac{D_2}{D_2 + U_2}$. So, based on the third rule's last point, the simplification of the mathematical formula:

$$1 - \frac{D_2}{D_2 + U_2} - \frac{U_2}{D_2 + U_2}$$

produced from the difference between the compared metrics derivation formulas is attempted and yields zero, so the compared metrics are finally inferred to be equivalent.

Constraint Programming and Dynamic Constraint Satisfation

Constraint Programming

Constraint Programming (CP) is the study of computational models and systems based on constraints. Due to its strong theoretical foundation and ability to solve real-hard problems, it has been widely used in areas such as planning, scheduling, and optimization, and is attracting widespread commercial interest.

In CP, a problem is solved by first stating constraints about the problem area and, consequently, finding a solution that satisfies all the constraints through the facilities of a *solver*. Thus, constraints in CP are used to declaratively state the problem without specifying a computational procedure to enforce them. They are generally expressed by a rich language that includes linear, non-linear, and logical combinations of them. Actually, this language expressiveness depends on the capabilities of the underlying solver.

A problem in CP is named as a Constraint Satisfaction Problem (CSP) and is expressed as a set of constraints. It is formally represented by a set of variables V, a set of domain of values D, and a set of constraints C. The domain of values can be boolean, integers, reals, enumerations or power sets and may be associated to one or more variables. Constraints are expressed as mathematical or symbolic (global) expressions over a subset of V, restricting these variables values. A CSP *solution* is an assignment in which each variable of V takes a value from its corresponding domain in D as long as no constraint in C is violated by this value. The set of all solutions of the CSP is the CSP's *solution space*. A CSP is *satisfiable* if it has a non-empty solution space, i.e. it has at least one solution. For instance, the CSP $(\{x,y\}, \{[0...2],[0...2]\}, \{x>y, y>0\})$ is satisfiable as it has the sole solution of $\{x \rightarrow 2, y \rightarrow 1\}$.

Constraints in CP are used actively through the *constraint propagation* mechanism to deduce infeasible values and delete them from the variable domains. Each constraint computes infeasible values for the variables it contains and "informs" other constraints via the variable sharing mechanism, which is used to propagate this information among all constraints. The above process stops only when new deductions cannot be made. Due to its incompleteness, the constraint propagation mechanism is associated with *tree search techniques* so as to discover solutions or prove optimality.

Dynamic Constraint Satisfaction

Dynamic Constraint Satisfaction (DCS) (Verfaillie & Jussien, July 2005) is a specific CP area concerned with handling dynamicity in constraint specification. In DSC, a *dynamic constraint satisfaction problem* (DCSP) is a sequence of CSPs, each one produced from some changes in the definition of the previous one. A change may affect any part of problem definition: variables, domains, constraints, constraint scopes (addition or removal of a variable in constraint's definition), or constraint definitions (e.g change in the mathematical expression). As all of these change types can be expressed as constraint additions or removals, a DCSP is a sequence $\{P_0, P_1, \ldots, P_i, \ldots, P_n\}$ where, for each i, $1 \leq i \leq n$, P_i is a CSP, C_{a_i} is a set of added constraints, C_{r_i} is a set of removed constraints, such as

$$C_{r_i} \subseteq P_i, \text{ and } P_i = P_{i-1} + C_{a_i} - C_{r_i}$$

There are two categories of approaches devised for solving DCSPs. *Proactive* approaches assume that the modeler provides to the system not only the constraints definition but also information about the possible changes and sometimes about their absolute or relative likelihood of occurrence. *Reactive* approaches use no information about the possible directions of the future changes but try to record, when solving, some potentially useful

information that will help them anticipate any possible change.

Reactive approaches try to reuse as much as possible the previous problem solving knowledge in order to solve the new problem. They are separated into *solution reuse* and *reasoning reuse* approaches. Solution reuse approaches try to reuse the previous solution in order to build the new one based on the assumption that as the previous CSP P_{i-1}, that is solved and has the solution S_{i-1}, is very close to the new one P_i, then a solution S_i of P_i can be searched for in the vicinity of S_{i-1}. Reasoning reuse approaches try to reuse the set I of implied constraints (constraints consequences) of CSP P_{i-1}, which was found to be consistent or inconsistent, based on the assumption that as P_{i-1} is very close to the new P_i then most constraints in I will remain valid in P_i. Thus, by recording the constraints in I that will certainly be valid and not producing them again, search efficiency is greatly favored.

Reasoning reuse techniques differ from each other only in the information they use to determine whether an implied constraint in I becomes questionable. This results in three families of methods: (1) graph-based, (2) justification-based, and (3) explanation-based methods. The latter two methods are more time and space consuming when producing implied constraints and their justifications or explanations. However, they exploit recorded information in such way that allows fewer constraints in case of justifications, and even no constraints in case of explanations, to be checked in order to maintain valid implied constraints.

QoS-Based Service Matchmaking

Two main techniques are used to perform QSM in the current research proposals. Both techniques enforce particular matchmaking metrics that formally describe the conditions under which two QoS specifications (i.e. QoS offer and demand) should match. Both techniques are also able to exploit QoS specifications defined by quite expressive languages or meta-models. The first technique uses subsumption reasoning to infer the match between QoS specifications based on the matchmaking metric adopted (Zhou, Chia, & Lee, 2004; Oldham, Verma, Sheth, & Hakimpour, 2006; Giallonardo & Zimeo, 2007). However, this technique is rather slow and appropriate only for QoS specifications containing just unary constraints (i.e. constraints involving one QoS metric/attribute) as it does not exploit constraint propagation mechanisms.

The second technique (Cortés, Martín-Díaz, Toro, & Toro, 2005; Degwekar, Su, & Lam, 2004; Kritikos & Plexousakis, 2009a) transforms the QoS specifications into one or more constraint models, according to the matchmaking metric adopted, and then uses a constraint solver to solve them. Based on the solving results, it is inferred if a match exists or not between the compared QoS specifications. Depending on the linearity of the constraints contained in the QoS models, different constraint solving techniques can be selected (e.g. mixed-integer programming (Schrijver, 1986) for linear constraints or CP if also non-linear constraints are involved) (Kritikos & Plexousakis, 2009a).

The second technique is more efficient as it is quicker and able to match n-ary constrained QoS specifications through its constraint propagation mechanisms. Thus, it is selected for performing QSM in the second chapter contribution. To this end, a small analysis of this technique follows.

According to the constraint solving technique, both QoS offers and demands are specified in a high-level language (e.g. QRL (Cortés, Martín-Díaz, Toro, & Toro, 2005) or OWL-Q), where the QoS metrics are either completely specified or referenced from common QoS catalogs that define them. Figure 1 shows a small example of the contents of one QoS offer and demand and one QoS catalog specified with the QRL language. Although QRL is not as expressive as some ontology-based languages such as OWL-Q, it was selected for economy of space reasons as it can express in a more compact way a QoS specification with respect to ontology-based languages.

After a QoS specification is issued to the QoS-based service matchmaker, it is transformed into a CSP which is checked for consistency, i.e. if it has any solution. If the CSP is inconsistent, then the specification is returned to the issuer. Otherwise, the specification is further processed. QoS offers are stored in the matchmaker, while QoS

Figure 1. An example of a QoS offer, demand, and a QoS catalog

```
catalog QoS{
AvgExTime{
 description: "Average Exec. Time";
 domain: integer [1,inf] second;
 property: ExecutionTime;
}
AvgAvail{
 description: "Average Availability";
 domain: real [0.0,1.0] percentage;
 property: Availability;
}
PR{
 description: "Service Price";
 domain real [0 inf] euro;
 property: Price;
}
}
```

a) QoS Catalog

```
using QoS;

requires{
AvgExTime>=3 and AvgExTime<=5;
AvgAvail>=0.95 and
AvgAvail<=0.999;
PR>=100 and PR<=300;
}
```

b) QoS Demand

```
using QoS;

requires{
AvgExTime>=3 and AvgExTime<=6;
AvgAvail>=0.96;
PR>=150 and PR<=275;
}
```

c) QoS Offer

Figure 2. The QoS-based service publication and matchmaking procedure for constraint-based matchmakers

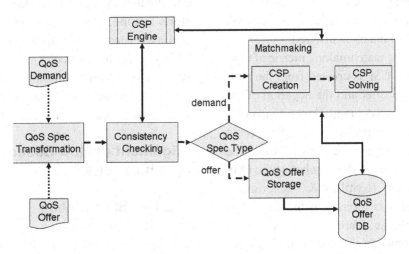

demands are compared with QoS offers according to the matchmaking metric adopted and then their results are returned. The publication and matchmaking procedure of a constraint-based matchmaker is depicted in Figure 2.

When matchmaking a QoS offer with a QoS demand, one or more CSPs are created from the two specifications and solved. In these CSPs, the same metrics are mapped to the same CSP variable. Depending on the results found from CSP solving, the matching is either inferred or not.

Figure 3 illustrates the CSP (having similar syntax with ILOG's OPL (http://www.ilog.com/products/oplstudio/)) that is produced from the QoS offer and demand of Figure 1 according to the matchmaking metrics of the works of Degwekar et al. (2004) and Cortés et al. (2005). According to the matchmaking metric of the first work, one CSP is produced from the compared QoS specifications, containing the constraints defined in both specifications. In this way, a match is inferred if there is a common solution between

Figure 3. The CSPs of the two matchmaking metrics

```
var int x1 in 0..inf;
var float x2 in 0.0..1.0;
var float x3 in 0.0..inf;

solveCSP{
  x1>=3;
  x1<=6;
  x2>=0.96;
  x3>=150;
  x3<=275;
  x1>=3;
  x1<=5;
  x2>=0.95;
  x2<=0.999;
  x3>=100;
  x3<=300;
}
```

a) Degwekar et al. metric

```
var int x1 in 0..inf;
var float x2 in 0.0..1.0;
var float x3 in 0.0..inf;

solveCSP{
  x1>=3;
  x1<=6;
  x2>=0.96;
  x3>=150;
  x3<=275;
  not(x1>=3 & x1<=5 & x2>=0.95 &
    x2<=0.999 & x3>=100 &
    x3<=300
  );
}
```

b) Cortés et al. metric

the QoS offer and demand. As can be seen from the corresponding CSP of Figure 3, indeed there is a common solution between the compared QoS specifications, so a match is inferred.

According to the matchmaking metric of Cortés et al. (2005), a CSP is created from the constraints of the QoS offer and the negation of the constraints of the QoS demand. Depending on the availability of the *not* operator in the CSP solving engine, either one or a series of CSPs may be created corresponding to the number of the QoS demand constraints (Kritikos & Plexousakis, 2009a). The match is inferred if the CSP(s) is (are) unsatisfiable, i.e. there is no solution to it (them). The rationale of this metric is that there is a match only if the QoS offer is conformant to the QoS demand, i.e. if it only contains solutions that are contained in the solution space of the QoS demand. The corresponding CSP of Figure 3 has a solution, so the match between the QoS offer and demand is not inferred.

CHAPTER CONTRIBUTIONS

This section provides an analysis of the various research contributions. These contributions concern the alignment of QoS-based service specifications, the proposal of a novel QoS-based WS matchmaking metric and of two algorithms realizing it, and the empirical evaluation of the proposed algorithms implemented using plain and eCP techniques. Each contribution is analyzed in its own subsection, while each subsection is separated into two sub-subsections: the first subsection explains what is the problem to be solved, while the second one analyzes this chapter's contribution towards solving the problem.

Before analyzing the chapter contributions, it is imperative to state that the first two contributions enhance and extend the publication and matchmaking procedure of a constraint-based QoS-aware service matchmaker in two main points, as can be seen in Figure 4. First, before a QoS specification

is transformed into a CSP, it is first aligned according to the contents of a QoS metric database/ store. Second, before any QoS offer is matched with a QoS demand, it is first enriched through the addition of constraints on QoS demand's metrics which were initially missing from the offer. As it will be demonstrated later on, these extensions increase the accuracy of the service matchmaker.

Alignment of QoS-Based Service Specifications

Problem Specification

The previous section indicated that many QoS meta-models have been proposed in the literature, each one used in one or few particular research prototypes. Thus, a QoS-based WS matchmaker should be able to align all QoS specifications taken out of various QoS repositories situated in other matchmakers/brokers or issued by the WS users in order to integrate these repositories and support any type of WS user that utilizes different QoS meta-models. So, QoS specification alignment algorithms have to be devised.

As QoS meta-models and languages use more or less similar concepts (Kritikos et al., 2010), it is adequate to use existing schema matching or ontology alignment algorithms in order to align the QoS specifications. However, the previous section indicated that the alignment of QoS specifications should also consider the metric descriptions or references in these specifications. Another reason for aligning QoS specifications based on metrics concerns the way QSM is performed by adopting the constraint solving techniques. A CSP is created from the QoS offer and demand, where the same QoS metric is mapped to the same CSP variable. Thus, in order not to reduce the accuracy of the QSM algorithm, the equivalence between QoS metrics of different QoS specifications or models should be inferred.

The current approaches on ontology alignment and schema matching are not able to cor-

Figure 4. The extended QoS-based service publication and matchmaking procedure for constraint-based matchmakers

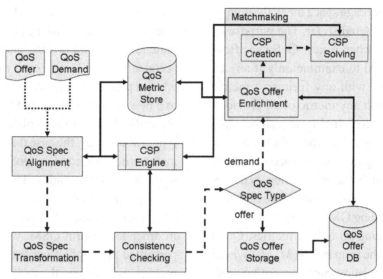

rectly infer if two QoS metrics defined through different specifications are equivalent due to two main reasons. First, some approaches can only map concepts that have concrete instances. However, the current QSD approaches specify concrete QoS metrics either at the concept or at the instance level. In the former case, QoS metrics do not have instances, so these approaches fail. In the latter case, these approaches can only be used for inferring if the QoS metric concepts in the QoS specifications are equivalent. Second, those approaches that use pure concept/schema-level information for specification alignment cannot infer if two concrete QoS metrics at the concept-level are equivalent. This is because they exploit only the concept/schema structure and not the actual semantic information in terms of the metric derivation formulas that describe the way a particular metric is derived from other metrics. For instance, they can infer that two metrics (e.g. *uptime* and *downtime*) are equivalent as they are derived from the same metric set (e.g. the *status* metric) without inspecting the actual way these two metrics are derived from this metric set.

Only one QoS metric matching algorithm has been proposed in the literature (Kritikos &

Plexousakis, 2006), which takes into account the semantics of QoS metrics in terms of their derivation formulas. This algorithm adopts OWL-Q and assumes that the input QoS (metric) specifications are described with this language. In this way and as it was indicated before, if QoS specifications are defined by different ontologies, it is assumed that ontology alignment algorithms are used to transform the QoS specifications to OWL-Q ones. However, this algorithm is not able to align QoS specifications.

The strategy followed to solve the above problems is to propose a novel QoS specification aligment algorithm that exploits the previous QoS metric algorithm in order to align QoS specifications in an efficient and cost-effective way, where metric-to-metric comparisons are minimal and the recursiveness of the third metric matching rule is avoided.

The Alignment Algorithm

The QoS specification alignment algorithm proposed (Kritikos, 2008) aims at aligning a new OWL-Q specification with all the previously processed ones through the use of the QoS metric matching algorithm. To this end, it relies on the facilities provided by a *QoS Metric Store* (QMS). QMS is a semantic storage space for all the unique QoS metrics encountered so far. The purpose of using QMS is that when a new QoS specification arrives, we need to examine only if any of its metrics matches with any (primary) metric in QMS and not with any metric of all previous specifications processed. In this way, all possible metric-to-metric comparisons are minimized and a common terminology across all processed specifications is enforced. In the end, the matched QoS metrics of this new specification will be replaced with the corresponding QMS metrics.

Apart from storing all unique metrics, QMS also stores facts of the form *match*(M_1,M_2), where *match* is a semantic relationship between QoS metrics denoting metric equivalence. This semantic relationship's domain contains *Primary* metrics, i.e. metrics used for performing the alignment task as their discovered equivalent metrics have to be aligned or transformed to them. This relationship's range contains *Secondary* metrics, i.e. metrics that cannot be used in the alignment task. In this way, when a QoS metric M of a new QoS specification has to be examined, one semantic query is first issued to check if the metric is already stored in QMS, what is its type, and its primary equivalent metrics (returned only for secondary metrics). If the metric is not unique and secondary, then we align it with its primary equivalent one. If the metric is unique, then it is stored in QMS and we try to find its equivalent metric through the QoS metric matching algorithm iterating over all primary metrics. Thus, if a new QoS metric M is found to be equivalent to a Primary metric M', then a fact in the form *match*(M, M') is inserted in QMS.

Two points have to be made about QMS and the metric matching. First, OWL-Q was extended appropriately through the definition of the *match* semantic relationship and the *isPrimary* boolean property defined for QoS metrics and indicating if the metric is primary or not. Second, we assume

that if a new QoS metric is equivalent to a secondary one, then it should also be equivalent to the primary metric that is equivalent to the secondary one. So, it is required to check if a new QoS metric matches only with primary metrics and not with secondary ones. However, it must be noted that when a primary metric is found to be equivalent to a new one, then the value type of the primary metric becomes the union of the two metrics value types. In this way, the case that a new QoS metric matches only a secondary QoS metric and not also a primary one is avoided. This means that while QoS specifications may be aligned immediately, only when we transform them to constraint models in order to perform QSM, we define the actual permitted range of values for the (primary) QoS metrics that become the model variables.

The QMS can be imagined as a forest of *metric derivation trees*. Each such tree contains QoS metrics that measure the same QoS property on the same service element/object (e.g. the service itself, one of its operations, etc.). It should be noted that the system maintains apart from the QMS a list of QoS properties that is dynamically updated whenever a new metric measuring a new QoS property is inserted, and a fixed list of service elements on which metrics can be applied.

In a metric derivation tree, there are two types of edges. *Derivation edges* connect the parent nodes to its children. They indicate that the parent metric is derived from its children through the use of a formula or function. As such, the leaves of a metric derivation tree represent resource metrics and have a level of one, while the nodes on the levels above represent composite metrics. The level of each composite metric equals the maximum level of its children plus one. Apart from derivation edges, *matching* edges connect equivalent metrics with each other, which can be on the same or different level. A simplified example of a metric derivation tree is given in Figure 5, where only derivation edges are displayed. This example shows how a QoS metric (denoted by the root node) measuring the average *execution time* of the whole service

Figure 5. A simplified example of a metric derivation tree

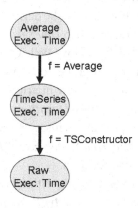

is derived from another metric, which represents a TimeSeries computed from raw execution time measurements provided by a resource metric, which is denoted by the tree leaf node.

The QoS specification alignment algorithm takes as input an OWL-Q specification Q in order to align it. Its aim is to align Q so as to contain references only to primary QoS metrics. To this end, each metric of Q that appears in Q's constraints is examined if it is primary or not. If not, then all references to this metric are updated to point to its equivalent metric. If the metric is new, then all its descendant metrics are examined from the bottom of its derivation tree to the top and the corresponding alignment actions are performed. In this way, all metrics are processed, including the ones that are indirectly referenced in Q as descendants of metrics participating in the constraints. Moreover, based on the way the alignment actions are performed it is guaranteed that primary metrics are derived only from primary metric descendants.

The algorithm's procedure is as follows:

For each QoS metric M_i of Q of level y that appears in the constraints of Q, from the lowest level until the upmost, find if M_i is already in QMS, based on the procedure described above.

- If yes, then:

  ◦ If M_i is primary, go to the next metric of Q.

  ◦ Otherwise, find the primary metric QMS_l that is equivalent to M_i. Then, perform the alignment of the Q's constraints from M_i to QMS_l. If M_i is a child of other metrics of Q that appear in Q's constraints, then align their derivation formula accordingly.

- Otherwise:

  1. Find the corresponding derivation tree T_k in QMS containing primary metrics QMS_l measuring the same QoS property on the same WS element as M_i.

  2. For each descendant metric M_{ik} of M_i of level x (which is not already present in Q's constraints), from the lowest level to the upmost, that has not been already processed from the alignment algorithm on Q, find if it is already in QMS.

     ▪ If yes, then:

If M_{ik} is primary, go to the next descendant metric of M_i.

Otherwise, find the primary metric M_{ik}' that is equivalent to M_{ik}. Then, align the derivation formula of the parents of M_{ik} accordingly.

     ▪ Otherwise, compare M_{ik} with those primary metrics QMS_l in T_k that have levels $x - 1$, x and $x + 1$ with the QoS metric matching algorithm.

If a match is found between M_{ik} and one QMS_l, then stop the search for the M_{ik} metric, insert into the QMS both the M_{ik} as a secondary metric and the fact *match*(QMS_l, M_{ik}), and align the derivation formulas of the parents of M_{ik}.

If no match is found at all, insert M_{ik} in QMS as primary.

  3. After all its descendant metrics have been processed, compare M_i with those primary metrics QMS_l in T_k that have levels $y - 1$, y and $y + 1$ with the QoS metric matching algorithm.

- If no match is found at all, put M_i in QMS as primary and go to the next metric of Q.
- Otherwise, if a match is found between M_i and one QMS_l, then stop the search for M_i, insert into the QMS both M_i as a secondary metric and the fact $match(QMS_l, M_i)$, and then perform the alignment of Q's constraints from M_i to QMS_l. If M_i is a child of other metrics of Q that appear in Q's constraints, then align their derivation formula.

The alignment of constraints and derivation formulas from M_i to QMS_l is performed by replacing M_i with the mathematical expression produced from the application of a scale-to-scale transformation function from the scale of QMS_l to the scale of M_i on QMS_l. Obviously, all references to M_i are now updated by pointing to QMS_l.

It should be noted that based on the real-world practice, the existing service instrumentation systems are not able to produce equivalent metrics belonging to levels with great difference (e.g. greater than three). That is why in this algorithm a metric is compared only with metrics that belong either to the same level or to one level up or down its own level.

A small example of the alignment algorithm's application is the following. Suppose that QMS is initially empty and that an OWL-Q specification Q_1 containing constraints on the previously referenced *Average Exec. Time* metric is issued (i.e. from the metric derivation tree example). The alignment algorithm would first insert the resource metric *Raw Exec. Time*, then the composite metric *TimeSeries Exec. Time* and finally the *Average Exec. Time* metric into the QMS as primary metrics. So Q_1 will not be actually affected and will still contain a reference to a primary metric derived only from primary metric descendants. Further, suppose that the *Average Exec. Time* metric has as

scale *MinutesDuration* and value type the real set [0.0, 2.0], while it is derived from the *TimeSeries Exec. Time* metric through the derivation formula $avg(Y)$, where Y is bound to *TimeSeries Exec. Time*. Finally, suppose that a new OWL-Q specification Q_2 is issued containing the constraint $X >= 100$, where X is bound to a new metric *AvgExecTime* that has as scale *Seconds-Duration* and value type the integer set [1, 120]. This new metric is also derived from the *TimeSeries Exec. Time* metric through the same formula.

When the alignment algorithm is executed on Q_2, it will discover that the *AvgExecTime* metric is new and its ancestor metrics are already contained in QMS as primary metrics. Then, it will discover that there is a match between *Average Exec. Time* and *AvgExecTime*, as these two metrics are composite, have compatible scales and value types, and are derived from the same metric through the same formula. So it will insert this match into QMS. Next, the algorithm will rebind X to the *Average Exec. Time* metric, which is the primary metric from the matched metric pair, and will transform the Q_2's constraint to the constraint $60 \cdot X >= 100$ as the scale-to-scale transformation function from *MinutesDuration* to *Seconds-Duration* is as follows: $f(X) = 60 \cdot X$. In other words, this scale-to-scale transformation function will be applied to the X variable and the result will be used to replace X in the Q_2's constraint. In addition, *AvgExecTime* will be inserted in QMS as a secondary metric. It is now obvious that Q_2 contains a new constraint that refers to a primary metric derived only from primary metric descendants.

Novel QoS-Based Web Service Matchmaking Metric and Algorithms

Problem Specification

As it was indicated in the previous section, QMS algorithms that adopt Constraint Solving techniques are better than ontology-based ones and rely on a particular matchmaking metric when matching a QoS offer with a QoS demand. However, such algorithms suffer from the following problems.

First, the matchmaking metric may be erroneous leading to accuracy problems. A matchmaking metric is a criterion dictating which QoS offers match a specific QoS demand. Thus, when applying it, two main categories of QoS offers are produced: *exact* and *fail*. However, a matchmaking metric may suffer from the false positives or false negatives effect or both. In this way, its accuracy is reduced. False positives are produced when a QoS offer is categorized as exact while does not actually match a QoS demand. False negatives are produced when a QoS offer is categorized as false while it actually matches a QoS demand.

Considering the matchmaking metrics discussed in the previous section, the Degwekar et al. metric is erroneous as it suffers from the false positives effect. To explain, when a QoS offer promises both solutions that are worse and equivalent to the ones requested by the QoS demand, it is matched with it. However, it should not match the QoS demand as it may provide worse performance than the one requested. Following the previous section's example, the QoS offer

promises that the service response time will be less or equal to 6 seconds while the QoS demand requests this response time to be less or equal to 5 seconds. As nothing guarantees the user that the service will respond to its request in less than 6 seconds, the QoS offer should not match the QoS demand. However, even the wrong results produced by applying this metric are useful during service negotiation, as the WS requester may come into an agreement with the WS provider to finally constrain the response time to be less than 6 seconds.

The matchmaking metric of Cortés et al. is better but suffers from the false negatives effect when WS requesters restrict the best values that particular metrics can take. Consider a slightly changed version of the example of Figure 1, which is given in Figure 6, where the QoS offer promises that response time will be less or equal to 5 seconds (instead of 6). While the best value (i.e. the lowest bound) of service response time should be constrained as it may have an impact on the quality of the service result produced, the best value of service availability should not be restricted as the service should be as available

Figure 6. Slightly changed version of the Figure 1 example, where the QoS offer's upper bound on average execution time has been altered

```
catalog QoS{
 AvgExTime{
  description: "Average Exec. Time";
  domain: integer [1,inf] second;
  property: ExecutionTime;
 }
 AvgAvail{
  description: "Average Availability";
  domain: real [0.0,1.0] percentage;
  property: Availability;
 }
 PR{
  description: "Service Price";
  domain real [0 inf] euro;
  property: Price;
 }
}
```

a) QoS Catalog

```
using QoS;

requires{
 AvgExTime>=3 and AvgExTime<=5;
 AvgAvail>=0.95 and
 AvgAvail<=0.999;
 PR>=100 and PR<=300;
}
```

b) QoS Demand

```
using QoS;

requires{
 AvgExTime>=3 and AvgExTime<=5;
 AvgAvail>=0.96;
 PR>=150 and PR<=275;
}
```

c) QoS Offer

as possible to its requesters. In this regard, the updated QoS offer matches the QoS demand as it promises even better solutions but according to the Cortés et al. metric it is a fail match as it provides a solution that is not requested by the QoS demand. Figure 7 shows the possible solution space of four QoS offers and one QoS demand and which QoS offers are considered as matches by which matchmaking metric. The discussion about which QoS metrics should have both lower and upper bounds or only one bound on the worse value will be continued later on.

Second, matchmaking metrics do not consider that a QoS offer may not provide constraints on some of the QoS demand metrics. Such a QoS offer is characterized as *incomplete*, while the ones that contain constraints involving all QoS demand metrics are characterized as *complete*. To this end, the existing realizations of the matchmaking metrics consider that incomplete QoS offers are handled in the same way as the complete ones and take an open world perspective where a QoS offer is examined based only on the constraints and metrics that it exposes. In this way, incomplete QoS offers that contain just one constraint involving only one metric can be placed in the exact category with complete QoS offers if their constraint conforms (matches) to the QoS demand constraints However, there can be cases

where such QoS offers can be quite worse than what is expected by the WS requester with respect to the values that the rest of the metrics can take. On the other hand, if the incomplete QoS offer is penalized to enter the fail category by considering that it may provide worse constraints on the QoS metrics that are missing, then there can be many cases where such decision ends up to be wrong.

Thus, based on the above analysis, none of the sketched solutions is (absolutely) correct due to the uncertainty of what happens to the rest of the performance of an incomplete QoS offer. This creates the need of devising a new approach that may possibly propose a compromised solution that lies between the sketched solutions, providing a fair and more correct way to categorize both complete and incomplete QoS offers, and takes into account both the WS providers and requesters' interests.

Third, there is no advanced result categorization. The simple categorization of QoS offers as matching and failing does not provide a great insight to the WS requester about how to further distinguish between a specific category's members. In particular, there is no way to distinguish about which exact QoS offers are better, i.e. they offer better solutions than the one expected. In this way, the user has to sort the offers himself and select the one that better suits his interests. Moreover, there is no way to distinguish between

Figure 7. Solution space for 4 QoS offers and 1 QoS demand and characterization of the exact matches produced by the matchmaking metrics of Degwekar et al. (2004) and Cortés et al. (2005)

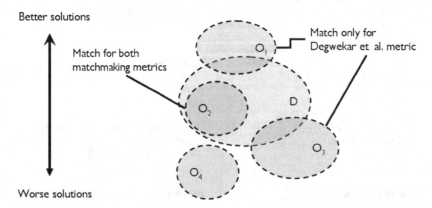

QoS offers violating all QoS demand constraints and the ones violating some of them. Such a distinction would be fruitful in case the QoS demand is over-constrained, i.e. it requests a better performance than the one that can be offered by existing services, as it could enable the user to concentrate on the QoS offers that violate some of the constraints of the QoS demand in order to take a rationale and compromised selection decision. Ideally, a fine-grained categorization would eliminate the need for performing service selection, but it could lead to a more time-consuming QSM process. Thus, a compromise should be made between the categorization granularity and the QSM time.

Fourth, the algorithms do not provide interesting results for over-constrained QoS demands. This can be possible in specific domains, or when users are not aware of the situation concerning service performance in their application domain. This is closely related to the previous problem as a better categorization of the failing results would reveal the results that are useful to the user. Thus, it is better that a QSM algorithm also proposes to users which failing QoS offers violate in the least possible way their QoS demand constraints so as to select them. Moreover, it would be advantageous to reveal which minimum constraint combinations have to be updated to enable the user to proceed with the appropriate QoS demand adjustments and make a new request that will result in the certain production of exact results.

The Matchmaking Metric and Algorithm

The above four problems have to be solved, as they influence the accuracy, effectiveness, and appropriateness of the constraint-based QSM metric and algorithms. This section aims at solving all of them by proposing QoS offer enrichment strategies, a novel QSM metric, and two algorithms realizing it.

QoS Offer Enrichment Strategies

The second problem, concerning the uncertainty of the incomplete QoS offers performance, can be partially solved by proposing QoS offer enrichment strategies that enrich QoS offers with constraints involving the missing QoS demand constraints. If such strategies are complemented by the application of an appropriate QSM metric, then the second problem can be completely solved. In the following, we analyze two QoS offer enrichment strategies and a possible way to combine them (Kritikos, 2008). It should be noted that the updates on the QoS offers have a local scope, i.e. they apply only for performing QSM with a specific QoS demand, unless their corresponding provider agrees to make them permanent. Of course, it would be interesting to save such updates and correlate them with the affected QoS offer, the strategy that enforced them, and possibly the reasoning steps behind these updates so as to re-use them when similar QoS demands are issued and not execute again particular QoS offer enrichment strategies.

The *Resource Exploitation Strategy* is the simplest strategy. According to this strategy, the (usually unary) constraints on the missing metrics are either provided from the corresponding WS provider by making an appropriate request or are derived from measurements coming from various known sources, including the actual service management system, third-parties measurement systems, and user feedback. Some source types are made known to the system either by the service provider, or are defined in particular QoS specification parts. Other sources constitute cooperating entities with the matchmaking system such as third-party measurement systems and user feedback and analysis systems. In addition, the matchmaker can act as a measurement or user feedback system itself and collect the required information.

Either directly or indirectly (i.e. when the WS provider supplies the additional constraints), statistical processing of the measurements is required. In particular, the measurements of those resource metrics that constitute the metric derivation tree of the missing composite metric are collected and propagated up to this metric by using mathematical and statistical functions. In case these measurements are not available for specific time periods or instances, then temporal database techniques are required for producing them.

As a concrete example of the application of this strategy, assume that a QoS offer does not contain constraints on metrics concerning the service reliability, availability, and reputation. Then, the service reliability could be produced by issuing the corresponding request to the service provider. The service availability could be measured by a third-party measurement system that performs an on-line testing of the service in a specific time period. Finally, the service reputation could be obtained by exploiting sophisticated techniques that collect the user feedback and evaluate it according to the user expectations.

A QoS offer enrichment becomes permanent only when the corresponding WS provider agrees with it and the additional information that is revealed. In this way, competitors can be prevented from exploiting this strategy in order to obtain sensitive information, such as the service complete performance or actual cost model, through the repeated issuing of QoS demands with different QoS metrics and constraints. An additional preventive action could be to block requests, either originating from the same source or being timely correlated, involving the same service with different QoS demands. Another disadvantage of this strategy is that it may be ineffective, i.e. it may not be able to derive constraints for all the missing metrics. The use of temporal database techniques remedies this problem but it cannot work when no measurements can be found for particular resource metrics.

Despite of its two main disadvantages, the major advantage of this strategy is that it provides unary constraints on the missing metrics. In this

way, the constraint-based QSM algorithms can solve the corresponding conformance CSPs in less time.

The *Mathematical Derivation* strategy aims at producing constraints by exploiting the relationships of the missing metrics with all the QoS offer metrics through the exploration of metric derivation trees.

The formal representation of the problem that this strategy tries to solve is as follows. Assume that there is a QoS offer O and a QoS demand D to be matched. Further, assume that there are M metrics in O and N metrics that are contained in D but are missing from O. The problem is how to alter O so as to enrich it with constraints that involve a metric N_k in N and one or more of the metrics in M. The two following cases are explored with decreasing order of significance in order to solve this problem:

1. A metric M_i is derived from a N_k metric or the opposite. For instance, M_i may be produced from metrics L and N_k by the expression f(x, y), where x is bound to L and y to N_k. Then, O will be altered by just adding the constraint $z = $ f(x, y), where z is bound to M_i, x to L and y to N_k. In this way, when a constraint c of D involving N_k is combined with all constraints of O (including the new one), then the values that both M_i and N_k can take will get more restricted. In the opposite case where N_k may be produced from metrics L and M_i by the expression g(x, y), where x is bound to L and y to M_i, O will be altered by adding the constraint $z = $ g(x, y), where z is bound to N_k, x to L and y to M_i. In both cases, N_k will be removed from N. However, the biggest issue is what happens with L. If L is missing (i.e. N_k is the only child of M_i) or is already contained in M or has a very small cardinality, then nothing remains to be done and the cardinality of N is reduced, which is the main object of research. Otherwise, L has to be added to N, so the cardinality

of N remains the same. The latter must be avoided at all costs as it can cause the indefinite execution of this strategy, so the offer's enrichment should not be enforced at this occasion. As another more concrete example, suppose M_i is *AvgServiceLatency* and N_k is *AvgExecutionTime*. In addition, suppose that the M_i's derivation formula is: $M_i = N_k + L$, where L is *AvgServiceQueueDelay*. Then, we will insert the derivation formula of M_i into O as a constraint and we may also add L to N. This will depend on the cardinality of L.

2. Metrics M_i and N_k are derived from the same child L. Then, we check the metrics derivation formulas in order to provide a constraint that involves them. For instance, if M_i is *Average Exec. Time* produced by the *TimeSeries Exec. Time* metric through the expression avg(x) and N_k is *Max Exec. Time* produced from *TimeSeries Exec. Time* with the expression max(x), then we can add to O the constraint $X <= Y$, where X is bound to *Average Exec. Time* and Y to *Max Exec. Time*. As it will not be always possible to derive such a constraint, we have put this case as second and not first.

It is quite obvious that this strategy is not as effective as the first because it will not always be possible to derive metric relationships between the metrics of the QoS demand that are missing from a QoS offer and the metrics contained in the QoS offer. Moreover, this strategy fails when a metric Nk in N has a derivation tree that is disjointed with all the derivation trees of the metrics in M.

There are three ways to combine the two strategies: two indicating sequential execution, where the missing metrics that one strategy fails to cover are given as input to the other strategy, and their interleaving. Moreover, it should be stated that all these combinations must be coupled with specific deadlines so that the offer enrich-

ment does not take significant time of the whole matchmaking process.

The most effective strategy combination is the one of interleaving, which exploits the two strategies in such a way that restrictive constraints involving missing metrics are quickly discovered. However, such combination is considered as a significant future step. In this chapter, the execution sequence of the resource exploitation strategy followed by the mathematic derivation one is proposed. This is because the resource exploitation strategy provides more restrictive constraints on the missing metrics with respect to the other strategy. Moreover, in this strategy there are two actual ways to obtain constraints on missing metrics, i.e. first the QoS offer's provider can choose which additional constraints he may reveal for the missing metrics and then the constraints for the remaining missing metrics can be derived from measurements. So, there is a considerable chance that many metrics may be covered.

Novel QoS-Based Service Matchmaking Metric

The first two problems of the constrained-based QSM algorithms, i.e. the erroneous matchmaking metrics and the categorization of incomplete QoS offers, are solved by introducing a novel matchmaking metric that is more accurate than the others and is able to deal with incomplete QoS offers in a more fair way. This metric also partially solves the last problem of returning interesting results for over-constrained QoS demands. A complete solution to the last two problems is offered by the algorithms realizing this metric.

The proposed matchmaking metric, which is called *Soft Conditional Conformance (SCC)*, is actually a small modification to the metrics of Cortés et al. (2005) and Kritikos and Plexousakis (2009a) that also requires the separation of the QoS demand constraints into *hard* and *soft*. Hard constraints should be met at all costs, while soft constraints do not cause a QoS offer penalization but they can be used for distinguishing between QoS offers of the same category, e.g. for further categorization of the basic categories of exact and fail matches. For this reason, soft constraints are not involved when applying this metric to a QoS offer and demand pair. In this way, as some QoS demand constraints are not considered during matchmaking, there is an increased chance that QoS offers may match an over-constrained QoS demand. However, this novel matchmaking metric partially solves the last problem because even if some constraints are neglected during matchmaking, this does not necessarily mean that the QoS demand will cease to be over-constrained.

Based on the SCC metric, a QoS offer and demand match if and only if the QoS offer metrics are a superset of those QoS demand metrics (which are called *hard*) that participate in hard constraints and each solution of the offer (with respect to the QoS demand hard metrics) is contained in the solution space of the QoS demand that is constructed by only considering the demand's hard constraints.

Let us now provide a more formal description of the SCC metric based on a specific notation that will be used in the rest of this section. Suppose that there are P QoS offers to be matched with one QoS demand D. We denote as C the number of constraints of each offer O and L the number of constraints of the QoS demand D, where K of these constraints are hard and L-K are soft. Further, we denote as M the number of metrics of each QoS offer and as N the number of metrics of the QoS demand, where N_{hard} of them are involved in the demand's hard constraints. Moreover, we denote as T_M^{C+1} the average execution time that a CSP engine takes to solve a CSP with M metrics and $C+1$ constraints, from which the C constraints are those belonging to the QoS offer and the other one is produced from the negation of a QoS demand constraint. Finally, we denote with P^O the CSP constructed from the QoS offer and with P_{hard}^D the CSP constructed from the N_{hard} metrics and the hard constraints of the QoS demand.

Based on the above assumptions and notations, the conformance of an offer O to D according to the SCC metric is given as follows:

$$conformance(O, D) \Leftrightarrow M \supseteq N_{hard} \wedge sat(P^O \wedge \neg P_{hard}^D) = false \quad (1)$$

where *sat* is a procedure returning true, when the CSP given as input is satisfiable, or false otherwise. The input CSP (i.e. $P^O \wedge \neg P_{hard}^D$) is constructed from the metrics M (of O which of course include the N_{hard} metrics), the logical combination of the constraints of O, and the negation of the logical combination of the constraints of D (where it is assumed that both O and D contain a logical combination of constraints).

As the SCC metric is an extension of the Cortés et al. metric, it could be expected that it may suffer from the false negative effect. However, by carefully categorizing as soft those QoS demand constraints that are problematic, e.g. when they provide bounds on the best values of particular QoS metrics, then we avoid providing false negatives. Thus, SCC exhibits perfect accuracy. For instance, by considering the example of Figure 6 that was given previously, the upper bound on availability of the QoS demand (i.e. AvgAvail <= 0.999) could be characterized as a soft constraint. In this way, the CSP constructed for assessing the

Figure 8. The conformance CSP constructed based on the example of Figure 6 and the SCC metric

```
var int x1 in 0..inf;
var float x2 in 0.0..1.0;
var float x3 in 0.0..inf;

solveCSP{
  x1>=3;
  x1<=5;
  x2>=0.96;
  x3>=150;
  x3<=275;
  not(x1>=3 & x1<=5 &
      x2>=0.95 & x3>=100 &
      x3<=300
  );
}
```

conformance between the QoS offer and demand would be the one of Figure 8. This CSP is unsatisfiable and as the QoS offer and demand contain the same metrics (where $N_{hard} = N$), there is a match between them. By inspecting, now, Figure 7 it can be seen that the SCC metric considers that both O_1 and O_2 offers match the demand D, which is actually the correct case.

The SCC metric takes the approach that incomplete QoS offers, which miss hard metrics of the demand, are penalized as fail matches. However, in conjunction with the QoS offer enrichment process, this metric can solve the incomplete offers problem in a more effective way. The reason is that while the QoS enrichment strategy enriches the incomplete QoS offers by inserting constraints on the missing metrics, the SCC metric does not consider those demand metrics that are involved only in soft constraints. In this way, by entering more metrics on an incomplete QoS offer and by not considering some QoS demand metrics, there is an increased chance that now the QoS offer is expressed at least with the same metric set as the QoS demand. Thus, the QoS offer may become complete, which is the actual object of research.

A simple optimization that could be proposed is to enrich the QoS offers only with respect to those missing metrics that are involved in the hard constraints of the QoS demand. However, it is useful to know the performance of a QoS offer also with respect to those missing metrics that are involved only in the soft constraints of the QoS demand in order to further categorize it. Thus, whether to perform such optimization depends on the granularity of the result categorization that has to be achieved.

Two Novel Algorithms Realizing the Soft Conditional Conformance Matchmaking Metric

We have implemented two novel QSM algorithms that realize the SCC metric. The first one is quick

and does not offer advanced result categorization, while the second is slower, offers advanced result categorization, and is able to produce interesting results for over-constrained QoS demands. Both algorithms work only for QoS demands expressed as a conjunction of unary constraints and rely on a specific formation of the conformance problem that is produced by analyzing Equation (1). As users often issue unary QoS demands, the proposed algorithms will work in the majority of all possible cases.

Suppose that a QoS demand D is expressed as a conjunction of the unary constraints c_1, c_2, ..., c_L where the constraints having an index from 1 to K are hard and the constraints that have an index from $K+1$ to L are soft. Then, equivalence (1) can be analyzed as follows:

$$conformance(O, D) \Leftrightarrow M \supseteq N_{hard} \wedge sat(P^O \wedge \neg P^D_{hard})$$
$$= false$$
$$\Rightarrow M \supseteq N_{hard} \wedge sat(P^O \wedge \neg(c_1 \wedge c_2 \wedge ... \wedge c_K))$$
$$= false$$
$$\Rightarrow M \supseteq N_{hard} \wedge sat(P^O \wedge (\neg c_1 \vee \neg c_2 \vee ... \vee \neg c_K))$$
$$= false$$
$$\Rightarrow M \supseteq N_{hard} \wedge sat((P^O \wedge \neg c_1) \vee (P^O \wedge \neg c_2) \vee ... \vee (P^O \wedge \neg c_K))$$
$$= false$$
$$\Rightarrow M \supseteq N_{hard} \wedge sat(P^O \wedge \neg c_1) = false \wedge sat(P^O \wedge \neg c_2)$$
$$= false \wedge ... \wedge sat(P^O \wedge \neg c_K) = false$$

Thus, there is match between an offer O and a demand D if the metrics of O are a superset of the hard metrics of D and all the K CSPs constructed from the CSP P^O of the offer and the negation of one of the hard constraints of the demand are unsatisfiable.

Before performing the actual matchmaking, the proposed SQM algorithms perform a small pre-processing step on D in order to correct the type (soft or hard) of the constraints involving particular metrics. Such a correction is necessary even in the case that users have separated their QoS demand constraints into soft or hard, as they may have wrongly set as hard a constraint such as the one on the upper bound of an *availability* metric. Thus, this step is necessary for simple and inexperienced users. On the contrary, this step is not required for experienced users who know exactly what they want from the performance of a service belonging to a particular type or applied to a specific domain, so we can consider that their QoS demand is absolutely correct and should be respected.

A matchmaking system can distinguish experienced users from inexperienced ones in various ways. First, by exploring the user history in terms of previous QoS demands and their success. Second, by having authentication and authorization mechanisms so as to distinguish experienced and significant clients/users from simple anonymous users. Third, by allowing users to indicate if their QoS demands must be exactly or more flexibly matched through correcting wrong constraint characterizations. The experienced users will indicate the first option, while most of the inexperienced users will indicate the second one as they will not be sure if their QoS demands are totally correct. Our approach has adopted the last way by allowing the QSM algorithms to receive a Boolean input parameter, which indicates whether the constraint pre-processing step must be performed.

The pre-processing step relies on characterizing first the type of metrics participating in the unary constraints of the demand and then fixing their corresponding constraints if needed. We can distinguish between the following metric types:

- **Sensitive Metrics:** For these metrics, both the upper and lower bounds on their values should be characterized as hard constraints. For example, the *refresh rate* metric concerns the rate at which the service should send updated information (e.g. vehicle traffic information) to the client. This metric is sensitive as both of its bounds should be respected. In particular, the lower bound should be respected to enable the user's application to properly consume the service's output (e.g. obtain information and load it to a map before it is updated). The upper bound should be respected to enable the user to obtain up-to-date information.

- **Semi-Sensitive Metrics:** For this type of metrics, the bound that restricts their worse value should be set as hard, while the other bound should be set as soft. This means that for positively monotonic metrics, the lower bound should be set as hard, while for negatively monotonic metrics the upper bound should be set as hard. As an example, availability is a semi-sensitive positively monotonic metric, so its lower bound should be set as hard, while if its upper bound exists, it should be set as soft. Indeed, WS requesters are highly interested in having an as highly available service as possible, so it is better that only the worse value of this metric has a hard bound.

- **Insensitive Metrics:** Such metrics should have only soft bounds on their values and they represent metrics that are not so important for users. As an example, constraints on *stability*, which measures the frequency with which the service interface and/or implementation is altered, should not play an important role for filtering services that are immediately consumed. So any constraint on this metric should be considered as soft.

As can be seen from the above characterization, a metric's sensitivity depends on the service type or the application domain. For example, the execution time of services that are not data-intensive has not an effect on the quality of the service output, so only the upper bound on execution time should be set as hard. In this case, execution time is a semi-sensitive metric. Moreover, it should be stated that the processing of semi-sensitive and especially of insensitive metrics may or surely results in having constraints on these metrics that are only soft. When this happens, these metrics are not used for assessing the SCC metric and this can result in de-characterizing particular QoS offers as incomplete with respect to the SCC metric, even if these offers do not have constraints on soft metrics of the QoS demand.

To avoid further confusion on the incompleteness matter, we distinguish between the following QoS offer types. A QoS offer is *SCC-complete* if it contains constraints on all the QoS demand hard metrics, while it is *SCC-incomplete* otherwise. In this respect, a QoS offer that is SCC-incomplete is also incomplete. However, an incomplete QoS offer is not necessarily SCC-incomplete. Moreover, a complete QoS offer is also SCC-complete but the opposite does not necessarily hold.

Finally, it should be noted that our approach does not impose significant requirements to users in terms of defining metrics. First, as a metric's sensitivity depends on the service type or application domain, users do not have to provide such information. The matchmaking system must have such knowledge, in terms of previous experience from matchmaking a specific service type or domain application rules, and enforce it. Second, users do not have to specify QoS metrics that have already been specified by other users or domain modelers. In fact, OWL-Q includes the specification of a set of domain-independent QoS metrics, as well as of a set of QoS metrics of a particular domain. Moreover, such information could be provided to the users demand authoring tools by issuing appropriate inquiries to respective QSM systems. When a required metric is not already defined, the users have to specify it along with the appropriate information such as the metric's monotonicity, which most of the times is obvious and independent of the service type or even the application domain (for domain-independent metrics). The only real specification effort the users have to provide concerns defining and characterizing constraints. Users must know exactly the service QoS they expect and which constraints must be satisfied at all costs.

Soft Conditional Conformance Algorithm (cond-conf for short)

This algorithm takes a straightforward approach in realizing the SCC metric. In this way, it is quicker

than the other one but fails to provide a more fine-grained categorization as it is only able to produce the exact and fail matching categories. Obviously, it is also not able to produce meaningful results for over-constrained QoS demands.

This algorithm first pre-processes the QoS demand in order to correct its constraints type. Then, it first checks if each QoS offer is SCC-complete. If not, the offer is characterized as a fail match and its processing ends. Next, the algorithm constructs a set of K CSPs, involving M metrics and containing the logical combination of the constraints of the QoS offer and the negation of one hard constraint of the QoS demand, and solves them one by one. If a CSP has a solution, then the QoS offer is characterized as fail. Otherwise, if all CSPs are unsatisfiable, then the QoS offer is characterized as exact.

Let us now theoretically analyze the time complexity of this algorithm for matching P QoS offers with one QoS demand. The QoS demand pre-processing may take $O(L)$ time, as all the demand constraints have to be processed (and each constraint processing takes a very small, unary time – $O(1)$). Checking for SCC-incomplete QoS offers will take $O(P \cdot (M + N_{hard}))$ time, as there are P QoS offers and checking each of them takes $M + N_{hard}$ time (i.e. iterating over all the offer metrics and the demand hard metrics). The worst time in the actual matchmaking is $O(P \cdot K \cdot T_M^{C+1})$, occurring when all QoS offers are SCC-complete as the cost of checking the conformance of each one (i.e. solving its CSPs) will be $O(K \cdot T_M^{C+1})$. On the other hand, the best time in the actual matchmaking is $\Theta(P)$, occurring when all QoS offers are SCC-incomplete so they just have to be characterized as fail.

Thus, in the worst case the algorithm will take $O(P \cdot K \cdot T_M^{C+1})$ time as the actual matchmaking time dominates over the time spent in the other steps. So, in the worst case the algorithm will scale quadratically on increasing sizes of both P and K. It must be noted that the time needed for solving a CSP will be almost stable with respect to the increase of M and C, as the solving time decreases with the increase on the constraint number and it increases with the increase on the variable number. It is expected that in the real-world K, M, and C are relatively constrained, so the only meaningful parameter affecting scalability is P. In the best case, this algorithm will take $O(P \cdot (M + N_{hard}) + P + L)$ time to execute, which can be further simplified as $O(P + L)$ if the information of which offer is (SCC-) incomplete is provided by the QoS offer enrichment process as input to this algorithm. Thus, in the best case, the algorithm will either scale quadratically on increasing sizes of both P and M or N_{hard}, or only linearly on P and L. However, as we expect that M and N_{hard} are relatively constrained in the real-world, the only meaningful parameter affecting scalability is again P.

Unary Algorithm

This algorithm offers advanced categorization of results with the cost of having to solve all the constraints of the QoS demand and not only the soft ones. In particular, it is able to categorize QoS offers in the following way, where a constraint violation occurs when the corresponding CSP (constructed from the QoS offer and the negation of this constraint) is satisfiable or even with the absence of the metric that this constraint involves from the QoS offer:

- *Super* matches are complete QoS offers that satisfy all the constraints of the QoS demand
- *Exact* matches are SCC-complete or even complete QoS offers that satisfy only the hard constraints of the QoS demand
- *Partial* matches are (SCC-) incomplete or (SCC-) complete QoS offers that satisfy some of the hard constraints of the QoS demand

- *Fail* matches are (SCC-) incomplete or (SCC-) complete QoS offers that do not satisfy any hard constraint of the QoS demand.

Apart from characterizing QoS offers, the *unary* algorithm is also able to sort the last three categories of matches in ascending order based on sort values that are produced from the number of QoS demand hard and soft constraints that they violate and on the weights that these violated constraints take. To this end, the following weights are introduced to the QoS demand constraints. Hard constraints get the weight of L, where L is a positive integer number and represents the total number of QoS demand constraints. Soft constraints get a weight from the set $[0.0, 1.0)$ of real numbers, where the higher the value, the greater the significance of the constraint. As it can be seen, a hard constraint gets a value that will never be equal to the sum of the values of all the soft constraints. This shows the significance of the hard constraints with respect to the soft ones, indicating that the violation of a hard constraint should never be traded even with the violation of all the soft constraints. In other words, when one QoS offer violates two hard constraints while another one violates only one hard and even all soft constraints, the first QoS offer will be rated greater than the second one so that the second offer will finally get a better position than the first.

The exact calculation of the sort value is as follows. When a QoS offer violates t hard constraints and k soft constraints, it will get a sort value of $t \cdot L + \sum\limits_{C \in Violated(L-K)} w_C,$ where $Violated(L-K)$ represents the set of violated soft QoS demand constraints. For example, suppose that L equals to 10 and a QoS offer violates 3 hard constraints and 2 soft constraints with weights 0.1 and 0.3, respectively. Then, the QoS offer will get a sort value of

$$3 \cdot L + 0.1 + 0.3 = 30.4 \,.$$

It should be noted here that the *unary* algorithm is not a full service selection algorithm as it is not able to rank all QoS offers but only those belonging to the three lower categories of matches. The ranking of the latter types of matches is actually a side-effect of knowing the type of constraints and inspecting which are violated. In addition, this algorithm ranks QoS offers based on the weight of the QoS constraints violated. The existing service selection algorithms rank QoS offers based on the weight a QoS metric has and its ranking function, which produces the metric's (partial) score according to the worse (or average) value this metric can take. Moreover, the *unary* algorithm does not require the existence of an additional requester-provided service selection model in order to perform the ranking but it exploits the extra information provided in the QoS demand in terms of the weights given to (soft) constraints. Finally, when QoS offers advertize values for a QoS metric that are not desired by the requester, full service selection algorithms penalize such QoS offers in the hardest possible way by giving them a zero partial score for the violated metric. On the other hand, the *unary* algorithm penalizes QoS offers first by downgrading them to a particular category (if it violates a hard constraint) and then giving them a higher weight. It also provides different penalties for violations occurring at the different bounds on a specific metric.

Apart from offering a more advanced result categorization, this algorithm is able to produce meaningful results for over-constrained QoS demands. In particular, when an over-constrained QoS demand is issued, the best results of the partial matching category are promoted to a new category called exact*. This category is between the exact and partial match categories. It has been created especially to contain those partial matches that satisfy in the best possible way the requester constraints. The term "best" indicates those partial results that have the smallest sorting number, i.e., they violate the least number of hard constraints and when other offers also violate the same num-

ber, they will surely have the less total weight of violated soft constraints with respect to these offers. These results deserve to be distinguished and represent the least number of updates that have to be performed in the QoS demand so as to surely have exact matches. By constructing a new category, the requesters do not confuse real exact matches with the partially promoted ones but are just aware that the contents of the new category could be potentially used to best satisfy their needs with respect to those belonging to the partial match category.

Another advantage of this algorithm is that it is able to report the complete list of QoS demand constraints that each QoS offer violates. In this way, users have a complete picture of which offers violate which constraints. So that they can decide which constraints to change if their QoS demand is over-constrained.

Let us now analyze this algorithm's time complexity. The QoS demand pre-processing is the same as the one spent in the first algorithm. The time needed for checking the offers' SCC-incompleteness is now $O(P \cdot (M + N_{hard} + L))$, as apart from checking which QoS demand metrics are missing, we have to check which corresponding constraints are violated and to add their weight to the offers' sort value. The worst time in the actual matchmaking is

$$O(P \cdot L \cdot T_M^{C+1} + P \cdot \log P),$$

occurring when all QoS offers are complete, as the cost of checking the conformance of each one (i.e. solving its CSPs) will be $O(L \cdot T_M^{C+1})$ and the time to insert each one in the right place of the appropriate category will be $O(\log P)$. On the other hand, the best time in the actual matchmaking is $\Theta(P)$, occurring when all QoS offers are totally incomplete (i.e. their constraints do not involve any metric of the QoS demand) so they just have to be characterized as fail and get the maximum possible sorting number.

Thus, in the worst case the algorithm will take $O(P \cdot L \cdot T_M^{C+1} + P \cdot \log P)$ time as the actual matchmaking time dominates over the time spent in the other steps. In this case, the algorithm scales quadratically on the increase of both P and L. Based on the previous algorithm's complexity analysis, the only meaningful parameter affecting scalability is P. In the best case, this algorithm will take $O(P \cdot (M + N_{hard} + L) + P + L)$ time to execute, which can be further simplified as $O(P \cdot (1 + L) + L)$ if the information of which offer is (SCC-) incomplete and which QoS demand metrics are missing from this offer is provided by the QoS offer enrichment process as input to this algorithm. So, in this case, this algorithm's complexity is similar to that of the previous one and its scalability is affected only by P.

As the worst and best case for each proposed QSM algorithm is different, we have to be very careful when comparing them. In the worst case of the *cond-conf* algorithm, the performance of the unary algorithm will vary from

$$O(P \cdot K \cdot T_M^{C+1} + P \cdot \log P),$$

when all the QoS offers that are surely SCC-complete are incomplete and do not involve any QoS demand soft metric, to

$$O(P \cdot L \cdot T_M^{C+1} + P \cdot \log P)$$

when all the QoS offers are complete. In this case, the performance of the *unary* algorithm will always be worse than that of the *cond-conf*.

In the best case of the *cond-conf* algorithm, the unary algorithm's performance will vary from $O(P \cdot (M + N_{hard} + L) + P + L)$, when all the QoS offers that are surely SCC-incomplete are incomplete and do not involve any QoS demand metric, to $O(P \cdot (L - 1) \cdot T_M^{C+1} + P \cdot \log P)$ when all QoS offers involve all the QoS demand metrics apart from one hard semi-sensitive metric. Thus, again the the *unary* algorithm's performance is worse than that of the *cond-conf*. In the average case (not with respect to a specific algorithm), we can expect that a QoS offer involves half of the QoS demand hard and soft metrics. So, the *unary* algorithm will take $O(P \cdot L / 2 \cdot T_M^{C+1} + P \cdot \log P)$ time, while the *cond-conf* one will take $O(P \cdot (M + N_{hard}) + P + L)$ time. Thus, the unary algorithm's performance will always be worse than the one of the *cond-conf*. This will be also empirically evaluated in the next subsection.

The functionality of our two proposed QoS-based WS discovery algorithms is demonstrated by supplying a simple example of their application to a set of four QoS offer CSPs P^i and one demand CSP P^D. Assume that all QoS specifications have the following three definitions: *execution time*:: $(0.0, 86400.0]$ ↓, *throughput*:: $(0, 100000]$↑, and *availability*:: $(0.0, 1.0)$↑, where all variables are actually mapped to semi-sensitive QoS metrics and the arrows show a metric's value monotonicity. These metric definitions will be mapped to a set of CSP variables: *execution time* will be mapped to the X_1 variable, *throughput* to X_2, and *availability* to X_3. Further, assume that the CSPs produced from the QoS specifications are show in Box 1.

Box 1.

$$P^1 : [\, X_1 \leq 10.0 \wedge X_2 \leq 100 \wedge X_2 \geq 50 \wedge X_3 \geq 0.9 \,],$$

$$P^2 : [\, X_1 \leq 4.8 \wedge X_2 \leq 50 \wedge X_2 \geq 40 \wedge X_3 \geq 0.95 \,],$$

$$P^3 : [\, X_1 \leq 16 \wedge X_2 \leq 40 \wedge X_2 \geq 30 \wedge X_3 \geq 0.98 \,],$$

$$P^4 : [\, X_1 \leq 16 \wedge X_2 \leq 50 \wedge X_2 \geq 40 \wedge X_3 \geq 0.98 \,], \text{ and}$$

$$P^D : [\, {}^{C_1 \wedge C_2 \wedge C_3 \wedge C_4, C_1 \equiv X_1 \leq 15, C_2 \equiv X_2 \leq 60, C_3}_{\equiv X_2 \geq 40, C_4 \equiv X_3 \geq 0.99} \,].$$

Moreover, assume that the WS requester did not provide weights to the constraints of his demand but the two algorithms have automatically given the weight of 4 to the hard constraints (i.e. C_1, C_3, and C_4) and the equal weight of 0.5 to all soft constraints (i.e. C_2).

Now, if we apply the *cond-conf* algorithm, it will provide the following results: Exact=[], Fail=[P^1, P^2, P^3, P^4]. So, this algorithm will return only fail matches as all QoS offers violate some of the hard constraints of the QoS demand. However, if we apply the *unary* algorithm, the results will be the following: Super=[], Exact=[(P^2,4, {$X_3 \geq 0.99$})], Partial=[(P^1, 4.5, {$X_2 \leq 60$, $X_3 \geq 0.99$}),(P^4, 8, {$X_1 \leq 15, X_3 \geq 0.99$})], Fail=[($P^3$, 12, {$X_1 \leq 15, X_2 \geq 40$, $X_3 \geq 0.99$})]. As it can be seen, this algorithm has promoted one partial result as exact as this result violates the least possible number of hard (1) constraints and no soft constraint with respect to the other ones. Moreover, it offers an advanced result categorization, which is more user-intuitive as the failing offers are separated into partial and fail. Finally, each result is accompanied by its sort value and the list of the constraints of the QoS demand that are violated.

Matchmaking Algorithms Implementation Details and their Empirical Randomized Evaluation

Problem Specification

Two main problems are the subject of research in this subsection. The first problem is concerned with the way the two proposed QSM algorithms match a set of QoS offers and one QoS demand. In particular, based on the analysis of the SCC metric, for each QoS offer a series of CSPs has to be first created by the two proposed algorithms and then solved. All these CSPs differ with each other only with respect to the removal of one constraint and the addition of another one. Thus, it would be interesting to search for a specialized DCS technique that could use the reasoning

knowledge from solving a previous CSP in order to solve the next one, as this technique could lead to enormous savings in execution time for the two QSM algorithms. Such savings can be of very high value for users. First, as the additional functional service matchmaking time should not be neglected. Second, as the QoS offer space is expected to grow enormously because service providers advertize more than one QoS offer for their services, the QSM time will be negatively affected. Thus, such savings could mitigate or eliminate this negative effect.

The second problem concerns the pragmatic evaluation of the two proposed algorithms. Apart from the theoretical comparison of the two algorithms, it is also interesting to investigate their performance under real or realistic circumstances. In this way, we can validate the results of the theoretical comparison or find reasons why these results do not hold in particular occasions.

The Explanation Constraint Programming Technique and the Empirical Evaluation

Each algorithm has to solve a particular set of CSPs in order to infer the match between two QoS specifications. However, when one CSP involving a QoS demand hard constraint is found to be feasible, it is not required to solve any other from the next CSPs. On the other hand, when all the CSPs involving a QoS demand hard constraint are infeasible, then there is a match. Thus, it would be interesting to speedup the solving procedure of a set of similar and infeasible CSPs. In this way, we resorted to the reasoning reuse techniques of DCS, as they can reuse the knowledge from solving a previous infeasible CSP in order to solve the new one. From the reasoning reuse techniques, the eCP one was finally selected for two main reasons: a) in eCP no constraints need to be checked to maintain valid implied constraints and b) there exists a free solving framework, called Choco (Laburthe, 2000), for normal and dynamic CSPs that uses explanation-based methods (a Java version of the Palm system (Jussien & Barichard, 2000)).

In result, our proposed *cond-conf* and *unary* matchmaking algorithms, which we denote as $CP_{cond-conf}$ and CP_{unary} respectively, were re-implemented in order to use the explanation-based methods of defining and solving CSPs of the Choco framework, producing in this way the algorithms denoted as $CP_{expl-cconf}$ and $CP_{expl-unary}$ respectively. In fact, Choco was used to implement all the CP algorithms that have been proposed, i.e. both CP and eCP ones. In this way, as the explanation-based mechanisms are built on top of the normal CP ones, we could run and experimentally evaluate our matchmaking algorithms in a fair manner without using different CSP engines for different types of CSPs (i.e normal and dynamic ones).

The second problem was solved by relying on an extension of the framework we have developed (Kritikos & Plexousakis, 2009a). This framework is able to conduct a series of experiments. In each experiment a series of tests is executed, where their number depends on the step of increase on one tuning parameter (e.g. a value from 10 to 90 with step 10 is translated to 9 tests) while the other tuning parameters are stable. The values of these tuning parameters are used to create random data in a controlled way and use it as input to a set of algorithms to be executed and evaluated according to specific metrics, such as the execution time, accuracy, and produced results size. Each test is executed many times (e.g. 20) producing many values for each metric assessed for every algorithm and then the average or minimum is registered depending on the metric assessed. So, after each test end, every algorithm has exactly one value registered for each metric.

The extension of this framework relied on the way the correct accuracy for the data created (i.e. QoS demand and offers) was calculated for each step, as the framework was assessing in a different way a QoS offer's correct category. As

this framework is configurable and can evaluate any QSM algorithm as long as it is implemented in Matlab, we created a wrapping Matlab code around our Java implementations, which included a straight-forward implementation of the Cortés et al. metric denoted as CP_{conf}. Moreover, in order to exploit the eCP solving facilities of Choco, our experiments were constrained to involve only integer-valued QoS metrics. We should state that the plain CP version of the *unary* algorithm was not included in the experiments. The pseudocode of the algorithms used in the experiments is provided in Appendix B.

Before presenting our experimental results, it must be highlighted that the speedup the $CP_{expl-cconf}$ and $CP_{expl-unary}$ algorithms had with respect to the other two algorithms is more related to the faster modeling of successive CSPs than to the actual explanation facility. This is because we have only used unary constraints in our experiments, so the explanation facility cannot offer anything but itself. In the near future, we plan to investigate the impact of n-ary constraints to the performance of our (e)CP-based matchmaking algorithms.

The faster modeling of successive CSPs in eCP is justified as follows. As it was mentioned before, all the algorithms have to solve a set of similar CSPs in order to infer if there is a match between a QoS offer and demand. However, for the first two algorithms (CP_{conf} and $CP_{cond-conf}$) that use plain CP techniques, the underlying constraint network after reaching a solution for a previous CSP could not be updated with the changes needed for the next CSP unless it was totally destroyed and restructured. In this way, each CSP from the set had to be created from scratch. In the worst case, the time needed for constructing these set of CSPs is

$$O(P \cdot L \cdot (M + (C + 1))) \text{ for } CP_{conf} \text{ and}$$
$$O(P \cdot K \cdot (M + (C + 1))) \text{ for } CP_{cond-conf}.$$

Thanks to the eCP technique the other two algorithms ($CP_{expl-cconf}$ and $CP_{expl-unary}$) exploited, they did not have to create a new CSP from scratch but only update the previous one and re-solve it. However, $CP_{expl\text{-}unary}$ had to create a new CSP whenever a previous CSP involving a demand soft constraint had a solution, as eCP can exploit only the knowledge of infeasible CSPs. Thus, in the worst case, the time needed for building/updating CSPs is $O(2 \cdot P \cdot K)$ for $CP_{expl\text{-}cconf}$ and $O(P \cdot (L - K) \cdot (M + (C + 1)))$ for $CP_{expl\text{-}unary}$. The CSP building/updating time was considered for all algorithms when calculating their execution time.

Due to space restrictions, we cannot report the results of all the experiments conducted. Instead, we will concentrate on presenting the first experiment results. In this experiment, the number of created QoS offers was increasing from 10 to 100, while the other tuning parameters were stable: the number of metrics involved in all QoS specifications was 10, the percentage of QoS offers that matched the QoS demand was 0.5, the percentage of super to all matching offers was 0.6, and the percentage of partial to all failing results was 0.5. The results of these experiments are depicted in Figure 9.

Concerning total matchmaking time, the $CP_{expl\text{-}cconf}$ was the best algorithm followed by the

algorithms of $CP_{expl\text{-}unary}$, $CP_{cond\text{-}conf}$ and CP_{conf} in decreasing order of performance. This was predicted as we were expecting first that *cond-conf* algorithm is always better than the *unary* algorithm and second that eCP-based algorithms will exhibit a better performance than their plain CP counterparts. Moreover, all the algorithms exhibited a linear increasing performance behavior. For the CP and eCP versions of the *cond-conf* algorithm and the CP_{conf} algorithm, this can be easily explained by observing that their time complexity depends on the number of constraints of the QoS demand and the number of QoS offers. As the first factor was stable and the other was increasing, we were expecting a linear behavior from them. However, a slightly different behavior was expected for the *unary* algorithm based on its time complexity. Instead, this algorithm has exhibited the same behavior as the others. This can be justified only by considering that the sorting time is considerably small and is dominated by the time needed for performing the actual matchmaking of all the QoS offers through the solving of their series of CSPs.

Concerning the accuracy of the QSM algorithms, all algorithms had perfect precision. However, while the *cond-conf* and *unary* algo-

Figure 9. A: Matchmaking time versus offer number; B: Precision versus recall

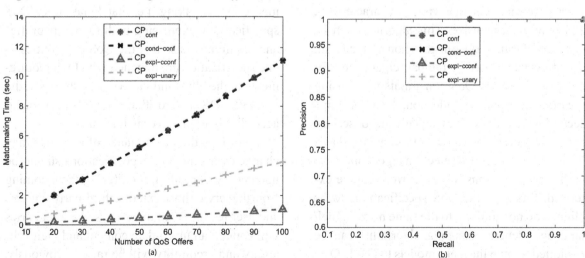

rithms had a perfect recall, the recall of the CP_{conf} algorithm was 0.6. This can be justified by the fact that the Cortés et al. metric suffers from the false negatives effect when the user-provided constraints are wrongly characterized, so it is able to return only the super matches as the QoS offers that actually match a QoS demand. The results clearly show that the two proposed QSM algorithms have a perfect accuracy, which is not influenced by wrong constraint characterizations, and this is a very crucial advantage with respect to the other algorithms that have been proposed in the literature.

FUTURE RESEARCH DIRECTIONS

In this section, we first show in which places of service research our work fits and then we discuss future and emerging trends.

The matchmaking of QoS metrics and the alignment of QoS specifications is part of the management of NFPs and their specifications, including the management of SLAs, so it directly contributes to these issues. Moreover, the implementation of the above functionalities can be exploited by corresponding tools and middleware for supporting NFPs and SLAs. Our novel QoS-based Web Service matchmaking algorithm advances the state-of-the-art by being perfectly accurate, even when user-constraints are wrongly characterized, and is more responsive. This algorithm can be exploited during service negotiation for matching the offers exchanged by the participants and for discovering which QoS constraints are causing the offers mismatch. In addition, the algorithm's second version provides an advanced service result categorization so it can be considered as a coarse-grained service selection algorithm.

There are various ways our work can be extended. First, in case QoS specifications to be aligned do not conform to the same meta-model/language, schema mapping algorithms can be exploited to map the meta-models to OWL-Q so that the QoS specifications and their attributes and metrics are transformed to OWL-Q ones. The transformed specifications can then be aligned by using the proposed algorithm.

Second, the use of Information Retrieval techniques for mapping the name of a QoS metric or attribute to the concept representing it in the corresponding QoS model. Such mapping techniques are useful for semantically enriching QoS specifications or monitoring facts coming from external sources that do not obey to a specific meta-model or just provide a QoS metric's name without actually defining it.

Third, various OWL-Q extensions are planned to be performed. OWL-Q will be extended to specify Process Performance Metrics (PPMs) (Wetzstein, Karastoyanova, & Leymann, 2008) and their corresponding constraints called Key Performance Indicators (KPIs). Such PPMs can be defined by other PPMs or QoS metrics. In this way, dependencies between metrics on the various service layers can be defined to be exploited during service monitoring and adaptation. Moreover, OWL-Q will be extended to become a novel SLA language by carefully solving the modeling inefficiencies of SLA languages such as the composite SLA specification. Finally, OWL-Q will be extended to specify the QoS capabilities and requirements of both service providers and requesters. In this way, it will allow for symmetric matchmaking, i.e. matchmaking of QoS specifications expressing both QoS capabilities and requirements so that the QoS capabilities of one specification are matched with QoS requirements of the other and vice versa. Obviously, the proposed QSM algorithm should be extended accordingly to provide such a feature.

Fourth, as the performance of a service may change over time, QoS specifications should be updated by exploiting monitoring facts coming from the service host, external third-party sources, and user feedback. In this way, service registries will contain an up-to-date content and their reliability and credibility will be raised. Obviously,

SLA management systems should also exploit such features to be informed of SLA violations and take appropriate adaptation actions such as SLA re-negotiation, service substitution, service reconfiguration, etc. In addition, it is imperative to be able to derive high-level monitoring facts from low-level ones or any useful fact even if the corresponding information is incomplete or slightly erroneous. Thus, more formal models and ways to combine monitoring information are needed so that the functionality of monitoring systems becomes added-value and more effective, enhancing as such the functionalities of service registries and SLA management systems when coupled with them.

Fifth, as a WS may advertise to support many QoS offers, a service registry may end up containing thousand or millions of QoS offers. In order to be effective and efficient, two main research directions should be pursued for reducing the matchmaking time. The first one is the creation of QoS offer taxonomies. In this way, when a QoS demand is issued, it should be only matched with the QoS offers contained in those taxonomies whose root elements match this QoS demand and not with all QoS offers. The second research direction is the distribution of the appropriate content and/or functionality of the service registry in order to parallelize the QSM process.

Finally, especially in domains where QoS demands can get over-constrained, it will be interesting to investigate the use of other constraint satisfaction techniques (e.g. semi-ring based constraint satisfaction (Bistarelli, Montanari, & Rossi, 1997) for performing QSM.

CONCLUSION

In this book chapter, a literature review on QoS-based WS description and matchmaking was performed, which showed three main problems that have to be solved. The first problem is that most QoS specifications and models are not aligned with each other, containing references or definitions to equivalent QoS metrics specified differently. For this reason, the first chapter contribution is the proposal of a novel procedure for aligning OWL-Q specifications that exploits our previously proposed QoS metric matching algorithm.

The second problem relies on the fact that the most promising QSM algorithms first transform the QoS specifications to be matched to one CSP, where the same metrics are mapped to the same CSP variable, and then solve this CSP to infer if there is a match. However, these algorithms do not distinguish between same degree-of-match QoS offers that do not contain constraints on a QoS demand's metric and those that do contain such constraints. Our second contribution solves this problem in two complementary ways. First, we propose QoS specification enrichment strategies that try to fill the QoS metrics gap between the compared QoS specifications by investigating various QoS metric relations and ways to represent them. Second, we take an open-world perspective where QoS offers not containing a demand's QoS metrics are not hardly penalized with respect to the equivalent (wrt. the matching) QoS offers that do contain them.

Finally, for the last problem, which concerns the accuracy of the matchmaking metric and the user-intuitive functioning in place of over-constrained QoS demands, we propose a novel matchmaking metric and a realizing algorithm that exploits the separation of user's QoS requirements into obligatory and optional ones so as to provide meaningful results even when the overall user's requirements are over-constrained. The QSM algorithm is implemented using both plain and explanation-based CP techniques. Its empirical evaluation shows that the explanation-based CP realization is faster from the plain CP one.

Apart from its exploitation in QSM, it has been shown that explanation-based CP techniques provide added functionality by checking the correctness of QoS specifications and SLAs

(Müller, Ruiz-Cortés, & Resinas, 2008). Moreover, as they reveal which constraints cause the mismatch between QoS specifications, they can be exploited during service negotiation to highlight the way one participant's offer has to be updated in order to match the other participant's offer. Thus, one future extension of our work could be to use explanation-based CP techniques in service negotiation. However, a series of other research directions can be also pursued, as it is revealed in the "Future Research Directions" section.

REFERENCES

Allen, P. (2006). *Service orientation, winning strategies and best practices*. Cambridge, UK: Cambridge University Press. doi:10.1017/CBO9780511541186

Anbazhagan, M., & Nagarajan, A. (2002, January). *Understanding quality of service for web services*. IBM Developerworks website. Retrieved from http://www-106.ibm.com/developerworks/library/ws-quality.html

Bach, T. L., Barrasa, J., Bouquet, P., Bo, J. D., Dieng, R., Ehrig, M., et al. (2004, August). *KnowledgeWeb European project deliverable D2.2.3: State of the art on ontology alignment*. Retrieved from www.starlab.vub.ac.be/research/projects/knowledgeweb/kweb-223.pdf

Baeza-Yates, R., & Ribeiro-Neto, B. (1999). *Modern information retrieval* (1st ed.). Addison Wesley. Paperback.

Berners-Lee, T., Hendler, J., & Lassila, O. (2001, May). The Semantic Web. *Scientific American*. Retrieved from http://www.scientificamerican.com/2001/0501issue/0501berners-lee.html

Bistarelli, S., Montanari, U., & Rossi, F. (1997). Semiring-based constraint satisfaction and optimization. *Journal of the ACM, 44*(2), 201–236. doi:10.1145/256303.256306

Booth, D., Haas, H., McCabe, F., Newcomer, E., Champion, M., Ferris, C., et al. (2002). *Web services architecture* (W3C Working Draft). W3C. Retrieved from http://www.w3.org/TR/ws-arch

Cappiello, C. (2006). Mobile Information Systems . In Pernici, B. (Ed.), *Infrastructure and design for adaptivity and flexibility* (pp. 307–317). Springer-Verlag.

Cappiello, C., Kritikos, K., Metzger, A., Parkin, M., Pernici, B., Plebani, P., et al. (2008, December). *A quality model for service monitoring and adaptation*. In Workshop on Monitoring, Adaptation and Beyond (MONA+) at the ServiceWave 2008 Conference. Springer.

Cliffe, O., & Andreou, D. (2009, 10 September). *Service matchmaking framework* (Public Deliverable N° D5.2a). Alive EU Project Consortium.

Cortés, A. R., Martín-Díaz, O., Toro, A. D., & Toro, M. (2005). Improving the automatic procurement of web services using constraint programming. *Int. J. Cooperative Inf. Syst., 14*(4), 439–468. doi:10.1142/S0218843005001225

Degwekar, S., Su, S. Y. W., & Lam, H. (2004). Constraint specification and processing in web services publication and discovery. In *ICWS* (pp. 210-217). IEEE Computer Society.

Frølund, S., & Koistinen, J. (1998). Quality of services specification in distributed object systems design. In *COOTS'98: Proceedings of the 4th USENIX Conference on Object-Oriented Technologies and Systems* (pp. 179-202).

Georgakopoulos, D., & Papazoglou, M. P. (2008). *Service-oriented computing*. MIT Press.

Giallonardo, E., & Zimeo, E. (2007). More semantics in QoS matching. In *SOCA: International Conference on Service-Oriented Computing and Applications* (pp. 163-171). IEEE Computer Society.

Jin, L., Machiraju, V., & Sahai, A. (2002, June). *Analysis on service level agreement of web services* (Technical Report N° HPL-2002-180). USA: Software Technology Laboratories, HP Laboratories.

Jussien, N., & Barichard, V. (2000, September). The Palm system: Explanation-based constraint programming. In *TRICS 2000: Proceedings of the Techniques for Implementing Constraint Programming Systems Workshop, Workshop of CP 2000* (pp. 118-133).

Keller, A., & Ludwig, H. (2003). The WSLA framework: Specifying and monitoring service level agreements for web services. *Journal of Network and Systems Management, 11*(1), 57–81. doi:10.1023/A:1022445108617

Klusch, M., Fries, B., & Sycara, K. (2009). OWLS-MX: A hybrid Semantic Web service matchmaker for OWL-S services. *Web Semantics: Science . Services and Agents on the World Wide Web, 7*(2), 121–133. doi:10.1016/j.websem.2008.10.001

Kritikos, K. (2008). *Semantic QoS-based Web service description and discovery*. PhD Thesis, University of Crete, Greece.

Kritikos, K., Pernici, B., Plebani, P., Cappiello, C., Comuzzi, M., & Benbernou, S. (2010). (Manuscript submitted for publication). A survey on service quality description. *ACM Computing Surveys*.

Kritikos, K., & Plexousakis, D. (2006). Semantic QoS Metric matching. In *ECOWS '06: Proceedings of the European Conference on Web Services* (pp. 265-274). IEEE Computer Society.

Kritikos, K., & Plexousakis, D. (2009a). Mixed-integer programming for QoS-Based Web service matchmaking. *IEEE Transactions on Services Computing, 2*(2), 122–139. doi:10.1109/TSC.2009.10

Kritikos, K., & Plexousakis, D. (2009b). Requirements for QoS-based Web service description and discovery. *IEEE Transactions on Services Computing, 2*(4), 320–337. doi:10.1109/TSC.2009.26

Laburthe, F. (2000, September). Choco: Implementing a cp kernel. In *TRICS 2000: Proceedings of the Techniques for Implementing Constraint Programming Systems Workshop, a Post-Conference Workshop of CP 2000*.

Lee, K., Jeon, J., Lee, W., Jeong, S.-H., & Park, S.-W. (2003, November). *QoS for Web services: Requirements and possible approaches*. World Wide Web Consortium (W3C) note. Retrieved from http://www.w3c.or.kr/kr-office/TR/2003/ws-qos/

Liu, Y., Ngu, A. H. H., & Zeng, L. (2004). QoS computation and policing in dynamic web service selection . In Feldman, S. I., Uretsky, M., Najork, M., & Wills, C. E. (Eds.), *WWW (Alternate Track Papers & Posters)* (pp. 66–73). ACM. doi:10.1145/1013367.1013379

Mabrouk, N. B., Georgantas, N., & Issarny, V. (2009, May). *A semantic end-to-end QoS model for dynamic service oriented environments*. In PESOS Workshop at ICSE 2009. IEEE.

Maximilien, E. M., & Singh, M. P. (2002). Conceptual model of web service reputation. *SIGMOD Record, 31*(4), 36–41. doi:10.1145/637411.637417

Müller, C., Ruiz-Cortés, A., & Resinas, M. (2008). An initial approach to explaining SLA inconsistencies. In *ICSOC '08: Proceedings of the 6th International Conference on Service-Oriented Computing* (pp. 394-406). Springer-Verlag. Oldham, N., Verma, K., Sheth, A., & Hakimpour, F. (2006). Semantic WS-agreement partner selection. In *WWW '06: Proceedings of the 15th International Conference on the World Wide Web* (pp. 697-706). ACM Press.

Plebani, P., & Pernici, B. (2009). URBE: Web service retrieval based on similarity evaluation. *IEEE Transactions on Knowledge and Data Engineering, 21*(11), 1629–1642. doi:10.1109/TKDE.2009.35

Ran, S. (2003). A model for web services discovery with QoS. *SIGecom Exch., 4*(1), 1–10. doi:10.1145/844357.844360

Rossi, F., van Beek, P., & Walsh, T. (2006). *Handbook of constraint programming (foundations of artificial intelligence)*. New York, NY: Elsevier Science Inc.

Sabata, B., Chatterjee, S., Davis, M., Sydir, J. J., & Lawrence, T. F. (1997). Taxomomy of QoS specifications. In *Words '97: Proceedings of the 3rd Workshop on Object-oriented Real-time Dependable Systems* (pp. 100-107). IEEE Computer Society.

Schrijver, A. (1986). *Theory of linear and integer programming*. New York, NY: John Wiley.

Stroulia, E., & Wang, Y. (2005). Structural and semantic matching for assessing Web-service similarity. *Int. J. Cooperative Inf. Syst., 14*(4), 407–438. doi:10.1142/S0218843005001213

Sumra, R., & Arulazi, D. (2003, March). *Quality of service for web services – Demystification, limitations, and best practices*. Retrieved from http://www.developer.com/services/article.php/2027911

Tian, M., Gramm, A., Naumowicz, T., Ritter, H., & Schiller, J. (2003). A concept for QoS integration in Web services. In *WISE Workshops (WISEW'03)* (pp. 149-155). IEEE Computer Society.

Tosic, V., Pagurek, B., & Patel, K. (2003). WSOL - A language for the formal specification of classes of service for web services . In Zhang, L.-J. (Ed.), *ICWS* (pp. 375–381). CSREA Press.

Verfaillie, G., & Jussien, N. (2005, July). Constraint solving in uncertain and dynamic environments: A survey. *Constraints, 10*(29), 253–281. doi:10.1007/s10601-005-2239-9

Wetzstein, B., Karastoyanova, D., & Leymann, F. (2008, June). Towards management of SLA-aware business processes based on key performance indicators. In *9th Workshop on Business Process Modeling, Development, and Support (BPMDS '08)*.

Zaremski, A. M., & Wing, J. M. (1997). Specification matching of software components. *ACM Transactions on Software Engineering and Methodology, 6*(4), 333–369. doi:10.1145/261640.261641

Zhou, C., Chia, L.-T., & Lee, B.-S. (2004). Daml-QoS ontology for Web services. In *ICWS '04: Proceedings of the IEEE International Conference on Web Services* (pp. 472-479). IEEE Computer Society.

ADDITIONAL READING

This section provides a set of references collected from prestigious journals and important conferences and workshops in order to assist the reader in further exploring the area of QoS-based WS description, selection, and composition. Concerning QoS-based WS description, some references are provided concerning requirements for QoS-based service description languages and the definition of QoS in various areas such as distributed systems, real-time applications, networks, and information systems. The latter references are useful for understanding the meaning of QoS in other types of applications. They are also useful for comprehending that some of the QoS parameters involved in such applications have been adopted in WS QoS models due to the nature of WSs, as WSs can be distributed, they use the network to obtain or send information, and they usually handle and process various types of information. This is also indicated by the definition of QoS provided in Section "Background", where QoS does not only characterize the service itself but also the entities used in the path from the service to its client. References for QoS-based service selection and composition are provided as these activities/processes are complementary to QoS-based service matchmaking and along with this activity provide the appropriate mechanisms for building QoS-aware service-based applications.

Ardagna, D., & Pernici, B. (2007). Adaptive Service Composition in Flexible Processes. *IEEE Transactions on Software Engineering*, *3*(6), 369–384. doi:10.1109/TSE.2007.1011

Benatallah, B., Sheng, Q. Z., Ngu, A. H. H., & Dumas, M. (2002). Declarative composition and peer-to-peer provisioning of dynamic web services. In *ICDE* (p. 297-308). IEEE Computer Society.

Canfora, G., Di Penta, M., Esposito, R., & Villani, M. L. (2005). QoS-Aware Replanning of Composite Web Services. In *ICWS '05: Proceedings of the IEEE International Conference on Web Services* (pp. 121-129). IEEE Computer Society.

Cardoso, J., Sheth, A. P., Miller, J. A., Arnold, J., & Kochut, K. (2004). Quality of service for workflows and web service processes. *Journal of Web Semantics*, *1*(3), 281–308. doi:10.1016/j.websem.2004.03.001

Clark, D. D., Shenker, S., & Zhang, L. (1992). Supporting real-time applications in an integrated services packet network: architecture and mechanism. *SIGCOMM Comput. Commun. Rev.*, *22*(4), 14–26. doi:10.1145/144191.144199

Cruz, R. L. (1995). Quality of service guarantees in virtual circuit switched networks. *IEEE Journal on Selected Areas in Communications*, *13*(6), 1048–1056. doi:10.1109/49.400660

Deora, V., Shao, J., Gray, W. A., & Fiddian, N. J. (2003). A quality of service management framework based on user expectations. In Orlowska, M. E., Weerawarana, S., Papazoglou, M. P., & Yang, J. (Eds.), *ICSOC* (*Vol. 2910*, pp. 104–114). Springer.

Georgiadis, L., Guérin, R., Peris, V., & Sivarajan, K. N. (1996). Efficient network QoS provisioning based on per node traffic shaping. *IEEE/ACM Transactions on Networking*, *4*(4), 482–501. doi:10.1109/90.532860

Jaeger, M. C., Mühl, G., & Golze, S. (2005, July). QoS-Aware Composition of Web Services: A Look at Selection Algorithms. In *ICWS 2005: IEEE International Conference on Web Services* (pp. 807-808). IEEE Computer Society.

Lee, Y. W., Strong, D. M., Kahn, B. K., & Wang, R. Y. (2002). Aimq: a methodology for information quality assessment. *Information & Management*, *40*(2), 133–146. doi:10.1016/S0378-7206(02)00043-5

Salamatian, K., & Fdida, S. (2001). Measurement based modeling of quality of service in the internet: A methodological approach. In *IWDC '01: Proceedings of the Thyrrhenian International Workshop on Digital Communications* (pp. 158-174). Springer-Verlag.

Sivashanmugam, K., Sheth, A. P., Miller, J. A., Verma, K., Aggarwal, R., & Rajasekaran, P. (2003). Metadata and semantics for web services and processes. In Benn, W., Dadam, P., Kirn, S., & Unland, R. (Eds.), *Datenbanken und informations systeme: Festschrift zum 60. geburtstag von gunter schlageter* (pp. 245–271). Hagen: FernUniversität in Hagen, Fachbereich Informatik.

Tosic, V., Esfandiari, B., Pagurek, B., & Patel, K. (2002). On requirements for ontologies in management of web services. In *CAISE '02/WES '02: Revised papers from the International Workshop on Web Services, E-business, and the Semantic Web* (pp. 237-247). Springer-Verlag.

Tosic, V., Ma, W., Pagurek, B., & Esfandiari, B. (2003). *On the dynamic manipulation of classes of service for xml web services* (Research Report N° SCE-03-15). Ottawa, Canada: Department of Systems and Computer Engineering, Carleton University. Available at: http://www.sce.carleton.ca/netmanage/papers/TosicEtAlResRepJune2003.pdf

Yu, T., & Lin, K.-J. (2005). Service selection algorithms for composing complex services with multiple QoS constraints. In Benatallah, B., Casati, F., & Traverso, P. (Eds.), *ICSOC* (*Vol. 3826*, pp. 130–143). Springer.

Zeng, L., Benatallah, B., Dumas, M., Kalagnanam, J., & Sheng, Q. Z. (2003). Quality driven web services composition. In *WWW '03: Proceedings of the 12th International Conference on World Wide Web* (pp. 411-421). ACM Press.

KEY TERMS AND DEFINITIONS

QoS-Based Service Description: The description of the service performance in terms of constraints on quality of service attributes and metrics.

QoS-Based Service Matchmaking: The process of matching QoS demands with QoS offers according to a specific matchmaking metric, where QoS demands are descriptions of the desired QoS service performance and QoS offers are descriptions of the offered QoS service performance.

QoS-Based Service Description Alignment: The process of aligning QoS-based Service Descriptions (i.e. QoS Offers and Demands) according to their equivalent QoS attributes and metrics.

Matchmaking Metric: A metric formally describing the conditions under which two QoS-based Service Descriptions (i.e. a QoS Offer and Demand) should match.

QoS Meta-Model: A meta-model specifies which quality concepts can be used in QoS-based Service Descriptions, what are their relationships, how they should be described and in which order or structure.

QoS Model: A QoS model comprises QoS categories, attributes, and metrics containing also the relations between these QoS entities and usually follows a specific structure.

APPENDIX: PSEUDO-CODE OF THE EVALUATED ALGORITHMS

```
//This function is used to match an Offer O and a Demand D according to the
//CPconf algorithm and return the matching object result
match CPconf(O,D){
  for (Constraint c in D)} //Iterate over all constraints in D
    c = negate(c); //Negate each constraint
    prob = constructCSP(O,c); //Construct the CSP of the offer O and the
                             //negated demand constraint
    result = engine.solveCSP(prob); //Solve the CSP
    //If CSP is feasible, O does not match D so create and return a fail match
object
    if (result = "feasible"){
      match = new Match(O,"fail");
      return match;
    }
  }
  //If all CSPs are infeasible, O matches D so create and return an exact
match object
  match = new Match(O,"exact");
  return match;
}
//This function is used to match an Offer O and a Demand D according to the
//CPcond-conf algorithm and return the matching object result
match CPcond-conf(O,D){
  //If the offers metrics are not a superset of those of the demand, create a
  //fail match object and return it
  if (!superSet(O.metrics,D.metrics)){
    match = new Match(O,"fail");
    return match;
  }
  for (Constraint c in D){ //Iterate over all constraints in D
    if (c.type == "hard"){ //Only if a constraint is hard, it is processed
                                  //similarly to the CPconf algo-
rithm
          c = negate(c);
          prob = constructCSP(O,c);
          result = engine.solveCSP(prob);
          if (result = "feasible"){
              match = new Match(O,"fail");
          return match;
      }
    }
```

```
   }
   match = new Match(O,"exact");
   return match;
}
//This function is used to match an Offer O and a Demand D according to the
//CPexpl-cconf algorithm and return the matching object result
match CPexpl-cconf(O,D){
   //If the offers metrics are not a superset of those of the demand, create a
   //fail match object and return it
   if (!superSet(O.metrics,D.metrics)){
     match = new Match(O,"fail");
     return match;
   }
   prev_c = null; //previous constraint
   result = null;
   for (Constraint c in D){
     if (c.type == "hard"){ //Only if a constraint is hard, it is processed
          c = negate(c);
          if (prev_c == null){ //If the first hard demand constraint is
                                          //processed, a new CSP must
be created and solved
             prob = constructCSP(O,c);
               result = engine.solveCSP(prob);
        }
        else{ //If the demand constraint is not the first one, then remove the
previous
             //constraint from the CSP, add the current one and resolve the
problem
          engine.removeConstraint(prev_c);
          engine.addConstraint(c);
          result = engine.resolve();
        }
       //If CSP is feasible, O doesn't match D so create and return a fail
match object
            if (result = "feasible"){
                match = new Match(O,"fail");
            return match;
          }
        prev_c = c;
     }
   }
   //If all CSPs are infeasible, O matches D so create and return an exact
match object
   match = new Match(O,"exact");
   return match;
```

```
}
//This function is used to match an Offer O and a Demand D according to the
//CPexpl-unary algorithm and return the matching object result
match CPexpl-unary(O,D){
  weight = 0; //the offer's weight
  type = "super"; //the offer is assumed to be "super" initially
  //a hard constraint's weight equals to the number of demand constraints
  hard_weight = D.constraints.size();
  //If the offers metrics are not a superset of those of the demand, then
  if (!superSet(O.metrics,D.metrics)){
    //get the weight of all constraints that involve a missing demand metric
    weight = getMissingMetricConstrWeight(O.metrics,D);
    //if the weight is greater than the weight of all hard constraints
    //then the offer's type is "fail"
    if (weight >= D.hard_constraints_size * hard_weight) type = "fail";
    //else if the weight is greater that the weight of a hard constraint, then
    //the offer's type is "partial"
    else if (weight >= hard_weight) type = "partial";
    else type = "exact"; //else the offer's type is "exact"
    //filter the demand to remove the constraints involving a missing metric
    D = filterDemand(D,O.metrics);
  }
  prev_c = null; //the previous constraint
  result = null;
  //variable storing the number of hard constraints currently violated
  hard_cons = 0;
  for (Constraint c in D){ //Iterate over all constraints in D
    c = negate(c);
    //if previous constraint is null, then either the first demand constraint
is
    //processed or the previous CSP was feasible, so a new CSP has to be cre-
ated
    //and solved
    if (prev_c == null){
      prob = constructCSP(O,c);
      result = engine.solveCSP(prob);
    }
    //if previous CSP was infeasible, remove previous constraint, add the new
one, and
    //resolve the CSP
    else{
      engine.removeConstraint(prev_c);
      engine.addConstraint(c);
      result = engine.resolve();
    }
```

```
    if (result = "feasible"){
       //If the CSP is feasible and the demand constraint was hard, then the
       //offer's type becomes "partial" and its weight is increased with the
       //hard_weight, while the hard_cons var is increased by 1
       if (c.type = "hard"){
          type = "partial";
          weight = weight + hard_weight;
          hard_cons++;
       }
       //If CSP is feasible and demand constraint was soft, then the offer's
weight is
       //increased, and if its type is "super" then it is downgraded to "exact"
       else {
          weight += c.weight;
          if (type == "super") type = "exact";
       }
       prev_c = null;
    }
    else prev_c = c;
  }
  //This condition checks if the offer belongs to the first three categories
  //So if it is satisfied, the appropriate matching object is created
  if (hard_cons == 0 || hard_cons != D.hard_constraints_size)
     match = new Match(O,type,weight);
  //Otherwise, the offer is a "fail" match and a respective object must be
created
  else
     match = new Match(O,"fail",weight);

  return match;
}
//This function is used to run any matchmaking algorithm according to the of-
fer list
//and demand given as input and provide as a result the matching categories
set
//IO Arguments: O_list->Offer list, D->Demand, algo->algorithm for matchmaking
two
//QoS specs, Matches-> matchmaking results
Matches runAlgo(O_list,D,algo){
  Exact = [];
  Fail = [];
  Matches = [];
  //The first three algorithms return 2 types of matches
  if (algo != CPexpl-unary){
     //Iterator over all offers and matchmake them with D
```

```
  for (Offer O in O_list){
    match = algo(O,D);
    //Depending on the type of match returned, put it to the appropriate
category
      if (match.type == "exact")
        Exact.add(match);
      else
        Fail.add(match);
    }
    //Add the filled in match categories to the Matches variable
    Matches.add(Exact);
    Matches.add(Fail);
  }
  else{ // Run the CPexpl-unary algorithm
    Super = [];
    Partial = [];
    //Iterator over all offers and matchmake them with D
    for (Offer O in O_list){
      match = algo(O,D);
    //Depending on the type of match returned, put it to the appropriate
category
      if (match.type == "super")
        Super.add(match);
      else if (match.type == "exact")
        Exact.add(match);
      else if (match.type == "partial")
        Partial.add(match);
      else
        Fail.add(match);
    }
    //Add the match categories to the Matches variable. The last three catego-
ries
    //are added after they are sorted according to the weight each match ob-
ject has
    Matches.add(Super);
    sort(Exact);
    Matches.add(Exact);
    sort(Partial);
    Matches.add(Partial);
    sort(Fail);
    Matches.add(Fail);
  }
  return Matches;
}
```

Chapter 11
Performance Modeling for Quality of Service Prediction in Service-Oriented Systems

Christoph Rathfelder
FZI Research Center for Information Technology Karlsruhe, Germany

Benjamin Klatt
FZI Research Center for Information Technology Karlsruhe, Germany

Franz Brosch
FZI Research Center for Information Technology Karlsruhe, Germany

Samuel Kounev
Karlsruhe Institute of Technology, Germany

ABSTRACT

With the introduction of services, systems become more flexible as new services can easily be composed out of existing services. Services are increasingly used in mission-critical systems and applications, and therefore, considering Quality of Service (QoS) properties is an essential part of the service selection. Quality prediction techniques support the service provider in determining possible QoS levels that can be guaranteed to a customer or in deriving the operation costs induced by a certain QoS level. In this chapter, we present an overview on our work on modeling service-oriented systems for performance prediction using the Palladio Component Model. The prediction builds upon a model of a service-based system, and evaluates this model in order to determine the expected service quality. The presented techniques allow for early quality prediction, without the need for the system being already deployed and operating. We present the integration of our prediction approach into an SLA management framework. The emerging trend to combine event-based communication and Service-Oriented Architecture (SOA) into Event-based SOA (ESOA) induces new challenges to our approach, which are topic of a special subsection.

DOI: 10.4018/978-1-61350-432-1.ch011

INTRODUCTION

With the introduction of service-oriented computing and virtualized cloud infrastructures, the dynamics of software systems at runtime and their flexibility increases. Services can be composed at runtime and infrastructure can be provisioned on demand. The new freedom to orchestrate services potentially from multiple providers gives software architects the chance to support business requirements with less in-house development and infrastructure. The challenge in Service-Oriented Architectures (SOA) to find functional interoperable services is a research topic since the rise of SOA. Solutions like the Universal Description, Discovery and Integration (UDDI) have already been available for a number of years.

Meanwhile, new challenges have cropped up. With the success of services and computing clouds, software architects who make use of those technologies, have to consider their restricted influence and control on those external services. But as services directly support business applications, their quality becomes important for the success of the whole enterprise. At this point, Service Level Agreements (SLAs) come into play. They are already well-established for computer centers, help desks and even non-computer-related industries. In the field of SOA, SLAs serve as a contract between the service consumer and connected service providers. Beyond the functional interoperability, the service provider guarantees a certain quality level for his services specified in the SLA. The service consumer again can act as service provider and offer a new orchestrated service.

The guarantee of a certain Quality of Service (QoS) level for a service specified in an SLA is an important aspect in service-oriented systems. Such guarantees may concern, for example, the response time and throughput of a service. SLAs determine the quality properties that can be expected from a provided service. SLAs are negotiated before a service is deployed and used by the customer.

The service consumer is only able to monitor the compliance of a QoS level on the granularity of service invocations. The operation and controlling of service internals and the detection and forecast of performance problems can only be done by the provider and is not accessible for the customer. Service providers create general offers for services as well as react on individual requests of potential customers. General and individual offers have to be based on sound data to ensure that services do not violate the guaranteed service levels. Additionally, service providers have to know in advance which infrastructure resources and external software services are required in order to fulfill a customer's request and estimate the resource demand induced by new applications on the hardware infrastructure. This knowledge allows them to estimate costs and to acquire necessary resources as well as optimize the overall resource utilization. This information helps, for example, to identify the optimal trade-off between costs and offered quality.

The prediction of performance attributes is a very complex task as the performance of a service depends on several factors. The number of concurrent service consumers and invocations as well as the used infrastructure resources the service is deployed on are two obvious influence factors. In case of a service composition, the performance of the composed service highly depends on the performance of the services it is composed of. Thus, a performance prediction technique for services has to consider all these aspects. Many different performance prediction techniques and models have been developed in the last years as surveyed in (Balsamo, Di Marco, Inverardi, & Simeoni, 2004; Koziolek, 2009). Often these approaches require expert knowledge to build and configure the prediction models or they do not consider all the necessary influence factors.

The Palladio Component Model (PCM) (Becker, Koziolek, & Reussner, 2009) is a design-oriented performance meta-model for modeling software systems. It allows an explicit capturing of service dependencies like dependencies on the service's usage profile and execution environment as well as external services. It provides support for a number of different performance analysis techniques including layered queueing networks (Koziolek & Reussner, 2008), stochastic process algebras (Happe J., 2008) and simulation models (Becker, 2008). In the PCM, models are parameterized. This enables reusing models for different usage scenarios and execution environments without changing the model of the service itself. This chapter bases on our earlier work on performance prediction in general and research results about using PCM based performance predictions in the context of service-oriented systems. After a short introduction into QoS prediction in those systems we introduce the PCM in more detail. We present a Palladio-based performance prediction integrated into an SLA management framework to support manual and automated prediction during SLA negotiation. While event-based communication is an emerging paradigm to build more loosely coupled and scalable service-oriented systems, we also present our work on extending the PCM to allow modeling and predicting systems using this paradigm. An outlook to current and future research directions as well as a short conclusion and summary completes the chapter.

BACKGROUND

In general, SLAs guarantee a range of quality attributes. Performance attributes like response time, mean throughput, or resource utilization are some of the more prominent ones. Predicting such performance attributes is one of the main targets of Performance Engineering as a discipline. It is of interest for researchers since a long time even before the advent of SOA. Performance prediction in general and for services and service compositions in particular is a complex activity since performance is influenced by at least four

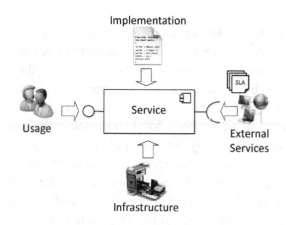

Figure 1. Influence factors on performance

factors as illustrated in Figure 1, which should all be considered by the prediction models.

It is obvious that the performance of a service is influenced by its implementation. In case of a service composition, the performance also depends on the performance of the external services that are used. In addition, the execution environment the service is deployed in has a big impact on the performance, too. For example, using a faster server might lead to a faster service execution. The last and often neglected influence factor is the service usage profile. Invoking a service once a minute or several times per second can make a big difference in the response time of a service. Especially, in a multi-user scenario where several customers use the same service with different guaranteed service levels or different services running on the same infrastructure. In such a case it is not possible to analyze the performance of each service separately. Due to these mutual interferences in such a scenario, specialized prediction techniques for service performance and resource utilization are required. As these predictions should be performed for each SLA negotiation, a highly automated tool support is required.

Performance prediction techniques can be categorized into simulation-based and analytical approaches; however this classification is no clear cut (Kounev, 2009). Simulation models are software programs that mimic the behavior of a system as requests arrive and get processed at the various system resources. Such models are normally stochastic because they have one or more random variables as input (e.g., the request interarrival times). The structure of a simulation program is based on the states of the simulated system and simulated resources (e.g. CPU) used by the system. The simulation programs record the duration of time spent in different states. Based on these data, performance metrics of interest (e.g., the average time a request takes to complete or the average system throughput) can be estimated at the end of the simulation run. The main advantage of simulation models is that they are very general and can be made as accurate as desired. However, this accuracy comes at the cost of the time taken to develop and run the models. Usually, many long runs are required to obtain estimates of needed performance measures with reasonable confidence levels. A comprehensive treatment of simulation techniques can be found in (Banks, Carson, Nelson, & Nicol, 2004) and (Law & Kelton, 2000).

Analytical models are usually less expensive to build and more efficient to analyze compared with simulation models. However, because they are defined at a higher level of abstraction, they are normally less detailed and accurate. Queueing networks and generalized stochastic Petri nets are perhaps the two most popular types of models used in practice. Queueing networks provide a very powerful mechanism for modeling hardware contention (contention for CPU time, disk access, and other hardware resources) and scheduling strategies. A number of efficient analysis methods have been developed for product-form queueing networks, a special subclass of queueing networks. The downside of queueing networks is that they are not expressive enough to model software contention and synchronization aspects accurately. Extended queueing networks (MacNair, 1985) and layered queueing networks (also called stochastic rendezvous networks) (Woodside, Neilson, Petriu,

& Majumdar, 1995; Woodside M.) provide some support for modeling software contention and synchronization aspects, however they are often restrictive and inaccurate. In contrast to queueing networks, generalized stochastic Petri nets can easily express software contention, simultaneous resource possession, asynchronous processing, and synchronization aspects. However, they do not provide any support for scheduling strategies. With queueing Petri nets (Bause, 1993; Bause & Buchholz, 1998), which combine the modeling power and expressiveness of queueing networks and stochastic Petri nets, this disadvantage can be eliminated. A major hurdle to the practical use of queueing Petri nets, however, is that their analysis suffers from the state space explosion problem limiting the size of the models that can be solved. Currently, the only way to circumvent this problem is by using simulation for model analysis (Kounev & Buchmann, 2006). All of the above performance prediction techniques have in common, that detailed knowledge about the used prediction models is required, so performance prediction could only be carried out by performance experts and not by each software developer.

Over the last fifteen years a number of approaches have been proposed for integrating performance prediction techniques into the software engineering process. Efforts were initiated with Smith's seminal work on Software Performance Engineering (SPE) (Smith, 1990). Since then, the performance engineering community has developed a number of architecture level performance meta-models. The most prominent examples are the UML SPT profile ((OMG), 2005) and its successor, the UML MARTE profile ((OMG), 2006). Both of them are extensions of UML as the de facto standard modeling language for software architectures. In addition, the OMG defined a general process for model-based performance predictions as illustrated in Figure 2 (Becker, 2008). The starting point of this process is a model that describes the software system itself using an established modeling language like the UML. General software models do not include any information specific to the performance characteristics of a software. This information is added in the next step. If the system is not implemented yet the resource demands are estimated. If an implementation is already available, for example in the case of a refactoring, measurements of the system can be used to gather the relevant information to annotate the model. The annotation can be done using one of the UML profiles mentioned before or using a meta-model designed specifically for this purpose such as the KLAPER model (Grassi, Mirandola, & Sabetta, 2005). Following this, the annotated software model is used as an input for a transformation into a model used by one of the performance prediction techniques already mentioned above. These models are then analyzed analytically or simulated. In a final step, the prediction results are returned as feedback for the original software model. A survey of model-based performance prediction techniques for software systems was published in (Balsamo, Di Marco, Inverardi, & Simeoni, 2004)

Architecture-level performance models are often built manually during system development and are used at design and deployment time to evaluate alternative system designs and/or predict the system performance for capacity planning purposes. In recent years, with the increasing adoption of component-based software engineering, the performance evaluation community has focused on adapting and extending conventional SPE techniques to support component-based systems which are typically used for building modern service-oriented systems (Bertolino & Mirandola, 2004). Due to the still emerging field of model-based performance prediction there is no standard model or standard tool for the specified process. Most of the available models and tools differ from each other in the performance factors captured by their model annotations. The performance specific meta-models also vary in their alignment with the UML syntax. For example, the domain specific language of the SPEED tool developed by Smith et al. (Smith, 1990) has no overlap with the UML, while the Palladio Component Model, which we will introduce in more detail later, is aligned with the UML syntax. The following list provides an overview of performance prediction approaches in the context of

Figure 2. Model-based performance prediction process

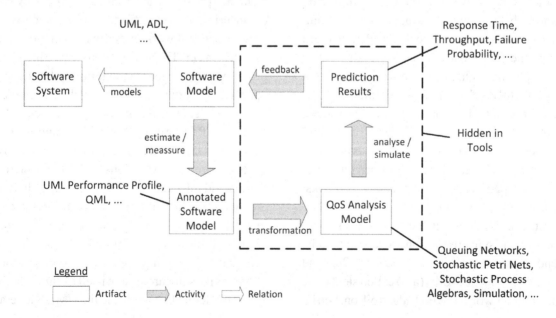

component-based systems. A recent survey of methods for component-based performance-engineering was published in (Koziolek, 2009).

- CB-SPE (Bertolino & Mirandola, 2004) applies the original SPE method of Smith et al. to component-based systems with the restriction that impacts of the internal processing and input parameters are not considered. Only probabilistic resource demands are used and the dependency on input parameters is not modeled.
- ROBOCOP (Bondarev, de With, Chaudron, & Muskens, 2005) is focused on the area of embedded systems. It is used to describe component internals in relation to the parameters of external services and resources. Due to the focus on embedded systems, resource parameters can only be specified as constant values and software layers are not supported at all.
- CBML (Wu & Woodside, 2004) presents an approach to use Layered Queueing Networks (LQN) to describe components from a performance point of view. Assembling a set of components is reflected in the assembly of the respective LQNs. The combined LQN is then solved to derive the overall performance properties of the system.
- PACC (Hissam, Moreno, Stafford, & Wallnau, 2002) is a conceptual framework to combine the performance properties of certified components and their assemblies. The weak point in this approach is that it provides only a conceptual framework and the quality of the prediction relies on the concrete method used for the prediction of the properties.
- SAPS (Balsamo & Marzolla, 2003) uses annotated UML models as input for performance predictions. The use of the well-known UML syntax for describing the system reduces the modeling complexity.

However, the approach lacks some tool support, which leads to a high modeling effort, as all annotations have to be done manually with compliance to the defined syntax.

One of the first approaches to combine the two worlds of Performance Engineering and Service-oriented Systems is presented in (Menascé & Dubey, 2007). This approach supports QoS brokering and service selection using analytic queueing models to predict the QoS of alternative services that could be selected under varying workload conditions. An approach to model the performance of composite SOA services composed by means of BPEL (Business Process Execution Language) was presented in (D'Ambrogio & Bocciarelli, 2007). Some further approaches based on simulation were proposed in (Song, Ryu, Chung, Jou, & Lee, 2005) and (Silver, Maduko, Jafri, Miller, & Sheth, 2003). In the first one, the control flow within a composed Web service is modeled using UML activity diagrams. Based on measurements under low load, the behavior of the composed service under high load is simulated and analyzed. The second approach uses a directed graph to model the process implemented by a composed Web service. This graph extended with the mean execution times of the used external services is the input to a simulation engine, used to derive the performance metrics under different load scenarios.

Within the Palladio approach (Becker, Koziolek, & Reussner, 2009), the two domains performance engineering and modeling of service-oriented systems with focus on QoS aspects are combined. We chose Palladio as our approach because it explicitly considers the four main performance influence factors as discussed earlier (see Figure 1). Especially the modeling of the system usage profile and its influence on the control and data flow throughout the architecture are accurately captured by the Palladio modeling approach, which allows for a more differentiated performance prediction with respect to usage profile changes.

The development of the Palladio Component Model (PCM) started in 2003 at the University of Oldenburg, and since 2006 it is continued at the Karlsruhe Institute of Technology (KIT) and the FZI Research Center for Information Technology. In the following, we provide a short overview of the most significant parts of the PCM. Further details about the PCM are given in (Becker, Koziolek, & Reussner, 2009) or can be found on the project website (KIT, 2010).

An Eclipse based modeling and prediction tool accompanies the PCM. This workbench includes graphical editors aligned with the UML syntax. Additionally, a simulation engine and several transformations into analytical prediction models exist as well as a visualization of the prediction results. Due to this integration of modeling, transformation, performance analyses and visualization, the performance evaluation of a system does not require any expert knowledge about the underlying prediction techniques. The system is modeled using a UML-like graphical syntax. The resulting models are automatically transformed either into simulation code or an analytical performance model, which is solved for the performance metric of interest. Finally, the results are visualized and presented to the user. As sketched in Figure 3, PCM supports the evaluation of different performance attributes, including response time, maximum throughput, resource utilization, and QoS levels. To realize these predictions, the Palladio approach provides a model for service-oriented systems that reflect the already mentioned four aspects implementation, service composition, deployment, and service usage as separated sub models. If the target service requires external software services outside the provider's domain, QoS annotations can be used to integrate quality levels into the prediction as they are guaranteed by SLAs.

In PCM, the implementation of services is specified in a component model called repository. The repository includes the interfaces (comparable to signature lists) that are provided or required by a service. Furthermore, the repository includes a description of the internal behavior of the provided services. The developer describes the internals of a service by means of a so-called Resource Demanding Service Effect Specification (RDSEFF). RDSEFFs define an abstract internal behavior with elements to specify the control flow as well as actions, which allow the specification of resource demands for internal processing or the invocation of external services.

In the composition model called System, the influence of external services and service composi-

Figure 3. Palladio approach

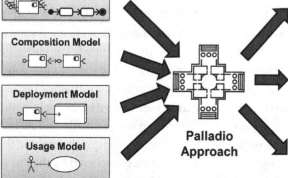
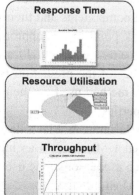

tions is reflected. The service is linked with other services that provide the required interfaces. Additionally, it is possible to specify extra-functional attributes of services as defined in SLAs. With these QoS annotations it is possible to consider the QoS levels of external services in the prediction without the need to model their internal behavior using an additional RDSEFF.

The influence of hardware resources is represented in the deployment model that consists of the ResourceEnvironment and the Allocation. The ResourceEnvironment includes a specification of the available hardware resources (like processor speed, network links, etc.). The allocation model specifies the deployment of services on hardware nodes.

The usage profile of the service is defined in the Usage model. This description comprises the type of workload issued to the system. The workload specifies for example how many users invoke the system or the interarrival time of invocations. Furthermore, the Usage model reflects the value of input parameters, as this can be a significant influence factor, too. For example, the response time of a service, that provides a conversion from word documents into PDF files highly depends on the size of the document respectively the number of pages. In the following section, we demonstrate the use of Palladio to model and predict the performance of a service-oriented system.

PERFORMANCE PREDICTION FOR SERVICE-ORIENTED SYSTEMS USING THE PALLADIO COMPONENT MODEL

As already mentioned, software performance prediction allows the a-priori evaluation of the quality of software services before they are actually deployed and executed. Prediction-results can be used by software service providers (1) to create general service offers, (2) to react to individual service requests of potential customers, and (3)

to optimize the cost induced by the hardware and external services used during runtime. Modeling service-oriented systems with the aim to conduct performance predictions is supported by the Palladio approach. This section presents the integration of a Palladio-based prediction into an SLA management framework within a Software-as-a-Service (SaaS) scenario. The last part of this section gives an overview of our current research on extending Palladio to support event-based communication, which is used increasingly in service-oriented systems.

Integration of Palladio into an SLA Management Framework

In the context of the European research project SLA@SOI (SLA@SOI, 2009), the Palladio approach is used as foundation to provide a performance prediction for software services integrated in an SLA management framework. The framework supports SLA negotiation, service provisioning, monitoring and adjustment across multiple layers (business, software, and infrastructure) and multiple provider domains (Comuzzi, Kotsokalis, Rathfelder, Theilmann, Winkler, & Zacco, 2009). Figure 4 shows the architecture of the available prediction tools and their integration into the SLA management framework. The architecture has been designed to support two envisioned scenarios, namely: (1) the manually controlled quality prediction during the service offering phase, and (2) the fully automated usage of the prediction during the SLA negotiation phase.

In the first scenario, a software service provider uses the prediction to determine feasible quality parameters for the software services to be offered. Prediction results are used for the creation of corresponding software SLA templates. The software service provider uses an integrated environment for the graphical creation of prediction models, the actual prediction, and the graphical visualization of prediction results (Figure 4, right-hand side).

Figure 4. Software performance prediction in SLA@SOI

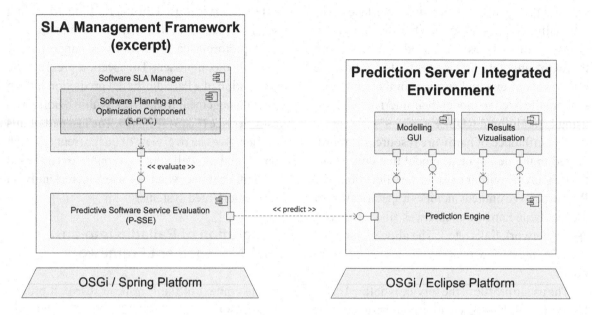

In the second scenario, prediction is performed automatically as part of the SLA negotiation process conducted by the SLA management framework. To this end, we have extended the prediction engine with a web service interface. Thus, the environment becomes a prediction server application, and prediction can be triggered programmatically. Within the SLA management framework, prediction is offered as a Service-Evaluation component for the case of predictive software service evaluation (P-SSE). It is invoked by the Software Planning and Optimization sub-component (S-POC) of the Software SLA Manager, in order to determine a proper reaction to a concrete SLA offer from a potential customer (accept, reject, or counter-offer). P-SSE invokes the prediction engine with a prediction model as input and retrieves the predicted response time as a result. Both scenarios use the same prediction engine; consistent results independent from the phase of application (service offering or service negotiation) are thus ensured.

Modeled Software-as-a-Service (SaaS) Scenario

The Open Reference Case (ORC) scenario was also developed within the European research project SLA@SOI. It is used as an open source demonstrator for a SLA management framework. The ORC is a service-oriented retail solution that can be used in a trading system as for example in a supermarket. It includes IT support for retail chains in general, covering enterprise headquarters (central management issues), stores (local management) and cash desks. Several enterprises, each with a certain number of stores are connected to a single service provider, supporting sales of goods with an IT system. This provider offers various services such as inventory management, credit card payment, preferred customer club card, and accounting.

The ORC service provider is connected to several external providers such as credit card institutes, wholesale centers, CRM supplier, etc. The services run on top of an IT infrastructure offered by a further provider. If the customer at the cash desk decides to pay with credit card, the card has to be validated and debited according to the summarized sales value. This requires an additional bank service provider, who offers this banking service to the ORC service provider. A more detailed explanation of this scenario and the system can be found in (Stopar, Hadalin, Rathfelder, & Klatt, 2011). The rest of this section focuses on the different sub-models of the PCM performance prediction model.

The sales process is supported by the inventory service and the payment service. The latter is a composition of two basic services: card validation service and payment debit service. The ORC service repository contains a specification of the components involved in the sales process, as well as the software components of the underlying legacy application (the trading system).

The ORC comprises 15 components – 8 service components and 7 legacy components. The service components include basic services (such as the inventory service) and composed services (such as the payment service).

Figure 5 illustrates the system view on the ORC service composition model, showing individual services and legacy components, as well as their composition. The system as a whole provides a set of interfaces (e.g., the payment interface), and requires a service interface (the bank interface), that indicates the need of a software service provided by an external software service provider.

As an example for a behavioral specification, Figure 6 depicts the control flow for the handlePayment() operation of the composed payment service. It is a composition of the card validation and payment debit services that in turn make use of the

Figure 5. Open reference case system model

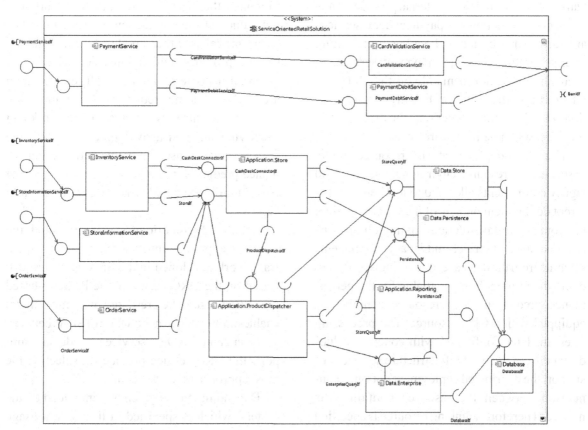

Figure 6. Payment service RDSEFF

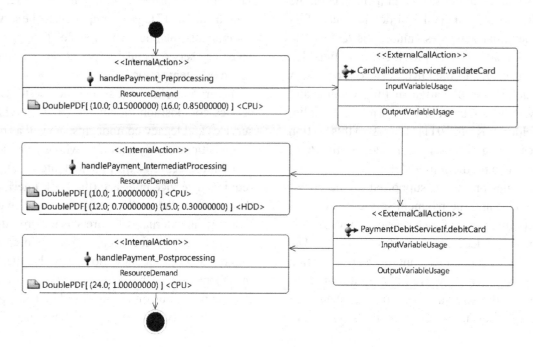

bank service offered by an external provider. Calls to the card validation and payment debit services are surrounded by internal actions representing internal processing of the payment service. In each internal action demands on the CPU and HDD are specified using probability density functions (PDF). In these functions, the probabilities for different value ranges are defined.

The ORC deployment and resource model describes the resource environment service and legacy components allocated to it. There are different deployment options of the ORC available: the complete retail solution running on one virtual machine, or service and legacy components separate from the database. Accordingly, different deployment models are available for the performance prediction. Each resource container is equipped with a CPU resource. The processing rates are later configured with concrete values derived from the used infrastructure services. To support the distributed deployment option, a connection between the resource containers is needed. Therefore, a linking resource is specified

to connect these containers. Latency and throughput values of the connection are specified. The usage model is either created by the software service provider, anticipating the behavior of potential customers, or dynamically created upon a concrete customer request. All operations are invoked concurrently with an open workload specifying an inter-arrival time, i.e., the time between two consecutive invocations. Performance prediction takes all interdependencies of concurrently executed service operations into account.

As already mentioned, we integrated the Palladio approach into the SLA management framework developed in the SLA@SOI project. Based on the ORC scenario, the Palladio-based predictions using the presented prediction model enables an automated negotiation of SLAs between a customer and an ORC service provider and supports the ORC service provider in selecting the most appropriate infrastructure.

Depending on the given maximal load on the system, which is specified in the SLA, a usage model is derived automatically and the simulation is started. The results are then aggregated and the mean value as well as several quantiles of the predicted response time are returned to the SLA negotiation component. In addition to this automated SLA negotiation, the Palladio prediction is used in several industrial use cases to evaluate the various QoS levels and eases the definition of SLA offers significantly. Currently, PCM is limited to service calls following the request/reply paradigm. Event-based communication following the Fire-And-Forget communication style is increasingly introduced in service-oriented systems. The modeling of such systems and the corresponding extensions of the PCM is part of the next section.

Extension of PCM to Support Event-Based SOA

The use of event-based communication within a SOA promises several benefits including more loosely coupled services and better scalability. However, the loose coupling of services makes it hard for system developers to estimate the behavior and performance of systems composed of multiple services. With the extension of the PCM presented in this section, we enable the design-oriented modeling of event-driven and service-oriented systems. Additionally, we describe a transformation of the introduced model extension to already existing model elements in the current version of PCM. The extension combined with the transformation enables the usage of existing analytical and simulative techniques while significantly reducing the modeling effort and complexity.

In the current version of PCM, only synchronous call-return communication between components is supported. As shown in (Happe, Becker, Rathfelder, Friedrich, & Reussner, 2009), it is however possible to define a performance equivalent model for asynchronous point-to-point communication using a combination of non-

synchronized fork actions and external service calls. Following this approach, asynchronous events are modeled using synchronous service calls and therefore a semantic gap between the system implementation and the architecture model is introduced. Moreover, the modeling effort of this workaround increases dramatically if event-based communication following the *Publish-Subscribe* paradigm is considered. To reduce this overhead and to eliminate the semantic gap, it is necessary to extend PCM with elements to model event-based communication semantically correct:

- **Events:** are the central element of event-based communication. In contrast to interfaces and method signatures, which include a set of parameters, events only specify the underlying data type. Similarly to method parameters, the event data can be considered when modeling a component's internal processing for a specific event type.
- **Event Sources:** mark a component to emit a certain type of events. For each emitted event type, the component must provide at least one event source. It is necessary to extend the RDSEFF with a new action called EmitEventAction allowing to instantiate and send events. This action is similar to an external service call. However, it does not block the client processing since it does not need to wait for any return values.
- **Event Sinks:** specify that a component is able to receive and process certain types of events. In analogy to event sources, each consumed event type induces an appropriate event sink. Only compatible event sources and sinks are allowed to be connected. Similar to provided interfaces that require the specification of RDSEFFs for each provided service, each event sink requires the specification of an event handler for every accepted event type. Event handlers are modeled similarly to ordinary component services using RDSEFFs.

The PCM meta-model with the extension presented above enables software architects to model their services with asynchronous many-to-many event-based communication. To feed the existing simulation and prediction methods, the new conceptual model elements have to be matched to the capabilities of the simulation and prediction methods. In service-oriented systems, the communication is often encapsulated by a communication middleware called Enterprise Service Bus (ESB). Each ESB has an implementation specific behavior and thus an influence on the performance of the whole service-oriented system, built on top of the ESB. To reflect the influence of the underlying communication middleware, the platform-independent model is transformed into a platform-specific model taking the platform's quality attributes into account.

To take advantage of the existing simulation and prediction methods, a model-to-model transformation substitutes the new event elements in the high-level model with elements that match the capabilities of the simulation and prediction methods (see Figure 7). In a second step, this platform-independent model is transformed to a platform-specific model. This is done by weaving a middleware model into the platform-independent one, in order to take the platform-specific quality attributes into account. Surveying the high-level, event-based connection in the meta-model leads to a chain of processing steps involved in reality. To facilitate the realistic quality prediction of the component interaction, an analysis of the possible steps has led to a conceptual chain of components involved. To separate between platform-independent and platform-specific parts, we introduced the chain of conceptual components for the overall data flow, and a middleware model for the resource demands.

Platform-Independent Model

In reality, if software communication comes down to the protocol level, it is often implemented with a synchronous infrastructure. Those systems realize the asynchronous behavior with intermediate components like queues and hubs. We used the same concept in the component chain architecture mentioned before. The concept enables modeling the intermediate chain based on components and processing descriptions already supported by the prediction methods of the PCM Workbench.

In the following, we describe this intermediate model in more detail.

To connect the components in the communication chain, the pipes and filters pattern is used. In the pipe, every component provides and requires the same interface derived from the event types of the replaced sinks and sources. Event sources and sinks are replaced with required and provided interfaces. Communication through operation interfaces is completely synchronous. To realize the asynchronous behavior, ForkActions decouple the individual control flow in the event distribution part. ForkActions can contain an arbitrary number of sub-control-flows, triggered without waiting for their response.

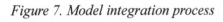

Figure 7. Model integration process

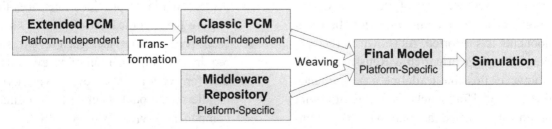

Figure 8. Model transformation

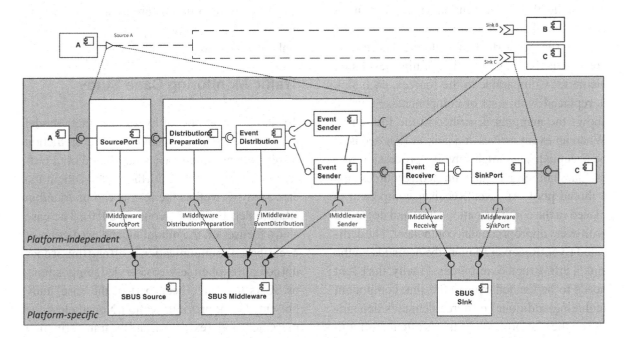

Figure 8 presents the mapping between a high-level source element and its low-level counterparts. Sources are transformed to sets of components. Each of them is responsible for a different concern in the event processing.

Component A is the original component emitting the event. To model the described operational communication chain, the source is replaced by a chain of components using synchronous operation calls. Strictly speaking, the component calls synchronously the SourcePort that takes care for the further processing. To represent the operational communication in the PCM model, the transformation replaces the original SourceRole of the source component with a required interface.

The SourcePort represents the client-side processing and communication of the event to the middleware. Such processing can include marshaling, queueing or similar actions. The SourcePort is deployed on the same system infrastructure as the source component it belongs to.

When a new event arrives at the middleware, some processing might be required at this point.

This processing takes place once per event and is independent of the number of recipients interested in the event. This processing can include middleware-side marshaling, security-checks, compression, and others depending on the underlying platform. To trigger the specific resource demands, the DistributionPreparation component is placed as the first in the middleware-side component chain.

The event-based communication is often used in an asynchronous, many-to-many relationship between components. To represent the processing sub-path for replication on the one hand, and decoupling, on the other hand, the EventDistribution component has been introduced. Its internal processing splits the control flow once for each downstream sink. From the quality prediction point of view, this component triggers the middleware demands specific to the distribution step.

When the middleware has replicated the events, it forwards them to the recipients. This step might include additional processing like compressions, transformations, filters, and others. The sending itself can have quality related resource demands. To handle this, an EventSender component is placed into the chain per recipient.

The second part of the intermediate model creation is the transformation of high-level sink elements. Comparable to the sources, each sink is replaced with a set of components. Figure 8 shows the mapping described in the following. When an event arrives at a sink, it first needs to be accepted. This might involve processing like de-marshaling or require limited resources like a thread pool. An EventReceiver component is placed in the communication chain and deployed with every appropriate sink component. The dedicated EventReceiver triggers the demands on the sink's infrastructure resources. Finally, the event needs to be handed over to the sink component including additional resource demands depending on the platform. While this is often in smooth transition to the event receiving, it is conceptual by separated to not limit the flexibility in the supported platforms. The SinkPort component represents the corresponding demands in the processing chain. The original sink component is modified to handle the incoming operation calls instead of the emitted events. The previous event sink is now replaced with a provided interface.

Platform-Specific Model

The available middleware products for event-based communication provide a wide range of event transmission methods. This includes central message hubs, peer-to-peer systems and a lot in-between. The mode of transmission and the platform used for it might have a big impact on the quality attributes of the overall system. The presented approach contains a fully automatic transformation, weaving an additional middleware model into the component chain described above.

To enable the weaving process, the middleware model has to provide predefined interfaces. There is one middleware interface for each member of the platform-independent component chain.

How many components are used to provide those interfaces in the middleware model is up to the architect. This could be one per Interface, three for sinks, middleware, and sources, or just one for all.

Traffic Monitoring Case Study

To show the applicability of our meta-model extension and the correctness of the prediction results, we present a case study based on a traffic monitoring system. Further details about the case study as well as the results can be found in (Rathfelder, Evans, & Kounev, 2010). The case study focuses on the modeling and prediction of event-based communication itself and thus it does not contain explicit services, service compositions or SLAs that have been part of the case study presented in the previous section. Nonetheless, the presented model extension and the transformation chain combined with the results of the first case study are also applicable to event-driven SOA. The traffic monitoring system was developed within the TIME project (Transport Information Monitoring Environment) (Bacon, et al., 2008) at the University of Cambridge. The application monitors the location of buses and the current state of traffic lights. Based on this information it is possible for example to optimize the traffic flow and to calculate traveling and arrival times. This application is of interest because of the required information about the state of traffic lights alongside the location information from buses that are, in many cases, not maintained by the same organization. Furthermore, the components can be deployed on different computing nodes with different resources. The involved resources range from embedded systems, running within a bus up to a central mainframe system for the traffic prediction. The implementation of this application uses the following four classes of SBUS services (Figure 9).

- **Bus Location Provider (the "ACIS component"):** The bus location provider uses

Figure 9. Traffic monitoring scenario

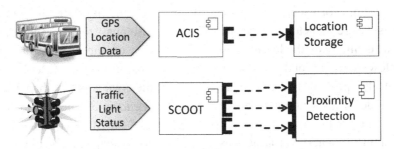

sensors to note the locations of buses and report them as soon as they change. In this case, GPS sensors coupled with a proprietary radio network are used.

- **Location Storage:** The location storage component maintains states for a set of objects that describe the most recent location reported for each of them. The input is a stream of events consisting of name/location pairs with timestamps, making a Bus Location Provider a suitable event source.

- **Traffic Light Status Reporter (the "SCOOT component"):** The city's traffic lights are controlled by a SCOOT system (Hunt, Robertson, Bretherton, & Winton, 1981), designed to schedule green and red lights to optimize the use of the road network. To control the lights, SCOOT knows whether each light is red or green and can transmit a stream of information derived from vehicle detecting induction loops installed in the road.

- **Proximity Detector:** This detector receives a stream of trigger events indicating when lights turn from green to red and vice versa; this stream is emitted by the SCOOT component. Upon such a trigger, the SCOOT component's Remote Procedure Call (RPC) facility is used to determine the location of the light that just turned red. This is collated with current bus locations to find out which buses are nearby.

The communication between services is handled by the SBUS (Stream BUS) middleware (Ingram, 2009). Messages are emitted from and received by endpoints and each endpoint is connected to one or more others. An endpoint specifies the schema of the messages that it will emit or accept. Each endpoint can be a client, a server, a source, or a sink. On the one hand, clients and servers implement RPC functionality, providing synchronous request/reply, and are attached in many-to-one relationships. On the other hand, event streams emitted by source endpoints are received by sinks in an asynchronous fashion. Due to the SBUS middleware, it is possible to distribute the components over several computing nodes as well as centralize them on one node without any changes of the components' implementation. Finding the maximal processable event rate for a given deployment option or a resource-efficient deployment scenario that still meets all SLA agreements regarding the event processing times is a complex task. Using performance prediction techniques eases the analysis of performance attributes for different deployment scenarios and event rates without prototypical implementations or test environments.

In order to derive the CPU demand for internal processing to be represented in the performance model and to calibrate the SBUS specific middleware repository, we extended the SBUS framework with several sensors collecting the time spent within a component itself. This extension has been done in the library to push events to the

SBUS wrapper as well as in the wrapper to trigger the receiving component. For each component, several experiments were conducted to measure the time spent in the component, the library, and the wrapper under low workload conditions. With these measurements, it is possible to estimate the individual resource demands without resource contention effects. The mean value over more than 10,000 measurements whose variation was negligible was taken as the estimated resource demand.

To demonstrate the model accuracy, we conducted several experiments with different deployment scenarios and compared measurements in our test bed with the prediction results. For each scenario, we run multiple measurements under increasing event rates resulting in increasing utilization levels of the system. We then compared the model predictions against measurements on the real system in order to evaluate the model accuracy. The selection of different deployment scenarios allows us to separate different possible influence factors like single-threaded implementations of components or the influence of concurrently running component instances.

- *Scenario 1.* As described above, the SCOOT component is connected to the Proximity Detector and the ACIS component is connected to the Location Storage component. To explore each of these interactions individually, we deployed ACIS together with Location Storage on one machine and SCOOT with Proximity Detector on another one. The prediction error is below 10% in most of the cases with exception of the cases under very low CPU utilization.
- *Scenario 2.* The first scenario did not include CPU contention effects since there were more CPU cores available than active threads running. In this scenario, we use the same setup as before but with multiple instances of the components. Each component is deployed in three instances resulting in 6

active threads per machine. In addition to considering CPU utilization, this time we also analyze the influence of CPU contention on the event processing times. With exception of the cases under very low load, the error was less than 5%.

- *Scenario 3.* The previous scenarios evaluated the SCOOT and ACIS interactions on separate machines. In this scenario, all four components are deployed on the same machine. Similarly to Scenario 1, we deployed only one instance of each component. As previously, with exception of the cases under very low load, the prediction error was below 5%. Even though in this case, we have four active threads (one per component), it was not possible to scale beyond a CPU utilization of 75%. This is because the computational load is not spread uniformly among the four threads and they are not running independently of one another (i.e., the Proximity Detector component is triggered by SCOOT and the Location Storage component is triggered by ACIS). As a result of this, not all four threads are always active at the same time and the 4 CPU cores cannot be saturated. The model predictions for the event processing times were of similar accuracy to those of the previous scenario.
- *Scenario 4.* In this last scenario, similarly to the previous one, we deployed all components on one machine, however, this time we used two instances of each component. The higher number of threads allows saturating the machine. Compared to the previous scenarios, the prediction error is slightly higher but still below 10% in most cases. Again, the predictions for the event processing times were similar.

In summary, the developed model proved to capture the system behavior well and provides accurate performance predictions under varying configurations and deployment scenarios. With a few exceptions, the modeling error was mostly below 10%. Using the model, we were able to predict the CPU utilization for a given event rate as well as the maximum event rate that can be sustained in a given deployment. In many cases, the maximum CPU utilization that could be reached was lower than expected due to the uneven distribution of the computational load among the active component threads. The model enabled us to accurately predict the maximum event rate that could be reached with a given number of component instances deployed on the physical machines. Furthermore, the model provided accurate predictions of the event processing times in scenarios with CPU contention. The developed model provides a tool for performance prediction and capacity planning that can be used to detect system bottlenecks and to ensure that the system is designed and sized to sustain its expected workload satisfying performance requirements.

FUTURE RESEARCH DIRECTIONS

In the future, the need for highly flexible and efficient systems will increase, therefore adaptability and re-configuration of systems and resources at runtimes is an important research topic. These systems will take use of automated built-in online performance predictions to enable a self-aware management of services and service compositions as well as of a distributed and shared infrastructure landscape. One part of our current and future research focuses on the idea to make architecture-level performance models like PCM usable at run-time. The newly founded Descartes research group (http://www. descartes-research.net) is working on enhancing PCM models to capture dynamic aspects of the environment and making them an integral part of the system (Kounev, 2010; Kounev, Brosig, Huber, & Reussner, 2010). To achieve this, the models should be integrated into the provided service. The execution environment should be enhanced with functionality to track dynamic changes and auto-

matically maintain those models during operation. The models can either be built manually during system design comparable to the SaaS scenario presented above or they are extracted at run-time based on online monitoring and measurement data as presented in (Brosig, Kounev, & Krogmann, 2009). These dynamic service performance models are continuously updated, refined and calibrated during operation based on online monitoring and measurement data.

The new models should be designed to encapsulate all information, both, static and dynamic, relevant to predicting a service's performance on-the-fly. This includes information about the service's software architecture, its workload and its execution environment. Due to the loose coupling and high distribution of service-oriented systems, the models of all involved services should be retrieved and combined by means of model composition techniques into a single architecture-level performance model. This architecture-level model encapsulates all information relevant to answering the performance questions. It will then be transformed into a predictive performance model by means of an automatic model-to-model transformation. A lot of different prediction models and techniques are available as surveyed in (Balsamo, Di Marco, Inverardi, & Simeoni, 2004; Koziolek, 2009), with different characteristics regarding accuracy, expressiveness, prediction speed, and required input data. The target predictive model type and level of abstraction as well as the solution technique will be determined on-the-fly based on the required accuracy and the time available for the analysis. Different model types like layered queueing networks, and queueing Petri nets as well as model solution techniques like exact analytical techniques and numerical approximation techniques will be exploited in order to provide flexibility in trading-off between prediction accuracy and analysis overhead.

The dynamic online performance prediction forms the basis for implementing techniques for self-aware performance and resource management in service infrastructures. Such techniques will be triggered automatically during operation in response to observe or forecast changes in service workloads. The goal will be to proactively adapt the system to such changes in order to avoid anticipated performance problems or inefficient resource usage. The adaptation will be performed in an autonomic fashion by considering a set of possible system reconfiguration scenarios (e.g., changing VM placement and/or resource allocations) and exploiting the online performance prediction mechanism to know the effect of such reconfigurations before making a decision. Model-based self-adaptation techniques have been studied in the software engineering and autonomic computing communities before. The use of dynamic architecture-level performance models at run-time for online performance and resource management however is a new research direction. The vision described above raises several big challenges that will be subject of long-term fundamental research. This includes abstractions for modeling performance-relevant aspects of services in dynamic virtualized environments, selection and generation of performance prediction models as well as their automated online extraction and calibration. Furthermore, techniques for self-aware performance and resource management guaranteeing SLAs while improving energy efficiency and lowering costs need to be considered in future research.

CONCLUSION

Meanwhile, the early challenges in service-oriented systems like the service fragmentation of a system or the detection of functional compatible services are more or less under control. However, new challenges have emerged like the management of non-functional properties of services especially in shared and cloud computing environments. Especially in business critical systems, guaranteed QoS (Quality of Service) levels became an important factor for the success of service-oriented computing. Determining and predicting the possible QoS-levels and deriving the requirements on the underlying infrastructure and external services are essential for an efficient and reliable operation of services.

As presented in this chapter, there is a large body of work on the prediction of software quality. This topic has grown according to the evolution of the software development itself. Meanwhile, it has reached an architectural level and is used to predict QoS-levels in service-oriented systems. The Palladio Component Model (PCM) is one of the advanced performance prediction approaches on the architectural level. Advantages of the PCM are its strong support for design-oriented modeling as well as the prediction under consideration of the system's usage, the used infrastructure and external services. Thanks to this, the PCM is feasible for the prediction of quality attributes in service-oriented systems. The integration of a Palladio-based performance prediction into an SLA management framework was demonstrated using a SaaS (Software-as-a-Service) scenario. Event-based communication is increasingly used in service-oriented systems. For this reason, this chapter included an extension of the PCM that enables the modeling and prediction of systems with event-based communication. Additionally, it provided details about a case study accomplished in co-operation of the Karlsruhe Institute of Technology and the University of Cambridge to proof the applicability and prediction accuracy of PCM in the context of an event-based distributed traffic management system installed in the City of Cambridge.

In the future, systems become increasingly dynamic and flexible. Thus, quality prediction of services and the deduction of the resource requirements to plan the infrastructure at design time is only a first step. As presented, there is already research ongoing which focuses on the about runtime management of quality models and attributes to enable the automatic adaptation and relocation of systems, especially in the field of cloud computing.

REFERENCES

Bacon, J., Beresford, A. R., Evans, D., Ingram, D., Trigoni, N., Guitton, A., et al. (2008). TIME: An open platform for capturing, processing and delivering transport-related data. *Proceedings of EEE Consumer Communications and Networking Conference.*

Balsamo, S., Di Marco, A., Inverardi, P., & Simeoni, M. (2004). Model-based performance prediction in software development: A survey. *IEEE Transactions on Software Engineering, 30*(5). doi:10.1109/TSE.2004.9

Balsamo, S., & Marzolla, M. (2003). A simulatrion-based approach to software performance modeling. *Proceedings of the 9th European Software Engineering Conference held jointly with 11th ACM SIGSOFT International Symposium on Foundations of Software Engineering.* ACM.

Banks, J., Carson, J., Nelson, B. L., & Nicol, D. (2004). *Discrete-event system simulation.* Prentice Hall.

Bause, F. (1993). *Queueing Petri nets - A formalism for the combined qualitytive and quantitative analysis of systems.* 5th International Workshop on Petri Nets and Performance Models. Toulouse.

Bause, F., & Buchholz, P. (1998). Queueing Petri nets with product form solution. *Performance Evaluation, 32*(4). doi:10.1016/S0166-5316(98)00005-4

Becker, S. (2008). *Coupled model transformations for QoS enabled component-based software design* (*Vol. 1*). Universitätsverlag Karlsruhe.

Becker, S., Koziolek, H., & Reussner, R. (2009). The Palladio component model for model-driven performance prediction. *Journal of Systems and Software, 82,* 3–22. doi:10.1016/j.jss.2008.03.066

Bertolino, A., & Mirandola, R. (2004). CB-SPE tool: Putting component-based performance engineering into practice. *Proceedings of the 7th International Symposium on Component-Based Software Engineering (CBSE 2004)* (pp. 233–248). Edinburgh, UK: Springer.

Bertolino, A., & Mirandola, R. (2004). CB-SPE tool: Putting component-based performance engineering into practice. In Crnkovic, I., Stafford, J. A., Schmidt, H. W., & Wallnau, K. (Eds.), *Component-based software engineering* (pp. 233–248). Springer. doi:10.1007/978-3-540-24774-6_21

Bondarev, E., de With, P., Chaudron, M., & Muskens, J. (2005). Modelling of input-parameter dependency for performance predictions of component-based embedded systems. *Modelling of Input-Proceedings of the 31st EUROMICRO Conference on Software Engineering and Advanced Applications* (pp. 36-43). IEEE Computer Society.

Brosig, F., Kounev, S., & Krogmann, K. (2009). Automated extraction of Palladio component models from running enterprise Java applications. *Proceedings of the 1st International Workshop on Run-time Models for Self-managing Systems and Applications (ROSSA 2009). In conjunction with Fourth International Conference on Performance Evaluation Methodologies and Tools (VALUE-TOOLS 2009).* Pisa, Italy: ACM Press.

Comuzzi, M., Kotsokalis, C., Rathfelder, C., Theilmann, W., Winkler, U., & Zacco, G. (2009). A framework for multi-level SLA management. *Proceedings of the 3rd Workshop on Non-Functional Properties and SLA Management in Service-Oriented Computing (NFPSLAM-SOC).* Stockholm, Sweden.

D'Ambrogio, A., & Bocciarelli, P. (2007). A model-driven approach to describe and predict the performance of composite services. *WOSP '07: Proceedings of the 6th International Workshop on Software and Performance* (pp. 78-89). New York, NY: ACM.

Grassi, V., Mirandola, R., & Sabetta, A. (2005). From design to analysis models: A kernel language for performance and reliability analysis of component-based systems. *Proceedings of the 5th International Workshop on Software and Performance* (pp. 25-36). Palma, Illes Balears, Spain: ACM.

Happe, J. (2008). *Predicting software performance in symmetric multi-core and multiprocessor environments*. Universitätsverlag Karlsruhe.

Happe, J., Becker, S., Rathfelder, C., Friedrich, H., & Reussner, R. H. (2009). Parametric performance completions for model-driven performance prediction. *Performance Evaluation, 67*(8).

Hissam, S. A., Moreno, G. A., Stafford, J. A., & Wallnau, K. C. (2002). Packaging predictable assembly. *Proceedings of the IFIP/ACM Working Conference on Component Deployment*. London, UK: Springer-Verlag.

Hunt, P., Robertson, D., Bretherton, R., & Winton, R. (1981). *SCOOT—A traffic responsive method of coordinating signals*. Technical Report LR1014, Transport and Road Research Laboratory.

Ingram, D. (2009). Reconfigurable middleware for high availability sensor systems. *Proceedings of the Third International Conference on Distributed Event-Based Systems*. ACM Press.

Kit, K. I. (2010). *Palladio approach*. Retrieved from http://www.palladio-aproach.net

Kounev, S. (2009). Software performance evaluation. In Wah, B. W. (Ed.), *Wiley encyclopedia of computer science and engineering. Wiley-Interscience*. John Wiley & Sons Inc.

Kounev, S. (2010). Emerging research directions in computer science. Contributions from the Young Informatics Faculty in Karlsruhe. In Pankratius, V., & Kounev, S. (Eds.), *Engineering of next generation self-aware software systems: A research roadmap*. Karlsruhe, Germany: KIT Scientific Publishing.

Kounev, S., Brosig, F., Huber, N., & Reussner, R. (2010). Towards self-aware performance and resource management in modern service-oriented systems. *Proceedings of the 7th IEEE International Conference on Services Computing (SCC 2010)*. Miami, FL: IEEE Computer Society.

Kounev, S., & Buchmann, A. (2006). SimQPN - A tool and methodology for analyzing queueing Petri net models by means of simulation. *Performance Evaluation, 63*(4), 364–394. doi:10.1016/j.peva.2005.03.004

Koziolek, H. (2009). Performance evaluation of component-based software systems: A survey. *Performance Evaluation, 67*(8).

Koziolek, H., & Reussner, R. (2008). A model transformation from the Palladio component model to layered queueing networks. *Performance Evaluation: Metrics* [Springer.]. *Models and Benchmarks, SIPEW, 5119*, 58–78.

Law, A. M., & Kelton, D. (2000). *Simulation modeling and analysis* (3rd ed.). New York, NY: McGraw Hill Companies.

MacNair, E. A. (1985). An introduction to the research queueing package. *Proc. of 17th Conference on WInter Simulation* (pp. 257-262). New York, NY: ACM.

Menascé, D., & Dubey, V. (2007). Utility-based QoS brokering in service oriented architectures. *IEEE International Conference on Web Services (ICWS 2007)*, (pp. 422-430).

OMG. (2005). *UML profile for schedulability, performance, v1.1*. Retrieved from http://www.omg.org/cgi- bin/doc?formal/2005-01-02

OMG. (2006, May). UML profile for modeling and analysis of real-time and embedded systems (MARTE).

Rathfelder, C., Evans, D., & Kounev, S. (2010). Predictive modelling of peer-to-peer event-driven communication in component-based systems. *Proceedings of the 7th European Performance Engineering Workshop (EPEW'10)*. University Residential Center of Bertinoro, Italy. Berlin, Germany: Springer-Verlag.

Silver, G. A., Maduko, A., Jafri, R., Miller, J. A., & Sheth, A. P. (2003). Modeling and simulation of quality of service for composite Web services. *Proceedings of the 7th World Multiconference on Systemics, Cybernetics and Informatics (SCI'03)*, (pp. 420-425).

SLA@SOI. (2009). *SLA@SOI project website*. Retrieved from http://www.sla-at-soi.eu

Smith, C. U. (1990). *Performance engineering of software systems*. Boston, MA: Addison-Wesley.

Song, H. G., Ryu, Y., Chung, T. S., Jou, W., & Lee, K. (2005). Metrics, methodology, and tool for performance-considered Web service composition. *Proceedings of the 20th International Symposium on Computer and Information Sciences (ISCIS 2005)* (pp. 392-401). Istanbul, Turkey: Springer.

Stopar, M., Hadalin, P., Rathfelder, C., & Klatt, B. (2011). D.B2b Reference Demonstrator. *Project deliverable SLA@SOI*, Retrieved from http://www.sla-at-soi.eu

Woodside, C. M., Neilson, J. E., Petriu, D. C., & Majumdar, S. (1995). The stochastic rendezvous network model for performance of synchronous client-server-like distributed software. *IEEE Transactions on Computers, 44*(1), 20–34. doi:10.1109/12.368012

Woodside, M. (n.d.). *Tutorial introduction to layered modeling of software performance*. Retrieved from http://www.sce.carleton.ca/rads/lqns/lqn-documentation/tutorialg.pdf

Wu, X., & Woodside, M. (2004). Performance modeling from software components. *SIGSOFT Softw. Eng. Notes, 29*(1), 290–301. doi:10.1145/974043.974089

KEY TERMS AND DEFINITIONS

Event Driven Communication: The communication between software components with asynchronously delivered data objects. A component emits the object, which is then delivered to all subscribed components.

Event-Based SOA (ESOA): An extension of the Service Oriented Architecture (SOA). In addition to the synchronous communication between services following the call and return behavior, services can also use event-driven communication.

Model Transformation: The conversion of a model to either another type of model or a textual artifact. In general, this is done automatically with specific transformation engines and transformation languages.

Performance Prediction: Prediction of quality attributes such as throughput, resource utilization, or timing effects. Model-based performance prediction is a type of prediction that uses a model as input for the prediction.

Service Level Agreement (SLA): Specification on a certain level of quality from both size, such as the usage profile and the expected quality properties.

Chapter 12
Service Selection Based on Customer Preferences of Non-Functional Attributes

Abhishek Srivastava
University of Alberta, Canada

Paul G. Sorenson
University of Alberta, Canada

ABSTRACT

With service-oriented systems driving the economies around the world there has been an exponential rise in the number and choices of available services. As a result of this, for most tasks there are a large number of services that can adequately cater to the requirements of the customers. Choosing the service that best conforms to the requirements from the set of functionally equivalent services is non-trivial. Research in the past has utilized the non-functional attributes of such services to select the best service. These efforts however make the assumption that the services with the best non-functional attributes are the ones that most closely conform to the requirements of the customer. This is not always true since the customer may sometimes prefer to settle for a slightly "inferior" service owing to price constraints. In this chapter, we apply the Mid-level Splitting technique to better assess the requirements of the customer and make a more judicious service selection. Furthermore, we also address the issue of assignment of weights to the various non-functional attributes of the services. These weights are reflective of the emphasis that the concerned customer wants to put on the various non-functional attributes of the service. These weights are normally assigned based on the intuition of certain expert personnel and are prone to human error and incorrect judgment. We utilize the Hypothetical Equivalents and Inequivalents technique to more systematically assign weights to the services based on customer preferences. The techniques are demonstrated with a real world example.

DOI: 10.4018/978-1-61350-432-1.ch012

INTRODUCTION

The major part of the so-called 'developed' and 'developing' economies in the world today is driven by services (Battilani & Fauri, 2007; Gallouj, 2002). This does not mean that services are replacing manufacturing based economies *per se*, rather services compliment manufactured products in what has been described as "servitization" of products (Vandermerwe & Rada, 1988). Manufacturing houses nowadays deliver 'bundles' to the customer that include the actual product along with supporting services with the goal of enhancing the customer experience. Besides such supporting services there are also 'pure' services such as a hotel service where the customer mainly pays to utilize the service. The penetration of the Internet in the daily lives of people also plays a big role in the proliferation of services. Vendors package their capabilities as web-services and conveniently transport these over the Internet to the customers.

The issue in such a scenario is service selection. With more and more services available, it is not unusual for more than one service to cater to the requirements of the customer. The customer has a choice to either select one of the functionally equivalent services at random or select the service that most closely conforms to his/her requirements. The latter task is non-trivial given the functional similarity of the available services. This task is further complicated by the availability of a large number of services and also by the multiple characteristic attributes of the services.

Research in the past has addressed the issue of service selection from functionally equivalent services making use of the non-functional attributes of the services (Ran, 2003; Kokash, 2005; Gao, & Wu, 2005). These approaches compare the available services on the basis of their non-functional attributes and the service that most closely conforms to the requirements of the customer is selected.

There are several challenges in this approach. First, services usually have more than one non-

functional attribute associated with them. Different non-functional attributes for the same service can be ranked differently when compared with the respective attributes of other competing services. For example, a service may have a higher value of reliability than another but a lower value in terms of security. How can one decide which of the two services is better? A lot of work has been done in addressing this problem and this is discussed in a subsequent section.

The second challenge in ranking services on the basis of their non-functional attributes is the main subject of this chapter and has to do with the perception of the customer of the various non-functional attributes. In the approaches thus far, it is assumed that the 'best' value for a non-functional attribute is what a customer always prefers. This however is not always true. A customer prefers a good value but not always the best as the best often entails a higher price. For example, while comparing two services on the basis of the non-functional attribute reliability, one service is found to have a reliability of 95% and another a reliability of 70%. All the previous approaches would rank the first service higher and it would be selected for the customer assuming that the customer always prefers the higher value. It is possible however that a certain customer might prefer a service of lower reliability in lieu of the lower price that he/she has to pay for the same. In this chapter, we utilize the 'Mid-level splitting' technique (Callaghan, & Lewis, 2000) to assess and better understand the customer perception of the various non-functional attributes of the service *vis-à-vis* the true value of the attribute. This enables service selection that conforms more closely to the requirements of the customer.

The third challenge in service selection using the non-functional attributes deals with the uneven emphasis that customers put on the various non-functional attributes of the service. For example, a customer may want to put greater emphasis on the reliability of a service than its security features. This would result in a different service selection than for a customer for whom security in the services is paramount. To address this challenge, the usual technique is to devise a 'weighting' scheme for the non-functional attributes. Our concern is that the usual technique to attach weights to the attributes is by intuition. We feel that greater user input is needed in determining these weights and therefore utilize the 'Hypothetical Equivalents and Inequivalents' method (Kulok, & Lewis, 2005) to assign weights to the non-functional attributes based on the requirements of the customer.

BACKGROUND

Service selection on the basis of non-functional attributes has received appropriate attention in previous research. Shuping Ran's paper is a pioneering work in this field (Ran, 2003). Ran proposes the use of an external Quality of Service (QoS) 'certifier' that certifies the QoS claims made by service providers on their respective services. The QoS values are then be incorporated into the 'UDDI' registry to facilitate more appropriate service selection. This approach has some limitations when the QoS claims made by service providers are dynamic. To have a certifier continuously assess these claims can become prohibitively expensive. The work is nevertheless significant in the sense that it gives a new direction to approaching the issue of service selection and is most relevant when non-functional attributes are changing slowly.

Closer to the work in this chapter, Godse *et al.* present a technique for service selection on the basis of the collective ratings of various non-functional attributes (Godse, Sonar, & Mulik, 2008). The non-functional attributes are grouped into clusters based on type similarity, and these clusters are the leaf nodes of a hierarchy. The hierarchy comprises the goal i.e. service selection as the root, and the factors leading up to the non-functional attributes as the intermediate levels. The elements at each level are compared

pair-wise to each other, and through a mathematical procedure, the pair-wise comparisons lead to a 'local' weight being assigned to each element. The element subsequently is assigned a 'global' weight by multiplying its local weight by that of its parent. The global weight thus calculated of each non-functional attribute, along with the degree to which the attribute is present in the candidate service, contributes to the ranking of the services and their subsequent selection.

Liu *et al.* present an 'extensible' model wherein the decision of which non-functional attributes are to consider for service selection is flexible (Liu, Ngu, & Zeng, 2004). The attributes considered depend on the service domain in question or possibly on the basis of customer preference. After the attributes to be considered are decided, the values of these attributes in the candidate services are arranged in the form of a matrix. This matrix is then made to undergo successive stages of normalization that finally yields values reflecting the extent to which the relevant non-functional attributes are present in each candidate service. Wang *et al.* have a similar approach to service selection with a few additions (Wang, Vitvar, Kerrigan, & Toma, 2006). First, their method takes into consideration linguistic expression of attributes such as 'slightly low', 'very low' etc. Second, their normalization procedure is different and the final result expresses the degree of the presence of attributes in the various candidate services as a value falling in the fixed range of 0 to 1.

Al-Masri *et al.* introduce the 'web service relevancy function (WsRF)' in their work (Al-Masri, & Mahmoud, 2007}. WsRF(ws_i) is a measure of the relevance of a web service ws_i to the requirements of the concerned customer. WsRF is calculated by first calculating the 'distance' of each non-functional attribute of the concerned service from the best respective value in the domain, and subsequently multiplying this distance with the weight (suggested by the customer) assigned to the attribute. These products are then summed over all the non-functional attributes of the service to give the WsRF value.

We feel these techniques are relevant but have an important restriction. They are all based on the premise that the preference of the customer with regard to each non-functional attribute is the same as the actual value of the respective attribute. In other words, it is assumed that only the best value of a non-functional attribute is desirable to customers. This is often not true. Customers certainly desire a good value of the non-functional attributes but not necessarily the best. In this chapter, we present a technique to capture the variation between the customer preference of an attribute and the actual attribute values. Liu *et al.* do incorporate the customer preferences in their technique but the role of the customer in their method is restricted to the selection of attributes.

Further, in this chapter, we use a technique to assign weights to the non-functional attributes that are again based on the preference of the customer. Most of the related work discussed assigns these weights in an intuitive manner that is often inconsistent. Godse *et al.* do have a systematic method of weight assignment but their method does not incorporate the customer as directly as ours does.

MAIN FOCUS OF THE CHAPTER

The challenges identified in the 'Introduction' of this chapter are taken up one by one in this section. The first challenge is in the ranking of services based on their non-functional attributes given that there are more than one attribute. A number of simple techniques are described in the first sub-section, which systemically progress from the most simple and perhaps least effective to the most complex and the most effective. The second sub-section deals with the next challenge, which is the issue of customer perception of the various non-functional attributes of the service not always aligning with the actual values of the attributes. The third sub-section addresses the challenge of

assigning weights to the various non-functional attributes in a systematic in conformance to the requirements of the customer. Finally, the last sub-section consists of a real world example to demonstrate how the techniques presented in this section can be used to make appropriate service selections.

Service Selection Where Multiple Non-Functional Attributes are Involved

Pair-wise comparison: The simplest service selection scheme where multiple factors are involved is 'Pair-wise comparison' (Salustri, 2005). In pair-wise comparison a pair of services is randomly selected from the group of candidate services. The service pair is compared attribute by attribute. For example, services A and B having the non-functional attributes: Accuracy, Response-time, and Security, need to be compared as shown in Figure 1. Service A is found to be better than service B in terms of Accuracy whereas service B is found to be better than service A in terms of both Response-time and Security. Service B is therefore found to be better than A on a larger number of attributes and so service A is 'eliminated'. Service B is then compared in a similar manner with another randomly picked service from the group of candidate services. This process continues until

Figure 1. Pair-wise comparison

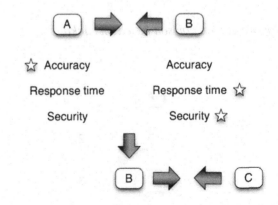

all the services are compared and the service that remains at the end is the one finally selected.

The pair-wise comparison method is very simple and straightforward. However, it also has a number of drawbacks. The comparisons may give rise to cyclic results. For example, B may be better than A, C better than B, and A better than C. Another drawback is that the attribute values are not taken into account during comparison. Continuing with our earlier example, service B may be better than A in terms of Response-time and Security only marginally, while A may be better than B by a large degree in terms of Accuracy, but still the service eliminated is A.

Ranking scheme: To address the problem of cyclic results, a ranking scheme is used for service selection. The ranking scheme is very simple and involves the comparison of all the candidate services together on the basis of their respective attributes. Each attribute is ranked in comparison with the other services and the service that has the smallest total rank is the one that is selected. The ranking scheme is demonstrated for a simple example in Figure 2.

Although the problem of cyclic results is solved using the ranking scheme, the problem of the attribute values not being taken into account persists. Even here a very large difference between the attribute values of services is as significant as a marginal difference.

Normalized rating: The problem of the values of the attributes not playing a significant part in

service selection is eliminated using the 'Normalized rating' scheme (Fernandez, Vallet, & Castells, 2006). The normalized rating scheme is also very simple. Here the non-functional attributes of each of the services are assigned a value between 0 and 1. The attribute of a service that has the best value among the attributes of all the candidate services is assigned a value of 1 whereas the attribute of the service that has the worst value is assigned a value of 0. All other attributes in between are assigned normalized values between 0 and 1 in proportion to their actual values relative to the two extreme values. This procedure is repeated for all the attributes. Finally each service gets a total value that is the sum of the normalized values of all its attributes. The service with the largest total value is selected. The normalized rating scheme is demonstrated through the simple example in Figure 3.

Customer Preference of the Non-Functional Attributes

The techniques discussed in the previous sections are based on the assumption that the service selected based on the 'best' values of the non-functional attributes is the one that is best for the customer. This is not always true. A customer may sometimes be interested in a relatively modest value of a non-functional attribute or attributes owing to price constraints. To facilitate a selection that more closely conforms to the requirements of the

Figure 2. Comparison based on ranking

	Accuracy	Response time	Security	Total
A	1	2	3	6
B	2	1	1	4 ☆
C	3	3	2	8

Figure 3. Normalized rating scheme.

	Accuracy	Response time	Security	
A	90%	0.4 sec	90%	
B	80%	0.2 sec	99%	
C	60%	1 sec	95%	

				Total
A	1	0.75	0	1.75
B	0.67	1	1	2.67 ☆
C	0	0	0.55	0.55

customer it is imperative to somehow determine the relation between the customer requirements and the actual attribute values.

We choose the 'Mid-level splitting' technique (Callaghan, & Lewis, 2000) to determine the relationship between the requirements of the customer with respect to a certain non-functional attribute and the actual value of the attribute. The Mid-level Splitting technique expresses this relationship by plotting a curve between the two. The technique involves an initial assessment of the range of the attribute values available. This range extends from the lowest (worst) attribute value available among the candidate services to the highest (best) value. This range is then split at its mid-point and the customer is queried on which of the two split parts is more significant. Depending on the customer's choice one of the parts is discarded and the other part is split at its mid-point. The customer is again asked to choose between the two parts. This process is repeated recursively until the customer says that both parts are equally significant. This gives us a point in the plot between the customer's requirements and

the actual attribute values. A simple example can explain the technique much better.

Assuming the three services shown in Figure 3 with the given values of the attributes are the candidate services. We use the mid-level splitting technique to determine the relationship between the customer preferences of the Accuracy attribute and the actual Accuracy values of the three services. First, the range of accuracy values is determined: the most accurate service in the example is service A with an accuracy of 90% and the least accurate is C at 60%. The Accuracy range available is therefore 60-90%. 60% is therefore assigned a value of 0 in terms of customer preference and 90% is assigned a value of 1 in terms of customer preference. To obtain the customer preference corresponding to 0.5 this range is now split at its mid-point to form two parts: 60-75% and 75-90%. The customer is then asked the following question:

Which range in Accuracy is more significant for you: 60% to 75% or 75% to 90%? The increase in price of the service if the first range is chosen is p_{11} to p_{12} and if the second range is chosen it is p_{21} to p_{22}.

A suitable algorithm for price needs to be used to come up with figures for p_{11}, p_{12}, p_{21}, and p_{22}. We do not dwell upon this subject in this chapter.

Assuming the customer replies by saying that 75% to 90% is the range that is more significant. The range of interest now becomes 75% to 90% and this range is now recursively split at its mid-point to form the parts 75-82.5% and 82.5-90% and the customer is asked the following question:

Which range in Accuracy is more significant for you: 75% to 82.5% or 82.5% to 90% ? The increase in price of the service ...

At this point, assuming the customer says that both the ranges are equally significant. The current mid-point: 82.5% therefore takes the value of 0.5 in terms of the customer preference. These points are plotted on the curve shown in Figure 4. Subsequently the range 60% to 82.5% is taken and recursively split and the customer asked questions in a similar manner to obtain the 0.25 equivalent of the customer preference. Similarly, the range 82.5% to 90% is recursively split to obtain the 0.75 equivalent of the customer preference. These points and further points if required are plotted as shown in Figure 4 to obtain the relationship curve between the customer preferences of the Accuracy attribute and the actual Accuracy values of the available services. Curves are obtained through a similar procedure for the other non-functional attributes of the services as well. These curves enable a service selection which conforms more closely to the requirements of the customer as will be demonstrated in the real world example described subsequently in this chapter.

One may argue that this approach to develop the preference curves entails a lot of effort on the part of the customer. While we agree with this, we would like to point out that such a customer

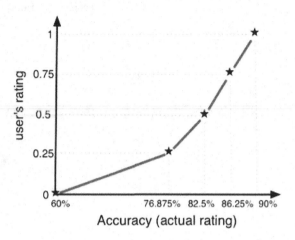

Figure 4. Customer's preference versus actual values of the accuracy attribute

specific curve should only be developed after the customer is shown a number of canonical curves and he/she is not satisfied (this is discussed with an example in the 'Real World Example' section). Furthermore, such curves should be developed for a customer only once and should be put into use in all subsequent requests by the customer.

Systematic Assignment of Weights to the Non-Functional Attributes

The third issue taken up in this chapter deals with assigning appropriate weights to the non-functional attributes in conformance to the requirements of the customers. The assignment of weights to the non-functional attributes is normally done in an intuitive manner wherein the concerned customer is asked a set of questions and based on the replies an expert personnel assigns appropriate weights. We feel that this technique is inconsistent and is overly dependent upon human expertise and judgment, which is prone to error. We therefore utilize the 'Hypothetical Equivalents and Inequivalents Technique' (HEIM) (Kulok, & Lewis, 2005) to assign weights to the non-functional attributes.

In this technique, a set of hypothetical candidate services each having random non-functional

Figure 5. List of hypothetical services

	Accuracy	Resp. time	Security
HS1	90	0.3	99
HS2	82.5	0.9	92.5
HS3	60	0.2	90
HS4	90	0.3	92.5
HS5	82.5	0.9	90
HS6	60	0.2	99
HS7	90	0.3	90
HS8	82.5	0.9	99
HS9	60	0.2	92.5
HS10	90	0.9	90

attributes are formed. For the purpose of demonstration, Figure 5 shows a list of hypothetical services with randomly assigned attribute values. The customer is shown these hypothetical services and is asked to rate comparatively as many of these services as possible in accordance with his/her requirements. Lets assume the customer feels that hypothetical service HS2 is more suited to his/her requirements than HS3, HS6 is better than HS5, and HS10 is worse than HS3.

The random attribute values of the hypothetical services are next traced on the relationship curve between the attribute values and the cus-

tomer preference of the attributes described in the previous sub-section. This gives the customer preference equivalent of the attribute values of the hypothetical services. An example of such values is shown in Figure 6.

Each non-functional attribute is assigned a weight variable w_1, w_2, and w_3. These weights are reflective of the emphasis that the customer puts on the three attributes relative to one another. The sum of the values assigned to the weight variables should always be 1 as shown in equation 1. The hypothetical equivalents and inequivalents technique seeks to assign values to these weight variables. Each hypothetical service is assigned a total customer preference weight which is a function of the weight assigned to the various non-functional attributes of the service and the preference value that the customer gives the respective attribute (as shown in the last column of Figure 6).

$$w_1 + w_2 + w_3 = 1 \qquad (1)$$

Based on the customer ratings of the hypothetical services described earlier *viz.* HS2 is better than HS3, HS6 is better than HS5, and HS10 is worse than HS3, a set of inequalities are formed as shown below in equation 2. These inequalities

Figure 6. List of hypothetical services (customer preference values)

	w_1	w_2	w_3	
	Accuracy	Response time	Security	Total
HS1	1	0.5	1	$w_1 + 0.5 \cdot w_2 + w_3$
HS2	0.5	0	0.5	$0.5 \cdot w_1 + 0.5 \cdot w_3$
HS3	0	1	0	w_2
HS4	1	0.5	0.5	$w_1 + 0.5 \cdot w_2 + 0.5 \cdot w_3$
HS5	0.5	0	0	$0.5 \cdot w_1$
HS6	0	1	1	$w_2 + w_3$
HS7	1	0.5	0	$w_1 + 0.5 \cdot w_2$
HS8	0.5	0	1	$0.5 \cdot w_1 + w_3$
HS9	0	1	0.5	$w_2 + 0.5 \cdot w_3$
HS10	1	0	0	w_1

use the total customer preference weight assigned to each hypothetical service as shown in the last column of Figure 6.

$$HS2 > HS3 \Rightarrow 0.5 * w_1 + 0.5 * w_3 > w_2$$

$$HS6 > HS5 \Rightarrow w_2 + w_3 > 0.5 * w_1$$

$$HS10 < HS3 \Rightarrow w_1 < w_2 \qquad (2)$$

Using these inequalities as constraints the technique seeks to optimize the objective function shown in equation 3. This objective function is based on the premise that the sum of the weights assigned to the non-functional attributes is 1. The objective function in equation 3 is optimized using techniques such as Linear Programming (Luenberger, 1984) or the Generalized Reduced Gradient Method (Hwang, Williams, & Fan, 1972). Optimizing the objective functions gives us the values of the weights assigned to the non-functional attributes.

Minimize $(1 - © w_i)^2 \qquad (3)$

A Real World Example

In this section, we will use a simple example and go through it step by step to clearly demonstrate the technique.

John Doe is planning a trip and he makes use of an online trip planner. The levels of functionality of this planner include: (1) a flight booking system, (2) a taxi booking system, (3) a hotel booking system, and (4) a combined payment system. Each level comprises a number of candidate services to choose from. Figure 7 shows the service domain for this system. The 0th level includes the 'logging-in', authenticity verification etc. The next three levels include the flight, taxi, and hotel booking functionalities respectively as mentioned above. The 4th level is the payment functionality, and finally the last level includes the 'logging-out' procedure.

For the sake of brevity and clarity, let us make a few simplifying assumptions. First, John has already completed the task of flight, and taxi booking and is about to decide on which of the various hotel booking services to use. The second

Figure 7. Example service domain.

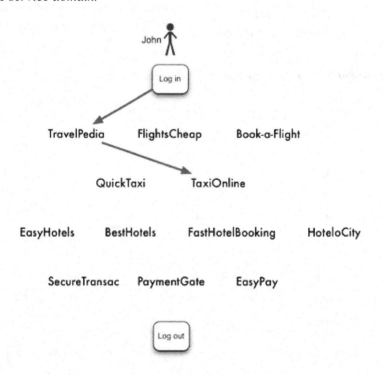

Figure 8. Example attribute values

	response time	ease of navigation	confidentiality
EasyHotels	1.2 sec	85%	95%
BestHotels	0.8 sec	55%	87%
FastHotelBooking	0.3 sec	70%	92%
HoteloCity	1.0 sec	95%	82%

assumption is that the selection is only on the basis of a few non-functional attributes.

Figure 7 shows the current state of the selection process. There are four hotel booking services available in the service domain: *EasyHotels*, *BestHotels*, *FastHotelBooking*, and *HoteloCity*. The non-functional attributes considered are: Response-time, Ease-of-navigation, and Confidentiality. The values of non-functional attributes

for each of the service instances are shown in Figure 8.

Customer's preference curves: John is first presented with a number of sample curves (possibly collected from past customers) representing the relationship between the variation in customer preference and the actual values of the attributes. These curves are shown in Figure 9. John selects curve (a) for Response-time, and

Figure 9. Example rating curves

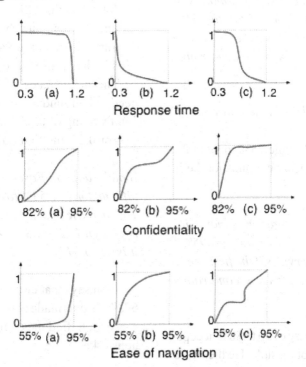

curve (c) for Confidentiality. Both of which show a high customer rating for a major part of the attribute range. He, however is particularly 'choosy' about Ease-of-navigation, and feels that none of the curves shown is to his liking.

The first task of the service selection system then is to form the curve for Ease-of-navigation which is specific to the liking of John Doe. The Ease-of-navigation values for the services have been expressed as a percentage with 100% representing the best value i.e. maximum Ease-of-navigation, and 0% representing the least Ease-of-navigation. The service instances available have the following values for Ease-of-navigation (from Figure 8): *EasyHotels* - 85%, *BestHotels* - 55%, *FastHotelBooking* - 70%, and *HoteloCity* - 95%. The best available value therefore is 95% which is made equal to a user rating of 1, and the worst value is 55% which is made equivalent to 0 for the customer. The next task is to calculate the Ease-of-navigation value which corresponds to John's rating of 0.5. The following query is put before John,

Which range in Ease-of-navigation is more significant for you, 55% to 75% or 75% to 95%? The increase in price of services if the first range is chosen is $0 to $2, and for the second range it is $2 to $20.

It may be noted that 75% is the mid-point of 55% and 95%.

John says, the second range 75% to 90% for him is more significant. The next question he is asked is,

Which range in Ease-of-navigation is more significant for you, 75% to 85% or 85% to 95%? The increase in price of services if the first range is chosen is $2 to $8, and for the second range it is $8 to $20.

John feels that a price rise of up to $8 is acceptable, but beyond that is not feasible. He therefore

Figure 10. John's specific rating (ease of navigation)

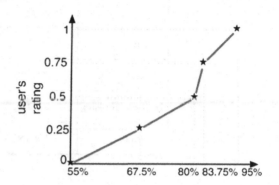

Ease of navigation (actual rating)

says the range between 75% to 85% is better. The next question that he is asked therefore is,

Which range in Ease-of-navigation is more significant for you, 75% to 80% or 80% to 85%? The increase in price of services if the first range is chosen is $2 to $4, and for the second range it is $4 to $8.

John says that either of the two ranges is good to him. At this point therefore, the mid-point of the range 80% is the value equal to John's 0.5. This is shown in Figure 10.

The next values of Ease-of-navigation that need to be found are those that are equivalent to John's rating of 0.25, and 0.75.

For 0.25, the first question asked is,

Which range in Ease-of-navigation is more significant for you, 55% to 67.5% or 67.5% to 80%? The increase in price of services if the first range is chosen is $0 to $1, and for the second range it is $1 to $4.

John says that either of these is good for him. 67.5% is thus made equal to 0.25 of John's rating.

Next, to find the equivalent of John's 0.75, he is asked:

Which range in Ease-of-navigation is more significant for you, 80% to 87.5% or 87.5% to 95%? The increase in price of services if the first range is chosen is $4 to $9, and for the second range it is $9 to $20.

John says he prefers the range 80% to 87.5%. John is then asked the following question,

Which range in Ease-of-navigation is more significant for you, 80% to 83.75% or 83.75% to 87.5%? The increase in price of services if the first range is chosen is $4 to $5, and for the second range it is $5 to $9.

John says it does not matter. The 0.75 for John is therefore set at 83.75%.

Generally for attributes like these that do not require a high degree of accuracy, 5 points of equivalence are sufficient to plot the curve between the customer's preference ratings and the actual attribute values. The curve for Ease-of-navigation is thus plotted specifically for John, as shown in Figure 10. The curves for the other attributes (Response-time, and Confidentiality) chosen by John from the group of canonical curves are shown in Figure 11.

Weight assignment to attributes: The next task is to assign weights to each of the non-functional attributes of the hotel booking services such that the weight is an indicator of the importance John gives to the respective attribute. Following the Hypothetical Equivalents and Inequivalents technique discussed in the previous sections, hypothetical services need to be formed and be presented to the customer.

A simple method to form hypothetical services is to take the values of every attribute corresponding to 0, 0.5, and 1 of the customer ratings and form different random combinations of the same. Referring to Figures 10, and 11, the attribute values corresponding approximately to 0, 0.5, and 1 of John Doe's preference ratings are: For Response-time, 0 ⇒ 0.3: 0.5 ⇒ 1.1: 1 ⇒ 1.2 (Figure 11);

Figure 11. John's chosen rating (response time, confidentiality)

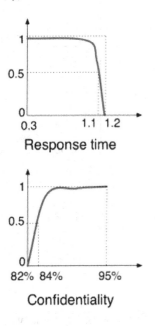

for Ease-of-navigation, 0 ⇒ 55%: 0.5 ⇒ 80% : 1 ⇒ 95% (Figure 10); and for Confidentiality, 0 ⇒ 82%: 0.5 ⇒ 84%: 1 ⇒ 95% (Figure 11).

These attribute values are then randomly combined to form a number of hypothetical services. Figure 12 shows 10 of these services with the actual attribute values, whereas Figure 13 shows

Figure 12. Hypothetical services

	Resp. time	Ease of navigation	Confidentiality
HS1	0.3	80%	95%
HS2	1.1	95%	84%
HS3	1.2	80%	82%
HS4	0.3	55%	84%
HS5	1.1	95%	82%
HS6	1.2	80%	95%
HS7	0.3	80%	82%
HS8	1.1	95%	95%
HS9	1.2	55%	84%
HS10	0.3	95%	82%

Figure 13. Hypothetical services with John's ratings, and weights

	w_1	w_2	w_3	
	Resp. time	Ease of navigation	Confidentiality	Total
HS1	1	0.5	1	$w_1+0.5w_2+w_3$
HS2	0.5	0	0.5	$0.5w_1+0.5w_3$
HS3	0	1	0	w_2
HS4	1	0.5	0.5	$w_1+0.5w_2+0.5w_3$
HS5	0.5	0	0	$0.5w_1$
HS6	0	1	1	w_2+w_3
HS7	1	0.5	0	$w_1+0.5w_2$
HS8	0.5	0	1	$0.5w_1+w_3$
HS9	0	1	0.5	$w_2+0.5w_3$
HS10	1	0	0	w_1

Figure 14. User equivalent of service attribute values.

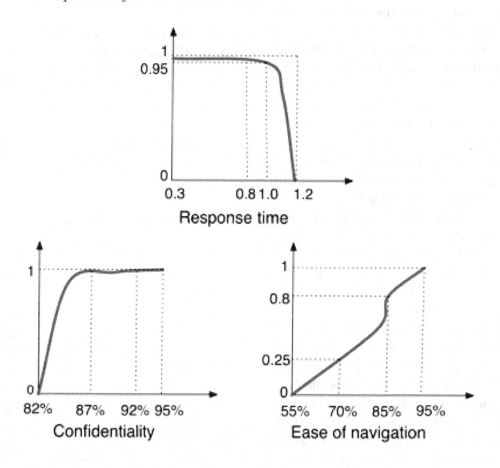

the same set of hypothetical values with John's preference rating for each of the attributes.

John is then presented with the hypothetical services table (the one shown in Figure 12) with the actual attribute values and is asked to comparatively rate as many of the services as he wants. John looks at these hypothetical services and feels: a) HS6 is certainly better than HS7, b) HS3 and HS5 are equally good, c) HS8 is worse than HS9. Using these preferences of John, the system obtains the following constraints from Figure 13,

$$HS6 > HS7 \Rightarrow w_2 + w_3 > w_1 + 0.5 * w_2$$

$$HS3 = HS5 \Rightarrow w_2 = 0.5 * w_1$$

$$HS8 < HS9 \Rightarrow 0.5 * w_1 + w_3 < w_2 + 0.5 * w_3$$

These constraints are then used in the optimization of the following objective function (from equation 3),

Minimize $(1 - © w_i)^2$

This optimization problem may be solved using one of various methods (Luenberger, 1984; Hwang, Williams, & Fan, 1972). For the purpose of illustration, lets assume that we solve the optimization problem and obtain the following values: $w_1 = 0.3$, $w_2 = 0.5$, and $w_3 = 0.2$.

These weight values are then used along with the user rating curves to calculate the total weight of each of the available services. To do this, first the user rating equivalent of each of the attribute values of the available hotel booking services are calculated from the rating curves. The attribute values in Figure 8 are traced on the user rating curves as shown in Figure 14.

The user rating equivalent of each of the attributes of the respective hotel booking services is shown in Figure 15. The total weight of each of the services is then calculated as follows: for example, for *EasyHotels*: Total-weight = 0*0.3 + 0.8*0.5 + 1*0.2 = 0.6.

The total service weights for all available services are shown in Figure 15. The service with the highest weight, *HoteloCity* is therefore found to be the most optimal for John Doe in terms of non-functional attributes and is therefore selected.

FUTURE RESEARCH DIRECTIONS

The service selection technique discussed in this chapter is noteworthy because it incorporates the customer perception of the non-functional attributes rather than the actual values. This is an innovative approach but it suffers from the constraint of being static in nature. The curves depicting the relation between the customer preference values and the actual values of the non-functional attributes are traced in advance and only then is the process of service selection carried out. We envisage a model which is much

Figure 15. Total service weight

	$w_1 = 0.3$	$w_2 = 0.5$	$w_3 = 0.2$	
	response time	ease of navigation	confidentiality	Total
EasyHotels	0	0.8	1	0.6
BestHotels	1	0	1	0.5
FastHotelBooking	1	0.25	1	0.625
HoteloCity	0.95	1	0	0.785 ☆

more dynamic in nature. Herein the customer should have the liberty of specifying his/her non-functional requirements 'on the fly' and the service selection model should make the selection accordingly. This is akin to a 'tuning knob' mechanism with a knob corresponding to every non-functional attribute. The customer should be able to turn this knob up or down depending upon the requirements and the model should make an appropriate selection. In our research we are developing such a model where service selection is part of a larger task of putting together service compositions dynamically. The customer specifies his/her non-functional requirements as a set of parameters and the model selects appropriate services accordingly. The goal is not to make optimal selections for each and every customer, which is not realistic given the resource constraints but to fulfill the non-functional requirements of all the customers as much as possible. This, unlike the technique described in this paper, is not a model that caters to requirements of individual customers.

The other limitation of the approach described in this chapter is that it is overly dependent upon the response of the customer to a set of questions. This is a risky proposition given that it is not unusual for customers to be incapable of consistently expressing their opinions. A relatively lay customer maybe unable to appropriately answer questions on his/her preferences and may as a result end up with a service far from his/her requirements. We feel future research should concentrate on assessing the preference of customers based on their past selection behavior rather than on the basis of their response to questions. Future research should take cue from this chapter on how to incorporate their findings into the process of service selection. Data mining techniques can be explored in eliciting trends in the selection behavior of customers and should try to relate this trend to the preference of the customers on the various non-functional attributes. Such an approach would be far more robust than the one outlined in this chapter and

would have a much larger possibility of closely conforming to the requirements of the customer.

CONCLUSION

The selection of services from a group of functionally equivalent ones using the non-functional attributes present several challenges as identified in this chapter. First and foremost, comparing services that have a large number of non-functional attributes is not straightforward. Solutions reviewed in this chapter range from simple techniques, such as pair-wise comparison, to relatively complex operations like normalized ratings.

Second, the techniques mentioned above and a host of other techniques from previous literature make service selections using the assumption that the 'best' service in terms of non-functional attributes is also the most preferred service for the customer. This is not always true. Utilizing the Mid-level splitting technique addresses the limitation of this assumption. The Mid-level splitting technique makes it possible to plot the curve between the preferences of the concerned customer with respect to a certain non-functional attribute and the actual values of the attribute. This enables selection of services that more closely conform to the requirements of the customer.

Finally, if we take into consideration a large number of non-functional attributes in assessing a service, the requirements that different customers have for these attributes can vary considerably. To address this problem, an expert can conduct interviews with the customer and based on the latter's response intuitively assigns weights to the attributes. This technique is simple and sometimes effective but is overly dependent on human judgment which is prone to error. The use of the Hypothetical Equivalents and Inequivalents method seeks to eliminate the dependence on the judgment of an expert by placing hypothetical service examples before the customer and simply asking him/her to rate these based on the requirements. The ratings of the customer then form the basis of weight assignment to the various non-functional attributes.

These techniques are generally simple and straightforward and also quite effective. The main drawback is that they are highly dependent upon the response of customers to various questions. A relatively naïve or careless customer poses a risk by responding inadequately and rendering the process ineffective. A solution to this problem is to determine the preference of the customer by systematically studying his/her actual behavior in the past rather than depending solely on his/her responses to queries.

REFERENCES

Al-Masri, E., & Mahmoud, Q. H. (2007). *Discovering the best web service.* International World Wide Web Conference/Poster paper.

Battilani, P., & Fauri, F. (2007). *The rise of a service-based economy and its transformation: The case of Ramini.* Ramini Centre for Economic Analysis, Working Paper Series.

Callaghan, A. R., & Lewis, K. E. (2000). A 2-Phase aspiration-level and utility theory approach to large scale design. *Proceedings of Design Engineering Technical Conferences and Computers and Information in Engineering Conference.*

Fernández, M., Vallet, D., & Castells, P. (2006). *Probabilistic score normalization for rank aggregation.* 28th European Conference on Information Retrieval.

Gallouj, F. (2002). *Innovation in the service economy: the new wealth of nations.* Edward Elgar Publishing.

Gao, Z., & Wu, G. (2005). *Combining QoS-based service selection with performance prediction.* IEEE International Conference on e-Business Engineering (ICEBE).

Godse, M., Sonar, R., & Mulik, S. (2008). *The analytical hierarchy process approach for prioritizing features in the selection of Web service.* Sixth European Conference on Web Services.

Hwang, C. L., Williams, J. L., & Fan, L. T. (1972). *Introduction to the generalized reduced gradient method.* Manhattan: Institute for Systems Design and Optimization, Kansas State University.

Kokash, N. (2005). Web service discovery with implicit QoS filtering. *Proceedings of the IBM PhD Student Symposium, in conjunction with the International Conference on Service Oriented Computing (ICSOC).*

Kulok, M., & Lewis, K. E. (2005). Preference consistency in multiattribute decision making. *Proceedings of Design Engineering Technical Conferences And Computers and Information in Engineering Conference.*

Liu, Y., Ngu, A. H. H., & Zeng, L. (2004). *QoS computation and policing in dynamic Web service selection.* International World Wide Web Conference.

Luenberger, D. (1984). *Linear and nonlinear programming.* Reading, MA: Addison-Wesley.

Ran, S. (2003). *A model for web services discovery with QoS.* ACM SIGecom Exchanges.

Salustri, F. A. (2005). *Pairwise comparison.* Retrieved from http://deed.ryerson.ca/~fil/t/pwisecomp.html

Vandermerwe, S., & Rada, J. (1988). Servitization of business: Adding value by adding services. *European Management Journal, 6*(4). doi:10.1016/0263-2373(88)90033-3

Wang, X., Vitvar, T., Kerrigan, M., & Toma, I. (2005). *Preference consistency in multiattribute decision making.* International Conference on Service Oriented Computing.

KEY TERMS AND DEFINITIONS

Customer Preferences: In this chapter, there is a greater emphasis on the values of non-functional attributes preferred or required by customers rather than the actual values of the attributes. For example, the service with the best reliability attribute is not necessarily considered the best choice. Rather the best choice is the service whose reliability conforms most closely to the preferences of the customer.

Hypothetical Equivalents and Inequivalents Method: This is another technique from Operations Research literature that enables the systematic assessment of weights (or emphasis) that the customer wants to assign to the various non-functional attributes of the service for the purpose of service selection.

Mid-Level Splitting Technique: This is a technique from Operations Research literature that enables plotting of customer preference values of non-functional attributes against the actual values of the same attributes.

Non-Functional Capabilities: The non-functional capabilities refer to characteristics of services that do not relate to their functional capabilities. The functional capabilities refer to the *what* functions the service is supposed to perform. The non-functional capabilities help in assessing *how well* the service performs these functions. The non-functional capabilities are usually the quality attributes of the service such as reliability, security, response-time etc.

Service Selection: In this chapter service selection implies selection from a group of services that are assumed to be identical in terms of their functional capabilities. The difference between the services and the criteria for selection are the non-functional capabilities.

Section 3
Service Contracts

Chapter 13
Reconciliation of Contractual Concerns of Web Services

Hong-Linh Truong
Vienna University of Technology, Austria

G.R. Gangadharan
IBM Research India, India

Marco Comerio
University of Milano-Bicocca, Italy

Vincenzo D'Andrea
University of Trento, Italy

Flavio De Paoli
University of Milano-Bicocca, Italy

Schahram Dustdar
Vienna University of Technology, Austria

ABSTRACT

There exist many works addressing service contracts fully or partially. They often mention the same notion with different languages and terminologies. This causes several problems in the specification, negotiation, and monitoring of contractual concerns in service-oriented environments, in particular in the Internet-scale and cloud computing environments. With the objective of reconciling contractual concerns, in this chapter, we will analyze the strengths and weaknesses of existing languages and standards for describing service contracts. We will present our research efforts for dealing with multiple contract specifications and semantics mismatching when identifying, specifying, negotiating, and establishing service contracts for service composition in the Internet and cloud computing environments. We will explore the issues of service contracts compatibility and present our solutions. Furthermore, we will analyze crucial points in monitoring and enforcement emerging contractual terms for Internet-based and cloud-based services that so far have not been in the research focus.

DOI: 10.4018/978-1-61350-432-1.ch013

INTRODUCTION

Web services aim at simplifying the interoperability and integration of services, developed by independent providers, for complex business processes by discovering and composing services distributed over the Internet. The building of such complex and valuable processes of multi-provider Web services relies on the efficiency of discovering the services and composing them. The Web services *discovery* will locate machine-processable descriptions of Web services that meet certain criteria. The Web service *composition* consists in combining the functionality of several discovered Web services in order to define composite services (Kuno et al, 2003). The increasing availability of Web services in the Internet and cloud computing environments that offer similar functionalities requires mechanisms to go beyond the pure functional discovery and composition of Web services. As a result, researchers have developed many solutions for enhancing Web service discovery and composition with the evaluation of multiple types of non-functional properties (NFPs) and applicability conditions associated with a Web service. These solutions play a crucial role in the establishment of mutual understanding about the business transaction between a provider (seller) and a consumer (buyer).

Currently, the mutual understanding between the service provider and the service consumer is established by several approaches across various application domains. Contracts, policies, licenses, and service level agreements (SLAs) are the most common approaches for expressing this understanding. Though there are some differences among contracts, policies, SLAs, and licenses, the common denominator is an identification for a belief of a business transaction between the service provider and the service consumer and thereby, commonly considered under the umbrella term `Service Contracts' or simply by `contracts'.

A contract is a legally binding exchange of promises or agreement between parties that the law will enforce. The contents of contracts may vary as the definition of contract is very broad in scope. A contract can include quality of service terms (e.g., response time and availability), legal terms (e.g., fair use and copyrights), intellectual rights terms (e.g., allowing or denying composition), and business terms (including financial terms such as payment and tax). Typically these terms are described in forms of conditions established on the basis of non-functional parameters. Both the provider and consumer can specify non-functional parameters associated with their services and their requests, in general, but contract terms will include specific conditions of non-functional parameters that are agreed by the provider and consumer for particular business transactions. As there is no single formal ontology or unique way of describing these terms, service providers and service consumers can represent these terms as they wish. This causes strong ambiguity and redundancies in terms descriptions, preventing the right interpretation of contract terms in multi-provider service-oriented environments.

In the literature, there exist many works fully or partially addressing service contracts, but they often mention the same concepts with different languages and terminologies. This requires guidelines and approaches for reconciling them to better collaboration between service providers, service consumers and service integrators. In most cases, current works do not consider the negotiation and establishment of contractual terms modeled by different specifications. However, such negotiation and establishment should be supported as service consumers are increasingly composing and utilizing services provided by different providers, each imposes a different meaning on contractual terms. In parallel, the trend of providing Software-as-a-service (SaaS) (Viega, 2009) and Data-as-a-Service (DaaS) (Dan et al., 2007;Truong et al., 2009) in the cloud demands a strong support for establishment, monitoring and enforcement of diverse contractual terms as in the SaaS/DaaS model typically each software usage is bound to a service contract. Addressing service contracts for composite services is important but this work is under-researched.

This chapter, based on an early discussion in (Truong et al., 2008), summarizes our observations, research outcomes and experiences in and discusses some future directions for dealing with the above-mentioned issues. We analyze the complexity of current contractual concerns, identify issues preventing the establishment of contractual concerns in the service composition, and propose guidelines for reconciling existing approaches to better collaboration between service providers, service consumers, and service integrators. While existing languages and techniques for service contracts are mainly designed for Web services, we will consider ``services'' in a generic view in which services are offered by software applications that can be invoked via software or services are performed by a human via a software interface. With this assumption, we will discuss common and differences in service contracts for generic services built based on Web services technologies.

The chapter is organized as follows: we will discuss an overview of service contracts in the next section. Then we will analyze the complexities of current contractual concerns and the possible issues due to these complexities. We present several research issues in the reconciliation of service contracts. Next, we present some of our research efforts that aim at tackling these research issues. Finally, we conclude the chapter and discuss future work.

SERVICE CONTRACTS: AN OVERVIEW

In the literature, the mutual understanding between providers and consumers is typically established by specifying policies, service level agreements, licenses, and contracts. We overview them in the following.

Policies establish a relationship between involved parties, specifying obligations and authorizations. Obligations specify the set of activities that an object must or must not perform on target objects and authorizations specify the set of activities that an object is permitted or prohibited to perform on target objects (Lupu & Sloman, 1997). Policies provide the means for specifying and modulating the behavior of a feature to align its capabilities and constraints with the requirements of its users (Kamoda et al, 2005).

A Service Level Agreement (SLA) contains technical data relating to the operation of services that implies the objectives with regard to a service consumer (Muller, 1999). An SLA, e.g. described by WSLA (Web Service Level Agreement) or WS-Agreement specifications, is a bilateral statement signed between a service provider and a service consumer, over the agreed terms and conditions of the given service. An SLA describes the minimum performance criteria a provider promises to meet while delivering a service and typically sets out the remedial action and any penalties that take effect if the performance falls below the promised standard. Thus, an SLA specifies the expected operational characteristics of a service in business oriented terms between a provider and a consumer, so that the characteristics can be measured, monitored, and managed (Lewis & Ray, 1999, Sahai et al, 2002). An SLA is often custom-made and negotiated between a consumer and a provider of a service. Templates for SLA specifications may vary with service providers. SLA negotiation can be a complex process as several terms and conditions related to performance criteria may involve in an SLA.

Service licensing includes all transactions between the licensor (e.g., service provider) and the licensee (e.g., service consumer) in which the licensor establishes the rights granted to the licensee when using some specific services for a specific tenure under predefined terms and conditions (Gangadharan et al, 2007). Licensing is perceived as a method for supporting technology transfer and as a mechanism for getting financial benefits. The objectives of a service license are as follows.

- To define the extent to which the service can be used, on the basis that any use outside the terms of the license would constitute an infringement.
- To have a remedy against the service consumer where the circumstances are such that the acts complained of do not constitute an infringement of copyrights.
- To limit the liability of service providers in case of failure of the service.

Optionally, a service license can include SLA terms. Thus, a service license can be broader than an SLA, protecting the rights of service providers and service consumers. The agreement between the service provider and the service consumer is bound to comply with license clauses, but in general, a license itself is a unilateral act of the provider and is not part of the negotiation.

In general, policies, SLAs, and licenses serve as a common denominator for specifying normative aspects of services and making business relationships between providers and consumers. Policies are commonly used for access control, quality of service, or other management tasks. Service licenses reflect the rights of providers to control how the service is distributed. Although policies and licenses are similar in that they govern what a service does, they are not the same. Typically, a SLA is a bilateral statement signed between a service provider and a service consumer, over the agreed terms and conditions of the given service. A SLA is often custom-made and negotiated between a consumer and a provider of a service. In case of a service license, the service provider and the consumer are bound to comply with license clauses, but the license itself is generally not part of the negotiation. As the literature describes several terms in a synonymous manner with less or more differences, we use a common terminology for referring to these diverse normative aspects describing non-functional properties. We describe a *contractual term* as an instance built as a constraint based on non-functional properties characterizing concerns associated with services and their data. We consider the terminology *contract* as a broader set including the terms of SLAs specified by WSLA or WSOL, the clauses of licenses specified by ODRL-S and the properties of policies specified in WS-Policy or WSPL (detailed in the later parts of this chapter).

Contractual concerns of services refer to functional/non-functional properties and business/management information of services. A service contract includes normative aspects that are agreed between the service consumer and the service provider who acted in compliance with the contract. A service contract is a complicated artifact surrounded with interdisciplinary research efforts. In general, the making of a service contract consists of the following phases.

- *Specification of (provisional) contractual terms:* Service providers and/or consumers can specify their provisional contractual terms. Contractual terms are fundamental aspects for service contracts. They basically describe the associated non-functional parameters of a service, covering QoS, business, legal, and intellectual rights issues related to the service usage. A provisional contractual term is basically a provisional constraint on a non-functional parameter; for example, the price for a pay-per-use is 5 Euros.
- *Negotiation and establishment of a contract:* During this phase, provisional contractual terms are negotiated and agreed contract terms are established between providers and consumers. In some specific situations, renegotiation of contracts is allowed.
- *Monitoring and enforcement of the contract:* In this phase, an agreed contract is

monitored and enforced. A set of metrics for measuring and evaluating contractual terms are considered by providers and/or consumers.

As there are several concerns associated with a service, the number of non-functional parameters can be very large or very domain-specific as well as the type of non-functional parameters can be diverse. Therefore, the specification and management of these non-functional parameters can be complex, making the specification, negotiation and establishment, monitoring and enforcement of service contracts complex. Furthermore, when we utilize several services from different providers, we will not deal with a single service contract described in a single specification, but multiple contracts represented in multiple specifications. Therefore, the number of non-functional parameters, types of non-functional parameters, the number of specifications to be used, etc., are increased and diverse. As a consequence, dealing with service contracts from multiple service providers will need techniques that are capable of managing diverse contractual terms, mapping them together, evaluating their compatibility as well as monitoring and enforcing these terms in one-to-multiple or multiple-to-multiple service interaction models. In the following, we will discuss the complexity of current contractual concerns.

COMPLEXITY OF CURRENT CONTRACTUAL CONCERNS

With an illustrative scenario inspired by the COMPAS project (The COMPAS Project, 2010) shown in Figure 1, we intend to give a sample of the complexity of contractual terms of today's multi-provider Web services and the requirement for reconciliation of contractual concerns. Assume that each Web service has a provisional contract (represented by $\{C_{XS}\}$) and a contract (represented as C_{XY} diagrammatically in a shaded

square) is established by through the contract negotiation in order to make two Web services to be compatible. The provisional contract specifies contractual terms that the service provider would like to have, but the contract is the final agreement between the provider and the consumer, based on the negotiation of provisional contracts. In Figure 1, the process flow is represented by arrowed dotted dash lines and contractual negotiations and establishments are represented by arrowed black lines.

We are considering a supply chain management scenario which involves multiple Web services from different providers. A *Request Service* issuing a purchase request to a *Purchase Order Service*. The *Purchase Order Service* has a provisional contract that includes an intellectual right term represented in $\{C_{PS}\}$. The order sent by this service is being processed by a *Purchase Processing Service* which has a provisional contract $\{C'_{AS}\}$. These contracts are negotiated and agreed upon the terms defined as C_{PA}.

Assume that a security-related QoS term has been associated with the *Purchase Processing Service* which has an impact on the provisional contract in $\{C_{AS}\}$. When the *Purchase Processing Service* interacts with the provisional contract $\{C'_{FS}\}$ of *Payment Service*, a new contract is established as C_{AF}.

A *Shipping Service* processes the *Payment Service* by establishing a contract C_{FT} satisfying contractual terms of $\{C_{FS}\}$ and $\{C'_{TS}\}$. The *Shipping Service* gives certain information about the transferred goods to a *Purchase Verification Service* by mutual contracts establishment. Similarly, the *Purchase Verification Service* sends the verified information about the goods ordered to the *Request Service*, to complete the process of requisition of order to receiving of goods.

In the above-mentioned scenario, there are several service providers. Each service provider has its own services, offers different provisional contracts, and is responsible for the negotiation of the contracts for its own services. On the other

Figure 1. Complexity of contractual concerns in services - a scenario based on COMPAS supply chain management

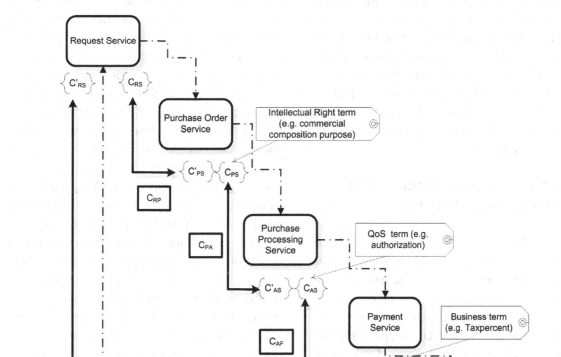

hand, there is a service integrator/consumer which would like to compose different services into a service composition. While the service providers might not be aware of each other, the integrator/consumer must deal with multiple providers. As in the Internet-scale and cloud computing environments each provider will have its own ways of specifying, negotiating and enforcing service contracts and its own ways will not be the same with that of others, to the service consumer there is a high level of complexity in representing and managing contracts for multi-providers services in the illustrated scenario. First, the current non-uniformity in contractual term specifications raises

the question of how to represent contractual terms so that they can interact. For example, in our scenario, the *Payment Service* specifies business term - including financial term - in $\{C_{FS}\}$. As today there is no common ontology for these terms of a contract, the financial term can be represented in the set of quality term by the *Shipping Service*. Second, as these terms can be represented in several XML-based languages, there exist several silos between contracts, SLAs, licenses, and policies. Consider that *Payment Service* represents the provisional contract in the WSLA framework and *Purchase Processing Service* represents the provisional contract in the SLAng. In this case, there are no defined regulations on how these contracts can communicate and establish a new contract. While some works, such as (Keller & Ludwig, 2002), proposed a solution for managing contractual terms across organizations, they mostly assume that all organizations use the same language/specification in describing contractual terms. Here we further examine cases in which organizations use different languages to model the contractual terms.

Issues on Contract Specification Languages and Standards

In the world of Web services, the Web service Description Language (WSDL) (Christensen et al, 2001) and its annotation are the standard way to describe what a service does. From a given WSDL specification and its annotation, the location of the service, the protocols supported by the service, and the functionalities provided in terms of incoming and outgoing messages can be known. Research focusing on languages for service contracts that aims to enhance and complete service description provided by WSDL is continually in progress. These languages/standards are mostly complementary to WSDL by addressing contractual concerns with varying levels of details.

We analyze major existing works, including the Web Service Level Agreement (WSLA) framework (Keller & Ludwig, 2003), WS-Agreement (Andrieux et al, 2007), SLAng (Skene et al, 2004), WSOL (Tosic et al, 2003), WS-Policy (Vedamuthu et al, 2007), Web Services Policy Language (WSPL) (Anderson, 2004), OASIS ebXML Collaboration Protocol Profile (CPP) and Collaboration Protocol Agreement (CPA) (OASIS, 2005), ODRL-S (Gangadharan et al, 2007), OWL-S (Martin et al, 2004) and WSMO (De Bruijn et al, 2005).

The Web Service Level Agreement (WSLA) framework (Keller & Ludwig, 2003) describes the complete life cycle of a Service Level Agreement (SLA) including SLA establishment by negotiation (signing of an SLA by signatory parties

for a given service offering), SLA deployment (checking the validity of the SLA and distributing it), Service level measurement and reporting (configuring the run-time system to meet a set of SLAs and comparing measured SLA parameters against the thresholds defined in the SLA), Management actions (determining SLA violations and corrective management actions to be taken), and SLA termination (specifying the conditions for termination). The WSLA framework enables to specify and monitor a wide variety of SLAs for Web services. Based on XML, the WSLA language defines a type system for the various SLA artifacts. An SLA in WSLA is comprised of parties (identifying all the contractual parties), service description (specifying the characteristics of the service and the observable parameters like service availability, throughput, or response time), and obligations (defining various guarantees and constraints to be imposed on SLA parameters).

The Web Services Agreement (WS-Agreement) (Andrieux et al, 2007) supports for establishing agreements between service providers and consumers, using (1) an extensible XML language for specifying the nature of the agreement, and (2) agreement templates to facilitate discovery of compatible agreement parties. The specification consists of three parts which may be used in a composable manner: a schema for specifying an agreement, a schema for specifying an agreement template, and a set of port types and operations for managing agreement life-cycle, including creation, expiration, and monitoring of agreement states.

SLAng (Skene et al, 2004) is a XML based language, for describing Service Level Specifications in the domain of distributed systems and e-business. This language has been modeled by Object Constraints Language (OCL) and Unified Modeling Language (UML) in order to define SLA precisely. SLAng formally defines SLA vocabulary in terms of the behaviour of the services and clients involved in service usage, with reference to a model of service usage.

The Web Service Offering Language (WSOL) (Tosic et al, 2003), a language for specifying constraints, management information, and service offering, provides different service levels defined by several classes of services. The same WSDL description with differing constraints (functional, non-functional, and access right) and managerial statements (price, penalty, and responsibility) is referred as "classes of service" of a Web service in WSOL. Consequently, different classes of services could vary in prices and payment models. WSOL offers several reusability elements to enable easier derivation of a new service offering from the existing offerings.

The WS-Policy (Vedamuthu et al, 2007) provides a general framework to specify and communicate (publish) policies for Web services. It is a model for expressing the capabilities, requirements, and general characteristics of a Web service as policies. The WS-Policy provides a base set of constructs that can be used and extended by other Web services specifications to describe a broad range of service requirements, preferences, and capabilities. The WS-Policy defines a policy as a collection of policy alternatives. In turn, each policy alternative comprises a collection of policy assertions. Each policy assertion indicates an individual requirement, capability or other property of a behavior.

The Web Services Policy Language (WSPL) (Anderson, 2004) is a policy language for expressing various aspects and features related to authentication, authorization, quality of service, quality of protection, reliable messaging, privacy, and application specific service options. WSPL specifies option choices for Web services in basic communication areas (reliable messaging, privacy, security, and so on). A WSPL policy is specified as a sequence of one or more rules, where each rule is an acceptable choice for satisfying the policy. WSPL policies list rules in the order of preference, with the most preferred listed first.

The OASIS ebXML specifies the contractual terms of a party by a Collaboration Protocol Profile (CPP) and the contractual agreement between two parties by a Collaboration Protocol Agreement (CPA) (OASIS, 2005). A CPP defines the capabilities of a party to engage in electronic business with other parties. In other words, a CPP defines what the parties can do (their services and activities) and how they can do. A CPA defines the capabilities that two parties need to agree upon to enable them to engage in electronic business for the purposes of the particular CPA. The CPA can merge the collaboration parties' CPPs into what they have selected to collaborate on and how they intend to do it.

The Open Digital Rights Language for Services (ODRL-S) (Gangadharan et al, 2007), a profile of the ODRL for Service Licensing, is a comprehensive language to represent exclusively the licenses for services, in a machine interpretable form. A license in ODRL-S describes information regarding the service being licensed, the extent to which the service could be used, accessed, and value added, on the basis that any use outside the scope of license would constitute an infringement, payment and charging terms, delivery terms (regarding quality of services and performance), acceptance terms, warranties, and limiting the liability of providers in case of failures, and the rights over future versions and over evolved services.

Current standards for semantic descriptions of services (e.g., OWL-S and WSMO) only marginally cover the specification of service contracts, limiting the support to the specification of sets of NFPs. The Web Ontology Language for Services (OWL-S) (Martin et al, 2004) supports only the specification of NFP in the *Service Profile* and their formalization in OWL. The Web Service Modeling Ontology (WSMO) (De Bruijn et al, 2005) approach allows the specification of a predefined set of NFPs. A closer look at the NFP set shows that many of them are used to express information about the description itself and not about the service. Moreover, these NFPs are not included in the WSMO logical model and thus reasoning on them is not possible.

Several research papers focus on solutions to overcome the current OWL-S and WSMO limitations. (Toma et al., 2007) propose to overcome the WSMO limitation by specifying NFP through axioms. (Kritikos et al, 2006) propose to fill the OWL-S gap by complementing it with a rich and extensible QoS model. (Giallonardo et al, 2007) define a model that allows service providers to advertise on the QoS offered, and service consumers to specify QoS requirements associated with an OWL-S profile.

Table 1 summarizes current support on service contracts with respect to QoS (e.g., performance, security, and dependability terms), business (e.g., financial terms), legal (e.g., jurisdiction place, warranty and limit of liability), and intellectual rights (e.g., share alike, commercial distribution, free). As shown in Table 1, existing approaches have addressed only few aspects (concerns and phases) associated with service contracts. Also, unfortunately, many of them address similar problems but speak in different languages and are not interoperable.

Following the umbrella term *'contractual concerns'*, the terms of a contract can describe quality of service, business, legal and intellectual rights conditions. Without a formal ontology or unique way of describing these terms, services can represent them as they wish, causing redundancies and misinterpretations in term description and leading to several issues in handling these contract terms. To give examples, let us illustrate the complexity in representing contractual terms in the said different languages with respect to our previous scenario.

Based on our classification of contract languages (Comerio, 2009), we group theses languages (see Table 2) and compare the complexity in representation among languages in the respective groups.

In our illustrated scenario, as different providers are participating, these providers could term contractual concerns in different ways.

When *Purchase Verification Service* specifies these terms, it introduces problems in negotiation and establishment of contracts with other services using WSLA or WSOL as these terms are not understandable and not supported by Type B or Type C or other Type A languages.

Though these two services specify similar quality of service conditions, there would be problems in automatic negotiations and composition of these services because these provisional contracts differ in language semantics and syntax.

Table 1. Current languages supporting contractual terms of services

Languages	Specifying			
	Quality of Service Terms	**Business Terms**	**Legal Terms**	**Intellectual Rights Terms**
Web Service Level Agreement (WSLA)	+	+		
WS-Agreement	+	+	+	
Web Service Offerings Language (WSOL)	+	+	+	
SLAng	+	+		
Web Services Policy Language (WSPL)	+			
WS-Policy	+			
Collaboration Protocol Profile and Agreement (CPP/CPA)		+		
Open Digital Rights Language for Services (ODRL-S)	+	+	+	+
Web Ontology Language for Services (OWL-S)	+			
Web Service Modeling Ontology (WSMO)	+			

Table 2. Current languages supporting contractual terms of services

Languages	Type and Description
ODRL-S, CPP/CPA	*Type A*: languages allowing the specification of predefined properties.
WSLA, WS-Agreement, WS-Policy, WSPL, SLAng, WSOL	*Type B*: languages allowing the specification of user-defined properties.
OWL-S, WSMO	*Type C*: languages allowing the specification of properties defined in user ontologies.

During the establishment of a contract, there arises misinterpretations due to non-unified/non-standard approaches in expressing contractual terms of the given two Web services.

Issues on Contract Negotiation and Establishment

In a business environment, a service provider specifies certain contractual terms which describe functional and/or non-functional properties of services. Service consumers also specify their expectation about functional and/or non-functional properties of their requested services. In a win-win business transaction, a provider and a consumer should agree upon contractual terms by negotiation and thereby establishing a contract.

Business and QoS are negotiable terms of a contract. Generally, consumers negotiate on these aspects with providers, using pre-defined templates. Negotiation refers to the comprising exchanges of offers and requests between the participating actors. The theoretical bases of SLA negotiation are provided in (Demirkan et al, 2005), identifying the requirements of a negotiation support system. A common understanding for the contractual terms among the negotiating parties is a critical issue in negotiation. To resolve this semantics issue in (Michael, 2002), template based negotiation is suggested (Grosof et al, 2002). The Policy-driven Automated Negotiations Decision-making Approach (PANDA) (Gimpel et al, 2003) automates the process of decision making within negotiation.

In our illustrated supply scenario, there are certain terms (such as legal terms like "non-commercial use") which cannot be measured by any means. However, these terms are significant in establishing a contract in the Internet and cloud environments. The definition of techniques to support negotiation between providers and consumers on legal and intellectual right terms is an open research challenge.

Exhibit 1. (contractual terms for intellectual rights and legal issues): Assume that Purchase Verification Service allows composition and offers indemnification rights. This can be expressed in ODRL-S as follows in the provisional contract of Purchase Verification Service.

```
<o-ex:permission>
      <sl:composition/>
</o-ex:permission>
<o-ex:requirement>
      <sl:indemnity>
         <sl:thirdpartyinfringementsclaims/>
      </sl:indemnity>
</o-ex:requirement>
```

Exhibit 2. (contractual terms for QoS): Assume that the provisional contract of Payment Service is specified in SLAng as follows

```
<Performance response_time="3"
successful_transactions="99"/>
Consider that Purchase Processing Service specifies QoS in WSOL as follows.
<wsol:QoSconstraint name=''MaxResponseTime''>
        <wsol:QoSname qname=''QoSns:responsetime''/>
        <wsol:QoStype typeName=''QoSns:max''>
        <wsol:qValue> 3 </wsol:qValue>
</wsol:QoSconstraint>
<o-ex:requirement>
            <sl:performance>
                <sl:responsetime> 3 </sl:responsetime>
            </sl:performance>
            <sl:reliability>
                <sl:availabilityrate> 99 </sl:availabilityrate>
            </sl:reliability>
</o-ex:requirement>
```

Issues on Contract Compatibility Evaluation and Composition

In the current service composition landscape, it is not so difficult for service consumers to compose different services based on published service interfaces. Existing composition tools allow service consumer to combine different services, potentially characterized by different service contracts. However, in order to define legal processes, there is a need to ensure that the service compositions do not include conflicting service contracts. This assurance cannot be given by a single provider and currently is not available in existing composition tools.

Incompatibilities among QoS, business, legal and intellectual rights terms specified in contracts of services involved in the composition have a strong impact on composite services and their execution. As an example, services offering incompatible copyrighted data and data distribution or in service coverage can cause inefficient composite service execution since their data are protected

by different rules and their coverage is limited to different world regions. Besides the evaluation of compatibility among service contracts, a unified contract for the composite service must be defined composing the contracts offered by the services involved in the composition. This unified contract specifies a recommended set of properties offered by the composite service. However, service contract compatibility and composition are complex activities since they must be evaluated according to the structure of the service composition. This is related to not only the control flow (i.e., the sequence in which the services are invoked) but also the data flow (i.e., the exchange of data between services) of the service composition.

While certain works (Zeng et al, 2004) (Aggarwal et al. 2004) address QoS-based compatibility for control flows, currently there is not a good understanding of how to check contract compatibility and composition for data, the input/output of services, whose contract terms are not always the same to that of the services. The consideration of both control and data flows is essential to perform an efficient Web service contract compatibility evaluation and composition.

Let us consider our scenario described in Figure 1 again, focusing on the interactions between the *Purchase Processing Service*, the *Payment Service* and the *Shipping Service*. The services follow a sequential execution and data are exchanged between the *Purchase Processing Service* and the *Payment Service* and between the *Purchase Processing Service* and the *Shipping Service*. As shown in Figure 1, C_{AS}, C_{FS}, and C_{TS} are the provisional contracts associated with the *Purchase Processing Service*, the *Payment Service* and the *Shipping Service*. To evaluate the compatibility of the availability time range term (i.e., the time range in which the service is available) in C_{AS}, the same term in only C_{FS} must be considered since the *Purchase Processing Service* and the *Payment Service* are executed one after the other. Vice versa, to evaluate the compatibility of the data ownership term (i.e., a license term stating how the data produced by the service are protected) in C_{AS}, the same term in C_{FS} and C_{TS} must be considered since the *Purchase Processing Service* data are managed by both the *Payment Service* and the *Shipping Service*.

Furthermore, past research has not focused on tools and algorithms dealing with contract compatibility evaluation when combining different services from different providers. Typically, they deal with only contract negotiation between consumer and service in a point-to-point manner. As a consequence, the definition of tools and algorithms dealing with service contract compatibility and composition evaluation considering data and control flows of the service composition appear to be an innovative research challenge.

Issues on Contract Monitoring and Enforcement

Consider a scenario where a service consumer is required to pay for a use of particular service through credit card. A message would be delivered to the service provider about payment from the customer. However, unless the credit card consortium informs about transaction, the provider cannot know whether it is paid and the amount of money paid for the use of a service by a customer. Business terms, being one of the important contractual terms, can be measured through an approach involving a third party who informs the provider on the moment of payment by a customer.

In general, many QoS terms are measurable. QoS terms can be measured at the consumer side to confirm whether the received QoS is in conformance with the QoS offered by providers. There can be contradictions in measurement, claiming the differences when a single QoS term is measured at both consumer side and provider side. There should be a consensus in measuring and monitoring of QoS and should be specified in a contract in indemnification clauses. However, there are some contractual terms (e.g., non-commercial use) which are difficult to monitor, if not impossible.

Most of the works in the area of service contracts focus on specifying and establishing contracts. The area of monitoring and enforcement of service contracts is given less attention

Table 3. Monitoring techniques for contractual terms

Contractual Terms	Methods of Measurement	Active Party
QoS terms	Sampling at regular intervals of time, querying through direct communication between provider and consumer	Consumer, Provider
Business terms	Notification through trusted third party approved services	Provider
Legal terms	Requires human involvement	Consumer, Provider
Intellectual rights terms	Requires human involvement	Consumer, Provider

by the community and is focused mainly on QoS terms and partially business terms for individual consumer-to-provider scenarios, not for cross-organizational scenarios. Current proposals on monitoring contractual terms are summarized in Table 3.

In the pioneering work of WSLA (Keller & Ludwig, 2003), the way of specifying, measuring, and monitoring the SLA parameters are described. Upon receipt of an SLA specification, the WSLA monitoring services are automatically configured to enforce the SLA. An event calculus based approach for monitoring SLAs in a utility computing scenario is presented in (Farrell, 2005). The recent work in (Skene et al, 2007) focuses on determining elements of SLAs that are monitorable at which degree. However, none of these approaches are sufficient to monitor completely contractual terms described by different specifications and associated with different services and to make decision strategies based on the outcome of monitoring.

RESEARCH ISSUES IN SERVICE CONTRACTS RECONCILIATION

Based on our analysis on service contracts, we have identified the following key research questions:

Research Issue 1: What Would be the Best Way to Manage Non-Functional Parameters and Service Contracts Associated with Service Instances Separately from WSDL?

Existing tools tend to assume that contracts can be annotated with service descriptions to facilitate the service discovery. However, a contract, if deployed in real business, will be associated with service instances. In particular, the concept of SaaS introduces various challenges to manage contracts associated with services because each

customer, in principle, would have a different contract for each service instance.

Research Issue 2: Can we Have a Single Language to Represent All Contractual Concerns? When there is no Unified Language, do the Existing Languages/Standards Satisfy the Requirement of Consumers for Representing Contractual Concerns?

Generally, all specification languages/standards focus on terms and conditions to be agreed by providers and consumers. Every language describes certain properties of services entirely. Unfortunately, at the time of writing, there is not a single language that fully supports all contractual terms. In the existence of multiple languages to represent contractual concerns, a unified set of standards for contractual terms is needed. To deal with multiple specifications, we can start from the consumer's point of view: we should provide a common language for the consumer to specify the requesting contractual terms. Such a common language can be used together with common ontologies for business, legal and intellectual terms. Based on consumer-specified contractual terms, we apply data integration techniques, such as schema mapping, meta-model and domain-specific languages, to query, evaluate and compare contractual terms given by different specifications/languages.

Interestingly, most of the present languages describing contractual concerns fail to represent hierarchical consumer preferences in contracts. For example, consider the following scenario where a consumer is interested in consuming a service with lesser cost and better response time. The consumer wishes to specify the order of preferences for the service by stating price as the priority term, i.e. the consumer wants to select a service with lower cost followed by higher response time. The present languages express contractual terms in a single level. Representing contractual terms in a hierarchical form (e.g., by a tree data structure) would be one simple solution but can enhance the description of consumer preferences and enable algorithms working on contractual terms to be more efficient. In this sense, the concept of constraints hierarchies (Borning et al, 1992) can be used to specify different preferences – mandatory and optional conditions - for selecting services (Guan et al, 2006).

Research Issue 3: Can we use Contract Negotiation/ Compatibility Algorithms, even though we do not have a Unified Specification Approach?

Presently, negotiation is mainly a manual process, and thus a full or partial automated contract negotiation is needed. Furthermore, in the case of composing services associated with different contracts, compatibility should be checked. However, this has so far attracted little attention.

Research Issue 4: Is Real Time Monitoring and Enforcement of the Contractual Concerns, in Particular, Legal and Intellectual Right Terms, of Dynamic Web Services Possible?

Though automated contract management and enforcement is highly desirable, it is obvious that many contractual terms cannot simply be monitored by the consumer and the provider in a fully automatic fashion, as assumed in most current work. A third party is needed in many cases, as discussed in (Keller & Ludwig, 2002). Moreover, for legal and intellectual right terms, besides third parties involvement, manual monitoring and enforcement will be required for contract enforcement. As a matter of facts, to support contract monitoring and enforcement in semi-automatic processes, the gap between technical contractual terms in business (human processing) level and in operational (machine processing)

level, as discussed in (Arenas & Wilson, 2008), has to be addressed.

TOWARDS SERVICE CONTRACTS RECONCILIATION

Addressing the said questions will need a lot of effort from the service community. There are some initial results on the reconciliation of service contracts. In the next sub-sections, we discuss some of our research efforts on addressing the said research issues.

Management of Non-Functional Parameters and Service Contracts

A common way to manage non-functional parameters and service contractual terms in Web services is to annotate service descriptions with these parameters and terms. Such parameters and terms will help to foster the service discovery and contract negotiation and selection. However, with the complexity of service and data concerns (Truong et al., 2009) and as these concerns evolve, this way of annotation is not scalable and cannot support runtime change of concerns well.

One way to deal with this problem is to consider the publishing and management of non-functional parameters and service contractual terms in the evolution of service changes. The SEMF (Service Evolution Management Framework) (Treiber et al., 2008), for example, proposed to manage different types of non-functional parameters and service concerns by using a data representation based on hierarchal Atom feeds. This model allows us to describe catalog of services where each service can have several types of concerns, such as QoS, licensing, interfaces, etc., managed by feeds. Furthermore, feeds, information entries, will be associated with temporal information and can link to external sources, thus allowing not only different types of parameters but also different specifications to be included. For example, domain-specific models can be described in RDF and OWL and linked to the Web service information. Exhibit 3. shows an example of data concerns linked with Web service description using SEMF.

While the model used by SEMF can foster a flexible way to describe contractual terms, it can, however, describe such terms at the service level only: such terms are specified for the whole service. Therefore, it will not be suitable for the management of contractual terms that are associated with service operations or individual data resources provided by services. This issue is particular important for DaaS (data-as-a-service)

which can be used to provide several data resources, each has a different contractual terms, e.g., like the Infochimps service (The Infochimp, 2010). This calls for another way to access and manage non-functional parameters and contractual terms to support also at the level of service operation and data resources.

Service Contract Mapping

In order to make service contracts comparable, techniques to map different service contracts described in different specifications and terminolo-

Exhibit 3. Example of using SEMF to managing different service and data concerns

```
<?xml version="1.0" encoding="UTF-8"?>
<feed xmlns="http://www.w3.org/2005/Atom">
    <id>urn:uuid:c7433422-49d6-4588-816d-c001cf00e9df</id>
    <updated>2008-03-25T16:28:15+01:00</updated>
    <title>USAddressVerification Service</title>
    <entry>
        <id>urn:uuid:4c44c6f7-7ee8-4b90-8348-931c1ef3d97e</id>
        <updated>2008-03-25T16:28:15+01:00</updated>
        <published>2008-03-25T16:28:15+01:00</published>
        <title>Interface</title>
        <summary>WSDL Interface </summary>
        <category label="Web Service Description" scheme="http://www.dmoz.org/
Computers/
        Programming/Internet/Service-Oriented_Architecture/Web_Services/
WSDL" term="Interface"/>
        <content type="application/wsdl+xml" src="http://ws.strikeiron.com/
USAddressVerification5?WSDL"/>
    </entry>
    <entry>
        <title>DaaS Concerns</title>
        <summary>Data Concerns</summary>
        <category label="Data Concerns"  term="DaaSConcern"/>
        <content type="application/xml" src="http://www.infosys.tuwien.ac.at/
prototyp/SOD1/

dataconcerns/samples/USAddressVerificationConcerns.xml"/>
    </entry>
</feed>
```

gies must be developed. In our view, the mapping of service contract specifications is not a static, but a dynamic process because specifications and terminologies as well as knowledge about them change over the time.

A possible solution to service contract mapping consists in performing semantic mediation based on ontology matching techniques (Euzenat & Shvaiko, 2007). However, the heterogeneity that characterizes service contract descriptions makes these techniques difficult to be applied. As a matter of fact, in some cases they cannot be applied since particular service contract descriptions (e.g., ODRL-S licenses) are not based on ontologies.

An alternative solution consists in performing the wrapping of service contract using a reference meta-model. An example of this solution is the Policy-Centered Metamodel (PCM) Wrapper (Comerio et al., 2009) that has been designed to support the semi-automatic mapping of ODRL-S, WSLA and WSOL contracts to PCM-based service contract descriptions. The PCM (De Paoli et al., 2008) has been chosen as common meta-model since it offers (1) expressive descriptions addressing qualitative contractual terms by means of logical expressions on ontology values and quantitative terms by means of expressions including ranges and inequalities and (2) structured descriptions by using the concept of *Policy* that aggregates different term descriptions into a single entity with an applicability condition. Moreover, as shown in (Palmonari et al. 2009), PCM-based service contracts allow for semantic mediation between contractual terms based on multiple ontologies (the evaluation and comparison of the PCM with other meta-models is out of the scope of this chapter.).

The PCM Wrapper provides support for two main activities:

- *Modeling and mapping service contract terminologies into a reference ontology:* since different contracts often utilize different terminologies, the definition of a ref-

erence ontology is needed. This ontology will contain semantic description of structures of service contract terms, their allowed values and the relationships among them. The description of techniques used by the PCM Wrapper to create the reference ontology is described in (Comerio et al., 2009).

- *Wrapping ODRL-S, WSLA and WSOL specifications to PCM Policy:* different techniques for performing the wrapping of a service contract in each type of language to PCM Policies are developed. For example, the wrapping of ODRL-S specifications is directly performed by applying fixed mapping rules since ODRL-S is characterized by a fixed profile model describing all the terms that can be in a service contract. For what concern specifications in WSLA and WSOL, the wrapping activity is more complicated since there is the necessity to handle the absence of knowledge (i.e., mapping rules) on specified terms, thus the service providers must define the mapping between their contract terms (i.e., text labels for WSLA and ontological concepts for WSOL) and concepts available in the reference ontology. Furthermore, lexical databases like WordNet could be integrated in order to support service providers to define mapping rules for identifying synonyms between text labels and ontological concepts defined in the reference ontology. Different types of ontology alignment tools could be also used to support the wrapping of WSOL specifications: (1) tools for defining a mapping between concepts in two different ontologies by finding pairs of related concepts (e.g., ANCHORPROMPT (Noy et al., 2003)) or by evaluating semantic affinity between concepts (e.g., H-MATCH (Castano et al., 2003)) and (2) tools for defining mapping rules to relate only relevant parts of the source ontologies (e.g., ONION (Mitra et al., 2001)).

Let us consider how the wrapping of a WSLA specification is performed: (1) parsing the specification in order to detect contract terms (i.e., SLAParameters); (2) searching the previously defined mapping rules related to the detected terms; (3) if mapping rules are not identified, use WordNet to identify a possible mapping between the SLAParameters and concepts available in the reference ontology and ask confirmation about the correctness of the mapping to the service provider; and (4) if the mapping is not correct or not available, ask to the service provider to perform the mapping manually.

Figure 2 illustrates the above-mentioned steps when wrapping the WSLA-based contract associated with the *Purchase Processing Service* of our scenario in Figure 1 that includes the following terms: *PrePayment = 9.99 Euros* and *ServiceUsage = "adaptation"* where *ServiceUsage* is a legal terms that can assume the value *adaptation* (i.e., the right of allowing the use of service interface only), *composition* (i.e., the right of service execution with the right of interface modification) or *deriva-*

tion (i.e., right of allowing modifications to the service interface as well as to the implementation of the service). In this example, a mapping rule for *PrePayment* already exists. On the contrary, the term *ServiceUsage* is not known and no rules are available. Moreover, no synonym relations are specified in WordNet between *ServiceUsage* and terms defined in the reference ontology. In order to handle this absence of knowledge, the service provider can navigate the ontology and map the SLAParameter *ServiceUsage* to any ontological concept. The result is that *ServiceUsage* is mapped to *Permissions*.

After this preliminary activity, the mapping proceeds considering the *Expressions* defined in each Service Level Objective of the WSLA specification. Each *Expression* follows the first order logic, including predicates and logic operators. According to the logic operators, different mapping rules can be applied. For example, In Figure 2, the logic operator *"And"* is used to specify the aggregation of two plain predicates stating conditions on *PrePayment* and *ServiceUsage*. The mapping to a PCM Policy consists of defining the concept instances related to all the plain predicates. The final result for the considered

Figure 2. Mapping between WSLA and PCM policy

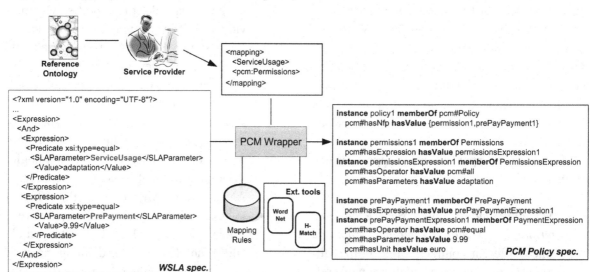

example is a PCM Policy containing: (1) an instance of Permissions characterized by an expression stating that the value *adaptation* is assumed (i.e., *pcm#hasOperator hasValue pcm#all; pcm#hasParameters hasValue adaptation*) and (2) an instance of PrePayPayment stating that the amount is equal to 9.99 Euros (i.e., *pcm#hasOperator hasValue pcm#equal; pcm#hasParameter hasValue 9.99; pcm#hasUnit hasValue euro*).

Although techniques proposed by the PCM Wrapper are promising for dealing with the heterogeneity of service contract languages, several limitations must be addressed in order to make the PCM Wrapper a practical and widely accepted solution for service contract mapping. First, the current version supports the mapping of a limited set of contract specification languages (i.e., ODRL-S, WSLA and WSOL). Second, currently the PCM Wrapper can be used only by service providers that are familiar with ontologies defined in the Web Service Modeling Language (WSML). Therefore a user-friendly support for ontology navigation and multi-language ontology definition are still open research issues. Finally, lexical databases and ontology alignment tools need to be integrated in a next version of the framework.

Service Contract Compatibility

With techniques to map different service contracts, it is possible to evaluate the compatibility between heterogeneous contracts associated with services to be composed into a composition. Our solution based on the SeCO2 framework (Comerio et al., 2009) also supports service composers to deal with service contracts in service composition. This framework takes as input a *composition description* (i.e., services involved in the composition, data and control flows) and produces the *compatibility results*: a list of identified incompatibilities among service contract terms. A contract is compatible with another contract if all contract terms are compatible. In order to produce compatibility results, SeCO2 utilizes the following resources:

- **SeCO Reference Ontology:** An extensible ontology contains semantic description of service contract terms, their allowed values, and the relations among them. The *SeCO Reference Ontology* is built based on the Policy-Centered Metamodel (PCM).
- **Contract Term Knowledge-Base:** A repository that contains additional information about properties described in the reference ontology. Among others, this repository contains the specification of the influences between each service contract term and *control* and *data flows*.
- **SeCO Policies:** Representing PCM-based WSML descriptions of service contracts including contract terms defined using the *SeCO Reference Ontology*.
- **Compatibility Evaluation Rules:** Rules for checking the compatibility between *SeCO Policies* of services involved in the composition. Each rule specifies how to evaluate the compatibility of a specific term defined in the reference ontology.
- **Composition Rules:** Rules for the service contract property composition. Each rule specifies how to evaluate a recommended value for a specific term to be included in a composite service contract.

Figure 3 shows (a) *setup-time* and (b) *run-time* activities supported by the SeCO2 framework. At setup-time domain experts are supported in the definition of rules to be applied in the compatibility evaluation and composition processes. The *Compatibility evaluation and composition rule definition* consists in defining a compatibility evaluation rule and a composition rule for each property specified in the *SeCO reference ontology*. This activity is performed considering data and control flows, as well as composition patterns, that can be associated with a service composition and using existing information in the reference ontology and in the contract term knowledge-base.

Figure 3. Setup-time (a) and run-time (b) activities in the SeCO2 framework

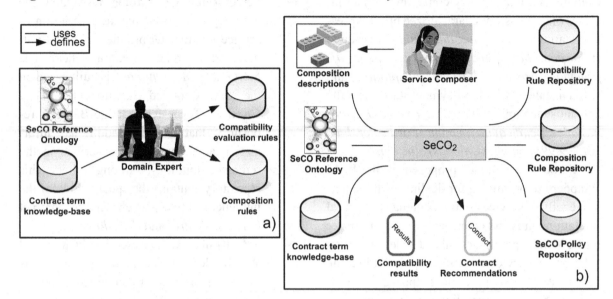

At run-time SeCO2 supports service composers offering the following functionalities: (1) *Composition description analysis*: analysis of the composition descriptions provided by the *Service Composer* in order to identify the services involved in the composition and data and control flows of the service composition; (2) *SeCO policy retrieval*: after having identified the services involved in the composition, their associated *SeCO Policies* are retrieved from the *SeCO Policy Repository*; (3) *Service contract compatibility evaluation*: contract terms are extracted from each *SeCO Policy* and evaluated according to the related *Compatibility evaluation rule* on the basis of the data and control flows of the service composition. Incompatibilities between service contracts are pointed out to the *Service Composer*; (4) *Composite service contract definition*: for each contract terms included in at least one of the retrieved *SeCO Policies*, the related *Composition rule* is executed considering data and control flows of the service composition. The result of each rule is included in the contract for the composite service.

Let us consider the provisional contracts C_{PS} and C_{AS} associated with the *Purchase Order Service* and the *Purchase Processing Service* of our supply chain management scenario in Figure 1. Let us assume that the two contracts present different *ServiceUsage* (i.e., the extent to which the service could be used, accessed, and value added, on the basis that any use outside the scope of license would constitute an infringement) terms. C_{PS} and C_{AS} specify *composition* and *derivation* as offered *ServiceUsage* terms respectively. The algorithm of SeCO2 will determine that C_{PS} and C_{AS} are compatible since *derivation* subsumes *composition*. For a complete compatibility analysis, the algorithm must know about the possible subsumptions, which imply a match that should occur, if the given contract clause is more permissive (accepts more) than the corresponding element in the other contract. For example, the subsumption rules for *ServiceUsage* are shown in Table 4.

There could also be a scenario when analyzing the compatibility of contracts where one of the contracts contains terms that the other contract does not. In certain cases, the absence of one or several of these terms does not affect the compatibility with the other contract. Further details about how the SeCO2 framework performs the contract

Table 4. Subsumption rules over ServiceUsage terms

Element 1	Element 2	Comparison	Redefinition
Derivation	Adaptation Composition	Derivation ⊃ Adaptation Derivation ⊃ Composition	Derivation Derivation
Adaptation	Composition Derivation	Composition ⊃ Adaptation Derivation ⊃ Adaptation	Composition Derivation
Composition	Adaptation Derivation	Composition ⊃ Adaptation Derivation ⊃ Composition	Composition Derivation

compatibility evaluation are in (Comerio et al., 2009).

The SeCO2 framework is an ongoing work in which service contract compatibility evaluation and composition rules are manually defined by domain experts. The support given by SeCO2 for automating this activity needs to be developed. Furthermore, only SeCO Policies defined in WSML can be evaluated. In order to manage different specifications, an enriched version of the PCM Wrapper (see the previous section) will be integrated into the framework.

CONCLUSION

In a dynamic market environment, the usage of Web services is based on contracts specifying the terms and conditions of using and provisioning of services. This chapter discusses the strengths and weakness of existing languages and standards for describing contracts in service-oriented computing. When the vision of software and data as a service is realized, service contracts are of paramount importance and we need to consider the interoperability of service contracts provided by different providers. Based on our study, we have suggested some guidelines and presented our solutions to reconcile the contractual concerns of Web services that could make the vision of service oriented computing more realistic.

We have discussed current approaches on the reconciliation of service contracts by focusing on the management of complex and diverse types of

contract terms, the mapping of contract terms and the evaluation of service contract compatibility. However, as we have discussed, still there are many issues to be solved in these approaches in order to support the establishment of service contracts in multiple service providers' environments. In particular, the management of non-functional parameters and contracts should cover also service operations and data resources as well, the wrapping of contract specifications should be linked with human tasks workflows and external semantic matching services, and the evaluation of service contract compatibility should also deal with data resources and data concerns.

In our reconciliation work, semi-automatic models and techniques for monitoring and enforcement of legal and intellectual property right terms have not been addressed. As stated in previous sections, contractual terms cannot simply be monitored by the service consumer and the service provider in a fully automatic fashion. A third-party *Authority Service* is the solution proposed in most works available in the literature (Keller & Ludwig, 2002; Smith & Ramakrishnan, 2003; Cardoso et al., 2009) for dealing with multiple types of contract specifications including QoS, business, legal and intellectual right terms. In our view, for what concerns QoS and business terms, the realization of an automatic contract monitoring is feasible and this has attracted a considerable research effort. However, how to monitor and enforce legal and intellectual right terms is very much open. In our opinion, the legal and intellectual right terms of a service contract cannot be enforced in an automatic manner. The primary reason for not enforcing is the fact that technology cannot protect freedoms such as "fair use". In other words, "fair use" cannot be coded. We believe that technological enforcement encumbrances the unplanned reuse of services. We want to encourage such use. And we, along with the vision of Creative Commons (Lessig, 2004), are concerned that the ecology for creativity will be stifled by the pervasive use of technology to "manage" rights. Copyrights should be respected, no doubt. But we prefer they be respected the old fashioned way — by people acting to respect the freedoms, and limits, chosen by the author and enforced by the law. Based on these observations, we state that for legal and intellectual right terms, only the realization of a semi-automatic contract monitoring is feasible. The service customer must manually communicate related monitoring data to the authority providing details about how the authority can verify them.

ACKNOWLEDGMENT

This work is partially supported by the European Union through the FP7 projects COIN and COMPAS and by the SAS Institute srl (Grant Carlo Grandi).

REFERENCES

Aggarwal, R., Verma, K., Miller, J., & Milnor, W. (2004). Constraint driven web service composition in meteor-s. In *Proceeding of the 2004 IEEE International Conference on Services Computing* (SCC 2004), (pp. 23–30).

Anderson, A. (2004). *Web services policy language (WSPL)*. In *Proceedings of the Fifth IEEE International Workshop on Policies for Distributed Systems and Networks* (POLICY'04), (pp. 189–192).

Andrieux, A., Czajkowski, K., Dan, A., Keahey, K., Ludwig, H., & Nakata, T. … Xu, M. (2007). *Web services agreement specification* (WS-Agreement). Grid Resource Allocation Agreement Protocol (GRAAP) WG. Retrieved from http://www.ogf.org/documents/GFD.107.pdf

Arenas, A., & Wilson, M. (2008). Contracts as trust substitutes in collaborative business. *IEEE Computer, 41*(7), 80–83.

Borning, A., Freeman-Benson, B. N., & Wilson, M. (1992). Constraint hierarchies. *Lisp and Symbolic Computation, 5*(3), 223–270. doi:10.1007/BF01807506

Cardoso, J., Winkler, M., & Voigt, K. (2009). A service description language for the internet of services. In *Proc. of the International Symposium on Service Science (ISSS 2009)*, March 2009.

Castano, S., Ferrara, A., & Montanelli, S. (2003). H-match: An algorithm for dynamically matching ontologies in peer-based systems. In *Proceedings of the 1st VLDB Int. Workshop on Semantic Web and Databases* (SWDB 2003).

Christensen, E., Curbera, F., Meredith, G., & Weerawarana, S. (2001). *Web services description language* (WSDL) 1.1. Retrieved from http://www.w3.org/TR/wsdl

Comerio, M., Truong, H. L., De Paoli, F., & Dustdar, S. (2009). Evaluating contract compatibility for service composition in the SeCO2 framework. In *Proceedings of International Conference on Service Oriented Computing* (ICSOC 2009).

Dan, A., Johnson, R., & Arsanjani, A. (2007). *Information as a service: Modeling and realization.* International Workshop on Systems Development in SOA Environments (SDSOA '07).

De Bruijn, J., Lausen, H., Krummenacher, R., Polleres, A., Predoiu, L., Kifer, M., & Fensel, D. (2005). *The Web service modeling language WSML* (D16. 1v0. 2). http://www.wsmo.org/TR/d16/d16.1/v0.21/20051005/

De Paoli, F., Palmonari, M., Comerio, M., & Maurino, A. (2008). A meta-model for non-functional property descriptions of Web services. In *Proceedings of the IEEE International Conference on Web Services* (ICWS 2008)

Demirkan, H., Goul, M., & Soper, D. (2005). Service level agreement negotiation: A theory-based exploratory study as a starting point for identifying negotiation support system requirements. In *Proceedings of the 38th Hawaii International Conference on System Sciences.*

Euzenat, J., & Shvaiko, P. (2007). *Ontology matching.* Springer-Verlag.

Farrell, A., Sergot, M., Salle, M., & Bartolini, C. (2005). Using the event calculus for tracking the normative state of contracts. *International Journal of Cooperative Information System, 4*(2).

Gangadharan, G. R., D'Andrea, V., Iannella, R., & Weiss, M. (2007). *ODRL service licensing profile (ODRL-S).* In *Proceedings of the 5th International Workshop for Technical, Economic, and Legal Aspects of Business Models for Virtual Goods.*

Giallonardo, E., & Zimeo, E. (2007). More semantics in QoS matching. In *Proceedings of International Conference on Service-Oriented Computing and Application* (SOCA'07), (pp. 163–171).

Gimpel, H., Ludwig, H., Dan, A., & Kearney, B. (2003). PANDA: Specifying policies for automated negotiations of service contracts. In *Proceedings of the First International Conference on Service Oriented Computing.*

Grosof, B., Reeves, D., & Wellman, M. (2002). Automated negotiation from declarative contract descriptions. *Computational Intelligence, 18*(4).

Guan, Y., Ghose, A. K., & Lu, Z. (2006). Using constraint hierarchies to support QoS-guided service composition. In *Proceedings of the IEEE ICWS*, (pp. 743–752).

Kamoda, H., Yamaoka, M., Matsuda, S., Broda, K., & Sloman, M. (2005). Policy conflict analysis using free variable tableaux for access control in Web services environments. In *Proceedings of the 14th International World Wide Web Conference* (WWW).

Keller, A., & Ludwig, H. (2002). Defining and monitoring service-level agreements for dynamic ebusiness. In *Proceedings of the 16th USENIX Conference on System Administration*, (pp. 189–204).

Keller, A., & Ludwig, H. (2003). The WSLA framework: Specifying and monitoring service level agreements for Web services. *Journal of Network and Systems Management, 11*(1). doi:10.1023/A:1022445108617

Kritikos, K., & Plexousakis, D. (2006). Semantic QoS metric matching. In *Proceedings of the European Conference on Web Services* (ECOWS'06), (pp. 265–274).

Kuno, H., Alonso, G., Casati, F., & Machiraju, V. (2003). *Web services - Concepts, architectures and applications*, 1st ed.

Lessig, L. (2004). The creative commons. *Montana Law Review*, (Winter): 1–13.

Lewis, L., & Ray, P. (1999). *Service level management definition, architecture, and research challenges.* In *Proceedings of the Global Telecommunications Conference* (GLOBECOM).

Lupu, E., & Sloman, M. (1997). *A policy based role object model.* In *Proceedings of the International Enterprise Distributed Object Computing Conference* (EDOC).

Martin, D., et al. (2004). Semantic markup for Web services. Retrieved from http://www.w3.org/Submission/OWL-S/

Michael, S. (2002). *Engineering electronic negotiations.* New York, NY: Kluwer Academic Publishers.

Mitra, P., Wiederhold, G., & Decker, S. (2001). *A scalable framework for the interoperation of information sources* (pp. 317–329). Stanford University.

Muller, N. (1999). Managing service level agreements. *International Journal of Network Management, 9,* 155–166. doi:10.1002/(SICI)1099-1190(199905/06)9:3<155::AID-NEM317>3.0.CO;2-M

Noy, N. F., & Musen, M. A. (2003). The prompt suite: Interactive tools for ontology merging and mapping. *International Journal of Human-Computer Studies, 59*(6), 983–1024. doi:10.1016/j.ijhcs.2003.08.002

OASIS. (2005). *ebXML CPP and CPA Technical Committee: Collaboration protocol profile and agreement specification version 2.1.* Retrieved from http://www.oasis-open.org/committees/ebxml-cppa/

Palmonari, M., Comerio, M., & De Paoli, F. (2009). Effective and flexible Nfp-based ranking of Web services. In *Proceedings of International Conference on Service Oriented Computing* (ICSOC 2009).

Sahai, A., Durante, A., & Machiraju, V. (2002). *Towards automated SLA management for Web services.* Technical Report HPL-2001-310 (R.1), Software Technology Laboratory, HP Laboratories, Palo Alto, USA.

Skene, J., Lamanna, D., & Emmerich, W. (2004). Precise service level agreements. In *Proceedings of 26th International Conference on Software Engineering* (ICSE).

Skene, J., Skene, A., Crampton, J., & Emmerich, W. (2007). *The monitorability of service-level agreements for application-service provision.* In *Proceedings of the 6th International Workshop on Software and Performance* (pp. 3–14).

Smith, T., & Ramakrishnan, L. (2003). Joint policy management and auditing in virtual organizations. In *Proceedings of the Fourth International Workshop on Grid Computing.*

The COMPAS Project. (2010). *Compliance-driven models, languages, and architectures for services.* Retrieved December 2010, from http://www.compas-ict.eu/

The Infochimps. (2010). Retrieved December 2010, from http://infochimps.org/

Toma, I., Roman, D., & Fensel, D. (2007). On describing and ranking services based on non-functional properties. In *Proceedings of the Third International Conference on Next Generation Web Services Practices* (NWESP '07), (pp. 61–66).

Tosic, V., Pagurek, B., Patel, K., Esfandiari, B., & Ma, W. (2003). Management applications of the Web service offerings language. In *Proceedings of the 15th Conference on Advanced Information Systems Engineering.*

Treiber, M., Truong, H. L., & Dustdar, S. (2008). SEMF - Service evolution management framework. In *Proceedings of the 34th EUROMICRO Conference on Software Engineering and Advanced Applications* (SEAA).

Truong, H. L., & Dustdar, S. (2009). *On analyzing and specifying concerns for data as a service.* In *Proc. of the 4th IEEE Asia-Pacific Services Computing Conference* (APSCC 2009), (pp. 87-94).

Truong, H. L., Gangadharan, G. R., Treiber, M., Dustdar, S., & D'Andrea, V. (2008). *On reconciliation of contractual concerns of Web services.* 2nd Non Functional Properties and Service Level Agreements in Service Oriented Computing Workshop (NFPSLA-SOC'08), co-located with The 6th IEEE European Conference on Web Services, Dublin, Ireland.

Vedamuthu, A., Orchard, D., Hirsch, F., Hondo, M., Yendluri, P., Boubez, T., & Yalcinalp, U. (2007). *Web services policy (WS-policy) framework.* Retrieved from http://www.w3.org/TR/ws-policy

Viega, J. (2009). Cloud computing and the common man. *Computer*, *42*, 106–108. doi:10.1109/MC.2009.252

Zeng, L., Benatallah, B., Ngu, A., Dumas, M., Kalagnanam, J., & Chang, H. (2004). QoS-aware middleware for web services composition. *IEEE Transactions on Software Engineering*, *30*(5), 311–327. doi:10.1109/TSE.2004.11

KEY TERMS AND DEFINITIONS

Contractual Terms: An instance built as a constraint based on non-functional properties characterizing concerns associated with services and their data. They basically describe the associated non-functional parameters of a service.

Non-Functional Parameters: Qualitative and quantitative parameters of a service covering QoS, business, legal, and intellectual rights issues related to the service usage.

Service Contract Compatibility: A process to verify whether there are no conflicting contractual terms among different contracts.

Service Contract Mapping: A process to map different service contracts described in different specifications and terminologies.

Service Contract Reconciliation: A process to reconcile the semantics and syntax of multiple service contracts specified in different languages.

Service Contract: A legal agreement between a service provider and service consumer that is enforced by the law.

Chapter 14
The Gross Interest:
Service Popularity Aggregation

Mohamed Hamdy
Ain Shams Universit, Egypt

Birgitta König-Ries
Friedrich-Schiller-University Jena, Germany

ABSTRACT

Service popularity, e.g., how often a service is requested, can be an important non-functional property determining the life-cycle of a service. To capture it, the requesting behavior of clients needs to be modeled. In this work, we introduce and discuss: the importance of the service popularity, a generalized requesting model that can capture the requesting behavior of clients, a service popularity measure called "Gross Interest," and a Gross Interest quantification method. Two extremely different sets of specifications for the proposed generalized requesting model which produce two different Gross Interest scenarios (rich and poor scenarios) are introduced and quantified. As an application example for the service popularity, we show a service replication protocol for Mobile Ad Hoc Networks (MANETs) which realizes and employs service popularity in its replication decisions.

INTRODUCTION

Realizing distributed applications based on Service Oriented Architectures (SOA) became recently very popular. Merging SOA with the up-growing semantic technologies enabled new dimensions of automation for the related core building blocks of SOA like service discovery, ranking, composition and execution. Selecting a suitable atomic service or a set of services is usu-ally based on the service ranking process. Service ranking is an important process which utilizes the service descriptions to determine an index of relevancy for a set of services regarding a service request. The ranking process generally uses two main categories of service description attributes which are *functional* and *non-functional*. While the functional and behavioral attributes describe respectively what the service does and how its functionalities are achieved, the non-functional attributes describe the restrictions and constraints

DOI: 10.4018/978-1-61350-432-1.ch014

on the provided service functionalities (Toma et al., 2007).

Matching a service offer for a specific service request is dependent on the deployed service ranking and matchmaking process. The early service ranking and matchmaking approaches focused only on the functional and behavioral attributes. Recently, a new generation of ranking approaches is starting to include the non-functional attributes in their decisions. Finding a way to balance the impacts of the functional and non-functional attributes is the key for achieving a better service ranking and more accurate matches (Hamdy et al., 2007).

Even if the descriptions of a specified service include the functional and typical non-functional attributes, they miss an important category of attributes, namely those aggregated attributes that the service can accumulate during its life time. This lack in descriptions can not be complemented or configured by an initial service offer. In fact, attributes like service popularity and trust represent an important set of attributes that can not originally (or at any other time) be specified by the service provider. Instead of that, it is accumulated, for example, from its clients requesting behavior.

The aggregated attributes represent a very important category of non-functional attributes which can not be easily described. From a provider perspective, the service popularity plays a great role. It is needed for a service provider in order to decide when it is supposed to enhance, replace or shut down a specified service. From a client perspective, for example, service popularity plays an important role in supporting the shown trust attributes of the service provider. Moreover, considering a set of competing services and providers, having such a computed service popularity attributes supports deploying better versions of services.

The concepts of service ranking and popularity may seem overlapping, but, imagine a distributed system with a SOA enabled application in which an un-interesting (i.e., unpopular) service is deployed

with a unique functionality. Should there ever be any request for this functionality by a system participant, this service will perfectly match, but this happens rarely. On the other hand, this service needs to be considered by the SOA core mechanisms like discovery and matchmaking adding to the effort required to perform them. Moreover, in some environments like unstable and mobile networks, this will be even more extreme, as there, services will frequently need to be replicated to ensure availability as required in many cases and applications. Replicating a service that is basically never used is clearly a waste of resources. From another perspective, both service ranking and popularity may be overlapping, if the service popularity reflects better functional, behavioral and non-functional service facilities. In that case, the better service offers will be more popular. In these cases, the service popularity that is being computed during the service operation will be not only be affected by the good attributes of the offered service, but will also prove these offers.

Since the aggregated attributes, namely service popularity, are absent in the service offer, the current service ranking and matchmaking approaches can not include them in the service selection. So, this missing integration between the service popularity and selection is required to overcome.

In order to have a measure for the service popularity, many candidate attributes can be considered. Examples are: the number of the requests that a service gains in a certain period of time, the trust values set by the different clients, the vitality (such as DHCP services) for the system participants and the service provider's stability and available resources. These can form individually or in combinations the main measurements behind the service popularity.

In this chapter, the concept of *Gross Interest* as a measure for the important non-functional property "service popularity" is introduced. Since, the *Gross Interest* is a non-functional measure based on the clients' requesting behavior which aggregates popularity of a certain service at a specific point in time, a general service requesting model is described and presented based on the request behavior modeling of (Hamdy & König-Ries, 2008b, Hamdy & König-Ries, 2009b).

The properties and abilities of this requesting model are described and analyzed. Based on the proposed generalized requesting model, a quantification method for the *Gross Interest* the Gross Interest.

The structure of this chapter is as follows: Section 1 presents the importance of the service popularity as a non-functional attribute. A generalized service requesting behavior model for a client is proposed with its criteria in Section 2. Moreover, the Gross Interest as a quantification for the service popularity is introduced. In Section 3, different specifications for the requesting behavior scenarios are proposed and analyzed. The effects of the service popularity and the Gross Interest on enhancing the service contents of a network are addressed and discussed in Section 4. Section 5 shows the advantages of applying a service popularity scheme in the context of service replication as an example case. Finally, the work of this chapter is summarized and the contribution are highlighted and presented in Section 6.

SERVICE REQUESTING BEHAVIOR

Based on the offered functionality of a specified service and how important this functionality is for all/some of the network participants (clients), a client forms his interest in this service. The client interest form the requesting behavior. From a service provider's perspective, aggregating the different clients' interest regarding the offered service in one measurement is vital. The term *Gross Interest* refers basically to the aggregated interest towards a specified service within a certain time.

Frequency of requests, amount of transported data and workload are a set of main factors that affect the service Gross Interest. Based on one (or a combination) of the mentioned factors, a service provider can estimate the popularity of his offered services. Moreover, in cases of presence of services with the same functionalities, the services can be ranked based on their interest or popularity. For the required popularity ranking process and in order to hold a common ranking for the different(same functionality) services, a reference value for the highest (possible to be achieved) Gross Interest should be determined and taken into consideration. In this section, a set of considerations for how to quantify the Gross Interest based on the number and frequency of the generated requests regarding a specified service are given. In order to quantify the Gross Interest, a generalized model that can capture any client requesting behavior regarding a specified service is introduced. Then, the important criteria of this requesting model is presented and discussed.

MODELING THE SERVICE REQUESTING BEHAVIOR

(Hamdy & König-Ries, 2008b, Hamdy & König-Ries, 2008a, Hamdy & König-Ries, 2009a) introduce a basic ``calling'' model which can describe the behavior of the generated requests regarding a specific service by a client. Based this, we propose here a generalization of this model is proposed. The generalized model can capture a wide set of different requesting behaviors by clients for many services. As depicted in Figure 2.1-A and B, any client requesting behavior regarding the offered service can be modeled a follows:

- As in Figure 2.1-A, the operation time of the service can be divided into a sequence requesting cycles from the perspective of clients.
- As in Figure 2.1-B, each of the requesting cycles consists of two periods: " left" active period in which the client performs requests to the service, and " passive" period

where the client pauses generating requests to the service.

- The active periods are composed of a number of units Us with a predefined length in time. The length and the number of these units N varies from cycle to cycle and depends on a given distribution for each requesting cycle.
- During the active periods, a requesting rate, $RequestRate$, describes the frequency of generating the requests. The value for the requesting rate varies from cycle to cycle and depends on a given distribution.
- The passive periods are composed of a number of units $U^d s$ with a predefined length in time. The length and the number of these units M is varying from cycle to cycle and dependent on a given distribution for each requesting cycle.
- The model specifications (U, U^d, N, M and $RequestRate$) for each requesting cycle are allowed to vary. Each of the clients may have its own specifications of requesting cycles sequences.

QUANTIFYING THE GROSS INTERESTS

Based on the previously introduced requesting model, a quantification of Gross Interest in terms of the expected number of active clients (those who perform actively requests to the service with the maximum possible requesting rate) is proposed. For simplicity of derivations, we assumed that the requesting model specifications (U, U^d, N, M and $RequestRate$) are fixed for all the requesting cycles.

As shown in Figure 2.1-B Let U be the time length of a requesting unit. Let n be the number of requesting units. Let U^d be the time length of a pausing unit. Let m be the number of the pausing units.

Case 1: In this case we assume that $U = U^d$. The Sum of all calling and pausing unites will be $m + n$. The probability for a client to be in an active period at a certain time $Prob(active)$ will be:

$$Prob(active) = \frac{n}{n + m} \qquad (1)$$

Considering the introduced requesting rate in our requesting model, since $RequestRate \in \{outcome(distribution(Rates))\}$, the probability for a client to achieve the maximum requesting rate at a certain time $Prob(active_{MaxRqst})$ will be:

$$Prob(active_{MaxRqst}) = \frac{n}{n + m} \times P(MaxRqst)$$

$$(2)$$

where $P(MaxRqst)$ is the probability for a client to have a $RequestRate = $ maximum request rate and $outcome(\ distribution(Rates)\ )$ is a function that produces the possible requesting rates. Therefore, the expected number of active clients who perform the maximum allowed requesting rate at a certain time Ex will be:

$$Ex = NetworkSize \times \frac{n}{n + m} \times P(MaxRqst)$$

$$(3)$$

Case 2: In which, see Figure 2.2-A and B, $U \neq U^d$ U^d units are supposed to be substituted by U units. Therefore, let us define R, which is the ratio of U^d to U where $R = \dfrac{U^d}{U}$ and so we substitute U^d by U. The new number of the new substituted U units is n^d and n^d replaces m where $n^d = R \times m$. The summation of all active and pause periods will be $n + R \times m$. For this Equation 2 should be modified to be:

$$Prob(active_{MaxRqst}) = \frac{n}{n + R \times m} \times P(MaxRqst)$$

$$(4)$$

and so Ex will be:

$$Ex = NetworkSize \times \frac{n}{n + R \times m} \times P(MaxRqst)$$

$$(5)$$

Since n and m are based on some distribution as mentioned before, they should be used as their expected values. Let Ex_n be the expected value of n and Ex_m be the expected value of m and so Ex, will be:

$$Ex = NetworkSize \times \frac{Ex_n}{Ex_n + R \times Ex_m} \times P(MaxRqst)$$

$$(6)$$

Definition: Based on the previously mentioned derivations the Gross Interest can be defined as: *The expected number of active clients connected to a specified service and performing the maximum allowed requesting rate at a certain time.*

Correlation to Service Popularity: Converging to the concept of service popularity, the expected Gross Interest can represent a common reference point. If the service providers know (based on experience, questionnaires, etc.) how the clients may access their services, based on the proposed requesting model, they can an approximate for the Gross Interest regarding an approximate for the Gross Interest regarding some services. Moreover, the Gross Interest for many services and service categories may be known in advance. In case of presence of competition among many providers who operate services with the same functionality in the same network, a provider can estimate how much interest is gained at his offered service. Not only from a perspective of a provider but also upon the level of the network, these same functionality services can be ranked reflecting their aggregated popularity.

CRITERIA OF THE GENERALIZED REQUESTING MODEL

The properties of the proposed generalized requesting model can be summarized as follows:

- Easy and clear abstract numeric based attributes to describe the requesting behavior of the clients. The quantification process of the requesting model can be generalized and different requesting specifications can be aggregated in the same computation style.
- Heterogeneity of specifications: Each requesting behaviors of the interested clients can be modeled individually. The resultant (maximum) Gross Interest is computable. Then, at a provider side, the number of requests that are really gained at any provider can reflect the relative popularity of the offered service. Moreover, the specifications are time varying which adds a dimension for the variant vitality (importance degree) of a service from a client perspective over the operation time of the network.
- The derivations introduced in Subsection 2.2 show that, as the number of the network participants increases, higher number of clients are active. In some environments like Web services in the Internet, the space of the network size is huge. Therefore, it is more suitable, in these cases, to tune down the weight of the network size, if any proposed computation method for a web service popularity in terms of Gross Interest.

GROSS INTEREST SCENARIOS AND QUANTIFICATIONS

If service providers care about the popularity of their offered services, they have to think firstly about estimating their offers' popularity. In this section, we give two extremely different sets of specifications for the proposed generalized requesting model. Based on the proposed computation method of the Gross Interest in Subsection 2.2, the expected number of active clients is computed as an indication for the service popularity. We care about the simplicity of the specifications in both of the proposed scenarios. Therefore, as derived in Subsection 2.2, the specifications are assumed to be fixed for all the service clients during the network operation time. Both scenarios represent pilot applications for the previously presented concepts of the service popularity, Gross Interest, and the generalized requesting model.

In order to quantify the Gross Interest in both scenarios, both the network size and the requesting rate should be specified. The network size may indicate the real number of the network participants or the expected size of the network participants who are targeted by a specified service. The network size varies from small numbers like in mobile ad hoc networks to very large numbers like in the Internet. As previously introduced, the weight of the network size need to be tuned in some cases. On the other hand, a suitable statistical distribution for the request rate should be specified. In our investigations, in order to have an estimation, we set the network size to be 25 participants and the requesting rate to be uniformly distributed between 0 and 3 requests per minute.

Scenario 1: Rich Gross Interest

In this Gross Interest scenario, a high number of frequent requests regarding a specific service is modeled as follows:

- U is 10 minutes.
- N is uniformly distributed between 1 and 5 units.
- U_d is 3 minutes.
- M is uniformly distributed between 0 and 4 units

Therefore, the expected number of E_x is about 5.2 clients a time, which is really high number compared to the network size.

Scenario 2: Poor Gross Interest

On the opposite of Scenario 1, this scenario models a low number of infrequent requests regarding a specific service as follows:

- U is 2 minutes.
- N is uniformly distributed between 1 and 3 units.
- U_d is 10 minutes.
- M is uniformly distributed between 0 and 4 units

Therefore, the expected number of E_x is about 1.0 clients a time, which is low number compared to the network size.

Comparing Scenarios: The specifications lead to long active periods in the first scenario versus short active periods in the second scenario and the short pause periods in the first scenario versus long pause periods in the second scenario. The two Gross Interest scenarios produce two extreme (high and low) number of clients expected to be active a time. Relatively, the resultant expected number of clients for both scenarios indicates a higher service popularity in the first scenario. If a normalization between the two expected values can be realized, then the first scenario of settings describes a very popular service while the second scenario describes a service with less interest by the client set.

The Role of the Requesting Rate: Gross Interest Ranges

One of the most important features of the proposed generalized requesting model it the requesting rate. Specifying the requesting rate can provide a service popularity categorization. By varying

Figure 1. Service requesting cycles from a client perspective

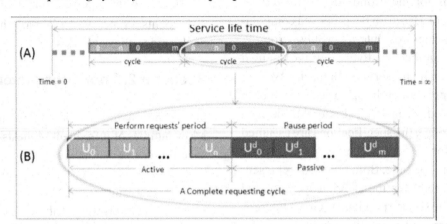

Figure 2. One complete requesting cycle

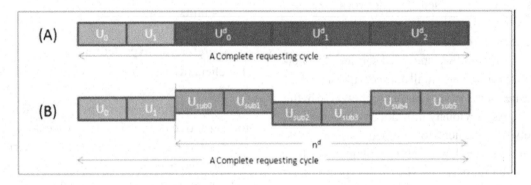

the requesting rate, different service popularities can be modeled. The clients of a specified service can be categorized into groups (client groups) based on the different specified requesting rate for the same Gross Interest scenario. Figure 1 illustrates this categorization in terms of client group. If the requesting rate varies between 0 and 1 requests per minute, this means that, at any time of the network operational time, there are two groups of more or less interested clients. The first group of client has clients with 0 requests per minute and the second group has clients with 1 requests per minute. In this category and based on the previous derivations in Subsection 2.2, E_x will be about 10.4 clients in the rich scenario and about 2.08 clients in the poor scenario. If the requesting rate varies between 0 and 3 requests

per minute, there are four groups of clients. The first group of client has clients with 0 requests per a minute, the second group has clients with 1 requests per minute, the third group has clients with 2 requests per minute, and the third group has clients with 3 requests per minute. In this category, the number of E_x will be about 5.2 clients in the rich scenario and about 1.04 clients in the poor scenario.

So, as depicted in Figure 1 and based on any proposed relative normalization for applying these client groups and in which scenario, we obtain here five different service popularities. On the highest top of the proposed popularity ranking arrow, the "always important" services. This category contains those services which are vital for the network participants during the entire

Figure 3. Service popularity ranges: Combination of requesting scenarios and different requesting rates

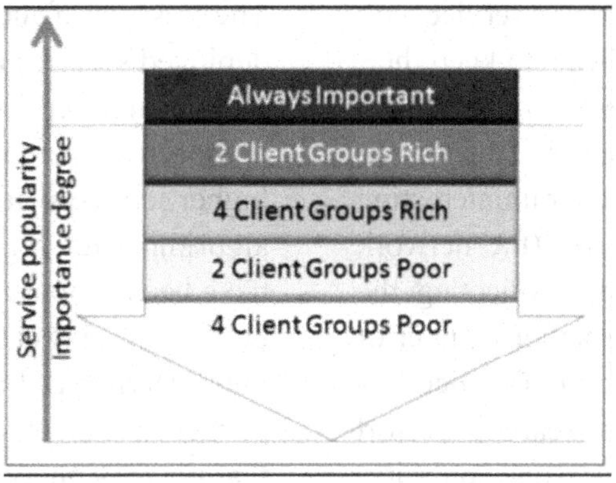

operation time of the network. Therefore, estimating the popularity for this category is not meaningful. Based on the computed Gross Interest, the order of the popularity of the rest of four categories are the "2 Client Groups Rich", "4 Client Groups Rich", "2 Client Groups Poor", then "4 Client Groups Poor".

The previous categorization can be done based on any other sets of specifications for the generalized requesting model. This categorization represents a practical try for ranking the popularity of services. By using such a categorization, a different requesting behavior have been modeled regarding a specified service or a set of services with same functionalities.

ENHANCING THE SERVICE CONTENTS

Service Content: What is meant by the "service content" is the collection of services (and their replicas if applicable and as required) to provide the required functionalities (in the interest scope of the network participants) of a specified network at a specified time. All the network participants can be service provider (depending on the type of services and their available resources). Each of these proposed service providers can provide arbitrary services. The important question about

the network performance is answered in terms of how the network participants access these services (in terms of some metrics like amount of transported data). The service popularity can play a great role here. The main concerns about what is important to be offered can be explained in terms of modeling the client requesting behavior and popularity. Involving the service popularity in the process of enhancing the service content is important.

In this section, the advantages which can be gained by applying any scheme (like the Gross Interest scheme) to grade and rank the service popularity are discussed. These advantages can be explained from different perspectives: (a) From a client perspective, based on semantics, the popular services' popularity can reflect a positive or negative effects on the service trust. Moreover, popular services are more likely to provide consistent results regarding the client requests, since they have been mostly and correctly called from a higher number of the society members. (b) From a service provider's perspective, by computing the Gross Interest of the proposed generalized requesting model, a service provider obtains an estimate of how often his service is called relative to the total Gross Interest.. As mentioned before, it can be used as a measurement to indicate how it is necessary to deploy a new version of a specified offered service. (c) From a network perspective, utilizing the network resources for the offered services can be saved. For example a service with longer process enforces the clients to keep their connected sessions to this service longer and then their resources are occupied longer. If the service providers are switching down their uninteresting services, the service repositories (the network parties who are responsible for collecting the service offers) will contain a smaller number of services' offers. Finding the required services offers in this case will require less searching effort and time. If such an election (based on popularity) is dynamically done, the network will be enabled to preserve the required service contents.

APPLICATION: THE SERVICE DISTRIBUTION PROTOCOL FOR MANETs (SDP)

Mobile Ad Hoc Networks (MANETs) represent the only feasible solution for communications in many applications and situations. Usage of ad hoc environments is varying from mobile networks in small offices to the most complex situations like in rescue and disaster recovery operations. The mobile nodes (network participants) are wireless equipped. Each can cover a certain transmission range. If two nodes are located close enough to each others, a wireless link between them might be formed. The mobile nodes operate without any centralized help or administration. The topology of a MANET is ever-changing, since all participants are allowed to move, join, and disjoin the network freely. In this network type, not only sharing of data is an important issue but also sharing of functionalities. Service orientation offers basis for ad hoc networks to achieve the required sharing of functionality. The challenges of applying SOA in MANETs have been introduced in (Hamdy & König-Ries, 2006). Many approaches have realized SOA in MANETs (Dia; Kozat and Tassiulas, 2003, Jorstad et al., 2005). MANETs are characterized by high dynamics in particular with

respect to the formation of network partitions. The presence of unconnected partitions makes the deployed services inaccessible to some network participants. Service replication is employed as an approach to overcome this problem and to ensure higher service availability. Several protocols and algorithms for service replication in MANETs have been proposed (Hauspie et al., 2001, Wang & Li, 2002, Jing et al., 2004, Dustdar & Juszczyk, 2007, Derhab & Badache, 2008). In general, all of these protocols and algorithms share a main feature: they query the lower network layer, e.g., the routing components, to obtain information. Besides being expensive and time consuming, these querying processes make the proposed protocols and algorithms architecture-dependent. The obtained information from the lower network layers are used in predicting the network partitioning behavior. Proactively, they try to push a service replica (copy of the service) in the ongoing to be formed new network partitions, once the partitioning behavior is detected. These protocols deal only with the ``always important" category services (see Figure 1). The services are required to be replicated whenever the network partitioning behavior is detected. The replication process is supposed to be done for all the service content. These protocols can not distinguish between the rarely used services and the popular ones. They replicate the services and pay the whole replication effort for each running service even if, it will be requested or not in the new forming partition.

Based on estimating the service popularity and modeling the client behavior regarding a specified service, the Service Distribution Protocol (SDP) (Hamdy & König-Ries, 2008b, Hamdy & König-Ries, 2009a, Hamdy & König-Ries, 2009b) provides an alternative for service replication in MANETs. It has been proposed to overcome this disadvantage of the other protocols. Its main contribution is to base the replication decision only on information of the service popularity.

This SDP feature enables it to be architecture independent. Unlike the other approaches, SDP needs no network status analysis or partition predication techniques. A replica is hosted by clients once they show enough interest (in terms of requesting behavior). The presence of a service-requesting behavior regarding a specific service is assumed. The assumed requesting behavior is modeled as in the proposed requesting model in Section 2.1.

Based on the importance degree of a specific service (popularity), which is time varying, SDP's replication decision is evaluated collaboratively among the service provider and its clients. The more interesting services are replicated more and kept active running. The client who achieves a number of requests during a certain time interval represents a candidate place for new replica allocation. Using the mobility of the mobile nodes, the interesting services prevail the network. The replication effort is oriented only for the interesting services of the whole service content. The service which looses its interests in terms of minimum number of gained requests are required to be hibernated (shutdown).

SDP provides two server election modes (Hamdy & König-Ries, 2009c), short and long election mode, to be used during the leader election processes, i.e., to determine whether and where to host or hibernate a replica based only on the number of gained requests (popularity). Mobile clients should find the best replica, in case of multiple concurrent running replicas, to direct their requests for. SDP assumes by using a suitable caching scheme the network prevalence in the network can be a popularity-based manageable.

Moreover, SDP can measure the resultant service distributions (distribution of the replicas over the different distinct network partitions) relatively to the assumed optimum service distribution situations based on replica allocation currentness ratios, which are computation methods that highlight the correctness of the service-replica prevalence process.

Requirements' Index: In SDP applications, the requirements' index have been introduced as a ser-

vice or replica attribute in (Hamdy & König-Ries, 2009b). It presents the possibility to create new meanings for the service popularity by combining it with other functional and non-functional service attributes. The objective behind this attribute is to combine the service popularity to the volume of requirements (resources perquisite) required to enable a client to host a replica of a specified service. Moreover, not only the functional requirement or resources are assumed to be combined to the service popularity by the requirements' index but also some non-functional attributes can be combined like fees for the forwarded replica or some operational constraints like the number of connected sessions (Hamdy & König-Ries, 2010).

CONCLUSION

In this chapter, the importance of the service popularity as a service non-functional attribute of services and its related issues have been addressed and discussed. The Gross Interest has been introduced as a proposed measurement for the service popularity. As previously mentioned, since the Gross Interest is based on a set of client's requesting behaviors regarding a specified service, a generalized requesting model that can capture a client requesting behavior has been introduced. Two sets of specifications (scenarios) for the proposed generalized requesting model have been described. A quantification method of the Gross Interest for these two groups of specifications showed how these scenarios are quite different from a service popularity perspective. More investigations have been given to highlight the role of the requesting rate of the proposed generalized requesting behavior. Finally, advantages of a case of applying a service popularity scheme in the context of service replication have been demonstrated.

REFERENCES

Derhab, A., & Badache, N. (2008). Self-stabilizing algorithm for high service availability in spite of concurrent topology changes in ad hoc mobile networks. *Journal of Parallel and Distributed Computing, 68*(6), 752–768. doi:10.1016/j.jpdc.2008.01.005

Diane. (n.d.). *Services in ad hoc networks* (research project). Retrieved from http://fusion.cs.uni-jena.de/diane/

Dustdar, S., & Juszczyk, L. (2007). Dynamic replication and synchronization of web services for high availability in mobile ad-hoc networks. *Service Oriented Computing and Applications, 1*, 19–33. doi:10.1007/s11761-007-0006-z

Hamdy, M., & König-Ries, B. (2006). Service-orientation in mobile computing - An overview. In *Proceedings of the Tools and Applications for Mobile Contents Workshop (TAMC2006) in Conjunction with the 7th International Conference on Mobile Data Management (MDM06)*, (p. 138). Nara, Japan. IEEE Computer Society.

Hamdy, M., & König-Ries, B. (2008a). *An extended analysis of an interestbased service distribution protocol for mobile ad hoc networks*. In the International Conference on Wireless Information Networks and Systems (WINSYS 2008), Porto, Portugal.

Hamdy, M., & König-Ries, B. (2008b). A service distribution protocol for mobile ad hoc networks. In the *Proceedings of the International Conference on Pervasive Services* (ICPS08), Sorrento, Italy.

Hamdy, M., & König-Ries, B. (2009a). Communications in computer and Information Science. In *ICETE 2008, CCIS 48: The service distribution protocol for MANETs- Criteria and performance analysis* (pp. 467–479). Berlin, Germany: Springer.

Hamdy, M., & König-Ries, B. (2009b). *Effects of different hibernation behaviors on the service distribution protocol for mobile networks and its replica placement process*. In International Workshop on the Role of Services, Ontologies, and Context in Mobile Environments (RoSOCM '09) in conjunction with the 10th International Conference on Mobile Data Management (MDM09), Taipei, Taiwan.

Hamdy, M., & König-Ries, B. (2009c). *Leader election modes of the service distribution protocol for mobile ad hoc networks*. In the fourth German Community Conference on Mobility and Mobile Information Systems (4. Konferenz Mobilitat und mobile Informationssysteme) (MMS 2009), Mueunster, Germany.

Hamdy, M., & König-Ries, B. (2010). *An interest-based load balancing mechanism for the service distribution protocol in Manets*. In the 8th International Conference on Advances in Mobile Computing and Multimedia (MoMM2010), Paris, France.

Hamdy, M., König-Ries, B., & Küster, U. (2007). Non-functional parameters as first class citizens in service description and matchmaking - An integrated approach. In *the International Conference on Service-Oriented Computing (ICSOC 2007) Workshops: The first International Workshop on Non Functional Properties and Service Level Agreements in Service Oriented Computing (NFPSLASOC2007), Revised Selected Papers*, (pp. 93-104). Berlin, Germany: Springer-Verlag.

Hauspie, M., Simplot, D., & Carle, J. (2001). *Replication decision algorithm based on link evaluation for services in Manet. Technical report*. France: University of Lille.

Jing, Z., Jinshu, S., Kan, Y., & Yijie, W. (2004). *Stable neighbor based adaptive replica allocation in mobile ad hoc networks. ICCS 2004, Lecture Notes in Computer Science* (pp. 373–380). Berlin, Germany: Springer.

Jorstad, I., Dustdar, S., & Thanh, D. V. (2005). Service-oriented architectures and mobile services. In the *3rd International Workshop on Ubiquitous Mobile Information and Collaboration Systems (UMICS), co-located with (CAiSE 05)*, (pp. 617-631). Porto, Portugal.

Kozat, U. C., & Tassiulas, L. (2003). *Network layer support for service discovery in mobile ad hoc networks*. In INFOCOM.

Toma, I., Roman, D., Fensel, D., Sapkota, B., & Gomez, J. M. (2007). A multi-criteria service ranking approach based on non-functional properties rules evaluation. In *Proceedings of the 5th International Conference on Service-Oriented Computing* (ICSOC 07), (pp. 435-441). Berlin, Germany: Springer.

Wang, K., & Li, B. (2002). Efficient and guaranteed service coverage in partitionable mobile ad-hoc networks. In *Proceedings of the IEEE Computer and Communications Societies Twenty-First Annual Joint Conference* (INFOCOM 2002), New York, USA.

KEY TERMS AND DEFINITIONS

Generalized Requesting Model: A model of clear and numeric based attributes to describe the requesting behavior of the clients.

Gross Interest: The aggregated interest towards a specified service within a certain time.

Requirements' Index: Presents the possibility to create new meanings for the service popularity by combining it with other functional and non-functional service attributes.

Service Content: The collection of services (and their replicas if applicable and as required) to provide the required functionalities (in the interest scope of the network participants) of a specified network at a specified time.

Service Popularity: An important non-functional property determining the life-cycle of a service carachterising how often a service is requested.

Chapter 15
Considering Quality of a Service in an Intentional Approach

Assia Ait-Ali-Slimane
Université Paris1 Panthéon Sorbonne, France

Manuele Kirsch-Pinheiro
Université Paris1 Panthéon Sorbonne, France

Carine Souveyet
Université Paris1 Panthéon Sorbonne, France

ABSTRACT

The success of service-based applications is based on service technologies such as Web services. Nevertheless, the benefits of the Service-Oriented Architecture (SOA) remain mainly at the software level, since business people are often unable to fully exploit its benefits due to their unfamiliarity with such software level technology. The intentional Service-Oriented Architecture (iSOA) suggests a move from the function-driven SOA to intention-driven SOA in order to provide service description understandable by business practitioners. However, such transposition from business to implementation level should also consider Quality of Service (QoS) aspects. In this paper, we propose modeling the Quality of intentional Service (QoiS) by introducing the quality goals and their qualitative and quantitative evaluation. We also propose populating the intentional service registry of the iSOA architecture with the QoiS description.

CONSIDERING QUALITY OF A SERVICE IN AN INTENTIONAL APPROACH

Service-Oriented Computing (SOC) is the computing paradigm that utilizes services as fundamental elements for developing software applications (Papazoglou et al., 2008). SOC relies on the

Service-Oriented Architecture (SOA) (Alonso et al., 2004) that is a way of reorganizing a portfolio of legacy applications into services that are self-describing computational elements, which are platform independent, accessible through standard interfaces and can be assembled in complex compositions based on standard messaging protocols. Service based applications are considered as support for Business-to-Consumer (B2C) interactions and Business-to-Business (B2B) collaborations.

DOI: 10.4018/978-1-61350-432-1.ch015

Services, usually referred as e-services, provide well-defined functionalities that allow users and applications to meet their functional requirements (Casati & Shan, 2001).

SOC is a way of designing a software system that is *function-driven* and it remains at the software level. Consequently, although business people are completely familiar with the notion of service, they are totally unable to fully exploit its benefits, since they are not familiar to such software level technology. SOC technology, such as WSDL (W3C, 2007) and OWL-S (W3C, 2004) is understandable by software professionals, but far to be easily comprehensible by business practitioners. Business practitioners use to reason in terms of business goals.

The *intentional Service-Oriented Architecture approach* (iSOA) (Rolland et al., 2009) suggests a progress from the function-driven SOC to intention-driven SOC in order to provide a service description understandable by business practitioners. The function-driven SOC focuses on a functional view of services, whereas the intention-driven SOC spells out the purpose, the intention behind a service. The main goal of iSOA is to fill the gap between high level business services, referred to *intentional service*, and low level software services. The iSOA approach proposes a higher abstraction level that allows business practitioners to publish, search and compose, in terms of goals and strategies, services that can be executed in the SOA level.

On both level (SOA and iSOA), the service selection remains an important challenge, especially, when a set of services fulfills the same functionality. Among these services, one will be eventually invoked by user, generally depending on a combined QoS evaluation. The QoS can be defined as a set of non functional properties related to software service such as performance, security, accuracy and fault tolerance mechanisms (O'Sullivan et al., 2002; W3C, 2003). On the business level, Fedosseev (2003/2004) describes QoS of business process as a set of qualitative and quantitative characteristics needed to meet the initial requirements of this process. On both levels, QoS stands for non-functional properties that the service provider can ensure and that are (or can be) demanded by the service user.

The QoS plays then an important role in the software service for different reasons (O'Sullivan et al., 2002; Aiello & Giorgini, 2004): (1) a service provider may offer the same functionality with differentiated QoS (for example different prices) and must therefore publish the different qualities for this same functionality; (2) a service requester may decide for a particular service based on its QoS properties; and (3) a service may depend on other services and it needs to be aware of the QoS of the collaborating services. Therefore, QoS becomes a main concern for providers and customers of a service.

Several works in the literature (Zeng et al., 2003; Herssens et al., 2008; Aiello & Giorgini, 2004; Penserini & Mylopoulos, 2005; Ma et al., 2009) propose QoS models. Certain authors (Zeng et al., 2003; Herssens et al., 2008) consider the QoS as a collection of metrics related to non functional properties of services. Zeng et al. (2003) proposes a QoS model to describe concepts of QoS such as execution price and execution duration, whereas Herssens et al. (2008) recommend using the Unified Modeling Language (UML) to enable QoS modeling. Requirement engineering community (Aiello & Giorgini, 2004; Penserini & Mylopoulos, 2005; Ma et al., 2009) propose to reason about non functional requirements, based on the qualitative framework (Mylopoulos et al., 1992), by considering the QoS as soft goal that a service can satisfied.

The expression of the QoS through the different metrics, as defined by (Zeng et al., 2003; Herssens et al., 2008), focuses on the implementation mechanisms of QoS, their computation and their monitoring. Other works such as (Aiello & Giorgini, 2004; Penserini & Mylopoulos, 2005; Ma et al., 2009) focus on the business process. However, an important gap remains between these approaches: business consideration on QoS remains often disconnected from their implementation counterpart.

We advocate that metrics used on the software level should be raised up the intentional level, in order to be understandable for business practitioners. In our point of view, QoS handling on iSOA should respect and follow an intention driven approach that makes QoS of software service more accessible to business practitioners (Ait-Ali-Slimane & Souveyet, april, 2008).

In this chapter, we propose to extend the original iSOA proposal (Kaabi et al., 2004; Rolland et al., 2009) to deal with the quality dimension. We propose: (1) a model to describe the *Quality of intentional Service* (QoiS), named ISM-q (Intentional Service Model extended to quality dimension*)* that considers QoiS as the set of the quality goals that an intentional service contribute satisficing; (2) a method for evaluating the QoiS associated with an atomic and aggregate service; (3) a XML description of ISM-q that allows publishing intentional service QoiS into the intentional service registry; and (4) the use of XQuery language to retrieve the services that meet users' requirements as considering QoiS. Our approach considers two main characteristics. First, we consider that the intentional service achieves a goal and can satisfices several quality goals (based on (Aiello & Giorgini, 2004; Penserini & Mylopoulos, 2005)). Second, we consider that the intentional service QoiS can be the high level abstraction of the software service QoS.

The chapter is organized as follows. Section 2 presents the related work. In Section 3, an overview of the ISM model is presented. In Section 4, we describe the ISM-q and the associated evaluation methods. The Section 5 illustrates the XML description of ISM-q that is published in the registry. Section 6 considers a query language for retrieving an intentional service considering its QoiS. Finally, Section 7 outlines conclusion and future works.

BACKGROUND

Maximilien and Singh (2004) identify selection of services as the step that enable differentiating the services whose provide similar functionality, by considering their QoS, such as performance, security and accuracy (Mani & Nagarajian, 2002; O'Sullivan et al., 2002; W3C, 2003).

The selection process supports several QoS models (Zeng et al., 2003; Herssens et al., 2008; Maximilien & Singh, 2004; Dobson et al., 2005; Toma et al., 2006; Ma et al., 2009) that enable providers and users to share the same concepts in the perspective of facilitating selection algorithm execution. Certain authors (Zeng et al., 2003; Herssens et al., 2008) consider the QoS as a collection of metrics related to non functional properties of services. Zeng et al. (2003) propose a QoS model to describe concepts of QoS such as execution price and execution duration, whereas Herssens et al. (2008) recommend using the Unified Modeling Language (UML) to enable QoS modeling. Another authors (Maximilien & Singh, 2004; Dobson et al., 2005; Toma et al., 2006) propose an ontology to describe the quality concepts. Practically, Toma et al. (2006) proposes extending the Web Service Modeling Ontology (WSMO) with QoS support by modeling QoS as quality attributes.

Requirement engineering community (Aiello & Giorgini, 2004; Penserini & Mylopoulos, 2005; Ma et al., 2009) propose to reason about non functional requirements, based on the qualitative framework (Mylopoulos et al., 1992), by considering the QoS as soft goal that a service can satisficed. Soft goals cannot be satisfied in a clear cut manner by opposition to hard goals for which this is possible. Soft goals are said satisficed within acceptable limits, related to a satisficing degree, by opposition to hard goals which can be said satisfied. Satisficing degree can be "very satisficed", "satisficed", "neutral", "not Satisficed" and "not at all satisficed", noted respectively by the symbols "++", "+", "?", "-", and "--".

The expression of the QoS through the different metrics and attributes, as defined by Zeng et al., 2003; Herssens et al., 2008; Maximilien & Singh, 2004; Dobson et al., 2005; Toma et al., 2006) focuses on the implementation level of QoS. It describes what a software service can provide as quality. However, it does not specify how the latter can meet the users' non functional requirements. Instead, works such as (Aiello & Giorgini, 2004; Penserini & Mylopoulos, 2005; Ma et al., 2009) focus on business process and non functional requirements of users. Nevertheless, they do not consider the software service QoS.

Moreover, the evaluation of QoS must be global in order to evaluate the QoS of composite services. Zeng et al. (2003) propose a global approach by introducing a set of aggregation function for the computation of the QoS of a composite service. Aiello and Giorgini (2004) recommend axioms that make the propagation of full and partial satisficing, whereas (Maximilien & Singh, 2004; Penserini & Mylopoulos, 2005; Toma et al., 2006; Herssens et al., 2008) do not consider the case of a global QoS.

The *intentional Service-Oriented Architecture* approach (iSOA) (Rolland et al., 2009) provides a service description understandable by users. The *Intentional Service Model* (ISM) enables describing services for service publishing, retrieval and composition in a goal driver manner. The intentional service focuses on the goal it allows to achieve rather than on the functionality it performs. Besides, atomic intentional services are operationalized by software services enabling fill the gap between the users' functional requirements and the software service.

Currently, ISM does not consider how to represent QoS eventually associated with an intentional service, neither with the corresponding operational service. We propose to extend the ISM to deal with the quality dimension in order to profit of the benefit of the iSOA approach while considering QoS issues, as defined in (Ait-Ali-Slimane & Souveyet, April, 2008).

INTENTIONAL SERVICES: THE ISM MODEL

In (Kaabi et al., 2004; Rolland et al., 2009) the authors introduce the concept of *intentional service*. An intentional service is defined as a service captured at the business level, in business comprehensible terms and described in a goal perspective. The intentional service focuses on the goal it allows to achieve rather than on the functionality it performs. Intentional services fill the gaps between the user functional requirements and the software services.

The intentional service model (ISM) is traditionally composed of three parts (Kaabi et al., 2004; Rolland et al., 2009), namely the *service interface*, the *service behavior* and the *service composition*, whose elements are represented in Figure 1.

The service interface describes the visible parts of a service that permits the fulfillment of a *goal*, given *an initial situation* and terminating in a *final situation*. Thus, *Make Room Booking* is a goal to make a reservation for rooms in a hotel. The achievement of this goal leaves the system in the state *Booking made*. If *Accept Payment* is the goal of a service, then the initial situation refers to the *booking* and *customer* classes, whereas the final situation comprises also the *payment* class. Similarly to SOA, in which service users search services based on their functional interface, iSOA approach considers that business agents find an intentional service by the goal it allows to fulfill. The goal related to an intentional service plays then the central role in the service retrieval, since the user (the business agent) will look for a service based on the goal it fulfills, a goal that should match his functional needs. In order to underline this point, we note an intentional service using its goal. For instance, the intentional service allowing to *Make Room Booking* is noted $S_{Make\ Room\ Booking}$.

The service behavior is specified through its *pre* and *post conditions* that are the initial and

Figure 1. Elements composing the intentional service model (ISM)

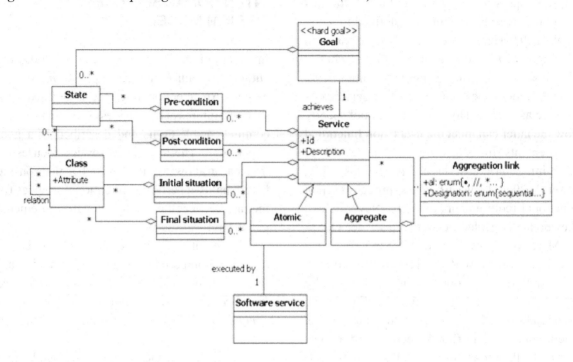

final sets of states characterizing the initial and the final situation, respectively. For instance, in the *Accept Payment* service example, <*booking. state='OK'∧customer.status='registered'*> and <*booking.state='paid'∧payment.status = 'done'* > are the pre and post-conditions, respectively.

Similarly to software services, intentional services can be composed. The service composition part on the ISM model indicates this possibility through two different kinds of services, namely the *aggregate* service and the *atomic* one. The former is composed of other services whereas the latter is not. *Atomic services* have goals that are *operationalized by software service* (see Figure 1). In contrast *aggregate services* have high-level goals that need to be decomposed in lower level services till atomic intentional services are found. Aggregation of services can involve *variants, i.e.* services which are alternative to the others or composites (see (Rolland et al., 2009) for more detail).

In the *iSOA* approach, services are defined in a goal-driven manner focusing on the '*whys*' of the functionality provided by the underlying software service. In other words, these compositions are represented by a set of aggregation links (•, //,⊗, v,* and ∪) (see Figure 1) indicating order or variability on service composition. Composition itself is goal-driven which are grounded in *XOR* (related to ⊗, and ∪), *OR* (related to v), *AND* (related to •, // and *) relationships among intentional services. However, the intentional service proposed by (Kaabi et al., 2004; Rolland et al., 2009) deals with the functional aspects of the service that are related to user functional requirements. Therefore, the notion of quality of service is not considered by the intentional service. We introduce in (Ait-Ali-Slimane et al., 2009) the notion of *quality goals* which enables capturing the user non functional requirements. This notion is used here in order to introduce a *quality dimension* on iSOA approach.

PROPOSAL OVERVIEW

We extend ISM model by considering that an intentional service should also be described by a quality dimension. This quality dimension is introduced in the ISM-q model through the QoiS (Quality of intentional Service) element, which introduces the quality properties of the intentional service. We consider that quality aspects can be captured by quality goals (Ait-Ali-Slimane et al., 2009).

The adoption of quality goals is not new. Other authors (Yu et al., 1995; Mylopoulos et al., 1992) have considered this notion. Mylopoulos et al. (1992) propose to handle quality goals as soft goals in a qualitative framework. The qualitative framework (Mylopoulos et al., 1992) is a goal-oriented approach for addressing non functional requirements such as security, performance and accuracy. We adopt the concepts of the qualitative framework, including the decomposition process, the contribution links and the evaluation process, in order to represent the non functional requirements and the QoiS as quality goals.

In order to make sure that quality goals are used uniformly by service providers and business users, we propose to combine quality goals in a quality referential. Although quality referential is out of the scope of this particular paper, we would like to underline the significance of building a quality referential in order to enable improving the quality consensus between users and service providers, corresponding to a specific domain.

The quality goals satisfaction is based on the concept of satisficing (Simon, 1981), which means a quality goal can be satisficed within acceptable limits (see (Mylopoulos et al., 1992; Chung et al., 2000) for more detail). The satisficing values can be qualitative one (Chung et al., 2000) or a quantitative one (Keller et al., 1990; Chung & Subramanian, 2001). The quality referential adopts a dual evaluation comprising a qualitative one and a quantitative one. The qualitative evaluation corresponds to the satisficing degree. The expres-

sions "*very satisficed*", "*satisficed*", "*neutral*", "*not Satisficed*" and "*not at all satisficed*", noted respectively by the symbols "++", "+","?", "-", and "--" correspond to the satificing degrees of the quality goal. We selected these notations for their understandability and readability for business users. However, as this satisficing scale is subjective we complement this evaluation by introducing the concept of *metric*. Each quality goal can be evaluated by one or more metrics which facilitate the quantification of the quality goal satisficing. Each metric has a set of *reference values* (corresponding to the quality of software services) that are associated with the qualitative scale (represented by satisficing degree). For instance, a quality goal *Confidentiality* can be associated with different metrics, such as *Fraud Rate* and *Security Level*. The *Fraud Rate* metric can be associated with a qualitative scale in which the satisficing degree "++" is obtained when the *Fraud Rate is lower than 0,02%*, whereas the satisficing degree "-" is obtained when the *Fraud Rate is greater than 1%*. The use of such metrics allows service providers to connect high level satisficing degree with corresponding operational measures performed by software services.

The quality referential is used by both sides: service providers and users. The former to describe the quality of theirs services, and the latter to express their non functional requirements.

Besides, intentional services can be atomic or aggregate. Aggregate services represent composition and variability on service definition. Thus, the quality (QoiS) of an atomic service is said *simple* and the quality of an aggregate service is said *global*: the simple QoiS reflects the contribution of an atomic service to the quality goals associated with it. It is calculated as a set of quality goals (q_j) that a service contributes satisficing and the related satisficing degree (d_j). The global QoiS results of a compilation of QoiS related to the constituent services of an aggregate service.

Hence, it is important to calculate the quality of the intentional service as a whole. The global

QoiS is based on the different kind of aggregation links binding aggregate and components services. In order to make use of the QoiS of an aggregate service in the selection algorithms, we propose calculating the $QoiS_{min\_max}$ corresponding to the set of quality goals (q_j) that an aggregate service contributes satisficing and the related satisficing degree (d_j). The calculation of $QoiS_{min\_max}$ depends on the aggregation link forming the global QoiS, namely composite quality or variant quality.

Every intentional service must be available in the intentional service registry. This enables retrieval of atomic and aggregate services and their adaptation to users' needs. Retrieval is based on goal matching that is, given a goal G, the registry searches a service that can satisfy this goal. In order to publish intentional service on an intentional registry, we adopt XML view of ISM-q. Such view represents all service dimensions: interface, behavior, composition and QoiS. Besides, we consider in this paper the possibility of using XQuery expressions in order to query registry, taking advantage of the quality description

of these services. Traditionally, iSOA approach considers that business users submit their requests through a user interface. In order to consider QoiS issues, such user interface should allow business users to express their preferences considering quality goals. In such preferences, business users can indicate what quality goals they expect from intentional services and the corresponding satisficing degree they consider as minimal. We call this user's quality context.

DEFINING THE QUALITY OF INTENTIONAL SERVICES (QoiS)

We define the quality of an intentional service (QoiS) as a set of quality goals that a service contributes satisficing and the associated satisficing degree. In this section, we present the ISM extended to QoiS (ISM-q) which models the QoiS aspects of different kinds of intentional services. We also present the evaluation and the calculation methods of these.

Figure 2. Intentional service model extended to QoiS (ISM-q)

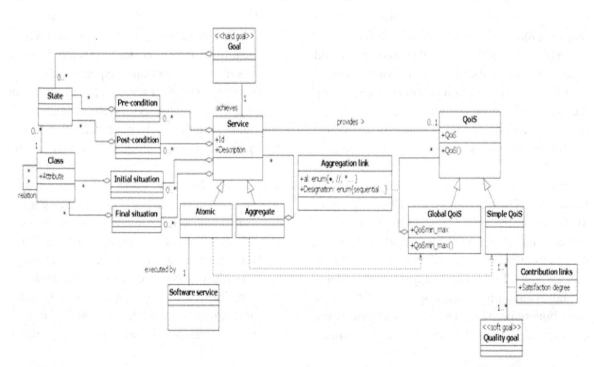

QoiS Description

In addition to service interface, service behaviour and service composition (see Figure 1), we consider that an intentional service should also be described by a quality dimension. The QoiS element shown in Figure 2 introduces this dimension, with the quality properties of the intentional service. This quality dimension introduces the quality goals and their qualitative evaluation on ISM-q (Ait-Ali-Slimane et al., 2009). We consider the *goal* (the goal element shown in Figure 2) associated with the service as a *functional hard goal*, and the *quality goal* (the quality goal element shown in Figure 2) as a *non functional soft goal*, capturing non-functional requirements that the service can contribute satisficing (Ait-Ali-Slimane & Souveyet, may, 2008). The goal satisfaction can be established through verification technique, whereas the quality goal satisfaction is subjective and cannot be established in clear cut manner (Mylopoulos et al., 1992; Jureta et al., 2006).

We propose using two models-oriented goal for identifying intentional services and their QoiS: a Map model (Rolland & Prakash, 2000) and a quality goal model. The Figure 3 presents an overview of both models.

The Map model (Rolland & Prakash, 2000) is used for modeling functional requirements as a map of goals (a hard goal). A map is a labeled directed graph with goals as nodes and strategies as edges. The map is capable of representing many strategies that can be used for achieving a goal. This map is used as an architectural style for determining business services and their composition (Rolland et al., 2009), by defining an intentional service as a section of the map (Kaabi et al., 2004). A Section is a triplet <*Source goal, Target goal, Strategy*> that represents a way to achieve the target goal from the source goal following the strategy.

The quality goal model represents criteria that services should meet. We propose that all service providers consult the quality referential to deter-

Figure 3. Map model, quality goal model and contribution links

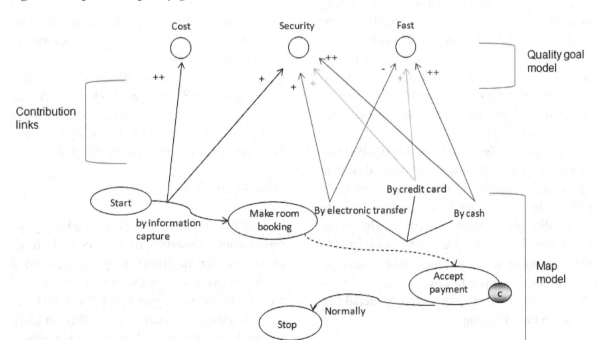

mine quality goals that theirs services can satisfice, enabling truthful descriptions in terms of QoiS.

Thus, the satisficing of those quality goals (soft goals) is encoded in the map. Their satisficing reflect the partial contribution of a service (map) towards (or against) a particular quality goal (Ait-Ali-Slimane & Souveyet, may, 2008). *Contributions links* are used to represent the links among the Map and the quality goal models, as showed by the "Contributions link" element in the Figure 2. The semantic of these links are based on the satisficing degree attribute in the Figure 2.

For example, Figure 3 describes the variant intentional service $S_{Accept\ payment}$. The identification of intentional services from the map model is detailed in (Kaabi et al., 2004). This service is composed of $S_{Accept\ payment\ by\ transfer}$, $S_{Accept\ payment\ by\ credit\ card}$ and $S_{Accept\ payment\ by\ cash}$. Among these variant services, the $S_{Accept\ payment\ by\ transfer}$ service contributes to make satisficing (+) a *Security* quality goal and contributes to not satisficing (-) a *Fast* quality goal.

The expression of a quality goal satisficing allows the service provider to indicate the quality level that their services can guarantee. Such degrees can then be matched with users' quality context. The integration of the quality dimension in the intentional service description aims at a user-centered selection of services. Although service selection is out of the scope of this paper, we define the intentional selection of services as the step that allows selecting services that satisfice user' quality context.

As shown in Figure 2, the quality (QoiS) of an atomic service is said *simple* and the quality of an aggregate service is said *global*: the simple QoiS reflects the contribution of the atomic service to the quality goals associated with it. The global QoiS results of a compilation of QoiS related to the constituent services of an aggregate service. Hence, it is important to calculate the quality of the intentional service as a whole. We detail this aspect in the following.

QoiS Evaluation

The QoiS of an intentional service is defined as a set of quality goals that a service contributes satisficing and the associated satisficing degree. As mentioned in the Figure 2, the service may define several QoiS. The QoiS can be a *simple QoiS* related to the *atomic service* or a *global QoiS* associated with the *aggregate service*. For instance, the service $S_{Make\ Room\ Booking}$ defines several QoiS that depend on the different variant services.

Simple QoiS

As shown in Figure 2, the QoiS of an atomic service (S_{at}) is said simple as it reflects the contribution of this service to satisficing quality goals. The Simple QoiS is calculated as a set of quality goals (q_j) that a service contributes satisficing and the related satisficing degree (d_j). We adopt the following structure, inspired from (Rohleder et al., 2009), to represent the simple QoiS:

$$QoiS(S_{at}) = S_{at}.\{<q_j,d_j>\} \qquad (1)$$

For example, the QoiS of the atomic services $S_{Accept\ Payment\ by\ electronic\ transfer}$ is expressed as follows: $QoiS(S_{AcceptPaymentbyelectronictransfer})= S_{Accept\ Payment\ by\ electronic\ transfer}.\{<Security,\ +>,<Fast,\ ->\}$. This QoiS defines that the service $S_{Accept\ Payment\ by\ electronic\ transfer}$ contributes to make "*satisficing (+)*" the *Security* quality goal and "*not satisficing (-)*" the *Fast* quality goal.

Global QoiS

In the *ISOA* approach, QoiS is defined in a goal-driven manner focusing on the '*whys*' of the quality values (non functional properties) provided by the software service. Such relationships are represented by the aggregation links (•, //,⊗, v,* and ∪), indicating order or variability on QoiS composition. Moreover, QoiS evaluation is itself grounded in *XOR, OR, AND* relationships among

QoiS of intentional services that compose an aggregate service (service components).

As shown in Figure 2, the QoiS of an aggregate service is said global as it results of a compilation of QoiS related to its components services. In other terms, the QoiS of an aggregate service (S) is calculated in a recursive manner, depending on the QoiS of components services.

The global QoiS calculation depends on the different kinds (composite and variant) of the aggregate service. As represented by the *Aggregation Link* element in the Figure 2, we propose to extend the semantic of the aggregation link to define the different kind of global QoiS. Given an aggregation link (*al: al* $\in \{\bullet, //, \otimes, v, *, \cup\}$) and a set of components services (S_n), we adopt a following generic structure, inspired from (Rohleder et al., 2009), to represent the global QoiS of the aggregate service (S_{ag}):

$$\text{QoiS}(S_{ag}) = al \, (\text{QoiS}(S_1), \text{QoiS}(S_2) \dots \text{QoiS}(S_n)) \tag{2}$$

We apply this structure to represent the different kinds of global QoiS related to the aggregate service. We detail this aspect in turn.

A *composite quality* is related to the composite service. It reflects a composition of the QoiS of its component services, corresponding to an AND relationship between the QoiS of the component services. The composition is denoted "$\bullet$", "$//$" or "$*$" symbol, depending on the kind of the composite service, respectively sequential, parallel or iterative. It is noted as:

$$\text{QoiS}(\bullet \, (S_1, S_2, \dots, S_n)) = \bullet \, (\text{QoiS}(S_1), \text{QoiS}(S_2) \dots \text{QoiS}(S_n))$$

For example, The QoiS of the composite service $S_{Make\,Confirmed\,Booking} = \bullet(S_{Make\,Room\,Booking}, S_{Accept\,Payment})$ is defined as the composition of the QoiS of both $S_{Make\,Room\,Booking}$ and $S_{Accept\,Payment}$. It is noted as:

$$\text{QoiS}(S_{Make\,Confirmed\,Booking}) = \bullet(\text{QoiS}(S_{Make\,Room\,Booking}), \text{QoiS}(S_{Accept\,Payment}))$$

Introduction of *variability* in quality modelling is justified by the need to introduce flexibility in quality goal satisficing and adaptability in intentional service execution. There are three types of *variant quality*, namely *alternative, choice* and *multi-path*.

An *alternative* variation corresponds to an XOR relationship between the QoiS of the alternative components, *i.e.* each QoiS of alternative component can be satisfied in exclusively way. The symbol "$\otimes$" is used to denote the alternative variation and it is noted as:

$$\text{QoiS}(\otimes \, (S_1, S_2, \dots, S_n)) = \otimes \, (\text{QoiS}(S_1), \text{QoiS}(S_2) \dots \text{QoiS}(S_n))$$

For example, The QoiS of the alternative service $S_{Accept\,Payment} = \otimes \, (S_{Accept\,Payment\,by\,electronic\,transfer}, S_{Accept\,Payment\,by\,credit\,card}, S_{Accept\,Payment\,by\,cash})$ is defined as the XOR relationship between the QoiS of both $S_{Accept\,Payment\,by\,electronic\,transfer}, S_{Accept\,Payment\,by\,credit\,card}$ and $S_{Accept\,Payment\,by\,cash}$. It is noted as:

$$\text{QoiS}(S_{Accept\,Payment}) = \otimes \, (\text{QoiS}(S_{Accept\,Payment\,by\,electronic\,transfer}),$$

$$\text{QoiS}(S_{Accept\,Payment\,by\,credit\,card}), \text{QoiS}(S_{Accept\,Payment\,by\,cash}))$$

A *choice* variation corresponds to an OR relationship between the QoiS of the alternative components. The difference between alternative and choice lies on the fact that the former implies exclusion of variants QoiS whereas the latter authorizes the selection of several of the choice when the variant QoiS is satisfied. The symbol "v" is used to denote the choice variation and it is noted as:

$$\text{QoiS}(v \, (S_1, S_2, \dots, S_n)) = v \, (\text{QoiS}(S_1), \text{QoiS}(S_2) \dots \text{QoiS}(S_n))$$

For example, The QoIS of the alternative service

$$S_{Investigate\ Candidate\ Booking} = v(S_{Investigate\ Candidate\ Booking\ on\ the\ Internet}, S_{Investigate\ Candidate\ Booking\ by\ visiting\ a\ travel\ agent})$$

is defined as the OR relationship between the QoIS of both $S_{Investigate\ Candidate\ Booking\ on\ the\ Internet}$ and $S_{Investigate\ Candidate\ Booking\ by\ visiting\ a\ travel\ agent}$. It is noted as:

$$QoIS(S_{Investigate\ Candidate\ Booking}) = v\ (QoIS(S_{Candidate\ Booking\ on\ the\ Internet}),\ QoIS(S_{Investigate\ Candidate\ Booking\ by\ visiting\ a\ travel\ agent}))$$

Finally a *multi-path* variation occurs when several QoIS compositions of an intentional service allow achieving the same intentional service and satisficing different quality goals. The multi-path is denoted "∪". It is noted as:

$$QoIS(\cup\ (S_1,\ S_2,\ ...,\ S_n)) = \cup\ (QoIS(S_1),\ QoIS(S_2)\ ...\ QoIS(S_n))$$

For example, let us define the QoIS of the multi-path service $S_{Make\ Confirmed\ Booking} = \cup (\bullet(S_{Make\ Room\ Booking}, S_{Accept\ Payment}),\ S_{Get\ a\ Rewarded\ Booking})$. Thus, there are two paths to providing the intentional service *Make a Confirmed Booking:* one by achieving the sequence of intentional services *Make a Booking* and Accept *payment*, and another by achieving the service *Get a Rewarded Booking*. Therefore the QoIS of $S_{Make\ Confirmed\ Booking}$ should consider the QoIS of the first path $QoIS(\bullet\ (S_{Make\ Room\ Booking}, S_{Accept\ Payment}))$ and the QoIS of the second path $QoIS(S_{Get\ a\ Rewarded\ Booking})$. It is noted as:

$$QoIS(S_{Make\ Confirmed\ Booking}) = \cup\ (QoIS(\bullet(S_{Make\ Room\ Booking}, S_{Accept\ Payment}),\ QoIS(S_{Get\ a\ Rewarded\ Booking})))$$

Previously, we present the definition of QoIS of an intentional service: a simple QoIS is related to the atomic service, whereas the global QoIS is related to the aggregate service. However the global QoIS specification remains not sufficient because it can-not be used by the selection algorithms that enable choosing among various intentional services (that achieve the same functional goal) those that meet user' quality context. For that, we propose in the next section to calculate the $QoIS_{min\_max}$ offered by the aggregate intentional service.

QoIS$_{min\_max}$ Calculation

We propose calculating the QoIS$_{min\_max}$ of an aggregate service in order to specify the set of quality goals that it contributes satisficing and the related satisficing degrees. The calculation of QoIS$_{min\_max}$ depends on the aggregation link forming the global QoIS, namely composite quality ("•", "//", "*") or variant quality ("⊗", "v", "∪"). Given an aggregate service (S_{ag}), we adopt a following generic structure to represent the QoIS$_{min\_max}$:

$$QoIS_{min\_max}\ (S_{ag}) = \{<Q,D>\} \tag{3}$$

The QoIS$_{min\_max}$ of the aggregate service S_{ag} corresponds to the set of quality goals Q and the related satisficing degrees D that a service S_{ag} contributes satisficing. The calculation of the QoIS$_{min\_max}$ is based on the propagation rules defined in the requirement engineering community (Chung et al., 2000). As its name indicates, the minimal and the maximal degrees are calculated (or propagated) in the case of a composite and a variant service, respectively.

In the case of a *composite quality* (for instance using the "•" operator), the rule R 1 is proposed. The notation of QoIS$_{min\_max}$ is based on the equation *(3)*. The QoIS$_{min\_max}$ is expressed as: (i) the union (∪) of quality goals (q_j) satisficed by the component services of the composite service *(S)*; and (ii) the minimum satisficing degree guaranteed by the component services per q_j. In the case of a composite quality (related to a composite service), the QoIS$_{min\_max}$ is calculated as follows:

$$Q = \overset{m}{\underset{j=1}{U}} q_j \quad \mathbf{R} \ 1$$

$$D = \min_{1 \le i \le n; 1 \le j \le m} d_{ij} / q_j$$

vice $\mathbf{S}_{\text{Make Confirmed Booking}}$. The QoiS of this service id specified as QoiS($\mathbf{S}_{\text{Make Confirmed Booking}}$)= • ($QoiS$ ($\mathbf{S}_{\text{Make Room Booking}}$), $QoiS$($\mathbf{S}_{\text{Accept Payment}}$)). The QoiS-$_{\text{min\_max}}$($\mathbf{S}_{\text{Make Confirmed Booking}}$) is computed as follows: (i) the set of quality goals the $\mathbf{S}_{\text{Make Confirmed Booking}}$ contributes satisficing, namely *Fast*, *Security* and *Cost*; and (ii) the minimum satisficing degree per quality goal: for instance $\mathbf{S}_{\text{Make Room Booking}}$ contribute to make "*satisficing (+)*" the *Security* quality, whereas $\mathbf{S}_{\text{Accept Payment}}$ contribute to make it "*not satisficing (-)*". Thus a minimum degree of *Security* quality is "*not satisficing (-)*". As a result, the QoiS$_{\text{min\_max}}$($\mathbf{S}_{\text{Make Confirmed Booking}}$) = {*<Fast,+>,<Security,->,< Cost,++>* }.

However, in the case of a *variant quality* (for instance using the "∪" operator), the rule R 2 is proposed. The notation of QoiS$_{\text{min\_max}}$ is also based on the equation *(3)*. The QoiS$_{\text{min\_max}}$ is also expressed as: (i) the union (∪) of quality goals (q_j) satisficed by the component services of the variant service *(S)*; and (ii) the maximum satisficing degree guaranteed by the component services per q_j. In the case of a variant quality (related to a variant service), the QoiS$_{\text{min\_max}}$ is calculated as:

$$Q = \overset{m}{\underset{j=1}{U}} q_j \quad \mathbf{R} \ 2$$

$$D = \max_{1 \le i \le n; 1 \le j \le m} d_{ij} / q_j$$

For instance, let us consider the QoiS$_{\text{min\_max}}$ of the variant service $\boldsymbol{S}_{\text{Accept Payment}}$. The QoiS of this service id specified as $QoiS$($\boldsymbol{S}_{\text{Accept Payment}}$)= ⊗($QoiS$ ($\boldsymbol{S}_{\text{Accept Payment by electronic transfer}}$), $QoiS$($\boldsymbol{S}_{\text{Accept Payment by credit card}}$), $QoiS$($\boldsymbol{S}_{\text{Accept Payment by cash}}$)). The QoiS$_{\text{min\_max}}$ ($\boldsymbol{S}_{\text{Accept Payment}}$) is computed as fol-

lows: (i) the set of quality goals the $\boldsymbol{S}_{\text{Accept Payment}}$ contributes satisficing, namely *Fast* and *Security*; and (ii) the maximum satisficing degree per quality goal: for instance $\boldsymbol{S}_{\text{Accept Payment by electronic transfer}}$ contribute to make "*not satisficing (-)*" the *Security* quality, whereas $\boldsymbol{S}_{\text{Accept Payment by credit card}}$ contribute to make it "*satisficing (+)*". Thus a maximum degree of *Security* quality is "*satisficing (+)*". As a result, the QoiS$_{\text{min\_max}}$($\boldsymbol{S}_{\text{Accept Payment}}$) = {*<Fast,+>,<Security,+>*}. More explicitly, this latter indicates that $\boldsymbol{S}_{\text{Accept Payment}}$ service provides the QoiS$_{\text{min\_max}}$ corresponding to "*satisficing (+)*" the *Fast* quality and "*satisficing (+)*" the *Security* one. This QoiS$_{\text{min\_max}}$ is depending of the chosen variant, namely $\boldsymbol{S}_{\text{Accept Payment by electronic transfer}}$, $\boldsymbol{S}_{\text{Accept Payment by credit card}}$ or $\boldsymbol{S}_{\text{Accept Payment by cash}}$.

The previous demonstrate the importance of calculating the QoiS related to the intentional service in order to differentiate the various services that achieve the same functional goal. The simple QoiS and the QoiS$_{\text{min\_max}}$ are both used to select among services those that meet users' quality context. Next section discusses the description of ISM-q that is published in the intentional service registry.

PUBLISHING THE QOIS

Every intentional service must be available in the intentional service registry. This enables retrieval of atomic and aggregate services and their adaptation to users' needs. Retrieval is based on goal matching; that is, given a goal G, the registry searches a service that can satisfy this goal. We consider, in the following, the issue of making available the QoiS descriptions in the registry. In order to publish intentional service on an intentional registry, we adopt XML view of *ISM-q*. Such view represents all service dimensions: interface, behavior, composition and QoiS. Figure 4 illustrates the XML Schema used to specify intentional service description in XML. It is worth noting that in this paper, we

Figure 4. XML schema of intentional service description

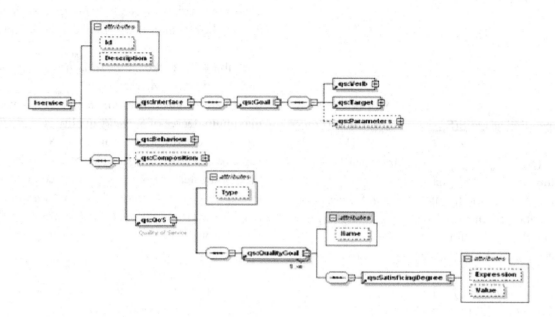

focus only QoIS dimension. Details concerning interface, behavior and composition can be found in (Rolland et al., 2009).

As shown in the Figure 4, the intentional service description considers the QoIS dimension of the intentional service additionally to the interface, the behavior and the composition ones. Such description allows service selection based on the QoIS provided by the service, in addition to goal it satisfies. In particular, the service provider can publish, for an atomic service, the simple QoIS associated with this service (Figure 4 element *qs:QoS* attribute *Type=SimpleQoS*). For an aggregate service, the service provider can publish the QoIS$_{min\_max}$ guaranteed by this service (Figure 4 element *qs:QoS* attribute *Type=GlobalMinQoS*). Each QoIS is composed of a set of quality goals (element *qs:QualityGoal* in Figure 4) satisfied by the intentional service and their corresponding satisficing degrees (element *qs:SatisficingDegree* in Figure 4).

The XML file presented in the Figure 5 specifies the QoIS of the atomic service $S_{Accept\ Payment\ by\ electronic\ transfer}$, which achieves the

goal *Accept payment* and contributes satisficing the quality goals *Security* ("+") and *Fast ("-")*. The XML file shown in the Figure 6 describes the QoIS$_{min\_max}$ associated with the aggregate service $S_{Make\ Confirmed\ Booking} = \bullet (S_{Make\ Room\ Booking}, S_{Accept\ Payment})$ that achieves the goal *Make Confirmed Booking* and contributes satisficing the quality goals *Security* ("-"), *Cost* ("++") and *Fast ("+")*. As one can observe on Figure 5 and Figure 6, the satisficing degrees proposed for each quality goal are described using a dual representation. Actually, in addition to the notation proposed on ISM-q, which indicates the satisficing degree using understandable expression for business agents, XML service description also includes a numeric value (attribute *value* in Figure 4). Such numeric values (*-2≤value≤+2, value* ∈ ℵ) translates the qualitative satisficing degree in such a way that queries involving such degrees can be easily executed. For instance, service $S_{Accept\ Payment}$ provides the quality goal *Security* with a satisficing degree of "+", which is translated to the value "*+1*" (Figure 5 line 15).

Figure 5. Example of simple QoiS

```
1    <?xml version="1.0" encoding="UTF-8"?>
2    <qs:Iservice xsi:schemaLocation="qs.xsd QoS_Iservice_QoS.xsd"
     xmlns:xsi="http://www.w3.org/2001/XMLSchema-instance" xmlns:qs="qs.xsd"
3    Id="http://www.booking.com/APet" Description="SAccept Payment by electronic transfer
4    ">
5    <qs:Interface>
6         <qs:Goal>
7           <qs:Verb Verb="Accept"/>
8           <qs:Target Target="Payment"/>
9           <qs:Parameters> Parameters="by electronic transfer" </qs:Parameters>
10        </qs:Goal>
11   </qs:Interface>
12   <qs:Behaviour>. . .            </qs:Behaviour>
13   <qs:QoS Type="SimpleQoS">
14      <qs:QualityGoal Name="Security">
15        <qs:SatisficingDegree Expression="Satisficed (+)" Value="+1"/>
16      </qs:QualityGoal>
17      <qs:QualityGoal Name="Fast">
18        <qs:SatisficingDegree Expression="Not Satisficed (-)" Value="-1"/>
19      </qs:QualityGoal>
     </qs:QoS>
     </qs:Iservice>
```

Figure 6. Example of QoiS$_{min\_max}$

```
1    <?xml version="1.0" encoding="UTF-8"?>
2    <qs:Iservice xsi:schemaLocation="qs.xsd QoS_Iservice_QoSmin.xsd"
...  xmlns:xsi="http://www.w3.org/2001/XMLSchema-instance" xmlns:qs="qs.xsd"
3    Id="http://www.booking.com/MCB"  Description="SMake Confirmed Booking">
4    <qs:Interface>
5         <qs:Goal>
6             <qs:Verb Verb="Make"/>
7             <qs:Target Target=" Confirmed Booking"/>
8             <qs:Parameters>. . .           </qs:Parameters>
9         </qs:Goal>
10   </qs:Interface>
11   <qs:Behaviour>. . .              </qs:Behaviour>
12   <qs:QoS Type="GlobalMinQoS">
13      <qs:QualityGoal Goal="Security">
14        <qs:SatisficingDegree Expression="Not Satisficed (-)" Value="-1"/>
15      </qs:QualityGoal>
16      <qs:QualityGoal Goal="Cost">
17        <qs:SatisficingDegree Expression="Very Satisficed (++)" Value="+2"/>
18      </qs:QualityGoal>
19      <qs:QualityGoal Goal="Fast">
20        <qs:SatisficingDegree Expression="Satisficed (+)" Value="+1"/>
21      </qs:QualityGoal>
22   </qs:QoS>
23   </qs:Iservice>
```

Figure 7. Example of query for an intentional service expressed in XQuery

```
for $x in //Iservice
let $g := $x/Interface/Goal
let $q := $x/QoS/QualityGoal
where $g/Verb/@Verb = "Make" and
    $g/Target/@Target = "Confirmed Booking" and
    ( ($q/@Goal = "Security" and $q/SatisficingDegree/@Value >= -1)
    or
      ($q/@Goal = "Cost" and $q/SatisficingDegree/@Value >=1 ) )
return $x
```

Moreover, the Figure 6 describes the QoiS$_{min\_max}$ of the aggregate service $S_{Make\ Confirmed\ Booking}$, including three different quality goals: *Security* (Figure 6 line 13), *Cost* (Figure 6 line 16) and *Fast* (Figure 6 line 19). For each quality goal, the satisficing degree is indicated. For example, the service described in Figure 6 supplies a quality goal *Security* with a satisficing degree *"Not satisfied (-)"* (Figure 6 line 14).

QUERYING INTENTIONAL SERVICES REGISTRY

Although query evaluation and service selection are out of the scope of this particular paper, we would like to underline the possibility of using XQuery expressions in order to query intentional service registry, taking advantage of the quality description of these services.

Traditionally, iSOA approach considers that business agents submit their requests through a user interface. In order to consider QoiS issues, such user interface should allow business agents to express their preferences considering quality goals. Through the user's quality context, business agents can indicate what quality goals they expect from intentional services and the corresponding satisficing degree they consider as minimal. The user's quality context will be used by the intentional service registry. We propose using a Multi-Criteria Decision-Making (MCDM) methods in order to select from several services those that meet the user's quality context. The MCDM

methods can deal with conflicting QoiS such as security and performance.

Based on the user's quality context, the user interface can form XQuery expression representing functional requirement formulated by the business agent as well as quality goals this agent demands. For instance, the Figure 7 presents a query for intentional service achieving the goal *Make confirmed booking* and providing *Security* and *Fast* quality goals with a minimal satisfaction degree "Not satisfied (-)" and "Satisfied (+)" respectively.

By considering XQuery for querying intentional registry, we focus on the advantages of using a standard query language. W3C XQuery standard is largely accepted by SOA community and offers a simple way of handling XML data (Innocenti, 2007), as the XML description proposed for intentional services.

CONCLUSION

In the last few years, the notion of service became a transversal notion that talks to technical software community as well as to business IT community. However, vocabulary used by these communities is not the same. For software community, services refer mainly to Web services and related technologies, with their technical constraints and implications. For business IT community, services based applications are considered as a support to improve cooperation between companies. In this context, the notion of intentional service is used to improve the service semantic by decreasing the gap between the users' requirements, considered by business IT community, and the software service, handled by software community. However, until now, ISM did not consider the quality dimension, but only functional requirements associated with intentional services. This chapter proposed an extension to the ISM specification by introducing the quality dimension.

Our contribution is varied. Firstly, we described the ISM extended to QoiS (ISM-q) and a whole evaluation methods enabling evaluating the global QoiS. Secondly, we recommend an XML description of the ISM-q in order to publish QoiS descriptions in the intentional service registry. Finally, we suggest the XQuery language to retrieve services considering their quality dimension.

As future work, we develop the selection algorithm by adopting the Technique for Order Preference by Similarity to Ideal Solution (Hwang & Yoon, 1981; Zavadskas, 1986) to select from several intentional services according to the users' quality context. Since the aggregate service supports variability in achieving the functional goal of user, we are investigating as future work how to configure this service according to the users' quality context. A prototype that supports intentional service selection and the configuration of an aggregate service is under development.

REFERENCES

W3C. (2003). *QoS for Web services: Requirements and possible approaches*. Retrieved from http://www.w3c.or.kr/kr-office/TR/2003/ws-qos/

W3C. (2004). *OWL-S: Semantic markup for Web services*. Retrieved from http://www.w3.org/Submission/OWL-S/

W3C. (2007). *Web service description language (WSDL) version 2.0 part 1: Core language*. Retrieved from http://www.w3.org/TR/wsdl12/

Aiello, M., & Giorgini, P. (2004). Applying the Tropos methodology for analysing Web services requirements and reasoning about qualities of services. *Journal for the Informatics Professional, 5*(4).

Ait-Ali-Slimane, A., Kirsch-Pinheiro, M., & Souveyet, C. (2009). *Goal reasoning for quality elicitation in the ISOA approach*. International Conference on Research Challenges in Information Science (RCIS), IEEE, Maroc.

Ait-Ali-Slimane, A., & Souveyet, C. (2008, May). *Une Approche Méthodologique Orientée But pour Eliciter les Qualités de Service comme des Aspects*. INORSIDE. France.

Ait-Ali-Slimane, A., & Souveyet, C. (2008, April). *A goal driven approach to deal with quality of service as potential aspects*. In Inter. Workshop on Advanced Information Systems for Enterprises (IWAISE'08), Algeria.

Alonso, G., Casati, F., Kuno, H., & Machiraju, V. (2004). *Web services: Concepts, architecture, and applications*. Springer Verlag.

Casati, F., & Shan, M. (2001). Dynamic and adaptive composition of e-services. *The 12th International Conference on Advanced Information Systems Engineering (CAiSE 00). Journal for Information Systems, 26*(3), 143–163. doi:10.1016/S0306-4379(01)00014-X

Chung, L., Nixon, B., Yu, E., & Mylopoulos, J. (2000). *Non-functional requirements in software engineering*. Kluwer Academic Publishers.

Chung, L., & Subramanian, N. (2001). Process-oriented metrics for software architecture adaptability. *In Proceedings of Fifth IEEE International Symposium on Requirements Engineering* (pp.310–311).

Dobson, G., Lock, R., & Sommerville, I. (2005). *QoSOnt: A QoS ontology for service-centric systems*. In Software Engineering and Advanced Applications. 31st EUROMICRO Conference.

Fedosseev, P. (2003/2004). *Composition of Web services and QoS aspects*. Seminar: Data Communication and Distributed Systems. Retrieved from http: //www.nets.rwthaachen. de/ content/ teaching/ seminars/sub/ 2003_2004_ws_docs/ WebServices.pdf

Herssens, C., Jureta, I. J., & Faulkner, S. (2008). Capturing and using QoS relationships to improve service selection. *In Proceeding of CAISE*, France.

Hwang, C.-L., & Yoon, K. (1981). *Multiple attribute decision making: Methods and applications*. Berlin, Germany: Springer.

Innocenti, C. (2007). SOA and the importance of XQuery. *The SOA Magazine, 10*. Retrieved from http: // www.soamag.com/I10/ 0907-3.pdf

Jureta, I. J., Faulkner, S., & Schobbens, P.-Y. (2006). A more expressive soft goal conceptualization for quality requirements analysis. *In Proceedings of 25th International Conference on Conceptual Modeling* (pp. 281-295).

Kaabi, R. S., Souveyet, C., & Rolland, C. (2004). *Eliciting service composition in a goal driven manner*. Int. Conf. on Service Oriented Computing (ICSOC), New York.

Keller, S. E., Kahn, L. G., & Panara, R. B. (1990). Specifying software quality requirements with metrics. In Thayer, R. H., & Dorfman, M. (Eds.), *System and software requirements engineering* (pp. 145–163). Washington, DC: IEEE Computer Society Press.

Ma, W., Liu, L., Xie, H., Zhang, H., & Yin, J. (2009). Preference model driven services selection. In *21st International Conference on Advanced Information Systems Engineering (CAISE'09)*, (pp. 216-230).

Mani, A., & Nagarajian, A. (2002). *Web services: Understanding quality of service for Web services*. IBM Developer Works. Retrieved from http://www-106.ibm.com/ developerworks/ library/ ws-quality.html

Maximilien, E. M., & Singh, M. P. (2004). A framework and ontology for dynamic Web services selection. *IEEE Internet Computing, 8*(5), 84–93. doi:10.1109/MIC.2004.27

Mylopoulos, J., Chung, L., & Nixon, B. (1992). Representing and using non-functional requirements: A Process-oriented approach. *IEEE Transactions on Software Engineering, 18*(6), 483–497. doi:10.1109/32.142871

O'Sullivan, J., Edmond, D., & Hofstede, A. T. (2002). What's in a service? Towards accurate description of non-functional service properties. *Distributed and Parallel Databases Journal - Special Issue on E-Services, 12*.

Papazoglou, M.-P., Traverso, P., Dustdar, S., & Leymann, F. (2008). Service-oriented computing: A research roadmap. *Int. J. Cooperative Inf. Syst., 17*(2), 223–255. doi:10.1142/ S0218843008001816

Penserini, L., & Mylopoulos, J. (2005). *Design matters for Semantic Web Services*. ITC-IRST, Technical report: T05-04-03.

Rohleder, C., Marhold, C., Salinesi, C., & Doerr, J. (2009). *Quality data model and quality control in the product lifecycle management*. International Conference on Product Lifecycle Management (ICPLM), Bath, Royaume Uni.

Rolland, C., Kirsch-Pinheiro, M., & Souveyet, C. (2009). *An intentional approach to service engineering. Transactions on Service Computing (IEEE-TSC), Special issue on REFS (Requirements Engineering for Services)*. IEEE.

Rolland, C., & Prakash, N. (2000). Bridging the gap between organizational needs and ERP functionality. *Requirement Engineering Journal*, 5(3), 180–193. doi:10.1007/PL00010350

Simon, H. A. (Ed.). (1981). *The science of the artificial* (2nd ed.). Cambridge, MA: The MIT Process.

Toma, I., Foxvog, D., & Jaeger, M. C. (2006). Modeling QoS characteristics in WSMO. In *Proceeding of the 1st Workshop on Middleware for Service Oriented Computing* (MW4SOC 2006).

Yu, E., Du Bois, P., Dubois, E., & Mylopoulos, J. (1995). From organization models to system requirements- A cooperating agents approach. In *Proc. 3rd Int. Conf. on Cooperative Information Systems (CoopIS-95)*, Vienna, Austria, (pp. 194-204).

Zavadskas, E. K. (1986). The method of ranking of construction-technological alternatives on the basis of the distance from the ideal solution. *In New construction technology for buildings and structures* (pp. 52-57). (in Russian)

Zeng, L., Benatallah, B., Dumas, M., Kalagnanam, J., & Sheng, Q. Z. (2003).Quality driven web services composition. In *Proceedings of the International WWW*.

KEY TERMS AND DEFINITIONS

Context Models: Informational models representing context information in a well-defined structure.

Context: Any information that can be used to characterize the situation of an entity (a person, place, or object considered as relevant to the interaction between a user and an application).

Context-Aware Services: Services of which description is enriched with context information related to non-functional requirements, describing the service execution environment or its adaptation capabilities.

Context-Aware Systems: Systems that are able to adapt their operations to the current context, aiming at increasing usability and effectiveness by taking into account environmental context.

Service Selection: The process allowing the identification of all services, among the available ones, that match functional and non-functional requirements.

Services: Independent entities, with well-defined interfaces, that can be invoked in a standard way, without requiring the client to have knowledge about how the service actually performs its tasks.

Similarity Measures: Measures used to compare the degree of similarity (or dissimilarity) between two concepts on a domain.

Chapter 16
WSARCH:
A Service–Oriented Architecture with QoS

Júlio Cezar Estrella
University of São Paulo, Brazil

Regina Helena Carlucci Santana
University of São Paulo, Brazil

Marcos Jose Santana
University of São Paulo, Brazil

Sarita Mazzini Bruschi
University of São Paulo, Brazil

ABSTRACT

This chapter aims at the design and implementation of a service-oriented architecture (SOA), named WSARCH – Web Services Architecture - which allows accessing Web Services using a combination of functional and non-functional aspects of Quality of Service (QoS). These QoS aspects, aiming at evaluating the performance of Web Services in order to achieve QoS in a service-oriented architecture, are identified and discussed. These QoS attributes were mapped to the components participating in a service-oriented architecture with QoS support. The proposed architecture provides the monitoring of service providers and the data obtained are used to locate the most appropriated service. The WSARCH can be used as an analytical platform for purposes of testing Web Services and understanding their behavior as well as an execution platform for building live systems. A prototype for the WSARCH was developed, and it can allow performance evaluation studies being conducted considering different components of the architecture, algorithms, protocols and standards. The proposal WSARCH is inserted into a context where it is important to define the way a SOA focusing on performance shall be designed, since the correct characterization of what to evaluate and how to evaluate.

DOI: 10.4018/978-1-61350-432-1.ch016

INTRODUCTION

Web Services have emerged as a technology that aims at improving the communication between applications through the service-oriented paradigm. A Web Service is defined by the W3C consortium as a software application that uses standard Internet protocols such as UDDI, WSDL, and SOAP to interact with other Web Services. The Web Services protocols have been proposed to describe, discover, connect, and integrate Web Services software providers based on different Web Servers. Web Services try to solve the problems of interoperability among different systems and applications using a Service-Oriented Computing (SOC) paradigm that utilizes services as fundamental elements for developing applications/solutions and a universal language such as XML. The potential of the service-oriented paradigm can be explored in areas such as education, where reliability, security and personalization of services and information are of primary concern in this endeavor (Hundling, 2006). Services can execute functions ranging from simple requests till complicated business processes. A Web Service composition for example can be mapped into a business process, composed of an arrangement of individual services that form a new, more complex service. Composition is one of the most important aspects in service oriented computing: the main idea is that when building a new service, one can rely upon existing services, which provide part of the needed operations. Several issues are related to this topic, such as the research on automating the composition process, the techniques for managing a composition and the relationship with software (and service) reuse (Andrea & Benatallah, 2006).

The choice of services that will compose a more complex service can involve many QoS parameters. The choice of a service that is not appropriated for building the composition can increase the response time of the service perceived by the user. Different versions of a particular service can perform the task required in a similar way but offering different QoS. Some versions of a service can execute quicker than others, or the invocation of a particular version can be more expensive. Therefore, a service composition designer needs to consider how to discover the best service to compose the complete service and improve the QoS perceived by the user. The definition of the services selection introduces an optimization problem (Ardagna & Pernici, 2005).

Although Web Services can improve the interoperability among applications, researchers involved with Web Services and SOA are still studying many issues, such as security, fault tolerance, semantic Web and others. Due to the integration of Web Services as a business solution in many enterprise applications, quality of service provided by Web Services is becoming relevant for both the service providers and the clients. Providers need to specify and guarantee the QoS of their Web Services in order to remain competitive and achieve the best attendance of the business processes. Furthermore, clients aim at having good performance (high availability, low response time, low latency and others).

Considering that many applications for distributed systems fail because they do not address aspects of QoS (Woodside & Menasce, 2006) and consequently QoS in Web services is essential to improve reliability and availability of services, the objective of this work is the design and implementation of a service-oriented architecture, named WSARCH - Web Services Architecture, which allows access to Web Services with QoS. The proposed architecture extends, with adaptations and improvements, other architectural models shown in the literature on Web Services. The main purpose of the WSARCH, which makes it different from other architectures, is to be an architecture developed in order to assist in evaluating the performance of Web Services considering QoS attributes. To enable the development of this architecture becomes necessary to define which attributes should be considered for this purpose. Thus, for the development of WSARCH is necessary to identify and to map the attributes of the various QoS components of a service-oriented architecture. An important point to achieve the goals of WSARCH is its architecture that considers the interaction between the components of a traditional SOA (Service Oriented Architecture) and also a Broker, responsible for the scheduling of SOAP messages between client, provider and service registry, considering QoS attributes.

The methodology used for the development of the project is the implementation of a WSARCH prototype. The prototype was developed in a modular form in order to enable different studies of performance evaluation. This prototype is validated through a performance evaluation experiment.

In this context this chapter is organized as follows: In section 2 the main related work about quality of services in Service Oriented Architecture is introduced. In order to improve the SOA paradigm and deal with some of its limitations, section 3 shows the prototype of a Service Oriented Architecture with QoS, in which the structure, main modules and entities are discussed. Section 4 presents the main guidelines that were applied to evaluate the performance of this architecture, which includes: test bed applications, environment configuration and experiment design. In Section 5 the results and contributions from the development of this work are presented. Finally, section 6 presents the conclusions and future work.

RELATED WORK

In Comuzzi & Pernici (2005), the authors have mentioned the creation of an automatic approach for the negotiation of Web Services using a Broker. In a Broker both the provider and the client can notify their preferences and negotiating strategies to achieve QoS based on the value of a set of parameters. The idea is that the Broker has a decision model of each provider, so that the client can interact directly with the Broker. The Broker

can simulate the behavior of the provider in the negotiation process without having contact with the provider every time the client makes a new QoS offer.

In Orta, Ruiz & Toro (2009) a simulation model related to capacity management for Web Services is presented. The main purpose of this model is to help managing the capacity allocated by Web Services providers to their clients in order to assure a Service Level Agreement (SLA). QoS issues have received attention in recent years, mostly in the communication network and also in the middleware communities (Tian et al., 2004) in which local metrics were defined without concerning on metrics for end-to-end services. It has been difficult to find proposals for direct negotiation of QoS in Web Services environments, especially when considering strategies with key aspect in defining a framework for automated negotiation.

The problem of adaptation based on QoS is considered in (Dorn et al., 2009). The authors address the problem of self-adaptation in service-oriented systems in internet-scale. When a system is subject to changes, services need to adapt, selecting as good as possible, the best services based only on some information of QoS. In general, the information is local and limited, which is not suitable when considering complex systems. In these systems, the global significance of the selection parameters changes dynamically. Therefore, the authors introduce a new metric to measure the distribution and the potential impact of service properties that affect these selection parameters and also present mechanisms for identifying the most important properties of an interaction based on aggregated data service.

Another important question is about QoS in Web Services Composition. In Yeom & Min (2005) it is presented a Web Service QoS Broker system that actively monitors QoS (availability, performance and reliability) of Web Services. With this information the user can select the Web Service that best suits his needs. The implementation of service composition automatically and efficiently is another problem when using Web Services in enterprise applications (Menasce, 2004), (Jaeger & Ladner, 2005), (Yeom & Min, 2005), (Jaeger, Muhl & Golze., 2005), (Zeng et al., 2005). The highly dynamic and distributed nature of Web Services often makes some service providers overloaded at certain times while others are idle. Based on the queuing theory, (Wang et al., 2004) presents a service selection and execution strategy to provide guarantees for QoS under limitation of the resources of the providers.

QoS metrics for selecting Web Services and providers also have been proposed in (Kalepu, Krishnaswamy & Loke, 2003). A measure of the trustworthy that the provider has achieved in relation to the levels agreed in the SLA is obtained by the authors quantifying the consistency of the level of compliance and introducing a new attribute called QoS Verity. An evaluation of the performance achieved is not presented in the article.

A Web Service Message Bus (wsBus) is presented in (Erradi &Maheshwari, 2005), aiming at improving QoS aspects in service oriented architectures and Web Services. The wsBus is a lightweight service-oriented middleware for reliable and fault tolerant Web Services interaction. On one hand the architecture design of wsBus is interesting but otherwise there is a poor performance evaluation of this architecture, that needs to be better evaluated.

WSARCH ARCHITECTURE

Although the basic model of SOA is implemented by means of Web Services concepts (such as service registration, discovery and load balancing of service requests), it is necessary an extension of this generic model to provide some important requirements. These requirements are essential for business-quality and include services facilities for ensuring consistency across the organization, high availability of services, security of non-public services and information, orchestration of mul-

tiple services as part of composite applications or metadata management, among other points (Papazoglou, 2005). Moreover some basic research is also necessary in order to reach a consensus about some key aspects. One of such key aspects should involve a common model for service descriptions, especially for the cases related to service discovery. For automated discovery these service descriptions need to be specified in a formal, computer readable way. Additionally, properties of services that are beyond technical interface specifications should be modeled (e.g., by including QoS properties) (Hundling, 2008).

The WSARCH (Web Services Architecture) is an architecture that allows the implementation and evaluation of all the requirement stated in the previous paragraph. The WSARCH allows studies considering the provisioning of QoS in different situations when a service is required (e.g., messages exchanged among the applications deployed). Some modules of QoS were considered in the architecture, besides a study of performance evaluation. The WSARCH and its components are presented in Figure 1.

The following steps are necessary for the execution of a request:

1. Client makes request to the Broker, which has updated information from the service provider (load, type of service, client class);
2. Based on the QoS information requested by the client of service, the Broker performs a search in a service repository in order to find the most appropriate service;
3. Broker gets the specification of appropriate service and information about the QoS of the service provider;
4. With the location of appropriate service in the repository services and information of the service providers (this QoS information is propagated periodically), the Broker chooses the best candidate provider (Service Selection);

Figure 1. WSARCH: Web services architecture

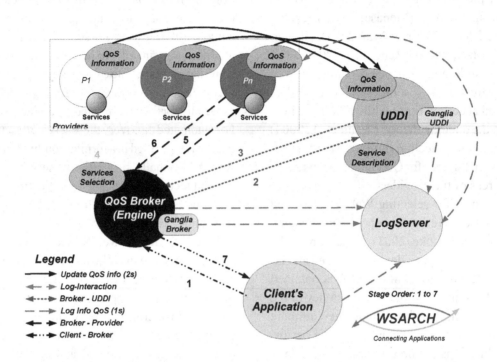

5.   After selecting the service, the Broker performs the request (invocation of Web Service) to the service provider;

After being made the request, the response is returned directly to the WSARCH Broker;

Finally, the response is sent to the client that originally requested the Web Service.

In addition to the steps relating to a service request, it is important to note that other activities occur in parallel with the request of the service client. The QoS information of service providers are updated periodically in the service registry Universal Description and Discovery Integration (UDDI) for each of the registered providers. The information is obtained through the use of the Ganglia Monitoring System (Massie, Chun & Culler, 2004) running in the service providers and also in the UDDI. The Ganglia also works if the UDDI is hosted by a third party and still allows the setting of permissions to access the information collected on the hosts. Service providers have slave monitors that collect and send information to a master monitor in the UDDI registry, so that the WSARCH Broker can use it as QoS information (performance index) for selecting the best service provider. Using this performance index the concept of Service Level Agreement (SLAs) becomes a key element. Although SLAs represent an additional responsibility for the service provider (it motivates the need of a SLA-Enforcement process in the WSARCH infrastructure) they can be seen as containers of the functional and non-functional properties that both parties (service consumer and the service provider) agree by specifying its rights and obligations during the interaction. It is essential to mention the role of the server log, which is responsible for storing all information about the WSARCH components in each experiment performed.

WSARCH Modules

The function of each WSARCH module is listed as follow:

- **Client Application:** The client application makes requests to the broker and specifies the QoS required;
- **Broker:** A number of sub-modules compose this module that it is responsible for offering information about QoS to the clients. When a SLA between client and service provider is established, the client can invoke the service directly to the service provider. One of the Broker sub-modules (QoS Manager) collects information that can be used to compute the response time for each service request and possibly other QoS attributes. Using such information, it is possible to incorporate two models (performance and price) into the Broker. The performance model returns a requirement describer. Pricing model is used to compute the price for service request depending on the required resources as specified in the resource describer and the pricing model.
- **Service Provider:** It contains the Web Services that will be requested by the client application. A classifier and an admission control compose this module. It has also a sub-module of QoS information, which sends messages to the Broker.
- **Log Server:** This module stores different information about the components of the architecture for each experiment, such as the time of interaction between the components of the architecture (search and selection time, WSDL (Web Services Description Language) parsing time, time taken to send requests from the broker to the provider, total execution time), information about the client request (name of service, selected provider, client identifica-

tion, identification of the execution related to an experiment), historical information about load and performance index of providers and broker, and others. Moreover, as the data experiments are stored into a relational database (MySQL Server), such information can be manipulated by using SQL commands in order to facilitate statistical analysis.

- **UDDI Server:** In most of the UDDI server proposed in the literature, this server is responsible for storing functional information of Web Services. For the purposes of WSARCH architecture the UDDI registry was modified to store dynamically non-functional information. In particular, non-functional information can be a QoS attribute used to describe some characteristic of an entity or component. The Ganglia Monitoring System (Massie, Chun & Culler, 2004) is used to collect the parameters related to the occupation of CPU and memory. The values of CPU and memory usage obtained by the monitoring tool are processed respectively in the CPU and the memory indices, which are normalized to build the performance index. This normalization enables that a new load index can be part of the index of performance. This index should be between the values of 0 and 1, meaning the closer to 0 the index is, the lower the overhead of the provider and the closer to 1, the greater will be the overhead. The performance index is sent periodically to the UDDI registry and associated with the WSDL of the service provider already registered. Thus, the index can be used by the Broker to select the best Web Service accordingly to the criteria desired by the client service. Different indices can be used by the WSARCH. The definition of performance indices should be based on the platform used and the QoS requirements defined by clients. Currently,

WSARCH implements an index when homogeneous service providers are considered and another one for heterogeneous service providers (Branco et al., 2006).

Additional Modules

Figure 2 presents a detailed WSARCH modular view, with the sub-modules that compose each one of the modules described in the previous section. In this section the client, broker and service provider sub-modules are detailed.

The Broker has all the sub-modules responsible for receiving the request; the definition of the provider that will perform the service and the routing of the request is as follows:

- **Client QoS Manager:** Receives a service request taking into account the parameters of QoS defined by the client application;
- **Search Manager:** Manages the research conducted by the UDDI registry, search-

ing for the type of service requested by the client application. Another function of this manager is to order the quality of service information (performance index) of the service provider and whether it has the suitable service.

- **Provider QoS Manager:** Receives information (processor, CPU load, memory, disk utilization) from the service provider through the search manager. The intermediary manager sub-module uses this information for further analysis.
- **Cache Module:** This module stores temporary information of the provider and its services. The advantage of using a cache is that a service previously consulted does not need to be searched again in the UDDI registry;
- **Provider QoS Descriptor:** Stores performance information in a standard format, collected and filtered by the QoS manager of service provider;

Figure 2. WSARCH: A modular view

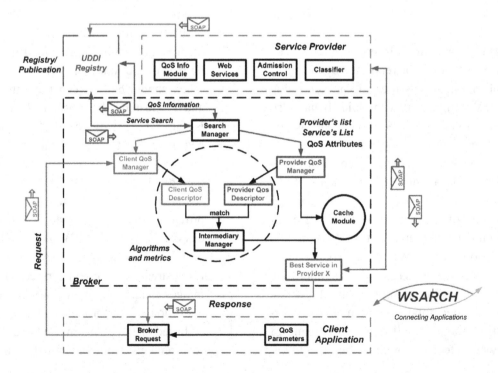

- **Client QoS Descriptor:** Uses QoS information obtained and filtered by the QoS manager of the service client;
- **Intermediary Manager:** Acts as an agent optimizer in order to realize the following tasks:
  - ○ Making the association of service (and characteristics) required by the client, with the availability of computing resources of providers running that service;
  - ○ Multiple providers to implement the same service can be available;
  - ○ Therefore, metrics and algorithms using the information of the QoS descriptors of the client and the provider to select the best possible service must be developed;
- **Best Service in Provider X (QoS Offer):** Must include the appropriate service that will be invoked by the WSARCH Broker.

The module that represents the client is shown with sub-modules as follow:

- **QoS Parameters:** Request (message) containing information (parameters) demanded by the client, in way that the requested service is executed adequately.
- **Broker Request:** Invocation of the service by the client through the Broker

The module representing the service provider presents the following components:

- **Provider QoS Information:** Is responsible for collecting information of performance of the service provider, in some periods. For example, memory utilization, CPU utilization, type of service in execution.
- **Web Services:** The service that will be invoked by the client.

- **Admission Control:** Controls the access to the service provider in order to avoid overloaded situation.
- **Classifier:** Used to classify the requests in accordance with the type of service requested.

WSARCH and QoS Attributes

When defining the attributes to be considered to achieve QoS in Web Services, it is important to verify how to apply QoS measures for both the client-side and the service provider side (Thio & Karunasekera, 2005). The use of QoS in Web Services presents a major relevance for allowing differentiation of similar services offered by different providers. The differentiation between the services offered by the providers offers to the customer the opportunity of choosing the most appropriate Web Service considering their requirements and of connecting to it at runtime.

This section discusses the attributes of QoS that should be mapped to allow that applications based on Web Services can communicate with quality. This mapping is particularly important because the convergence of application running on the web is currently usual. Therefore, the QoS offered to clients should be carefully addressed. Thus, the interaction between QoS and all the entities (client, provider and broker) has to be characterized.

The QoS attributes considered in the WSARCH architecture can be split in non-transactional and transactional attributes. Sections 3.2.1 and 3.2.2 present the most significant attributes considered. The WSARCH modules involved with the attribute considered are shown into parenthesis. Table 1 summarizes the relationship between WSARCH entities and QoS.

Table 1. WSARCH entities and QoS attributes

QoS Attributes	WSARCH Modules			
	Client	Provider	QoS Broker	UDDI
Response Time	X			
Throughput		X	X	X
Memory	X	X	X	X
Message Compression	X	X		
Network Latency	X	X	X	X
Service Composition	X	X	X	X
Availability		X	X	X
Service Cost			X	
Reliability		X	X	X
Service Class		X	X	
Provider Load		X	X	X
Latency		X	X	X
Reputation	X		X	
Security	X	X		X
Atomicity		X		X
Consistency		X		X
Isolation		X		X
Durability		X		X

Non-Transactional QoS Attributes

Non-transactional QoS refers to the attributes when single requests are considered. The most relevant attributes are:

- **Response Time (Client):** Very important when trying to assess what impact is visible to the client about the performance of the system and also features of the communication network. This response time can be the total response time, involving communication network in conjunction with the application, or only the time necessary for that particular service being completed;
- **Throughput (Provider, Broker, UDDI):** The ability of a particular service provider will present in terms of execution per time unit. This attribute depends on other factors, such as the capacity of processing, available memory, disk speed and application characteristics;
- **Main memory (Client, Provider, Broker, UDDI):** Both the amount of memory available and the access time are important in the response time returned to different applications;
- **Compression of messages (Client, Provider):** Compression of messages (Wu et al., 2003) is used to reduce the transmission time of messages exchanged between the entities. An appropriate heuristic that signalizes when to compress or not to compress a SOAP message in a SOA environment is discussed in Estrella et al. (2008).
- **Network Delay (Client, Provider, Broker, UDDI):** The transmission time required to receive the response from service

execution. The bandwidth attribute is also essential to the broker because it will decide whether a service should be invoked when a client uses lower bandwidth than usual.

- **Services Selection (Client, Provider, Broker):** Due to the dynamic nature of Web Services it is necessary to identify and implement techniques for selecting the most appropriate services based on requirements of QoS, especially when composing business processes;

- **Availability (Provider, Broker, UDDI):** The unavailability of a service can lead to problems during services composition. For example, to finalize a service composition, with proper QoS, a particular service needs to be available. The unavailability can be either due to software or hardware. To improve the availability of services in software it is suggested the use of optimization algorithms. Regarding the hardware unavailability, techniques such as Linux-HA (Linux High Availability) can be used. Linux-HA provides basic capacity for high availability (used in a wide range of platforms, supporting thousands of websites in critical mission in the world);

- **Cost of service (Broker):** Cost analysis is a key aspect to check the feasibility of establishing a quality of service for an application. The Web Services have different characteristics and the computation cost for each service will depend on those characteristics;

- **Reliability (Provider, Broker, UDDI):** Service selection that best fits the needs of the application;

- **Service Class (Provider, Broker):** A service class is a collection of Web Services with individual common functionality but different nonfunctional properties. For example, two services can accomplish the same task but differ in the value of a particular attribute of QoS. As the variety of business functionality is enormous it is impossible to formulate a concrete definition of the term. For example, some service read data, other write data, others might have access to one or multiple back ends and others perform complicated workflows. There is no sense to deal with all of them in the same way. The best way is to categorize the services when common differences between their properties become clear.

- **Server load (Provider, Broker, UDDI):** Number of service providers and the amount of simultaneous requests for each type of service. The quality of service perceived by the client may suffer degradation if there are not mechanisms that control the amount of requests supported by a service provider. In a real environment the service provider cannot directly expose their load for security reasons, but may present a metric for an external entity (broker) to indicate how it is loaded at any given moment. External entities can be configured to access this metric.

- **Latency (Provider, Broker, UDDI):** Time between the arrival of requests and response dispatch.

- **Reputation (Client, Broker):** Web Service reliability measure. It can be evaluated trusting on the experience of the client on a particular service.

- **Security (Client, Provider, UDDI):** This attribute can be used in interactions in which the components of WSARCH exchange secure information. Improper use of security measures or lack of them can degrade the system performance.

QoS Transactional Attributes

Transactional QoS refers to the level of reliability and consistency when transactions are executed.

These attributes are fundamental to maintain the Web Service integrity (Mani & Nagarajan, 2002) and are discussed briefly in this chapter. Firstly, it is considered the classic ACID properties (Atomicity, Consistency, Isolation, Durability). Further studies should be conducted to verify the need of applying other transactional attributes (presented in some works in the literature with different objectives) in the scope of WSARCH.

- **Atomicity (Provider, UDDI):** In an atomic transaction, all the stages necessary for their execution should be completed, otherwise the initial consistent state of the system is restored;
- **Consistency (Provider, UDDI):** A system should be in a consistent state before and after the transaction execution;
- **Isolation (Provider, UDDI):** The results of a transaction should be visible to other transactions only when it is committed. A transaction should run as if it was unaware of the occurrence of other ones;
- **Durability (Provider):** Once a transaction completes, the changes finalized should never be lost.

PERFORMANCE EVALUATION OF WSARCH ARCHITECTURE

Aiming at validating the proposed architecture and the attributes presented in the previous section, a prototype of the WSARCH was developed. The prototype allows carrying out performance evaluation studies, considering different components of the architecture, algorithms, protocols and standards. The purpose of this section is to describe the configuration considered for the prototype and the experimental design used to validate the WSARCH architecture. The validation adopts two approaches. The first is used to demonstrate that the architecture is functioning as designed through an analysis of the WSARCH behavior

(Section 5.1). Completing the verification of the WSARCH operation, sections 5.2 and 5.3 show how the Broker and the Log Server influence on the performance achieved by the services. The second approach aims at demonstrating how the proposed architecture achieves its goal of being a tool that enables performance evaluation of Web Services with QoS (Sections 5.4, 5.5 and 5.6).

The dynamic nature of both the architecture WSARCH and the prototype developed make possible the evaluation of a considerable number of experiments. Some possibilities were chosen to illustrate here how the proposed architecture works.

Environment Configuration

For a proper evaluation of the performance of a computer system, it is essential to know the elements of hardware and software used in the experimentation, since these elements may have a significant influence on the results. For hardware elements were considered processing units multicore (all homogeneous), used for processing messages on both client and service providers. Table 2 details the computing infrastructure used in the prototype. Seven processing units act as service providers, one processing unit acts as a record of information services, eight units of clients and one unit acts as the broker of the architecture. There is also one processing unit that corresponds to the log server, which stores information (at runtime) of all components during the experiments.

Table 3 describes the software elements used in the development of the architecture. For the software were used Java virtual machines, engines, SOAP message processing, server and client applications, Broker for routing SOAP messages, and some auxiliary applications. Table 3 emphasizes the software elements used as support tools and applications built effectively for the WSARCH design and implementation.

Table 2. Hardware elements used in the prototype

	Amount	Type
Service Provider	7 units	Intel QuadCore Q6600 2GB of RAM, HD 120GB, 7200 RPM
UDDI	1 unit	Intel QuadCore Q6600 2GB of RAM, HD 120GB, 7200 RPM
Broker	1 unit	Intel QuadCore Q9400 8GB of RAM, HD 500GB, 7200 RPM
Clients	8 units	4 units (Intel QuadCore Q9400 4GB of RAM, HD 750GB, 7200 RPM) e 4 units (Intel QuadCore Q6600 4GB of RAM, HD 320GB, 7200 RPM)
LogServer	1 unit	Intel QuadCore Q9400 4GB of RAM, HD 500GB, 7200 RPM

Experiment Design

Planning the experimental design is a key stage in the performance evaluation of computer systems and is not trivial since it is necessary to define what data, what amount and what condition the data should be collected during an experiment.

For the planning of an experiment, it is important to obtain the maximum information with the minimum number of experiments. Thus, it is possible to reduce considerably the effort that would be applied to make the experiments. A proper analysis of experiments also helps to separate the effects of various factors that may affect the performance. Furthermore, it is possible to determine whether a factor has significant effects on the performance, or whether the observed difference is simply because of not controlled parameters or variations caused by random errors of measurement (Jain, 1991). There are many terms used during the initial design and analysis of experiments, such as the response variable, factors, levels and interaction. The response variable represents the behavior of the system evaluated. The factors are

Table 3. Software elements

Name	Description
Apache Axis2 1.5.1	SOAP message engine processor
Apache Tomcat 6.0.20	Servlet Container
JUDDI 0.9	Java implementation of the OASIS UDDI Specification
Java Virtual Machine 1.6	Java Virtual Machine
Ganglia 3.1.2	Monitoring system distributed and scalable
MySQL Server 5.1	Management System Database (DBMS) used by JUDDI and also by the Broker WSARCH
WSARCH-Broker	Broker Architecture WSARCH
WSARCH-LoadInfoColetctor	Application developed to standardize the information obtained from the Ganglia Monitoring System
WSARCH-GeneralLoadIndex	Application developed to compose a load index to be used by the Broker in the selection of services
WSARCH-Client	Client applications developed for testing the Architecture
CPU-BoundApp	Application – CPU bound

Table 4. Factors and levels for the experiments

Factors	Levels
Log	ON/OFF
Workload - Time between request	3seg / 0 – 3seg / 0 – 1seg
Workload - Number of processes	1 / 6
Service Differentiation Algorithm	Classification / RSV
Service Execution Time	0,001seg / 3seg / 6seg
Client Type	50% Gold, 50% Bronze / 100% Gold / 100% Bronze

the system characteristics that affect the response variables. The values that a particular factor can assume are called levels. The interaction shows the dependence between factors.

In addition, the experimentation can be performed following three different designs: simple, full factorial and fractional factorial (Jain, 1991). In a simple design, an initial configuration is considered and one factor is changed at a time. This design does not allow the evaluation of the interaction between factors. In the full factorial design all combinations considering all factors and levels are used. The main problem with this approach is the computational cost because it generates a large number of experiments. The fractional factorial design considers a fraction of the full factorial design.

The WSARCH validation considered several experimental projects. Most of these projects follow the simple factorial design, since the goal of the performance evaluation of the WSARCH prototype was to check the operation of the components and the influence of isolated factors in the response variable chosen in the experiments. The verification of the interaction between all factors was not the objective at this stage of the performance evaluation. As the WSARCH is a distributed architecture and involves several components, many factors can and should be considered on performance evaluation in future studies.

The experiments presented in this chapter was conducted for the purpose of considering six

aspects of the prototype of WSARCH, i.e. validation of the architecture, overload generated by the use of the Log Server, overload generated by the use of the Broker, the influence of the workload, verification of the processing time on service providers and evaluation of the algorithms for service differentiation. To achieve these objectives, the factors and levels described in Table 4 were defined.

For all experiments were performed five executions used to determine the mean, standard deviation (SD) and the confidence interval of 95% according to the T-Student table. The number of executions has been set considering the need for significant difference among the confidence intervals of the experiments that involves the comparison of results. Table 5 summarizes all the experiments.

The experiment Exp001 refers to an initial experiment to highlight the functioning of the WSARCH architecture. The experiments Exp002 and Exp003 were performed to determine how Log Server could influence the results obtained with the execution of the experiments. The experiments Exp004 and Exp005 present the behavior of the architecture by varying the time between requests. The experiment Exp006 verifies how the processing time in service providers can influence the average response time perceived by the client application. The experiments Exp007 and Exp008 evaluate different algorithms for routing/ scheduling messages implemented in the Broker. For all experiments were considered eight clients

Table 5. Experiments

	Exp001	Exp002	Exp003	Exp004	Exp005	Exp006	Exp007	Exp008
Number of Clients	8	8	8	8	8	8	8	8
Client Type	50% Gold, 50% Bronze	100% Gold	100%Gold	50% Gold, 50% Bronze	50% Gold, 50% Bronze	100% Bronze	50% Gold, 50% Bronze	50% Gold, 50% Bronze
Number of processes	1	1	1	1	6	1	6	6
Service execution time	6s	3s	3s	0,001s	0,001s	0,001s	3s	3s
Time between requests	3s	0 – 3s	0 – 3s	0 – 3s	0 – 1s	0 – 3s	0 – 1s	0 – 1s
Algorithm (broker)	Classification	Classification	Classification	Classification	Classification	Classification	Classification	RSV(5G, 2B)
Log Information	Yes	Yes	No	Yes	Yes	Yes	Yes	Yes

and seven service providers. Each process considers the implementation of 200 service requests. All services are considered CPU-Bound. In this study, the Cluster behavior was characterized as Free, which indicates that during the experiments only the deployed applications in the service provider were running, without any influence of other external application. All clients were synchronized by time aiming at starting at the same time on each experiment using the Cron software. Cron is a time-based job scheduler in Unix-like operating systems used to schedule jobs to run automatically at a certain time or date. All experiments were executed with the QoS information of service providers updated periodically every 1-second in the service registry Universal Description and Discovery Integration (UDDI) for each of the registered providers.

In the experiments presented in this chapter, the workload is characterized by the time between requests and by the number of active processes per client. In these experiments, it was chosen to keep fixed the number of clients since other two factors are already being considered to characterize the

workload. A full characterization of the workload in Web Services is being considered in a specific work that investigates different factors that can influence the WSARCH performance.

For the initial prototype of the WSARCH architecture both client and service provider were implemented using the SOAP message API called Apache Axis2. The service used for the validation tests is characterized by performing a mathematical calculation which consumes CPU and returns a response to service client after processing it. The client application that accesses the service provider needs to pass as parameters the name of the service, the operation of the service, the processing time and a client class. The broker receives the parameters and selects the service provider, based on information from the UDDI and from a performance index associated with the client class that most closely matches the requirements of the client. After this selection, the broker will forward the request to the selected provider, which processes the service and then returns the response to the client.

ANALYSIS OF RESULTS

This section presents some results obtained with the WSARCH prototype. The experiments presented were conducted for the purpose of considering six aspects of the WSARCH prototype. The first aspect to consider is the validation of the architecture and the demonstration that the prototype achieves the objectives presented in the WSARCH specification. This validation is done through tests that follow the guidelines suggested by (Sargent, 2005) for validation of models. In the second aspect it is investigated if the Broker, on which relies almost all the WSARCH execution, can become a bottleneck in the system during the exchange of information over the components of the architecture. This assessment is presented in Section 5.2. The third aspect considered is the quantification of the overhead generated by the use of the LogServer. As WSARCH aims at evaluating the performance of service-oriented architectures, it is necessary to collect information about the time involved in completing each stage of treatment for a service. This assessment, described in Section 5.3, quantifies the overhead generated in this collection. Sections 5.4 to 5.6 refer to tests of validation of the WSARCH architecture for variation of the factors presented in Table 4. The fourth aspect considers the influence of the workload imposed on the architecture and is discussed in Section 5.4. The fifth part deals with the processing time in the service provider and this aspect is characterized in Section 5.5. Finally, it is considered the use of algorithms for differentiation of services implemented to make the scheduling/routing of messages in the WSARCH architecture.

Initial Tests

The results from the first test of the WSARCH architecture operation do not have comparative purposes and also there is no concern regarding the performance of the system. The main objective is the validation of the prototype, verifying if the information is being correctly propagated and if the architectural components are well integrated. Several experiments were performed in order to evaluate the behavior of the WSARCH. In those experiments were considered different levels to the factors defined. In all cases, it was possible to demonstrate the adequate behavior of the WSARCH. An experiment that shows a typical behavior of the WSARCH is examined aiming at demonstrating the operation of the architecture.

The first scenario analyzed refers to the experiment Exp001, using the classification algorithm. The testbed application is CPU-Bound, with half of its clients being for the Bronze Class as shown in Figure 3 and half of them as Gold Class, according to Figure 4 where each client runs a process that sends 200 requests.

The time between requests considered in this experiment is constant and equal to 3 seconds (uniform distribution). The application run takes about 6 seconds. As the experiments considered 7 service providers, there are not overload on service providers leading to a proper distribution of clients into them. Furthermore, this parameterization facilitates the evaluation of the results, aiming at validating the architecture. The graphs of Figures 3 and 4 show the distribution of requests according to the classification algorithm for each of these providers in the experiment. The average attendance for both Bronze and Gold clients has remained balanced for all providers, as it was expected due to the parameterization considered. The classification algorithm does not consider any resource reservation and only distributes requests according to the performance index. This means that considering all the providers, the one that provides the best index, i.e. closer to 0 (zero), will be chosen to process the requests of Gold class clients. In contrast, the provider with the performance index closer to 1 (one) will be chosen to process the requests of Bronze class clients. Several other experiments were made and also help to show that WSARCH presents the ex-

Figure 3. Requests: Client (broker) x provider

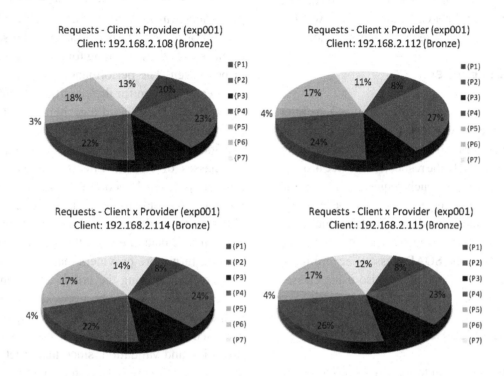

Figure 4. Requests: Client (gold) x provider

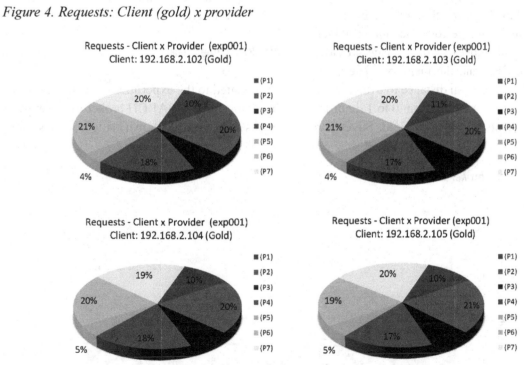

pected behavior. These experiments also validate the behavior of the architecture, and allow other conclusions as discussed in the next sections.

WSARCH Broker

The WSARCH Broker acts as a router/scheduler of SOAP messages received from the clients of the Web Services. All requests are reviewed before being forwarded to the respective service providers that can execute such requests. The criteria for routing/scheduling messages can be based on algorithms implemented in the Broker, which have distinct characteristics such as the selection using the contents of the SOAP message according to some header information and also using classes of applications.

Broker Service Selection Algorithm

In the initial Broker prototype two algorithms were implemented: the first one is called Classification Algorithm (CA), which only selects service providers based on a performance index (which is composed of indices of the service provider for both the CPU and the memory). The algorithm uses the Euclidian distance to evaluate the performance index ranging from 0 to 1, in order to classify clients into classes Gold, Silver and Bronze. The Gold class will be served when the performance index is close to 0 (zero). For clients in the Bronze class, the performance index should be close to 1 (one) signaling for the worst feature to be chosen. The performance index closer to the mean is chosen for the classification into the Silver class. The second algorithm called RSV (Resource Reservation Algorithm) is a variant of the first one, which goal is to reserve a resource for classes of clients. Clients will have their requests processed according to the number of providers available for each class of clients. The clients of the Gold class will have more providers available than clients of the Silver class and these in turn more providers than clients of the Bronze class. Among the providers assigned to this class it chooses the best provider according to the performance index. The two algorithms proposed in this work aimed at the WSARCH execution and validation, since the structure of the Broker software enables the construction of new algorithms for routing/scheduling messages more effectively.

Broker Overhead

Still related to the experiment Exp001, a typical behavior of the WSARCH broker for all experiments in this study is shown in Figure 5. It is noted

Figure 5. Typical broker behavior

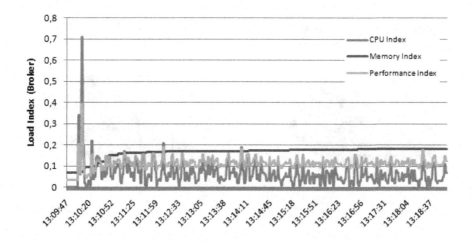

that the workload imposed on the Broker architecture causes no degradation on the performance of the architecture. Both indices, ICcpu (CPU) and ICmemory (Memory) are presented. The variations of CPU and memory measured in the broker architecture are derived in the same way on service providers, so that the broker can use them to select the best Web Service in accordance with the client class.

The graph in Figure 5 shows that at the beginning of the experiment has some variation in rates of CPU and memory. After some time, the rates are stabilized at low levels (less than 0.15). Even during the warm-up the rates do not exceed 0.24. Table 6 complements the information from the graph in Figure 5 which shows the behavior of the Broker architecture in three separate experiments. The data of mean and standard deviation (SD) show that even occurring variation in the data entry for Web Services (Exp002 and Exp004), the variation in the time between requests (for Exp004 and Exp005) and the variation in the number of clients, the Broker architecture does not suffer overload in terms of CPU and memory, which shows a performance index near zero.

In general, dropping the initial range (initial warm-up of the experiment) the performance index of the WSARCH Broker was below 0.1. Note as well that the main contribution to the increase/decrease in the performance index is the factor memory, since this feature is massively used by XML message processors to extract information from the SOAP messages sent/received by clients and service providers. The behavior shown in the results confirms that the Broker does not represent a bottleneck for the WSARCH architecture.

Log Overhead

All activities of the components of the WSARCH architecture, including processing time in the service providers, response time of requests from clients, search time, time of services selection, parser time, among others, are stored in a Log-Server. It is important to note that the inclusion/exclusion of LogServer does not compromise the functioning of the architecture. That is, if the LogServer is excluded, the interactions between the components remain the same. However, to evaluate the overall performance of the architecture and its components was essential to include the LogServer that stores information about time, processing, flow, etc. The inclusion of a LogServer generates an additional overload (S) in the activities of the WSARCH, as can be seen in the heuristic presented in equations 1, 2, 3 and 4.

$$S_{BROKER} = S_{ACCESSBroker} + S_{QOSCalc} \qquad (1)$$

$$S_{WSARCH} = S_{BROKER} + S_{LOG} \qquad (2)$$

$$S_{SOA} = S_{UDDI} + S_{PARSER} + S_{ACCESSProvider} \qquad (3)$$

$$S_{TOTAL} = S_{SOA} + S_{WSARCH} \qquad (4)$$

According to equations 1 to 4 it is possible to observe that the additional overhead generated by LogServer can be obtained from the difference between S_{WSARCH} - S_{BROKER} and observed in the

Table 6. Mean and standard deviation for broker behavior

	Exp002		Exp004		Exp005	
	Mean	**SD**	**Mean**	**SD**	**Mean**	**SD**
CPU Index	0,0185	0,0111	0,02531	0,01229	0,03490	0,02962
Memory Index	0,0885	0,0021	0,14740	0,01980	0,16572	0,02610
Performance Index	0,0535	0,0057	0,08635	0,01249	0,10031	0,2246

Figure 6. WSARCH architecture with LogServer (ON/OFF)

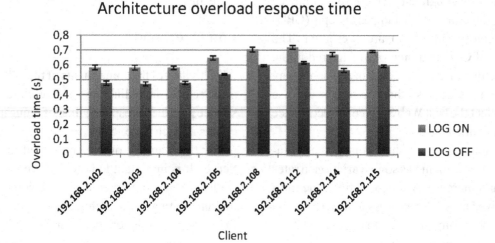

results presented in the graph in Figure 6, related to experiments Exp002 and Exp003.

The overload of the LogServer is generated on the basis of various approaches to writing information in a relational database that stores all data from experiments. Table 7 summarizes the percentage increase in the WSARCH overhead and highlights that the maximum influence of the LogServer on the overhead time of the architecture does not exceed 23%.

In general, this overhead does not affect the processing time of SOAP messages in service providers as noted in the graph of Figure 7, but the total response time perceived by the client of the architecture. Analyzing the graph in Figure 7, the conclusion is that there is no statistical difference between the time of the experiment with the LogServer enabled or disabled.

Response Time on Service Providers

The results discussed in this Section are for two experiments in which the processing in service providers suffers variation. The experiment Exp002 corresponds to an application that runs 3 seconds on average while the experiment Exp006

Table 7. Mean and standard deviation of WSARCH behavior related to LogServer

	LOG (ON)		LOG (OFF)		% of Increase
	Mean	SD	Mean	SD	
192.168.2.102 (Gold)	0,5827	0,0152	0,4769	0,0142	22,19
192.168.2.103 (Gold)	0,5818	0,1590	0,4733	0,0130	22,92
192.168.2.104 (Gold)	0,5809	0,0112	0,4803	0,0104	20,93
192.168.2.105 (Gold)	0,6470	0,0135	0,5373	0,0050	20,41
192.168.2.102 (Bronze)	0,7035	0,0158	0,5963	0,0058	17,98
192.168.2.112 (Bronze)	0,7179	0,0012	0,6156	0,0074	16,60
192.168.2.114 (Bronze)	0,6712	0,0142	0,5652	0,0129	18,74
192.168.2.115 (Bronze)	0,6922	0,0077	0,5940	0,0077	16,53

Figure 7. WSARCH behavior related to processing time in service providers

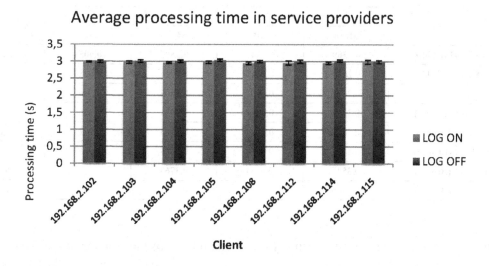

corresponds to an execution time of 0.001 second in the service provider. The values of execution time are determined according to an input parameter sent by the client application, so that when the SOAP message is stripped off in the provider, the parameter sent by the client is used by the service in execution. The service receives the parameter and makes a computation that indicates high CPU usage.

The conclusion obtained from the experiments conducted in this phase, maintaining the same flow of requests for the two experiments, is that the processing time in providers has little influence on the overhead imposed by the architecture as shown in Figure 8. The data relating to Exp006 experiment show that in this situation, the overhead is higher in relation to the data from the experiment Exp002. This is because the service capacity of the Broker architecture is high in terms

Figure 8. WSARCH overload related to variation of processing time in service providers

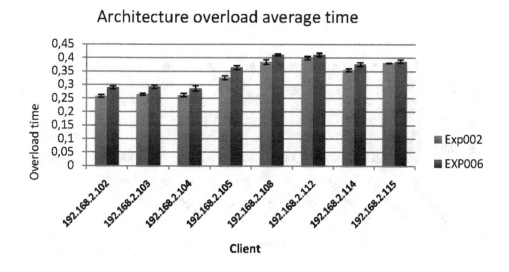

Table 8. Mean and standard deviation of WSARCH behavior related to variation of requests time

	Exp002		Exp006		% of Increase
	Mean	**SD**	**Mean**	**SD**	
192.168.2.102 (Gold)	**0,2569**	**0,0049**	**0,2895**	**0,0054**	**12,70**
192.168.2.103 (Gold)	0,2644	0,0040	0,2921	0,0057	10,44
192.168.2.104 (Gold)	0,2611	0,0061	0,2863	0,0091	9,68
192.168.2.105 (Bronze)	0,3262	0,0074	0,3631	0,0068	11,32
192.168.2.102 (Bronze)	0,3846	0,0086	0,4103	0,0034	6,68
192.168.2.112 (Bronze)	0,3992	0,0054	0,4109	0,0062	2,93
192.168.2.114 (Bronze)	0,3541	0,0054	0,3763	0,0070	6,29
192.168.2.115 (Bronze)	0,3806	0,0009	0,3867	0,0057	1,61

of computational resources (CPU and memory) as discussed in Section 5.2.2.

The influence of processing time in the system overhead is more evident in Table 8, which presents data regarding the mean, and SD of the experiments discussed. When the processing time is increased by three thousand times, the system overload has increased by less than 12.7%. This is due to the fact that the overhead to execute the services has little influence on the processing time of the request.

The average response time is modified in proportion to the processing time, since it is a component of the response time. That is, when the processing time increases, the logic is that the response time perceived by end user (client) also increases, as shown in the graph in the Figure 9.

Workload Influence

In order to show the behavior of the WSARCH architecture considering the change in workload two experiments were carried out. In the first experiment (Exp004), the time between requests follows a uniform distribution between 0 and 3s with only one active process per client sending

Figure 9. Mean response time of WSARCH for different clients

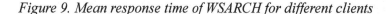

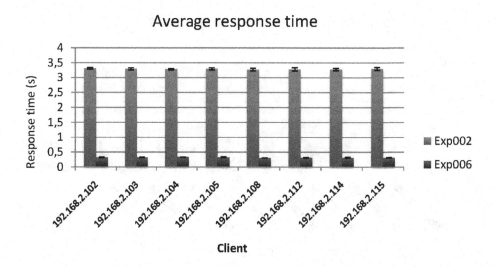

Figure 10. WSARCH overload according to response time variations between requests

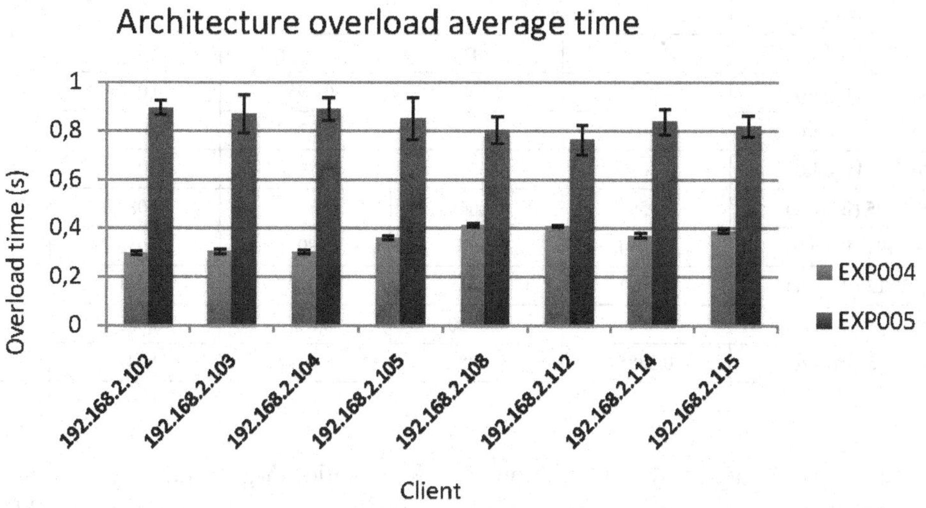

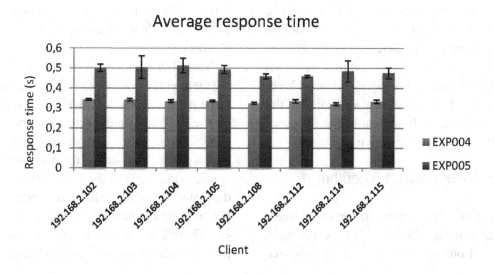

Architecture overload average time

requests to the Broker. The experiment Exp005 presents a time between requests following a uniform distribution between 0 and 1s and six active processes by clients sending requests to the Broker.

Aiming at evaluating the influence of the workload on the results of the architecture, the overload and the average response time were analyzed. The graph in Figure 10 shows how

the architecture has a larger overhead when the workload is increased.

In turn, the graph of Figure 11 highlights how the variation of the time between requests caused a negative impact on the average response time for each client participating in the experiment.

In Table 9, the behavior of the mean and SD for five executions for each of the participating clients of the experiments are presented. In addition, it is shown that the percentage increases in

Figure 11. Average response time for experiments Exp004 and Exp005

Average response time

Table 9. Mean and standard deviation of WSARCH behavior related to variation of requests time

	Exp004		Exp005		% of Increase
	Mean	**SD**	**Mean**	**SD**	
192.168.2.102 (Gold)	0,2975	0,0083	0,8952	0,0308	200,90
192.168.2.103 (Gold)	0,3033	0,0107	0,8708	0,0793	187,10
192.168.2.104 (Gold)	0,3016	0,0088	0,8904	0,0473	195,17
192.168.2.105 (Bronze)	0,3591	0,0068	0,8507	0,0860	136,85
192.168.2.102 (Bronze)	0,4094	0,0072	0,8035	0,0564	96,26
192.168.2.112 (Bronze)	0,4081	0,0038	0,7627	0,0613	86,86
192.168.2.114 (Bronze)	0,3690	0,0100	0,8373	0,0536	126,93
192.168.2.115 (Bronze)	0,3885	0,0087	0,8194	0,0421	110,89

relation to the overhead caused by the variation of the time parameter among the request and also due to the number of active processes.

For the results presented were considered an average of five executions with a confidence interval of 95% according to the T-Student table. In the next section the results of message scheduling algorithms will be detailed.

Message Scheduling Algorithm

An important test also conducted to validate the WSARCH architecture considers algorithms of routing/scheduling messages. The implemented algorithms have simple features and work as proof of concept to verify the occurrence of service differentiation. Due to the modular characteristic of the WSARCH architecture, new scheduling algorithms can be implemented in the Broker architecture considering techniques such as, artificial intelligence, ontologies, semantic Web, among others. In the context of validation of the architecture, one configuration of the Resource Reservation Algorithm (RSV) is discussed.

Resource Reservation Algorithm

In connection with implementation of the algorithms of routing/scheduling, one experiment was carried out based on the use of Resource Reservation Algorithm. The experiment Exp008 uses 5 providers for clients of Gold class and 2 providers for clients of Bronze class.

The results illustrate effectively the services differentiation with the usage of the resource reservation algorithm, since there are differences in relation to the amount of resources for the Gold class and Bronze class, as shown by the graphs of Figures 12 and 13.

The redistribution of resources must contribute to a better quality of service for clients of Gold class by improving the total response average time, SOA overload time, and the processing time in service providers in relation to clients of the Bronze class.

In the graph of Figure 14 it is visible the service differentiation to clients in respect of the Gold Class when compared with clients of the Bronze Class.

The differentiation also appears when analyzing the average time of SOA elements, according to the graph in Figure 15. Considering the overload on the WSARCH architecture, as shown in the graph in Figure 16, it is observed that the average time is greater for clients of the Bronze class when compared to those of the Gold Class. Clients in the Gold Class were performed on machines with better hardware, according to data from Table 2, contributing to the increase in overhead when it is considered clients of the Bronze class and re-

Figure 12. Resource reservation algorithm with 2 provider of bronze class

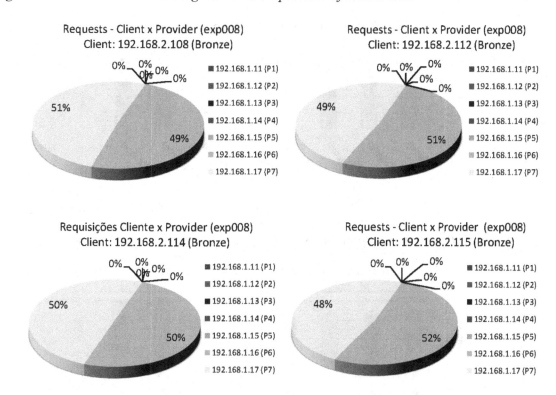

Figure 13. Average response time for experiments Exp004 and Exp005

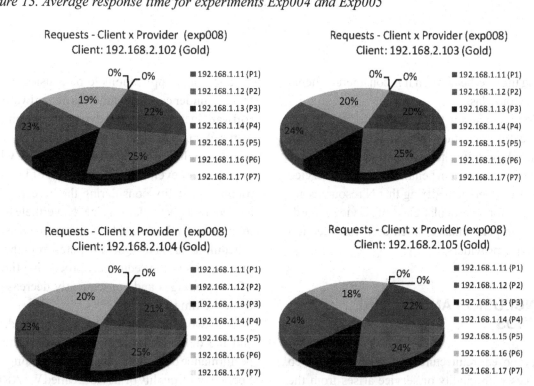

Figure 14. Service differentiation for different clients

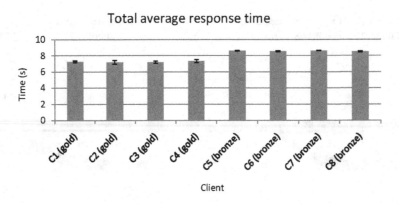

Figure 15. Service differentiation considering SOA elements

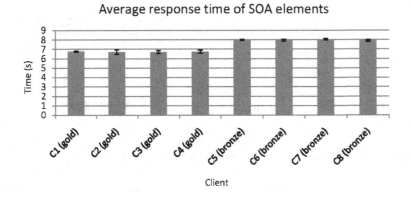

ducing the overhead when it is considered clients of the Gold class.

Complementing the results referring to the service differentiation, the data described in Figure 17 show how the distribution of resources made by the algorithm penalizes a class of service against another, considering that N resources are available for a particular class of service according to the performance index used for selection of service providers.

CONCLUSION AND FUTURE TRENDS

The proposed architecture for the provision of Web Services with quality of service arises from the need to allow applications to be considered differently under certain conditions of hardware and software in a complex and dynamic environment as the Web. An original SOA for Web Services does not include a SOAP messages Broker, which in practice prevents the applications of having a minimum quality considering the perception of a client of a particular service. Nevertheless, the inclusion of a Broker and techniques of messages scheduling based on QoS attributes from the service providers can reduce the processing time of SOAP messages and consequently decrease the response time.

This work presented the results of validation and the demonstration of how to evaluate the performance of an architecture for providing Web Services with quality of services called WSARCH.

Figure 16. Service differentiation considering WSARCH overload

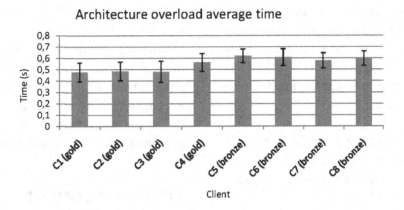

Figure 17. Service differentiation considering the mean response time

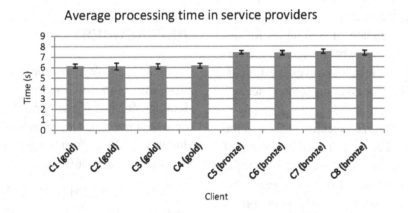

Initially were discussed the configuration of the environment and validation tests involving hardware and software parameters, an experimental design according to the validation of the architecture, the overhead generated by the new components added in an original SOA and the algorithms for differentiation of services. The integration of a broker of services within an original SOA structure has also been properly approached. It is important to emphasize that the results presented in this work provide a basis for comparisons with new algorithms that can be implemented in the Broker architecture, other propagation techniques of non-functional QoS requirements between

the components of the architecture, among others. The WSARCH uses the functional and the non-functional requirements to distribute the services among the providers. The use of both the functional and non-functional requirements is a starting point when handling with non-functional issues in service oriented and particularly highly distributed environments. Unlike other proposals found in the literature and referred to in this work and many others not mentioned here, the WSARCH has been designed and implemented and some results were presented.

In the performance evaluation many situations were discussed: Broker overload, LogServer overhead, processing time in service providers, workload and service differentiation algorithms used to schedule SOAP messages to appropriate service providers according to a QoS attribute defined in the experiments. As the WSARCH has a modular structure, new improvements can be implemented, such as:

- The creation of service level agreements (SLA) between clients and providers and how will be the behavior of the architecture with these SLAs;
- The implementation and testing of new scheduling algorithms for the message broker;
- The establishment of a mechanism for the generation of different workloads aiming at studying the behavior of WSARCH;
- The implementation of techniques for negotiating requests between service providers and clients, which involves creating algorithms for processes requests in service classes;
- The incorporation of security aspects in the interactions between the components of WSARCH architecture. Security is a topic that was not explored in the original proposal of the architecture and it is important to consider this aspect for the evolution of the architecture, since this is of fundamental importance for the exchange of secure messages between Web Services from different organizations;
- The investigation of mechanisms for fault tolerance associated with the components of the architecture; the inclusion of a module for dynamic service composition, in order to deal with issues such as the evolution of services (changes, updates) and how it can degrade the quality of service needed to make business processes more robust and reliable.

Based on experience in modeling and implementing a SOA with QoS support, it is possible to highlight that the main difficulties are related to two levels: the first level involves the mapping of performance problems in service-oriented environments (XML parsers, message processing engines, etc.) and the second level involving the setting and configuration of the computing environment for the tests presented in this chapter.

ACKNOWLEDGMENT

This chapter provides an overview of work that has been fully supported by the FAPESP (São Paulo Research Foundation), grant 06/55207-5

REFERENCES

Andrea, V. D., & Benatallah, B. (2006). Report from the composition group. In F. Cubera, B. J. Kramer, & M. P. Papazoglou (Eds.), *Service oriented computing (SOC), number 05462*. Retrieved January 1, 2011, from http://drops.dagstuhl.de/opus/volltexte/2006/520

Ardagna, D., & Pernici, B. (2005). Global and local QoS constraints guarantee in web service selection. In *Proceedings of the IEEE International Conference on Web Services (ICWS'05)*. IEEE CS Press.

Branco, K., Santana, M., Santana, R., & Bruschi, S. (2006). PIV and WPIV: Performance index for heterogeneous systems evaluation. In *2006 IEEE International Symposium on Industrial Electronics,* volume 1, (pp. 323–328).

Comuzzi, M., & Pernici, B. (2005). An architecture for flexible web service qos negotiation. In *EDOC '05: Proceedings of the Ninth IEEE International EDOC Enterprise Computing Conference*, (pp. 70–82). IEEE Computer Society.

Dorn, C., Schall, D., & Dustdar, S. (2009). A model and algorithm for self-adaptation in service-oriented systems. *European Conference on Web Services*, (pp. 161–170).

Erradi, A., & Maheshwari, P. (2005). A broker-based approach for improving web services reliability. In *ICWS '05: Proceedings of the IEEE International Conference on Web Services*, (pp. 355–362). IEEE Computer Society.

Estrella, J. C., Santana, M. J., Santana, R. H. C., & Monaco, F. J. (2008). Real time compressing soap messages in a SOA environment. In: *SIGDOC '08: Proceedings of the 26th Annual ACM International Conference on Design of Communication*, (pp. 163–168). New York, NY: ACM.

Hundling, J. (2006). Towards a meta-model for service properties. In F. Cubera, B. J. Kramer, & M. P. Papazoglou (Eds.), *Service oriented computing (SOC), number 05462*. Retrieved January 1, 2011, from http://drops.dagstuhl.de/opus/volltexte/2006/529

Jaeger, M. C., & Ladner, H. (2005). Improving the QoS of WS compositions based on redundant services. In: *NWESP '05: Proceedings of the International Conference on Next Generation Web Services Practices*, (p. 189). IEEE Computer Society.

Jaeger, M. C., Muhl, G., & Golze, S. (2005). Qos-aware composition of web services: A look at selection algorithms. In *ICWS '05: Proceedings of the IEEE International Conference on Web Services*, (pp. 807–808). IEEE Computer Society.

Jain, R. K. (1991). *The art of computer systems performance analysis: Techniques for experimental design, measurement, simulation, and modeling*. Wiley.

Kalepu, S., Krishnaswamy, S., & Loke, S. W. (2003). Verity: A QoS metric for selecting Web services and providers. In *International Conference on, Web Information Systems Engineering Workshops*, (pp. 131–139).

Mani, A., & Nagarajan, A. (2002). *Understanding quality of service for Web services*. Retrieved January 1, 2011, from http://www.ibm.com/developerworks/library/ws-quality.html

Massie, M. L., Chun, B. N., & Culler, D. E. (2004). The Ganglia distributed monitoring system: Design, implementation, and experience. *Parallel Computing, 30*(7). doi:10.1016/j.parco.2004.04.001

Menasce, D. (2004). Response time analysis of composite web services. *IEEE Internet Computing, 8*(1), 90–92. doi:10.1109/MIC.2004.1260710

Orta, E., Ruiz, M., & Toro, M. (2009). A system dynamics approach to web service capacity management. In *European Conference on Web Services*, (pp. 109–117).

Papazoglou, M. P. (2005). Extending the service-oriented architecture. Retrieved January 1, 2011, from http://arno.uvt.nl/ show.cgi?fid= 106521

Sargent, R. G. (1999) Validation and verification of simulation models. In: *WSC '99: Proceedings of the 31st Conference on Winter Simulation*, (pp. 39–48). New York, NY: ACM.

Thio, N., & Karunasekera, S. (2005). Automatic measurement of a QoS metric for Web service recommendation. In *ASWEC '05: Proceedings of the 2005 Australian conference on Software Engineering*, (pp. 202–211). IEEE Computer Society.

Tian, M., Voight, T., Naumowicz, T., Ritter, H., & Schiller, J. (2004). Performance considerations for mobile web services. *Elsevier Computer Communications Journal, 27*(1), 1097–1105.

Wang, X., Yue, K., Huang, J. Z., & Zhou, A. (2004). Service selection in dynamic demand-driven web services. In: *ICWS '04: Proceedings of the IEEE International Conference on Web Services*, (p. 376). IEEE Computer Society.

Woodside, M., & Menasce, D. A. (2006). Guest editors' introduction: Application-level QoS. *IEEE Internet Computing, 10*(3), 13–15. doi:10.1109/MIC.2006.49

Wu, C.-H., Su, D.-C., Chang, J., Wei, C.-C., Lin, K.-J., & Ho, J.-M. (2003). The design and implementation of intelligent transportation Web services. In *IEEE International Conference on E-Commerce Technology (CEC'03)*, (pp. 49-52).

Yeom, G., & Min, D. (2005). Design and implementation of web services QoS broker. In *International Conference on Next Generation Web Services Practices*, (pp. 454–455).

Zeng, L., Benatallah, B., Dumas, M., Kalagnanam, J., & Sheng, Q. Z. (2003). Quality driven web services composition. In *WWW '03: Proceedings of the 12th international conference on World Wide Web*, (pp. 411–421). New York, NY: ACM.

KEY TERMS AND DEFINITIONS

Message Scheduling: it is an activity performed by an element named broker (scheduler) of a distributed system that makes use of contexts of messages or any kind of information that can be used to determine priorities.

Performance Evaluation: Technique used to evaluate the performance of computer systems.

Quality of Service: Ability to offer greater quality assurance for applications in a specific area of work.

Service Differentiation: It is one of the mechanisms for implementing flexibility in Service-Oriented Architecture involving information quality, security and costumer segmentation.

SOA: Service Oriented Architecture.

Web Services: Services implemented in Application Servers.

Workload: The amount of work assigned to or expected from a worker in a specified time period. In the WSARCH domain refers to the amount of requests sent per unit time to the broker architecture by the clients.

Chapter 17
Business Continuity Management of Business Driven IT Landscapes

Ulrich Winkler
SAP Research Belfast, UK

Wasif Gilani
SAP Research Belfast, UK

ABSTRACT

Businesses and enterprises depend more than ever on Information and Communication Technologies (IT) landscapes. Business processes are vulnerable to disruptions caused by failures in IT landscapes. Business Continuity Management addresses this problem and tries to identify potential threats and determine strategies and responses to overcome or mitigate a possible business disruption.

The overall objectives of this book chapter are (a) to provide an introduction of Business Continuity Management, (b) to discuss the importance of business continuity in a service-oriented IT environment, (c) highlight and discuss major challenges and approaches to translate business requirements and objectives down to BCM related service level terms and metrics and (e) identify requirements, such as modelling methodologies or analyses, to enable such translations.

INTRODUCTION

New emerging technologies, such as virtualisation, web-services and cloud computing have created whole new business ecosystems, in which business processes depend more than ever on IT services provided by partner organisations.

Often, disruptions in services delivery affect immediately thousands of business customers and consumers. For example, on January, 4th 2010, *SalesForce,* a company offering online enterprise support services, experienced an outage for over an hour which effected 68'000 business customers (Miller, 2010). Another example would be *Paypal*, a service to process online payments. *Paypal* was down for 4.5 hours worldwide on August, 4th

DOI: 10.4018/978-1-61350-432-1.ch017

2009. *Paypal* usually processes 2'000 USD per second for its customers.

Disruptions do not only have a financial impact or cause damage to reputation; they may also have legal consequences. In particular key industrial sectors, such as energy, gas, oil, pharmacy or finance, have to demonstrate business continuity competence, which is sometimes required by regulations and laws. An interesting study to quantify IT business continuity risks at Essent Netwerk, a Dutch electricity and gas distributer, revealed, that a four hour outage of an IT landscape would cost 5 million EUR, and might result in a withdrawal of the licences to operate, which would be even worst (Wijnia & Nikolic, 2007).

Business Continuity Management addresses these problems and aims to:

- Identify potential threats to business processes, IT system, services and operations,
- Assess the business impact of an adverse event, estimate probabilities and compute risk exposures,
- Determine strategies and responses to these threats, and model a business continuity plan to overcome or mitigate a possible business disruption.

In service-oriented systems, where business support systems and solutions are provided by partner organisations as services, the Business Continuity Manager has to further define *Service Level Agreements (SLA).*

However, in order to define adequate SLAs the Business Continuity Manager faces several challenges. First he has to understand the business, business processes and the impact of business disruptions. He has to take not only financial indicators into consideration, but also other non-financial Key Performance Indicators (KPIs), such as customer churn rate, customer satisfaction, etc, other business objectives/targets and legal obligations, e.g. BASEL II (Basel Committee on Banking Supervision, 2005) or Sarbanes Oxley (107th Con-

gress, 2002). Second, he has to determine various Business Continuity Metrics for every business process and business function. For example the Business Continuity Manager has to determine the Maximum Tolerable Outage Time (MTO) of a given business process. Third, the dependency and risk graph is used to translate business-level BCM metrics down to Service Level Agreements terms and penalties. For example the MTO of a business process is translated down to *Return Time Objective* (RTO) or *Recovery Point Objective* of services the process depends on. SLA penalties can be derived from the estimated business impact.

BACKGROUND

Business Continuity Management is standardised by the British Standards Institution (BSI) and formally defined as follows:

A holistic management process that identifies potential threats to an organization and the impacts to business operations that those threats, if realized, might cause, and which provides a framework for building organizational resilience with the capability for an effective response that safeguards the interests of its key stakeholders, reputation, brand and value-creating activities (Smith, 2002)

The business continuity lifecycle is a closed-loop and comprises four groups of activities, which are (1) understanding the organisation, (2) determining Business Continuity Strategies, (3) developing and implementing a BCM response, and (4) exercising, maintaining and reviewing BCM arrangements.

All four activities are organised by a fifth activity, the BC Program Management, which initiates business continuity related projects, assigns responsibilities, observes and manages activities, conducts training, and provides documentation.

The remainder of this chapter is organised as follows: we use these four activities of the Business Continuity lifecycle to provide background information, discuss related work, controversies, problems and open research challenges that need to be addressed. Then, we talked about two distinguish, but complementary analysis methodologies deployed by Business Continuity Management, followed by a discussion of three current research projects. Hereby we will focus on non-functional properties and their importance for Business Continuity Management and Information Systems. We also aim to identify open problems that hinder Business Continuity Manager to conduct thorough analysis and to develop non-functional requirements for business processes and IT landscapes. We close this chapter with a condensed summary of open problems and issues.

UNDERSTANDING THE ORGANISATION

This activity aims to provide information that enables Business Continuity Managers to (1) identify critical business processes, stakeholders, assets, resources and internal/external dependencies (2) identify potential threats to critical business values and business performance and (3) assess and evaluate potential damages or losses that may be caused by an adverse event to critical business processes. Business Continuity Managers refer to these activities as *Business Impact Analysis* and *Dependency and Risk Analysis (DA/RA)*.

Business Impact Analysis: The Business Impact Analysis (BIA) is a crucial tool used by a business continuity manager to better understand the business of an organisation. The overall objectives of BIA are to (1) identify critical business processes, business values, important performance objectives and (2) assess and evaluate potential damages or losses to these critical performance values, financial and non-financial alike. Essentially, BIA is sensitivity analysis that systemati-

cally evaluates how changes in the behaviour of business processes affect non-functional properties of a business. Nowadays this is done in a manual fashion where the business continuity managers tend to gather information about business processes via questionnaires and interviews (Heng, 2008). Afterwards impact analysis is done using standard office tools, such as Microsoft Excel. This manual approach is time-consuming, cumbersome and error-prone, in particular for large enterprises. Large and globally operating enterprises deploy up to hundreds of different business processes, spanning different functional areas of an enterprise. Some of these business processes are complex and not all processes are well documented and IT supported. Business processes can change and evolve over time or can exist in regional variants. For example, Coca Cola's business process management program includes over 50 cross-functional business processes in 36 variants, involving 6500 users in all functional areas (Silver, 2009). Business continuity managers are not able to develop a current, accurate and complete analysis solely based on interviews and questionnaires; they require tooling, analysis and modelling support that integrates business process management and business impact analysis.

Besides (implicit) obligations towards customers, organisations and businesses often have legal obligations towards governments or regulation bodies. In particular financial, pharmacy, healthcare or gas and oil industries have strict obligations to demonstrate business continuity competence. As stated previously, Wijnia and Nikolic, 2007, identified a potential disruption in a specific business process of ESSENT NETWERK. This disruption could have been ignored from the financial perspective, but from the legal perspective the government could have withdrawn the license to operate from the company effectively taking ESSENT NETWERK out of business. Although laws and regulations are of importance for businesses and business continuity, these are out of scope for this chapter. However, we provide a list of relevant laws, regulations and selected publications in the section [sec:Further Readings].

Dependency and Risk Analysis: The business continuity manager does not only has to understand the effects of an adverse incident on a business, he also has to understand dependencies among business processes, dependent resources and possible root-causes of an adverse incident.

To carry out a dependency and risk analysis the business continuity manager has to identify stakeholders, assets, resources and relations to external parties on which a business process depends. Furthermore, he needs to understand and analyse the nature and significance of dependencies. For example, the analyst needs to understand how a broken air-conditioning unit may affect the datacentre and servers deployed in that datacentre.

Business Continuity Strategies

First, the business continuity manager has to understand, estimate, and quantify risk probabilities of threats. Second, he has to determine the acceptable minimum level of business process operations to mitigate the business impact. He also has to specify acceptable timeframes (BCM metrics) in which a normal level of operations has to be restored, such that the organisation can continue to deliver products and services.

Return Time Objective and *Recovery Point Objective* are examples of BCM metrics. The Recovery Point Objective (RPO) defines "the maximum amount of data loss an organization can sustain during an event". It is also the point in time (prior to outage) in which systems and data must be restored to (Spremic & Popovic, 2008). Return Time Objective (RTO) defines the "target time for resumption of product, service or activity delivery after an incident" (BSI, 2006). In addition there exist other BCM related metrics; some are commonly used in Business Continuity Management, others are organisation or business specific. A discussion and overview about BCM related metrics is given in (Asnar & Giorgini,

2008; Spremic & Popovic, 2008; Brooks et al., 2007; Harper, Lawler & Thornton, 2005).

Development and Implementation of Business Continuity Responses

The business continuity manager can put four responses against a risk in place: to remove a risk, to mitigate the adverse effects of a risk, to transfer the risk responsibility to third parties, or to do nothing at all and simply accept the risk. The business continuity manager has to develop a *recovery plan* if a decision is made not to accept the risk. The recovery plan details the steps to be taken to maintain or restore business operations to defined levels of operations within given timeframes. A business process manager should also be able to analyse a recovery plan. He has to prove that a recovery plan is valid. Furthermore, he has to make sure that the recovery plan is robust and is less dependent on uncertain estimations made in the dependency and risk model. This could be achieved by sensitivity analysis. A recovery plan might depend on resources and might be vulnerable to threats itself. Therefore, a business continuity manger should be able to model and analyse dependencies and threats to recovery plans in a similar way as he is able to do with business processes. The business continuity manger also has to make sure that recovery plans are dead-lock or live-lock free.

If the business continuity manager decides to transfer the risks to third parties or if a business process depends on external service providers in the first place, the Business Continuity Manager may specify *Service Level Agreements*. This means, he has to detail objectives encoded in a SLA and he has to specify penalties in case the service provider is not able to fulfil the agreements made. The exact penalties (or incentives) should be derived from the Business Impact Analysis. The manager needs a methodology to translate business level BCM metric and objectives down to individual ICT elements BCM objectives. For example, he needs to translate the RTO of a business process to RTOs of external services.

Mitigation strategies for IT systems would actually influence the IT landscape layout. For example, the Business Continuity Manager could demand a minimum number of redundant servers, hot-standby or cold-standby solutions and fail-over switches. In dynamically provisioned environments, such as cloud computing, the Business Continuity Manager may place a reservation for certain amount of virtual infrastructure that can be dynamically provisioned if required. Again, these requirements would be encoded in *Service Level Agreements* (sometimes also called Operational Level Agreements) that have to be negotiated with the IT department or respective service provider. Besides technical parameters, the Business Continuity Manager also has to define and negotiate IT support services, such as IT help desk services, first, second, and third line support response times, etc.

Exercising, Maintaining and Reviewing BCM Arrangements

These activities enable the organisation to demonstrate that business recovery plans are complete, coherent, current and correct. Exercising and reviewing helps business continuity managers to understand the organisation better (that closes the loop) and gives them opportunities to identify improvements in business recovery plans, business continuity strategies and business impact analyses.

ISSUES RELATED TO BUSINESS IMPACT ANALYSIS

In this section academic and industrial approaches to model and analyse resource dependencies, failure propagation and recovery models are reviewed.

In order to understand, how an impact on the performance of a business can be estimated and evaluated, one has to understand how a business

derives and defines its business performance characteristics, parameters and policies. In the following section we provide insights into how performance characteristics of businesses are derived and implemented. We also highlight issues related to the translation and decomposition process of non-functional business process properties.

Business Performance and Non-Functional Properties of Businesses

An organisation can be treated as a *System*. A System has functional and non-functional properties. The functional properties (or the behaviour) of system specify *what* a system is supposed to do. Non-functional properties can be used to specify *how well* a system is supposed to perform its primary function. In cases of organisations and businesses the functional property would be to *deliver products or services to customers*. Non-functional properties are, for example, to deliver products and services in *good quality* or to *increase the annual revenue*. These non-functional properties of a business are often called performance objectives. These objectives are identified and postulate in a process called *Strategy Making* (Thompson et al., 2010).

A business strategy is a distinctive high-level view of an organisation's mission and future path. The strategy making process produces a refined hierarchy of three strategies; *the business strategy*, the *functional area strategy* and the *operational area strategy*. This hierarchy is shown in Figure 1. The overall business strategy is usually defined by chief and senior executives and clarifies the visions for an entire organisation. A business strategy could, for example, contain statements as "to increase the annual revenue by x% and to gain y% percent market share". The functional area strategy, developed by heads of functional areas (e.g. production or sales/distribution), refines a business strategy with aspects of the respective functional area and provides details about how

Figure 1. Relationship among various Strategies, KPIs and business enabling resources. Note, that this Figure shows a very simplified and limited version of a business level KPI and Strategy hierarchy. Similar, but complete and coherent KPI hierarchy maps are provided and discussed by (Bansal, 2009)

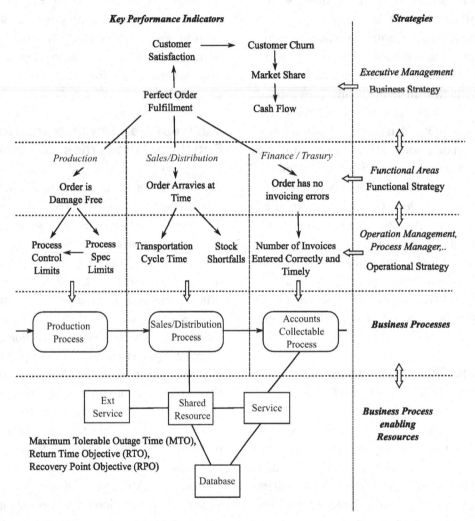

the overall business strategy can be achieved. Functional strategies would contain statements like "to deliver the right product to the right customer at the correct time". The functional strategy is further refined into the operational strategy by business process owners, operation managers and domain experts. They add operational details such as staffing plans, resource allocation plans, etc.

Strategy Making Process

The Strategy Making Process, which is essentially a translation, de-composition and refinement process, produces not only strategies, but also a set of distinctive performance indicators (often called *Key Performance Indicators*) and fixed targets (objectives) for every strategy. These indicators and objectives convert a strategy vision into tangible performance targets, or for that matter, into non-functional properties of a business. After completion of the strategy making process, an organisation possesses a set of *business, functional* and *operational indicators and objectives.* A common methodology to derive business and functional objectives is the Balanced Score Cards methodology (Maisel, 1992). Operational KPIs are defined by respective business functions using appropriate methods. For example, Stochastic Process Control is a common tool in production and manufacturing to derive operational KPIs. Stochastic Process Control uses statistical methods to define indicators for business processes, such as the Process Capability Index and related control and specification limits (Oakland, 2002).

The Business Impact Analysis itself is a part of this translation process as it derives BCM KPIs for business processes from other operational and functional KPIs. BCM KPIs are therefore operational level KPIs as well.

Business Level Key Performance Indicators

Key Performance Indicators are classified along two dimensions. The first dimension distinguishes between *financial* and *non-financial* KPIs. Examples for financial KPIs are *Cash Flow, Return of Investment* or *Revenue Margins.* Examples for non-financial KPIs would be *Customer Satisfaction, Perfect Order Delivery* or *Customer Churn Rate.* The second dimension classifies KPIs as *lagging* or *leading* KPIs. Lagging KPIs can be used to make statements about *past* performance. Financial KPIs are often lagging KPIs as they indicate how well a business performed up today. Leading KPIs, on the other hand, are used to indicate *future* performance and therefore indicators of future financial success or loss. For example, if customers are not satisfied with the delivery of an order (indicated by a low *Customer Satisfaction Index*), they might go to competitors (indicated by a high *Customer Churn Rate*) and this will eventually lead to losses in revenue. This is proven by research which shows importance of customer focus and customer satisfaction (Balasubramanian,

Konana, & Menon, 2003), (Kim, Ferrin, & Rao, 2008). Furthermore, mangers distinguish between *long-term* and *short-term* objectives. Short terms objectives are usually operational and functional level objectives and define how a business should perform at a day-to-day, weekly or monthly basis. Long-term objectives, on the other hand, define targets that have to be achieved within several months or years. Business objectives are usually long-term objectives.

Due to the translation and refinement in the Strategy Making Process, Key Performance Indicators and Objectives form relationship among each other, as shown in Figure 1. For example, the Supply Chain Operational Reference (Poluha, 2007) defines (among 150 other KPIs) the *Perfect Order Fulfilment* KPI. This KPI reflects the performance of a supply chain process and is defined as: the correct product is delivered to the correct customer, to the correct place, in the correct condition, in the correct quantity with the correct documentation. Note, that this KPI spans various different functional areas, such as production, sales/distribution and finance. For each functional area the Perfect Order Fulfilment KPI can be further translated and de-composed into operational indicators, such as production process quality parameters or requirements for sales/distribution processes. The Perfect Order Fulfilment KPI, on the other hand, influences the Customer Satisfaction Index, which itself has an impact on the Customer Churn Rate. A low Customer Churn Rate is required to gain Market Shares which leads eventually to gains in revenue (observed via the *Cash Flow* KPI). This KPI hierarchy is shown in Figure 1.

Current approaches to conduct Business Impact Analysis usually focus on financial and short-term impact. To the best of our knowledge no generic BCM analysis implementation exists that takes non-financial or leading indicators into account or estimate long-term impact. This, however seems to be a general problem, as noted by Moura, Sauve, & Bartolini, 2007. They authors state, that the underlying financial models utilised in research for business driven IT management are sometimes insufficient and to some extend "naive". However research exists that contributes to this field of knowledge by investigating in special aspects and scenarios (Sadique, Adams, & Edmunds, 2008; Snyder & Shen, 2007)

It has to be noted, that the aforementioned translation process is not necessarily formal and well-defined as it would be required for automated translations. Often, KPIs and objectives are educated guesses made by experienced human experts solely relying on their expertise. Even if the relationship among KPIs is apparent, it does not necessarily mean that there exists a sound mathematical model to compute the influence of KPIs on each other. For example, managers are interested in finding out how variations in the Perfect Order Fulfilment KPI can influence the Customer Satisfaction Index. Perfect Order Fulfilment is a well defined KPI that can be easily computed from data available in business logs and enterprise databases. As this KPI is standardised it is even possible to compare the perfect order fulfilment rate of various different businesses and organisations with each other. The Customer Satisfaction Index on the over hand, is business specific, and is subject to human judgement and is influenced by customer expectations (Fornell, Johnson, Anderson, Cha, & Bryant, 1996). It takes some effort to develop a significant and representative Customer Satisfaction Index for a business. This is usually done via interviews, polls or questionnaires. As stated above, there exists an evident, but not necessarily easy to specify relationship between these two KPIs.

In general, models and methodologies to translate business level KPIs (including long-term, short term, financial, non-financial, leading and lagging KPIs) to operational KPIs, BCM Metrics, IT system requirements, etc. is an interesting research area. In particular, modelling customer expectations and behaviour with regard to system failures and outages is a major challenge (Hess Jr., Ganesan, & Klein, 2003), (Magnini, Ford, Markowski, & Jr, 2007), (Hedrick, Beverland, & Minahan, 2007).

Issues Related to Dependency and Risk Analysis

Apart from the impact estimation on business values, the Business Continuity Manager has to identify risks, failures, and failure effects to IT systems that may lead to potential disruptions in business. Business Continuity Managers refer to this analysis as Dependency and Risk Analysis (DA/RA). DA/RA is very close to reliability engineering, a well researched area. Fault-Tree Analysis (FTA) or Failure Modes, Effects, and Critical Analysis (FMECA) are two methodologies commonly deployed to carry out DA/RA (Brall, 2010).

Failure Modes, Effects, and Critical Analysis (FMECA) (FMECA, 1980) was developed by a military research project, and is a standard to determine the impact on function, mission success, personal safety and performance that may could arise from failures in systems. FMECA uses a systematic approach to analyse systems. First the system under consideration has to be defined. Second, the system is decomposed in smaller elements, e.g. components and the dependencies among components are documented. Third, for each system component potential failure modes are identified. Each failure mode is evaluated in terms of the worst potential consequences which may result and a severity classification category is assigned, detectability, severity and occurrence. This enables a priority ranking and a Risk Priority Number is assigned to every failure mode. The goal is to identify failure modes that are hard to detect, very severe and very likely to occur.

Although the main objective of FMECA is to eliminate failure modes in early design phases, the standard says about itself: "Probably the greatest criticism of the FMECA has been its limited use in improving designs. The chief causes for this have been untimeliness and the isolated performance of the FMECA without adequate inputs to the design process." FMECA analysis failures one-by-one and does not consider combination of them. However, a thorough BCM dependency and risk analysis should consider possible combinations, for example an earthquake may cause a fire and a power breakdown as well. FMECA also does not evaluate combination of systems, e.g. a database with or without a primary backup server. Furthermore, FMECA provides no means to model failures caused by environmental events, e.g. earthquakes, which are often the primary focus of BCM analysis. BCM mangers are also interested in quantified analysis of timely behaviour of resources. FMECA provides no means to analysis this aspect.

Fault Tree Analysis (FTA) (FTA, 2006) is a technique used in reliability engineering to determine combinations of failures in a system that could lead to undesired event at system level. The modelling process starts with the undesired event (e.g. "valve is closed") and is broken down into a fault tree. Each fault is analysed in more detail (e.g. "valve is closed due to human errors", "valve is closed due to hardware failure") and if necessary broken down again, until a reasonable level of understanding has been achieved (e.g. "valve is not opened by operator after last test" or "valve is closed because of malfunctioning switch"). The logical relationship between faults is defined by logical "gates", such as AND, OR, XOR and NOT. Probabilities are assigned to basic events and the overall likelihood of an undesired event can be calculated.

Although a fault tree analysis is able to provide a better estimation of the probability of adverse events to occur, such an analysis is not able to model the dynamic behaviour of systems since Boolean gates are not able to capture the order in which events occur, nor is it possible to model time constraints, such as dead-lines. This limits the application of FTA in BCM to very simple analyses.

Issues Related to IT Landscape Planning

IT landscape is a set of services, hardware, software and facility elements arranged in a specific configuration, which serves as a fabric to support the business operation of an enterprise. *IT Landscape planning* is the process of determining an optimized IT landscape.

It has to be noted, that the terms *IT landscape* and *IT landscape planning* are widely accepted in industry, but are not as common in research and academia.

In order to conduct a complete and coherent DA/RA, Business Continuity Manager needs a complete picture of an IT landscape. However, IT landscapes are complex and therefore it is hard to form such a complete picture. Different modelling techniques are used to describe ICT landscapes. For example, at the infrastructure layer, the Common Information Model (CIM) is used to model systems, networks, applications and services. Software components, at the software layer, are often modelled using the Unified Modelling Language (UML). Proprietary modelling techniques are often deployed as well. For each layer domain specific tools are available that support modelling, analysis and planning. These tools produce independent, but conceptually related models and model artefacts, which could be utilized for a comprehensive DA/RA.

Furthermore, IT Landscapes are adaptive systems. They evolve over time. New servers and systems are added with time, software is updated on regular basis, while obsolete systems are decommissioned. In dynamic provisioned environment, such as cloud computing, IT landscape deployment layouts can be altered within minutes. As pointed out by Wijnia in (Wijnia, 2007) even small changes in an IT landscape layout can cause severe problems and may invalidate existing BCM arrangements. Hence, Business Continuity Manager needs automated methodology, which supports him to consolidate and correlate various different IT landscape models for a DA/RA. Winkler (Winkler et al, 2010) proposed a model-driven framework for BCM which integrates business process modelling and IT management. This approach enables automatic consolidation of information from various data sources, such as IT landscape models.

On the other hand, Business Continuity Management should contribute to the IT landscape planning process. For instance, BCM requirements, derived from Business Impact Analysis and DA/RA, could be translated into respective IT landscape requirements and deployment options. These observations are shared by (A. Moura, Sauvé, & C. Bartolini, 2007). They concluded that there exists a complexity problem and that "the complexity of modelling the interactions, incident, problem, [. . .] and continuity management has not been tackled yet". The authors also state that the modelling and analysis of "how IT affects the business [...] is a good research problem to think about." The SAP IT Business Continuity Management team acknowledges these problems as well and confirmed that existing methodologies and technologies for Business Impact Analysis and Dependency Modelling are not sufficient enough to meet the needs of IT Business Continuity Management. Winjia (Wijnia & Nikolic 2007) concluded that IT Business Continuity Management should become a part of IT landscape planning in the first place.

As stated previously, Business Continuity Managers have to demonstrate that their analyses are complete, coherent, current, effective and efficient. This is required by external reviewers if an organisation wants to become BCM certified. However, this is a major challenge for large and distributed IT landscapes and globally operating enterprises.

Another interesting question and research challenge is to quantify completeness, effectiveness ("are we doing the right thing?") and efficiency ("are we doing things right?") of BCM arrangements. Currently, there has been little research done in this area related to Business Continuity Management and IT landscape planning. However, we want to highlight the work of (Boehmer, Brandt, & Groote, 2009). The authors presented a model to evaluate the performance of business continuity plans. In order to do so they introduced KPIs to measure, define and compute the effectiveness and economic efficiency of business continuity plans.

EXISTING RESEARCH PROJECTS

In this section we discuss three research projects, which aim to provide tooling and analysis support for Business Continuity Management. We discuss advantages of these approaches and outline open issues.

Risk Aware Process Evaluation (ROPE)

The ROPE framework, developed by (Jakoubi, Tjoa, & Quirchmayr, 2007), aims to combine business process modelling with risk and business continuity management. ROPE diagrams consist of three layers: the business process layer, the Condition, Action, Resource and Environment (CARE) layer and the Threat Impact Processes (TIP) layer. The business process layer models business process activities. A CARE layer element describes resources (e.g. "personal computer") and an environment (e.g. "office") needed by a business activity in a simplified fault-tree-like structure. The top-element of this fault-tree structure is the business activity. At the time of writing, the ROPE framework only considers resource availability and resource utilisation as modelled aspects. If the fault-tree evaluates to false, the associated business activity is *on hold* and therefore the business process does not proceed.

The TIP layer models three kinds of processes: threat processes, detection sub-processes and countermeasure processes. A threat process step is linked against a set of resources or an environment of a CARE element and makes those resources or environment unavailable. If a threat activity (e.g. "virus") makes the associated resource set unavailable (e.g. "personal computer") and, if the fault-tree of the CARE element evaluates to false, the associated business activity is paused. A threat process does not proceed by itself and is paused at each single threat activity. The detection sub-process and the countermeasure sub-process processes are linked against single threat activities. A countermeasure activity releases threat-activities in such a way that the threat-process is able to proceed. If the threat-process reaches its final state, a threat has been removed.

The ROPE framework has some novel features. First, it uses workflows models for all four activities: to model business processes, to model threats, to describe detection behaviour and to model countermeasure activities (A. Zalewski, Sztandera, Ludzia, & M. Zalewski, 2008). This allows business process manager to model all activities using the same concept. Second, it assigns resources and business activities and enables resource dependency modelling and resource multiplicities modelling. Last, business processes, threats, and countermeasure processes are independent process models, but are capable of influencing each other. This eases the modelling phase since every process can be modelled independent of each other.

However, ROPE has few limitations. First, the simplified fault-tree dependency model does not allow the analysis of temporal failure propagation. Second, ROPE only delays business process activities; there is no means to model situations where certain business process activities have to be repeated due do an adverse event. This is needed in order to analyse the backlog caused by an adverse event, e.g. if a database failed and data has to be re-entered manually. Third, ROPE does not provide any means to model effects. An adverse event always makes a set of resources completely unavailable. ROPE does not consider other adverse event characteristics, e.g. an adverse event might gradually decrease a resource's performance. An effect-model should also be used to model the effects of n-out-of-k system on dependent resources. For example, if two out of five air-conditioning units fail, then the sever room will overheat within two days. If all air-conditioning units fail the sever room will overheat within five minutes. Fourth, threat processes can be combined in ROPE, but they do not interact with each other. This makes it hard to create advanced risk scenarios where, for example, threats trigger or enable each other. Last, countermeasure process models do not have resources assigned. Therefore it is not possible to model scenarios in which an adverse event may affect the countermeasure process itself. These scenarios are needed to detect dead-locks or live-locks; for example a login-server might be unavailable, but the administrator depends on the availability of this particular login-sever to resolve the problem (one of the problems encountered in the ESSENT NETWERK study).

Model Driven Performance Engineering (MDPE) Workbench

The MDPE workbench, developed by Fritzsche et al. aims to provide end-to-end business performance related decision support (Fritzsche, Johannes, Cech, & Gilani, 2009). Business performance related decision support is used to estimate resource consumption and utilisation, response times of business process tasks and to determine the optimal work force needed to guarantee a certain business process throughput, etc. The authors stated that MDPE Workbench can be utilised to perform Business Impact Analysis. The authors noted that nowadays companies deploy different tools and platforms for modelling business processes. The reason for this is that organisations grow and evolve over time. They acquire new companies and merge with other businesses. After a business takeover it can take several years, until all business lines and sectors within one organisation are using the same tools. Thus end-to-end performance related decision support is needed to plan and analyse business processes, to assign resources, to estimate sales order requests or to answer what-if planning questions.

In order to realise end-to-end decision support spanning multiple business process modelling environments, the MDPE workbench provides (1) a pivot performance model, called Tool Independent Performance Model (TIPM) and (2) utilises model driven technologies, such as model transformations and model annotations. In a first step, the user uses graphical tools provided by the MDPE workbench to annotate business processes (the target model) with performance related information. In a second step, model transformations are used to transform the annotated information together with process model into the TIPM format. In a third step, a model transformation chain transforms the TIPM data into the input format for various different analysis tools, such as simulation engines, analytical problem solvers or optimisation frameworks. In a last step, after a run of all analysis tools, the analysis results are brought back and decorated on the original target models for the benefits of the business process planner.

The MDPE approach has several advantages. First, it allows the business process planer to add performance related decision support – hence Business Impact Analyses - to arbitrary business process modelling tools. Second, the pivot performance model allows to integrate and to run various different analyses with little effort. This is an important aspect, as current enterprise grade business process modelling tools do not provide support for business continuity analysis.

The MDPE workbench can be used to conduct a simple BIA; for example to simulate unavailable resources or resources with limited operation time. However, it does not provide a means to model the behaviour of resource (e.g. the behaviour of work force or customers) in case of a disaster. This is essential to understand the impact on non-financial KPIs or to estimate back-log. Second, TIPM only supports a single layer of resources

directly associated with the business process steps; therefore TIPM does not provide any means to analyse interactions between resources or to model recovery plans. The support for defining custom measurements (e.g. Perfect Order Fulfilment) in TIPM is weak, since it requires implementation effort. To analyse temporal failure propagation through multi resource layers is not possible since TIPM does not permit to model multi-resource layers in the first place. It is not possible to conduct a Dependency/Risk Analysis using the MDPE workbench. For more information please see: http://www.mdpe.org

Tropos Goal-Risk Framework

In his doctoral thesis Asnar, (2009) developed the Tropos Goal-Risk (GR) Framework for requirement analysis and risk assessment for critical socio-technical systems, such as Air Traffic Management. This GR framework has some interesting features. First, it provides means to model combinations of failures similar to FTA. Second, it provides semantics to model other aspects, such as time dependencies, treatments and assets, which are useful for Business Continuity Management. In fact, Asnar and Giorgini (2008b) demonstrated that the GR framework could be used to analyse and compare the effectiveness and cost-efficiency of different treatment strategies.

However, the analysis does not provide means to determine business impact nor does it provide means to determine BCM metrics, such as RTO. Furthermore, the treatment analysis is not sufficient to model complex examples. The example provided in (Asnar & Giorgini, 2008b, Fig 2, p5) models a database failure with an outage time of exactly three hours. Business continuity management normally assumes a distribution of outage time, mostly estimated by a three-point-estimation (minimal outage time, most-likely outage time and worst-case outage time) to fit a beta-distribution. Treatments in GR can be modelled by reducing likelihood and/or reducing the time period of disruption. In the example a treatment is modelled as well. The treatment ("backup-server") reduces the likelihood of the database to fail by 90%, but does not provide any means to model the behaviour of a switch from primary to backup database server, nor does provide means to model why a switch fails. Also, steps of treatments are not detailed and hence are not well suited to model and analyse recovery plans. Furthermore, the algorithm proposed in Asnar & Giorgini, (2008b) only selects a combination of possible treatments; the algorithm does not propose treatment levels, e.g. proposals that a backup-server should reduce the risk by 99% to guarantee certain level of business continuity. For more information see also: http://www.troposproject.org

SUMMARY AND FUTURE RESEARCH

In this chapter we provided an introduction into Business Continuity Management. We showed the business continuity management lifecycle and discussed the importance of business continuity in a service-oriented IT environment. We used the four activities of the Business Continuity lifecycle to provide background information, and discussed related work and open research challenges. Below we detail problems that have not been addressed within this chapter and point out potential solutions and future research directions.

Business Impact Analysis

Current approaches focus on financial KPIs solely and do not consider non-financial, leading indicators into account. Therefore, derived Business Continuity Metrics are not well aligned with business strategies. Future work should consider financial, non-financial, leading and lagging indicators. Furthermore, if applicable, the impact analysis should span all three layers of business level KPIs.

Modelling People Behaviour

People are essential elements and resources in business processes, ICT landscapes and are crucial for recovery plans. Furthermore, as noted in (Machiraju, C. Bartolini, & Casati, 2004), human resources usually cost higher than hardware or software. Hence, any ICT Business Continuity management should take interaction with people and people costs into consideration.

Single-Box vs. Fine-Grained Business Process Models Approach

Due to the complexity and missing tooling/analysis support, Business Continuity Managers treat business processes as single entities and do not go into details. For example, Business Continuity Manger would treat a business process as a "single box" rather than breaking this process down and conduct an impact analysis at process activity level, which would be required for a fine-granular Business Impact Analysis.

Rigorous Definition of Metrics

Not all business level KPIs and BCM metrics are well defined. Often, only an implicit definition is given. Rigorous and well defined metrics are needed to automate Business Impact Analysis and KPI/SLA translations. Also, the relationship between metrics needs to be defined in a rigorous manner.

Model and Tool Diversity

Different modelling techniques are used to describe business processes, Risks, SLAs, KPIs and IT landscapes. This adds additional complexity to IT Business continuity analysis. Future work should address model diversity and provide solutions to integrate heterogeneous models.

IT Complexity

IT landscapes are complex adaptive systems comprising hardware, software, facility and human components. ICT landscapes evolve over time; for example new servers are added or software is upgraded. No single person has a complete understanding of all involved ICT landscapes nor can one oversee all dependencies among ICT elements. This is a key problem that hinders a thorough Dependency and Risk Analysis.

Multi-Level Resource Dependency, Multi-Layer Risk Management, Risk Break Down Modelling

The dependency models should support arbitrary kinds of layered resources (e.g. business process resources, ICT elements, human resources). Resource behaviour and temporal aspects of dependencies are important. The "ripple" effect of temporal failure propagation through resource layers is one subject of analysis. Furthermore, it should be possible to model and analyse combined failure modes since threats may influence, foster or trigger one another.

Fault Propagation

Small changes in an operational ICT landscape may have severe consequences. To estimate the business impact, a full understanding of the behaviour and analysis of all interactions, between processes, applications and hardware has to be performed.

Multi-Paradigm-Analysis and Optimisation

Besides the Business Impact Analysis and the Resource and Dependency Analysis, following analysis, planning and optimisation methodologies should be considered:

- **Single point of failure:** Business Continuity Manager should be able to identify and spot single point of failure with regard to business continuity planning in an ICT landscape or recovery plan.
- **What-If-Questions:** Business Continuity Manager should be able to simulate different scenarios and should be able to compare different recovery plans.
- **Dead-Lock:** It should possible to detect dead-lock or live-lock situations in recovery plans.
- **Sensitivity Analysis:** Business Continuity Manager should be able to analyse variation and uncertainty in the dependency, threat and recovery plan models. The manager should be able to demonstrate that a recovery plan is robust and is valid even for uncertain risk assumptions.
- **SLA Translation and Multi-Objective-Optimisation:** A methodology is needed to translate business level BCM metrics and KPIs to individual ICT elements BCM objectives, for example to translate RTO of a business process to the RTO objective of an air-conditioning unit. Furthermore ICT level BCM metrics need to be optimised; for example to identify the maximum tolerable outage time for given ICT elements with acceptable costs and minimised risks.
- **Formal Methods:** Currently, Monte-Carlo simulation based approaches are common to perform Business Impact Analysis. However, simulations have the disadvantage that they are not able to identify worst-case scenarios. A current research trend is to deploy formal methods, such as process algebras to address this problem.

REFERENCES

Asnar, Y. (2009). *Requirements analysis and risk assessment for critical information system*. PhD Thesis, University of Trent.

Asnar, Y., & Giorgini, P. (2008a). Analyzing business continuity through a multi-layers model. *Proceedings of the 6th International Conference on Business Process Management*. Springer.

Asnar, Y., & Giorgini, P. (2008b). Analyzing business continuity through a multi-layers model. *Proceedings of the 6th International Conference on Business Process Management*. Springer.

Balasubramanian, S., Konana, P., & Menon, N. M. (2003). Customer satisfaction in virtual environments: A study of online investing. [Institute for Operations Research and the Management Sciences.]. *Management Science, 49*(7), 871–889. doi:10.1287/mnsc.49.7.871.16385

Bansal, S. (2009). *Technology scorecards: Aligning IT investments with business performance* (p. 336). John Wiley & Sons.

Basel Committee on Banking Supervision. (2005). *International convergence of capital measurement and capital standards (BASEL II)*. Basel, Swizerland: Author.

Boehmer, W., Brandt, C., & Groote, J. F. (2009). Evaluation of a business continuity plan using process algebra and modal logic. *2009 IEEE Toronto International Conference Science and Technology for Humanity (TIC-STH)* (pp. 147-152). IEEE. doi: 10.1109/TIC-STH.2009.5444515

Brall, A. (2010). Reliability analysis - A tool set for improving business processes. *2010 Proceedings - Annual Reliability and Maintainability Symposium (RAMS)*, (pp. 1-5). IEEE. doi: 10.1109/RAMS.2010.5447983

Brooks, C., Leung, C., Mirza, A., Neal, C., Qiu, Y. L., Sing, J., et al. (2007). *IBM system storage business continuity solutions overview*. IBM, International Technical Support Organization. Retrieved from redbooks.ibm.com

BSI. (2006). *Business continuity management 2006: Code of practice (BS ISO)*. British Standards Institution.

FMEC. (1980). *MIL-STD-1629A: Procedures for performing a failure mode, effects and criticality analysis*. Washington, DC: Department of Defense, United State of America.

Fornell, C., Johnson, M. D., Anderson, E. W., Cha, J., & Bryant, B. E. (1996). The American customer satisfaction index: Nature, purpose, and findings. *Journal of Marketing, 60*(4), 7..doi:10.2307/1251898

Fritzsche, M., Johannes, J., Cech, S., & Gilani, W. (2009). MDPE workbench - A solution for performance related decision support. *Proceedings of the Business Process Management Demonstration Track, CEUR Proceedings*.

FTA. (2006). *IEC 61025 ed2.0 - Fault tree analysis (FTA)*. Geneva, Switzerland: International Electrotechnical Commission.

Harper, M. A., Lawler, C. M., & Thornton, M. A. (2005). *IT application downtime, executive visibility and disaster tolerant computing*. CITSA, 2nd International Conference on Cybernetics and Information Technologies, Systems and Applications.

Hedrick, N., Beverland, M., & Minahan, S. (2007). An exploration of relational customers' response to service failure. *Journal of Services Marketing, 21*(1), 64–72..doi:10.1108/08876040710726301

Heng, D. G. M. (2008). *Conducting your impact analysis for business continuity planning* (2nd ed.).

Hess Jr., R. L., Ganesan, S., & Klein, N. M. (2003). Service failure and recovery: The impact of relationship factors on customer satisfaction. *Journal of the Academy of Marketing Science, 31*(2), 127-145. Sage Publications. doi: 10.1177/0092070302250898

Jakoubi, S., Tjoa, S., & Quirchmayr, G. (2007). Rope: A methodology for enabling the risk-aware modelling and simulation of business processes. *ECIS, 15th European Conference on Information Systems*, 1596-1607.

Kim, D., Ferrin, D., & Rao, H. (2008). A trust-based consumer decision-making model in electronic commerce: The role of trust, perceived risk, and their antecedents. *Decision Support Systems, 44*(2), 544–564..doi:10.1016/j.dss.2007.07.001

Machiraju, V., Bartolini, C., & Casati, F. (2004). Technologies for business-driven it management. In *Extending Web services technologies: The use of multi-agent approaches.* Kluwer Academic Publishers. doi:10.1007/0-387-23344-X_1

Magnini, V. P., Ford, J. B., Markowski, E. P., & Honeycutt, E. D. Jr. (2007). The service recovery paradox: Justifiable theory or smoldering myth? *Journal of Services Marketing, 21*(3), 213–225.. doi:10.1108/08876040710746561

Maisel, L. S. (1992). Performance measurement: The balanced scorecard approach. *Journal of Cost Management, 6*(2), 47–52.

Miller, R. (2010). Salesforce.com hit by one hour outage. Retrieved from http://www.datacenter-knowledge.com/archives/2010/01/04/salesforce-com-hit-by-one-hour-outage/

Moura, A., Sauvé, J., & Bartolini, C. (2007). Research challenges of business-driven IT management. *The Second IEEE/IFIP International Workshop on Business-Driven IT Management (BDIM)*, (pp. 19–28).

Moura Antao Sauve, J., & Bartolini, C. (2007). Research challenges of business-driven IT management. *2nd IEEE/IFIP International Workshop on Business-Driven IT Management*, (pp. 19-28). IEEE. doi: 10.1109/BDIM.2007.375008

Oakland, J. S. (2002). *Statistical process control* (p. 464). Butterworth-Heinemann. Retrieved from http://www.amazon.co.uk/Statistical-Process-Control-John-Oakland/dp/0750657669

Poluha, R. G. (2007). *Application of the SCOR model in supply chain management* (p. 480). Cambria Press. Retrieved from http://www.amazon.co.uk/Application-Model-Supply-Chain-Management/dp/1934043230

Sadique, M. Z., Adams, E. J., & Edmunds, W. J. (2008). Estimating the costs of school closure for mitigating an influenza pandemic. *BMC Public Health, 8*, 135..doi:10.1186/1471-2458-8-135

Silver, B. (2009). *SAP NetWeaver BPM.* White Paper.

Smith, D. J. (2002). *Business continuity management: Good practice guidelines.* The Business Continuity Institute.

Snyder, L. V., & Shen, Z. J. M. (2007). Managing disruptions to supply chains. *Frontiers of Engineering: Reports on Leading-edge Engineering from the 2006 Symposium*, October, (p. 139). The National Academies.

Spremic, M., & Popovic, M. (2008). Emerging issues in IT governance: Implementing the corporate IT risks management model. [World Scientific and Engineering Academy and Society] [WSEAS] [Stevens Point, Wisconsin, USA.]. *WSEAS Transactions on Systems, 7*(3), 219–228.

Thompson, A. A. with Gamble, J. E., Jr. (2010). *Essentials of strategic management: The quest for competitive advantage* (p. 592). McGraw-Hill Higher Education.

Wijnia, Y., & Nikolic, I. (2007). Assessing business continuity risks in IT. *2007 IEEE International Conference on Systems, Man and Cybernetics*, (pp. 3547-3553). IEEE. doi: 10.1109/ICSMC.2007.4413845

Winkler, U., Gilani, W., Fritzsche, M., & Marshall, A. (2010). A model-driven framework for process-centric business continuity management. *2010 Seventh International Conference on the Quality of Information and Communications Technology* (pp. 248-252). Porto. doi: 10.1109/QUATIC.2010.46

Zalewski, A., Sztandera, P., Ludzia, M., & Zalewski, M. (2008). Modeling and analyzing disaster recovery plans as business processes. In *Computer Safety, Reliability, and Security* (vol. 5219, pp. 113-125). Berlin, Germany: Springer. doi: 10.1007/978-3-540-87698-4

ADDITIONAL READING

Armbrust, M., Fox, A., Griffith, R., Joseph, A., Katz, R., Konwinski, A., et al. (2009). Above the clouds: A Berkeley view of cloud computing. EECS Department, University of California, Berkeley, Tech. Rep. UCB/EECS-2009-28.

Avizienis, A., Laprie, J., Randell, B., & others. (2001). Fundamental concepts of dependability. Technical Report Series, University of New Castle

Boehmer, W. (2009). Survivability and Business Continuity Management System According to BS 25999. Third International Conference on Emerging Security Information, Systems and Technologies, 142-147. IEEE. doi: 10.1109/SECURWARE.2009.29.

Balaouras, S., Yates, S., & Herald, A. (2009). Businesses Take BC Planning More Seriously. Reproduction (pp. 1-14). Forrester.

Bonafede, E., & Giudici, P. (2007). Statistical models for business continuity management. *Journal of Operational Risk, 2*(4), 79–96.

Brandt, C., Hermann, F., & Engel, T. (2009). Modeling and reconfiguration of critical business processes for the purpose of a Business Continuity Management respecting security, risk and compliance requirements at Credit Suisse using algebraic graph transformation. 13th Enterprise Distributed Object Computing Conference Workshops (pp. 64-71). IEEE. doi: 10.1109/EDOCW.2009.5332015.

Brown, W., & Nasuti, F. (2005). Sarbanes-Oxley and Enterprise Security: IT Governance - What It Takes to Get the Job Done. *Information Systems Security, 14*(5), 15–28..doi:10.1201/1086.10658 98X/45654.14.5.20051101/91010.4

Carvajal-Vion, J., & Garcia-Menendez, M. (2003). Business Continuity Controls in ISO 17799 and COBIT. *The European Journal for the Informatics Professional, IV*(6).

Chen, Y., Iyer, S., Liu, X., Milojicic, D., & Sahai, A. (2007). SLA Decomposition: Translating Service Level Objectives to System Level Thresholds. Fourth International Conference on Autonomic Computing (ICAC'07), 3-3. Ieee. doi: 10.1109/ICAC.2007.36.

Dillon, R. L., & Mazzola, J. B. (2010). Management of disruption risk in global supply chains. *Journal of Research and Development (Srinagar), 54*(3), 1–9. doi:.doi:10.1147/JRD.2010.2044674

Edgeman, R. L., Bigio, D., & Ferleman, T. (2005). Six Sigma and Business Excellence: Strategic and Tactical Examination of IT Service Level Management at the Office of the Chief Technology Officer of Washington, DC. *Quality and Reliability Engineering International, 21*(3), 257–273..doi:10.1002/qre.635

Gerber, M., & Vonsolms, R. (2005). Management of risk in the information age. *Computers & Security, 24*(1), 16–30..doi:10.1016/j.cose.2004.11.002

Graupner, S., Rolia, J., & Edwards, N. (2007). *Deriving IT Configurations from Business Processes: From the Business Process to the Grounded Model.* HP Invent.

Grillo, A. (2003). *Information systems Auditing of Business Continuity Plans.* The European Journal for the Informatics Professional (IT Contingency Planning and Business Continuity, 4(6), 12-16.

Haworth, D., & Pietron, L. (2006). *Sarbanes-Oxley: Achieving Compliance by Starting with ISO 17799*. Information Systems Management, 23(1), 73-87. Taylor & Francis. Doi: 10.1201/1 078.10580530/45769.23.1.20061201/91775.9.

Hayes, T., Chatterji, S., Hwang, K., Lainhart, J. W., Penri-Williams, H., Eddy Schuermans, et al. (2008). *Aligning COBIT 4.1, ITIL V3 and ISO/ IEC 27002 for Business Benefit*. IT Governance Institue.

Hiles, A. (2010). *The Definitive Handbook of Business Continuity Management*. John Wiley & Sons.

Hubbard, D., & Evans, D. (2010). Problems with scoring methods and ordinal scales in risk assessment. IBM Reseach and Development, 54(3), 2:1-2:10.

ISO/IEC. (2005). ISO/IEC 27002:2005(E) *Information technology - Security techniques - Code of practice for information security management*. Security (Vol. 2005). International Organization for Standardization and International Electrotechnical Commission.

Jacobs, S. (2006). Current trends in regulatory impact analysis: the challenges of mainstreaming RIA into policy-making. *Jacobs and Associates, 30*, 1–52.

Jakoubi, S., Neubauer, T., & Tjoa, S. (2009). A Roadmap to Risk-Aware Business Process Management. In Computing (pp. 23-27). doi: 10.1109/ APSCC.2009.5394145.

Jakoubi, S., Tjoa, S., Goluch, G., & Quirchmayr, G. (2009). A Survey of Scientific Approaches Considering the Integration of Security and Risk Aspects into Business Process Management. 2009 20th International Workshop on Database and Expert Systems Application, 127-132. Ieee. doi: 10.1109/DEXA.2009.71.

Kepenach, R. J. (2007). Business Continuity Plan Design. In Second International Conference on Internet Monitoring and Protection (ICIMP 2007) (pp. 27-27). Ieee. doi: 10.1109/ICIMP.2007.11.

Kimball, M. S., Sahm, C. R., & Shapiro, M. D. (2008). Imputing Risk Tolerance From Survey Responses. *Journal of the American Statistical Association, 103*(483), 1028–1038.. doi:10.1198/016214508000000139

Lewis, W., Watson, R. T., & Pickren, A. (2003). An empirical assessment of IT disaster risk. *Communications of the ACM, 46*(9), 201.. doi:10.1145/903893.903938

Li, H., Theilmann, W., & Happe, J. (2009). (Manuscript submitted). SLA Translation in Multi-Layered Service Oriented Architectures. *Status and Challenges.*

Machiraju, V., Singhal, S., Arlitt, M., Beyer, D., Graupner, S., Pruyne, J., et al. (2005). Quartermaster-a resource utility system. Integrated Network Management, 2005. IM 2005. 2005 9th IFIP/IEEE International Symposium on, 265-278.

Madni, A. M., & Jackson, S. (2009). Towards a Conceptual Framework for Resilience Engineering. *IEEE Systems Journal, 3*(2), 181–191..doi:10.1109/ JSYST.2009.2017397

Petriu, D. B., & Woodside, M. (2006). An intermediate metamodel with scenarios and resources for generating performance models from UML designs. *Software & Systems Modeling, 6*(2), 163–184.. doi:10.1007/s10270-006-0026-8

Ray, B., & McAuliffe, K. (2010). Preface: Business Integrity and Risk Management. *Journal of Research and Development (Srinagar), 54*(3), 1–2.. doi:10.1147/JRD.2010.2044842

Rodriguez, A., Fernandez-Medina, E., & Piattini, M. (2007). A BPMN Extension for the Modeling of Security Requirements in Business Processes. IEICE TRANSACTIONS on Information and Systems, 90(4), 745-752. IEICE. doi: 10.1093/ ietisy/e90.

Sadgrove, K. (2005). *The complete guide to business risk management*. Risk Management. Gower Pub Co.

Sauve, J. Moura, a., Sampaio, M., Jornada, J., & Radziuk, E. (2006). An Introductory Overview and Survey of Business-Driven IT Management. 2006 IEEE/IFIP Business Driven IT Management, 00(c), 1-10. Ieee. doi: 10.1109/BDIM.2006.1649205.

Sauve, J., Marques, F., Moura, A., Sampaio, M., Jornada, J., & Radziuk, E. (2005). Sla design from a business perspective. [Springer.]. *Lecture Notes in Computer Science, 3775*(8), 72. doi:10.1007/11568285_7

Tjoa, S., Jakoubi, S., Goluch, G., Kitzler, G., Goluch, S., Quirchmayr, G., et al. (2010). A Formal Approach Enabling Risk-aware Business Process Modeling and Simulation. IEEE Transactions on Services Computing, 1-14. doi: 10.1109/TSC.2010.17.

Tjoa, S., Jakoubi, S., Goluch, G., & Quirchmayr, G. (2008). Extension of a Methodology for Risk-Aware Business Process Modeling and Simulation Enabling Process-Oriented Incident Handling Support. 22nd International Conference on Advanced Information Networking and Applications (aina 2008), 48-55. Ieee. doi: 10.1109/AINA.2008.81.

Tjoa, S., Jakoubi, S., & Quirchmayr, G. (2008). Enhancing Business Impact Analysis and Risk Assessment Applying a Risk-Aware Business Process Modeling and Simulation Methodology. 2008 Third International Conference on Availability, Reliability and Security, 179-186. Ieee. doi: 10.1109/ARES.2008.206.

van der Aalst, W., Nakatumba, J., Rozinat, A., & Russell, N. (2008). Business process simulation: How to get it right? In Technical Report BPM-08-07.

Wallhoff, J. (2004). *Combining ITIL with COBIT and ISO/IEC 17799: 2000*. Scillani Information AB.

Wan, S. H. (2008). Adoption of business continuity planning processes in IT service management. In 2008 3rd IEEE/IFIP International Workshop on Business-driven IT Management (pp. 21-30). IEEE. doi: 10.1109/BDIM.2008.4540071.

zur Muehlen, M., & Rosemann, M. (2005). Integrating risks in business process models. Proceedings of the 2005 Australasian Conference on Information Systems (ACIS 2005), Manly, Sydney, Australia

KEY TERMS AND DEFINITIONS

Business Impact Analysis: Aims to (a) identify critical business processes, stakeholders, assets, resources and internal/external dependencies and (b) assesses and evaluates potential damages or losses at business level that may be caused by a threat to IT landscape.

Dependency and Risk Analysis (DA/RA): Aims to identify dependencies among business processes, resources and services, and possible root-causes of adverse incidents.

IT Business Continuity Management: A management process that identifies potential threats to an organisation's IT landscape and the impacts to business operations that those threats, if realized, might cause. IT BCM aims to build operational resilience with the capability for an effective response that safeguards an IT landscape and business operations.

IT Landscape: A set of hardware, software and facility elements, arranged in a specific configuration, which serves as a fabric to support the business operation of an enterprise.

SLA Translation: The process of translating business level BCM metrics and KPIs to BCM objectives for individual IT elements.

Section 4
SLA Governance

Chapter 18
Semantic Modelling of Resource Dependability for SLA– Based Service Governance

Martin Hall-May
IT Innovation Centre, UK

Ajay Chakravarthy
IT Innovation Centre, UK

Thomas Leonard
IT Innovation Centre, UK

Mike Surridge
IT Innovation Centre, UK

ABSTRACT

In this chapter we present a survey of research work related to the semantic modelling of security, semantic SLA modelling, and the current state of the art in SLA-based system governance. Based on this survey, and after observing the essential aspects needed to semantically model an SLA, we first propose a semantic model of resource dependability. This model can be used to semantically encode in SLA the service commitments (to customers) and resource capacity (from suppliers) in terms of usage, performance, and other QoS characteristics that represent non-functional properties. On the basis of this model, we propose a flexible approach to SLA-based system governance that allows for elastic provisioning of resources (by autonomic processes) that meet NFP requirements. This approach can be used to monitor and manage services such that they meet (and continue to meet) agreed levels of QoS.

INTRODUCTION

ICT systems today are increasingly composed of a set of resources that span multiple organisations; that is, they comprise a combination of in-house locally managed resources and 3rd party services

that are often used under the terms of a contractual agreement. At one extreme, the system can be rapidly composed through ad hoc discovery and composition of services for short-term inter-enterprise collaboration on a specific project. At the other extreme, an organisation may use a value chain that comprises services provided by known suppliers through long-standing business

DOI: 10.4018/978-1-61350-432-1.ch018

relationships. In both cases (and all those that lie on the continuum in between), service providers today are conscious of the need to manage access to, use of, and performance of their own services, as well as the adequate provision of the resources (which are themselves services) that underpin them, in order to meet (and continue to meet) their individual business goals, even in the face of failure or underperformance of services. To do this requires service providers to describe the Non-Functional Properties (NFPs, especially dependability characteristics) of their services and to agree the Quality of Service (QoS) that consumers of the service can expect (as well as their associated obligations). This Chapter reviews the current state-of-the-art in terms of modelling NFPs and will show that capturing these in a structured fashion does not adequately address today's loosely coupled cross-organisational systems, in which the inter-dependencies, resources and threats to their NFPs (e.g. performance and availability) change dynamically. In this Chapter we present solutions to modelling resource dependability in a semantically tractable way through extending a base dependability metric ontology; encoding QoS commitments (as metric constraints) in bilateral Service Level Agreements (SLAs); monitoring QoS according to these SLAs to determine aggregate service commitments and resource capacity; and managing service behaviour through local service adaptation, as part of a governance framework that can be used to maintain end-to-end (system-level) properties and to balance trade-offs between competing dependability attributes.

CHAPTER STRUCTURE

This Chapter contains the following four parts:

1. An analysis of relevant background;
2. A proposed solution to semantic modelling of resource dependability;
3. A flexible approach to SLA-based system governance; and
4. A discussion of future directions.

In this Chapter, we present a survey of research work related to semantic modelling of security, semantic SLA modelling, and the current state of the art in SLA-based system governance. This Chapter provides an overview of existing approaches in two areas: (1) tools and approaches to model and analyse security, risk and vulnerabilities of IT landscapes and (2) SLA modelling, SLA negotiation and deployment. The former gives an understanding of the risk to which a provider of ICT services may be exposed, while the latter provides a means to model these and capture how the dynamics of the runtime system can indicate the presence of a threat and effectiveness of mitigation strategies.

The review is followed by a proposal for a semantic model of resource dependability. This approach aims to encode service commitments to customers and resource capacity in a semantic driven way.

On the basis of this model, we then propose a framework for elastic service provisioning that allows services to be deployed in such a way that they can be managed to meet the stated QoS requirements.

The Chapter concludes with a list of future research directions.

BACKGROUND

In a typical security modelling approach, a system is described as a collection of assets or resources, which typically include computers, networks and data. These have properties such as confidentiality, integrity and availability, which are important to the organisation operating the system. They also have vulnerabilities whereby these properties can be undermined.

We need a more general set of dependability attributes to express the behaviour of resources even if accessed across organisational boundaries, and to manage their run-time composition to meet (potentially changing) requirements. Moreover, the collection of resources will itself change as inter-organisational relationships are formed and broken, or discarded as untrustworthy.

In order to address whole-system requirements, it is necessary to model distributed ICT systems as interconnected services, including dependencies that may cross organisational boundaries. This allows the interconnections to be adapted during run time through agile service composition or re-composition to address the needs of a dynamically changing environment.

The existing research in this area is reviewed below and does not adequately address the following issues, solutions to which will be put forward in this Chapter:

- Inter-dependencies between loosely coupled systems that may be operated by different organisations;
- Dynamic changes to resources and assets, their inter-dependencies and threats; and
- The link between organisational risk management and ICT security and management policies.

Grid-based deployments are classically focused on providing applications and storage, typically measured in CPU time and storage capacity. As explained above, today's systems, comprising chains of services, require guarantees on end-to-end properties that go beyond the traditional model of non-recoverable usage. SLAs are bilateral agreements that encode the terms of the business relationship with respect to service provider constraints and consumer obligations.

The existing work in the area of SLA-based governance does not adequately address the fact that there exist dependability requirements for 'systems of services' that manifest only at the system-level from individual service behaviour, and which require policy to map to local management actions. We propose an approach to this based on a SLA- and policy-based management framework in this Chapter.

Semantic Modelling of Security

The following review is based on two of the most recent papers from Secure Business Austria and their collaborators at Vienna University of Technology. (Fenz & Ekelhart, 2009) describe the security ontology developed by the group, and indicates how it can be used to capture and exploit expert knowledge about security threats and controls. (Ekelhart, Fenz, & Neubauer, 2009) describe a software tool for exploiting the ontology in real-world security analysis.

The group's basic premise is that risk management should be conducted by business stakeholders, but that they also need access to security expertise (about threats, vulnerabilities and controls) that they typically do not have. To address this and maintain business continuity it is necessary to engage a security expert throughout the process. This expert is typically expensive and can become a single point of failure in the risk management process. The solution is to encode the necessary security expertise as an ontology, and to provide user-friendly tools that exploit this ontology to make risk analysis by business stakeholders feasible. In this review we describe new and existing challenges which are not met by the SBA work.

Security Ontology

The security ontology is described in (Fenz & Ekelhart, 2009). The ontological model was based initially on the NIST Handbook (National Institute of Standards and Technology, 1995). The ontology was then populated by analysing the guidelines and checklists from the German IT Grundschutz Manual (BSI, 2004), supplemented by other sources such as ISO/IEC 27001 (ISO, 2005). Although the IT Grundschutz Manual was selected as the most suitable starting point for the work, it is clear from the paper that it does not conform to the NIST 800-12 security model, and many adjustments must have been needed. For example, the IT Grundschutz Manual does not distinguish between threats and vulnerabilities, so it was necessary to manually classify concepts to map them to the NIST model.

The security ontology includes about 500 concepts associated with the following basic concepts and relationships:

- Organisations, one of which is the organisation whose risks are being analysed;
- Tangible and intangible assets owned by organisations, and security attributes (e.g. confidentiality, integrity, etc) needed for business operation;
- Threats to these asset security attributes;
- Vulnerabilities through which the assets would be compromised;
- Controls that may be implemented to mitigate these vulnerabilities.

The security ontology should be used alongside an enterprise ontology that captures:

- Places at various levels (from towns down to individual rooms);
- Organisational roles;
- Staff and other organisations that may fill these roles;

Once the organisation and its assets and controls have been modelled, the relationships can be used to find threats and vulnerabilities. It is also possible to capture aspects like the severity of vulnerabilities, effectiveness of controls, the impact of asset loss, the probability of threats arising in each place within the organisation, etc.

The main strength of the security ontology is that it allows recursive relationships to be defined, to capture several important security issues:

- Linkages between different threats, in which the manifestation of one threat gives rise to others, e.g. a physical break-in brings the threat of physical attack on assets in the same place;
- The ways in which controls depend on uncompromised assets, which may or may not have been present independently of the control, e.g. a fire-fighting procedure may depend on smoke alarms;
- The ways in which assets depend on each other, e.g. a certification authority may depend on a data store.

Given these (and other) relationships, it is possible to extract a list of threats for a given set of assets, find their vulnerabilities and possible controls, etc. This is done using Pellet to extract inferences based on the basic ontological axioms and relationships, and either SPARQL or the Protégé OWL API to extract instance information (e.g. to find which assets may be compromised by a given threat).

The paper provides hardly any detail on how security properties are quantified and taken into account. For example, control effectiveness is barely mentioned, though in (Ekelhart, Fenz, & Neubauer, 2009) it becomes clear this is modelled via the probability of a vulnerability leading to an asset compromise once subject to a threat. The only aspects that are discussed are characterised via a three-point Likert scale (Likert, 1932).

The main weakness of the security (and enterprise) ontologies is that they are unable to address any dynamic aspects of security risk management, e.g. changes in assets or organisational structure, or the temporal aspects of vulnerabilities. The evaluation by security analysts identified a specific aspect of dynamic behaviour: the fact that the severity of an asset compromise is often related to its duration. In typical service deployments today, there is often a far more dynamic situation, in which assets and business relationships can change during operation. Neither situation is addressed in the reviewed papers – the authors say the system is designed for static risk analysis only.

Tooling

The tooling from SBA is the Automated Risk and Utility Management (AURUM) framework, as described in (Ekelhart, Fenz, & Neubauer, 2009). There are some differences in terminology between this paper and (Fenz & Ekelhart, 2009) – here the term 'resources' is used extensively. This seems to be equivalent to the term 'assets' from the latter paper. However, since complete equivalence cannot be checked, we will use the term 'resources' with the unproven belief that it is a synonym for 'assets'.

AURUM provides user interfaces to guide a user (a business stakeholder who presumably is not a security expert) through a risk management procedure. The tool supports the NIST SP 800-30 risk management standard (Stoneburner, Goguen, & Feringa, 2002), via ten phases of analysis:

- **System Characterisation:** capturing the organisational structure, resources (assets) and implemented controls;
- **Threat Identification:** discovering threats to the system as characterised;
- **Vulnerability Identification:** discovering vulnerabilities through which these threats can compromise system resources (assets);
- **Control Analysis:** analysing which vulnerabilities are addressed by controls;
- **Likelihood Determination:** finding the probability that a vulnerability will be exploited by a threat, given the a priori probability of each threat and other potentially triggering threats;
- **Impact Analysis:** working out the impact from each threat based on the impact of in-

dividual asset compromises that could be caused by each threat;

- **Risk Determination:** working out the overall risk level for each asset, given the likelihood of each threat and the impact of each asset compromise;
- **Control Recommendations:** proposing controls to address threats, taking account of which controls are already implemented;
- **Control Evaluation and Cost/Benefit Analysis:** working out the cost and benefit of combinations of proposed controls, based on criteria defined by the stakeholders.
- **Control Selection:** selecting between the most cost-effective combinations of controls found by the control evaluation process.

Many of these phases are supported by semantic queries and semantic inference over the security and enterprise ontologies to filter information (including questions) presented to the user, or to propose controls, etc. The final step is described as a decision support system that presents consequences of user decisions via graphical displays of costs and benefits, and the potential for user decisions to change these.

Much of the paper's content is a discussion of how AURUM differs from two other German tools: GSTool (BSI) and CRISAM (Calpana). The comparison can be summarised as follows:

The security ontology is used as a substitute for security expertise, providing a database of threats, vulnerabilities and controls and their relationships. This allows the tool to filter and present relevant information to users who may not otherwise know which vulnerabilities and controls are relevant to their organisation, etc. The relationship to the NIST risk management approach is clear, and the sources of information encoded in the ontology are given. The analysis supported is described but not in detail, presumably because of SBA commercial sensitivities.

Table 1. Comparison of risk management tools

Phase	GSTool	CRISAM	AURUM
System characterisation	Manual inventory	Manual inventory	Automated network scanning
	Extensive resource catalogue, arbitrary extensions possible	Limited resource catalogue, no extensions possible	Consistent and extensible resource catalogue based on ontological models
	No support for existing controls inventory	No support for existing controls inventory	Guided modelling of existing controls based on resource inventory
Threat identification	Extensive threat catalogue from IT Grundschutz Manual	No threat catalogue	Uses extensive threat catalogue based on multiple sources
Vulnerability identification	No vulnerability catalogue	No vulnerability catalogue	Extensive vulnerability catalogue incorporated into the ontology
Control analysis	No support for existing controls inventory	No support for existing controls inventory	Can model existing controls
	Manual analysis via control questions per resource	Manual analysis via control questions per resource groups	Automatic analysis of modelled controls
Likelihood determination	No modelling of threat probabilities	No modelling of threat probabilities	Mathematical modelling of location-dependent threat probabilities
	No consideration of existing controls	No consideration of existing controls	Takes account of modelled controls
Impact analysis	Based on confidentiality, integrity and availability requirements entered manually per resource	Based on manual assessment of control effectiveness per resource requirement	Based on automated reasoning to compute impact of modelled threats per resource
Risk determination	Based on checklists only	Based directly on control effectiveness responses	Risks are determined from threat likelihood and consequent impact
	No support for threat probabilities, so risks cannot be traced to find causes	No support for threat probabilities, so risks cannot be traced to find causes	Risks can be traced to specific threats
	Uses comprehensive threat catalogue from IT Grundschutz Manual	No links to specific control standards or implementations	Linked via security ontology to standards
Control recommendations	Describes controls using natural language from IT Grundschutz Manual	No support for control recommendations	Describes controls using formal and natural language from security ontology
Control evaluation and cost/benefit analysis	No direct support for control effectiveness analysis	Control effectiveness is specified manually by the user	Control effectiveness is calculated based on user-specified objective functions
Control selection	No direct support apart from natural language presentation of controls	No direct support	Graphical display of control effectiveness to assist user decisions

Semantic SLA Modelling

A service level agreement is a legal contract that specifies the minimum expectations and obligations that exist between a service provider and a service customer. Modelling semantic SLAs provides means for capturing and managing SLA/SLM (service level management) data in support of business-oriented SLM objectives. (Ward,

Buco, Chang, & Luan, 2002) highlight the main advantages of semantic SLA modelling as follows:

1. It aids in the development of extensible external representations for SLA data and SLA/SLM linkage;
2. It aids in the design of physical data models for this data. (such as schemas for relation database management stores); and
3. It allows the creation of object-oriented programming models as well as APIs for accessing SLA/SLM data.

Ward, Buco, Chang, and Luan's SLA Model

The SLA model specification in (Ward, Buco, Chang, & Luan, 2002) allows for information flows between the SLA semantic elements. Here qualified service level measurement data is generated after applying qualifying rules and algorithms to the raw service level measurement data. The qualification rules are extracted from the contract. Unqualified inclusion/exclusion data such as customer approved downtime and maintenance window start/stop time are also taken in account. The generation of qualified measurement data is crucial in order to prevent the use of unqualified data in the service level evaluation process or to complex corrections being applied at the service level evaluation phase. The overall SLA refund/reward algorithm is composed from an accumulation of individual service level guarantee (SLG) refund data sets which are organised into service categories. It uses these service categories along with SLA wide policy statement to compute the actual refund/reward due to the customer.

The SLA semantic model contains service package graphs which are composed of service packages and transition triggers which reside between the service category refund/reward data and the SLA refund/reward algorithm, these service package graphs allow the model to capture contractual agreements on how quality standards

and SLA refunds/rewards details can change. This model was created after performing an in depth analysis of nine commercial SLA contracts/templates comprising of over 100 service level components and has been validated against 40 other e-business outsourcing SLA contracts since it was designed.

The SLAs produced using the above approach are static for the contract period and are applied equally to the overall traffic between the end-user and the network, regardless of the different service levels required by different applications. This implies that dynamic negotiation of QoS requirements specified by the service level specification within an access network is not possible.

Web Service Modelling Ontology

Semantic modelling of service level agreements (SLA) and quality of service (QoS) characteristics has been done in the past using the Web Service Modelling Ontology (WSMO) (Roman, et al., 2005). This was done with the intention of providing QoS-aware service oriented architectures. Semantic SLA modelling using WSMO focuses principally on automated service mediation and on the service execution infrastructure (Toma, Foxvog, & Jaeger, 2006). By adding semantic descriptions to service parameters it is possible for agents to discover and rank services automatically by applying semantic reasoning. Using service mediation it is also possible to translate between user requirements and service offerings. The WSMX (Haller, Cimpian, Mocan, Oren, & Bussler, 2005) environment enables the provision of these services on demand.

The WSMO initiative has focused its QoS modelling efforts on capturing the requirements from a service consumer point of view more precisely so as to ensure a continuous level of QoS. Work done by Toma et al (2006) involves extending the WSMO ontology to include QoS and non-functional properties and treat them as normal attributes for semantic web services and goals. With the QoS properties as part of the logical model of the Web Service Markup Language (WSML), it is possible to reason and infer new knowledge from these descriptions. All non-functional properties are defined through the use of relations where the range of the relation is not constrained to class instances.

The non-functional properties proposed by WSMO are divided into two main categories. The properties such as reliability, scalability and security capture the constraints over a service's functional behaviour and behavioural aspects. NFPs such as contributor, creator and date are additional metadata to provide description of a service. However since these properties are only provided as attribute value pairs, reasoning supported over the non-functional properties is very limited.

OWL-Q

Other efforts in the area of semantic modelling for SLA include OWL-Q (Kritikos & Plexousakis, 2006), which is an upper level ontology extending OWL-S for describing QoS for web services. The OWL-Q ontology is defined using various facets which are developed and expressed independently. Each of these facets serves a specific purpose in the ontology. For example the connecting facet is used for linking the OWL-Q ontology to a higher level OWL-S ontology; the QoS metric facet is used for defining the QoS metric instances; the function, measurement directive and schedule facets are used for the measurement of metrics; and the unit facet describes the unit of a QoS metric.

The OWL-Q approach proposes a way to infer equivalences between differently named QoS parameters that are semantically equivalent. Constraint-based programming is used to perform the matchmaking of compatible offers. Selection is performed by means of a weighted composition of utility functions, which balance the best and worst scenarios to compute the utility value. However, these user preferences are not seman-

tically defined in the OWL-Q ontology (García, Ruiz, & Ruiz-Cortés, 2009).

onQoS Ontology

Research work carried out by (Giallonardo & Zimeo, 2007) describes a QoS ontology 'onQoS', which is an openly available OWL ontology for QoS and evaluates it in a QoS-aware matching environment. The ontology can be used for specifying the QoS advertisements by service providers and the QoS requirements by service consumers in the form of templates. The main concepts of the ontology include QoSParameter which is a measurable QoS characteristic or feature, QoS-Metric which is a type of measurement and relates to a QoS parameter, MeasurementProcess is the process by which numbers of symbols are assigned to QoS parameters according to a given set of rules. Other main concepts include Scale which defines the nature of the relationship between a set of values and ScaleValue which is the number or symbol that identifies a category in which the QoS parameter can be placed. The ontology is subdivided into three categories. The Upper Ontology which describes the QoS ontological language. The upper ontology contains the upper level vocabulary needed in order to provide the most appropriate information for formulating and for answering QoS queries. The middle ontology defines the standard vocabulary of the ontology such as QoSParameters, QoSMetrics and QoSScales. Various metrics such as Elementary Metrics, Derived Metrics and Internal, External, Nominal, Ordinal, Numeric, Ratio and Interval Metrics are defined in this layer. The low ontology encodes the concepts, properties and constraints of a specific domain. These concepts belong to those of a real world application. (Giallonardo & Zimeo, 2007) have also developed matching algorithms using the Pellet reasoner to perform automated web service matching using the QoS metrics.

Green's SLA Ontologies

Green proposes an SLA formalisation using OWL and SWRL (Green, 2006). Green's work was developed as part of defining the service level agreements in the telecommunications domain in a machine understandable format. A Unit ontology was formalized to model the units of metrics which can be used to compare metrics and also support any operations on these metrics. The Time Unit ontology is an extension of the Unit ontology and is based in the domain of temporal comparisons. Other ontologies which were formalized as part of this process included the Temporal Ontology, The Network Metrics Ontology and the Currency Ontology. The SLA ontology specifies only the bare minimum requirements for an SLA and is designed to be sub classed for a specific domain. It consists of two main classes: the SLA Class, which specifies properties such as the period of validity of an SLA together with a number of obligations that services place on the SLA; and the Service Obligation Class, which describes a single service obligation on an SLA. The QDINE SLA Ontology is a specialized ontology which imports the SLA ontology and refines it by adding additional properties such as has Violation which is restricted to the instances of Violation Model. The Violation model formalizes the various violations which can occur on an obligation.

The abstraction layer necessary to deal with different level of QoS parameters is not available in Green's ontology models. There is a lack of generic concepts to describe the QoS parameters and their metrics. Only network level parameters are specified. The QDINE ontologies make use of rules to perform QoS matching. The ontologies themselves are not used directly (using axioms etc.) to assist in the matching process.

WSLA

The WSLA specification is designed to capture service level agreements in a formal way to en-able automatic configuration of both the service implementing system and of the service providing organization as well as the system that is used to supervise the agreed quality of service (Ludwig, Keller, Dan, King, & Franck, 2003). A service level agreement specified using WSLA will consists of the description of parties and their roles and the action interfaces they expose to other parties of the contract. A specification of the service level parameters against which guarantees are applied. These SLA parameters are specified using metrics which define how to measure an item. Additionally WSLA also contains a representation of the parties' obligations; these are expressed as service level objectives. SLOs contain a formal expression of the guaranteed condition of a service in a given period. WSLA defines the agreed performance characteristics and the way to evaluate and measure them between a service and the application using it. During the runtime management of a WSLA a measurement function receives the measure metrics from the systems instrumentation and measures its system parameters according to the instruction set given in the measurement directives of a WSLA. The measurement function is also responsible to collect higher level metrics. A condition evaluation function then evaluates the guarantees of the WSLA as defined in the agreement. A management function is responsible for implementing actions which are invoked when WSLA guarantees are violated. Various MeasurementDirectives are defined in the WSLA specification. These define how parameter values are to be measured by the organization that makes a metric's value available. The measurement directive for a particular metric corresponds to a data item that is exposed by the instrumentation of a service. A few examples of simple measurement directives include ResponseTime, NetworkLatency, CPUSpeed etc.

However the WSLA specification does not define or implement the end to end QoS management capability. The specification also lacks facilities for complete QoS estimation, management and monitoring for processes.

Unified QoS Ontology

Efforts by (Dobson, 2006) have tried to produce a unified QoS/SLA ontology which is applicable to QoS-based web service selection, QoS monitoring and QoS adaptation. Past research by (Tosic, Esfandiari, Pagurek, & Patel, 2002) and (Tian, Gramm, Naumowicz, Ritter, & Schiller, 2003) has focused on the need for having a QoS ontology for web service selection. In the context of a service level agreement, quality is only a part of the SLA hence the unified QoS ontology should include additional terms in order to define a semantic SLA. Pre-existing concepts such as Guarantee/ Agreement, Advertisement and User request are imported from the QoS profile. A Service Level Objective concept is added with two derived concepts: Capability Offer and Requirement, the fulfilment of these offers is verified using rules. Other additional concepts include Actors, Assessment (Match/Mismatch) for quality assessment. Business value, Assertion Specification and Cost Model information. The relationship information between these concepts has also been modelled into the SLA ontology. An SLA must include the service provider, service requester and measurement partners, as well as define the price of the Service etc. A full list of the requirements for an SLA ontology can be found in (Dobson, 2006).

This approach does not deal with user-driven and semi-automatic definitions of SLA mappings. The automation is required to enable negotiations between inconsistent SLA templates. Also the approach does not facilitate user driven definition of publicly available SLA templates.

SLA-Based System Governance

System governance (in a service-oriented architecture) is concerned with managing the relationship between service providers and service consumers.

It is important to recognise that this is a two-sided process. The service provider should manage their commitments to provide services, and manage how the services are provided so they meet their commitments. The service consumer also has to manage their relationships with service providers, and manage how they use services from those providers to meet their needs.

On each side, management decisions are based on a local 'context': a body of information about the relationship (e.g. the commitments made to the other party), and other things that may affect the relationship (e.g. the availability of resources, the existence of other relationships and commitments that may compete for those resources, the availability of competing services from other providers, the consumer's overall requirements for the system in which the service will be used, etc). A subset of the context on each side will be known to the other party, and this includes the content of any service level agreement between the two parties, as shown in Figure 1.

This notion of system/service management using bilateral SLA is used in GRIA (Service Oriented Collaborations for Industry and Commerce), which was developed in the NextGRID project (NextGRID), and includes the notion of private information that is not shared. Note that the situation shown in Figure 1 applies even before an SLA is negotiated between the two parties – they each have a context in which the (potential)

Figure 1. Service provision and consumption: Shared vs. private management context

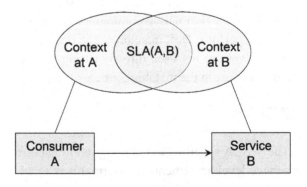

SLA is considered, and some of this is shared. SLA negotiation is the process whereby the parties make commitments in terms of the shared information, and once made, these commitments become an important (but not the only) factor driving their respective management decisions.

In GRIA, the service provider first creates an SLA template describing which services are offered to the consumer, the quality of service, and how much and how often the consumer will have to pay for their use. This is published, so it becomes part of the context shared with any consumer. However, the SLA template also contains some 'hidden' terms which are not included in the published version, and these describe the resources needed by services to deliver an SLA based on the template, A service provider may define and publish many different SLA templates. Templates may be tailored to individual customers and access to the templates restricted accordingly, or several different general templates may be defined with a variety of level of service and price to give the customer some choice. In GRIA, a consumer who wants to negotiate an SLA has to choose an SLA template from a suitable provide, and ask them (via a web service message) for an SLA based on that template. The provider then decides whether to grant or deny the request – this is known as a discrete offer negotiation.

Service Level Agreements

Differentiated Services (DiffServ) use a low-level approach in an attempt to provide QoS guarantees by classifying network traffic. (Bouras & Sevasti, 2005) attempt to address end-to-end SLAs on top of DiffServ. The SLA is described as being divided into two parts — the administrative/legal part plus the Service Level Specification (SLS). Each SLS comprises a Service Level Object (SLO), which defines parameters and their values that are guaranteed by the service.

The above approach makes the assumption that bilateral SLAs are more permanent than end-to-end SLA, which may need to be dynamically negotiated using existing SLAs and torn down within a short time frame. An *e2e* SLA is composed from the aggregation of a chain of bilateral SLAs. However, an end-to-end ("e2e") SLA specification requires the *a priori* negotiation of all bilateral SLAs. This means it is of limited use for *ad hoc* workflows, which may be initiated before it is known whether a key service can be provided. It is also very brittle, in that the failure to meet any one agreement fails the whole chain, and makes no provision for renegotiation.

In contrast to DiffServ, there are a large number of increasingly high level ways to represent SLAs. Several languages have been developed to represent SLAs, including SLAng (Skene, Lamanna, & Emmerich, 2004), WSOL (Tosic, Pagurek, & Patel, 2003), QuA (Amundsen, Lund, Eliassen, & Staehli, 2004), WSLA (Ludwig, Keller, Dan, King, & Franck, 2003), QSL (Teyssié, 2006) and QML (Frølund & Koistinen, 1998)(Becker, 2008). Most of the existing work on SLA specification has fed into or been superseded by the current WS-Agreement standard (Andrieux, Czajkowski, Dan, Keahey, & Ludwig, 2007). The following summarises the salient characteristics of existing SLA representations:

- **SLAng:** a domain-specific language expressed using an EMOF metamodel (an extension to UML) with OCL constraints that include reliability, availability and timeliness.
- **Web Service Offering Language (WSOL):** an extension to WSDL that formally describes the QoS offerings of services, where one service may make multiple offerings.
- **Quality of service-aware component Architecture (QuA):** an architecture in which components exchange QoS information to support "service planning" such that the overall system QoS requirements

are satisfied. There is no formal concept of the agreement between components.

- **Web Service Level Agreements (WSLA):** an unambiguous specification of SLAs that are monitorable in a distributed environment The WSLA specification defines an agreement between three named parties: the service provider, the consumer and a third, supporting, party. The use of such a tri-partite agreement is considered to be outmoded and not representative of actual business agreements.

WS-Agreement is a specification developed by the Grid Resource Allocation Agreement Protocol (GRAAP) working group of the Open Grid Foundation (OGF). This specifies an XML schema and a protocol for establishing a bilateral agreement, including the specification of agreement templates. The specification is intentionally generic and domain-specific parameters must be defined. The negotiation protocol is also very simple. Extensions, such as WS-Agreement Negotiation (Ziegler, Wieder, & Battré, 2008) allow for counter-offers and re-negotiation. There is also work on using a suitable QoS ontology of domain concepts to allow consumers to discover services that satisfy their QoS requirements using WS-Agreement (Oldham, Sheth, Hakimpour, & Verma, 2006).

GRIA is the only (known) open source technology to fully support bilateral SLA including shared and private context models. The SLA model used in GRIA is designed to include QoS constraints and bounds that have to be honoured by the service provider. The model focuses on capacity management rather than on dynamic provisioning decisions (Boniface M., Phillips, Sanchez-Macian, & Surridge, 2007). The GRIA SLA model is not based on a semantic model. However, a GRIA SLA represents (enforceable) constraints on service behaviour from a provider's perspective, while providing a statement of capability from a consumer's perspective.

Semantic Modelling of Resource Dependability

Semantic models of the critical infrastructure, including its ICT services, can be used to identify failure and underperformance (such as caused by faults in or attack on the service), to increase human awareness of the potential risks and/or to allow automated mitigation of them. Semantics allows information and services to be described in such a way that makes them amenable to machine-based interpretation and reasoning. Thus when a failure (or a threat of failure) is detected, governance components can take autonomous or semi-autonomous (human-directed) action to manage the consequences, including changing the interdependency relationships between services.

In this Chapter, we present a service model and a base-metric ontology which can be used by service providers to give a domain-specific semantic description of their services. We explain the underlying mathematical model and show how this allows us to aggregate service-level measurements in order to provide system-wide Key Performance Indicators (KPIs).

Service Consumers, Providers, Resources and Tasks

A service is implemented by a service provider and made accessible to service consumers. The service uses resources (made available as services) from suppliers who may be external to the service provider. In this approach we assume that services are made available only under a service level agreement (SLA) between a service provider and a service customer who is typically also a service consumer. Each service provider will therefore have zero or more 'consumer SLA' with customers relating to the consumption of its services, and 'supplier SLA' with resource suppliers. Resources should have a common representation in terms of supplied services with a supplier SLA, even if the resource is in-house and the supplier SLA is simply a description of its expected properties.

When a consumer uses a service, the context for each related set of interactions is called a task. For example, in a service to provide cleaning of aircraft, each occasion when an aircraft is cleaned may be a task. In this context the consumer may make requests to schedule the cleaning (i.e. specify when the aircraft will be available and ready for cleaning), to inform the cleaners that the aircraft is ready and cleaning can start, and to obtain estimates of when the cleaning will be completed. The task allows these requests to be related to each other, and the service will need to support a means for attaching the context to each request – e.g. by using the WS-Resource specification. Note that we do not call such a context a 'resource' to avoid confusion with the above definition of a resource as something supplied to and used by a service.

A service provider refers to tasks associated with the use of its services by consumers as 'consumer tasks'. Tasks associated with the use of supplied resources by its services are called 'supplier tasks'. If the service is implemented as a workflow, the individual steps in the workflow are referred to by the service provider as 'activities', and typically several activities may be associated with the same supplier task.

Services that are available to consumers are implemented via a service *hosting container*. This container is accessible only to the service provider and can be used to create services associated with each consumer SLA. The consumer can use the services to create tasks, and because each service is associated with only one SLA, each task can only be associated with one SLA.

Service Behaviour, Measurement and Metrics

A behaviour is anything a service does that we may wish to measure or agree commitments about. Typically this will be something that happens over time or at some particular time – e.g. how often

and when a service is used, how much work it does, how quickly it responds to certain events, etc.

A metric refers to measurements of some behaviour of interest. Values obtained by measuring a service can only be interpreted if we know what they refer to and how they were measured. Typically a metric will be referenced by a URI which is associated with the behaviour of interest, the measurement procedure (if this matters), and the units of measurement (if the values are not dimensionless).

A measurement procedure should deliver data relating to a particular metric, from a particular service (or group of services), in a particular context (e.g. a particular user or SLA, etc). Any measurement should be associated with an absolute (wallclock) time at which it is valid. If the measurement is of some event then this time will be the time of the measured event. If it relates to some continuous behaviour, the measurement time will be the time up to which the behaviour is reflected in the value returned by the measurement.

Quality of service (QoS) is measured by a service provider about the services it provides to others. For example, the number of times a service is used by a consumer as measured by the provder of the service is a QoS measurement. QoS measurement procedures can be embedded into the implementation of any service, and should deliver this data as required. Quality of Experience (QoE) is measured by a service consumer about the services it uses (whether provided in-house or by others). QoE measurement procedures can be embedded into workflows that use the measured services. Note that service providers can report QoS to consumers, and consumers can report QoE to service providers (see Figure 2). The terminology refers to the origin of measurement data, not where it is used.

Service Management and Commitments

The management and governance of services should control service behaviour, and hence con-

Figure 2. QoS/QoE terminology

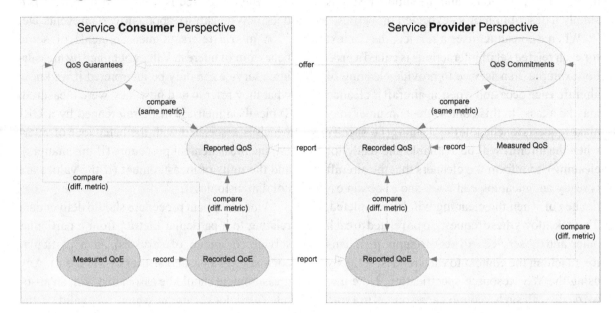

trol what values are obtained in QoS (and ideally QoE) measurements. Controlled behaviour is defined via constraints on particular metrics for a particular service (or group of services) in a particular context and possibly at particular times or time intervals. Constraints arise in two ways:

- In management policies defining behaviour that should trigger specific management actions; and
- In service level agreements to define commitments on what behaviour is acceptable and if not what consequences should follow.

In both cases, constraints refer to metrics (and hence behaviour) and define the range of values that is acceptable (i.e. no action need be taken). If the behaviour does not meet the constraint then the consequences are applied. In a management policy this is a management action initiated by the service provider, e.g. to change the security policy or allocate more resources to the service. Note that the action occurs only after the behaviour has transgressed the constraint. In an SLA term,

the consequence is typically a remedial action or loss of rights for whichever party is responsible for ensuring the constraint is not violated. For example, if a service provider fails to deliver the service with acceptable QoS, they may have to pay a fine or lose the right to bill the customer, while if a consumer uses the service too much they may have to pay a surcharge or lose the right to access the service in future.

Metric Model

The metrics required to monitor and manage resource dependability are as follows:

- **Absolute Time:** the wall clock time at which some event happens
- **Elapsed Time:** the time interval between some triggering event and some specified response;
- **Counter:** the number of times some event occurs;
- **Minimum, Maximum and Mean Elapsed Times:** simple measures of the distribu-

tion of Elapsed Time for collections of responses;

- **Elapsed Time Compliance:** the proportion of elapsed times for a specified set of responses that do not exceed a specified limit;
- **Non Recoverable Usage and Usage Rate:** the amount that a resource is used, typically measured in terms of the time for which it was used, and where appropriate also the usage rate (or intensity);
- **State:** the state of a service;
- **State Occupancy:** the time for which a service is in a particular state (or not in that state).
- **Data Error:** the error of data supplied compared to the reference value to which it relates;
- **Data Accuracy:** the error of data supplied as a proportion of the data precision;
- **Data Accuracy Compliance:** the proportion of items in a specified set of data whose accuracy is not worse than a specified limit;
- **Data Precision:** the precision bands for data, which may need to be considered as a metric so it can be constrained as a condition for the application of accuracy metrics.
- **Auditable properties:** of a service, which are usually represented as a State metric, but which cannot be measured, only asserted.

These metrics represent 'base classes' that capture the physical and mathematical nature of certain kinds of service behaviours and measurements. The intention is that users of the ontology create subclasses referring to specific types of service behaviour. For example, if we have a service that provides aircraft cleaning, we may define:

1. The number of consumer tasks created for the service, i.e. the number of occasions when cleaners will attend and clean any aircraft (subclass of Counter);
2. The number of requests for estimates of the completion time for cleaning tasks (subclass of Counter);
3. The amount of time the service is able to receive and process requests for new consumer tasks (subclass of State Occupancy);
4. The amount of time the service is able to receive and process requests for the estimated completion time for existing consumer tasks (subclass of State Occupancy);
5. The elapsed time until the start of cleaning since the cleaning was scheduled and the aircraft became available (subclass of Elapsed Time)
6. The proportion of elapsed times for cleaning tasks provided by the service that are up to a specified limit (subclass of Elapsed Time Compliance);
7. The proportion of scheduled times when aircraft are supposed to be available whose accuracy is within a specified limit (subclass of Accuracy Compliance);
8. The accuracy of the estimates for when cleaning will be finished (subclass of Accuracy).

The SLA may include commitments by the customer to limit the number of consumer requests for cleaning tasks and completion time estimates – constraints on metrics (1) and (2) respectively. They may also agree to a limit on the proportion of cleaning tasks for which the aircraft was not available at the scheduled time – a constraint on metric (7).

The provider may then commit to limit the availability of the service is to process each type of request – constraints on metrics (3) and (4). The provider may also guarantee how accurate their estimates for cleaning completion time will be – a constraint on metric (8), and of the proportion of cleaning tasks that take longer than some bound – a constraint on metric (7).

The provider may also specify management policies that are not agreed with the customer. For example, they may define policies to call more cleaners to work if the number of cleaning tasks grows – a constraint on metric (1), and/or the elapsed times for starting to clean become too large – a constraint on metric (5).

Note that it is frequently necessary to construct compound constraints by combining simpler constraints. For example, the guarantee about how often the cleaners start promptly may be conditional on the number of cleaning tasks remaining within bounds and the proportion of aircraft that are not available on schedule is not too high. Or one may wish to call an extra cleaning team if there are more than 20 cleaning tasks, but only if you currently have less than 5 cleaning teams available. To handle these situations do this, one can use logical 'AND', 'OR' and 'NOT' operators to combine a primary constraint with conditions, so the overall constraint is satisfied if the primary constraint is satisfied, or any of the conditions is not satisfied.

Metric Classes and Ontological Relationships

The classes of metrics described above clearly have some relationships:

- Elapsed times may be sub-intervals of other elapsed times, in which case it is meaningful to define a new elapsed time metric based on the larger interval but excluding the smaller;
- Min/max elapsed times are based on elapsed times;
- Mean elapsed times and elapsed time compliance are based on elapsed times and also a counter for the number of responses whose elapsed time is included;
- Data accuracy is equal to the data error relative to its precision;

- Data compliance is based on data accuracy and also a counter for the number of data items whose accuracy is included;
- Non-recoverable usage and usage rate metrics come in related pairs;
- Min/max usage rates are based on non-recoverable usage rates;
- State occupancy is a special case (subclass) of non-recoverable usage, where the usage rate is always 1 or zero, and the state it relates to is one of the possible values of a state metric;
- Auditable property is a special case of state, whose value cannot be measured but only confirmed through audit.

These relationships should be captured in properties of each class, and are illustrated in Figure 3.

Mathematical Relationships

Metrics may be related to each other through mathematical equations. Consider the case of ElapsedTime above. This metric just signifies how long it takes for some event to occur in response to some stimulus. It can be measured by recording the time when the stimulus arises, then checking the time when the subsequent event is observed and finding the difference.

Subclasses of this metric would be used to refer to particular responses, e.g. the time taken to process and respond to each type of request supported by each type of service, or the time taken for some internal resourcing action to occur such as cleaners arriving at an aircraft after it was scheduled and available. It should be possible to ask a consumer task for the elapsed times of all responses corresponding to the metric, and possibly to ask for the same thing in a wider context (e.g. from a service or service container).

Constraints on such metrics signify how long it should take for some response. There are two types of constraints:

Figure 3. Metric base classes and relationships

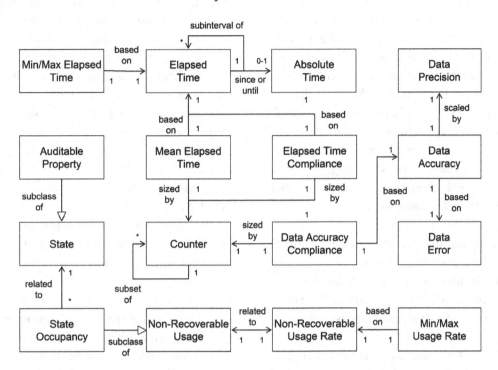

- An upper limit on the elapsed time, encoding a lower limit on the performance of a service, which is often used in SLA commitments as well as management policies;
- A lower limit on the elapsed time, which is typically used only in management policies to trigger actions to reduce the resource available if a service over-performs.

If there are many events of the same type, one may wish to define a single constraint that applies to all the responses, so if any breaches the constraint the whole set is considered to do so. This allows one to test the constraint more efficiently by checking only the fastest and slowest response in the set.

Sometimes it may be appropriate to define constraints that include more than one response time. For example, suppose a service supports aircraft refuelling but the amount of fuel supplied (and hence the time spent actually pumping fuel) is specified by the consumer – as shown in Figure 4.

In this situation the service provider cannot guarantee the total response time T(i), because they have no control over the amount of time C(i) for which the fuel will actually flow into the aircraft. But they can control how long it takes

Figure 4. Service response times

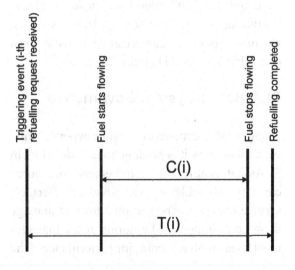

for a fuel browser to reach the aircraft after the refuelling request is received, and how long it takes to connect and disconnect the fuelling hoses and get clear after fuelling is completed, etc. So the service provider may prefer to specify a constraint on the difference between the two elapsed times. Anything that is constrained should be a metric (to keep the SLA and policy constraint logic and schema simple), so in this situation one should define a new metric which might be called something like 'fuelling operation time'. One then has two options to obtain its value:

- Measure it directly so values are returned by the measurement procedure; or
- Define rules specifying the relationship between the new metric's value and the other metrics whose values are measured.

In Figure 4 we should define three metrics:

1. The total response time for a job execution service;
2. The computation time for jobs executed by the service;
3. The delay in executing the job at the service.

All three of these metrics should be subclasses of elapsed time. The last of them could be measured directly in the usual way, but alternatively we could derive its value from those of (1) and (2) through semantic reasoning. To support this, we must capture the numerical relationship via a rule relating (3) to (1) minus (2).

SLA-Based System Governance

Using the above model of resource dependability, we explain how it is possible to encode NFPs in SLAs that relate resource requirements to resource capacity and enable a service provider to offer their service to consumers, and monitor and manage these commitments. Monitoring at the management level involves identifying performance of the service according to defined metrics. Monitoring at the governance level involves allowing consumers to make a choice based on the trustworthiness of a service provider. This is achieved through the certification of services by accredited bodies (and their associated trust chain, i.e. we believe what they say), which provides consumers with evidence on which to make a trust decision (rather than making an arbitrary decision or having the service forced upon them). Such evidence supports the claim that the service provider can fulfill the SLA.

We propose a governance framework that is installed by a service provider and which comprises the following three components:

- An SLA manager that manages commitments with down-stream customers;
- A resource manager that manages local resources and commitments with up-stream suppliers (the 'underpinning contract' in ITIL terminology (Office of Government Commerce)); and
- A service manager that helps to balance customer commitments with supplier commitments and takes action according to a human-defined management policy.

Challenges to Existing SLA-Based Service Management

Existing service oriented infrastructures (SOI), as exemplified by GRIA, provide a simple model of a service provider, an organisation that has some (fixed) resources of known capacity, which runs services that operate by using those resources, and makes commitments to customers (in SLA) regarding the usage of those services. Given this simple model, the main use cases supported by GRIA include the following:

1. Service provider defines the nature and capacity of resources, via usage rate metrics such as the number of CPU, the capacity

of storage devices, network bandwidth, software licences, etc.

2. Service provider defines SLA templates, encoding usage limits via metrics such as the number of service tasks, the number of frames rendered, CPU time consumed, etc.

3. Service provider publishes (or withdraws) SLA templates via their SLA manager.

4. Customer discovers published SLA templates by querying the provider's SLA manager.

5. Customer negotiates an SLA based on a published SLA template by requesting the SLA from the service provider's SLA manager (in the context of the SLA template).

In use case (2) above, each usage limit represent a commitment by both parties. The service provider is saying 'I will make sure this level of usage is possible', provided the customer agrees that 'I won't use more than this'. In practice, the service provider enforces the limit by refusing service requests that would cause the limit to be exceeded, and destroying long-running tasks once the limit is reached.

In use case (5) the SLA is issued if the customer is trustworthy (has a trade account and credit with the service provider), and the service provider's resources are sufficient for the prescribed usage. To check this, a simple comparison is made between the total usage commitments in all extant SLA plus the proposed new SLA, and the capacity of resources:

$$\sum_{i \in S'} \frac{L_{ij}}{r_{ij}} \leq \sum_{k \in R} C_{kj}, \forall j \in M \quad (1)$$

Here M is the set of usage rate metrics describing the available resources. R is the set of resources, whose capacity is specified as an upper limit C_{kj} for each resource k and metric j. S' is the set of existing SLA plus the proposed new SLA, L_{ij} is

the upper limit specified for metric j in SLA i, and r_{ij} is the contention ratio for this limit or 1 if no contention ratio is specified. If an SLA limit specifies cumulative usage, a corresponding usage rate limit is found by dividing the total permitted usage by the time interval to which the limit applies. If an SLA specifies both usage rate and cumulative usage limits, the one with the higher L_{ij}/r_{ij} should be used in the summation.

In the current state of the art (as reviewed above), such as GRIA (Service Oriented Collaborations for Industry and Commerce), the SLA limits seen by the customer are expressed in terms of service usage metrics that are meaningful to them. For example, the SLA may say they can render 1000 high definition video frames per day. Resource capacity may be specified using quite different metrics chosen by the service provider, such as the number of 3 GHz CPU cores available. These metrics may not mean anything to the customer, and if they do, the service provider may not want the customer to know how much resource they will need to deliver the SLA. Thus it is possible that none of the metrics used to describe resource capacity are used in the SLA terms, so that the left hand side of inequality (1) gives zero for every resource capacity metric.

To get around this, inequality (1) is applied not only to the SLA terms seen by the customer, but also to the associated management policies (private terms) defined in the corresponding SLA template. Thus a service provider can specify an SLA template for up to 1000 frames per day, and also specify a hidden policy committing them to use up to one 3 GHz CPU core subject to a contention ratio of 2 (the contention ratio indicates that the core is needed half time). If their capacity is 100 of these cores, they could have up to 200 SLA corresponding to this template.

This approach works reasonably because of several key simplifications:

- All resources are in house, their capacity is known and specified to the system in advance by the service provider – any changes in capacity must be handled manually;
- Resource capacity is expressed in terms of usage rate limits (possibly with contention), for usage metrics chosen by the service provider;
- Commitments made by the service provider to customers in SLA are also expressed in terms of usage limits (usage rate or total usage), for metrics chosen by the service provider;
- The comparison of customer commitments with resource capacity is done by comparing the limits using the same metrics on both sides;
- If this comparison should not be visible to the customer, it is encoded on the SLA side using private terms.

In current service-oriented ICT deployments and usage scenarios, we typically have a more complex situation in which the above approach cannot work, since:

- Customer commitments are likely to include other QoS terms (representing performance, dependability, etc) as well as limits on usage;
- Resource capacity is therefore also a more sophisticated concept, describing the ability of a resource to support usage in the presence of other QoS constraints (reflecting performance, dependability and aspects such as the level of risk to the service provider);
- Resources may elastically provisioned from external (upstream) service providers, so their total capacity is not known in advance, and may be changed automatically by management actions (e.g. nego-

tiating new supplier SLA with upstream providers);
- Resources provisioned in this way will be specified in a supplier SLA, using metrics chosen by the supplier that may not even be known in advance by the service provider;
- The comparison between customer commitments therefore cannot be done using the same metrics for both.

The net result of this is that the comparison between customer commitments and resource capacity cannot be done by simply comparing limits for the same metrics on both sides. Even using private SLA terms for resourcing implications of customer commitments will not work because some resources represent the use of upstream services under SLA that use different metrics chosen by their supplier. Finally, because the resourcing approach can be elastic and under autonomic control, it is not even possible to estimate the capacity of the service provider to deliver a type of service in advance.

The challenge is to support customer commitments and management policies that go beyond mere usage limits. We must also support the use of external resources, which in principle can be changed dynamically through automatically triggered SLA negotiation or termination. However, in this flexible value chain the comparison between commitments and capacity (including externally supplied capacity) is complex. This is partly due to the fact that all resources are treated as services, and some capacity measures are (pre-)defined for every service. We require a single, well-defined model that covers all requirements for aggregating commitments and resource capacity. Using this model it is possible to support distinct management objectives for upstream and downstream services, as well as elastic customer services whose capacity is not pre-defined and depends only on upstream/in-house resources.

Proposed Approach and Terminology

Actors and Services

To address the more general case outlined above, we must clarify the terminology and metrics used by a service provider, and then define a generic approach to policy- and model-driven management that can meet our needs.

The first concern is to define the actors:

- The *service provider* is the (natural or legal) person providing services and operating the service management framework;
- A *consumer* is a (natural or legal) person who consumes one or more services provided by the service provider;
- A *customer* is a (natural or legal) person who makes an agreement (a *consumer SLA*) with the service provider for the provision of services to one or more consumers (possibly including the customer);
- A *supplier* is a (natural or legal) person who makes an agreement (a *supplier SLA*) with the service provider for the provision of services by the supplier.

Commitments made by the service provider in agreements with customers are known as *consumer commitments*, while those made to the service provider in agreements with suppliers are known as *supplier commitments*. Obligations placed on consumers in agreements with customers are known as *consumer obligations*, and where such obligations appear in supplier SLA they are known as *supplier obligations*. A typical consumer obligation might be an undertaking to pay for services used, or to keep usage within some limit.

There also exist scenarios in which a service provider uses services as a consumer, where the service operator is not one of their suppliers – i.e. the service is not accessible to the service provider under any supplier SLA. For this reason, we propose the following terminology:

- A *downstream service* is a service provided by the service provider to (downstream) consumers;
- An *upstream service* is a service used by the service provider to provision a downstream service.

The terms upstream and downstream refer only to whether the service provider is providing a service or whether they are consuming a service. There is no longer any reference to the business relationships under which the service is provided or consumed. Upstream services may be provided by suppliers (with whom the service provider has an SLA), or by another party specified by the consumer. A typical example of this is when a consumer uses a (downstream) computational service from the service provider, and has to specify an (upstream) data storage service to which the computational service will send its output.

It is also possible for an upstream service to be another service from the same service provider – whether specified by the consumer or used internally by the service provider. In such cases, the second service is both downstream (as seen by the service provider) and upstream (as seen by the first service). It turns out to be useful to model these two views of the second service separately, as discussed below.

Resources and Capacity

Having defined upstream and downstream services, it is possible to define a terminology for resources. These are the means by which downstream services are implemented, and represent the service provider's assets and capacity to deliver downstream services.

For the purposes of service management, we should model downstream services separately from the resources that determine their capacity. Anything that restricts the amount or quality of downstream services operated by the service provider should be modelled as a resource. This should mean that no downstream service has an intrinsic capacity, and the ability of the service provider to meet consumer commitments can be determined from the capacity of its resources.

It is important to distinguish between an upstream service (i.e. a service used to deliver a downstream service), and the resource it represents. The service provider does not always 'own' the upstream service, so we cannot consider the service itself as an asset. However, the right to use the service (possibly within some limits) is an asset, and as far as the governance framework is concerned, that is what should be modelled as a resource.

The operation of downstream services may also depend on other assets (e.g. computers, networks, and non-IT assets) that are controlled by the service provider and are not accessed via upstream services. These must also be modelled as resources if their capacity is to be taken into account by the governance framework when managing services and commitments.

This leads to the following terminology to describe resources:

- **Supplier Resources:** these represent upstream services (for which the service provider is a consumer), whose suppliers have commitments to the service provider related to their usage and other QoS characteristics;
- **Client Resources:** these represent upstream services specified by a consumer, which are accessible to the service provider's downstream services, but about which the service provider has no commitments from any supplier;
- **In-House Resources:** these represent internal assets that enable the operation of a consumer service.

Note that a supplier resource represents the supplier commitments (in its SLA) to the service provider, and not the supplied upstream service itself. A client resource represents the obligation

of a consumer to enable access to a suitable upstream service, and not the upstream service itself.

All resources must be available to the downstream services on which they depend, but how this is achieved depends on the nature of the resource. The first two types of resources have to be invoked by the downstream service in order to use them. For supplier resources, the way to do this is by making the corresponding upstream service available for discovery and incorporation into the downstream service workflow. For client resources, this is not necessary because the upstream service will be specified by a consumer via the functional interface of the downstream service they are using. Where a downstream service is deployed on a resource (rather than invoking the resource), which is often the case with in-house resources, this can be done by making the resource available for discovery by a downstream service factory.

The capacity of any resource may vary over time. Some in-house resources may have variable capacity that can be actively managed by the governance framework (e.g. a pool of workers who can be called to work by SMS when needed or a job queue for computational cluster whose priority can be changed by sending a message to the cluster management system). The governance framework should be able to do these things automatically without human intervention, if appropriate. Other in-house resources (e.g. a high capacity data storage system) may have fixed capacity, meaning that changes can only be made by humans acting outside the governance framework.

The service provider (and hence the governance framework) cannot manage the capacity of individual supplier resources directly, as that can only be done by the operator of the corresponding upstream services. The service provider can change the number of supplier services available to them, or scale of allowed usage, by negotiating or terminating supplier SLAs. It can also decide when and how supplier resources will be used by its own downstream services. The governance framework should be able to do these things automatically without human intervention, if appropriate.

The service provider cannot manage the capacity of a client resource, nor even decide when or how they are used, because the right to use the corresponding upstream service is delegated to them by consumers for use in delivering a particular service to them. The service provider can specify the capacity that a client resource should have by obliging the consumer to specify upstream services that provide this capacity. This would need to be done in the consumer SLA. Thus a ground handling service provider may define their consumer SLA with airlines to contain:

- **Consumer Commitments:** the service can be used up to 20 times per day and will turn around each aircraft in under 60 minutes;
- **Consumer Obligations:** the service will not be used more than 20 times in a day, and the consumer will provide access to the airline's fuelling service, which must complete fuelling each aircraft within an agreed time once asked to start by the ground handler.

Here, the downstream service is the ground handling service, which depends on a refuelling service specified by the consumer (in addition to any in-house and supplier resources). The right to access this service is modelled as a client resource, and the capacity of that resource is defined as part of the consumer obligation to provide those access rights (in italics). The reason we need to model consumer-specified upstream services as client resources is so we can associate a capacity specification with them, and check whether the upstream service meets this specification.

Interdependent Services

Where a service provider's downstream service uses one of its other services as a resource, there are two possibilities:

- If the second service was specified by the consumer, it is treated as a client resource – as the use of the second service is based on commitments to a customer;
- If the second service is used because the service provider chose to resource the first service that way, the second service is treated as a supplier resource.

In the second case, the service provider should model the relationship between the two services by an SLA with itself. When modelling the resources available to the first downstream service, the second service is modelled as a supplier resource, the SLA is taken as the supplier SLA, and the upstream service is treated as though it were external so its resourcing is not an issue. The second service is modelled separately as a downstream service with its own resource requirements, in which the SLA is treated as a consumer SLA, and the downstream client is treated as though it is external.

Metrics and Models

Finally, we need to address the fact that the service provider (and hence the governance framework) will need to work with three different sets of metrics:

- **Customer Metrics:** chosen by the service provider, used to define and report on QoS commitments in consumer SLA, in terms likely to appeal to the customer;
- **Resource Metrics:** also chosen by the service provider, used to define and measure the capacity of resources (including consumer SLA obligations defining client resources), in terms that help with resource management;
- **Supplier Metrics:** chosen by external suppliers, used to define and report on QoS commitments in supplier SLA, in terms likely to appeal to the service provider.

The service provider does not choose the metrics for supplier commitments, and has to reflect customer preferences in its choice of metrics for consumer commitments, so these may not coincide with the metrics they use for resource management. This means we will need to define mapping functions:

- From customer metrics to resource metrics, used to find the resources needed (described by resource metrics) to support a given set of consumer commitments (described by customer metrics);
- From supplier metrics, used to determine the resource(s) provided (described by resource metrics) by a given set of supplier commitments (described by supplier metrics).

In practice, capacity mapping functions will also need to take account of the reported Quality of Service (QoS) and the observed Quality of Experience (QoE) for the resource in question. We may also sometimes need inverse functions to calculate the consumer commitments we could meet with a given resource, or the supplier commitments we need to provide a given capacity. These mapping functions will necessarily incorporate models of how downstream (and possibly upstream) services actually work.

Example Scenarios

Data Preservation

Figure 5 shows an example data preservation scenario, which illustrates the distinction between

Figure 5. Film preservation scenario: Commitments, services and resources

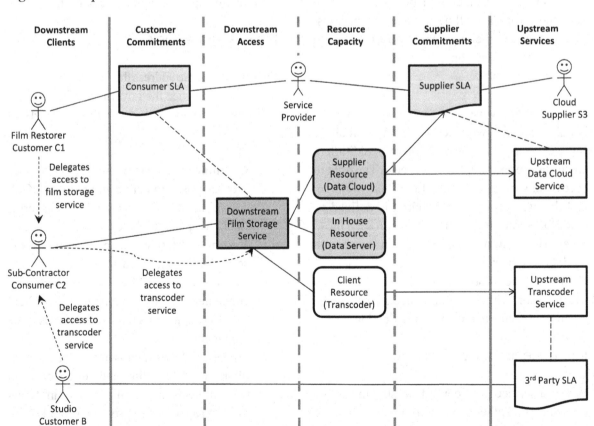

upstream and downstream services, and between services and resources via a simple value chain:

1. The customer is a film restorer, for whom the useful metrics are the number of feet of film they can store, the speed of serial access, and the number of feet lost per decade.
2. The downstream service offered by the service provider is for long-term digital film storage, and the SLA is expressed using the customer's preferred metrics. The consumer can upload film in any format, but must give the service provider access to a trans-coding service to be used for ingest processing.
3. The service needs two types of resources: a trans-coding service specified and provisioned by the consumer which must meet a minimum processing speed requirement, and digital media storage which may be an in house resource or an external supplier resource.
4. The service provider also offers other digital media services to a broader market, and they quantify their in-house digital media storage resources in terms of the number of frames stored, the speed of random access, and the number of frames corrupted per year.
5. The service provider also uses a cloud storage provider to handle peak loads. They address a general storage infrastructure market, and their SLA defines storage in terms of the number of GBytes stored, the access latency and bandwidth, and the bit degradation rate.

In Figure 5, the film restorer/archivist C1 negotiates an SLA with the service provider, who thereby commits to providing access to a consumer service for film storage. However, the SLA obliges the consumer to specify a suitable trans-coding service (i.e. one with adequate performance) to fulfil the functional interface of the downstream film storage service. The restorer delegates access to the service to a sub-contractor C2, who specialises in digitising analogue film stock, so they can digitise and upload a film. This subcontractor is a start-up partly financed by studio B, who provides them with free use of a trans-coding service (from a 3rd party supplier) as part of their investment. The subcontractor C2 can now use the film storage service, specifying that it use the 3rd party trans-coding service paid for by B.

The consumer service in Figure 5 has no intrinsic capacity, only commitments as specified in the consumer SLA (or several SLA – see below). In principle it can calculate what it needs to meet its commitments – just digital media storage resources with a certain capacity and performance, given that the consumer must fulfil the requirement for a trans-coding service. The digital media storage resources could come from an in-house resource, or from an external cloud storage service. The cloud storage resource is represented by a supplier resource, whose capacity (as seen by the service provider) is described using the same metrics as the in-house resource and the service requirements. This capacity is determined from the commitments in the supplier SLA agreed by the service provider with the external cloud supplier S3. The governance framework can then easily check how much resource is needed, and manage whether to use the in-house storage resource, the external cloud storage, or a mixture of the two.

Ground Handling

The following scenario is of interest because the 'turnaround' of an aircraft after landing at an airport determines when the aircraft will be ready to take off again for its next flight. Predictions of aircraft ready time are needed by the air traffic control network for safe and efficient operation of European airspace and airport runway capacity. EUROCONTROL has specified a Collaborative Decision Making (CDM) process for air traffic management operations, including Airport Collaborative Decision Making (A-CDM) to exchange information between airports and air traffic controllers. System governance in this

Figure 6. Ground handler scenario: Interdependent services

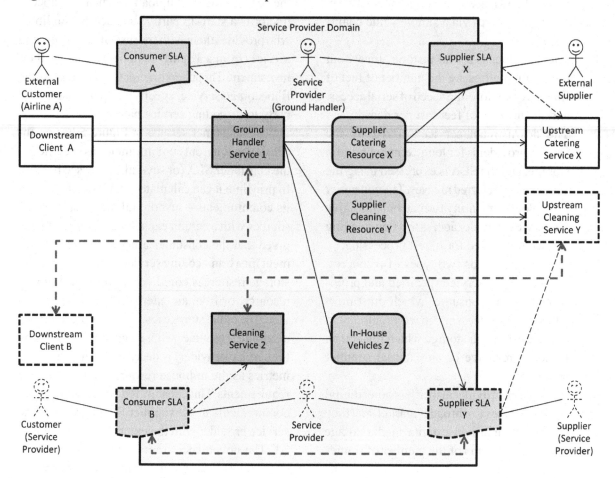

scenario is concerned with managing the dependability of information services used to implement A-CDM at an airport

Figure 6 shows the second example scenario in which a Ground Handler offers a downstream Ground Handling service to airlines. To deliver this service, it sends a redcap to the aircraft in a vehicle. A redcap is a Ground Handler employee who provides 'on the spot' management of services provided to the aircraft. The redcap orchestrates two ramp services: a catering service and a cleaning service. The Ground Handler also operates its own cleaning service, provided by sending a team of cleaners to the aircraft in a separate vehicle.

Here, the Ground Handling Service 1 is a downstream service with an external customer (an airline), who accesses the service under con-

sumer SLA A via Client A (actually the airport A-CDM system, acting on its behalf). To meet its commitments under this SLA, the Ground Handling service uses in-house resource Z representing a vehicle pool, and two supplier resources X and Y. The first represents the service provider's right to use an upstream catering service X under supplier SLA X. The second represents its right to use Cleaning Service 2 which is also operated by the service provider. However, in supplier resource Y, Service 2 appears as a notionally externally upstream cleaning service Y, accessed under a supplier SLA Y as shown. Resources X and Y represent the commitments of suppliers rather than upstream services X and Y themselves, so they are independent of the resources needed to deliver services X and Y. For this purpose, it does not matter that supplier SLA Y is agreed by the service provider with themselves, or that upstream service Y is really also the downstream Cleaning Service 2.

The dashed items in Figure 6 indicate models representing an item that is really internal to the service provider, but is modelled separately from a different viewpoint so the management model can be simpler overall. The dashed arrows indicate how these externalised models relate to other viewpoints for the same items. The model of Cleaning Service 2 can thus be considered as totally separately from Service 1. In the model for Service 2, consumer SLA B defines the commitments to a service customer, who accesses the service via client B. Service 2 uses the in-house vehicle pool represented by resource Z to meet this commitment. It does not matter that client

B is actually Downstream Service 1, or that the consumer SLA B is identical to supplier SLA Y, agreed by the service provider with themselves.

By specifying expectations of Service 2 in SLA Y = SLA B, the interdependency between the two services is broken for modelling purposes. If these expectations are set too high, the aggregated commitments from consumer SLAs A and B may overload the in-house vehicle pool Z. If the expectations of Service 2 are set too low, supplier resource Y may be insufficient to meet the commitments for Ground Handling Service 1. But in that case, the service provider could seek an alternative (e.g. external) supplier for upstream cleaning services, and scale back Cleaning Service 2 so its vehicles can be used by Redcaps.

Figure 7. Classes and relationships

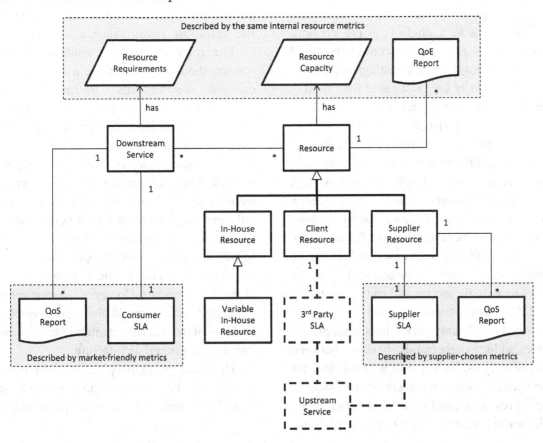

Indicative Structure

Figure 7 provides an indicative structure for classes and their relationships and (some) attributes, capable of modelling the scenarios described by Figure 5 and Figure 6.

The downstream service class is now shown to have commitments under zero or one consumer SLAs, and zero or more QoS reports describing how it behaved (e.g. how much it was used, how it responded, etc). A downstream service with no SLA represents an unmanaged service. It will deliver service at whatever service level it can manage with the available resources, to any consumers who can access. A service with an SLA represents the case where the service provider negotiates an SLA with a customer, and deploys a separate service to meet its commitments to each of its customers, accessible only in the context of the corresponding SLA.

It is possible for a service provider to negotiate multiple SLA with different customers, enabling access to a single (e.g. pre-existing) service. However, in practice consumers would then need to provide some distinguishing context (e.g. a security key) associated with its SLA when they access the service, so their access can be accounted for under the right SLA. We can therefore model this situation as a collection of services with different contextualised endpoints, each associated with a single SLA, but using a common set of resources. It is also possible for a service provider to negotiate a single SLA allowing access to multiple services, but for simplicity we will assume that in such cases the SLA can be decomposed into separate pieces, each of which applies to a single service and can be treated as the SLA for that service.

Each downstream service uses multiple resources, and a resource can also be shared between multiple services. The resource is a base class, for which derived classes represent client resources, supplier resources, and variable or fixed capacity in-house resources. Each resource will have a description of its capacity, and zero or more QoE reports describing how it behaved in relation to its capacity. Supplier and client resources are associated with an upstream service, while in-house resources represent in-house assets that do not need to be accessed as services. Supplier resources also have an associated supplier SLA defining the supplier's commitments to the service provider with respect to the associated upstream service, and zero or more QoS reports describing how the service behaved with respect to its SLA commitments.

Resource Capacity and Requirements

Resource Requirements

The resources needed by a service provider should be described as a set of resource types, each of which has a usage constraint (total usage over some period) and other constraints on characteristics like usage rate, performance, etc.

The requirements for each downstream service should in general be a function of its customer commitments. The function will be associated with a downstream service type, and provide the mapping between customer-friendly commitment metrics and the service provider's internal resource description and management metrics. Where all services of the same type will have the same (fixed) commitments (i.e. there is only one SLA template which never changes), the service requirements will also be constant. In this special case the mapping function may return the known requirements without referring to the commitments. However, the requirements mapping function should always be treated as a function of the service commitments, so it can fit into a more general architecture.

The requirements mapping function represents a model for the corresponding service type. It may also be helpful to have an inverse mapping function, able to calculate the QoS a service can deliver, given the capacity of available resources.

Resource Capacity

The capacity of a resource should be expressed as a set of constraints on usage rate, just as in GRIA, except that constraints may also be specified for performance and other characteristics. For a fixed capacity in house resource, these constraints will be specified by a human user when they register the resource with the governance framework. Other types of resource must provide an interface to get their current capacity. In practice, all resources should provide such an interface even if the resource has fixed capacity, so they can fit into the proposed architecture in a consistent way.

The most interesting case is the supplier resource, whose capacity will initially be based on the commitments from the supplier SLA. Since the supplier commitments may use different metrics than the service provider, a mapping function will also be needed here to compute the capacity constraints from the SLA terms. In principle, this capacity mapping can also take account of any QoS and QoE reports for the resource. Suppose a supplier SLA says a service will be available 99% of the time, but the reported QoS was only 98% availability, and the QoE was 95% availability. This indicates that the upstream service failed to meet its own commitments, or that the service provider and supplier measure availability in different ways, or that the supplier is dishonest, etc. In such cases, the mapping function might return a capacity specification of 95% availability. Of course, one must take care not to use QoE data in this way where it is inappropriate. For example, one should not assume the availability will be only 95% in future if the past performance was due to a network outage that was not the supplier's fault, and is now resolved.

Client resources have no supplier SLA or reported QoS that is visible to the service provider, so no mapping function is needed. When the consumer specifies a client resource, the service provider must assume its capacity is whatever the service will need. Ideally the service provider should define this requirement in the consumer SLA as an obligation, making the consumer responsible for specifying an upstream service that can meet the requirement. The service provider cannot choose when to use a client resource, so the actual capacity will only be of interest if the client resource prevents the consumer service from meeting its commitments. To keep track of this, the service provider must model the associated upstream service as a resource with the required capacity, and maintain QoE records that show whether or not it delivered this capacity, allowing the service to report a 'not my fault' error if appropriate.

The capacity mapping function for a supplier resource represents a model of the corresponding supplier relationship. It may also be helpful to have an inverse mapping function, able to calculate the QoS commitments a service provider should negotiate, such that the associated upstream service delivers a required resource capacity.

Aggregation

Typically one would aggregate resource requirements and capacity before checking whether the latter is sufficient to meet the former.

1. Service resource requirements should be calculated per service, and then aggregated over all services that use a given resource pool. Usage requirements should be summed, while other requirements should be combined by taking the worst case (highest quality) limit over all the services.

2. Resource capacity should be calculated per resource, and then aggregated over all resources in a pool. The usage limits from each resource should be added to get the usage limit for the pool. Other limits should be

combined by taking the worst case (lowest quality) limit over all the resources.

While contention ratios are a useful concept, their use often confuses developers and users of services, so it is proposed that the model be usable without them. To achieve this, the usage limits over a period should be lower than the peak usage rate times the length of the period. This indicates that while the resource must be able to deliver a specified peak load, the average load is much less and so the resource could be shared. For this to work, we have to think of usage rate limits as a constraint on which resource can be used, and not related to the usage at all.

Given this, we can express the balance between requirements and capacity as follows:

$$\sum_{r \in S'} L_{ij} \le \sum_{k \in R'} C_{kj}, \forall j \in M' \tag{2}$$

where now M' is the set of usage metrics (excluding usage rate metrics), L_{ij} are the resource requirements derived from the set S' of all SLA including a proposed new SLA, and C_{kj} is the capacity of resource k for metric j. Note however that the sum is now over a subset of resources k∈R', for which:

$$L_{ij}^u \ge C_{kj} \ge L_{ij}^1 \forall i \in S', \forall j \notin M' \tag{3}$$

In this expression, j now covers all the remaining (non-usage) metrics including usage rates, performance, etc. R' is defined as the set of resources whose capacity C_{kj} for these metrics is within the required range.

This basically means we add the usage limits as before (over a suitable period), but we only consider resources that have the necessary performance and other characteristics. The procedure is as follows:

- Use the capacity mapping function to find the resource capacity Ckj for each resource;
- Use the requirements mapping function to find the resource requirements Lij arising from each SLA;
- Use (3) to determine which resources can be used to meet these commitments;
- Use (2) to decide whether those resources have sufficient capacity to meet the requirements.

If we have different types of SLA with different non-usage requirements, it is possible that some resources may be useful for only some SLA. In that case, one should consider the requirements coming from each type of SLA in turn, starting with the most demanding. As each type of SLA is added, the usage requirements will grow but more resources will be able to meet them.

For example, if we have Gold, Silver and Bronze SLAs representing different service levels (in the obvious order), one would:

- Use (3) to find the set of resources able to support Gold users, then use (2) to check if requirements associated with Gold SLA are met;
- Use (3) to find the set of resources able to support Silver users (which should include those able to support Gold users), then use (2) to check if requirements associated with Gold and Silver SLA are met by this larger set of resources;
- Use (3) to find the set of resources able to support Bronze users (which should include those able to support Gold or Silver users), then use (2) to check if requirements associated with all SLA are met by this largest set of resources.

This approach assumes that resources are allocated to services using the least capable resource that can still satisfy the non-usage requirements. If enough high-end resources are available to satisfy

Gold SLA commitments, but some are allocated to a Bronze service, then a Gold-level service could fail through having to use low-end resources. In general, it is possible to have several different SLA templates that are served by different intersecting but not fully overlapping subsets of the resources. Such cases are complex and difficult to manage, and should be further explored if we need to support them.

Obviously, one can also segregate SLA and associated resource requirements to simplify the calculations where different SLA refer to different types of services, etc.

FUTURE RESEARCH DIRECTIONS

Future work in semantic SLA management will include making the metric model more expressive to efficiently encode the relationships between QoS metrics and the business requirements to infrastructure ones. The use of semantic rules, such as SWRL (Horrocks, Patel-Schneider, Boley, Tabet, Grosof, & Dean, 2004) and an underlying reasoner (e.g. Pellet, FaCT++) to automatically derive new metrics will also be considered. Fuzzy logic rules using OWL based interference engines and usage based analyzers will provide essential input for decision making systems. This will allow for metrics to be derived from the core metrics reported by a single service and for metrics to be derived from core metrics reported from more than one service. The aim of this is to avoid re-implementing the service whenever requirements for usage reporting (e.g. for use in SLA) change.

For example, if a service is created or procured that counts and reports the number of jobs runs per day, but the service operator would like to constrain the number of jobs run *per hour*, it would mean recoding the service logic. If the service simply reports the number of jobs run (since the creation of the task), then we can define a metric that represents the number of jobs run in an hour, which is calculated by the usage store at the end of

each hour from the measurements in the previous hour and stored as a new metric. This allows a service provider to offer two SLAs: for example, one which constrains JobsPerHour, the other of which constrains JobsPerDay. These two metrics are derived from the values of JobsRun, which is the only metric reported by the job service.

An alternative solution is to provide an interface to the usage store that allows the SLA service to query all the measurements needed to create the new metric. This has the advantage that a service provider could let consumers query services to create their own metrics that it does not already report. However, it is unlikely that a service provider would allow this level of access to the service's reporting data (plus, it would increase the amount of traffic between components). It is likely that such an interface (for querying detailed usage data) will be required anyway, but should only be used for deductive *post facto* analysis to determine the cause of an identified service failure.

Defining these new metrics is part of the service configuration. A service describes the metrics it can measure through an ontology (derived from the base metric ontology). These are core metrics and can be reported 'as is' or manipulated to produce a derived metric. A derived metric can be:

i.   A function of two or more metrics, or
ii.   A subset of the measurements (typically those within a particular time period).

In the case of (1), it is not clear when the derived metric is calculated. For example, if the job service reports TotalJobRunTime and #JobsRun, dividing the former by the latter will give MeanJobRunTime. However, if we calculate the mean upon receipt of a new measurement report for TotalJobRunTime, without waiting for a new #JobsRun report, then we would produce an erroneous value.

In the case of (2), the usage store should calculate the value of the derived metric at the end of the time period. Of course, there are cases in which an ongoing metric (such as the length of a job run) will overlap two (or more) adjacent time periods. Then it should be defined which period the measurement should contribute to: the period in which the activity started, the period in which it ended, or 'sliced' across all periods in which the activity took place (e.g. 3.34 jobs run between 09:00-10:00).

Figure 8 shows a simple example of a metric derived from two metrics that a data service reports. The data service ontology describes AmountUploaded and AmountDownloaded as subclasses of NonRecoverableUsage and partitions of AmountTransferred. If the partitioning is complete (i.e. there is no other class other than these two) then a reasoner can work out Amount-Transferred as the sum of AmountUploaded and AmountDownloaded

It is often useful to create a metric that applies a criterion to each of a set of measurements against a threshold and represents the ratio of measurements that meet the threshold to those that do not (e.g. percentage of uploads today less than 100MB; percentage of ingest jobs that complete in under 30 minutes). According to the metric ontology introduced in this Chapter, these are called compliance metrics.

The value of the compliance metric is the ratio of the measurements that satisfy the criterion to the total number of measurements in the period.

Figure 8. AmountTransferred as a derived metric

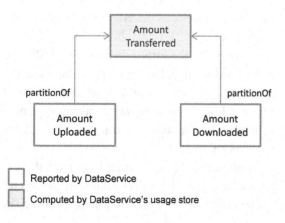

These two measurements (of type Counter) can be reported by the service, but could also be inferred through the relationships in the ontology. For example, the service reports IngestTime (ElapsedTime) each time an ingest job completes and adds one to the NumIngestJobs (Counter). NumIngestJobsUnder30Mins can be calculated from IngestTime and a constant threshold. The compliance metric is then equal to NumIngest-JobsUnder30Mins/NumIngestJobs. This is recalculated every time a job completes.

Deriving Metrics across Multiple Services

In a service's ontology, a service is subclassed from the class Service (or a child of this). For example an ImageService is a subclass of Service, and a SwirlService is a subclass of ImageService. A service is used to create tasks. In the case of a service that executes code, these are Jobs, whereas for a service that stores data, these may be a DataStager. A service ontology describes the classes of metrics that a service is expected to report. The metrics are subclassed from the base metric ontology, which includes relationships to other base metric classes (e.g. MeanElapsedTime is *basedOn* ElapsedTime and *sizedBy* a Counter). If these can be interpreted correctly, it allows us to infer the values for metrics not directly reported by the service. For example, consider the ontology in Figure 9. This combines the ontology from a PaintJobService with that of a SwirlJobService. The black squares are metrics reported by the services, while the grey are those defined in the ontology but not reported. The values of these can be inferred.

Figure 9 shows an example of deriving a new metric from the combined ontologies of two related services. An ImageService provides Image-Jobs and a SwirlService provides SwirlJobs. A metric NumSwirlJobs is reported by the swirl

Figure 9. Combined metric ontology from a paint job service and a swirl job service

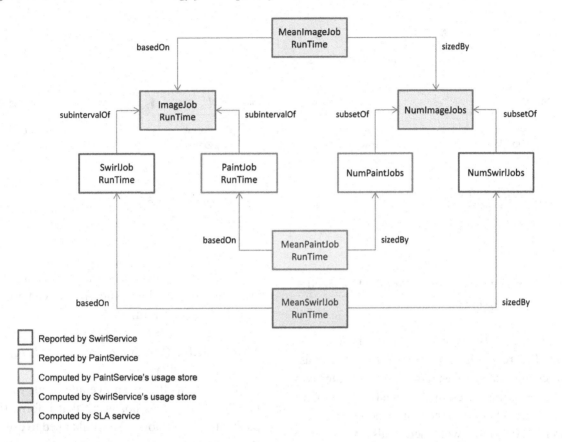

service, while a PaintService reports a metric NumPaintJobs. If these metrics are both subclasses of NumImageJobs, it would be tempting to claim that an SLA offering both a PaintService and a SwirlService could constrain NumImageJobs, whose value is the sum of NumPaintJobs and NumSwirlJobs. However, although this gives the correct result in this case, it uses specious reasoning. Consider a metric MeanImageJobRun-Time with two subclasses MeanSwirlJobRunTime and MeanPaintJobRunTime. Values for the superclass cannot be calculated from the sum of its subclasses, and there is insufficient information to otherwise calculate it.

The metrics MeanPaintJobRunTime can be computed by the paint service's usage store, while the metric MeanSwirlJobRunTime can be computed by the swirl service's usage store. However,

the metrics referring to image jobs span multiple services, so no individual service's usage store has sufficient information to infer the value. Therefore the inference must be done at the SLA service.

SWRL supports Math 'built-ins' that allow mathematical operations and comparisons to be specified in rules. In order to populate derived metric classes with values derived from instances of other (core) metric classes, it is necessary to store each measurement of a particular metric as an instance of that metric class in the ontology. This may prove to be unscalable given how many measurements will be stored, but no experiments have yet been carried out.

The following examples show how SWRL (and SQWRL) can be used to calculate values for derived metrics.

Figure 10. Inferring new relationships

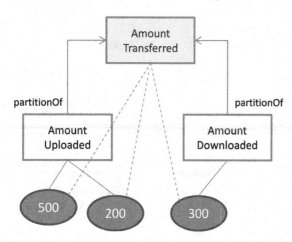

Figure 11. Creating a new individual

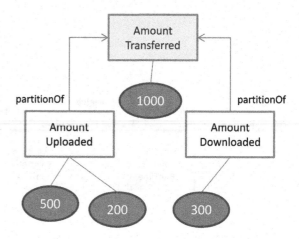

1. AmountTransferred = AmountUploaded + AmountDownloaded (ever)

There are two ways of doing this. The first (see Figure 10) is to define two rules that classifies individual measurements of the latter two classes as instances of AmountTransferred. In this way, every instance of AmountUploaded and of AmountDownloaded is also an instance of AmountTransferred:

AmountDownloaded(?x) →
AmountTransferred(?x)

AmountUploaded(?x) →
AmountTransferred(?x)

The second way is to use SQWRL to query the sum of all measurements of AmountUploaded and AmountDownloaded. Then the Protégé API can be used to create a new individual of class AmountTransferred, whose value is equal to the sum (see Figure 11). However, SQWRL does not allow computed values to be inserted back into the ontology. This is because "such a mechanism could invalidate OWL's open world assumption and lead to nonmonotonicity" (O'Connor, 2010).

2. MeanPaintRuntime (ever)

To create the average of a number of measurements of class PaintRuntime, we can use the following SQWRL rule:

PaintTime(?x) ∧ hasValue(?x, ?v) ∧ sqwrl:makeBag(?b, ?v) ∧ sqwrl:avg(?avg, ?b) → sqwrl:select(?avg)

This returns the mean average of all values, but (as above) does not insert that information back into the ontology. We would need to use the Protégé API to create a new individual of class MeanPaintRuntime, whose value is the result of executing the above rule.

3. MeanPaintRuntime (today)

It should be possible to use SQWRL's 'group by' function to get the mean average for measurements relating to a specific day/hour/arbitrary block of time.

4. MeanImageJobRuntime (today)

As in (1), we can use SWRL rules to create new associations between instances of PaintRuntime, SwirlRuntime and ImageJobRuntime. Then, as in (2) and (3), we can compute the average of these.

Other future directions of research include the implementation of more complex policies for issuing rewards and penalties in case of task migration when there are violations in the SLA and not enough resources to supply will form part of the future work activities. Integration and compatibility with existing SLA standards like WSLA and WS-Agreement is also required for better interoperability between resources implementations. The next step for this research is to prove the concept of the semantic SLA management model in real-life applications.

CONCLUSION

Existing approaches to service usage and capacity management are not sufficient for the way in which SOA is used today, because:

- Resources may be elastically provisioned via autonomic processes, meaning the capacity of resources available to a service provider is not fixed;
- Service commitments and resource capacity are no longer concerned only with usage but also performance and other QoS characteristics;
- Different metrics may be needed to describe QoS commitments to customers, resource capacity, and QoS commitments for externally supplied services used as resources.

It is proposed that a different approach is required, based on a service provider's viewpoint as a middle-man in a service value chain. In this approach:

- Consumer SLAs encode commitments by the service provider for the delivery of services to consumers;
- Downstream services are the means whereby consumers can initiate processes executed by or using service provider resources: they have no intrinsic capacity;

- Resources are used to deliver services: their capacity determines the capacity of the services that use them;
- Upstream services are the means whereby a service provider can initiate processes using resources from other organisations;
- Supplier SLAs encode commitments by external suppliers to deliver upstream services to the service provider utilising their own resources.

Upstream services in effect act like resources, whose capacity is based on supplier commitments or consumer obligations to the service provider. This leads to modelling of resources via three sub-classes:

- In-house resources represent resources owned by the service provider, which may have fixed or variable capacity;
- Supplier resources represent the use of upstream services based on SLA commitments from a supplier;
- Client resources represent the use of upstream services specified by a service consumer via a downstream service's functional interface, which may have to satisfy some capacity obligations encoded in the consumer SLA for the downstream service.

Three different sets of metrics are used to model the characteristics of these different entities:

- Consumer metrics: for modelling consumer service commitments and QoS;
- Resource metrics: for modelling resource capacity and QoE;
- Supplier metrics: for modelling supplier service commitments and reported QoS.

Only the first two of these sets of metrics are chosen by the service provider, and even these may be different so the terms in consumer SLA are appealing and comprehensible to customers.

Mapping functions will therefore be needed to derive resource requirements from consumer SLA commitments and resource capacity from supplier SLA commitments (and other information) respectively.

The mapping giving resource requirements as a function of supplier commitments constitutes a model of the service implementation. It should reflect aspects like the efficiency of implementation for service processes, etc. Note that services have no intrinsic capacity – how much service they can deliver depends on the capacity of resources at their disposal, in a way that depends on the inverse of the resource requirements mapping function.

The mapping giving resource capacity as a function of supplier commitments constitutes a model of supplier reliability and trustworthiness. It can take account of the reported QoS and the measured QoE, as well as the supplier commitments as defined by their SLA terms. In general, the capacity of any resource may be similarly adjusted if the measured QoE indicates that a previously calculated capacity is too inaccurate.

The capacity of client resources should be defined as a consumer obligation in the consumer SLA. It is therefore not necessary to model the capacity of client resources, or to include them in the resource requirements of a service, as they should always be sufficient.

To compare resource requirements with resource capacity, a more general approach is required, in which non-usage requirements are also considered. This can be done by taking the non-usage requirements as a specification of which resources could be used to provision services under each type of SLA, and checking the usage capacity of just those resources against the usage requirements for that type of SLA.

ACKNOWLEDGMENT

The research leading to these results has received funding from the European Community's Seventh Framework Programme under grant agreement no. 225336, SERSCIS.

REFERENCES

Addis, M., Lowe, R., & Norlund, C. (2008). *A service oriented approach to online digital audio-visual archives.* 2008 Networked and Electronic Media Summit.

Ahsant, M., Surridge, M., Leonard, T.A., Krishna, A., & Mulmo, O. (2006). Dynamic trust federation in Grids. *4th International Conference on Trust Management, LNCS 3986/2006.* Pisa, Italy: Springer.

Amundsen, S., Lund, K., Eliassen, F., & Staehli, R. (2004). *QuA: Platform-managed QoS for component architectures.* White Paper, Simula Research Laboratory.

Andrieux, A., Czajkowski, K., Dan, A., Keahey, K., & Ludwig, H. (2007). *Web services agreement specification.* Grid Resource Allocation Agreement Protocol Working Group. Open Grid Forum.

Ashri, R., Payne, T., Marvin, D., Surridge, M., & Taylor, S. (2004). Towards a semantic Web security infrastructure. *Semantic Web Services 2004 Spring Symposium Series.* Stanford, CA: AAAI.

ASPIC Best Practices Committee. (2000). *A White Paper on service level agreement.* Application Service Provider Industry Consortium.

Avellino, G., Boniface, M., Cantalupo, B., Ferris, J., Matskanis, N., & Mitchell, W. (2008). *A dynamic orchestration model for future internet applications.* ServiceWave.

Becker, S. (2008). Quality of service modeling language. In *Dependability Metrics* (*Vol. 4909*). LNCS. doi:10.1007/978-3-540-68947-8_7

Beco, S., Cantalupo, B., Giammarino, L., Matskanis, N., & Surridge, M. (2005). OWL-WS: A workflow ontology for dynamic grid service composition. *1st IEEE International Conference on e-Science and Grid Computing* (pp. 148–155). IEEE Computer Society.

Benkner, S., Engelbrecht, G., Middleton, S. E., Brandic, I., & Schmidt, R. (2007). End-to-end QoS support for a medical grid service infrastructure. *New Generation Computing, 25*(4).

Boniface, M., Phillips, S. C., Sanchez-Macian, A., & Surridge, M. (2007). Dynamic service provisioning using GRIA SLAs. *1st Non Functional Properties and Service Level Agreements in Service Oriented Computing Workshop*. Vienna, Austria.

Boniface, M. J., Phillips, S. C., & Surridge, M. (2006). *Grid-based business partnerships using service level agreements*. Cracow Grid Workshop. Cracow, Poland.

Bouras, C., & Sevasti, A. (2005). Service level agreements for DiffServ-based services' provisioning. *Journal of Network and Computer Applications, 28*(4), 285–302. doi:10.1016/j.jnca.2004.07.001

BSI. (2004). *IT Grundschutz Manual. Federal Office for Information Security*. BSI.

BSI. (n.d.). *GSTOOL*. Retrieved Aug 26, 2010, from http://www.bsi.bund.de/gstool/

Calpana. (n.d.). *Corporate risk application method*. Retrieved August 26, 2010, from http://www.crisam.net

De Roure, D., & Surridge, M. (2003). *Interoperability challenges in Grid for industrial applications*. Ninth Global Grid Forum Semantic Grid Workshop. Chicago IL, USA.

Dobson, G. (2006). *Towards unified QoS/SLA ontologies*. Third International Workshop on Semantic and Dynamic Web Processes.

Ekelhart, A., Fenz, S., & Neubauer, T. (2009). *AURUM: A framework for supporting information security risk management*. 42nd Hawaii International Conference on System Sciences, HICSS2009. Los Alamitos, CA: IEEE Computer Society.

Fenz, S., & Ekelhart, A. (2009). *Formalizing information security knowledge*. ACM Symposium on Information, Computer and Communications Security. New York, NY: ACM Press.

Frey, N., Matlus, R., & Maurer, W. (2000). *A guide to successful SLA development and management*. Strategic Analysis Report, Gartner Group Research.

Frølund, S., & Koistinen, J. (1998). *QML: A language for quality of service specification*. Technical Report HPL-98-10, Software Technology Laboratory, Hewlett Packard.

Giallonardo, E., & Zimeo, E. (2007). More semantics in QoS matching. *IEEE International Conference on Service-Oriented Computing and Applications* (pp. 163–171). Washington, DC: IEEE Computer Society.

Green, L. J. (2006). Service level agreements: An ontological approach. *Eighth International Conference on Electronic Commerce*, (pp. 185–194).

GRIA. (n.d.). *Service oriented collaborations for industry and commerce*. Retrieved August 27, 2010, from http://www.gria.org/

Hall-May, M., & Surridge, M. (2010). Resilient critical infrastructure management using service oriented architecture. *International Workshop On Coordination in Complex Software Intensive Systems*. Krakow, Poland.

Haller, A., Cimpian, E., Mocan, A., Oren, E., & Bussler, C. (2005). *WSMX - A semantic service-oriented architecture*. International Conference on Web Services. Orlando, Florida, USA.

Herenger, H., Heek, R., Kubert, R., & Surridge, M. (2008). *Operating virtual organizations using bipartite service level agreements*. Grid Middleware and Services: Challenges and Solutions at 8th IEEE International Conference on Grid Computing. Springer.

Hiles, A. (1999/2000). *The complete IT guide to service level agreements - Matching service quality to business needs*. Brookfield, CT: Rothstein Associates Inc.

Horrocks, I., Patel-Schneider, P. F., Boley, H., Tabet, S., Grosof, B., & Dean, M. (2004). *SWRL: A Semantic Web rule language combining OWL and RuleML*. W3C Member Submission 21 May 2004.

ISO. (2005). *ISO/IEC 27001:2005. Information technology – Security techniques – Information security management systems – Requirements*. International Organization for Standardization.

Jacyno, M., Payne, T. R., Watkins, E. R., Taylor, S. J., & Surridge, M. (2007). *Mediating Semantic Web service access using the semantic firewall*. UK e-Science Programme All Hands Meeting. Nottingham, UK.

Kritikos, K., & Plexousakis, D. (2006). Semantic QoS metric matching. *European Conference on Web Services* (pp. 265–274). IEEE Computer Society.

Likert, R. (1932). A technique for the measurement of attitudes. *Archives de Psychologie*, *140*(1), 1–55.

Ludwig, H., Keller, A., Dan, A., King, R. P., & Franck, R. (2003). *Web service level agreement (WSLA) language specification v1.0*. IBM Corporation.

McArdle, M., Leonard, T., Surridge, M., & Watkins, R. (2007). *Cross-middleware interoperability in distributed concurrent engineering*. International Grid Interoperability and Interoperation Workshop. Bangalore, India.

Middleton, S. E., Surridge, M., Nasser, B. I., & Yang, X. (2009). *Bipartite electronic SLA as a business framework to support cross-organization load management of real-time online applications*. Delft, The Netherlands: Euro-Par Real Time Online Interactive Applications on the Grid.

Mitchell, B. (2009). *QoS provisioning and orchestrating processes within an SOA*. Integrated Formal Methods Workshop on Formal Methods and SOA. Düsseldorf, Germany.

National Institute of Standards and Technology. (1995). *An introduction to computer security – The NIST handbook*. National Institute of Standards and Technology Special Publication 800-12.

NextGRID. (n.d.). *EC IST Project 511536 — The next generation Grid*. Retrieved from http://www.nextgrid.org

O'Connor, M. (2010). *SQWRL*. Retrieved August 28, 2010, from http://protege.cim3.net/cgi-bin/wiki.pl?SQWRL

Office of Government Commerce. (n.d.). *Information Technology infrastructure library version 3: Service design — Service level management*.

Oldham, N., Sheth, A., Hakimpour, F., & Verma, K. (2006). Semantic WS-agreement partner selection. *15th International Conference on World Wide Web*, (pp. 697–706).

Rana, O. F., Bunford-Jones, D., Hawick, K. A., Walker, D. W., Addis, M., & Surridge, M. (2001). *Resource discovery for dynamic clusters in computational Grids*. 15th International Parallel & Distributed Processing Symposium. San Francisco, CA, USA.

Roman, D., Keller, U., Lausen, H., Bruijn, R. L., Stollberg, M., & Polleres, A. (2005). Web service modeling ontology. *Applied Ontology*, *1*(1), 77–106.

Skene, J., Lamanna, D., & Emmerich, W. (2004). Precise service level agreements. *26th International Conference on Software Engineering* (pp. 179–188). Edinburgh, UK: IEEE Computer Society Press.

Snelling, D. F., Anjomshoaa, A., Wray, F., Basermann, A., Fisher, M., Surridge, M., et al. (2007). *NextGrid architectural concepts*. CoreGRID.

Stoneburner, G., Goguen, A., & Feringa, A. (2002). *Risk management guide for information technology systems*. National Institute of Standards and Technology Special Publication 800-30.

Sturm, R., Morris, W., & Jander, M. (2000). *Foundations of service level management*. SAMS.

Surridge, M., Marvin, D., Ashri, R., Payne, T., & Denker, G. (2004). *Semantic Web service interaction protocols: An ontological approach*. Third International Semantic Web Conference. Hiroshima, Japan.

Surridge, M., Payne, T. R., Taylor, S. J., Watkins, E. R., Leonard, T., Jacyno, M., et al. (2006). *Semantic security in service oriented environments*. UK e-Science Programme All Hands Meeting.

Teyssié, C. (2006). UML-based specification of QoS contract negotiation and service level agreements. *International Conference on Networking, International Conference on Systems and International Conference on Mobile Communications and Learning Technologies*, (p. 12).

Tian, M., Gramm, A., Naumowicz, T., Ritter, H., & Schiller, J. (2003). A concept for QoS integration in Web service. 1st Web Services Quality Workshop. Rome, Italy.

Toma, I., Foxvog, D., & Jaeger, M. C. (2006). *Modelling QoS characteristics in WSMO*. 1st Workshop on Middleware for Service Oriented Computing. Australia.

Tosic, V., Esfandiari, B., Pagurek, B., & Patel, K. (2002). *On requirements for ontologies in management of Web Services*. International Workshop on Web Services, E-Business and the Semantic Web.

Tosic, V., Pagurek, B., & Patel, K. (2003). *WSOL — A language for the formal specification of various constraints and classes of service for Web Services*. International Conference On Web Services.

Upstill, C., & Surridge, M. (2003). *Grid security: Lessons for peer-to-peer systems*. 3rd IEEE Conference on P2P Computing.

Verma, D. (1999). *Supporting service level agreements on IP networks*. McMillan Technology Series.

Wang, Y., D'Ippolito, R., Boniface, M., Qian, D., Cui, D., & Jiang, J. (2008). Cross-domain middlewares interoperability for distributed aircraft design optimization. *IEEE Fourth International Conference on eScience*, (pp. 485-492).

Ward, C., Buco, M. J., Chang, R. N., & Luan, L. Z. (2002). A generic SLA semantic model for the execution management of e-business outsourcing contracts. *Third International Conference on E-Commerce and Web Technologies*, (pp. 363-376).

Ziegler, W., Wieder, P., & Battré, D. (2008). *Extending WS-agreement for dynamic negotiation of service level agreements*. CoreGRID Technical Report TR-0172.

ADDITIONAL READING

Addis, M., Lowe, R., & Norlund, C. (2008). *A Service Oriented Approach to Online Digital Audiovisual Archives*. Networked and Electronic Media.

Ahsant, M., Surridge, M., Leonard, T. A., Krishna, A., & Mulmo, O. (2006). Dynamic Trust Federation in Grids. *4th International Conference on Trust Management. LNCS 3986/2006.* Pisa, Tuscany, Italy: Springer.

Ashri, R., Payne, T., Marvin, D., Surridge, M., & Taylor, S. (2004). Towards a Semantic Web Security Infrastructure. *Semantic Web Services 2004 Spring Symposium Series.* Stanford, CA, USA: AAAI.

ASPIC Best Practices Committee. (2000). *A White Paper on Service Level Agreement.* Application Service Provider Industry Consortium.

Avellino, G., Boniface, M., Cantalupo, B., Ferris, J., Matskanis, N., & Mitchell, W. (2008). *A Dynamic Orchestration Model for Future Internet Applications.* ServiceWave.

Beco, S., Cantalupo, B., Giammarino, L., Matskanis, N., & Surridge, M. (2005). OWL-WS: A Workflow Ontology for Dynamic Grid Service Composition. *1st IEEE International Conference on e-Science and Grid Computing* (pp. 148–155). IEEE Computer Society.

Benkner, S., Engelbrecht, G., Middleton, S. E., Brandic, I., & Schmidt, R. (2007). *End-to-End QoS Support for a Medical Grid Service Infrastructure.* New Generation Computing.

Boniface, M. J., Phillips, S. C., & Surridge, M. (2006). Grid-Based Business Partnerships using Service Level Agreements. *Cracow Grid Workshop.* Cracow, Poland.

De Roure, D., & Surridge, M. (2003). Interoperability Challenges in Grid for Industrial Applications. *Ninth Global Grid Forum Semantic Grid Workshop.* Chicago IL, USA.

Frey, N., Matlus, R., & Maurer, W. (2000). *A Guide to Successful SLA Development and Management.* Strategic Analysis Report, Gartner Group Research.

Hall-May, M., & Surridge, M. (2010). Resilient Critical Infrastructure Management using Service Oriented Architecture. *International Workshop On Coordination in Complex Software Intensive Systems.* Krakow, Poland.

Herenger, H., Heek, R., Kubert, R., & Surridge, M. (2008). Operating Virtual Organizations Using Bipartite Service Level Agreements. *Grid Middleware and Services: Challenges and Solutions at 8th IEEE International Conference on Grid Computing.* Springer.

Hiles, A. (1999/2000). *The Complete IT Guide to Service Level Agreements - Matching Service Quality to Business Needs.* Brookfield, Connecticut, USA: Rothstein Associates Inc.

Jacyno, M., Payne, T. R., Watkins, E. R., Taylor, S. J., & Surridge, M. (2007). Mediating Semantic Web Service Access using the Semantic Firewall. *UK e-Science Programme All Hands Meeting.* Nottingham, UK.

McArdle, M., Leonard, T., Surridge, M., & Watkins, R. (2007). Cross-middleware Interoperability in Distributed Concurrent Engineering. *International Grid Interoperability and Interoperation Workshop.* Bangalore, India.

Middleton, S. E., Surridge, M., Nasser, B. I., & Yang, X. (2009). *Bipartite electronic SLA as a business framework to support cross-organization load management of real-time online applications.* Delft, The Netherlands: Euro-Par Real Time Online Interactive Applications on the Grid.

Mitchell, B. (2009). QoS Provisioning and Orchestrating Processes within an SOA. *Integrated Formal Methods Workshop on Formal Methods and SOA.* Düsseldorf, Germany.

Rana, O. F., Bunford-Jones, D., Hawick, K. A., Walker, D. W., Addis, M., & Surridge, M. (2001). Resource Discovery for Dynamic Clusters in Computational Grids. *15th International Parallel & Distributed Processing Symposium.* San Francisco, CA, USA.

Snelling, D. F., Anjomshoaa, A., Wray, F., Basermann, A., Fisher, M., Surridge, M., et al. (2007). NextGrid Architectural Concepts. *CoreGRID*.

Sturm, R., Morris, W., & Jander, M. (2000). *Foundations of Service Level Management*. SAMS.

Surridge, M., Marvin, D., Ashri, R., Payne, T., & Denker, G. (2004). Semantic Web Service Interaction Protocols: An Ontological Approach. *Third International Semantic Web Conference*. Hiroshima, Japan.

Surridge, M., Payne, T. R., Taylor, S. J., Watkins, E. R., Leonard, T., Jacyno, M., et al. (2006). Semantic Security in Service Oriented Environments. *UK e-Science Programme All Hands Meeting.*

Surridge, M., Taylor, S., De Roure, D., & Zaluska, E. (2005). Experiences with GRIA — Industrial Applications on a Web Services Grid. *First International Conference on e-Science and Grid Computing* (pp. 98–105). IEEE Press.

Upstill, C., & Surridge, M. (2003). Grid Security: Lessons for Peer-to-Peer Systems. *3rd IEEE Conference on P2P Computing.*

Verma, D. (1999). *Supporting Service Level Agreements on IP Networks*. McMillan Technology Series.

Wang, Y., D'Ippolito, R., Boniface, M., Qian, D., Cui, D., & Jiang, J. (2008). Cross-Domain Middlewares Interoperability for Distributed Aircraft Design Optimization. *IEEE Fourth International Conference on eScience*, (pp. 485-492).

KEY TERMS AND DEFINITIONS

Consumer: Someone that sends requests to one (or more) services.

Customer: Someone who is responsible for requests sent to one (or more) services.

Quality of Experience (QoE): The level of service experienced by a consumer in its use of one (or more) services.

Quality of Service (QoS): The level of service provided by a service in processing and responding to requests.

Resource: An asset (e.g. another service) used by one (or more) services when processing and responding to requests.

Service: A means for a service provider to receive, process and respond to requests from consumers.

Service Governance: The processes and mechanisms needed to coordinate and manage the use of IT-related activities and resources to meet the operative and strategic goals of the company providing the services.

Service Level Agreement (SLA): A bilateral agreement that encodes the terms of the business relationship between a service provider and a customer.

Chapter 19
Negotiation of Service Level Agreements

Peer Hasselmeyer
NEC Laboratories Europe, Germany

Bastian Koller
High Performance Computing Center Stuttgart, Germany

Philipp Wieder
TU Dortmund University, Germany

ABSTRACT

Non-functional properties are an essential constituent of service level agreements as they describe those quality-of-service parameters that are not related to the actual function of a service. Thus, non-functional properties let providers create distinguishing service offers and let consumers discriminate between various offers that provide the same function. The negotiation of non-functional properties is how service level agreements are commonly established. This chapter introduces various forms, models, specifications, and realizations of service level agreement negotiation to provide a broad background of the current state-of-the-art. Although different in various details, the described systems share a number of common features. Based on them, a holistic architecture is defined combining previous work into one coherent framework. The architecture is applicable to different negotiation models and protocols, and covers all functions of the negotiation phase. Based on this architecture, particular challenges and areas of future work are motivated. These mostly revolve around increasing the acceptance of service level agreement negotiation and enhancing interoperability.

INTRODUCTION

In a service-oriented IT landscape, where more and more essential business functions are outsourced to external parties, management and control of the IT services externally procured are of paramount importance to ensure that the promised service quality is actually provided. Such control can only be exerted by having appropriate contracts in place that clearly state the agreed upon performance, legal, financial, and regulatory properties of the services provided and consumed. One method for expressing electronic contracts is through service level agreements (SLAs) (Marilly, Mar-

DOI: 10.4018/978-1-61350-432-1.ch019

tinot, Betge-Brezetz & Delegue, 2002). Such SLAs typically contain functional descriptions of what the service is and how it is to be accessed. In addition, SLAs contain descriptions of non-functional properties (NFPs) in the performance, legal, financial, and regulatory categories (Lee & Ben-Natan, 2002).

Service level agreements are used throughout the lifecycle of service-oriented systems. They are an important tool for providing, procuring, and operating electronic services. For the different purposes in service-oriented systems, SLAs are expressed through different, often domain-specific formalisms and representations. To this end, a number of different frameworks for service-level management exist, which cover different management aspects of service-oriented system operation (Parkin, Badia & Martrat, 2008).

The establishment of electronic contracts and SLAs requires the reconciliation of the needs of the service customer and the constraints of the service provider. This reconciliation is achieved with some form of negotiation between providers and customers. Negotiation can be seen as part of the service selection process where the result is a binding agreement between the two parties that provides solid guarantees on non-functional properties to the customer to base their business on and information to the service provider to plan and optimize service provisioning and revenue.

At present, contracts between service providers and customers are established in a mainly manual fashion, making the negotiation process lengthy, resource-intensive, and difficult to manage. With the abundance of services expected for future service markets and the associated dynamism of service interrelations, such a manual process will need to be partly, if not fully, automated. SLA negotiation is a method to reach such automation and is therefore expected to be an essential tool for the future service market.

In this chapter, we focus on SLA negotiation as the means to establish a common understanding between service provider and service customer

regarding the non-functional properties of service delivery. We therefore first introduce in Section "Service Level Agreements" what definition of SLAs we adhere to and where in the lifecycle of an SLA negotiation actually takes place (as outlined in Section "The SLA Lifecycle"). Following this, in the "Background" Section we present a selection of SLA models, protocols, and frameworks to provide the necessary background for the reader to understand and be able to discuss our solution as described in Section "A Proposal for a Generic Negotiation Architecture". We finally complete this chapter with a discussion of potential research directions in the area of SLA negotiation for the purpose of providing ideas for future work.

Service Level Agreements

A multitude of SLA application domains, specifications, and frameworks exist, just like definitions of what an SLA actually represents and contains. For our work and hence this chapter we follow the TeleManagement Forum, which defines an SLA as,

[a] formal negotiated agreement between two parties, sometimes called a service level guarantee [...], it is a contract (or part of one) that exists between the service provider and the customer, designed to create a common understanding about services, priorities, responsibilities, etc. (Lee & Ben-Natan, 2002, p. 3).

Part of this common understanding is formed by the functional and non-functional properties of a service, collectively referred to as the *terms* of the SLA. Functional properties specify what a service is doing, e.g. performing a finite-element analysis. Non-functional properties describe various quality aspects that the service fulfills, e.g. a minimum resolution of 0.1 mm in relation to the analysis mentioned before.

Negotiations are used to adjust the properties of an SLA to suit both parties. They generally only cover the non-functional properties of the service, as services that do not offer the required functions are most likely not considered for negotiation in the first place. Functional properties may nevertheless be negotiable. But experience shows that functional requirements are most often hard, and are, as a result, used to pre-select those service providers that offer the respective function. It is obvious that a customer looking for a finite-element analysis service does not see any need to negotiate with a printing service provider. But the distinction of the functional properties is not always that clear. In the end, the business objectives of the individual parties lead to the separation of negotiable and non-negotiable properties. In addition to the structured NFP descriptions assumed throughout this chapter, we foresee future systems to accept also free-text descriptions of desired services.

In addition to the definition of an SLA, we introduce a number of terms that we refer to throughout the chapter: SLA template, offer, counter-offer, bid, and SLA precursors. The service provider creates *SLA templates*. They describe the product, i.e. the service, including all its functional and non-functional properties. As such, SLA templates are used to advertise services to customers and they therefore lay the foundation for a common understanding of the services and their quality. There may be a one-to-many relationship between a service and its associated templates as a provider may offer the same service with different non-functional properties like price, performance, availability, or penalties. With respect to the structure, the SLA template normally follows the formal description of the actual SLA. This implies that a non-negotiable SLA template is identical to the actual SLA as far as the non-functional properties are concerned (for further information on non-negotiable SLAs see the Sections "Accept/Reject" and "Discrete Offer").

An *offer* represents a non-binding version of a service level agreement currently under negotiation. With respect to the definition quoted above,

the offer is the foundation to create a common understanding of the service quality. It can be considered as the first iteration of a contract. Offers can be identical to SLA templates in which case they contain the same functional and non-functional properties. Any subsequent offer that is based on a preceding offer we call a *counter-offer*. Although a counter-offer is structurally not different from an offer, we make this distinction to stress the relation between two offers where one, the counter-offer, is an iteration of (and therefore based upon) the other.

While offers and counter-offers are exchanged during bipartite negotiations, *bids* are used in auctions. They serve the same purpose as (counter) offers, namely the specification of parameters of the proposals for SLAs. In contrast to offers, bids are binding, as they must be observed once accepted.

All SLA-related documents that are not yet agreed upon, i.e. templates, bids, offers, and counter-offers, are collectively referred to as *SLA precursors*.

The SLA Lifecycle

SLAs are closely related to the services they pertain to. SLAs therefore follow a similar lifecycle as services and their lifetimes and lifecycles are closely related. A structured approach towards the management of the different lifecycle phases is essential to facilitating and streamlining the implementation of service level management. Ideally, the definition of the lifecycle phases is independent of the domain the SLA is actually used in. Although there is no universally agreed definition of the SLA lifecycle, the one introduced by the TeleManagement Forum in (TeleManagement Forum, 2005) is frequently applied to building service-oriented systems.

Figure 1 shows the lifecycle of an SLA as defined by the TeleManagement Forum. It consists of the six phases development, negotiation, implementation, execution, assessment, and

Figure 1. The SLA lifecycle according to the TeleManagement Forum (TeleManagement Forum, 2005)

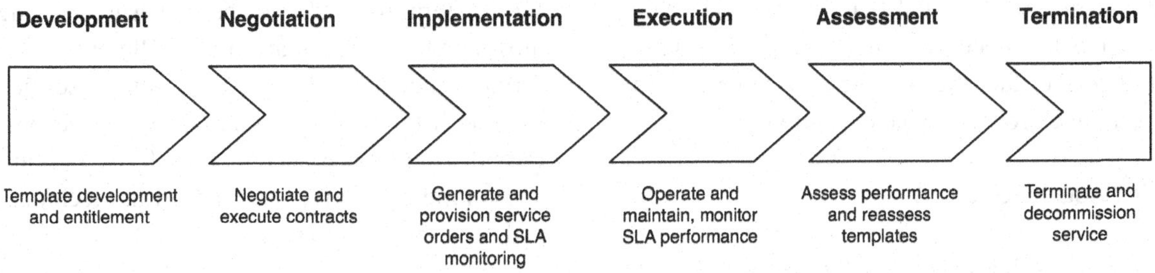

Development	Negotiation	Implementation	Execution	Assessment	Termination
Template development and entitlement	Negotiate and execute contracts	Generate and provision service orders and SLA monitoring	Operate and maintain, monitor SLA performance	Assess performance and reassess templates	Terminate and decommission service

termination. SLAs usually pass through these phases in lock-step with their associated services. Deviations are possible, for example, in case an SLA is developed after the service it relates to has been implemented. Depending on the application scenario, phase transitions may not be visible, or phases may even be skipped, but in the general case, this lifecycle is applicable. As this chapter focuses on negotiation of SLAs, the emphasis is put on the negotiation phase. To put the negotiation phase into context within the overall SLA lifecycle, the six phases are briefly outlined in the following paragraphs.

SLA Template Development

In the initial phase of the SLA lifecycle, the service and its associated SLA templates are being developed. In case the provider has the respective service in place already, SLA templates will be developed as an add-on to the service. With the broad adoption of SLAs in future service markets, SLA template development will become an essential aspect of service development.

According to Lee and Ben-Natan (2002), the SLA template itself should contain, from a "purely contractual standpoint" (p. 17), the following items: the agreement definition, i.e. parties, service access points and contract terms and conditions, the service definition, performance metric definitions, measurement definitions, correction definitions, and reconciliation definitions. Included are functional and non-functional aspects of the

service and SLA templates can therefore be seen as blueprints for yet-to-be-negotiated contracts.

Contract Negotiation

Once a service provider and a service consumer discovered each other to potentially engage in business transactions, they need to reach a binding agreement regarding the service to be delivered and the remuneration to be paid. To get there, the customer and the provider negotiate the service delivery terms. Although functional requirements might also be a matter of negotiation, in most cases the customer's functional requirements are fixed and only non-functional properties are negotiated. The result of the negotiation phase is either an agreed upon and ready-to-execute SLA, i.e. a contract, or nothing. In the latter case, the consumer may look for other providers to negotiate with, change her requirements, or wait for a later point in time where the preconditions for a negotiation may have changed.

Implementation

The implementation of an SLA includes the instantiation, configuration and provisioning of the service instances which are needed to fulfill the contract between the service consumer and the service provider. In contrast to the phases described before, work in the implementation phase is usually performed per service instance, including all means to monitor, measure, report, and assure performance. Affected is not only the service itself, but also auxiliary services that provide the necessary monitoring information and control facilities for the service provider to guarantee proper service execution.

Service Execution

During service execution the service provider has to deliver what has been contractually agreed upon as the result of the negotiation process: the service according to the service level agreement. How this is achieved is at the sole discretion of the provider. The provider will usually rely on auxiliary services and functions that allow to measure and control the non-functional properties specified in the SLA. It is essential in this phase to monitor the performance of the service, measure and record it, and, in parallel, assess the performance as described in the next phase. In case the SLA is breached, monitoring and assessment may trigger immediate actions to maintain the properties agreed upon.

Performance Assessment

Assessment of the service's performance happens during service execution and after service termination as part of the decommissioning phase. The gathered information helps both service provider and service consumer to assess whether their business objectives are met. For both parties, monitoring, evaluation, and potentially the application of corrective measures are essential in this phase. In addition, service providers may re-assess their SLA templates to counter repeated breaches of particular SLA terms or to increase revenue.

Service Termination and Decommissioning

This final phase in the SLA lifecycle includes the termination of the service (and the auxiliary services) as well as its decommissioning. The service terminates due to certain triggers. The most common causes are the fulfillment of the service, and some SLA violation during service runtime. In both cases, the service provider decommissions the service, accompanied by accounting and billing of service use, and a final technical and economic assessment.

Non-Functional Properties

Service level agreements contain, among other things, the non-functional properties of the associated service. NFPs can cover different aspects of service access, including performance, legal, financial, and regulatory properties. A common way to specify NFPs is by an identifier and a value or a value range. The identifier uniquely specifies the semantics of the property. The semantics include specifications of various aspects, potentially including what the property refers to (e.g. network bandwidth), the syntax of the property's value (e.g. floating point), the unit the property is specified with (e.g. Mbps), where it is measured (e.g. at the connection between the data center and the transport network provider), whether/how values are averaged (e.g. sliding window over the last five seconds, calculated every one second), and others, depending on the property.

Property values in SLAs are either concrete values or ranges of values, usually specifying a maximum or a minimum value for the property. Examples of concrete values are prices, e.g. "monthly price = €100.00", or Boolean values, e.g. "ISO27001 certification = true". Value ranges are useful for many quality aspects, where only minimum and/or maximum values are required and any performance "better" than the limit does not affect the functionality of the service, but may increase the customer's satisfaction. Examples are "bandwidth >= 1Mbps", "processing time <= 5ms", or "transactions per second >= 2000".

The NFPs must be encoded in some way in order to be processable by machines. As described above, NFPs are basically name-value pairs, where the values can be value ranges in addition to concrete values. The various SLA specification methods have defined different methods for encoding NFPs in SLAs. As NFPs are mostly domain-specific, the specific identifiers to use inside SLAs are usually not defined in SLA specification frameworks. They rather provide extensibility mechanisms that allow adding the particular domain-specific NFPs. Of course, the NFP specification mechanism must follow some basic rules and principles to be usable inside a particular SLA framework.

The SLA frameworks also provide mechanisms to combine NFPs inside an SLA. Combinations usually provide the common Boolean functions of and, or, and exclusive-or.

BACKGROUND

This Section introduces existing work in the area of SLA negotiation. First, models of negotiation are introduced, including bilateral negotiations and auctions. These were developed independently of SLAs or electronically supported business and exist for a much longer time. Still, they form the basis for any kind of negotiation, including electronically supported SLA negotiation. Next, specifications for realizing SLA negotiation using the described models in a computer-supported environment are described. Implementations of such protocols are then examined in the third part of this section.

Negotiation Models

Negotiation models are descriptions of how a contract between one or more sellers of goods, resources or services and one or more buyers of such products can be established. The major part of establishing a contract is reaching an agreement (i.e. a common understanding) on the terms of the contract. This is accomplished by negotiations between the buyer and the seller who have different requirements and constraints. Negotiations come in different forms and involve diverse procedures. The models most relevant to service-related research and development are introduced in this section.

Accept/Reject

Probably the easiest negotiation protocol is the "Accept/Reject" protocol. In this protocol the seller advertises his goods to potential customers. Buyers select the things they would like to purchase and announce their choice to the seller. The seller then decides on whether to accept or reject the deal. In this process, none of the parameters of the deal are negotiable. The seller can only accept or reject whatever choice the buyer has made. The offer will usually have to be the same as the seller's advertisement, as he will otherwise not agree to the offer. As this is the common procedure in self-service supermarkets, this protocol is also termed the "supermarket approach".

Formally, the displaying of goods is considered an "invitation to treat" in contract law (Burrows, 2009). The buyer is then making a binding offer to the seller who can accept or reject it. The result of this negotiation is either a contract for exchanging goods for money, or nothing.

Mapped to the SLA world, an SLA template is the equivalent of an invitation to treat, as it is a (more or less) public display of the offering of the seller. The buyer then submits an SLA offer. If accepted, the negotiation process results in an SLA, which is a binding contract agreed upon by both parties. The contract usually stipulates that the described services are provided to the customer who in turn has to provide some form of payment.

As noted before, none of the parameters are negotiable. Translated to SLAs, this means that none of the terms can be changed and the SLA template, the offer, and the final SLA all contain the same non-functional properties. The SLA templates are therefore said to be non-negotiable.

Figure 2. The discrete offer model (left) and the invite-tender model (right)

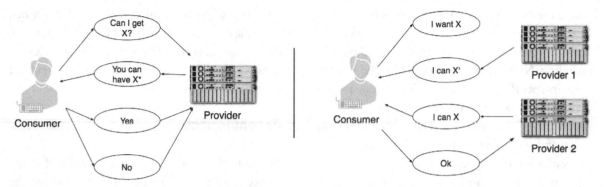

Discrete Offer

The discrete offer model, as depicted in Figure 2, follows the so-called "take-it-or-leave-it" approach (Hasselmeyer, Koller, Schubert, & Wieder, 2008b). Sometimes also referred to as "one-phase-commit" model, it assumes that service providers have a pre-defined set of service offers, which are accessible to customers. Once a customer receives a service offer, this negotiation model foresees that he agrees to one of the offers but has no flexibility to modify any of the terms.

This model is quite similar to the accept/reject model introduced before. The main difference is that the roles of who provides a binding offer and who finally accepts or rejects an SLA are reversed. For the accept/reject model, the consumer makes a binding offer and the provider decides on acceptance/rejection. In the discrete offer model, the provider makes a binding offer and the consumer accepts or rejects it.

Invite-Tender

The invite-tender model moves away from the accept/reject protocol in which consumers look around for appropriate service providers. For the invite-tender model, the service consumer specifies his requirements and publishes this specification to the "outside world" to be found by service providers. Providers interested in provid-ing the needed service can send tenders on this invitation. The tenders are then reviewed by the consumer, potentially adapted and sent back to the provider who can send in new tenders. In general this follows a similar approach to the multi-phase (n-phase) negotiation and could be realized by a symmetric protocol. Figure 2 shows a customer following this model with two service providers sending in tenders. In the example, service provider 2 offers exactly the desired service so that no further negotiation needs to take place.

Multi-Phase (n-phase) Negotiation

As mentioned before, the discrete offer model is rather inflexible and therefore not sufficient in all business cases. More flexibility can be achieved by extending the discrete offer approach to several rounds of negotiation. In the beginning, the concept is similar to the discrete offer model with a request and a potential offer following. Now, instead of either agreeing to or rejecting the offer, the customer has the possibility to adapt the offer and to send it to the provider as a counter-offer, who can also modify the counter-offer and send it back (as shown in Figure 3).

This process happens repeatedly and might run indefinitely, which is the biggest concern of the opponents of this model. However, when realized in a proper way, there are mechanisms and decision points for both customer and service

Figure 3. Multi-phase negotiation

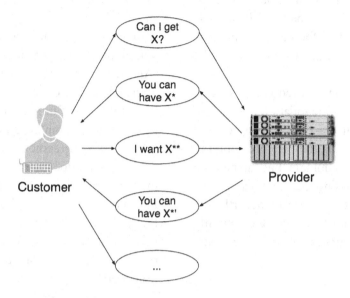

provider to stop this negotiation, either with or without an agreement.

English Auction

The model of the English Auction realizes a first-price, open cry, ascending auction (Nabi & Nadeem, 2009). It starts with a price set by the auctioneer, followed by bids that constantly increase the price. If no further bid is received within a certain amount of time, the highest bidder is awarded the goods. This process ensures that the price is increased until only one participant is left who pays the highest price.

Dutch Auction

In contrast to the English Auction, the Dutch Auction starts with a high price, which then is decreased subsequently (Lie & McConnell, 1998). Lowering the price continues until one of the participants is willing to pay the current price, or a pre-defined price is reached (the minimum acceptable price as defined by the seller in advance) in which case the item is not sold. In principle, the Dutch Auction

is a very simple and quick protocol, as it needs only one bid to finish the auction.

Vickrey Auction

William Vickrey proposed an adapted auction model, based on the principle of hidden offers – the Vickrey Auction (Vickrey, 1961). Similar to the English Auction, the participant with the highest bid wins. However, in this adapted form, he only has to pay the second highest price. The advantage of this model is that the participants are encouraged to bid a realistic price instead of bidding above or below their real valuation.

SLA-Related Negotiation Protocols

This section introduces specifications of computer-processable models and communication protocols that can be used to realize certain negotiation models with the help of machines. For making SLA negotiations accessible to computers, service level agreements must be encoded in some electronic format that can be processed by a computer. Furthermore, the communication between the negotiation partners must be defined in an unambiguous way. Depending on the desired degree of automation, other parts of the models need to be specified as well, for example computer-"understandable" languages for describing the terms inside SLAs.

The specifications introduced in this section cover the automation of negotiation to different degrees. All of them are designed to be used generically, meaning that they are not bound to a particular application domain, but can be used for any application. Using the specifications for a particular application scenario nevertheless requires additional artifacts, most commonly descriptions of properties of the targeted domain.

WS-Negotiation

WS-Negotiation is an XML-based language, which was proposed by Hung, Li, and Jeng (2004) as basis for agreement establishment between customers and service providers. The specification is split in three parts: Negotiation Message, Negotiation Exchange, and Negotiation Decision Making.

The Negotiation Message part describes the format of the exchanged information between customer and service provider. Even though planned, an enhancement of the message description with definitions of schema and semantics was not yet published.

Message exchanges are following the Negotiation Protocol, which covers bilateral multi-phase negotiations. The rules provided for negotiation define the protocol to be a repeated exchange of offers and counter-offers, i.e. a multi-phase negotiation model is followed.

Finally, the Negotiation Decision Making part is representing decision processes that are based on the strategies of the individual users. The strategies are aligned with each negotiation participant's preferences and by that they are specific to each participant and therefore not defined in the specification.

WS-Agreement

Although not primarily aimed at being a negotiation protocol specification, WS-Agreement (Andrieux et al., 2007) is mentioned here as it offers basic SLA creation mechanisms and as its SLA structure definition is used by other activities to realize more complex forms of SLA negotiation.

The WS-Agreement specification defines SLAs as XML documents divided into two parts: the context and the terms. The context contains information about the parties acceding to the SLA. For the terms, WS-Agreement only specifies that part's structure, but not the terms themselves. It relies on other XML languages to define appropriate terms. Terms are separated into functional ("service description terms") and non-functional terms ("guarantee terms"). Individual terms can be combined by methods defined by WS-Agreement; basic logic operators are available, including "and", "one or more", and "exactly one".

In addition to the structure of SLAs, WS-Agreement defines a structure for SLA templates. It is basically equivalent to the SLA structure, with the addition of a (potentially empty) constraints section that specifies certain provider restrictions on the terms inside to-be-negotiated SLAs. Examples for such constraints are the maximum number of transactions and the minimum price.

WS-Agreement defines a simple interface for establishing SLAs. The interface allows one party to send an SLA offer to another party who can then accept or reject it. Through this, WS-Agreement allows the implementation of the accept/reject or the discrete offer model as described before.

Service Negotiation and Acquisition Protocol – SNAP

The SNAP protocol was published by Czajkowski et al. to present a protocol for remote management of service level agreements across the borders of different resource providers (Czajkowski et al., 2002). The main focus of this work is on enabling resource reservation and provisioning by negotiating single service level agreements across multiple administrative domains (and by that referring to different resources).

Within the SNAP concept, the cross-domain issue is addressed by introducing three types of service level agreements:

- TSLAs (Task Service Level Agreements) cover the execution of an activity (task). Within this construct information about service steps and resource requirements is contained.
- RSLAs (Resource Service Level Agreements) cover the rights to consume a resource but not necessarily what the resource will be used for. Here, the resource is characterized by its abstract service capabilities.
- BSLAs (Binding Service Level Agreements) cover the use of a resource for a task. This task is then either defined directly by a TSLA or a unique identifier, which allows its application to a RSLA.

SNAP was published in 2002, but did not find the desired acceptance in the community. There were some basic implementations, e.g. the implementation of a resource broker based on SNAP by Haji, Gourlay, Djemame, and Dew (2005) using a three phase commit protocol. However, the biggest weakness of SNAP is its generality, as this gives too many degrees of freedom to implement it easily (Sahai, Graupner, Machiraju, & Van Moorsel, 2003).

The Contract Net Protocol

Contract Net is a protocol used in multi-agent systems (Smith, 1980). It supports distributed problem solving by task sharing between several participants. Once a big task needs to be solved, the problem is broken down into different subtasks, which are distributed to other participants. In this model, an invitation to tender is generated for each of the sub-tasks. Based on this, bids are received from potential contractors (agents) and the winning ones get the tasks to execute.

FIPA Contract Net Protocol

The Foundation for Intelligent Physical Agents (FIPA, a standards body in the agent-technology area) proposed a specification on top of the Contract Net Protocol as depicted in Figure 4. The FIPA Contract Net Protocol (CNP) (FIPA Technical Committee Communication, 2002a) foresees a single round of bids. Once a deadline has been reached, all bids are evaluated and the winners get the tasks.

Figure 4. The FIPA contract net protocol

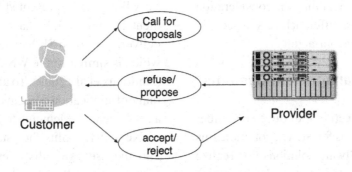

FIPA Iterated Contract Net Protocol

An adaptation of the CNP is the FIPA Iterated Contract Net Protocol (ICNP) (FIPA Technical Committee Communication, 2002b), which realizes an approach allowing for several bids by one bidder. By that, it is possible to have several bidding rounds, one after the other (depending on the pre-defined values of the auctioneer).

The Combinatorial Contract Net Interaction Protocol

Another adaptation of the Contract Net Protocol is the Combinatorial Contract Net Protocol (Karaenke, & Kirn, 2010). This protocol was developed and implemented in 2009 within the context of the BREIN project. It extends the CNP to support reverse combinatorial multi-attribute auctions over multiple tiers, specifically BREIN supply chain levels. The protocol allows the evaluation of subcontracts to enable the creation of better binding proposals.

The protocol is labeled "combinatorial" as it provides three different combination possibilities: Combination of tasks, of attributes and of tiers. Combination of tasks allows providing offers for not only one, but several tasks. They can be described with AND or XOR operators, where the latter allows the customer to accept only a part of the tasks and not necessarily the complete proposal. Combination of attributes was introduced to allow for multi-attribute auctions with an enhanced winner determination. Finally, the combination of tiers is enabling the consideration of dependencies across different levels, especially for the purpose of subcontracting.

Service Level Management Systems

While the previous section introduced a number of models and protocols for SLA negotiation, this section describes software solutions that realize SLA negotiation and integrate it into larger service level management frameworks. The selection covers a broad range of the current state-of-the-art in service level management systems, which are primarily targeted at distributed service infrastructures.

We do not intend to provide the full picture of SLA-based negotiation frameworks, as this would require a book on its own. We therefore selected five of the projects we have been or are working for and which show a broad enough use of negotiation models and protocols. For further systems we refer to the literature referenced in the Additional Reading section.

One central objective of all the systems we cover in this chapter is automation of SLA negotiation to the greatest possible extent. To achieve this, the frameworks provide complex technical solutions that fully embrace SLA negotiation. The examples show that the research efforts have resulted in a sizable body of implementations and experiences with them. In addition, it highlights that many aspects still remain to be explored fully.

NextGRID

The focus of the NextGRID project was on developing an architectural blueprint and reference implementations for the next generation of Grids (Snelling et al., 2008). Part of these activities was an SLA Management Framework, which was conceptually presented within the overall architecture and was verified with an implementation based on the Globus Toolkit 4 (Foster, 2005) and GRIA.

NextGRID aligned its developments with the SLA lifecycle as presented by the TeleManagement Forum (TeleManagement Forum, 2005), delivering its own SLA schema (Snelling, 2007), which is similar to the WS-Agreement structure (Andrieux et al., 2007). To allow its use in a wide range of application domains, the schema contains a set of generic elements to provide flexibility.

NextGRID splits the establishment of SLAs into the use cases discovery, negotiation, and agreement (Koller, Snelling, Hasselmeyer, &

Tserpes, 2008). Separating negotiation and agreement allows the model to cover single-phase as well as multi-phase negotiations by skipping or including the negotiation phase. The agreement protocol (Hasselmeyer, 2008a) was implemented in a prototype following the discrete offer protocol (Mersch et al., 2008). Multi-phase negotiation has not been covered in this project.

Akogrimo

The Akogrimo (Access to Knowledge through Grid in a mobile World) project aimed at developing a middleware for fixed, nomadic and mobile citizens by merging results from the Grid and the network domains (Laria, 2007).

Service level agreements and their management provided the basis for addressing quality-of-service-related issues and guarantees to cover the dynamicity of the Akogrimo environment on two layers – Grid and network. It was not in the focus of the project to provide its "own" SLA schema, therefore the decision was taken to base the work on WS-Agreement as it was fitting the project needs best. Besides this, WSLA terms were embedded in the WS-Agreement frame to specify the properties of the services more clearly and in a standardized way. With respect to negotiation

protocol, the project follows the discrete offer protocol.

BREIN

The European BREIN project's objective was to apply methods and technologies from artificial intelligence, intelligent systems, and the semantic web to evolve Grid infrastructures towards electronic business platforms.

BREIN has realized an SLA negotiation architecture based on agents and semantic capabilities. This architecture is depicted in Figure 5. The system uses a multi-phase negotiation model, which is based on the combinatorial contract net protocol.

BREIN uses negotiation agents on both consumer and provider side, which represent and act on behalf of the respective party (and therefore realize the respective negotiation model). The consumer agent is connected to an editor, which supports SLA negotiation through specification of SLA requirements and business objectives. The provider's editor in addition provides information about SLA templates. Together with a resource manager and a relationship manager, the service provider's negotiation agent can decide to either accept or reject an SLA offer, or to make a counter-offer instead. To increase interoperability, a *Semantic Translator* is used to translate,

Figure 5. The BREIN negotiation architecture (Hasselmeyer et al., 2008b)

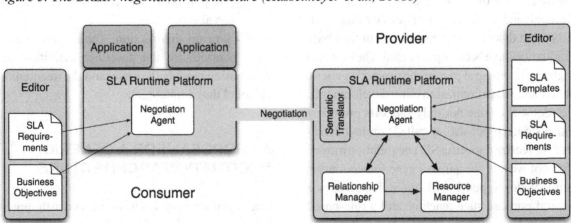

based on a global ontology, incoming SLA offers to a format processable by service providers internally and, vice versa, offers into the customer terms.

The representation of functional and non-functional properties in BREIN was based on a merge of WS-Agreement (as a frame) and WSLA to specify the terms.

This schema was then extended with semantic annotations (leading to Semantic Annotated SLAs, SA-SLA specification) to allow for domain specific flexibility and interoperability of terms (Kotsiopoulos, Soler Jubert, Tenschert, Benedicto Cirujeda, & Koller, 2008; Kotsiopoulos, Munoz Frutos, Koller, Wesner, & Brooke, 2009).

SLA@SOI

SLA@SOI is a European project that aims at creating a framework to integrate service level agreements into a service-oriented IT-landscape (Comuzzi et al.,2009) On the vertical axis, SLA@SOI differentiates between three different service layers, namely the infrastructure, software and business layers. All interactions between services of the different layers and between services within the software and the infrastructure layers are governed by SLAs. The framework supports the complete SLA lifecycle as introduced in Section "The SLA Lifecycle".

SLA@SOI contains a configurable protocol engine capable of handling arbitrary negotiation protocols and models. At the time of writing (mid-2011), the discrete offer model and multi-phase negotiation have been implemented. The protocol engine is an integral part of the project's generic SLA manager. In contrast to other developments, the protocol engine not only supports providers and customers, but also so-called "protocol writers". To realize a specific SLA negotiation model, protocol writers specialize a generic negotiation protocol developed by SLA@SOI that uses a general purpose state machine and a rule-based approach to encode negotiation protocols.

SLA4D-Grid

SLA4D-Grid is a project funded by the German ministry of education and research. It develops a service level management framework for the German national academic Grid, the D-Grid (Freitag & Wieder, 2011). D-Grid currently features over 30.000 CPU cores and five petabytes of storage distributed all over the country. The major development challenge is the heterogeneous software and service base, which has to be supported by "horizontal" developments including SLA negotiation. As a case in point: D-Grid supports the three different Grid middleware suites gLite, Globus, and UNICORE.

To realize a service level management framework without developing the functionally equivalent service stacks three times, SLA4D-Grid uses a generic component that supports the complete SLA lifecycle as described in Section "The SLA Lifecycle". For SLA negotiation, this component implements the WS-Agreement standard (Andrieux et al., 2007) and follows the current proposal for a multi-phase negotiation protocol based on WS-Agreement (Wäldrich, 2010). The non-functional service properties used within SLA4D-Grid contracts depend on the actual usage scenario that is realized on top of the service management solution. One example scenario, an Infrastructure-as-a-Service system, differentiates the various service instances by NFPs like availability, support hours, price, or service interruption intervals.

To sum up this section, Table 1 contains a short overview of the described activities, the negotiation models they use, and the negotiation protocol they implement.

A PROPOSAL FOR A GENERIC NEGOTIATION ARCHITECTURE

The negotiation approaches described in the previous section are addressing different, often multiple

Table 1. Service level management systems and their negotiation models and protocols

Framework	Model	Realized Protocol
NextGRID	**Discrete offer**	**NextGRID negotiation**
Akogrimo	Discrete offer	WS-Agreement
BREIN	Invite-Tender, discrete offer	Combinatorial Contract Net Protocol
SLA@SOI	Designed to be used with different models	Generic proprietary protocol
SLA4D-Grid	Multi-phase negotiation	WS-Agreement Negotiation (Wäldrich, 2010)

parts of the overall negotiation process. Although they differ widely in their purpose and functionality, architectural blueprints can be developed that are applicable generically. In this section, we first discuss the issues that occur realizing such an approach. Then, we discuss the negotiation architecture from two different perspectives: data flow architecture and component model.

Issues, Controversies, Problems

SLA negotiation is a healthy field of research with participation from different institutions and backgrounds. Work is performed on different layers from fundamental research on negotiation models to implementations in specific application domains. This section introduces and discusses a number of issues that have been addressed in various ways but that are not yet solved in a commonly agreed way.

Choice of Negotiation Model and Protocol

As can be seen from the large variety of negotiation models and protocols, there is no consensus on which method is best suited for the negotiation of service level agreements. And indeed, some models are better suited for particular scenarios than others. For time-critical negotiations, e.g. for urgent computing (Cope & Tufo, 2008), bilateral negotiations, potentially using a simple take-it-or-leave-it approach, seem to be most appropriate,

while an auction might give better results in terms of price, if enough time and resources are available to hold that auction. As the example showed, the selection of the most appropriate negotiation scheme does not depend on the function of the resources to which access is negotiated. Rather, the circumstances of the use of the resources govern the choice of the best negotiation model.

So far, decisions on the negotiation model have been made once at the design time of a system taking the anticipated circumstances into account. Although such systems work fine in the environment they were developed for, adapting them to changing circumstances or placing them in an environment different from the initially expected one cause major redesigns of the system or simply render them unusable.

Currently available SLA negotiation protocols and middleware suites are generically applicable, in the sense that the protocols and implementations can be reused across particular applications and application domains. They are nevertheless bound to the specific negotiation model and protocol that they specify or implement. Changing that model or protocol is usually prohibitively resource-intensive. And this is without even considering dynamically changing the negotiation model or protocol on-the-fly.

From the development of generically applicable SLA negotiation protocols and middleware one can derive the trend towards increased abstraction from lower level implementation details. Extending that trend into the future, one possible route could (and in the eyes of the authors, should) be the abstraction from the actual negotiation model and protocol used. The architecture described in this section is generic enough to allow its use with different negotiation models and protocols.

NFP Descriptions

Interoperability between negotiation partners can only be achieved if the terms inside SLAs and SLA precursors are known to and understood by all the partners. So far, most if not all deployments of automated SLA negotiation have used their own terms, or at least worked with their own specific selection of existing term description languages. As a result, these systems only work amongst themselves, making the inclusion of external participants difficult or even impossible.

The problem has a number of aspects all contributing to the difficulty of interoperability. Basically, every SLA protocol, middleware, and application comes with its own description mechanism for terms. This is particularly true for systems that are designed and developed for one particular scenario. In case of middleware and protocols aimed at generic use, the languages for describing single terms are not mandated. But even in this case, the language for combining individual terms (i.e., "A and B", "C or D", "exactly one of E, F, G", etc.) is pre-defined, restricting interoperability to the same protocol or middleware. But even when using the same generic negotiation protocol or middleware, the applications use different description languages for the terms inside the SLA, again defeating interoperability.

So far, no language for individual NFPs or for term combination has generally been accepted as common practice. Only the Job Submission Description Language (JSDL) (Savva, 2005) comes close to being a de-facto standard as it is commonly used for resource reservations in the high-performance computing domain (Rasheed et al., 2003).

On one hand, being open to all kinds of terms and to any description language is important to enable re-usable protocols and middleware for SLA negotiation. On the other hand, broad acceptance of negotiation systems may have been delayed by the openness due to the associated uncertainty of future usability. The authors expect that de-facto standards will emerge with the maturation of the field. To drive this trend forward proactively, application domain experts should be encouraged to engage in discussions on standardizing term description languages and their use in SLAs and SLA negotiation.

Property Reconciliation

Negotiation of SLAs relies on reconciling client requirements and provider constraints. Finding ranges of values that are acceptable to both parties is the basis for all kinds of SLA negotiation. Most of the existing negotiation systems use program code that is specifically tailored to reconcile the properties of the SLAs and SLA precursors that are to be used in their environments.

Again following the path of increased generality and abstraction, values and value ranges for SLA terms should be processed independent of the particular term they are contained in. Research conducted by the authors confirmed that reconciliation is possible for simple types of values. Simple types are in particular integer and floating point values and ranges of such values. Reconciliation of string values (other than equality) and complex, interdependent data items is much harder and generically applicable description languages are not readily available.

Semantic models might be a viable solution to reconcile requirements and constraints. The use of semantic annotations to service level agreements, for example, could be of high value for the representation of non-functional properties. The BREIN project has evaluated such an approach, resulting in a specification for semantic annotations of service level agreements (Kotsiopoulos et al., 2008).

This specification provides annotation mechanisms that enhance SLA descriptions with pointers to semantic concepts, which are captured in more expressive domain-specific ontologies (represented in languages such as OWL or WSML). To this end, domain stakeholders have to to produce a set of related ontologies, which apply to the different levels of the service landscape. Such a set of ontologies is in general based on a number of core ontologies, which can be extended for certain use cases to describe the non-functional properties, service profiles, resources, and general issues of the respective domains.

Although first efforts like the one described here already exist, an evaluation (and realization) of the integration of semantic models into the SLA lifecycle (and thus into the negotiation process) is still to be done.

Integration

The SLA negotiation components need to be integrated with the applications they work with. Depending on the SLA-awareness of the application, two conceptually different models are possible.

In case of being SLA-aware, applications can use functions of the SLA middleware directly. On the client side, an application can trigger SLA negotiation on demand and it will let the middleware know when it needs to make use of the guarantees stated in the SLA. On the server side, the application would notify the SLA middleware of the constraints for SLA properties. Integration of SLA middleware and SLA-aware applications is tight, as the application needs to contain explicit calls to the SLA middleware.

For SLA-unaware applications, SLAs need to be established outside the application and SLAs need to be bound to application traffic in some way. Commonly, an SLA negotiation user interface external to the actual application is used to create SLAs. This tool can be generic and is therefore usable for all kinds of applications and SLAs. The tool interacts with the SLA middleware and establishes SLAs under the control of a user.

The tool then needs to associate the established SLA with the application it has been agreed for. The association can happen in different ways, depending on the technologies used by the application. Web Service invocations can, for example, be augmented by a reference to an SLA by the Web Services middleware used. Another possibility is to tag traffic for a certain destination address with an SLA-specific marker. For all these solutions some interception mechanism must be available that allows modifying the communication between the client and the provider.

So far, most system implementations have leaned towards the second solution, enhancing existing applications with SLA negotiation capabilities. Although some service interaction protocols have been redesigned to accommodate SLA capabilities, the back-end systems have usually been reused from existing systems.

The direct use of SLA negotiation capabilities by service providers and clients is expected to be of benefit in particular because of its tighter integration. Clients can come bundled with requirements for their guaranteed operation, obviating the need for external description of such requirements. A similar argument applies to the provider side, where management is simplified by the need to manage just one (integrated) application, instead of two interlinked ones (the application itself and the associated SLA negotiator).

The architecture described below does not further explore the differences between those two models. It can be used in both of them. It is nevertheless important to note that the integration of SLA negotiation and applications is influenced by the complexity of the SLA negotiation application programming interface (API). So far, the APIs have been rather complex. A simplified API should be developed to increase adoption.

Data Flow Architecture

Architectural artifacts that are solving parts of the issues described above have been developed and are presented in this section. Although the individual pieces were developed separately, they have been integrated and are described within the scope of the coherent architecture here. The data flow is first described in this section, while a break-down into components is shown in the following section.

An abstract data flow architecture for SLA negotiation systems is shown in Figure 6. The two actors in the model are a client and a provider. Both participants in a negotiation have a *negotiation engine* that executes the negotiation protocol. Although both engines are similar in purpose, their behavior is strictly bound to the stakeholder they serve. This reflects the different roles of the stakeholders in many negotiation protocols. For example, in English auctions there is a clear distinction between bidders and auctioneer.

The choice of negotiation model does not affect the data flow model as the same information flows into and out of the negotiation engine, independent of the negotiation model. The interacting negotiation engines must have a common negotiation protocol in order to be able to communicate. The selection of protocol is assumed to happen out-of-band before starting the actual negotiation. Methods for selecting the protocol include manual configuration, automated configuration according to information received during service discovery, and automated negotiation. In the latter case, bootstrapping of such negotiations is required and resorts to one of the other methods.

The negotiation engines are steered by information provided by the parties they represent. As indicated in Figure 6, clients supply information on requirements, preferences, and selection rules to their negotiation engines, while providers pass on constraints, templates, and selection rules.

Clients' *requirements* state conditions that the non-functional properties contained in a future SLA need to fulfill. Examples of such requirements are "the bandwidth must be at least 10Mbps", "the price must be below $10 per month", and "the service provider must be ISO27001-certified". The requirements represent a minimum level of compliance and are therefore non-negotiable. The requirements can be split into two groups: quality-of-service related and business related. Quality-of-service-related requirements are needed for the application to run properly. A streaming audio/video application might require a certain minimum bandwidth and maximum jitter to work adequately. Business-related requirements are not needed for using the service as such, but are related to business aspects. For example,

Figure 6. Data flow architecture

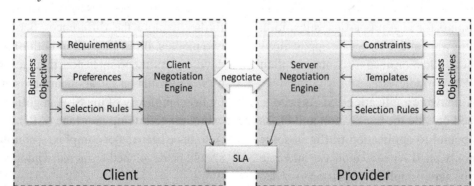

in order to be profitable, a client might need to specify a maximum amount of money to spend on a particular service.

Preferences, on the other hand, state wishes of the client. These express what the client prefers, in case it has a choice. Examples of preferences are "minimize the prize", "maximize throughput", and "prefer providers based in Europe". Such preferences can only be observed when the client has the choice among at least two providers whose SLAs would fulfill all of the client's requirements.

Selection rules on the client side are similar to preferences, but rather than being applicable to properties inside SLAs, they are rules governing provider selection independent of an SLA's contents. Examples of selection rules are "select provider A, even if he is 20% more expensive than the cheapest provider", "do not do business with provider B", and "always use provider C on the weekend".

All three types of information needed to steer SLA negotiation are partial representations of the client's *business objectives*. Together they form a computer-processable externalization of those objectives. Structuring them according to the three given categories allows for their independent evolution and separate representation. This is particularly important as complexity and maturity of the categories are different. Specifically, expressing requirements is most advanced, while expressing selection rules is the least advanced of the three, as the variety of potential rules is extremely large.

The different types of information on the client side have equivalents on the provider side. The analog to requirements are constraints on the provider side. *Constraints* are restrictions that non-functional properties of future SLAs need to observe. Example constraints are "the bandwidth must be less or equal to 100Mbps", "the price must be at least $5 per month", and "the client must have a bank account in the US". Similar to the client's requirements, the constraints can

be separated into quality-of-service-related and business-related ones.

Templates are service advertisements with pre-defined content. Although not strictly necessary, the content usually consists of a set of property settings preferred by the provider. The templates might or might not be used as the basis for negotiation. Parts of a template's content are negotiable and can be modified by the client during negotiation, if the chosen negotiation model allows this.

Selection rules on the provider side are similar to the ones on the client side. They can contain restrictions and preferences on the set of clients. Examples of these rules are "give 10% discount to client A", and "do not do business with client B", and "clients must have a credit rating of at least B+".

All the abovementioned types of information are potentially dynamic and can change over time. In particular the service provider's constraints are susceptible to adjustments. An obvious example is the current utilization of the resources on offer. If the load is low, the price might be low, while it is higher during times of peak utilization. A client's requirements (e.g. on price or delivery date) can change similarly with the urgency of the need for a service.

During negotiation, clients' requirements and providers' constraints are reconciled and SLA properties fulfilling both requirements and constraints are found. At the same time, selection rules are observed and preferences fulfilled as far as possible. The result of a successful negotiation is the *SLA* that has been agreed upon by both parties. The negotiation process must ensure that both parties' copies of the SLA are identical and contain what the parties agreed upon. Mutual (cryptographic) signatures on the SLA are one way to ensure this. In case no agreement was reached, the negotiation process terminates without a usable output.

Although Figure 6 only shows a single client and a single provider, it is often the case that clients and providers are engaged in multiple parallel negotiations. In this case, each negotiation process is modeled as an independent instance of the data flow architecture.

In case of negotiating access to combined resources from multiple providers, it is assumed that there is a mediator who acts as the single instance a client is negotiating with. The mediator in turn engages in multiple parallel negotiations with the providers responsible for the individual parts. Although modeled as one interaction with a mediator, co-scheduling of resources can be realized in different ways. One viable alternative to an external mediator is the coordination of the multiple negotiation sessions by the client itself, potentially using a two-phase-commit-like protocol to ensure all-or-nothing semantics for the negotiated resources.

Component Model

The data flow architecture described how data is flowing through the system while being operated on. The component model shows the components of the system that perform that processing. The component model of a generic SLA negotiator is shown in Figure 7. The architecture is independent of the negotiation model, the negotiation protocol, and the application domain.

The figure shows that a number of components are shared between client and provider. On top of that, there are a number of additional components on the provider side that deal with connecting SLA negotiation with the resources to which access is negotiated. The business objectives play a special role in the diagram, as they are no components in the component architecture per se, but rather data artifacts as described previously. They are shown here to make the link from the data flow architecture to the component model visible.

The client has four functional components. The *protocol engine* is the component that is involved in the communication with the provider. It is specific to the protocol being spoken between the negotiation partners. It may use a signer component to digitally sign documents if instructed to do so by the SLA manager.

The *SLA manager* coordinates the process of SLA negotiation. Upon external request it starts a negotiation session. It uses the protocol engine component to talk to candidate providers. The set of candidate providers is known at the negotiation stage, either through explicit configuration or via some service discovery protocol.

The most important task of the SLA manager is to decide on how to progress the negotiation. It has access to the business goals in terms of re-

Figure 7. Component model

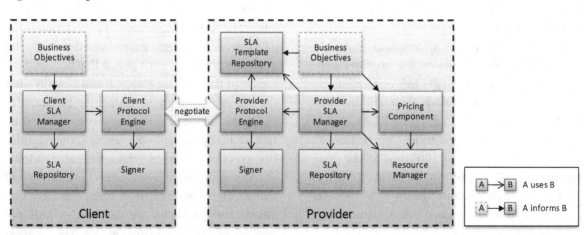

quirements, preferences and selection rules, and it receives information about the current offers from the protocol engine. It takes all this information into account and decides on how to proceed. For bilateral negotiations, the current offer can be accepted, a new counter-offer can be created, or negotiations can be terminated. For auctions, the SLA manager may announce the current price level and select the winner as soon as all necessary bids have been received.

In case an SLA is established, the manager stores the signed SLA in the *SLA repository* for further reference. Stored SLAs are used on the client side mainly to later on claim access to the reserved resources.

The *signer* is an optional component that electronically signs SLAs. Signatures on SLAs are needed to indicate agreement to an SLA and can be used as a non-repudiation mechanism in case of later dispute. Depending on the negotiation model and requirements, this component might be left out in simple setups.

The provider has four components similar to the client, plus three additional ones. The four components it has in common with clients serve the same purpose as their equivalents on the client side. As they have partly different functions, a distinction is made between the client-side components and their counterparts on the provider side. Although both client-side and provider-side *protocol engines* execute a particular negotiation protocol, they take on different roles within the negotiation process, e.g. the buyer and the seller roles.

The *signer* component can be the same as on the client side. The *SLA repository* can also be the same component as on the client side, although it is used in a slightly different way on the provider side. Specifically, the stored SLAs are used to reserve and provision resources in accordance with their contents. Upon resource access, the provider verifies the association between SLA and requested resources and ensures the contractual use of the resources. Both functions need the

SLA repository to get access to SLA terms and conditions.

The *provider SLA manager* deals with more jobs than its counterpart on the client side. As its client-side equivalent, it also coordinates the negotiation process. To adequately perform this role, the provider SLA manager needs to be aware of the capabilities and state of the resources it negotiates access to. It therefore communicates with the resource manager and coordinates resource access schedules. The SLA manager makes use of the pricing component in order to determine prices for SLA offers according to the business objectives.

The *pricing component*'s responsibility is to determine prices for SLA offers/bids. The pricing depends on the business objectives of the provider. The pricing model can be static or dynamic. In case of it being dynamic, it can depend on many external factors, with the most common being the utilization of resources. The pricing component therefore interacts with the resource manager in order to learn the current and future load on the resources.

The *resource manager* coordinates access to the resources it is responsible for and which are offered to customers via SLA negotiation. It keeps a schedule of agreed access commitments and can therefore estimate current and future utilization of the resources. It provides such information to the SLA manager and the pricing component, which can then allow or deny access and determine appropriate resource prices, respectively.

In addition to the SLA repository, which holds agreed-upon SLAs, the provider has an *SLA template repository*, which holds templates for SLA negotiation. These templates are handed out to potential clients upon request by the protocol engine. The templates are usually created manually by the provider according to his business objectives and are then stored in the template repository.

All the mentioned components are part of a generic architecture and are used independent of the negotiation model, negotiation protocol and application domain. In particular, the architecture is applicable to both bilateral negotiations as well as auctions. Depending on the negotiation model, different protocol engines and SLA managers need to be developed and used. The other components are independent of the negotiation model and do not need to be adapted to a particular negotiation model.

FUTURE RESEARCH DIRECTIONS

The previous section already discussed a number of issues that have been addressed in various ways but that have not yet a generally accepted solution or best practice. Finding the "best" solution or criteria for selecting particular options will remain of interest for some time to come. Besides these issues, a number of challenges and open problems are discussed in this section. Their state is not as mature as the ones introduced before and they therefore require more research effort. Some of the challenges might not even have a generally applicable or usable solution.

Dynamic Negotiation Model Selection

A major problem with the existing middleware solutions is that once they are released the effort required to adapt them to other negotiation models or protocols is prohibitively large. Accordingly, the simplest solution, which is followed by many activities, is to develop a new system for each and every new use case from scratch, throwing most of the existing components away.

One important research issue in the SLA negotiation area is to develop concepts and methods for encouraging reuse of middleware components in different environments. A re-thinking of the current approaches towards the realization of such systems needs to take place to provide a basis for more adaptive systems.

One radical improvement over existing solutions could be to significantly raise the level of abstraction. Basically, applications that need access to services with certain non-functional guarantees want to specify the services they need and the service quality levels. They do not want to be bothered with how negotiation proceeds or even what negotiation model or protocol is used. As mentioned before, the selection of negotiation model and protocol depends on the usage environment, not the functions of the applications and services themselves. The selection should therefore be moved outside of the applications and application developers should not see or be bothered with peculiarities of the negotiation middleware.

Recently, a plug-in approach was presented allowing abstraction from the actual negotiation logic to be used for Grids and Clouds (Koller, 2009; Wieder, Hasselmeyer, & Koller, 2010). Applications interact with a negotiation middleware that selects the actual negotiation logic and implementation to be used. The applications do not know which implementation is used as the interface to the middleware is always the same. Implementations of negotiation models, protocols and logic are created in the form of plug-ins, which realize certain functions pre-defined by the middleware. Such plug-ins can be replaced dynamically at run-time and are selected according to properties of the current environment.

The plug-in approach so far only exists at a conceptual level. Suitable abstractions of the negotiation process need to be found and appropriate interfaces both on the side of the applications and on the side of the plug-ins need to be defined. Whether a level of abstraction covering negotiation models ranging from bilateral negotiations to auctions can be found remains to be shown by future research.

Representation of Business Objectives

The complete SLA negotiation process is driven by business objectives in some form. As stated before, the maturity of specification formalisms for the different categories of business objectives varies. Representing requirements and constraints is already rather mature while there are no declarative specification mechanisms for general selection rules. This problem transcends the domain of SLA negotiation and is ideally addressed in a more holistic way as it potentially impacts all aspects of electronic business.

The separation of business objectives into the aspects requirements/constraints, preferences, templates, and selection rules is only a pragmatic first step to bridge the time until complete modeling of business aspects is available and commonplace. As even the modeling of these specific aspects is by no means mature yet, it is expected that holistic modeling is still some ways away. The pragmatic separation might therefore prevail for quite some time.

Negotiation Broker

Adding SLA negotiation capabilities to client and server applications requires a certain amount of effort. Not only need the applications be augmented with calls to the SLA middleware, the SLA middleware itself needs to be selected and later on maintained. Maintenance costs in particular can be high if updates occur frequently.

One way to cut maintenance costs is to outsource negotiation to an external service. The external service is called a *negotiation broker*. The broker is operated by an independent party and takes care of negotiation on behalf of a service client or provider. With this model, maintenance of the SLA middleware on the client and provider side is not necessary as it is being taken care of by the broker's operator.

The negotiation broker contains all the components as shown in the component model (cf. Figure 7) with the exception of the business objectives. As elaborated in (Hasselmeyer, Qu, Koller, Schubert, & Wieder, 2006), the broker needs enough information to steer its negotiation behavior to best represent the party on whose behalf it operates. This requires the transfer of business objectives in some form. Besides running into the unsolved problem of representing the business objectives (see above), this is a potential privacy problem as business objectives are usually securely guarded company secrets. Giving out such information to an external broker is a potential risk. It is an open question how much information needs to be given out and how much of a privacy problem that is.

Outsourcing negotiations on the client-side is deemed less problematic than on the provider side. On the client side, requirements and preferences (and maybe some further selection rules) need to be transferred to the broker. On the provider side, in addition to static constraints, templates and selection rules, access to dynamic resource information must be given to the broker as SLAs can only be established if enough resources are available, which needs to be checked at SLA establishment time. Worse yet, if dynamic pricing of resources is desired, the broker needs access to the pricing policies. It is of yet unknown for which resources such outsourcing of negotiation is acceptable.

Confidence in Automated Decision Making

The main goal of SLA negotiation research is to automate the negotiation phase as much as possible. There has been quite some progress on the technical side, but acceptance of SLA negotiation has been slow so far. Besides numerous technical problems, one main question is how far humans trust the decision-making capabilities of machines. Having machines negotiate SLAs inherently involves automated decision-making: decisions on the price, decisions on the suitability of SLAs, and decisions on who to contract.

Although large parts of business are now conducted with the help of computers, large business deals are still negotiated face-to-face. Delegating negotiations of such deals to machines still seems rather far-fetched. As experience with automated negotiation is nearly non-existent, one does not want to give away control of important business transactions. The authors believe that with increasing (positive) experience from low-value transactions automated negotiations will be gaining in acceptance and increasingly higher-valued transactions will be supported or conducted completely by automated negotiation systems.

Making this possible needs a few breakthroughs on the technical side, in particular with regard to the intelligent and trustworthy handling of terms inside SLAs. Current systems can only deal with very limited sets of non-functional properties in SLAs. The set of understood properties needs to be extended and the interrelation of various properties needs to be specified. Furthermore, the negotiation systems need to be able to tell which properties they understand and which they don't in order to guarantee that they do not agree to unwanted terms.

CONCLUSION

SLAs are deemed an important tool for the future service market. They offer service users guarantees for their service access while they allow service providers to better plan resource assignment. Their establishment is currently mostly a manual process making it slow and expensive. Speeding up the process and significantly reducing its costs require automation of the complete SLA lifecycle, including the negotiation phase.

SLA negotiation has been introduced in this chapter. Various models of negotiation were described, protocols and middleware suites implementing such models were detailed, and

a comprehensive architecture encompassing the described systems was presented. The chapter showed the vast amount and variety of work conducted in this area. Yet, it also showed that most implementations focus on only a particular application domain or a small subset of the SLA negotiation process. Middleware suites do offer a certain degree of generality, but often shift the hard parts to extensions not provided by the middleware.

At the heart of negotiation are the terms of the SLA describing functional and non-functional properties. Negotiation is about finding sets of values for the terms that satisfy both the service customer and the provider. A good understanding of the meaning and implications of the terms is therefore required on both sides. So far, existing work has always focused on particular application domains using their own specific sets of NFPs and NFP description languages. Reusing such hand-coded implementations or interoperating with them is difficult and costly. Standardized sets of terms have so far not emerged but are needed to increase adoption of SLAs and SLA negotiation.

The other major point of variability in the negotiation process is the negotiation model used. So far, all implementations are bound to one specific hard-coded negotiation model. Having opted for a particular model makes participating in trade with partners using other models impossible without a major reimplementation of the application. Worse still, negotiation models can be realized with various protocols, but implementations only realize one particular protocol, rendering interaction with components speaking a different protocol impossible.

Replacing negotiation models and protocols, even dynamically at run-time, seems possible, but has not been tried so far. Research in this direction appears to be fruitful and could pave the way towards broad adoption of SLAs and SLA negotiation.

Another important research topic is the simplification of integration of SLA negotiation into services and applications. One solution could be outsourcing negotiation to external SLA brokers. Breakthroughs in the area of modeling and encoding business objectives are required to make full outsourcing possible.

Based on the discussions in this chapter, it can be seen that SLA negotiation has already come a long way and interesting work has been done, is currently being done, and the open research issues outlined in this chapter promise that interesting work will continue to be done in the future. SLAs and their negotiation are important cornerstones of electronic business and their broad adoption is expected to increase pervasiveness of electronic business, speed up trade, and improve market efficiency.

REFERENCES

Andrieux, A., Czajkowski, K., Dan, A., Keahey, K., Ludwig, H., Nakata, T., & Xu, M. (2007). *Web services agreement specification (WS-Agreement)*. The Open Grid Forum, Specification GFD-R-P.107. Retrieved September 8, 2011, from http://www.ogf.org/documents/GFD.107.pdf

Burrows, A. (2009). *A casebook on contract* (2nd ed.). Oxford, UK: Hart Publishing.

Comuzzi, M., Kotsokalis, C., Rathfelder, C., Theilmann, W., Zacco, G., & Winkler, U. (2009). A framework for multi-level SLA management, *3rd Workshop on Non-Functional Properties and SLA Management in Service-Oriented Computing (NFPSLAM-SOC '09)* (pp. 187-196). New York, NY: Springer.

Cope, J., & Tufo, H. M. (2008). Adapting Grid services for urgent computing environments. In Cordeiro, J., Shishkov, B., Ranchordas, A., & Helfert, M. (Eds.), *ICSOFT (PL/DPS/KE)* (pp. 135–142). INSTICC Press.

Czajkowski, K., Foster, I. T., Kesselman, C., Sander, V., & Tuecke, S. (2002). SNAP: A protocol for negotiating service level agreements and coordinating resource management in distributed systems. In Feitelson, D. G., Rudolph, L., & Schwiegelshohn, U. (Eds.), *Job scheduling strategies for parallel processing* (pp. 153–183). Berlin, Germany: Springer-Verlag. doi:10.1007/3-540-36180-4_9

FIPA Technical Committee Communication. (2002a). *FIPA contract net interaction protocol specification, FIPA specification SC00029H*. Geneva, Switzerland: Foundation for Intelligent Physical Agents.

FIPA Technical Committee Communication. (2002b). *FIPA iterated contract net interaction protocol specification, FIPA specification SC00030H*. Geneva, Switzerland: Foundation for Intelligent Physical Agents.

Foster, I. (2005). Globus toolkit version 4: Software for service-oriented systems. In *Network and Parallel Computing (IFIP International Conference, NPC 2005), LNCS 3779* (pp. 2-13). Berlin, Germany: Springer-Verlag.

Freitag, S., & Wieder, P. (2011). The German Grid initiative D-Grid - Status quo and future perspectives. In Yang, X., Wang, L., & Jie, W. (Eds.), *Guide to e-science: Next generation scientific research and discovery*. New York, NY: Springer.

Haji, M. H., Gourlay, I., Djemame, K., & Dew, P. M. (2005). A SNAP-based community resource broker using a three-phase commit protocol: A performance study. *The Computer Journal, 48*(3), 333–346. doi:10.1093/comjnl/bxh088

Hasselmeyer, P. (2008a). NextGRID SLA negotiation schema. *The NextGRID Project*. Retrieved September 8, 2011, from http://www.nextgrid.org/GS/management_systems/SLA_management/NextGRID_SLA_negotiation_profile.pdf

Hasselmeyer, P., Koller, B., Schubert, L., & Wieder, P. (2008b). Added value for business through econtract negotiation. In Cunningham, P., & Cunningham, M. (Eds.), *Collaboration and the knowledge economy: Issues, applications, case studies* (Vol. 5, pp. 641–648). Amsterdam, The Netherlands: IOS Press.

Hasselmeyer, P., Qu, C., Koller, B., Schubert, L., & Wieder, P. (2006). Towards autonomous brokered SLA negotiation. In Cunningham, P., & Cunningham, M. (Eds.), *Exploiting the knowledge economy: Issues, applications, case studies* (Vol. 3, pp. 44–51). Amsterdam, The Netherlands: IOS Press.

Hung, P. C. K., Li, H., & Jeng, J.-J. (2004). WS-Negotiation: An overview of research issues. In *Hawaii International Conference on System Sciences, vol. 1* (p. 10033b).

Karaenke, P., & Kirn, S. (2010). A multi-tier negotiation protocol for logistics service chains. *Proceedings of the 18th European Conference on Information Systems (ECIS 2010)*. Retrieved September 8, 2011, from http://web.up.ac.za/ecis/ECIS2010PR/ECIS2010/Content/Papers/0068.R1.pdf

Koller, B. (2009). Towards optimal creation of service level agreements. In P. Cunningham, & M. Cunningham (Eds.), *eChallenges e-2009 Conference Proceedings*. IIMC International Information Management Corporation Ltd.

Koller, B., Snelling, D., Hasselmeyer, P., & Tserpes, K. (2008). *NextGRID SLA management use cases*. The NextGRID Project. Retrieved September 8, 2011, from http://www.nextgrid.org/GS/management_systems/SLA_management/NextGRID_SLA_usecases.pdf

Kotsiopoulos, I., Munoz Frutos, H., Koller, B., Wesner, S., & Brooke, J. (2009). A lightweight semantic bridge between Clouds and Grids. In P. Cunningham, & M. Cunningham (Eds.), *eChallenges e-2009 Conference Proceedings*. IIMC International Information Management Corporation Ltd.

Kotsiopoulos, I., Soler Jubert, I., Tenschert, A., Benedicto Cirujeda, J., & Koller, B. (2008). Using semantic technologies to improve negotiation of service level agreements. In Cunningham, P., & Cunningham, M. (Eds.), *Expanding the knowledge economy: Issues, applications, case studies* (Vol. 4, pp. 1045–1052). Amsterdam, The Netherlands: IOS Press.

Laria, G. (Ed.). (2007). *Consolidated report on the implementation of the application support services layer*. The Akogrimo project. Retrieved September 8, 2011, from http://www.akogrimo.org/modules87ce.pdf?name=UpDownload&req=getit&lid=123

Lee, J. J., & Ben-Natan, R. (2002). *Integrating service level agreements – Optimizing your OSS for SLA delivery* (1st ed.). Indianapolis, IN: Wiley Publishing, Inc.

Lie, E., & McConnell, J. J. (1998). Earnings signals in fixed-price and Dutch auction self-tender offers. *Journal of Financial Economics, 49*(2). doi:10.1016/S0304-405X(98)00021-X

Marilly, E., Martinot, O., Betge-Brezetz, S., & Delegue, G. (2002). Requirements for service level agreement management. *IEEE Workshop on IP Operations and Management* (pp. 57-62).

Mersch, H., Wieder, P., Koller, B., Murphy, G., Perrot, R., Donachy, P., & Anjomshoaa, A. (2008). Improving business opportunities of financial service providers through service level agreements. In D. Talia, R. Yahyapour, & W. Ziegler (Eds.), *Grid middleware and services – Challenges and solutions* (pp. 397-408). New York, NY: Springer Science+Business Media, LLC.

Nabi, M. G., & Nadeem, A. (2009). A formal model for English auction protocol. In R. Y. Lee, W. Du, H.-K. Kim, & S. Xu, (Eds.), *Proceedings of the 2009 Seventh ACIS International Conference on Software Engineering Research, Management and Applications* (pp. 119-126). Washington, DC: IEEE Computer Society.

Parkin, M., Badia, R. M., & Matrat, J. (2008). *A comparison of SLA use in six of the European Commission FP6 projects*. Institute on Resource Management and Scheduling, CoreGRID – Network of Excellence. CoreGRID Technical Report TR-0129.

Rasheed, H., Gruber, R., Keller, V., Wäldrich, O., Ziegler, W., Wieder, P., Kuonen, P., Sawley, M., Maffioletti, S., & Kunszt, P. (2003). *IANOS: An intelligent application oriented scheduling middleware for a HPC Grid*. Technical report, TR-0110, Institute on Resource Management and Scheduling, CoreGRID - Network of Excellence.

Sahai, A., Graupner, S., Machiraju, V., & Van Moorsel, A. P. A. (2003). Specifying and monitoring guarantees in commercial Grids through SLA. In *Cluster Computing and the Grid* (pp. 292–299). IEEE Computer Society.

Savva, A. (Ed.). (2005). Job submission description language (JSDL) specification, version 1.0. *The Open Grid Forum*, Specification GFD-R.056. Retrieved September 8, 2011, from http://www.ogf.org/documents/GFD.56.pdf

Smith, R. G. (1980). The contract net protocol: High-level communication and control in a distributed problem solver. *IEEE Transactions on Computers, C-29*(12), 1104–1113. doi:10.1109/TC.1980.1675516

Snelling, D. (2007). *NextGRID SLA schema*. The NextGRID Project. Retrieved September 8, 2011, from http://www.nextgrid.org/GS/management_systems/SLA_management/NextGRID_SLA_schema.pdf

Snelling, D., Anjomshoaa, A., Wray, F., Basermann, A., Fisher, M., Surridge, M., & Wieder, P. (2008). NextGRID architectural concepts. In Priol, T., & Vanneschi, M. (Eds.), *Towards next generation Grids* (pp. 3–14). Berlin, Germany: Springer.

TeleManagement Forum. (2005). SLA management handbook: *Vol. 2. Concepts and principles - GB917 v2.5*. Morristown, NJ: The TeleManagement Forum.

Vickrey, W. (1961). Counterspeculation and competitive sealed tenders. *The Journal of Finance, 16*(1), 8–37. doi:10.2307/2977633

Wäldrich, O. (Ed.). (2010). *WS-Agreement negotiation*. The Open Grid Forum. Retrieved September 8, 2011, from http://ogf.org/Public_Comment_Docs/Documents/2011-03/WS-Agreement-Negotiation+v1.0.pdf

Wieder, P., Hasselmeyer, P., & Koller, B. (2010). Towards service level management in Clouds. In P. Cunningham, & M. Cunningham (Eds.), *eChallenges e-2010 Conference Proceedings*. IIMC International Information Management Corporation Ltd.

ADDITIONAL READING

Bichler, M., & Kalagnanam, J. R. (2006). Software Frameworks for Advanced Procurement Auction Markets. *Communications of the ACM, 49*(12), 105–108. doi:10.1145/1183236.1183239

Conitzer, V. (2010). Making Decisions Based on the Preferences of Multiple Agents. *Communications of the ACM, 53*(3), 84–94. doi:10.1145/1666420.1666442

Goswami, K., & Gupta, A. (2008). Resource Selection in Grids Using Contract Net. *16th Euromicro Conference on Parallel, Distributed and Network-Based Processing*, 105-109. IEEE Computer Society.

Gray, J., & Lamport, L. (2006). Consensus on transaction commit. *ACM Transactions on Database Systems, 31*(1), 133–160. doi:10.1145/1132863.1132867

Hasselmeyer, P., Mersch, H., Koller, B., Quyen, H.-N., Schubert, L., & Wieder, P. (2007). Implementing an SLA negotiation framework. In Cunningham, P., & Cunningham, M. (Eds.), *Expanding the knowledge economy: Issues, applications, case studies* (*Vol. 4*, pp. 154–161). Amsterdam, The Netherlands: IOS Press.

Lamport, L., Shostak, R., & Pease, M. (1982). The Byzantine Generals Problem. *ACM Trans. Program. Lang. Syst., 4*(3), 382–401. doi:10.1145/357172.357176

Lin, K. J. (2008). E-Commerce Technology. *IEEE Internet Computing, 12*(1), 60–65. doi:10.1109/MIC.2008.10

Ludwig, A., Braun, P., Kowalczyk, R., & Franczyk, B. (2006). A Framework for Automated Negotiation of Service Level Agreements in Services Grids. In Bussler, C., & Haller, A. (Eds.), *Business Process Management Workshops* (pp. 89–101). Berlin, Germany: Springer. doi:10.1007/11678564_9

McKee, P., Taylor, S., Surridge, M., Lowe, R., & Ragusa, C. (2007). Strategies for the Service Market Place. In Veit, D., & Altmann, J. (Eds.), *Grid Economics and Business Models* (pp. 58–70). Berlin, Germany: Springer. doi:10.1007/978-3-540-74430-6_5

Ordanini, A. (2006). What Drives Market Transactions in B2B Exchanges? *Communications of the ACM, 49*(4), 89–93. doi:10.1145/1121949.1121953

Ouelhadj, D., Garibaldi, J., MacLaren, J., Sakellariou, R., & Krishnakumar, K. (2005). A Multiagent Infrastructure and a Service Level Agreement Negotiation Protocol for Robust Scheduling in Grid Computing. In Sloot, P. M. A., Hoekstra, A. G., Priol, T., Reinefeld, A., & Bubak, M. (Eds.), *Advances in Grid Computing* (pp. 651–660). Berlin, Germany: Springer.

Pichot, A., Wäldrich, O., Ziegler, W., & Wieder, Ph. (2009). Towards Dynamic Service Level Agreement Negotiation: An Approach Based on WS-Agreement. In Aalst, W., Mylopoulos, J., Sadeh, N. M., Shaw, M. J., Szyperski, C., & Cordeiro, J. (Eds.), *Web Information Systems and Technologies* (pp. 107–119). Berlin, Germany: Springer. doi:10.1007/978-3-642-01344-7_9

Quan, D. M., & Kao, O. (2005). SLA Negotiation Protocol for Grid-Based Workflows. In Yang, L. T., Rana, O. F., Di Martino, B., & Dongarra, J. (Eds.), *High Performance Computing and Communcations* (pp. 505–510). Berlin, Germany: Springer. doi:10.1007/11557654_59

Seidel, J., Wäldrich, O., Ziegler, W., Wieder, P., & Yahyapour, R. (2008). Using SLA for Resource Management and Scheduling - A Survey. In Talia, D., Yahyapour, R., & Ziegler, W. (Eds.), *Grid Middleware and Services - Challenges and Solutions* (pp. 335–347). New York, NY, USA: Springer.

Tamma, V., Phelps, S., Dickinson, I., & Wooldridge, M. (2005). Ontologies for supporting negotiation in e-commerce. *Engineering Applications of Artificial Intelligence, 18*(2), 223–236. doi:10.1016/j.engappai.2004.11.011

Varian, H. R. (2008). Designing the Perfect Auction. *Communications of the ACM, 51*(8), 9–11. doi:10.1145/1378704.1378708

Wolski, R., Plank, J. S., Bryan, T., & Brevik, J. (2001). G-commerce: Market Formulations Controlling Resource Allocation on the Computational Grid. In *Proceedings of the 15th International Parallel and Distributed Processing Symposium*. San Francisco, CA, USA.

Zhao, F. (Ed.). (2006). *Maximize business profits through e-partnerships*. Hershey, PA: IRM Press.

KEY TERMS AND DEFINITIONS

Negotiation Framework: Contains a set of software components that work together to achieve SLA negotiation. Besides description of the components themselves, the framework contains specifications of how the components interact.

Negotiation Model: A description of a set of actors and rules detailing how negotiation of SLAs is proceeding.

Negotiation Protocol: A specification of a set of messages and rules that encode the informa-tion transferred and the conditions when message exchanges happen.

Non-Functional Properties (NFPs): Param-eters in SLAs that express the properties of the service an SLA relates to. They are the subject of negotiation.

Service Level Agreements (SLAs): Electronic contracts that govern access to services.

SLA Negotiation: Used to establish electronic contracts between a number of parties that satisfy the requirements and constraints of all the partners.

Chapter 20
A Framework for Multi-Level SLA Management

Wolfgang Theilmann
SAP Research, Germany

Sergio Garcia Gomez
Telefonica Investigacion y Desarrollo, Spain

Davide Lorenzoli
CITY University, UK

Christoph Rathfelder
FZI Research Center for Information Technology, Germany

Thomas Roeblitz
Dortmund University of Technology, Germany

Gabriele Zacco
Fondazione Bruno Kessler, Italy

ABSTRACT

Service-Oriented Architectures (SOA) represent an architectural shift for building business applications based on loosely-coupled services. In a multi-layered SOA environment the exact conditions under which services are to be delivered can be formally specified by Service Level Agreements (SLAs). However, typical SLAs are just specified at the customer-level, and there are no established formalisms for service providers to translate and manage those SLAs, i.e. to understand how customer-level SLAs translate to metrics or parameters at the various layers of the IT stack.

In this chapter we present a technical architecture for a multi-level SLA management framework. We discuss the fundamental components and interfaces in this architecture and explain the developed integrated framework. Furthermore, we show results from a qualitative evaluation of the framework in the context of an open reference case. Last, we elaborate on important future directions for the area of SLA management.

DOI: 10.4018/978-1-61350-432-1.ch020

INTRODUCTION

The paradigm of *Service-Oriented Architectures (SOA)* has changed the way IT-based systems are built (Papazoglu & Heuvel, 2007). Initially SOA was mainly applied to restructure the IT stack within an organisation. More recently it has also evolved as a common paradigm for cross-organisational service landscapes where services are considered as tradable goods. Consequently, services operate under a strong business context where service customers can expect services to be provided under well-defined and dependable conditions and with clearly associated costs.

Service Level Agreements (SLAs) are a common way to formally specify the exact conditions (both functional and non-functional behaviour) under which services are or shall be delivered. However, the current SLAs in practice are just specified at the customer-level interface between a service provider and a service customer. Customer-level SLAs can be used by customers and providers to monitor whether the actual service delivery complies with the agreed SLA terms. In case of SLA violations, penalties or compensations can be directly derived.

Customer-level SLAs do not allow service providers to either plan their IT landscapes according to possible, planned or agreed SLAs; nor do they allow understanding of why a certain SLA violation might have occurred. The reason for this is that SLA guarantee terms might not be explicitly or directly related to actual performance metrics or configuration parameters. This makes it difficult for service providers to derive proper configuration parameters from customer-level SLAs and to assess (lower-level) monitoring metrics against customer-level SLAs. Overall, the missing relation between customer-level SLAs and (lower-level) metrics and parameters is a major hurdle for managing IT stacks in terms of IT planning, prediction or adjustment processes and in accordance with possible, planned or actual SLAs.

As part of the European Research project SLA@SOI (SLA@SOI, 2010), we developed the vision to use the paradigm of SLAs for managing a complete IT stack in correlation with customer-level SLAs which are agreed at the business level. This complies with the current technical trend to apply the paradigm of service-orientation across the complete IT stack, i.e. infrastructure/platform/software as a service, but also with the organisational trend in IT companies to organise different departments as service departments, providing infrastructure resources, middleware, applications or composition tools as a service. SLAs will be associated with multiple elements of the stack at multiple layers, e.g. SLAs for elements of the physical/virtual infrastructure, middleware, application and process-level. Such internal SLAs describe the contract between the lower-level entities and higher-level entities consuming the lower ones. More precisely, the SLAs specify the required or agreed performance metrics but also the related configuration parameters.

The scenario of multi-level SLA management is relevant in many different contexts, where either a chain of service level providers contributes to the delivery of an eventual service or services within single providers are of such a complex nature that their proper management requires the splitting of the service into layers (and chains) of internal sub-services. As a set of complementary use case scenarios, the project SLA@SOI investigates in particular the following four industry scenarios: ERP hosting, where complex enterprise applications are managed via layers of internal services, Enterprise IT, where IT resources are to be delivered to multiple competing internal customers along business priorities, Service Aggregation, where value added services are composed of lower level IT and telco services, and eGovernment, where social services are composed of different human and IT-based services.

This paper presents the detailed conception and implementation of a multi-level SLA management framework and it is built on a previous discussion of a purely conceptual architecture (Theilmann, Yahyapour, & Butler, 2008). The remainder of this chapter is organised as follows. Section 2 discusses the state of the art. Section 3 introduces the developed framework while Section 4 provides evaluation results in the context of a case study. Section 5 concludes with a brief summary and outlook.

BACKGROUND

The ambition to create a multi-level SLA management framework requires the integration of concepts from a large variety of disciplines and areas. We summarise the most important related work along the areas of modelling, negotiation, planning, monitoring, and adjustment of SLAs. Then, we briefly refer to efforts that apply SLA management in Grid and Cloud computing. Other related aspects such as eContracting, service composition or autonomic management are omitted due to space restrictions.

SLA modelling is about the formal description of SLAs and other related artefacts (e.g. software and infrastructure) that matter within the overall SLA management process. WS-Agreement (Andrieux, et al., 2007) is the prevalent standard for expressing SLAs. It defines a representation of SLA templates with terms free to modify, SLA offers based on these templates, and agreements themselves. While WS-Agreement focuses on specifying a general framework for SLA descriptions other approaches proposed very detailed specification mechanisms, such as the logic-based approach by (Paschke & Bichler, 2008).

SLA negotiation and planning concern the actual interaction protocol used between service customers and providers and the reasoning to determine actual SLAs a provider can agree to, respectively. WS-Agreement provides only a "single-shot" protocol, which is the one adopted in our framework. Relevant extensions can be found in the literature (Frankova, Malfatti, &

Aiello, 2006) and it is our intent to apply M-to-N, multi-round (re-)negotiation techniques in upcoming releases.

SLA planning (Hui, Theilmann, & Happe, 2009) relates to (performance) prediction and SLA translation techniques. Prominent approaches in this area rely on (layered) queueing networks (Chen, Iyer, Liu, Milojicic, & Sahai, 2008) for translating SLA terms into low-level system thresholds or Petri nets (Bodenstaff, Wombacher, Reichert, & Jaeger, 2008) analysing cost and resource usage of service compositions. Distinguishing aspects of our framework are the flexible support of different scenarios, e.g. service composition styles, and the clear separation of concerns between involved parties, e.g. preventing universal knowledge to be assembled in one place.

SLA monitoring and adjustment is about the monitoring of an SLA-governed system and the interpretation of monitoring events against agreed SLAs. Research on service-based systems monitoring has so far focused only on mechanisms for monitoring properties expressed in first-order temporal logic languages, e.g. Event Calculus, either event-based (Spanoudakis & Mahbub, 2006) or based on the instrumentation of the service execution environment, e.g. the BPEL Process (Baresi & Guinea, 2005). Distinguishing aspects of our framework are the automated derivation of monitoring rules from SLAs and the integration between monitoring and related (autonomic) control actions in reaction to detected violations.

Projects focusing on Grid computing (and more recently, Cloud computing) have researched the topic of SLA management from a more holistic perspective. Research on Grid computing focuses mainly on SLA negotiation (Czajkowski, Foster, Kesselman, Sander, & Tuecke, 2002) and SLA-based scheduling (Ouelhadj, Garibaldi, MacLaren, Sakellariou, & Krishnakumar, 2005). A more complete SLA management framework is presented in (Hasselmeyer, Koller, Schubert, & Wieder, 2006) in the context of High-Performance Computing. This work extends further than negotiation, with configuration and execution. A holistic approach to SLA Management is central within the NextGrid project (Snelling, et al., 2007). However, this work is more conceptual and describes only functional requirements. Additionally, (Parkin, Badia, & Martrat, 2008) provides a more elaborate review of how SLA management is taking place in six large European projects.

As regards SLAs for Cloud computing, research results are only starting to appear in literature, and are mostly related to the problem definition and requirements analysis for supporting users with SLAs (Buyya, Yeo, & Venugopal, 2008). The main problem in SLAs for Cloud computing, and at the same time the main difference with existing solutions, is that it is harder to identify the exact service, and the lines between its functional and non-functional properties are becoming very thin.

SLA MANAGEMENT FRAMEWORK

The primary goal of the SLA management framework is to support service and infrastructure providers (the latter are a specialization of the former ones) to manage the lifecycle of their services based on the notion of SLAs. Complementing this there are tools for supporting software providers to assist the engineering of predictable software components.

The design and implementation of our SLA management framework is based on the conceptualisation presented in (Theilmann, Yahyapour, & Butler, 2008) and the lessons learned from a rapid prototype presented in (Comuzzi, Theilmann, Zacco, Rathfelder, Kotsokalis, & Winkler 2009). The conceptualisation includes the following core concepts:

- The four roles of service customer, software provider, service provider and infrastructure provider;

- The three layers of business, software, and infrastructure management;
- A service lifecycle model including design, negotiation, provisioning, operation, i.e. monitoring and adjustment, and decommissioning;
- Conception of relevant basic data store entities covering design-time and run-time data for the various layers and roles; and
- Conception of functional flows for the lifecycle phases of negotiation, provisioning, and operation.

Data Models

In order to communicate, the components of the SLA@SOI Architecture make heavy use of two models that reflect the essential data structures in the system. The *SLA(T) model* describes SLAs for the communication within and among SLA Managers, as well with external providers. The *Service Construction Model* provides and collects information necessary to create a new instance of a service (for a particular SLA). In the following, we provide an overview of both models.

SLA(T) Model

The SLA and SLA Template model (SLA(T) model) extends pure functional service descriptions to allow for the expression of non-functional service properties and quality of service (QoS) guarantees. The SLA(T) Model is part of a larger model hierarchy, including primitives, basic expressions, service descriptions, standard terms and business terms.

At the lowest level of the hierarchy are the Primitive (Ground) Terms on which everything else is built. Building on the Primitives are a handful of Ground Expressions, supporting annotations, and the generic expression of constraints, events, and functions. These expressions support extension/customisation through standard vocabularies, in which specific terms, and semantics

Figure 1. Overview of the model hierarchy including the SLA(T) model

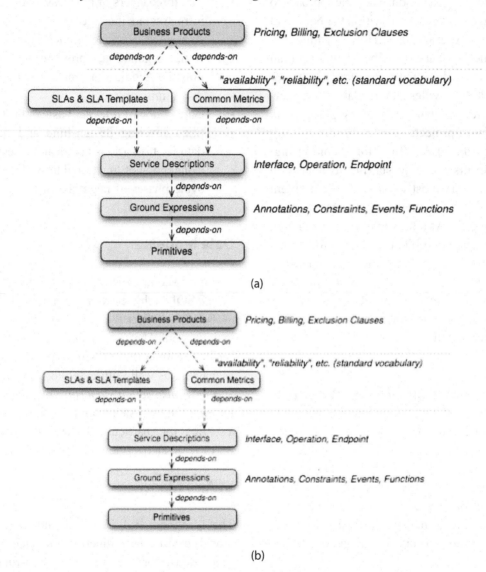

can be defined. Above this is a generic Service Description model, providing a means to describe the functional properties (interfaces, operations, and endpoints) of services. The main body of the present specification defines the SLA(T) Model, which builds on the Service Description level to allow for the expression of non-functional service properties and quality of service (QoS) guarantees.

The SLA(T) Model provides the basic structure of an SLA(T), but leaves the specification of particular QoS terms open, supporting extension

through standard vocabularies. A set of default QoS terms are provided as a standard vocabulary of Common Metrics. At the highest level is a Business SLA(T) Model, which builds on the SLA(T) Model and Common Metrics to model business-specific information, such as business terms (i.e. support), offer, constraints, pricing, penalties, billing details, termination and exclusion clauses.

Basically, an SLA is a set of agreements between two (or more) parties. These agreements are expressed by terms each of which denotes guarantees made by, or obligations on, the various parties. Each agreement term comprises an optional constraint expression specifying the conditions under which the agreement term holds (i.e. a precondition on the term). If no preconditions are specified then it is assumed the term holds for the entire effective duration of the SLA. Guarantees defined in the agreement are either guaranteed states or guaranteed actions.

A *guaranteed state* is a guarantee made by one of the parties to the agreement, that a certain state of affairs will hold, e.g. service level objectives (SLOs) or targets for key-performance indicators (KPIs). The state of affairs is defined by a constraint expression. A *guaranteed action* is an action that one of the parties to the SLA is obligated to perform (or may perform, or is forbidden from performing) under certain, specified circumstances.

For example, the expression mean(completion_ time(S)) < 20 ms states that for operation S of the target service the customer requires a mean completion time below 20 ms. A precondition like mean(arrival_rate(S)) < 200.0 rpm ensures an upper bound for its usage by giving a mean arrival rate of 200 requests per minute.

Service Construction Model

The *Service Construction Model (SCM)* is inspired by the management of services (cf. Section 3.2) and SLA concepts sketched above. We introduced the SCM to ease the communication between different components, responsible for the core SLA management, the management of services, and the quality evaluation of possible service offerings. Service Managers can use the SCM to manage multiple implementations of the same service. Furthermore, the SCM allows different components to access and add information about a potential service instance.

Figure 2 illustrates the basic concepts of the SCM. The core classes of the SCM (Service Type, Service Implementation, Service Builder, and Service Instance) represent the different stages in a service's life cycle.

Figure 2. Overview of the service construction model

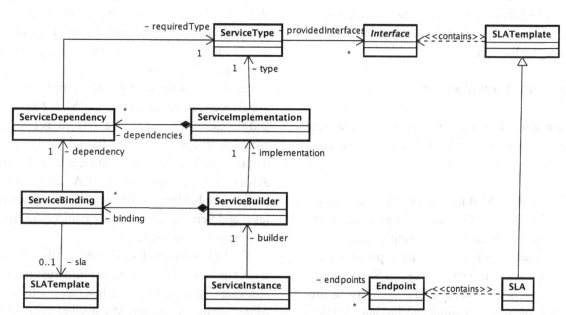

A *Service Type* specifies the functional interfaces a service provides. Service Types can be realized by multiple *Service Implementations* that specify i) the artifacts of the implementation (such as software components, or executables) and ii) the dependencies of the artifacts on other services. For example, a software service "InventoryService" may depend on infrastructure services that host its virtual machines. Such dependencies are expressed in terms of *Service Dependencies*.

Service Builders hold information about resolved dependencies of a Service Implementation. For this purpose, a *Service Binding* relates a Service Dependency to an SLA Template or one of its specializations (SLA and Business Product). The SLA Template contains all information necessary to evaluate and access a service outside the domain of an SLA Manager. The SLA Template includes quality constraints and, after the SLA has been agreed, endpoints of the service.

Finally, a *Service Instance* models the actual runtime entity representing a service. The Endpoints of a Service Instance either refer to a running and accessible service or point to the location where the service will be available according to the time constraints defined in its SLA.

In the following we now show a concrete technical architecture which implements the previous conceptualisation.

Technical Architecture

The primary functional goal of our SLA management framework is to provide a generic solution for SLA management that

1. supports SLA management across multiple layers with SLA (de-)composition across functional and organizational domains;
2. supports arbitrary service types (business, software, infrastructure) and SLA terms;
3. covers the complete SLA and service lifecycle with consistent interlinking of design-

time, planning and run-time management aspects; and

4. can be applied to a large variety of industrial domains.

In order to achieve these goals, the reference architecture is based on three main design principles. First, we put a strong emphasis on a clear separation of concerns, by clearly separating service management from SLA management and by supporting a well layered and hierarchical management structure. Second, a solid foundation in common meta models for SLAs as well as their relation to services and the construction of actual service instances is an important aspect to support clear semantics across different components of the framework. Third, design for extensibility is a key aspect in order to address multiple domains. Therefore, we clearly distinguish between generic solution elements and places where domain-specific logic/models need to be provided.

Figure 3 illustrates the main components of the SLA@SOI framework and their relationships.

The framework communicates to external parties, namely customers who (want to) consume services and 3rd party providers which the actual service provider might rely upon. Relationships are defined by stereotyped dependencies that translate to specific sets of provided and required interfaces. Figure 3 shows one *possible* setup of the framework.

In order to achieve a good generalization of the framework architecture, the SLA Manager and the Service Manager are defined as general components that can be specialised for different domains (software, infrastructure, etc.). In Figure 3, we chose an example where SLA Managers are realized for business, software and infrastructure level and Service Managers are realized for software and infrastructure level.

On the highest level, we distinguish the Framework Core, Service Managers (infrastructure and software), deployed Service Instances with their Manageability Agents and MonitoringEventChan-

Figure 3. Architecture overview: Example application of the framework for a three level service and SLA hierarchy

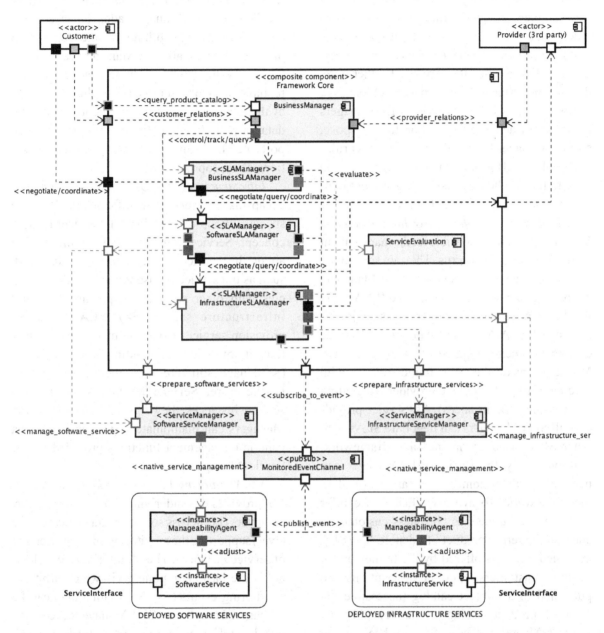

nels. The Framework Core encapsulates all functionality related to SLA management. Infrastructure- and Software Service Managers contain all service-specific functionality. The deployed Service Instance is the actual service delivered to the customer and managed by the framework via Manageability Agents. Monitoring Event

Channels serve as a flexible communication infrastructure that allows the framework to collect information about the service instance status.

In the following, we briefly describe the main components of our framework and their interactions.

The *BusinessManager* controls all business information and communication with customers (<<customer_relations>>) and providers (<<provider_relations>>). For example, it realizes the customer relation management (CRM) necessary to efficiently sell the services. Furthermore, the BusinessManager governs the (Business-, Software-, and Infrastructure-) SLAManagers (<<control/track/query>>). For this purpose, an SLAManager has to adhere to business rules defined by the BusinessManager ('control') and have to inform the BusinessManager about their current status and activities ('track').

The *(Business-, Software- & Infrastructure-) SLAManagers* are responsible for the management of all SLA-related concerns. They are specialisations of a generic SLA Manager. SLA Managers are responsible for the negotiation of SLAs, and for the SLA Management of services subject to SLAs. All SLA Managers can act as "service customers"; negotiating SLAs with other SLA Managers inside the same framework, or with external (3rd party) service providers (including other framework instances). As "service providers" all SLA Managers can negotiate SLAs with other SLA Managers in the same framework. However, only the BusinessSLAManager can negotiate with customers who are external to the framework. To avoid confusion, we refer to external customers as "business-customers", and use the term "product" to denote the (SLA governed) services offered by the framework to business-customers. Product descriptions are published in a product catalog (accessible via <<query_product_catalog>>) maintained by the BusinessManager. Once an SLA has been agreed with a customer, it is the responsibility of the Business Manager to send reports on SLA status to the customer and to provide a unique access point to query historical consolidated information about his products consumption linked with the specific SLAs. All negotiation and reporting interactions are captured by the <<negotiate/ query/coordinate>> relation. These interactions are equally used at business-level for the customer interaction (<<negotiate/coordinate>>) where the BusinessSLAManager adds business-level considerations (e.g. billing) to the negotiation protocol. Finally, all SLA Managers can consult ServiceEvaluation to evaluate *a-priori* the potential quality of a service (<<evaluate>>). This evaluation can be based on prediction, historical data, or predefined quality definitions, and supports the SLA Manager in finding service realisations of appropriate quality.

Infrastructure- and SoftwareServiceManager encapsulate all service-specific details. Both are specialisations of the abstract ServiceManager concept. Service Managers provide information about the service implementations supported, such as the service realisation and its dependencies with other services (<<prepare_software/ infrastructure_services>>). SLA Managers provision services using the management functionality of their corresponding ServiceManager (<<manage_software/infrastructure_service>>). Furthermore, Service Managers control the service instances they have provisioned. SLA Managers can manipulate service instances via generic management functions provided by the ServiceManager.

The *MonitoringAdjustment Management System* provides the underlying fabric across different layers (i.e. across software and infrastructure layer) supporting the monitoring and management of service instances. The MonitoringEventChannel is the basic component via which arbitrary monitoring events (e.g. SLO violations) can be propagated to relevant SLA Managers. Access to this channel is realized via the <<publish_event>> and <<subscribe_to_event>> interaction stereotypes. ManageabilityAgents support the actual configuration and management of service instances. The access to Manageability Agents for SLA Managers is always mediated via a specific Service Manager. Due to the service-specific nature, the interactions between Service Managers and Manageability Agents is represented by the <<native_service_management>> stereotype which is not further refined by this architecture.

Last, two additional component types form part of the monitoring system: sensors, and reasoners. A *Sensor* component collects information form a service and sends it to reasoners. A *Reasoner* component receives sensors information an process it to detect and/or predict SLA violations.

Interactions

The *negotiation/planning sequence* starts with a customer querying for available products and SLA Templates (<<query_product_catalog>>) and eventually registering himself with the provider (<<customer_relations>>). The actual negotiation is then started by the customer via <<negotiate/coordinate>>. The framework manages the negotiation request in a hierarchical manner across different SLA Managers, again using the same <<negotiate/coordinate>> interaction. Each SLA Manager checks with its Service Managers for possible service implementations (<<prepare_[T]_services>>). For each possible implementation it resolves required dependencies to lower-level services with the next level SLA Manager (<<negotiate>>), evaluates possible combinations of service implementations and service bindings via the ServiceEvaluation (<<evaluate>>) and, finally, returns a set of feasible SLA offers to the customer (or the higher-level SLA Manager). Once an agreement has been established (again via <<negotiate>>) relevant resources are booked on all layers (<<prepare_[T]_services>>).

In general, the *provisioning sequence* is automatically triggered by the respective SLA Managers according to the service start times specified in the agreed SLAs. It is executed via the respective Service Managers (<<manage_[T]_service>>) who take care of the creation of service instances (if necessary), their configuration as well as the set up of a responsible ManageabilityAgent. Alternatively, provisioning might be also explicitly triggered by a customer (<<coordinate>>). Suc-

cessful provisioning is eventually reported back to customers via the reporting mechanisms of <<customer_relations>>.

The *monitoring/adjustment sequence* typically starts with the detection of an SLA violation by the monitoring system. SLA Managers evaluate these violations and initiate adjustment actions via the Service Managers (<<manage_[T]_service>>) who use the respective ManageabilityAgent to execute the corresponding adjustment actions. Furthermore, SLA Managers report violations to the BusinessManager (<<control/track/query>>) who decides whether the customer needs to be informed (<<customer_relations>>) and/or a renegotiation may be initiated (<<negotiate>>).

The examples above illustrate the interplay of the framework components. However, the flexibility of the framework allows many different variants, such as provider initiated negotiation processes or different order of planning steps.

Further details on this architecture, in particular the detailed structure of a generic SLA manager and a couple of industrial adoption examples are discussed in (Theilmann, Happe, Kotsokalis, Edmonds, Kearney, & Lambea, 2010).

Integration Foundations

The integration approach, that glues together the components of the technical architecture to generate the SLA@SOI platform, is based on two main aspects. The first aspect is the general need for a flexible and open integration of the components; the second aspect is the adoption of a common approach, based on de-facto standards, for the modeling of the solutions devised within the different components of the framework.

The adoption of a flexible and open integration approach derives from the need of being able to dynamically compose the framework so to satisfy the requirements of the different domains in which the platform is executed. Depending on the scenario in which the platform is meant to provide its SLA management capabilities, the SLA@SOI framework can be composed using a set of core building blocks plus a set of domain-dependent components. The former ones provide general purpose SLA management capabilities; the latter ones supply those ad-hoc SLA management features that necessarily depends on the peculiar characteristics of the application in which the platform is used. Even more, the adoption of a plugin-based integration approach, as the one used in the SLA@SOI solution, determines the possibility of adapting, modifying and enriching the platform, in terms of its components, also during its run-time execution. Such an integration feature gives the chance of provisioning new potentials to the SLA management framework, even without the need of restarting it. The technology used for achieving this high level of flexible and dynamic modularity is the model proposed by the Open Source Gateway initiative (OSGi) (OSGi, 2010).

The adoption of de-facto standards is another important aspect of the framework integration. In particular, the adoption of the WS-Agreement (Andrieux, et al., 2007) standard, with its definition of a signalling protocol for establishing SLAs, guarantees a solid foundation for building a SLA modelling solution that is shared across the platform modules. Finally, it is worth mentioning that the solution adopted for the management of infrastructure services is based on the Open Cloud Computing Interface (OCCI) (OGF OCCI-WG, 2010) standards, a state-of-the-art models for the management of infrastructure resources. OCCI has been used to implement the interfaces and the models through which the Infrastructure-ServiceManager exposes its functionalities to clients thus abstracting the low-level details of the provisioning system supported and facilitating the SLA-enabling of other OCCI-compliant provisioning systems. OCCI opens up the possibility of an interesting brokerage scenario for the Infrastructure SLA Manager should it be aware of multiple OCCI-compliant infrastructure services.

PROTOTYPE IMPLEMENTATION AND CASE STUDY

The described framework architecture has been fully implemented and has been evaluated against a reference application, the so-called Open Reference Case (ORC). This section briefly sketches the structure of this application, explains the related SLA hierarchy that we established, and provides results from a qualitative evaluation.

Open Reference Case

The ORC is a service-oriented software system supporting a retail chain scenario. The ORC extends the Common Component Modelling Example (CoCoME) (Rausch, Reussner, Mirandola, & Plášil, 2008), which represents a component-based trading system dealing with the various aspects of handling sales at a supermarket. This includes the interaction at the cash desk with the customer, including product scanning and payment, as well as accounting the sale at the inventory.

Figure 4 illustrates the bindings between the different stakeholders involved in the ORC use case. The Service Provider offers the ORC as *Software as a Service* (SaaS) solution to a number of different customers. Thus the service provider negotiates an SLA with each customer. A dedicated Software Provider is responsible for the development and the maintenance of the ORC, which runs on top of a cloud-based IT infrastructure offered by an Infrastructure Provider. The Software Provider may not provide all services. Hence, it may need to integrate services from external suppliers such as a bank, wholesale centre, or CRM supplier. The quality of the services offered by the Service Provider to the customer depends on the quality of the integrated services and the resources provided by the Infrastructure Provider. In order to guarantee to the customer a certain quality level, the Service Provider therefore has to negotiate SLAs with the the External Supplier and the Infrastructure Provider.

Figure 4. ORC stakeholders

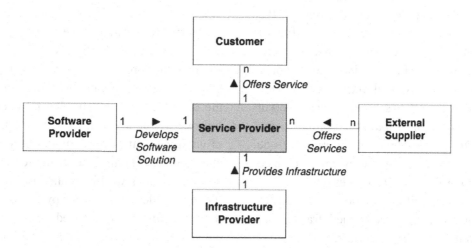

As illustrated in Figure 5, the ORC provides the four services interfaces **InventoryServiceIf**, StoreInformationServiceIf, OrderServiceIf, and PaymentServiceIf implemented by the respective components. InventoryService, StoreInformationService, and OrderService use the functionality provided by the component Inventory, that encapsulates the database access. The PaymentService is a composite service implemented using BPEL. If a customer wants to pay with credit card, the PaymentService uses two external services, namely PaymentDebitServiceIf and CardValidationServiceIf offered by an external bank to validate and debit the card.

The service provider should be able to offer the ORC to small super markets as well as large

Figure 5. ORC architecture overview

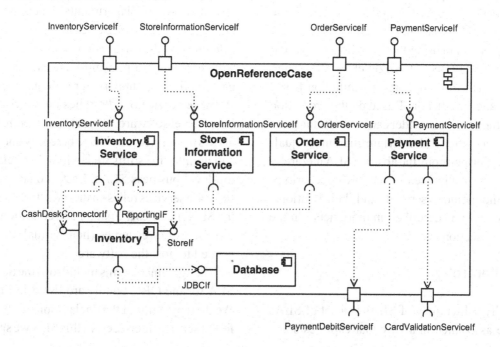

enterprises with several stores and several thousand customers per day. For this reason, the Service-Provider can choose among different deployment options, i.e., *all in one*, with the service containers, BPEL engine, and database running on the same virtual machine; *separated database*, with the database running on a different virtual machine; and *separated database and BPEL engine*. These deployment options can be run on one single server or on several virtualized servers with different hw resources (e.g., processor speed, number of processors, or amount of available memory) operated by the infrastructure provider in its cloud-based IT infrastructure.

To demonstrate the SLA framework in the ORC scenario, some ORC specific configurations, adaptations, and extensions are required. To enable the management of the ORC a manageability interface was designed and developed. This ORC specific management extension includes an instrumentation of the services that monitors the start and stop of service calls. This was realized by implementing additional message handlers, which intercept each received and sent SOAP message. Additionally, the design-time performance prediction, which is part of the negotiation module, requires an ORC specific model that reflects the structure and behaviour of the ORC. This model was implemented using the Palladio Component Model (PCM) (Becker, Koziolek, & Reussner, 2009), which also supports a simulation-based performance prediction. Based on the prediction results, the Service Provider can calculate the price for a service offer with a certain guaranteed quality level. Furthermore, the abstract SLA hierarchy needs to be instantiated in the ORC scenario to reflect the included services and their relations. This hierarchy is described in more detail in the following section.

SLA Hierarchy

Generally, a hierarchy of SLAs is a set of SLAs that are associated in a way that captures some kind of dependency of one on another. This kind of association / dependency is not always straightforward. It may be the case that the reduced capacity of a provider forces it to rent capacity from another provider, to serve its clients as per the standing agreements. In a different scenario, the dependency might be due to a request for fail-over redundancy, in which case the failure of an agreement of the provider may not affect at all the agreements of its customer. Dependencies may just as well be related to functionality that a provider cannot offer by default, and that therefore must be outsourced.

SLA dependencies may also be internal to a single provider. This is the case where a department of a provider relies on another department of the same provider, in order to accomplish its tasks. Very often this has to do with a business department relying on the IT department, for back-office or other functions.

In our evaluation we use the ORC scenario described above with one single provider which has 2 internal departments (software IT department and infrastructure department) relying on each other via internal SLAs.

Figure 6 illustrates the realized SLA hierarchy. It shows the departmental layers where the top-level business SLA describes the complete offered Retail-as-a-Service solution, including software but also relevant business aspects (legal conditions, support agreements, etc.). The software service bundle relies on a hierarchy of lower-level software services. The hierarchy here allows the service provider to precisely understand and monitor his software landscape in relation to top-level business SLAs. Last, the collection of software services relies on the infrastructure where the SLA specifies the nature and conditions of the infrastructure resources (here virtual machines) needed to host the software.

The agreement terms included in the Software-SLA for the ORC bundle are listed in Figure 7. We thereby omitted the declaration of all the different service interfaces. In this SLA we specified

Figure 6. Implemented SLA hierarchy

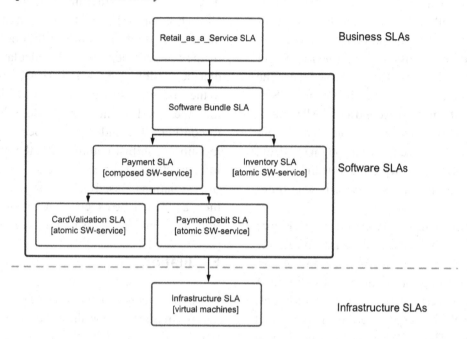

Figure 7. ORC SoftwareSLA

```
agreement_term{
    id = ORC_CustomerConstraintPayment
    guaranteed_state{
        id = ORCThroughputConstraintPayment
        arrival_rate(ORCPaymentService/PaymentServiceOperation) < "100" tx_per_s
    }
}

agreement_term{
    id = ORC_CustomerConstraintInventory
    guaranteed_state{
        id = ORCThroughputConstraintInventory
        arrival_rate(ORCInventoryService/bookSale) < "900" tx_per_s
    }
}

agreement_term{
    id = ORC_ResponseTimePayment
    guaranteed_state{
        id = ORCResponseTimePaymentState
        completion_time(ORCPaymentService/PaymentServiceOperation) < "100" ms
    }
}

agreement_term{
    id = ORC_ResponseTimeInventory
    guaranteed_state{
        id = ORCResponseTimeInventoryState
        completion_time(ORCInventoryService/bookSale) < "100" ms
    }
}
```

a guaranteed completion time of less then 100 ms for the PaymentService as well as for the InventoryService. As the completion time of a service is influenced by its usage we defined an upper limit of service invocations for both services. The customer is allowed to invoke the Inventory Service up to 900 times per second and the PaymentService up to 100 times per second. The Inventory Service is invoked for each bought good and the PaymentService only once. For this reason the limit of the Inventory Service is nine times higher.

The listing of the Infrastructure SLA in Figure 8 again only includes the agreement terms for the defined virtual machine, as they are most important and interesting parts of the SLAs. In this SLA we cover two very important quality attributes, namely reliability respectively availability and performance. The SLA guarantees a mean time to failure (MTTF) of 455000 hours and a mean time to repair (MTTR) of 3 hours. This corresponds to an availability of the VM of 0.998%. In addition, the infrastructure includes a specification of the performance relevant attributes of the virtual machine. The specification includes the number

of cores for the virtual machine as well as the CPU speed of 3 GHz and the amount of available memory. This information is on the one hand used by the Software department to calculate and predict the possible QoS levels that can be guaranteed to the customer using this virtual machine and on the other hand by the infrastructure department to configure the underlying hypervisor and the monitoring infrastructure. With the monitoring infrastructure it is possible to detect and forecast SLA violations. Based on this information adjustment action can be executed. A detailed description of this monitoring is part of the next section.

Evaluation

Our experiments with the SLA Framework cover the two main scenarios already described in Section 3.3.

For the negotiation and provisioning scenario, we experimented with different SLA templates, deployment options and infrastructure options. We decided to differentiate services starting from the highest service layer, the business services layer, and we adopted the widely used metaphor of *gold*, *silver* and *bronze* class services. Hence, we run our experiments with three distinguished business level SLA templates. Although the three SLA templates provide default values, the customer in our scenarios should be able to request individual non-functional properties, i.e. completion times and arrival rates (as *qualifying condition*) for each service operation accessible by the customer. Note, that the *qualifying condition* is understood as "customer obligation" within an SLA, meaning that if the arrival rate of service requests is higher than agreed, the service provider is no more bound to sustain the agreed completion time. In this case it is simply the customer who violated the SLA. At the software level we used individual templates for each service in order to support flexible service composition and provisioning, and to gain fine grained SLA hierarchies as depicted in Figure 6. The infrastructure template allows resource

Figure 8. ORC infrastructure SLA

```
agreement_term{
    id = Reliability
    guaranteed_state{
        id = MTTRState
        mttr(VM_Access_Point) < "10" hrs
    }
    guaranteed_state{
        id = MTTFState
        mttf(VM_Access_Point) > "5000" hrs
    }
}

agreement_term{
    id = Performance
    guaranteed_state{
        id = VM_CORES
        vm_cores(VM_Access_Point) = "4"
    }
    guaranteed_state{
        id = VM_CPU_SPEED
        cpu_speed(VM_Access_Point) = "3" GHz
    }
    guaranteed_state{
        id = VM_MEMORY_SIZE
        memory(VM_Access_Point) = "4096" MB
    }
}
```

configuration (comprising multiple virtual machines) and enables the service provider to request guarantees from the infrastructure provider on various virtual resources, such as CPU or memory. We realized different deployment options for our reference application allowing different distributions over several independent virtual machines operated by the Infrastructure Provider. In these deployment options for example, the database can be separated from the application logic or the BPEL engine running the composite service can be separated from the basic services.

The core of the actual negotiation procedure is now the translation of terms along the SLA hierarchy, the evaluation of different composition/deployment/infrastructure options and the selection of the best suited ones. The basic element to this procedure is a prediction service which, based on a PCM model (Becker, Koziolek, & Reussner, 2009) of the ORC, can simulate the non-functional behaviour of all these options. Taking the results of this prediction, the SLA hierarchies of possible solutions are associated with terms on their non-functional behaviour and costs. Last, the negotiation component selects the cheapest option that still satisfies the requested top-level SLA. Experiments show the feasability of this approach and the selection of well-suited system setups which realize the requested customer SLAs in a cost efficient manner.

On the selected composition/deployment/infrastructure option the check for monitorability operation is performed by MonitoringManager (MM), an inner component of SLAManager. It checks whether the selected option is monitorable (fully or partially) or not. MM check for monitorability output is a monitoring system configuration which tells how to configure the required monitoring system components in order to monitor a given SLA with respect to a selected composition/deployment/infrastructure option.

Monitoring system components are: sensors, effectors, and reasoners. A Sensor component collects information form a service and sends

it to reasoners. A Reasoner component receives sensors information a process it to detect and/or predict SLA violations. An Effector component interacts with services to change their behaviors.

The check is based on the concept of monitoring feature, that is the ability of a monitoring system component to provide or consume information. For instance, in order to monitor a service CPU utilisation CPU measurements must be available. The ability to provide CPU utilisation data is a monitoring feature. A service can be designed to be monitorable, i.e., it provides operations for retrieving information about its functioning, or another component (a sensor) retrieves and makes this data available. In general we talk about a list of monitoring features belonging to a service. As sensors belong to the information providers side, reasoners belong to the information consumer one. A reasoner monitoring feature is the ability to process data, e.g., by providing operations for evaluating boolean expressions or computing other kind of functions. For instance, a reasoner can provide a monitoring feature named *lessEqualTo* to evaluate the boolean expression $a \leq b$ where a and b are decimal numbers.

The MM checks whether an SLA can be monitored (fully or partially) with respect to a list of monitoring features belonging to the chosen services and the available reasoners. For instance, let's consider the scenario in which a service has been selected for a given SLA and a sensor S collects service information. Moreover, in our scenario a reasoner R has been deployed. Figure 9 shows the CPU utilisation guaranteed state, part of an SLA, which defines the constraint *CPUUtilization* $\leq$ 90% over CPU utilisation.

Sensor S advertises *CPUUtilization* monitoring feature through which it provides information about the service CPU utilisation. Reasoner R advertises the *lessEqualTo* monitoring feature for evaluating boolean expressions.

MM checks whether an SLA guaranteed condition can be monitored. With respect to our scenario, MM checks if the service itself or a sen-

Figure 9. SLA fragment representing the guaranteed state CPUUtilisation ≤90%

```
<slasoi:State>
    <slasoi:ID>CPUUtilisationState</slasoi:ID>
    <slasoi:Constraint>
        <slasoi:TypeConstraintExpr>
            <slasoi:Value>
                <slasoi:FuncExpr>

<slasoi:Operator>commonTerms#CPUUtilization</slasoi:Operator>
                    <slasoi:Parameter>
                        <slasoi:ID>CPU_Access_Point</slasoi:ID>
                    </slasoi:Parameter>
                </slasoi:FuncExpr>
            </slasoi:Value>
            <slasoi:Domain>
                <slasoi:SimpleDomainExpr>

<slasoi:ComparisonOp>coremodel#greater_than</slasoi:ComparisonOp>
                    <slasoi:Value>
                        <slasoi:CONST>
                            <slasoi:Value>90</slasoi:Value>

<slasoi:Datatype>units#percentage</slasoi:Datatype>
                        </slasoi:CONST>
                    </slasoi:Value>
                </slasoi:SimpleDomainExpr>
            </slasoi:Domain>
        </slasoi:TypeConstraintExpr>
    </slasoi:Constraint>
</slasoi:State>
```

sor can provide *CPUUtilization* information and if there exists a reasoner to evaluate the expression *CPUUtilization* ≤ 90%. In our case, sensor S provides CPU utilisation information and reasoner R can consume that information and check for guaranteed condition violations, therefore the SLA is monitorable.

If an SLA is monitorable, MM creates a monitoring system configuration that will be dispatched to the sensors, effectors, and reasoners necessary to monitor the SLA. In our scenario, the configuration dispatched to sensor S set it up to send CPU utilisation measurements to reasoner R. The configuration dispatched to reasoner R contains a monitoring specification to setup R to evaluate the boolean expression $a \leq b$ where a are the CPU utilisation run-time values sent by S and b is the constant constraint 90%.

Once the monitoring system is setup SLAs start being monitored and their violations are reported. SLA violations can be used for charging the party

who violated the SLA or to adjust the scenario, e.g., re-negotiating the terms of an SLA.

For what concerns the monitoring and adjustment scenario, a software layer monitoring result event (MRE), e.g. too high average response time of an operation call, is identified by the name of the guarantee term and the unique id of the SLA to which the guarantee term belongs. This information is sufficient for the Adjustment module to retrieve the violated SLA and the related SLA hierarchy and to decide eventual control actions. Since infrastructure SLAs only report the identifiers of the virtual machine images on which the services are being executed, a violation at the infrastructure layer can not be defined in terms of ids of the SLA and the guarantee term. Infrastructure violations report the id of the resource on which the violation has occurred and information on the parameter, e.g. CPU or memory utilisation, which has been violated.

An example of a typical violation at the software layer is reported in Figure 10. The viola-

Figure 10. Software layer SLA violation

```
<EventPayload>
    <MonitoringResultEvent>
        <monitoredSLA>
            <slaID>SLA_PaymentService-UUID-550e8400-e29b-41d4-a716-446655440003</slaID>
        </monitoredSLA>
        <GuaranteeTerm>CompletionTime_Request_Gterm</GuaranteeTerm>
    </MonitoringResultEvent>
</EventPayload>
```

Figure 11. Infrastructure layer SLA violation

```
<EventPayload>
  <infrastructureMonitoringEventType>
    <infrastructureId>3f44be0c-bf0c-48a9-9947-1fa3924c83ee</infrastructureId>
    <resourceId>e268ea71-feb0-4d7c-a9ea-ce56353e357c</resourceId>
    <infrastructureProperties>
      <infrastructureParameter xsi:type="ns3:CPUUtilization" description="Functional">
        <utilization value="99.5"/>
      </infrastructureParameter>
    </infrastructureProperties>
  </infrastructureMonitoringEventType>
</EventPayload>
```

tion refers to the guarantee term on the average completion time of the operation bookSale of the service InventoryService in the ORC. Figure 11 shows a violation at the infrastructure layer. The violation refers to the parameter CPUUtilization in a specific virtual machine, identified by the element infrastructureId. In particular, the CPU utilisation in the example has exceeded the threshold value of 99.5%.

Adjustment actions have been realised at various layers relying on the analysis done within the adjustment module. SLA violations may result from faulty customer behaviour, e.g. where a customer exceeds the SLA-agreed maximum workload. In this case a message is sent via the eContracting module to the customer, to inform him/her about this.

Concerning the infrastructure, Adjustment may trigger the re-provisioning of the virtual machines on which services are executed. In particular, if the Adjustment receives a violation of the software-level guarantee term on a service operation completion time and, at the same time, a violation of the CPU utilisation on the virtual

machine on which the service is executed, then it commands the Infrastructure to re-provision the virtual machine on which the service is executing with a higher CPU share.

Concerning the software layer, the corrective action implemented at the current stage is the reconfiguration of the BPEL engine in which composite services are executed. The reconfiguration is triggered when a software-level guarantee term on completion time of an operation of a composite service is violated, and when it is not possible to find a corresponding infrastructure violation of the virtual machine where the service is executed. The Adjustment detects, in this case, that the problem belongs to the BPEL engine in which the service is executing; the reconfiguration of the engine involves the increase of thread pool of the composite service for which the violation has been detected.

Last and if no other adjustment action can be detected, violations are reported as faults of the service provider and the customer is informed accordingly, including the acceptance of possibly agreed penalties.

CONCLUSION AND FURTHER DIRECTIONS

This paper presents a technical architecture and implementation for a multi-level SLA management framework. We discussed the fundamental components and interfaces in the architecture. The framework dynamics were described via two fundamental scenarios, which cover the core SLA management lifecycle including negotiation, provisioning, monitoring and adjustment. Furthermore, the main technical and integration aspects of the developed framework have been described. The framework has been successfully applied within the context of a reference application. The qualitative evaluation includes a description of the actually realised SLA hierarchy and the details about the concrete scenario steps. Further evaluations in other use case domains have been conducted in the areas of ERP Hosting (Theilmann, Happe, Winkler, & De Magrans, 2010), EnterpriseIT, Service Aggregation, and eGovernment (SLA@SOI, 2010).

We also identified several future directions which are important to address in order to leverage the full potential of integrated SLA management.

One important area is about *model-based translation of SLA terms*. Conceptually, top-down translations should support the restriction of the search space for possible SLA templates. Bottom-up translations should support the eventual term evaluation and assessment in a multi-objective optimization approach. With our current approach the knowledge about the translation of SLA terms between different layers is either decoded within a domain-specific planning module or within a service evaluation module. Some of these are described in a rather hard-coded domain-specific way. Future research should address general translation models for SLA terms which can be specified by domain experts without any need for programming. Based on such models, the framework could automatically decide on the most efficient planning and optimization approach to follow.

Another promising future direction is about *harmonizing autonomic with SLA-driven management*. While SLA-driven management is based on centrally (SLA-)provided management policies, autonomic management aims at decentralized policies and system adjustments. The challenge is here to harmonize both perspectives and finding the optimal tradeoff that combines the efficiency of decentralized management operations and the transparency of central ones.

Currently, the framework natively supports bilateral negotiation only. For advanced scenarios, *multilateral negotiation* is needed. Today such scenarios only may be realized by specific implementations of the BusinessManager (cf. Figure 3). Support for multilateral negotiation requires a standardized protocol (e.g., based on WS-Agreement) and mechanisms for transactional behaviour of all particpants including the flexible handling of faults in a transaction.

From the Business perspective of SLA management, there are several issues that are important to be addressed. First, the aggregation of multiple services with different SLA(T)s requires, beyond a simple aggregation of them, a real *merge of compatible guarantee terms from different services* into unique terms. For instance, the response time guarantee term of the aggregated service must be a smart combination of the guarantee terms from the component services, and so must be the risk assessment and the penalties associated to their breach. Therefore, further research is needed on integrating business rules (and their management) with the SLA model and the business terms. Second, Business SLA negotiation is also a major objective. Beyond basic negotiation of guarantee terms, the information from *customer and provider profiles* (preferences, previous negotiations, etc.), together with other business relevant information, should be used to drive the negotiation process. Eventually, we envisage a complete business negotiation framework which will include renegotiation and multilateral negotiation as described above.

One infrastructure-specific future direction that has been identified is the opportunity for a *standard addressing low-level infrastructure monitoring.* Such an initiative would, in conjunction with OCCI, facilitate a much cleaner separation of concerns between infrastructure management and potentially arbitrary third party infrastructure provider implementations. Without such a standard, monitoring feature discovery, configuration and runtime integration needs to be explicitly implemented for each infrastructure provider supported.

Last but not least, the area of *business performance* provides a huge potential for further research. The goal here is to manage the eventual performance of business activities in conjunction with SLAs of enabling services. Such analysis would allow to understand exactly the tradeoff between business benefits and technical capabilities and to manage business IT stacks accordingly.

REFERENCES

Andrieux, A., Czajkowski, K., Dan, A., Keahey, K., Ludwig, H., & Nakata, T. (2007). *Web services agreement specification (WS-Agreement). Open Grid Forum.* OGF.

Baresi, L., & Guinea, S. (2005). *Towards dynamic monitoring of WS-BPEL processes. Service-Oriented Computing - ICSOC 2005. LNCS 3826* (pp. 269–282). Amsterdam, The Netherlands: Springer.

Becker, S., Koziolek, H., & Reussner, R. (2009). The Palladio component model for model-driven performance prediction. *Journal of Systems and Software, 82*(1), 3–22. doi:10.1016/j.jss.2008.03.066

Bodenstaff, L., Wombacher, A., Reichert, M., & Jaeger, M. C. (2008). Monitoring Dependencies for SLAs: The MoDe4SLA Approach. *IEEE International Conference on Services Computing. 1*, pp. 21-29. Honolulu, USA: IEEE Computer Society.

Buyya, R., Yeo, C. S., & Venugopal, S. (2008). Market-oriented cloud computing: Vision, hype, and reality for delivering IT services as computing utilities. *10th IEEE International Conference on High Performance Computing and Communications, HPCC 2008* (pp. 5-13). Dalian, China: IEEE.

Chen, Y., Iyer, S., Liu, X., Milojicic, D., & Sahai, A. (2008). Translating service level objectives to lower level policies for multi-tier services. *Cluster Computing, 11*(3), 299–311. doi:10.1007/s10586-008-0059-6

Comuzzi, M., Theilmann, W., Zacco, G., Rathfelder, C., Kotsokalis, C., & Winkler, U. (2009). A framework for multi-level SLA management. *Proc. of ICSOC/ServiceWave Workshop NF-PSLAM 2009:* (pp. 187-196).

Czajkowski, K., Foster, I. T., Kesselman, C., Sander, V., & Tuecke, S. (2002). SNAP: A protocol for negotiating service level agreements and coordinating resource management in distributed systems. *Job Scheduling Strategies for Parallel Processing, 8th International Workshop, JSSPP 2002. LNCS 2537,* (pp. 153-183). Edinburgh, UK: Springer.

Frankova, G., Malfatti, D., & Aiello, M. (2006). Semantics and extensions of WS-agreement. *Journal of Software, 1*(1), 23–32. doi:10.4304/jsw.1.1.23-31

Hasselmeyer, P., Koller, B., Schubert, L., & Wieder, P. (2006). Towards SLA-supported resource management. *High Performance Computing and Communications, Second International Conference, HPCC 2006. LNCS 4208,* (pp. 743-752). Munich, Germany: Springer.

Hui, L., Theilmann, W., & Happe, J. (2009). *SLA translation in multi-layered service oriented architectures: Status and challenges.* Universität Karlsruhe.

OGF OCCI-WG. (2010). *OGF Open Cloud Computing Interface Working Group.* Retrieved December 9, 2010, from http://www.occi-wg.org/

OSGi. (2010). *OSGi Alliance: OSGi.* Retrieved December 9, 2010, from http://www.osgi.org/

Ouelhadj, D., Garibaldi, J. M., MacLaren, J., Sakellariou, R., & Krishnakumar, K. (2005). A multi-agent infrastructure and a service level agreement negotiation protocol for robust scheduling in Grid computing. *Advances in Grid Computing - EGC 2005, European Grid Conference. LNCS 3470,* (pp. 651-660). Amsterdam, The Netherlands: Springer.

Papazoglu, M. P., & Heuvel, W.-J. (2007). Service oriented architectures: Approaches, technologies and research issues. *The VLDB Journal, 16*(3), 389–415. doi:10.1007/s00778-007-0044-3

Parkin, M., Badia, R. M., & Martrat, J. (2008). *A comparison of SLA use in six of the European Commissions FP6 projects.* Institute on Resource Management and Scheduling. CoreGRID-Network of Excellence.

Paschke, A., & Bichler, M. (2008). Knowledge representation concepts for automated SLA management. *Decision Support Systems, 46*(1), 187–205. doi:10.1016/j.dss.2008.06.008

Rausch, A., Reussner, R., Mirandola, R., & Plášil, F. (2008). *The common component modeling example: Comparing software component models* (Vol. LNCS 5153). Springer. SLA@SOI. (2010). *SLA@SOI project: IST-216556, empowering the service economy with SLA-aware infrastructures.* Retrieved December 9, 2010, from http://www.sla-at-soi.eu

Snelling, D. F., Anjomshoaa, A., Wray, F., Basermann, A., Fisher, M., & Surridge, M. (2007). NextGRID architectural concepts. *Towards Next Generation Grids* [Rennes, France: Springer.]. *Proceedings of the CoreGRID Symposium, 2007,* 3–13.

Spanoudakis, G., & Mahbub, K. (2006). Non-intrusive monitoring of service-based systems. *Int. J. Cooperative Inf. Syst., 15*(3), 325–358. doi:10.1142/S0218843006001384

Theilmann, W., Happe, J., Kotsokalis, C., Edmonds, A., Kearney, K., & Lambea, J. (2010). A reference architecture for multi-level sla management. *Journal of Internet Engineering, 4*(1).

Theilmann, W., Winkler, U., Happe, J., & Magrans de Abril, I. (2010). Managing on-demand business applications with hierarchical service. *Proc. of 3rd Future Internet Symposium (FIS 2010), Berlin, September 20-22, 2010, LNCS, Vol. 6369.* Springer.

Theilmann, W., Yahyapour, R., & Butler, J. (2008). Multi-level SLA management for service-oriented infrastructures. *Proceedings of the 1st European Conference on Towards a Service-Based Internet* (pp. 324-335). Madrid, Spain: Springer-Verlag.

KEY TERMS AND DEFINITIONS

Adaptive Infrastructures: An IT infrastructure that can be dynamically adapted.

e-Contracting: An electronic way of negotiating and finalizing contracts.

Non-Functional Properties: A property of an (IT) component/service/system that goes beyond its primary functional objective (e.g. performance, usability, etc.).

Service Level Agreement (SLA): A contract specifying the conditions under which a service is (to be) delivered.

Service-Oriented Infrastructure (SOI): An IT infrastructure that exposes its resources and capabilities as a service.

Chapter 21
Framework for Managing Features of Open Service Ecosystems

Toni Ruokolainen
University of Helsinki, Finland

Lea Kutvonen
University of Helsinki, Finland

ABSTRACT

The recent increased use of Internet, social media, and networked business mark a development trend where software-based services flow to the open market for enabling service-oriented networked business. Our vision is that in the future, organizations and individuals collaborate within open service ecosystems. An open service ecosystem is characterized especially by the autonomy of its entities, its evolution with respect to available services and collaboration types, and dynamic establishment of collaborations. For facilitating collaboration establishment in open service ecosystems features of services and cooperation facilities, and feature inter-dependencies need to be governed rigorously. Towards this purpose we have established a framework for unambiguous description of service ecosystem features. The framework comprises a conceptual model which provides especially a categorization of features, and a formalization of the conceptual model as a meta-model for service ecosystems. We show that the corresponding feature categories have their specific roles and semantics as part of different ecosystem elements and in different phases of service ecosystem processes.

INTRODUCTION

The recent increased use of Internet, social media, and networked business mark a development trend where software-based services flow to the open market. Technological approaches like SaaS, SOA, and Web Services present tools and architectures for this: they provide protocols for accessing remote functionality encapsulated to a business-relevant units, declared available though service registries and manifests of service functionality, requirements for messaging platform support, information representation and semantics, and

DOI: 10.4018/978-1-61350-432-1.ch021

choreography (protocol) for exchanges in utilising the service.

However, this situation is uncontrolled and uncontrollable in several ways. First, the trustworthiness of the services marketed is unknown, as there is no guaranteed knowledge (facts) about their properties. The clientele is left to rely on declarations by the service providers. The declarations carry several risk aspects. The semantic of the declaration may be obscure due to the lack of shared vocabulary for describing service behaviour in functional and nonfunctional aspects exists. Furthermore, the declarations can be biased, as the cost of inaccurate declarations is not sufficient as an incentive.

Second, the interoperability between independently developed services is immature, especially in terms of nonfunctional properties. There is no commonly accepted framework for functionality and selectable properties or property management for those functions. Middleware platforms have built-in support for various transparency properties (e.g., location and access, data representation, transactionality) and various security technologies (e.g., encryption, non-repudiation), but as the groupings of properties differ, the interworking challenges still exist. Furthermore, the concepts of nonfunctional properties commonly refer to platform services, but in modern social networking and inter-enterprise collaboration scenarios, business and user oriented properties (such as policies for governing joint behaviour, pricing schemes, privacy preservation declarations) are relevant requirements.

Third, the current platforms weakly support collaboration management or concepts required for it. Concepts of contracts, parties, authority and ownership, policies and breaches of contracts causing sanctions are necessary for the different kinds of networked collaborations.

As a partial solution to these challenges, software ecosystems have become popular as a means for producing software applications more efficiently for heterogeneous clientele with varying requirements. A software ecosystem is typically based on a software platform provided by an organization. The platform is then used by internal and external developers for implementation of applications (Bosch & Bosch-Sijtsema, 2010). Software ecosystem strategy is utilized by companies such as Amazon [1] or Nokia [2] for establishing communities of developers and clientele over their own corresponding platforms.

While the software ecosystem approach emphasises the software production challenges, the open use of services from the open marketplace is stressed by service ecosystem approaches. A service ecosystem is an environment for creating and managing service-based collaborations, such as virtual organizations or service mash-ups, from services provided by a community of service providers. Service ecosystems exist currently especially in form of platform provider specific Software-as-a-Service (SaaS) -environments. The typical service ecosystems available currently are closed, meaning that the methods and technologies used for providing new services are pre-determined by the hosting environment, and service compositions and collaboration networks are determined statically during service development. Such closed ecosystems can not be applied in domains where services are to be provided and managed by autonomous entities, or when service collaboration networks are to be established dynamically on demand.

The challenge still remains to provide an environment where several service-oriented software engineering (SOSE) methodologies and distributed teams could produce services that easily can be organised into collaborations managed by dynamic contracts, because linkage between these two sides is missing.

The main architecture design must address a more complex situation where the clientele and the ecosystem itself have potential conflicts of interest in details, but still, the members of the ecosystem have incentives for collaboration both at business network level and ecosystem introduction, control and evolution levels.

Instead of considering nonfunctional features as a single, uniformly directed domain of research, there is definite need to address separately three levels: (1) business collaboration aspects, (2) service properties, and (3) collaborative management of communication technology usage in specific cases. For the business collaboration aspects, the declaration of vocabulary and behaviour requirements is directed by companies and consortia focusing on issues including business processes, legal systems, business models. For service properties, the aspects to be managed will be implemented mainly as software – and thus design choices depend on the software engineering practices used – but the management of quality, business issues and user interaction aspects need to be aligned across the service ecosystem with the needs of the business collaboration level. Further, the communication technology needs to be governable though shared vocabulary with the level above, although the facilities are provided and designed by platform service producers.

Our vision in the CINCO group (Collaborative and Interoperable Computing research group, http://cinco.cs.helsinki.fi) is that in future, organizations and individuals collaborate within open service ecosystems for enabling service-oriented networked business. An open service ecosystem is characterized especially by the autonomy of its entities, its evolution with respect to available services and collaboration types, and dynamic establishment of collaborations. In an open service ecosystem the service providers and clients are not bound to a shared development platform. Instead, each ecosystem member may utilize methods and technologies that suit best their own needs. A set of global infrastructure services are then used for service publication and discovery, as well as dynamic establishment of service-based collaboration networks (Kutvonen, Ruokolainen, Ruohomaa, & Metso, 2008). An open service ecosystem is based on the service-oriented architecture (SOA) architectural style with service brokering and dynamic binding facilities, but requires more sophisticated infrastructure services for enabling interoperable service collaboration.

The contribution of this Chapter is built up in steps. First we introduce the service ecosystem framework that merges the concepts for service-oriented software engineering and eContracting in such a way that ecosystem level evolution is facilitated. This provides the environment in which, as the second step, the enhanced concepts of ecosystem features can be connected to the relevant primary targets, i.e. service, collaboration and communication. Once the concepts are introduced, the third step provides the processes necessary for evolving the open service ecosystem understanding and usage of the features. This text provides insight for the Pilarcos ecosystem work, and as new contribution, introduces the feature management method within the Pilarcos ecosystem frame. Thus the text reflects the CINCO group vision that in future, individual users, enterprises or public organizations can easily compose new services from open service markets, or establish temporary collaborations with complex peer relationships. Furthermore, these contract-governed collaborations can be managed by all involved parties. All this is supported by a global infrastructure with facilities for interoperability control and contract-based community management (establishment, control and breach recovery) among autonomous organization; this infrastructure also takes responsibility of governing trust and privacy-preservation issues. The support environment is complemented with service-oriented software engineering practices that enable semantic and pragmatic interoperability management.

Section 2 introduces the open service ecosystem, while Section 3 elaborates on the ecosystem spanning from technical platforms to business-oriented needs of managing inter-enterprise collaborations. Section 3 demonstrates the conceptual model and its formalization as a meta-model hierarchy, and how the necessary concepts can be organised to achieve the goals of synchronous management of the three levels of issues described above. Section 4 proceeds then to discuss management of features in several service ecosystem processes: service ecosystem life-cycles, eContracting, and ecosystem evolution. Section 5 discusses the benefits of the framework, while conclusions are given in Section 6.

OPEN SERVICE ECOSYSTEM

We propose open service ecosystems as a coherent solution for the challenges of interoperability and collaboration management, met in the phases of service production and utilisation through collaborations, and innovation of new types of collaborations and services. Most of the challenges arise from the inherent and necessary independence of actors involved, including collaboration partners, parties engineering services, clients, and platform providers.

In terms of operational time composability of services and facilities of inter-enterprise collaborations, a key point is sufficient, automated support for interoperability. Interoperability concept covers technical, semantic and pragmatic interoperability aspects. Technical interoperability is concerned with connectivity between the computational services, allowing messages to be transported from one application to another. Semantic interoperability means that the message content becomes understood in the same way by the senders and the receivers. This concerns both information representation and messaging sequences. Pragmatic interoperability captures the willingness of partners to perform the actions needed for the collaboration. This willingness to participate refers both to the capability of performing a requested action, and to policies dictating whether it is preferable for the enterprise to allow that action to take place.

At the design and engineering time concerns include efficient production and maintenance of service software with clear, published interfaces and behaviour descriptions. While the direct production concern is how to extend model-based methodologies to distributed team environment, an even more pressing is the need of producing exploitable, composable services that can be managed in such a way that interoperability can be achieved at operational time. Behind these two problem areas remains the problem of changing business models and changing computing and communication platforms: both the production and operational systems should be tolerant for changes.

Against this background we define a service ecosystem as an environment for creating and managing service-based collaborations, such as virtual organizations or service mash-ups, from services provided by a community of autonomous entities. In future service-oriented networked business, organizations and individuals collaborate within service ecosystems. Currently there are several emerging service ecosystems in the domains of business and technology. Software ecosystems (Bosch & Bosch-Sijtsema, 2010) are utilized by enterprises for producing software applications more efficiently for heterogeneous clientele with varying requirements. Software ecosystems can be characterized as product centric service ecosystems. Different kinds of electronic business networking environments, such as eCommerce platforms, supply chains, and virtual organizations, can be considered as collaboration and process centric service ecosystems. Cloud computing platforms, such as provided by Amazon, Google, or Salesforce, are resource centric service ecosystems. Finally, community and individual centric service ecosystems are realized by social networking platforms such as Facebook, LinkedIn or MySpace. The maturity of these ecosystems vary from closed software systems to open collaboration systems with ad hoc collaboration models.

For us, the open service ecosystem is characterized especially by its evolution with respect to available services and collaboration types, and dynamic establishment of collaborations. Indeed, the purpose of the ecosystem is to provide infrastructure, tools and vocabulary for independent entities (people, organisations, collaborations) to create new collaborations, utilising the already existing services from the ecosystem. This is in contrast to a common goal in related work (e.g., ECOLEAD (Rabelo, Gusmeroli, Arana, & Nagellen, 2006), CrossWork (Mehandjiev & Grefen, 2010)) for creating a shared space with a shared incentives of the members. In open service ecosystems the initiators of collaborations each have their private incentives and conflicts of interest are to be expected, and resolution of such conflicts need to be supported.

The open service ecosystems are defined by a conceptual framework and a set of life cycles:

- The conceptual framework provides a vocabulary and an ontology for defining the properties of services, collaborations and entities in the ecosystem.
- A service ecosystem life cycle declares which kinds of activities are expected from the ecosystem participants to support the operation of the ecosystem. Foundational ecosystem life cycles, which exist in every service ecosystem, include a *service life cycle* and a *collaboration establishment life cycle*. Additional life cycles can be associated with a service ecosystem depending on the requirements of the domain of interest, such as *ecosystem evolution life-cycle*.

The service life cycle addresses steps of service innovation, modeling, production and utilisation. Therefore, the service-oriented software engineering methodologies and instruments must produce modules that exploit the facilities of the ecosystem infrastructure for efficient and dependable service delivery (i.e. service publication, discovery, selection, location and binding).

The collaboration establishment life cycle relies on artifacts defining the content of contracts, and infrastructure mechanisms for dynamic establishment of safe, interoperable service collaborations taking qualitative requirements into consideration. The ecosystem evolution life-cycle allows the concept base and infrastructure service base to be enhanced and modified while the ecosystem is utilised. This evolution then allows existing SOSE methods and eContracting methods to facilitate the new innovations.

The Pilarcos ecosystem illustrated in Figure 1 can be considered as a concretization of the ecosystem framework. The Pilarcos architecture views inter-enterprise collaboration as a loosely-coupled, dynamic constellation of business services. The constellation is governed by an eContract that captures the business network model describing the roles and interactions of the collaboration, the member services, and policies governing the joint behavior (Kutvonen, Metso, & Ruohomaa, 2007, Kutvonen, Ruokolainen, & Metso, 2007).

The Pilarcos architecture for the open service ecosystem comprises of

1. The participating enterprises, with their public business service portfolios exported (Kutvonen, Ruokolainen, Ruohomaa, & Metso, 2008);
2. Business-domain governing consortia, with their public models of business scenarios and business models expressed as exported business network models (comprising a set of business process descriptions and compulsory associations between roles in them, and governing policies about acceptable behavior)(Kutvonen, 2002);
3. A joint ontology about vocabulary to be used for contract negotiation, commitment and control (Metso & Kutvonen, 2005, Ruokolainen & Kutvonen, 2006, 2007b);
4. Legislative rules to define acceptable contracts (Metso & Kutvonen, 2005);

Figure 1. A schematic view of the Pilarcos service ecosystem life-cycles

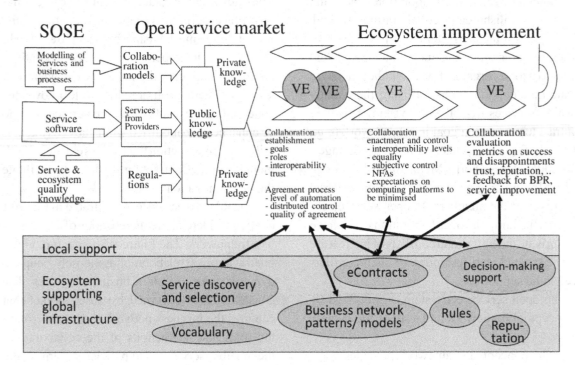

5. Technical rules to define conformance rules over all categories of meta-information held as collaboration and interoperability knowledge (Ruokolainen, 2009, Ruokolainen & Kutvonen, 2007a);

6. Infrastructure services to support partner discovery and selection, contract negotiation and commitment to new collaborations, monitoring of contracted behavior of partners, and breach detection and recovery services; these services especially include trust aspects in decision-making on commitment and breaches (Kutvonen, Metso, & Ruohomaa, 2007, Kutvonen, Ruokolainen, & Metso, 2007);

7. Reputation information flow, collected from past collaborations (Ruohomaa & Kutvonen, 2008, Ruohomaa, Viljanen, & Kutvonen, 2006).

Figure 1 illustrates the ecosystem life-cycles. On the left, meta-information repositories and flows are shown to be created by the publishing and exporting processes denoted above as items 1 and 2. The repositories in particular contain public information about the available business network models, available services and reputation information about the available services. This information is stored in globally federated repositories, applying strictly specified structuring and conformance rule (Kutvonen, 2004) created by the processes listed above as items 3, 4 and 5. The information is in turn utilized by the ecosystem infrastructure functions listed as item 6, e.g. service discovery and selection, eContracting functions, monitoring of business services and reporting of experience on the services when a collaboration terminates. These functions are further described below.

On the right, the life-cycle of independent collaborations is shown to flow from establishment to evaluation at the dissolution phase. The infrastructure functions provide support for the four phases of the collaboration: establishment, agreement, enactment and control, and evaluation. In the Pilarcos framework the collaboration establishment is a multi-lateral process involving a collaboration initiator and one or more service providers that have published their services in the service ecosystem.

Service discovery and selection supports the collaboration establishment phase. It is based on public business network models describing the collaborations, and public service offers made by service providers (Kutvonen, Metso, & Ruohomaa, 2007, Ruokolainen & Kutvonen, 2007b). The business network models capture the best practices of a given field, and they are built from formally defined service types. The task of producing these models and types naturally falls to consortia and standardization bodies.

Service selection includes automated static interoperability checking, which ensures that the service offers fit the model of the collaboration, and have terms that are compatible with other offers being selected into the proposed business network. As service discovery and selection is separate from contract negotiations, it can be done without access to sensitive information; this makes it possible to have this task implemented as a third-party service (Kutvonen, Metso, & Ruohomaa, 2007).

Automated eContract establishment supports the agreement phase of the collaboration (Kutvonen, Metso, & Ruohomaa, 2007). The business network model and the proposed service offers to populate the roles in it are processed by an automated contract negotiation infrastructure, which is controlled locally by each collaboration partner. Contracts are based on templates specific to the collaboration model, and the terms of service provision given in service offers form the basis of negotiations. The negotiated eContract includes a model of the business process of the collaboration, as well as the finalized terms of service in the form of accepted service offers.

Monitoring supports the enactment and control phase of the collaboration in particular (Kutvonen, Metso, & Ruokolainen, 2005). It is done by each collaborator to protect local resources, keep track of the progress of the collaboration, and to ensure that partners follow the collaboration model. The business network model and service provision terms set by the negotiated eContract form the specification of correct behavior in the collaboration, which becomes relatively straightforward to monitor.

Experience reporting supports the evaluation phase of the collaboration, and connects to the monitoring service during the enactment of the collaboration (Ruohomaa & Kutvonen, 2008, Ruohomaa et al., 2006). Experience reporting forms the core of social control in the open service ecosystem. As contract violations are detected by monitors, they are published to other actors as well: it is important to create a direct reputation impact to privacy and data security violations in order to limit the damage that misbehaving actors can achieve in other collaborations.

For evaluating the ecosystem approach, a set of prototype infrastructure services has been implemented in the Pilarcos interoperability middleware (Kutvonen et al., 2008). Systematic performance testing of the framework has been conducted in the context of the Pilarcos interoperability middleware. The results show that the approach is feasible performance-wise (Metso & Kutvonen, 2005). The conceptual framework and the corresponding metamodels has been scrutinized during their development with architectural analysis. For example, a threat analysis has been conducted with respect to privacy issues (Moen et al, 2010).

As can be detected experimenting with the Pilarcos type of ecosystem, the ecosystem features have several roles within service ecosystems. They are used as qualitative service features, for example during service discovery and selection. During collaboration establishment they are considered as contractual artifacts that are negotiated between entities willing to establish service-based collaborations. Finally, they are deployable products, that is artifacts created by someone using a specific process, which are put into use during collaboration enactment. Furthermore, while the set of possible service ecosystem features is open and can not be predetermined or enumerated due to their context dependency and evolution of an open service ecosystem, their usage can be disciplined by deliberate management facilities. These facilities involve design and deployment of the features, as well the operational time facilities for governing their utilization.

FEATURES IN SERVICE ECOSYSTEMS

Service ecosystem is a socio-technical complex systems where autonomic entities collaborate with each other over a service-oriented computing environment. The service-oriented computing environment provides infrastructure services for establishing interoperable collaborations. Collaborations are enabled by cooperation facilities, such as communication channels, that are set up during collaboration establishment for arbitrating activities and knowledge between ecosystem members. In service ecosystems the different features of entities and cooperation facilities affect the structure, behaviour and qualities of service-based collaborations.

For facilitating collaboration establishment processes and other service ecosystem processes the features and their inter-dependencies need to be governed rigorously. Towards this purpose we have established a framework for unambiguous description of service ecosystem features. The framework comprises a conceptual model which provides especially a categorization of features, and a formalization of the conceptual model as a meta-model for service ecosystems. In the following we describe the categorization of service ecosystem features. As we will see, the categorization does not actually contain a notion of non-functional features. Different features in service ecosystems govern activities taken in different phases of ecosystem life-cycles: so-called cooperative features defining intensions of legal entities are used for decision making in the preparatory phases of collaboration establishment, whereas so-called extra-functional features declare qualitative features of interaction and communication. All service ecosystem features have active roles during collaboration establishment processes (e.g. virtual organization establishment).

In this Section we discuss the characteristics of service ecosystem features and their management. We first define what we mean with feature management and discuss related problems, and activities. We then provide a categorization of service ecosystem entities and cooperation facilities that are utilized for enabling service-based collaborations. After that we define a categorization of ecosystem features. The categorization is derived from the identification of ecosystem entities and cooperation facilities, and requirements stemming from foundational ecosystem life-cycles, such as collaboration establishment life-cycles. The categorizations and the conceptual framework describing relationships between the kinds of ecosystem entities, cooperation facilities, and their features are formalized in a service ecosystem meta-model. UML class diagrams (Object Management Group, 2005) described in this Chapter illustrate parts of a larger modelling framework (Ruokolainen, 2009) for managing service ecosystem knowledge. Finally, we provide a discussion of the semantics for service ecosystem features. We perceive that each feature category is associated with a distinguishing semantic framework.

Managing Service Ecosystem Features

Managing features of software systems is problematic: features may have complex dependencies with each other, they can be defined at different abstraction levels, and interpretation of their meaning or importance can be subjective. In addition to these generic problems, more specific challenges are introduced for feature management in open service ecosystems. In open service ecosystems new kinds of features emerge following the demands of the individual members and the domain of operation. This dynamism of the knowledge landscape must be addressed by mechanisms that allow extension of the feature ontologies. Due to the autonomy of ecosystem members feature management can not be centrally controlled. Instead, features should be managed using a federated approach where feature descriptions can be shared between ecosystem members and utilized efficiently in the local systems. Finally, for guaranteeing interoperability during dynamic collaboration establishment processes, features should be provided with rigorous and unambiguous semantics.

Features can have several kinds of inter-dependencies. When addressing features at the same level of abstraction, features may have horizontal interactions with each other. Behavioural features of business services can be affected by security features requiring key-exchange protocols, for example. Another example of horizontal feature interaction is the potential conflict between performance and security features: introduction of communication encryption may increase the response time of business service. Features at the same level of abstraction may require other features to function correctly: introducing message encryption feature on a communication endpoint is typically not valid without introducing an decryption feature on the other communication endpoint. Finally, features may have direct conflicts with each other (e.g. monitoring of communication vs. privacy preservation), be mutually exclusive (e.g. different message encryption schemes), or have some domain specific dependencies with each other.

Features are defined in different levels of abstraction for decreasing the complexity of their description and for achieving loose coupling between business and technology. In this setting features defined at a higher level of abstraction

are instantiated at a lower level of abstraction by a collection of more specific features. For example, at the business level a feature requirement for communication confidentiality is declared. This high-level feature can be implemented at a lower level of abstraction by an appropriate combination of features representing strong encryption and privacy. Further down the abstraction chain, the feature of strong encryption can be implemented by providing a feature that represents usage of RSA algorithm with 1024 bit key length, for example.

Especially in open service ecosystems the subjectivity of interpretation of feature intensions has to be addressed carefully. Without a shared understanding about the meaning of ecosystem features, identification and selection of eligible features, and analysis of feature interoperability are impossible. For this purpose, means for categorizing service ecosystem features must be provided. The categorization is utilized for classifying available features such that features providing required characteristics of business services and communication can be efficiently identified. Such feature categorization provides a basis for an ontology of service ecosystem features. In addition to prescribing feature categories, such ontology should also provide means for defining horizontal and vertical feature dependencies.

For increasing the elasticity and sustainability of the service ecosystem, an ontology describing service ecosystem features must be dynamically extensible. Especially, it should be possible to introduce new kinds of feature categories on demand. A modelling framework that is based on the powertype pattern (see e.g. (Gonzalez-Perez & Henderson-Sellers, 2006)) or some other means for dynamic type definition should be used. While it may be sufficient in other contexts to use ontologies for simply describing features, such as has been done for example in (Kabilan et al., 2007) or (Kassab, Ormandjieva, & Daneva, 2009), this is not sufficient in open service ecosystems. Instead, feature definitions need to be provided also with prescriptive definitions for reducing ambiguity in feature interpretation, and for enabling efficient feature implementation in ecosystem member organizations. Feature intensions in service ecosystem domain ontologies can be formalized as meta-models and models (Ruokolainen, 2009).

However, even defining both the descriptive and prescriptive characteristics of features is not sufficient in open service ecosystems. While such an ontology provides some guidance especially for the selection and development of required features, from the interoperability management perspective these descriptions are incomplete. What is still missing from this setting is rigorous semantics providing unambiguous interpretation of feature intensions and dependencies. This deficiency can be approached with abstract platform thinking and by providing proper semantics for the different categories of features.

An *abstract platform* represents the support that is assumed by platform-independent models of a distributed application (Almeida, Dijkman, Sinderen, & Pires, 2004). In open service ecosystems abstract platforms are made explicit by models that prescribe the characteristics of interaction and communication. From feature management perspective, these models provide a mechanism for prescribing the effects that certain features have on interaction and communication. More over, feature dependencies can be characterized with respect to abstract platform models, such as descriptions of communication channels. For example, it can be described that two specific features can not be bound simultaneously to a communication channel.

Semantics for features in service ecosystems should be formalized by using proper, category specific semantics. Behavioural features of services can be formalized using Petri-nets, process algebra, or finite state automata, for example. Structural features of communicated information can be formalized based on different type systems. Policies and business rules, which are kinds of non-functional features, can be formalized as temporal or deontic constraints over service behav-

iour. Different alternatives for formalizing feature semantics are discussed below, after introducing the feature categories of service ecosystems.

Service Ecosystem Entities and Cooperation Facilities

Features in service ecosystems specify the characteristics of ecosystem entities and abstract platform components. An entity has its own existence and has an identity (e.g. a unique identifier, address, name, or URI) which can be used for referring to and identifying the corresponding entity. Examples of service ecosystem entities are organizations, individuals, business services, and service endpoints. We consider entities and features as the primary artifacts in service ecosystems, and meaning of an entity is prescribed by the features it possesses. Abstract platform components are called in this framework as *cooperation facilities*, since they provide elements that are needed for realizing interaction and communication in service ecosystems. Denotation of a cooperation facility comprises a selection of features.

A diagram illustrating the relationships between entity kinds and features, as well as the top-level categorization to functional and legal entity kinds is given in Figure 2. The notions of *Concept* and *Intension* are foundational parts of the service ecosystem meta-model which enable ontological and linguistic meta-modelling practices (Ruokolainen, 2009).

Functional entities provide the essential activities, behaviour, and interactions for realizing collaboration in service ecosystems. Functional entities comprise endpoint, information, behavioural and service entity kinds, as illustrated in Figure 3. The intensions of functional entities are prescribed by *functional features*.

Endpoint entities represent interaction endpoints in the system. Their features declare what kind of interaction semantics is to be used, e.g. remote procedure calls or publish-subscribe. Information entities represent information contents

Figure 2. Ecosystem entity kinds

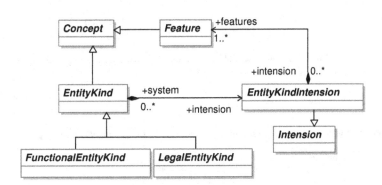

Figure 3. Functional entity kinds

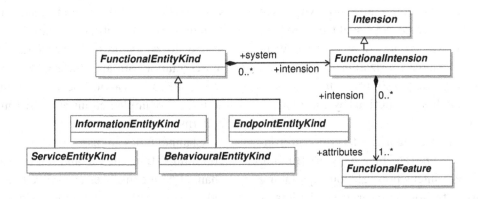

available in the system with the corresponding features describing business document structures, for example. Behavioural entities' intensions compose behavioural patterns that are supported for realizing collaborations in the ecosystem. We may have behavioural entities that define simple message exchange patterns (MEPs) of the web services architecture (Web Services Architecture Working Group, 2004) or behavioural entities that declare more complex business protocols, as in the case of the Pilarcos service ecosystem (Kutvonen, Ruokolainen, et al., 2008, Ruokolainen & Kutvonen, 2007b). Finally, service entities represent the actual services available in the system. Service entities are further classified to two distinct categories: business services and infrastructure services. Business services are used in the busi-

ness networks for realizing collaboration activities. Infrastructure services, such as business service discovery services or populators (Kutvonen, Ruokolainen, et al., 2008), are used for realizing service ecosystem life-cycle activities.

Service providers, consumers, clientele and other real-life actors are represented in service ecosystems by the concept of legal entity. Legal entities are categorized to individuals and organizations, as illustrated in Figure 4. The intension of a legal entity kind is defined by a collection of *cooperative features*. A cooperative feature can prescribe policies a legal entity must conform to, or declare a reputation mechanism for evaluating the trustworthiness of a legal entity.

Cooperation facilities provide elements for describing the abstract platform of a service eco-

Figure 4. Legal entity kinds

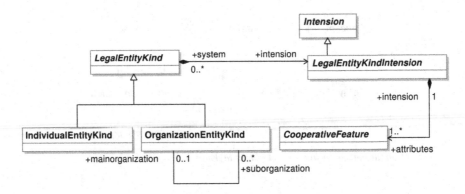

system. These abstractions provide representations for interaction and communication which are agnostic with respect to the actual technological platforms (e.g. web services or other middleware platform) used. The categorization of cooperation facilities is illustrated in Figure 5. Intensions of cooperation facilities are defined by a set of *facility features*.

There are two categories of cooperation facilities: channel types and binding types. Binding types represent interaction relationships taking place between two or more service endpoints. A binding type provides an abstraction for declaring interaction characteristics, such as if interaction is to be taken in a one-to-one or one-to-many setting. Binding types provide especially an abstraction for interception mechanisms that can be utilized for adaptation (e.g. mappings in different representation formats), exogenous coordination (e.g. notifications about specific communication activities), or implementing enterprise integration patterns.

Channel types are used for declaring abstract communication media and their features. A channel type comprises an ordered set of channel phases. Each phase represents an individual activity that must be taken for propagating the

Figure 5. Cooperation facilities

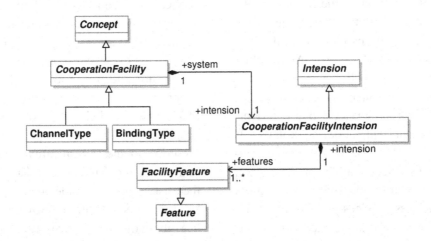

communication payload from one interaction endpoint to another.

Categorization of Service Ecosystem Features

To facilitate interoperability management in service ecosystems it becomes essential to unambiguously specify ecosystem features. As was discussed above, a specification of ecosystem features must declare both descriptive (ontological) and prescriptive (engineering) characteristics of the features. In the following, we introduce a descriptive categorization of service ecosystem features. The categorization is based on definition of ecosystem entities and cooperation facilities. Especially, most of the feature categories are declared for providing intensions for the entities and cooperation facilities. In addition, qualitative features affecting the functionality of entities and cooperation facilities are provided with appropriate categories.

The categorization of service ecosystem features identifies five different categories, namely (1) functional features, (2) facility features, (3) cooperative features, (4) contractual features, and (5) extra-functional features. The categorization is illustrated in Figure 6. Functional features declare intensions of functional entity kinds, while cooperative features are associated with legal entity kinds. Facility features provide meaning for the cooperation facilities. Cooperative, contrac-

tual and extra-functional features are qualitative features of legal entity kinds, business services and operations, and cooperation facilities, correspondingly. In the following we discuss the non-functional part of this categorization; features associated with semantics of functional entities such as business services, information or service endpoints are not discussed further in this Chapter.

Facility features define the characteristics of cooperation facilities and thus, the abstract platform. There are two categories of facility features, namely binding port types and channel phases, as illustrated in Figure 7. Binding port types are used for specifying the intensions of binding types. Each binding port type represents an endpoint of an interaction relationship. A binding port type can be associated with an endpoint entity kind (e.g. a service endpoint), or another binding port type. These different associations of binding port types provide representations for typical interaction and exogenous coordination patterns, correspondingly. The intension of a channel type is declared by an ordered set of *channel phases*. The ordering is provided by the *predecessor*-association inherited from the concept of *Event*. Each channel phase declared in a channel type is associated with a binding port type defined in a binding type. This effectively makes the set of channel phases a bipartite collection, each phase now belonging to a set associated with one of the two binding port types defined in a binding type.

Figure 6. Service ecosystem feature categories

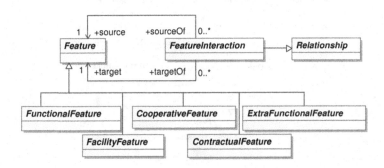

Figure 7. Facility features

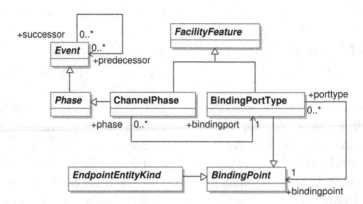

Cooperative features represent a category of service ecosystem features that define the intensions of legal entities. Legal entities are characterized by the rules they must conform to, and means for judging their trustworthiness in a service ecosystem community. As illustrated in Figure 8, the characteristics are represented by the concepts of *Policy* and *ReputationKind*. Cooperative features are utilized in the decision making phase of collaboration establishment processes for evaluating the feasibility of a potential service provider. During the operation of a business network community the rules declared by cooperative features are monitored dynamically. Finally at the dissolution phase of a community the reputation of community members can be updated corresponding to the quality of their performance (Kutvonen, Metso, & Ruohomaa, 2007).

Policies are further classified to legislation, policy frameworks and business models. Legislation comprises legal acts that must be obeyed by the corresponding kind of legal entities. Policy frameworks comprise operational policies, or practices, that are characteristic for a certain kind

Figure 8. Cooperative features

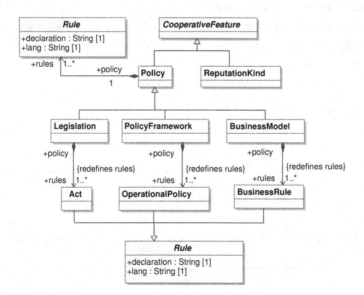

Figure 9. Contractual features

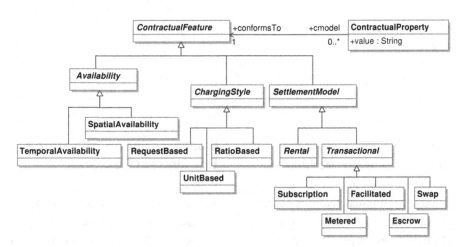

of organization or individual. Operational policies regulate the use of business functionality and knowledge provided by a legal entity, such as an enterprise. For example rules addressing accessibility, authorization, trust and privacy with respect to the provided business services and information are typical examples of organizational policies. Business models are collections of business rules, which are declarative statements defining or constraining some aspect of a business. Different kinds of reputation models or criteria, such as recommendations or ratings, can be categorized under the concept of *ReputationKind*.

Cooperative features address the pragmatic interoperability issues, that is policies and methods of decision-making on collaborations, such as risk, business value, trust and reputation. Again, there is need to define policies that are commonly understandable but dependent on all business domains involved. Collaborative properties especially are subject to business service owners' autonomic intentions. For collaborative properties to be truly usable within an open business service ecosystem, facilities for identity, trust and reputation management should also exist, since assertions of cooperative features can not usually be validated in advance.

Contractual features represent qualitative characteristics of business services and their operations. Contractual features comprise availability constraints and different charging styles, in addition to different models for settling about the service usage, as illustrated in Figure 9. Contractual features are instantiated to contractual properties. A contractual property is a declaration of a concrete value or value constraint over some contractual feature. For example, response time can be considered as a temporal availability feature with values declared in milliseconds; now the corresponding property can be for example a declaration of constraint *"response time must be less than 200 ms"*.

Contractual features address especially the semantic interoperability concerns related to the qualitative characteristics of business services and operations. Contractual features are agreed upon during the negotiation phases of collaboration establishment life-cycles. The features and property values that have been agreed upon negotiations are used during the operational phase of the community as monitoring criteria. If the agreed qualities are not met, compensations or other mechanisms for recovering from the contract breach can be used. Contractual features are controllable by the business service provider and

Figure 10. Extra-functional features

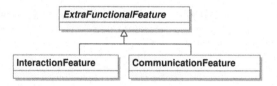

modifying these features requires business administrative authority over the service. More over, for enabling loosely coupled and dynamic business collaborations, contractual features should be dynamically configurable in the local systems.

Extra-functional features represent qualitative characteristics of cooperation facilities. We identify two categories of extra-functional features: interaction features and communication features, as illustrated in Figure 10. Interaction features are bound to binding types and they represent interaction characteristics, such as functionality related to messaging and encoding. Communication features are bound to channel types and represent functionality such as encryption, decryption or monitoring of behaviour. Communication features must be introduced in certain order to be feasible, that is they can have mutual ordering dependencies: information monitoring must be executed before encryption, for example.

Extra-functional features address semantic and technical interoperability issues relevant for managing the dependability of the underlying communication platform. These features are controllable by the service realisation provider by using the computational platform. Modifying these features requires technical administrative authority over the local communication platform, and they are closely intertwined with the computational services administered within administrative domains. Extra-functional features manifest static aspects of interaction and communication that are selectable during service binding and collaboration contract establishment.

Characteristics of Service Ecosystem Features

The feature categories presented above represent characteristics of distinctive ecosystem elements. From the set of categories we can identify two groups of categories: (1) intensional features, and (2) qualitative features. Intensional features specify intensions of ecosystem entities and cooperation facilities. That is, the group of intensional features includes functional, facility and cooperative features. Rest of the feature categories, namely contractual and extra-functional features, can be characterized as qualitative features, since they are used for specifying qualitative features of business services and cooperation facilities.

Especially, there is a difference in the usage of intensional features and qualitative features. Intensional features are declared statically over the corresponding subjects, that is entity kinds and cooperation facilities. By contrast, qualitative features are bound dynamically to their targets, such as business services or communication channels. Qualitative features are bound with a mechanism of *property binding*. A property binding is a relationship between a property subject (e.g. a business service) and a property declaration, as illustrated in Figure 11.

A property object can be either a set-based constraint, such as *PropSomeOf* or *PropNoneOf*, a contractual property (applicable over business services or service operations) or an extra-functional feature (applicable over cooperation facilities). The set based constraints give means for declaring different property variations, such as

Figure 11. Property binding model

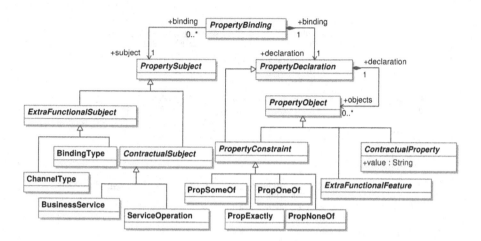

different service pricing policies, for example. During the population phase of the eContracting life-cycle, the properties required by a business network are matched against those declared by service providers. The *PropOneOf* constraint means that any single one of the given properties must be same and supported by a provided services. Constraint *PropSomeOf* means that a number of the given values must be the same but not necessarily all. *PropExactly* means that all properties must be the same. *PropNoneOf* is an exclusive range and means that none of the given values are suitable.

The categorization also constitutes a family of semantic domains: each feature category is associated with distinctive semantic frameworks. Functional features can be formalized by using a selection of semantic frameworks. For formalizing behavioural features, such as service conversations, formal methods based on Petri-nets (Hamadi & Benatallah, 2003), process algebras (Salan, Bordeaux, & Schaerf, 2004), or finite-state machines (Berardi, Calvanese, Giacomo, Lenzerini, & Mecella, 2003) can be used. Structural features, such as business document typing, can be formalized with appropriate typing schemes addressing XML (Simeon & Wadler, 2003, Hosoya, Vouillon, & Pierce, 2005), for example.

Facility features are used for specifying the semantics of binding types and channel types. In each service ecosystem there are some principles how communication channels can be constructed, for example. These rules can be provided with axiomatic semantics which *"involves rules for deducing assertions about the correctness or equivalence of programs and corresponding parts"* (Zhang & Xu, 2004). Axiomatic semantics is a kind of semantic framework which is used especially for formalizing programming languages. In the context of service ecosystems the cooperation facilities are associated with domain-specific axiomatic semantics. The corresponding rules constrain the construction of channel types and binding types, and provide criteria for their correctness.

Cooperative features are utilized for establishing feasible service provisioning relationships, and for governing the usage and operation of business services. Declarative business rules can be formalized with conceptual graphs (Valatkaite & Vasilecas, 2003) or defeasible logic (Antoniou & Arief, 2002), for example. Operational policies (e.g. privacy preservation) or other normative rules can be formalized, at least to some extent, with different modal logics. Modal logics, such as temporal, deontic or epistemic logics, are

Figure 12. Instantiating a contractual feature

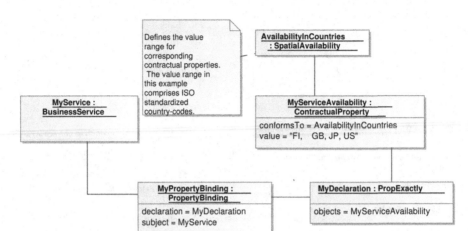

utilizable for declaring operational policies over business services, for specifying obligations and permissions over legal entities, and for defining privacy policies, for example (see e.g. (Lupu & Sloman, 1999, Luo, Tan, & Dong, 2009, Benbernou, Meziane, & Hacid, 2007)).

Contractual features are bound to business services and service operations for characterizing their business capabilities. This category includes features such as service availability (e.g. declarations that a service is available during business hours or within a geographical location), charging style (e.g. per business operation or intensity of use), and different models for settling about service use (e.g. rental or subscription). Contractual features are negotiated during eContract establishment; the negotiations are typically bilateral. The properties accepted in negotiations are put in service-level agreements.

The distinguishing characteristics of contractual features is that they are instantiated to concrete values. These values are called *contractual properties*. A contractual feature is considered as a type definition which defines the acceptable value range for the corresponding kinds of properties. An simplified example of contractual feature instantiation is given in Figure 12. The example is illustrated as UML class diagram

(Object Management Group, 2005) with instance specifications of the classes presented previously.

In this example, *AvailabilityInCountries* is defined as a kind of a *SpatialAvailability*; this is declared with a *conformsTo* relationship. Contractual features define especially the acceptable value ranges for the corresponding properties. In this case, the acceptable values are lists of ISO standardized country codes [3] (this declaration is provided only as an informal comment in the example). The contractual property named *MyServiceAvailability* declares that a contractual subject, i.e. a business service or operation, is available in Finland, United Kingdom, Japan and United States. Finally, the contractual subject is bound with the *PropertyBinding* concept to a business service with the name of *MyService*.

In addition to contractual features, the extra-functional features are a category of qualitative features that can be bound dynamically. Extra-functional features are bound with the property binding mechanism to cooperation facilities, that is binding types and channel types. In distinction to contractual features that were instantiatable to contractual properties, extra-functional features do not have such a direct typing relationship. Instead, extra-functional features are made concrete by transformations between abstraction levels, e.g.

Figure 13. Example of representing an extra-functional feature with model transformation

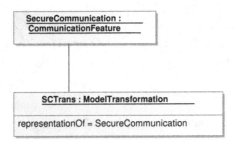

from business level requirements to technology level artifacts.

In this framework, the semantics of extra-functional features are given as model transformations. The model transformations take as an input a cooperation facility and produce a cooperation facility with the required feature implemented by appropriate channel phases, for example. We clarify the characteristics of extra-functional features with a simple example. In this example an extra-functional feature for secure communication is addressed. Within the knowledge base of the service ecosystem exists a declaration for an extra-functional feature named *SecureCommunication*; this is illustrated in Figure 13. More over, a model transformation has been published, named *SCTrans*, which is declared as a *representation of* (Favre, 2004) the *SecureCommunication* feature.

In this example we assume that the intensions of cooperation facilities are modeled using a meta-model described in Figure 14. The meta-model is a simplified and streamlined version of the meta-models defined in (Ruokolainen, 2009). The meta-model is an Ecore meta-model of the

Figure 14. A simplified Eclipse Ecore meta-model prescribing intensions of cooperation facilities

```
import ecore : 'http://www.eclipse.org/emf/2002/Ecore#/';

package facilities : facilities = 'http://cinco.org/cooperationfacilities'
{
  class NamedElement
  {
    attribute name : String[1];
  }
  class ChannelType extends NamedElement
  {
    property features : ChannelPhase[+] { composes };
  }
  class ChannelPhase extends NamedElement
  {
    property predecessor : ChannelPhase[*];
    property bindingport : BindingPortType[1];
  }
  class BindingType extends NamedElement
  {
    property features : BindingPortType[+] { composes };
  }
  class BindingPortType extends NamedElement, BindingPoint
  {
    property bindingpoint : BindingPoint[1];
  }
  class BindingPoint;
  class EndpointEntityKind extends NamedElement, BindingPoint;
}
```

Eclipse Modeling Framework (The Eclipse Foundation, 2010a) declared in XText-based (The Eclipse Foundation, 2010b) concrete textual syntax. The metamodel defines seven classes with appropriate properties for describing cooperation facilities.

The *SCTrans* model transformation can be defined using the QVT model transformation language (*Meta Object Facility (MOF) 2.0 Query/View/Transformation Specification*, 2005), for example. Such description of the model transformation is given in Figure 15. The model trans-

Figure 15. SCTrans model transformation defined in QVT language

```
modeltype FACIL "strict" uses facilities('http://cinco.org/cooperationfacilities');

transformation SCTrans(in input : FACIL, out output : FACIL);

main() {
  input.rootObjects()[FACIL::ChannelType]->map channel2SecureChannel();
}

-- Returns the channel phases that do not have any predecessors.
query FACIL::ChannelType::firstPhase() : OrderedSet(FACIL::ChannelPhase) {
  return self.features->select(e | e.predecessor->isEmpty());
}

-- Returns the channel phases that do not have any successors.
query FACIL::ChannelType::lastPhase() : OrderedSet(FACIL::ChannelPhase) {
  return self.features->select(e | -- Select channel phase 'e' from the result
    not self.features->exists(p | -- if there is no 'p' such that
      p.predecessor->includes(e) -- 'e' is a predecessor of 'p'
    )
  );
}

-- Maps a ChannelPhase to a ChannelPhase (simple copy)
mapping FACIL::ChannelPhase::mapChannelPhase() : FACIL::ChannelPhase {
  name := self.name;
  bindingport := self.bindingport;
  predecessor := self.predecessor;
}

-- Maps a ChannelType to another ChannelType with encryption and decryption
-- phases in phase sequence beginnings and ends, correspondigly.
mapping FACIL::ChannelType::channel2SecureChannel() : FACIL::ChannelType {
  init { var feats := self.features; }

  name := self.name.concat('WithSecurity');

  self.features->forEach(a | true) {
    -- First copy the channel phase to the new channel type.
    features += a->map mapChannelPhase();

    if(self.firstPhase()->includes(a)) then {
      -- This is first phase in sequence
      var enc := object FACIL::ChannelPhase { -- Create the encryption phase.
        name := a.name.concat('Encryption');
        bindingport := a.bindingport;
      };
      -- Set encryption phase a a predecessor of the first channel phase.
      a.resolveoneIn(FACIL::ChannelPhase::mapChannelPhase, ChannelPhase).
        predecessor := enc;
      features += enc;
    } else {
      if(self.lastPhase()->includes(a)) then {
        -- This is last phase in sequence
        var dec := object FACIL::ChannelPhase { -- Create the decryption phase
          name := a.name.concat('Decryption');
          bindingport := a.bindingport;
          -- Set the last phase as the predecessor of the decryption phase
          predecessor := a;
        };
        features += dec;
      } endif;
    } endif;
  }
}
```

formation effectively adds encryption and decryption phases to the channel phase sequences contained in any channel type conforming to the meta-model defined in Figure 14. Encryption phases are introduced before every initial phase of channel sequences induced by the *predecessor* reference. Decryption phases are introduced after each final phase of channel sequences.

Extra-functional features may induce a series of model transformations, or transformation chains. In this setting, the application order of the transformation is essential, since the corresponding features can have mutual dependencies that have to be respected, or there are several abstraction levels in use.

MANAGING FEATURES IN SERVICE ECOSYSTEM PROCESSES

Service ecosystems involve several processes where feature management activities take place. The ecosystem processes include those of service-oriented software engineering processes, ecosystem evolution, service ecosystem life-cycles. Service-oriented software engineering processes utilize domain-specific methodologies suitable for producing service artifacts. The artifacts include service implementation components and models defining different features of services, service collaborations and cooperation facilities. By ecosystem evolution we mean the "meta-life-cycle" of service ecosystems from their design and initiation to operation, and their progressive development, especially with respect to available features, during

their operation. Finally, ecosystem life-cycles are processes which prescribe especially processes for collaboration establishment. Service delivery or product life-cycles, among others, could be prescribed in as service ecosystem life-cycles depending on the domain and objectives of the corresponding ecosystem.

Feature management activities in the preceding processes can be characterized as comprising of (a) feature identification and selection, (b) feature concretization, (c) feature introduction, and (d) feature coordination. These activities are enacted in different phases of the ecosystem processes and have their distinguishing interpretations. Manifestations of feature management activities in service-oriented software engineering, eContracting and ecosystem evolution processes are illustrated in Table 1.

The actors and the visibility of produced artifacts are different in each of the processes illustrated in Table 1. In service-oriented software engineering processes ecosystem members act typically as individuals for producing local, private artifacts such as implementation components. In service ecosystem life-cycles, such as the eContracting process, a collection of ecosystem members constitute a community which shares knowledge about the characteristics, i.e. features, of the collaboration. Finally, in ecosystem evolution the members of the ecosystem introduce new, public and globally available knowledge into the service ecosystem; this knowledge includes especially features and their categories.

In service-oriented software engineering processes feature identification is provided by

Table 1. Feature management activities in service ecosystem processes

	SOSE	eContracting	Evolution
IDENTIFICATION	Requirements engineering	Population	Domain analysis
CONCRETIZATION	Feature specification	Negotiation	Ecosystem modeling
INTRODUCTION	Feature implementation	Binding	Feature publication
COORDINATION	Deployment & configuration	Monitoring	Knowledge management

requirements engineering activities. Identified features are made concrete by feature specifications which define the descriptive (i.e. ontological) and prescriptive (i.e. engineering) characteristics of the features. The set of identified features can then be formalized with a service ecosystem modeling language (Ruokolainen, 2009). New ecosystem features are introduced locally by implementing them in platform specific technologies. Finally, ecosystem features are coordinated by deployment and configuration activities which weave feature implementations with provided business services, communication components, or other feature implementation components.

In ecosystem evolution the fundamental features and their categories are identified by a domain analysis. The domain analysis is executed during the initial design of the service ecosystem. Domain analysis is *"process by which information used in developing software systems is identified, captured and organized with the purpose of making it reusable when creating new systems"* (Prieto-Díaz, 1990). When this definition of domain analysis is put into the context of service ecosystems, "software systems" are considered as service collaborations, and "creation of new systems" means establishment of new service collaborations.

During the design of a new service ecosystem the foundational features, the abstract platform, and their inter-dependencies are identified during a domain analysis process. The results of the domain analysis are used for modeling the features of the service ecosystem. Feature concretization is implemented thus during ecosystem modeling. During the operation of service ecosystem new features can be introduced by ecosystem members by publishing feature models. Infrastructure services providing knowledge management functionality are used for such model publication. Ecosystem specific knowledge base, which includes especially the feature models, is coordinated by knowledge management activities enacted by infrastructure services. These activities maintain the knowledge base consistency needs for enabling establishment of interoperable service collaborations.

In the following, we describe more thoroughly the role of feature management activities in collaboration establishment life-cycles, taking the eContracting process of the Pilarcos service ecosystem (Kutvonen, Ruokolainen, et al., 2008, Kutvonen, Metso, & Ruohomaa, 2007) as an example.

eContracting

Service ecosystems are provided with a collaboration establishment life-cycle. A collaboration establishment life-cycle defines a process for preparing necessary agreements and facilities required for service-based cooperation between community members. In the context of the Pilarcos framework (Kutvonen, Ruokolainen, et al., 2008, Kutvonen, Metso, & Ruohomaa, 2007) this process is known as *eContracting*. During eContracting processes features are managed during population, negotiation, configuration, operation and dissolution phases, as illustrated in Figure 16. Phase specific activities, such as service discovery in the population phase or monitoring in the operation phase, are taken for managing business network and service features; the activities are enacted in cooperation by legal entities and infrastructure services. Each phase is also associated with a collection of business services which is refined or utilized in the corresponding eContracting phase.

An eContracting life-cycle starts with a population phase where a business network model is filled with services matching the criteria of the selected business network and those set by the initiator of the population phase (Kutvonen, Metso, & Ruohomaa, 2007). Population phase utilizes infrastructure services available in a service ecosystem for realizing necessary activities; the population activities themselves are enacted by a infrastructure services known as a populator (Kutvonen, Ruokolainen, et al., 2008). Service discovery mechanisms provided by the infrastruc-

Figure 16. Phases in an eContracting life-cycle

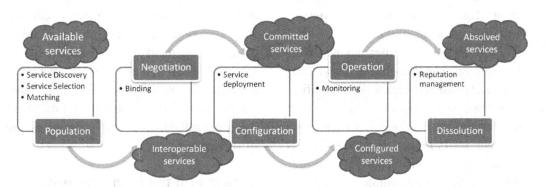

ture services are first used for identifying services that can be potentially accepted for a specific business network. The primary criteria for service discovery is the functional features associated with services, e.g. behaviour and structure.

Service discovery activity provides a set of services that are technically compatible with the corresponding business network model. The primary purpose of the service selection activity is to guarantee technical and semantic interoperability. Each service passing the service selection criteria should be at least technologically and behaviourally compatible with the given form of collaboration. In addition to interoperability criteria, both collaboration itself and its initiator may require certain level of initial trust and reputation from corresponding service providers. Infrastructure service providing trust and reputation management mechanisms (Kutvonen, Metso, & Ruohomaa, 2007), are utilized for this purpose.

In the population phase a set of collaboration proposals are established from a selection of services and and a business network model that characterizes the structure and requirements of the collaboration (Kutvonen, Ruokolainen, & Metso, 2007a, Kutvonen, Metso, & Ruohomaa, 2007). Semantic interoperability is addressed further by the population phase especially with respect to the non-functional features of the services and requirements set by the collaboration. Compatibility

between different features are matched; for this purpose, constraint satisfaction algorithms can be used (Kutvonen, Metso, & Ruohomaa, 2007). As a final outcome of the population phase, a set of collaboration contract proposals is provided. The services included in the proposals are guaranteed to be interoperable with each other.

While the population phase addresses technical and semantic concerns of interoperability, negotiation phase is utilized especially for addressing the pragmatic interoperability aspects. As an example of pragmatic interoperability aspects, expression of the entities' willingness to collaborate, are considered during the negotiation phase. Cooperative features are utilized especially for such decision making. First of all, the policies associated with the kinds of legal entities are used as the principal criteria for selecting members for business networks to be established. Secondly, reputation of legal entities is used for further judging the eligibility of an entity as a member in the business network.

The negotiation phase enables autonomic ecosystem members to resolve and bargain about the contractual features of the collaboration. The negotiations result in formulation of a collaboration contract which states the responsibilities for each participating entity, the structure of the collaboration, and features expected from the corresponding cooperation facilities, such as communication channels. The collaboration contract is then used for managing the operation of the collaboration (Kutvonen, Ruohomaa, & Metso, 2008, Metso & Kutvonen, 2005).

In service binding the features agreed upon during the preceding negotiations are introduced as more concrete, usually technology specific, declarations. Especially, cooperation facilities are refined with the required extra-functional features; more over, features in higher abstraction levels are instantiated to lower abstraction levels using model transformations, for example.

After a successful binding service providers are equipped with declarations that can be used locally for configuring the technological platforms. Models of the cooperation facilities declared during service binding can be utilized for configuring systems in local administration domains. Models of extra-functional features can be used for generating appropriate implementation components, such as communication interceptors or adapters. More over, models representing cooperative features can be utilized for feeding the local business rule engines with appropriate rules.

During the operation phase the use of features is coordinated with monitoring mechanisms. Especially, contractual properties are used for service-level monitoring of both external (e.g. detecting contract breaches) and internal services. Finally, in the dissolution phase especially the reputation features of legal entities are coordinated. The reputation of entities are updated in accordance to the corresponding kind of reputation system.

DISCUSSING THE FRAMEWORK

Due to the dynamism of the environment and autonomy of entities special emphasis must be imposed on controlling and maintaining interoperability knowledge in open service ecosystems. During collaboration establishment processes information is required especially about the features of ecosystem members, provided services, and available cooperation facilities. In the previous

Sections we have described a framework for enabling management of service ecosystem features. In this Section, we discuss impacts of this work on the management of non-functional features in open service ecosystems. After that we introduce a selection of related work with comparison to our framework and a brief analysis on future research directions in the area of model-driven management of service ecosystem features.

Impacts on the Management of Service Ecosystem Features

The framework presented in this Chapter provides a well-defined classification of service ecosystem features. We have shown that the corresponding feature categories have their specific roles, as part of different ecosystem elements and in different phases of service ecosystem processes. We have intentionally avoided the use of term "non-functional feature". First of all, the meaning of a non-functional feature or property is ambigous. It's definition as "any other feature than functional" does not get us too far in their management. In this framework, we have first analyzed the components that act in service ecosystems and then defined the features in accordance to the categorization of entities and cooperation facilities (Ruokolainen, 2009). Secondly, features in service ecosystem are all functional in a sense that they are used for decision making, negotiation, or supporting service interactions in the different phases of service ecosystem processes.

Based on the categorization of the foundational entities, a feature categorization has been defined. The characteristics of the corresponding categories are summarized in Table 2. In this characterization two groups of features are distinguished. The three feature categories on the top of the table (functional, facility and cooperative features) can be considered as intensional feature categories, since they are used for specifying the intensions of service ecosystem entities and cooperation facilities. Two remaining categories,

Table 2. Overview of the service ecosystem features

	TARGET	SEMANTICS	EXAMPLES
FUNCTIONAL FEATURES	Functional entity intension	Various frameworks (e.g. for operational or structural features)	Service behaviour; business document structures
FACILITY FEATURES	Cooperation facility intension	Axiomatic	One-to-one interaction; communication monitoring
COOPERATIVE FEATURES	Legal entity intension	Various logics (e.g. temporal, deontic, epistemic logics)	Corporate form definitions; domain specific business rules; information privacy laws
CONTRACTUAL FEATURES	Business service and operation qualities	Denotational	Availability of business services; price per operation call
EXTRA-FUNCTIONAL FEATURES	Interaction and communication qualities	Translational (transformations over cooperation facilities)	WS-* / REST –style messaging; communication security

contractual and extra-functional, specify qualities of provided business services and the abstract platform. Categories are first characterized with respect to the target of the feature definitions in the corresponding category. Secondly, the kind of semantics utilizable for formalizing the features is given. Finally, some characteristic examples of concrete feature definitions are provided for each of the categories.

The framework discussed in this chapter is based on a conceptualization of service ecosystem elements and formalization of the corresponding concepts with a formal meta-model (Ruokolainen, 2009). The meta-model can be considered as a *domain specific meta-modeling language* (Zschaler, Kolovos, Drivalos, Paige, & Rashid, 2010) for service ecosystems. The corresponding meta-modeling language is used for defining the fundamental elements of a service ecosystem prescribing life-cycles, entities and features. Additional domain specific concepts are also included in the resulting service ecosystem models. A service ecosystem model is then utilized for generating service ecosystem specific engineering artifacts. The set of artifacts includes meta-models for describing concept intentions; one such meta-model describing cooperation facilities was illustrated in context of the example given in Section 4. The set of meta-models generated from

a service ecosystem model actually constitutes a *family of domain specific languages (DSLs)*. In addition to DSLs, skeletons for ecosystem specific infrastructure services can be generated from the ecosystem model; these include especially model repositories for maintaining information about entities, cooperation facilities and their features.

This work provides facilities for enhancing interoperability management and software engineering support in service ecosystems. For enhancing interoperability management in service ecosystems, this work formalizes a top-level ontology for declaring service ecosystem specific features. Such interoperability knowledge is utilized in service ecosystem life cycles for guaranteeing interoperable operation of service-based collaborations. Interoperability knowledge includes information about features and their mutual dependencies, and their applicability with respect to different models of collaboration, for example.

From the software engineering support perspective this work provides a comprehensive definition of the entities and features identifiable from service ecosystems. Thus, a unifying framework for defining vocabularies enabling engineering knowledge exchange about service artifacts is provided. Knowledge repositories based on a unified ecosystem model and maintaining corresponding feature information can then be utilized by developers for sharing information and enabling global software engineering practices. Especially, formalization of service ecosystem concepts as models and meta-models makes it possible for enabling development tool interoperability by integration of software engineering processes and domain specific languages through the ecosystem models and knowledge repositories.

We can analyze the impacts of this work by considering different actors in service ecosystems and what level of support is provided for their activities. First of all, the framework discussed in this Chapter enables efficient development of domain specific service ecosystems. The domain specific meta-modeling language behind this framework is used for modeling the service ecosystem. Service ecosystem modeling can be utilized by information system providers in requirements gathering and design processes in cooperation with their clients. After an appropriate service ecosystem model has been designed, the resulting model is utilizable for producing ecosystem specific meta-models, corresponding DSLs and model repositories. Model-driven engineering principles are exploited for efficient generation of these artifacts.

Secondly, the framework provides means for individual service providers to join selected service ecosystems in a more flexible manner. The collection of tools, methods and modeling languages are typically specific for individual service providers based on their expertise, experience and practice. When joining a new service ecosystem, a service provider must possibly adopt new kinds of methods, tools or languages to provide services in conformance with the ecosystem. Such an intrusive adoption of new practices and expertise makes joining new service ecosystems an expensive process. However, explicit service ecosystem models, such as provided by this framework, can provide more efficient means for such adaptation by conceptual unification: organization specific languages (and tools) can be mapped to the ones used by the ecosystem.

Such mappings can be formalized as weaving models (Bézivin et al., 2005) and further utilized for efficient implementation of model integration (Jossic et al., 2007).

Finally, the framework presented in this Chapter can be exploited by modeling and software engineering tool providers. The domain specific meta-modeling language for service ecosystems provides means for developing coherent families of domain-specific languages, or DSLs. Traditionally DSLs are developed one language at a time. However, in service ecosystems several languages need to be used in conjunction to describe the different viewpoints (e.g. legal entities vs. functional entities) in the service ecosystem. In the single-language-at-a-time model the correspondences between languages and consistency between viewpoints may become hard to handle due to complex dependencies between features. In this framework these complexities can be handled more efficiently, since the correspondences are formalized in the service ecosystem model. The model can be used for generating the abstract syntaxes of the individual DSLs in the corresponding language family, and especially, for creating explicit correspondence descriptions between the elements of the DSLs. Correspondences between individual viewpoint languages can be formalized with use of QVT, for example (Romero, Jaén, & Vallecillo, 2009).

Research Issues in Model-Driven Management of Service Ecosystem Features

The framework presented in this paper utilizes model-driven engineering principles for modeling and managing features in open services ecosystems. Similar approaches have been introduced before for example in (Jonkers et al., 2005). The authors introduce a method for integrating functional models with non-functional ones in the context of model-based service development processes. In their work, the authors make a distinction between two modeling spaces for non-functional features, namely design and analysis space. Design space comprises modeling languages and tools for describing non-functional features. Analysis space consists of specification languages and notations which are applicable for formalizing the semantics of the non-functional features of interest. Horizontal transformations are then used for propating information between a design space and a corresponding analysis phase. Vertical model transformations are used for model refinement within the modelling spaces in the traditional model-driven engineering sense. Similarly, (Köllmann et al., 2007) presents an approach for managing several Quality of Service (QoS) dependability dimensions. This approach applies model-driven development and aspect-oriented techniques for detaching the QoS aspects from software specifications. Graph transformations are then utilized for weaving the QoS aspects to QoS independent models. The approach of (Jonkers et al., 2005) for attaching domain-specific semantics for non-functional features can be utilized in the framework presented in this Chapter. Also, the approach of (Köllmann et al., 2007) for providing translational semantics for non-functional features can be used. Our approach is more specific in a sense that it is targeted for open service ecosystems. Especially, our approach formalizes the inter-dependencies and roles between different "non-functional" and functional features in service ecosystems. We have, to a certain degree, fixed the semantic for different features in service ecosystems. We see that such constraints over the feature categories, their definitions and usage are needed for enabling feature management in various service ecosystems.

In (Ameller, Cabot & Franch, 2010) the authors report current state of model-driven engineering approaches for managing non-functional requirements in software engineering processes. They make a remark based on a literature survey that in general non-functional requirements are not addressed in model-driven engineering methods.

Towards enhancing the situation they envision a general framework that integrates non-functional requirements management into model-driven software engineering process, and identify research issues related to their framework. In their framework proposal the authors utilize a platform-independent model (PIM) for representing the functionality and non-functional requirements of a system. This PIM is then analysed against a knowledge base containing information about available non-functional, architectural and technological features and solutions. Based on this analysis a model transformation is created which transforms the PIM to an architectural model. The architectural model describes an architecture that implements all the functionality of the system in a way that satisfies the non-functional requirements whose satisfaction depends on the decisions made at the architectural level (Amellers, Cabot & Franch, 2010). The architectural model is then analyzed agaTints the knowledge base and a second model transformation is applied. The model transformations takes the architectural model as an input and produces a platform-specific model (PSM). The PSM follows the architectural guidelines expressed in the architectural model but also takes into account non-functional requirements depending on technological choises. Finally, a model to text transformation can be applied for generating technology specific code from the PSM. The approach proposed by Amellers, Cabot & Franch (Amellers, Cabot & Franch, 2010) can be aligned with our approach. In our framework the knowledge about service ecosystem features is available in specific knowledge repositories. This knowledge is based on the categorization of the features and the corresponding metamodels presented in this Chapter. The metamodels introduced in this Chapter are part of a larger metamodel which formalizes the foundational elements of service ecosystems (Ruokolainen, 2009). This service ecosystem metamodel can be considered as a model for architectural models in the sense of (Amellers, Cabot & Franch, 2010).

It is used as a basis for defining platform-independent models that specify all requirements of service-based collaborations and their elements. In addition to architectural issues, the service ecosystem metamodel includes technology-oriented knowledge in form of cooperation facility features and extra-functional features, as discussed in the previous sections.

More generally the framework behind the work presented in this Chapter is related to research conducted in the areas of large-scale SOA systems, their modeling and corresponding service-based middleware platforms. There are a few European research initiatives and projects that have similar goals with this respect. NESSI (*Networked European Software & Services Initiative)* is a European Technology Platform dedicated to software and services (Lizcano et al., 2010). As part of its research activities, the NESSI consortium is developing the NESSI Open Service Framework (NEXOF) which is described as "a coherent and consistent open service framework leveraging research in the area of service-based systems" (NESSI Consortium, 2009). In comparison to the reference architecture developed as part of the NEXOF, our service ecosystem framework is more focused on the knowledge management side of service ecosystems, and explicitly provides means for extending domain models of specific ecosystems with new concepts.

The SeCSE (*Service Centric System Engineering*) is an EU Integrated Project of the 6th Framework Program that aims for developing processes, methods and tools to develop service-oriented systems (Colombo et al., 2005). The SeCSE project provides a conceptual model for service oriented systems describing actors, entities and activities relevant to the service domain, and relationships between them. While the conceptual model of SeCSE addresses the various steps (e.g. publication, discovery, composition and monitoring) of the service-centric system creation process, the primary purpose of the model is to provide a common understanding for human readers about the main concepts involved (Colombo et al., 2005). The primary purpose of our framework and the corresponding conceptual model is to facilitate the infrastructure services and tools needed for instrumenting service ecosystems.

The framework presented in this chapter includes several topics for further research; a selection of these are discussed below. The framework implicitly proposes an approach for modeling service-oriented systems with a family of feature-specific languages. Each of the are used for defining different aspects of the system, and the overall model defining the service ecosystem is utilized for guaranteeing coherency of the language family and consistency between different languages. Utilizing such a language family for operating in a service ecosystem necessitates appropriate modeling tools and methodologies. From modeling tools perspective, several notations have been developed for describing different kinds of features in software systems (e.g. Object Management Group, 2005; Amellers, Cabot & Franch, 2010). However, simply providing a notation for feature modeling is not sufficient. What is still lacking from most of the modeling tools is the capability analyze feature interactions and effects of introducing cross-cutting concerns in system models. Towards this purpose, research should be conducted especially in the areas of analysing viewpoint correspondences and consistency based on semantics frameworks defined for corresponding domain-specific languages. Feature interactions are likely to introduce interactions between the different semantics frameworks (e.g. between operational semantics of business processes and declarative semantics of business rules); this is a research topic that should be investigated more in the future. From the methodological viewpoint, engineering processes and methods should be developed that are applicable for distributed development taking place in open service ecosystems and that utilize multi-viewpoint modeling practices. Knowledge sharing facilities provided by shared, global knowledge repositories should be also integrated to corresponding software engineering tools.

Modeling of service ecosystem features is only the first phase in their application. Especially in open service ecosystems models are utilized for configuring, adapting and governing the operation of the system. Such a models-at-runtime –approach (e.g. Blair, Bencomo, & France, 2009) involves in itself several new research challenges, the most foundational one being that of maintaining the causal relationship between the model and the running system. Maintaining the causal relationship becomes problematic especially in open service ecosystems, where individual services are maintained by autonomous service providers and access to the underlying technological systems are restricted due to security related and competitive reasons. In the Pilarcos framework (Kutvonen et al., 2008) we have especially covered issues related to maintaining a coherent view over the service collaborations between autonomous partners.

CONCLUSION

Open service ecosystems present means to solve many collaboration management and interoperability control problems. Indeed, the ecosystem concept reveals that there is notably different interest domains within the feature concept family: business control needs, service control needs, and configuration needs on communication channels between services. Although the presently arising software and service ecosystems forward the business domain significantly, there are still severe problems to be solved:

- Trustworthiness of service offers,
- Interoperability control automation, and
- Collaborative, systematic methods for dynamic collaboration management.

These issues cannot be resolved unless the open service ecosystems are able to bind together

- The service-oriented software engineering methodologies that are responsible of providing business network models serving as eContract templates and thus providing evaluated rules for detecting illegal, unwanted, or low quality services;
- Operational time collaboration management, including service selection advised with trustworthiness predictions, eContract forming, monitoring of contract breaches, and feedback on the experiences gained.

This chapter has shown how a consistent knowledge base for maintaining features in open service ecosystems can be provided, thus creating a life link between the engineering and operational environments. Furthermore, the knowledge base structure must allow for declaration of new concepts and new relationships between concepts, thus facilitating further evolution of the ecosystem without disturbance in the already existing collaborations. The framework allows multiple different kind of ecosystems to be established, and controlled either as isolated, or federated, for cases of competing or collaborating ecosystems.

REFERENCES

Almeida, J. P., Dijkman, R., Sinderen, M. v., & Pires, L. F. (2004). On the notion of abstract platform in MDA development. In *EDOC '04: Proceedings of the Eighth IEEE International Enterprise Distributed Object Computing Conference* (pp. 253–263). Washington, DC: IEEE Computer Society.

Ameller, D., Cabot, J., & Franch, X. (2010). Dealing with non-functional requirements in model-driven development. In *Requirements Engineering Conference (RE), 2010 18th IEEE International* (pp. 189-198). Washington, DC: IEEE Computer Society.

Antoniou, G., & Arief, M. (2002). Executable declarative business rules and their use in electronic commerce. In *SAC '02: ACM Symposium on Applied Computing* (pp. 6–10). New York, NY: ACM Press.

Benbernou, S., Meziane, H., & Hacid, M. S. (2007). Run-time monitoring for privacy-agreement compliance. In *ICSOC '07: Proceedings of the 5th International Conference on Service-Oriented Computing* (pp. 353–364). Berlin, Germany: Springer-Verlag.

Berardi, D., Calvanese, D., Giacomo, G. D., Lenzerini, M., & Mecella, M. (2003). Automatic composition of e-services that export their behavior. In *ICSOC '03: Proceedings of the First International Conference on Service-Oriented Computing* (Vol. 2910, pp. 43–58). Berlin, Germany: Springer.

Bézivin, J., Jouault, F., Rosenthal, P., & Valduriez, P. (2005). Modeling in the large and modeling in the small. In *Model Driven Architecture* (*Vol. 3599*, pp. 33–46). Berlin, Germany: Springer. doi:10.1007/11538097_3

Blair, G., Bencomo, N., & France, R. B. (2009, October). Models@run.time. [Washington, DC: IEEE Computer Society.]. *Computer, 42*(10), 22–27. doi:10.1109/MC.2009.326

Bosch, J., & Bosch-Sijtsema, P. (2010). From integration to composition: On the impact of software product lines, global development and ecosystems. *Journal of Systems and Software, 83*(1), 67–76. doi:10.1016/j.jss.2009.06.051

Colombo, M., Di Nitto, E., & Di Penta, M. distante, D., & Zuccala, M. (2005). Speaking a common language: A conceptual model for describing service-oriented systems. In Benatallah, B., Casati F. & Traverso, P. (Ed.), *Service-Oriented Computing – ICSOC 2005,* (vol. 3820, pp. 48-60). Berlin, Germany: Springer.

Favre, J.-M. (2004). Foundations of model (driven) (reverse) engineering: Models - Episode I: Stories of the Fidus Papyrus and of the Solarus. In Bézivin, J. & Heckel, R. (Ed.), *Language engineering for model-driven software development,* (vol. 04101). Schloss Dagstuhl, Germany: Internationales Begegnungs- und Forschungszentrum für Informatik (IBFI).

Gonzalez-Perez, C., & Henderson-Sellers, B. (2006). A powertype-based metamodelling framework. *Software and Systems Modeling, 5,* 72–90. doi:10.1007/s10270-005-0099-9

Hamadi, R., & Benatallah, B. (2003). A Petri net-based model for web service composition. In *CRPITS'17: Proceedings of the Fourteenth Australasian Database Conference on Database Technologies 2003* (pp. 191–200). Darlinghurst, Australia: Australian Computer Society, Inc.

Hosoya, H., Vouillon, J., & Pierce, B. C. (2005). Regular expression types for XML. *ACM Transactions on Programming Languages and Systems, 27*(1), 46–90. doi:10.1145/1053468.1053470

Jonkers, H., Iacob, M. E., Lankhorts, M. M., & Strating, P. (2005). Integration and analysis of functional and non-functional aspects in model-driven e-service development. In *Proceedings of the Ninth IEEE International EDOC Enterprise Computing Conference.* Washington, DC: IEEE Computer Society.

Jossic, A., Didonet Del Fabro, M., Lerat, J., Bézivin, J., & Jouault, F. (2007). Model integration with model weaving: A case study in system architecture. In *Proceedings of the 2007 International Conference on Systems Engineering and Modeling (ICSEM'07)* (pp. 79–84). IEEE.

Kabilan, V., Johannesson, P., Ruohomaa, S., Moen, P., Herrmann, A., & Åhlfeldt, R.-M. (2007). Introducing the common non-functional ontology. In *Enterprise Interoperability II — New Challenges and Approaches* (pp. 633–646). London, UK: Springer.

Kassab, M., Ormandjieva, O., & Daneva, M. (2009). An ontology based approach to non-functional requirements conceptualization. In *International Conference on Software Engineering Advances (ICSEA)* (pp. 299–308). Washington, DC: IEEE Computer Society.

Kutvonen, L. (2002). Automated management of interorganisational applications. In *Proceedings of the Sixth International Enterprise Distributed Object Computing Conference (EDOC'02)*. Washington, DC: IEEE Computer Society.

Kutvonen, L. (2004). Challenges for ODP-based infrastructure for managing dynamic B2B networks. In A. Vallecillo, P. Linington, & B. Wood (Eds.), *Workshop on ODP for Enterprise Computing (WODPEC 2004)* (pp. 57–64).

Kutvonen, L., Metso, J., & Ruohomaa, S. (2007, July). From trading to eCommunity management: Responding to social and contractual challenges. *Information Systems Frontiers (ISF) -. Special Issue on Enterprise Services Computing: Evolution and Challenges, 9*(2-3), 181–194.

Kutvonen, L., Metso, J., & Ruokolainen, T. (2005, November). Inter-enterprise collaboration management in dynamic business networks. In On the Move to Meaningful Internet Systems 2005: CoopIS, DOA, and ODBASE: OTM Confederated International Conferences, CoopIS, DOA, and ODBASE (Vol. 3760, pp. 593–611). Berlin, Germany: Springer. doi:10.1007/11575771_37doi:10.1007/11575771_37

Kutvonen, L., Ruohomaa, S., & Metso, J. (2008, September 8–10). Automating decisions for inter-enterprise collaboration management. In *Pervasive collaborative networks. IFIP TC 5 WG 5.5 Ninth working conference on virtual enterprises, september 8–10, 2008, Poznan, Poland* (pp. 127–134). Springer.

Kutvonen, L., Ruokolainen, T., & Metso, J. (2007, January). Interoperability middleware for federated business services in Web-Pilarcos. *International Journal of Enterprise Information Systems, Special issue on Interoperability of Enterprise Systems and Applications, 3*(1), 1–21.

Kutvonen, L., Ruokolainen, T., Ruohomaa, S., & Metso, J. (2008, October). Service-oriented middleware for managing inter-enterprise collaborations. In A. Gunasekaran (Ed.), Global implications of modern enterprise information systems: Technologies and applications (pp. 208–241). Hershey, PA: IGI Global. doi:10.4018/978-1-60566-146-9.ch012doi:10.4018/978-1-60566-146-9.ch012

Köllmann, C., Kutvonen, L., Linington, P., & Solberg, A. (2007). An aspect-oriented approach to manage QoS dependability dimensions in model driven development. In L. Ferreira Pires & S. Hammoudi (Ed.), *The 3rd International Workshop on Model-Driven Enterprise Information Systems (MDEIS 2007)* (pp. 85-94). INSTICC Press.

Lizcano, D., Jiménez, M., Soriano, J., Cantera, J. M., Reyes, M., & Hierro, J. J. ... Tsouroulas, N. (2008). Leveraging the upcoming internet of services through an open user-service front-end framework. In *ServiceWave '08: Proceedings of the 1st European Conference on Towards a Service-Based Internet* (pp. 147-158). Berlin, Germany: Springer-Verlag.

Luo, X., Tan, Z., & Dong, R. (2009). Automatic verification of composite web services based on temporal and epistemic logic. In *WGEC '09: Proceedings of the 2009 Third International Conference on Genetic and Evolutionary Computing* (pp. 693–696). Washington, DC: IEEE Computer Society.

Lupu, E. C., & Sloman, M. (1999). Conflicts in policy-based distributed systems management. *IEEE Transactions on Software Engineering, 25*(6), 852–869. doi:10.1109/32.824414

Mehandjiev, N., & Grefen, P. (Eds.). (2010). *Dynamic business process formation for instant virtual enterprises*. Springer. doi:10.1007/978-1-84882-691-5

Meta Object Facility (MOF). (2005, 11 November). *2.0 query/view/transformation specification*. (Final Adopted Specification – ptc/05-11-01).

Metso, J., & Kutvonen, L. (2005, September). Managing virtual organizations with contracts. In *Workshop on Contract Architectures and Languages (CoALa2005)*.

Moen, P., Ruohomaa, S., Viljanen, L., & Kutvonen, L. (2010). *Safeguarding against new privacy threats in inter-enterprise collaboration environments*. (Report No. C-2010-56). Helsinki, Finland: University of Helsinki, Department of Computer Science.

NESSI Consortium. (April, 2009). *NESSI open framework - Reference architecture – RA model V2.0*. Retrieved December 17, 2010, from http://www.nexof-ra.eu/sites/default/files/D6.2_v1.0.pdf

Prieto-Díaz, R. (1990). Domain analysis: An introduction. *SIGSOFT Software Engineering Notes, 15*(2), 47–54.

Rabelo, R. J., Gusmeroli, S., Arana, C., & Nagellen, T. (2006). The ECOLEAD ICT infrastructure for collaborative networked organizations. In *Network-centric collaboration and supporting frameworks* (*Vol. 224*, pp. 451–460). Springer. doi:10.1007/978-0-387-38269-2_47

Romero, J. R., Jaén, J. I., & Vallecillo, A. (2009). Realizing correspondences in multi-viewpoint specifications. In *EDOC '09: IEEE International Enterprise Distributed Object Computing Conference* (pp. 163–172). IEEE.

Ruohomaa, S., & Kutvonen, L. (2008, March). Making multi-dimensional trust decisions on inter-enterprise collaborations. In *Proceedings of the Third International Conference on Availability, Security and Reliability (ARES 2008)* (pp. 873–880). IEEE Computer Society.

Ruohomaa, S., Viljanen, L., & Kutvonen, L. (2006, March). Guarding enterprise collaborations with trust decisions — The TuBE approach. In *Interoperability for Enterprise Software and Applications. Proceedings of the Workshops and the Doctoral Symposium of the Second IFAC/IFIP I-ESA International Conference: EI2N, WSI, IS-TSPQ 2006* (pp. 237–248). ISTE Ltd.

Ruokolainen, T. (2009, June). *Modelling framework for interoperability management in collaborative computing environments* (Tech. Rep. No. C-2009-9). Department of Computer Science, University of Helsinki. (Licentiate's thesis)

Ruokolainen, T., & Kutvonen, L. (2006, September). Addressing autonomy and interoperability in breeding environments. In L. Camarinha-Matos, H. Afsarmanesh, & M. Ollus (Eds.), Network-centric collaboration and supporting frameworks (Vol. 224, pp. 481–488). Helsinki, Finland: Springer. doi:10.1007/978-0-387-38269-2_50doi:10.1007/978-0-387-38269-2_50

Ruokolainen, T., & Kutvonen, L. (2007a, September). Managing non-functional properties of inter-enterprise business service delivery. In *Non Functional Properties and Service Level Agreements in Service Oriented Computing Workshop (NFPSLA-SOC) (co-located with the 5th International Conference on Service Oriented Computing, ICSOC 2007)*.

Ruokolainen, T., & Kutvonen, L. (2007b, April). Service typing in collaborative systems. In Doumeings, G., Müller, J., Morel, G., & Vallespir, B. (Eds.), *Enterprise interoperability: New challenges and approaches* (pp. 343–354). Springer.

Salan, G., Bordeaux, L., & Schaerf, M. (2004). Describing and reasoning on Web Services using process algebra. In *ICWS '04: Proceedings of the IEEE International Conference on Web Services* (p. 43). Washington, DC: IEEE Computer Society.

Simeon, J., & Wadler, P. (2003). The essence of XML. In *POPL '03: Proceedings of the 30th ACM SIGPLAN-SIGACT Symposium on Principles of Programming Languages* (pp. 1–13). New York, NY: ACM Press.

Object Management Group. (2005, August). *Unified modeling language: Superstructure.*

The Eclipse Foundation. (2010a). *Eclipse modeling framework website.* Retrieved December 17, 2010, from http://www.eclipse.org/modeling/emf/.

The Eclipse Foundation. (2010b) *Xtext - Language development framework.* Retrieved December 17, 2010, from http://www.eclipse.org/Xtext/.

Valatkaite, I., & Vasilecas, O. (2003, September). A conceptual graphs approach for business rules modeling. In *Advances in Databases and Information Systems* (Vol. 2798).

Web Services Architecture Working Group. (2004, February) *Web Services Architecture.* W3C Working Group Note 11 February 2004. http://www.w3.org/TR/ws-arch/

Zhang, Y., & Xu, B. (2004). A survey of semantic description frameworks for programming languages. *SIGPLAN Notifications*, *39*(3), 14–30. doi:10.1145/981009.981013

Zschaler, S., Kolovos, D., Drivalos, N., Paige, R., & Rashid, A. (2010). Domain-Specific Metamodelling Languages for Software Language Engineering. In M. van den Brand, D. Gasevic, & J. Gray (Eds.), *SLE'10: Software Language Engineering* (Vol. 5969, p. 334-353). Springer Berlin / Heidelberg.

KEY TERMS AND DEFINITIONS

Feature Management: Includes (1) identification, (2) concretization, (3) introduction, and (4) coordination of service ecosystem features in service ecosystem processes.

Intensional Feature: Specifies the intension (meaning) of an ecosystem entity or a cooperation facility.

Qualitative Feature: Specifies qualitative characteristics of business service and operations, and cooperation facilities.

Service Ecosystem Feature: Characteristics of a service ecosystem entity, cooperation facility, a business service or operation, or interaction and communication.

Service Ecosystem Process: A life cycle or a choreography taking place in a service ecosystem. Ecosystem entities act in prescribed roles in service ecosystem processes.

Service Ecosystem: Comprises of (a) entities acting in domain specific roles (e.g. as providers and consumers of specific services), (b) services available for enabling collaboration and co-creation in the ecosystem, and (c) infrastructure for realizing service engineering, delivery and governance.

ENDNOTES

[1] Amazon EC2: http://aws.amazon.com/ec2/
[2] Nokia Ovi: http://www.ovi.com/
[3] http://www.iso.org/iso/country_codes/iso_3166_code_lists.htm

Chapter 22
Aiding Compliance Governance in Service-Based Business Processes

Patrícia Silveira
University of Trento, Italy

Carlos Rodríguez
University of Trento, Italy

Aliaksandr Birukou
University of Trento, Italy

Fabio Casati
University of Trento, Italy

Florian Daniel
University of Trento, Italy

Vincenzo D'Andrea
University of Trento, Italy

Claire Worledge
Deloitte Conseil, France

Zouhair Taheri
PricewaterhouseCoopers Accountants, The Netherlands

ABSTRACT

Assessing whether a company's business practices conform to laws and regulations and follow standards and SLAs, i.e., compliance management, is a complex and costly task. Few software tools aiding compliance management exist; yet, they typically do not address the needs of who is actually in charge of assessing and understanding compliance. We advocate the use of a compliance governance dashboard and suitable root cause analysis techniques that are specifically tailored to the needs of compliance experts and auditors.

The design and implementation of these instruments are challenging for at least three reasons: (1) it is fundamental to identify the right level of abstraction for the information to be shown; (2) it is not trivial to visualize different analysis perspectives; and (3) it is difficult to manage and analyze the large amount of involved concepts, instruments, and data. This chapter shows how to address these issues, which concepts and models underlie the problem, and, eventually, how IT can effectively support compliance analysis in Service-Oriented Architectures (SOAs).

DOI: 10.4018/978-1-61350-432-1.ch022

INTRODUCTION

Compliance generally refers to the conformance to a set of laws, regulations, policies, best practices, or service-level agreements. *Compliance governance* refers to the set of procedures, methodologies, and technologies put in place by a corporation to carry out, monitor, and manage compliance. Compliance governance is an important, expensive, and complex problem to deal with:

It is *important* because there is increasing regulatory pressure on companies to meet a variety of policies and laws (e.g., Basel II, MiFID, SOX). This increase has been to a large extent fueled by high-profile bankruptcy cases (Parmalat, Enron, WorldCom, the recent crisis) or safety mishaps (the April 2009 earthquake in Italy has already led to stricter rules and certification procedures for buildings and construction companies). Failing to meet these regulations means safety risks, hefty penalties, loss of reputation, or even bankruptcy (Trent, 2008).

Managing and auditing/certifying compliance is a very *expensive* endeavor. A report by AMR Research (Hagerty et al., 2008) estimated that companies would have spent US$32B only on governance, compliance, and risk in 2008 and more than US$33B in 2009. Audits are themselves expensive and invasive activities, costly not only in terms of auditors' salaries but also in terms of internal costs for preparing for and assisting the audit – not to mention the cost of non-compliance in terms of penalties and reputation.

Finally, the problem is *complex* because each corporation has to face a large set of compliance requirements in the various business segments, from how internal IT is managed to how personnel is trained, how product safety is ensured, or how (and how promptly) information is communicated to shareholders. Furthermore, rules are sometimes vague and informally specified. As a result, compliance governance requires understanding/ interpreting requirements and implementing and managing a large number of control actions on a variety of procedures across the business units of a company. Each compliance regulation and procedure may require its own control mechanism and its own set of indicators to assess the compliance status of the procedure (Bellamy et al., 2007).

If we look at how every-day business is being conducted at an operative level, we note that technologies like web services and business process management systems have largely proved their viability for organizing work and assisting and orchestrating also human actors involved in business processes. The adoption of the so-called *service-oriented architecture* (SOA) to conduct business (eased by technologies such as SOAP, WSDL, and HTTP) has further affirmed the analogy between web service technologies and common business practices, turning the traditional, heavyweight and monolithic software approach into flexible and reconfigurable service ecosystems. One of the advantages of this kind of ecosystem is that they suddenly allow one to obtain fine-grained insights into runtime aspects, e.g., message exchanges, events, and process progress states, which can only hardly be accessed in traditional legacy systems. As we will see in this chapter, in our work we specifically leverage on this potential in order to check compliance of service-based business processes.

Interestingly, despite these novel opportunities, compliance is to a large extent still managed by the various business units in rather ad-hoc ways (each unit, line of business, or even each business process has its own methodology, policy, controls, and technology for managing compliance) and without leveraging on the new transparency of electronic business (Sloane et al., 2006). As a result, nowadays it is very hard for any CFO or CIO to answer questions such as: *Which rules does my company have to comply with? Which processes should obey which rules? Which processes are following regulations? Where do violations occur? Which processes do we have under control?* (Cannon & Byers, 2006). Even more, it is hard to do so from a perspective that not only satisfies the company but also the company's *auditors,* which is crucial as the auditors are the ones that certify compliance.

In light of these challenges, in this chapter we provide the following contributions:

- We provide a *conceptual model for compliance and for compliance governance dashboards* that covers a broad class of compliance issues. We identify the key abstractions and their relationships that are necessary to establish the dashboard's role of single entry point for compliance assessment.

- We define a *user interaction and navigation model* that captures the way the different kinds of users can interact with the dashboard, to minimize the time to access the information users need and to make sure that key problems do not remain unnoticed.

- We show how reporting on compliance can be complemented with a simple but effective instrument for the identification of *root causes* of compliance violations. While the up-to-date awareness of the compliance state of a company is useful to take operative decisions on how to deal with non-compliance, root cause analysis is important to understand how to improve current practices for the future.

- We combine the above *broadness with simplicity and effectiveness*. The challenge here is to derive models and interaction paradigms that, despite being broad, remain simple and useful/usable. If the abstractions are not carefully crafted and kept to a minimum, the dashboard and analyses will be too complex and remain unused.

- We derive a suite of solutions that are in line with the *criteria and approach that auditors have* to verify compliance. In this chapter, this last contribution is achieved "by design", in that the model is derived

also via a joint effort of two of the major auditing companies and reflects the desired method of understanding of and navigation among the various compliance concerns.

- We describe the *implementation* of our prototype tools and describe some concrete examples of how such have been applied in the context of our research.

Next, we describe a real-world scenario that highlights the need for compliance governance and root cause analysis in the context of healthcare. Then, we abstract the requirements deriving from the scenario into a set of conceptual models, describe the design of our Compliance Governance Dashboard (CGD), and show how the collected data can also be used for root cause analysis. We describe the implementation of our prototype system, discuss related works, and, finally, conclude the chapter, also providing some hints about our future research directions.

SCENARIO

Let us consider the case of a drug reimbursement process in the healthcare domain. The process is the case study in one of our European Union projects, where we cooperate with Hospital San Raffaele (Milan, Italy), which runs the process shown in Figure 1. The overall purpose of this process, from the hospital's point of view, is to obtain reimbursements from the Italian Health Authority for the drugs dispensed to outpatients (i.e., patients that are not hospitalized). In order to obtain the reimbursement, there are many compliance requirements imposed by the Health Authority, among which we mention privacy preservation in personal information processing, separation of duties, and the adherence of standard template of dispensation reports.

The core process that generates the information that needs to be sent to the Health Authority occurs inside the Ward. The process starts when a

Figure 1. Summary of the direct drug reimbursement process

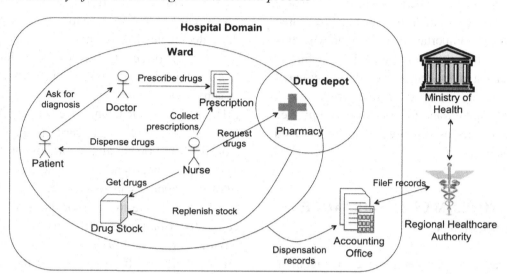

patient visits the hospital's ward to consult a doctor. After diagnosing the patient, the doctor prepares a drug prescription that is delivered to a nurse, who is in charge of dispensing the prescribed drugs to the patient. If the amount of drugs is going below a certain threshold, the nurse issues a drug request to the central pharmacy of the hospital, which must replenish the ward's drug stock in no later than 48 hours. The execution of this process is fully supported by the ward's SOA-based information system, and all progress events generated during process executions are recorded in an event log for later inspection.

While the process above is executed daily, the preparation of the *FileF records* for drug reimbursement is a monthly task. That is, at the end of each month, the *Dispensation records* (extracted from a database of dispensations) are collected from the various wards of the hospital and the corresponding *FileF records* to be sent to the *Regional Healthcare Authority* are created. The *Accounting Office* is the responsible for starting this process and creating the *FileF records*. These reports consist in simple text files (known as *FileF*) in which data about the dispensations are included. Examples of data included in these files are *hospital identification, patient, doctor,*

dispensed drug and quantity, and *amount in Euros.* Whenever the report is ready, it is sent to the *Regional Healthcare Authority*, which checks the quality of the report against some compliance requirements imposed on dispensation reports. For instance, one compliance requirement that decides whether a dispensation can be reimbursed or not regards the completeness and correctness of records: no *null* or incorrect data are tolerated in any field. If there are such problems in the report, the *Regional Healthcare Authority* sends a feedback to the hospital indicating the number and type of errors found for each record of the file, and, in turn, the hospital must correct them so as to get the reimbursement. This is the last chance the hospital has to receive the reimbursement, if the data is not correct that time the money will not be re-passed to the hospital by the *Ministry of Health*.

The complete reimbursement process is complex, and not complying with the above requirements can be costly. Therefore, in order to better control the compliance of the reimbursement process, the hospital wants to implement an early warning system that allows the hospital's compliance expert to have updated information on daily compliance issues, e.g., in form of indicators, reports, or predictions on the compliance of its processes. In addition, in case of repeated problems, it is important to understand why they happen and how they can be solved for the future. However, manually analyzing the data in the event log is time consuming and also error-prone but, still, the hospital wants to improve its compliance in order not to lose money for not reimbursed drug dispensations.

THE PROBLEM OF COMPLIANCE MANAGEMENT

To characterize the compliance management problem intuitively introduced above, we now generalize the problem in terms of two models of its most important concepts, their relationships, and the dynamics that describe their adoption in practice.

Concepts and Terminology

Despite the increasing awareness of compliance issues in companies and the recognition that part of the compliance auditing task can be easily automated, i.e., assisted by means of software tools ((Evans and Benton, 2007), (Sloane, 2006) and (Trent, 2008)), there is still a lot of confusion around (e.g., lack of dedicated tools to monitor compliance, unclear natural language compliance rules that need to be transformed in lines of code to check compliance, among others). This is especially true for the IT community, which would actually be in charge of aiding compliance governance with dedicated software. To help thinking in terms of auditing, in the following we aim to abstract a wide class of compliance problems into a few key concepts that are also the ones understood by auditors. The resulting model does not cover all possible compliance problems, but our goal is to strike a balance between coverage and simplicity. The model is illustrated in Figure 2.

We read the model from the top-left corner: The *Compliance Source* entity generalizes all those documents that regulate or provide guidelines for the correct or good conduct of business in a given business domain. Common examples of compliance sources are legislations (e.g., MiFID, The Electronic Commerce Directive), laws (e.g., SOX, HIPAA), standards (e.g., CMMI, CoBIT, ISO-9001), and contracts or SLAs. Typically, a compliance source defines a set of rules or principles in natural language, which constrain or guide the way business should be conducted. *Complying* with a source means satisfying its rules and principles. Yet, a company might be affected by only some of the rules or principles stated in a given source. The selection of the pertaining ones represents the *requirements* for compliance management, commonly expressed in terms of control objectives and control activities. A regulation expresses multiple requirements, and a requirement might relate to one or more compliance sources.

Assessing compliance demands for an interpretation and translation of the requirements provided in natural language in an actionable rule description (especially in the case of principle-based regulations) (Giblin et al., 2006), (Namir & Stojanovic, 2007). This is modeled by the *Compliance Rule* entity, which represents actionable rules expressed either in natural language (using the company's terminology and telling exactly how to perform work) or, as desirable in a formalism that facilitates its automated processing (e.g., Boolean expressions over events generated during business execution). Rules are then grouped into *policies*, which are the company-internal documents that operatively describe how the company intends achieving compliance with the selected requirements. Typically, policies represent a grouping of the requirements into topics, e.g., security policies, QoS policies, and similar.

At a strategic level, compliance is naturally related to the concept of risk. Non-compliant situations expose a company to risks that might be

Figure 2. Conceptual model of compliance management

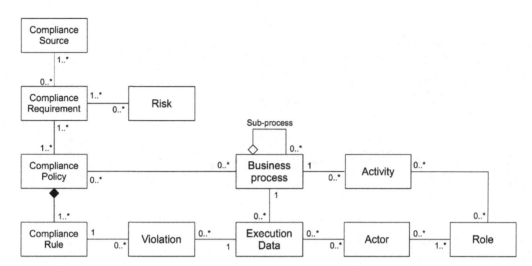

mitigated. For example, a non-encrypted message that is sent through the network might violate a security compliance rule, which, in turn, might put at risk sensitive information. Risk mitigation is the actual driver for internal compliance auditing. The *Risk* entity represents the risks a company wants to monitor; risks are associated with compliance requirements. For the evaluation of whether business is executed in a compliant way or not, we must know which rules must be evaluated in which business context. We therefore assume that we can associate policies with specific *business processes* (though this can easily be generalized to the case of projects, products, and similar). Processes are composed of *activities*, which represent the atomic work items in a process.

The actual evaluation of compliance rules is not performed on business processes (that is, on their models) but on their concrete executions, i.e., their instances. Executing a business process means performing activities, invoking services, and tracking progression events and produced business data (captured by the *Execution data* entity). In addition, e.g., separation of duties, it is necessary to track the *actors* and *roles* of execution of activities. When the evaluation of a rule for a process/activity instance is negative,

it corresponds to *violations*, which are the core for the assessment of the level of compliance of a company.

The model in Figure 2 puts into context the most important concepts auditors are interested in when auditing a company. The actual auditing process, then, also looks at the dynamic aspect of the compliance management problem, that is, at how the company decides which compliance sources are pertaining, how it implements its business processes, how it checks for violations, and so on. In short, the auditing process is embedded in a so-called compliance management life cycle, which we discuss next.

THE COMPLIANCE MANAGEMENT LIFE CYCLE

In everyday business, a company is subject to a variety of different compliance sources. It is up to the company to understand, select, and "internalize" them that affect its business, thus producing a set of internal policies (*internalization* phase in Figure 3). The latter then drive the design of the company's business practices, yielding a set of business processes that are possibly designed

Figure 3. The compliance management life cycle with phases, products, and actors

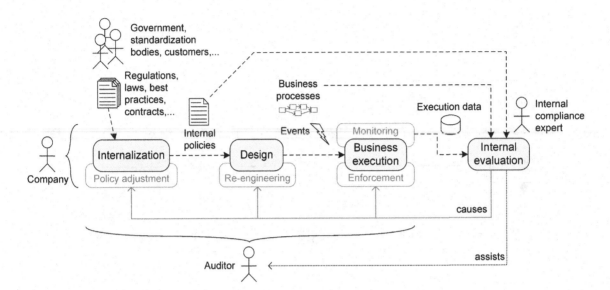

compliantly (*design* phase), meaning that they are designed to respect the internal policies. To provide evidence of the (hopefully) compliant execution of designed business processes, the company also defines a set of events, often also called "controls" or "control points".

Process and event definitions are consumed in the business execution phase, where the company's employees perform the tasks and duties specified in the process models. Ideally (but not mandatorily), this execution is assisted by software tools such as workflow management or business process execution systems, also able to collect compliance-specific evidence and to generate respective execution events (the execution data), which can be stored in an audit trail or log file for evaluation.

The *internal evaluation* phase serves a twofold purpose: First, it is the point where collected data can be automatically analyzed to detect compliance violations. Indeed, designing compliant processes is not enough to assure compliance, as in practice there are a multitude of reasons for which deviations from an expected business process might happen (e.g., human factors, system downtimes).

Some of such problems can be detected during runtime, resulting in the generation of respective events; some of them can only be detected after execution by means of, e.g., data mining or root cause analysis techniques applied to tracked runtime data. Second, the internal evaluation is the moment where a company-internal expert (auditor) may inspect and interpret the tracked evidence to assess the company's level of compliance. The outcome of this internal evaluation might be the enforcement of corrective runtime actions (e.g., sending an alert), the re-engineering of process designs (e.g., to consider design flaws) or the adjustment of the internal policies (e.g., to cope with inconsistent policies).

Note that the internal evaluation does not yet certify a company's level of compliance; it rather represents an internal control mechanism by means of which the company is able to self-assess and govern its business. For the certification of compliance, an external auditor, e.g., a financial auditor, physically visits the company and controls whether (1) the company has correctly interpreted the existing regulations, (2) business processes have been correctly implemented, and, finally, (3) business processes have been executed according to the policies. In practice, external audits are based on statistical checks of physical documents. In addition to unavoidable statistical errors, a certified level of compliance is further subject to the auditor's assessment and, therefore, also contains a subjective component.

REPORTING ON COMPLIANCE

To aid the internal evaluation and to help a company pass external audits, a concise and intuitive visualization of its compliance state is paramount. To report on compliance, we advocate the use of web-based CGDs, whose good design is not trivial (Few 2006, Read et al. 2009). For example, in order to provide useful dashboards it is important to understand and solve complex issues like: (1) what the typical information auditors expect to find is; (2) how large amounts of data can be visualized in an effective manner, and how data can be meaningfully grouped and summarized; and (3) how to structure the available information into multiple pages, that is, how to interactively and intuitively guide the user through the wealth of information. Each page of the dashboard should be

concise and intuitive, yet complete and expressive. It is important that users are immediately able to identify the key information in a page, but that there are also facilities to drill-down into (i.e., ask for more) details.

Designing CGDs requires mastering some new concepts in addition to those discussed above. Then, the new concepts must be equipped with a well-thought navigation structure to effectively convey the necessary information. Here, we do not focus on how data are stored and how rules are evaluated; several proposals and approaches have been conceived so far for that (see the Related Work Section), and we build on top of them.

A Conceptual Model for CGDs

In Figure 4 we extend the conceptual model (Figure 2) to capture the necessary constructs for the development of a CGD (bold lines and labels represent new entities and their respective inter-relations). The extensions aim at (1) providing different *analysis perspectives* (in terms of time, user roles, and organizational structures), (2) *summarizing* data at different levels of abstraction, and (3) enabling drill-down/roll-up features (from aggregated data to detailed data, and vice versa).

Figure 4. Conceptual model of the CGD

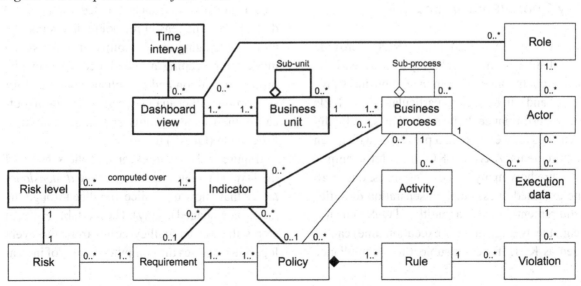

The *Dashboard view* entity represents individual views over the compliance status of the company. A view is characterized by the user role that accesses it, e.g., IT specialists, compliance experts, managers, or similar. Each of these roles has different needs and rights. For instance, managers are more interested in aggregated values, risk levels, and long time horizons (to take business decisions); IT personnel are rather interested in instance-level data and short time spans (to fix violations). A view is further characterized by the *time interval* considered for the visualization of data (e.g., day, week, month, or year), also providing for the historical analysis (e.g., last year) and supporting different reporting purposes (operative, tactical, strategic). Finally, a view might be restricted to only some of the *business units* in the company, based on the role of the user. Business units can be composed by other business units, forming a hierarchical organizational structure. In summary, views support different summarization levels of the overall available data, ranging over multiple granularity levels.

The described model extension aims at relating general compliance concepts with concepts that are specific to the design of dashboards. The model is general and extensible, so as to allow for the necessary flexibility to accommodate multiple concrete compliance scenarios.

Key Compliance Indicators

Key Compliance Indicators (KCIs) provide compliance experts with highly aggregated view on the compliance performance of business processes and can be seen as particular type of KPIs (Key Performance Indicators) that specifically measures how compliant a process is with given requirements. A typical KCI may, for example, measure how many process instances, out of all the executed ones, satisfy a separation of duties requirement; but also a traditional QoS indicator (e.g., the average process execution time) can be seen as KCI, if we are subject to a compliance

requirement regarding QoS (e.g., deriving from a contract with the customer). As we will see, KCIs also provide a starting point for finding the root causes of non-compliance.

The main sources of process execution and compliance data are the *event logs* generated by the execution of service-based business processes. Therefore, let us first conceptualize the key ingredients characterizing event logs, as we perceive them for our analysis. An *event* is a tuple $e = <t, s, ts, d, p_1, ..., p_n, B>$, where t is the type of the event (e.g., *ProcessStart, ActivityExecuted, Violation*), s is the source that generates the event, ts is a timestamp, $p_1, ..., p_n$ is a set of properties (e.g., event message header properties such as correlation data, process instance identifier or similar), and B is the body of the event message (e.g., containing business data needed for the computation of an indicator). Using this data, events can be grouped together by their process instance and ordered by timestamp, forming this way traces. A *trace* is a sequence of events $T_i = <e_{i1}, e_{i2}, ..., e_{in}>$, where i refers to a process instance identifier and n is the number of events that compose the process instance. This way, an *event log* can be expressed as a set of traces $L = \{T_1, T_2, ..., T_k\}$, where k is the total number of traces.

The events in the log are processed by Extract-Transform-Load (ETL) flows, in order to store them into a data warehouse (DW), which is modeled using a compliance-oriented dimensional data model. The reason for doing this is that we aim at leveraging the capability of dimensional models for keeping a conciliated view on the process execution and compliance data, and for supporting further analysis, e.g., by means of root-cause analysis algorithms or Online Analytical Processing (OLAP) tools.

Figure 5 shows an excerpt of the schema of the DW. The tables in white are the *dimensional tables* that allow us to slice and dice through the *fact tables* (shaded in gray). The fact table F_Event stores the events as they come from the event log, F_KCI stores the computed values of indica-

Figure 5. *Simplified schema of the data warehouse model*

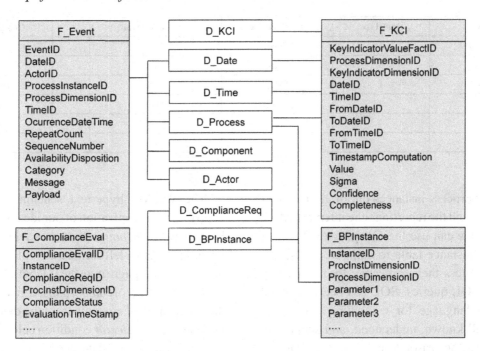

tors, F_BPInstance, the instances of processes, and F_ComplianceEval, the compliance status of process instances as computed, for instance, by the compliance checking algorithms adopted in the context of the EU projects COMPAS[1] or MASTER[2].

The F_BPInstance table deserves a further explanation, as it constitutes an *abstraction* of the process execution data, and the basis for computing indicators and performing root-cause analysis. In our DW model, each business process *BP* has its own F_BPInstance table, or, as we call it, *process instance table* (e.g., in our scenario we have a F_DrugDispensationInstance table that corresponds to the drug dispensation process of the hospital). In these tables, each row corresponds to an instance of the associated process, while columns (i.e., parameters of the process instance table) correspond to business data that are of interest for the analysis of each process.

Table 1 shows a conceptual view on the process instance table for the drug dispensation process, where each row corresponds to a single drug dispensation. The *DrugType* column refers to the

type of drug, *ErrPerData* indicates whether there was an error in the information about the patient, *ErrCompData* tells us if there was an error in any other complementary data, and *Compliant* tells us whether the dispensation was free of error. These parameters are obtained from the attributes of the events that are part of the event trace. Sometimes, the parameter values can be directly extracted from events without modifications (e.g., the *DrugType* parameter), while in other cases the values are obtained by performing aggregation/computations over a set of events and attributes of process instances (e.g., the *Compliant* parameter).

Finally, it is worth to mention that in order to populate the DW, the ETL usually needs to access other sources of data such as user management systems and human task managers (e.g., to fill the table D_Actor in Figure 5), which are the main data providers for dimension tables, as opposed to event logs, which provide mostly the evidences of process executions.

KCIs can be easily specified by using the available information in Table 1. For example, a KCI may be defined as the percentage of non-

Table 1. Example of a process instance table for the drug dispensation process

InstanceID	DrugType	ErrPerData	ErrCompData	...	Compliant
38769	**1**	**False**	**False**	**...**	**True**
32537	6	True	False	...	False
27657	1	False	False	...	True
32547	2	False	True	...	False
35340	1	False	False	...	True
....	....	....	....	...	....

compliant process instances out of all instances in the DW (and the reporting time interval). More precisely, we can use the *Compliant* column of a process instance table to compute KCIs, and we can express their respective formulas using standard SQL queries. SQL has been designed also as a language for computing aggregates and is well known, understood, and supported, so there was no reason to come up with another language. Yet, the ease with which we are able to express KCIs stems from the abstraction we made on the process execution data by using the so called process instance tables.

Navigation Design

We now focus on the *dynamic* aspect of the dashboard, i.e., on how to structure the interaction of users with the dashboard, and on how users can explore the data underlying the dashboard application. Specifically, on top of the conceptual model for CGDs, we now describe how complex data can be organized into hypertext pages and which navigation paths are important.

For this purpose, we adopt the Web Modeling Language (WebML) (Ceri et al. 2002), a conceptual modeling notation and methodology for the development of data-intensive web applications. We use the language for the purpose of illustration only (we show a simplified, not executable WebML schema) and intuitively introduce all the necessary constructs along with the description of the navigation structure.

The WebML hypertext schema (Figure 6) describes the organization of our ideal web CGD. It consists of five *pages* (the boxes with the name labels in the upper left corner), Compliance Home being the home page (note the H label). Each page contains a number of *content units*, which represent the publication of contents from the data schema in Figure 5 (the *selector* condition below the units indicates the source data entity). Usually, there are many *hyperlinks* (the arrows) in a hypertext schema, representing the possible navigations a user might perform, but for simplicity, we limit our explanation to only those links that represent the main navigation flow. Links carry *parameters*, which represent the selection performed by the user when activating a link (e.g., the selection of a process from a list). For the purpose of reporting on compliance, we define a new content unit (not part of the WebML), the *compliance drill-down* unit, which allows us to comfortably show compliance data in a table-like structure (see the legend in Figure 6 and the examples in Figure 7).

Let's examine the CGD's structure (Figure 6): The home page of the CGD provides insight into the compliance state of the company at a glance. It shows the set of most important indicators (Main indicators *multidata* unit) and a set of indicators grouped by their policy (IndByPolicy *hierarchical index* unit). Then, we show the (BUnits/C. Sour.) unit that allows the user to drill-down from business units to processes and from compliance sources to policies. A click on one of: (1) the processes lead the user to the ComplianceSourc-

Figure 6. WebML hypertext schema structuring the navigation of CGD concepts and data

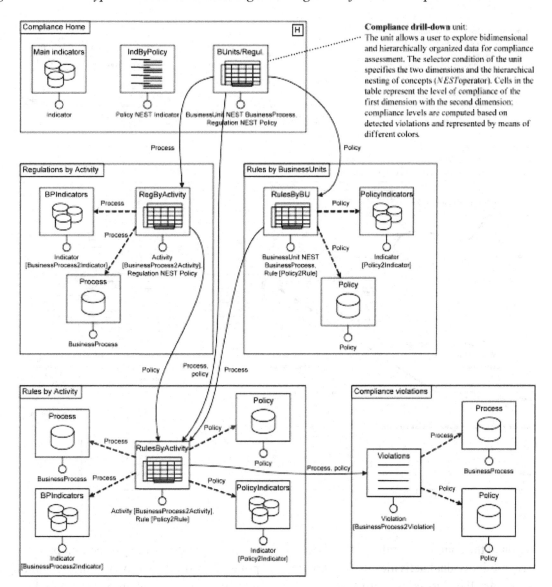

es by Activity page; (2) compliance source leads her to the ComplianceRules by BusinessUnits page; and (3) the cell of the table leads her to the ComplianceRules by Activity page. After the selection of a process, in the ComplianceSources by Activity page the user can inspect the compliance state of each activity of the selected process with the given compliance sources and policies (CSourByActivity), a set of related indicators (BPIndicators unit; the unit consumes the Process parameter), and the details of the selected process

(Process *data* unit). Similar details are shown for policies in the ComplianceRules by BusinessUnits page, which allows the user to inspect the satisfaction of individual compliance rules at business unit or process level (ComplianceRulesByBU). A further selection in the compliance drill-down units in these last two pages or the selection of a cell in the BUnits/C.Sour unit in the home page leads the user to the ComplianceRules by Activity page, which provides the user with the lowest level of aggregated information. It visualizes the

Figure 7. Example CGD screenshots of our prototype implementation

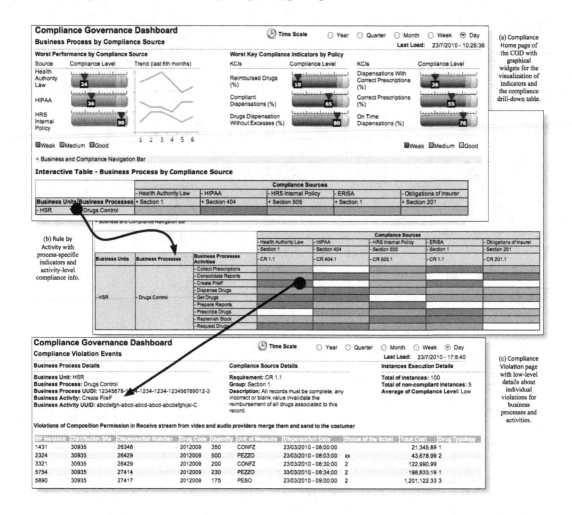

satisfaction of the compliance rules of the chosen policy by the individual activities of the chosen process (ComplianceRulesByActivity), along with the details of the chosen policy and process and their respective indicators. A further selection in this page leads the user to the Compliance Rule Violations page, which shows the details of the violations related to the chosen process/policy combination at an instance level in the Compliance Rule Violations *index* unit.

The navigation structure in Figure 6 shows one of the possible views over the data in Figure 5, e.g., the one of the internal compliance expert. Other views can easily be added. Each page provides a different level of summarization (overview,

process-specific, policy-specific, process- and policy-specific, violation instances), guiding the user from high-level information to low-level details. The time interval to be considered for the visualization can be chosen in each of the pages.

CGDs in Practice

Figure 7 illustrates some screenshots from our prototype CGD. The screenshots show views that clarify and consistently present our ideal CGD. Figure 7(a) shows the Compliance Home page (Figure 6), Figure 7(b) the Rules by Activity page, and Figure 7(c) the Compliance violations page.

Compliance Home concentrates on the most important information at a glance, condensed into just one page (compare with Figure 7). It represents the highest granularity of information. The three colored indicators (top left) are the most relevant, showing the most critical non-compliant compliance sources. The gray indicators (right) report on the compliance with KCIs. In the bottom, there is the interactive compliance drill-down table containing the compliance performance of business units and processes (rows) in relation to compliance sources and policies (columns). The user can easily reach lower levels of granularity by drilling down on the table or navigating to pages. For instance, the Rules by Activity page condenses lower level information concerning all the activities of the Drugs Control business process and the compliance requirements of all compliance sources adopted by the hospital. The colors of the cells represent the compliance performance of each combination. For instance, the Create FileF business activity presents a critical situation regarding the compliance requirement CR 1.1 of the Healthy Authority Law (red cell) and weak performance regarding CR 505.1 (yellow cells). Due to size and visibility constrains each compliance source contains just one policy and compliance requirement, however the real implementation uses more than this.

A drill-down on the red cell, for instance, leads us to the Compliance violations page, which provides the lowest level of abstraction in form of a table of concrete, registered violations of the selected compliance requirement. The page illustrates the main information that must be reported to assist internal and external auditors. The data in the particular page reports all violations of the Create FileF activity in Drugs Control business process of the HSR business unit, detected considering CR 1.1 of the Healthy Authority Law - Section 1. Each row of the table represents a distinct violation and the columns contain the typical information required by auditors, e.g., business process instance, distribution site, dispensation number, drug code, quantity, unit of measure, dispensation date, status of the ticket, total cost, and drug typology.

The amount and position of the graphical widgets for indicators, tables, summaries, and other visual metaphors are chosen in accordance with our short-term memory and the convention of most western languages that are read from left to right and from top to bottom (Few 2006).

ANALYZING NON-COMPLIANCE

While *checking* the compliance of business process instances means determining whether the process instances are compliant or not at the individual event trace level, *analyzing* non-compliance of business process executions, i.e., understanding and explaining the underlying reasons of non-compliance, needs to be performed over a set of traces in order to be able to derive meaningful knowledge that can be used to improve processes for future executions.

Incidentally, labeling event traces as compliant or non-compliant, which is the main goal of compliance checking, is very similar to *classifying* data tuples, a data mining practice that is well-studied in literature (Grigori et al., 2004). There are several algorithms that can help in performing this analysis, among which we choose decision trees, as they are good for knowledge discovery where neither complex settings nor assumptions are required (Grigori et al., 2004), and they are easy to interpret and analyze. In this section, we discuss how we address the issue of compliance analysis through decision trees, going from data preparation to the actual building and interpretation of the decision tree.

Preparing the Analysis

In the previous section, we introduced our DW model, which constitutes the basis for our CGD and the root cause analysis. Preparing the analysis therefore means selecting which data, out of the huge amount of events stored in the DW, are suitable for identifying root causes for non-compliance. We also introduced the idea of having process instance tables, one per process, in which we store those process parameters that are used for computing indicators. Recall that each tuple in a process instance table represents a particular instantiation of the process under consideration and that each instance comes with its compliance label. Now, considering that we are interested in analyzing non-compliance problems for process instances, it is interesting to note that the process instance tables initially conceived for the computation of indicators also contain the data we are searching for. In fact, by defining a set of indicators for each process (and the events and data attributes that are necessary to compute them), the compliance expert implicitly performs a pre-selection of the data that are most likely to be related with compliance issues. The availability of the compliance label for each instance indicates that the best choice for the root cause analysis is to use the process instance tables to feed the decision tree mining algorithm, as their data naturally fits the typical input format of these kinds of algorithms.

For instance, considering again the process instance table shown in Table 1, one way of building the training tuples for the decision tree is to use the *Compliant* column as the *class attribute* (leaf nodes) for the decision tree, while *ErrPerData* and *ErrCompData* can be used as the attributes on which the algorithm defines the split points (for internal nodes). This way, the training tuples can be represented as,

<ErrPerData, ErrCompData, **Compliant**>

The set of training tuples can be easily obtained through trivial SQL queries, and the retrieved result set can be used directly to feed the decision tree algorithm. Note that, as in the case of the specification and computation of the KCIs,

the task of building the training tuples is greatly facilitated by the abstraction provided by the process instance tables.

Understanding Key Factors

The algorithm we use in our prototype implementation for building decision trees is J48 (a Java implementation of the C4.5 algorithm) (Witten & Frank, 2005), one of the algorithms that comes with the Weka library (Hall et. al.,), which we use for our implementation.

As in any decision tree, the internal nodes contain the criteria used for classifying tuples. The leaf nodes, instead, contain the classes to which tuples are classified. For instance, if we choose the *Compliant* column of Table 1 as the class attribute, we will obtain a decision tree where the leaf nodes contain the *compliance outcomes* for the paths drawn from the root of the tree. However, nothing prevents us from choosing any other parameter of the process instance table as the class attribute when searching for the root causes of non-compliant process executions.

For instance, as part of the validation of this approach, we performed experiments on a dataset of more than 30000 drug dispensations performed between January and April of 2009 in the hospital described in the Scenario section. To this end, a process instance table with around 25 relevant parameters was build for the drug dispensation process, among which the parameters shown in Table 1 were included. Since the dependence of the *Compliance* column on the *ErrPerData* and *ErrCompData* columns was fairly obvious (but still, proven with our tools), we narrowed our analysis by considering only those process instances that were not compliant. After exploring some combinations of parameters, we found out that there was a relation between the *ErrCompData* and *DrugType* parameters. More precisely, we found that 393 drugs dispensations out of around 30000 had some error, among which 173 had errors of the type *ErrCompData* and 220 errors of the type *ErrPerData*. While the decision tree was not able to tell us anything that was really significant about errors of the type *ErrPerData*, it was able to find something useful for the errors of the type *ErrCompData*, as shown in Figure 8. More precisely, the decision tree discovered that 137 out of 173 (79%) erroneous process instances corresponded to drugs of the type 2 (DrugType=2), which are drugs for ambulatory usage, while the rest (21%) corresponded to drugs of the type 6, 9 and 11.

Since the *ErrCompData* refers to error in the dispensation data (such as the drug code, quantity and unitary price), this may be an indication that, for example, this type of drugs is dispensed at ease, and thus, a better monitoring or compliance enforcement need to be carried out on the controls related to this compliance requirement.

Predicting Compliance States

While decision trees are generally perceived as simple classifiers, we however use them rather for discovering and understanding better the root causes of undesirable behaviors. Furthermore, we advocate the use of decision trees also for predicting the potential outcomes of process instances that are still running. In fact, each decision point in a tree corresponds to an event (or better to an attribute of an event). So, if during process execution an event that corresponds to a decision point is generated, this allows performing predictions on the likely outcome (in terms of compliance) of the process instance: it suffices to inspect the path in the tree determined by the registered event to identify the instances' likely compliance label.

Figure 8. Decision tree computed over instances of the drug dispensation process

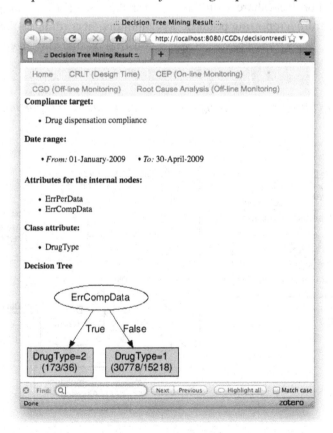

Thus, in the case of predictions of non-compliant behaviors, enforcement actions can be enacted in order to align process executions, whenever possible, to the corresponding compliance requirements. This is particularly useful in cases when the process has several tasks and long running times that span, e.g., over several hours. Also, the prediction is particularly useful in the case compliance is enforced manually, because it allows the compliance expert to better focus his effort on those process instances that are likely to be non-compliant, leaving out compliance ones.

IMPLEMENTATION

The above described concepts are a joint result of the Compas and Master projects, which involve Deloitte and PricewaterhouseCoopers as industrial and auditing partners and who participated in the design of the user interfaces and validated the design models. Both projects share a similar functional architecture from a reporting point of view (Figure 9).

Figure 9 depicts such architecture, in which events are emitted and published, during business process execution, on an Enterprise Service Bus (ESB), then stored in an Event Log to be Extracted, Transformed, and Loaded (ETL) in the DW. After that, compliance assessment routines are executed over the registered data in order to assess the compliance of the tracked event traces and to calculate KCIs. Finally, the CGD and the Root Cause Analysis components access the DW in order to retrieve the relevant compliance performance information to be showed to compliance experts and internal/external auditors. The CGD is set on the top of the DW (optimized for reporting purposes) that implements the data schema depicted in Figure 5. Although the navigation structure described in Figure 6 has been developed on top of the conceptual data model in Figure 4, implementing the CGD on top of the DW does not affect the logic behind the conceived navigation structure, which represents a best practice for the rendering of compliance information to auditors, according to the experience of the industrial partners involved in the projects.

Figure 9. Functional architecture for logging business executions and reporting on compliance

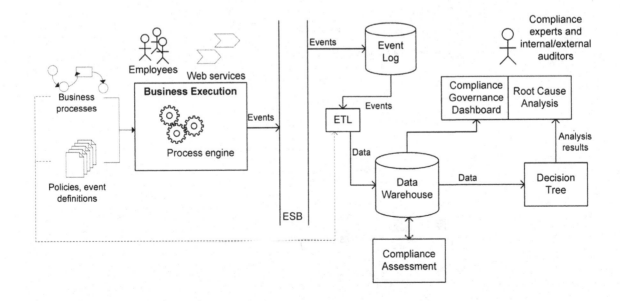

Figure 10. Web applications involving the implementation of the CGD

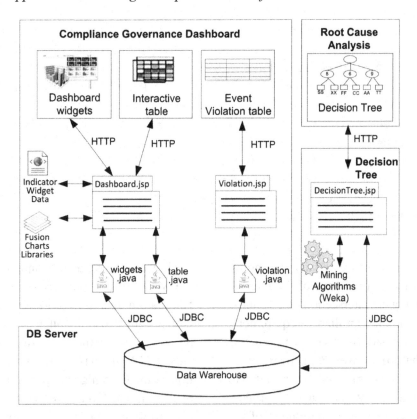

The front-end of the CGD is an interactive web application implemented according to Figure 10 and composed of JSP pages. *Dashboard.jsp* is responsible for loading the dashboard widgets and the interactive table as illustrated in Figure 7(a) and 7(b). Each time this page is loaded, i.e., at the first access or when a new time scale is selected, it invokes the *widgets.java* class, which runs a set of pre-defined, parameterized SQL queries over the DW, filled with variable input parameters (e.g., time scale and business level) representing user selections. Exhibit 1, for example, shows a typical query used to retrieve the necessary data to render indicators in their colorful or gray UI widgets. These graphical representations of indicators are implemented using Fusion Widgets V3 (www. fusioncharts.com) flash libraries, which require XML files as input (*Indicator Widget Data*) and

render their content into HTML divisions (<div>) of the dashboard page.

When loading the dashboard into the client browser, also the content of the interactive table is updated according to the same parameters and the functions contained in *table.java*. In addition, the rows of the interactive table are also refreshed when a new business or compliance perspective is selected, e.g., via a mouse click. This table is fed with the DW data based on two SQL queries, one that brings all the data associated with business process and the other with business process activities. In both cases, the results of the query are locally stored on the client side as hash table objects, which allow us to dynamically show or hide their content in an HTML table according to the selected business and compliance perspectives.

The *Violation.jsp* page shows the lowest level information (events) and can be accessed through

Exhibit 1. Percentage of non-compliance for a given sources in a pre-defined time interval

```
SELECT Req.Source_Name AS Name,
       ROUND(100*(Count(*)-Sum(Proc_Inst.CausedViolation))/Count(*)) AS Value
FROM D_Date, F_BPInstance Proc_Inst
INNER JOIN F_ComplianceEvaluation Evaluation ON Proc_Inst.BPInstance_Key =
Evaluation.BPExecutionKey
JOIN D_ComplianceRequirement Req ON Req.ComplianceRequirement_Key = Evalua-
tion.ComplianceRequirement_Key
WHERE(D_Date.Calendar_Date_Key = Evaluation.Calendar_Date_Key) AND        (D_
Date.System_Date >= to_date('startDate', 'DD/MM/YYYY')) AND (D_Date.System_
Date < (to_date('endDate', 'DD/MM/YYYY')+1))
GROUP BY Req.Source_Name ORDER BY Value ASC;
```

the interactive table, more specifically via a mouse click on one of the colored cells of the interactive table rendering the intersection of a business process activity and a compliance requirement. White cells correspond to activity-requirements combinations that do not have compliance requirements to be checked, thus no events associated to them are stored in the DW. The business process activity and the compliance requirement of the clicked cell are passed as parameters to the classes of the *violation.java* class that connects to the DW and retrieves the respective events. Similar to the previous approach, the *Violation.jsp* file also adopts an SQL query as depicted in Exhibit 2.

The *decision tree* page guides the user in the process of decision tree mining for root cause analysis and prediction. In this process, the page helps users in choosing the parameters of interest for building the decision tree. More precisely, it helps users in selecting the attributes for the internal nodes, the class attributes to which tuples will be classified, the time range used for filtering process instances, among other parameters of the algorithm used for the mining task. Once these parameters have been selected, *DecTree.jsp* processes the instances from the process instance table (stored in the DW) in order to prepare the training tuples that will be used to feed the mining algorithm. The concrete algorithm used for building the decision tree is J48 and we rely on Weka

(Hall et. al. 2009) as the supporting library for the whole mining process as it is a well-known and mature data mining library. Note, however, that we can choose any other decision tree mining algorithm among the ones available in Weka. We choose J48, which is an open source implementation of the C4.5 algorithm, due to its popularity and the fact that this is a well-understood algorithm for building decision trees. In addition, it is equipped with features such as continuous number categorization and missing value handling, which are key features when doing classification on data coming from realistic settings.

All pages of the CGD were developed using Eclipse Java EE IDE for Web Developers, and the DW runs on Oracle 11g. An example of the CGD web portal as used in the Compas project is available at http://compas.disi.unitn.it:8080/CGDs/main.jsp selecting the CGD tab. From the same start page it is also possible to access the decision tree component by selecting the Root Cause Analysis tab.

RELATED WORK

Compliance has been investigated in several contexts yielding a variety of approaches. In the following, we discuss related work in four areas that fall in the context of this paper, namely,

Exhibit 2. SQL query used to retrieve all the low-level events associated to a specific compliance requirement and business process activity

```
SELECT
    eb.BPInstance_Key,
    e.BPActivityExecutionKey,
    bpe.EventKey,
    bpe.EventType,
    bpe.BEvent_Source,
    to_char(dd.System_Date, 'YYYY/MM/DD HH:mm:ss') AS EventTimestamp
FROM F_ComplianceEvaluation e JOIN B_BusinessEventBridge eb
    ON e.BPActivityExecutionKey = eb.BPActivityInstance_Key AND
        e.BPExecutionKey = eb.BPInstance_Key
                            JOIN D_Date dd
    ON dd.Calendar_Date_Key = e.Calendar_Date_Key
                            JOIN F_Event bpe
    ON bpe.eventKey = eb.BEvent_Key
WHERE
bpe.eventType != 'ComplianceViolationEvent' AND
e.BP_Key = 'BP_Key' _ AND
e.BPActivity_Key = 'BPActivity_Key' AND
e.ComplianceRequirement_Key = 'CompReqKey' AND
NVL(e.ServiceInstance_Key, 0) = NVL(eb.ServiceInstance_Key, 0 AND
e.IsViolation = 1 AND
dd.System_Date >= to_date('startDate','DD/MM/YYYY') AND
dd.System_Date < (to_date('endDate', 'DD/MM/YYYY')+1)
```

compliance modeling, compliance dashboards, Business Activity Monitoring (BAM), and data mining techniques.

Most of the compliance modeling efforts have been done with the aim of checking compliance at design time, and, therefore, the resulting models consist in formalisms for expressing low-level rules for the compliance requirements (Awad & Weske, 2009), (Liu et al., 2007), (Lu et al., 2007). Typically, they are based on formal languages to express compliance requirements (e.g., Business Property Specification Language, Linear Temporal Logic) and simulations to prevent errors at runtime (e.g., finite state machine, Petri nets). For instance, in Liu et al. 2007 the problem of static (i.e., before process execution) compliance checking of process models against compliance rules is addressed by expressing the models in pi-calculus and the corresponding rules in linear temporal logic; then, model checking techniques are used to determine whether a process model complies with the rules or not. In Brunel et al. 2007, policies are modeled and checked as deontic sentences (i.e., rules are of the form *"it is obligatory that X..."* or *"it is permitted that Y..."*); then, a system can be compliant even if violations occur, in which case, a second-level set of rules might be applied, for which, again, compliance needs to be checked. A similar modeling technique is presented in Saqid et al. 2007, in which Format Contract Language (FCL), a combination of defeasible logic and deontic logic, is used to express normative specifications. Once the FCL specification is built, control tags can be derived from it and used to annotate the process model so that control concerns can be visualized in the process model space. In this context, just few approaches address *compliance monitoring at runtime*. For instance, Trinh et al. 2009 monitor time constraints during the execution of process activities, using UML Timing Diagrams to specify constraints and Aspect Oriented Programming to control executions. Chung et al. 2008 check if the user-defined process is compliant to pre-defined ontology and a specific model, in which compliance requirements are described. An IBM research group (Giblin et al., 2006) advocates the use of the REALM (Regulations Expressed As Logical Models) metamodel to define temporal compliance rules and the Active Correlation Technology to check them. That way, it can detect duplicate events or compute a user-definable function, which checks whether a function exceeds some threshold.

To the best of our knowledge, there are no works on dashboards that specifically address the problem of visualizing compliance concerns. However, there are some works that, in part, deal with the problems we address in this paper. For example, Bellamy et al. 2007 studies the problem of designing visualizations (i.e., the representation of data through visual languages) for risk and compliance management. Specifically, the study is focused on capturing the exact information required by users and on providing visual metaphors for satisfying those requirements. In Chowdhary et al 2006, the business performance reporting is provided in a model-driven fashion. The framework provides: data model, navigation model, report template model, and access control model, which jointly help designing a business performance dashboard. However, none of mentioned approaches provides suitable navigation models supporting different analysis perspectives, summarization levels, and user roles.

Business Activity Monitoring (BAM) has gained a lot of attention during the last decade, and many tools have been proposed to support it

(e.g., IBM Tivoli, HP Business Availability Center, Nimbus, Oracle Business Activity Monitoring). BAM aims at providing aggregated information suitable for performing various types of analysis on data obtained from the execution of activities inside a business. For example, tools such as Oracle BAM, Nimbus and IBM Tivoli aim at providing its users with real-time visual information and alerts based on business events in a SOA environment. The information provided to users comes in the form of dashboards for reporting on KPIs and SLA violations. The compliance management part of these tools (if any) comes in the form of monitoring of SLA violations, which need the SLA formal specifications as one of its inputs. In our work, we take a more general view on compliance (beyond SLAs, which are a special case to us) and cover the whole lifecycle of compliance governance, including a suitable dashboard for reporting purposes. Although, such tools still do not have the capability to process and interpret *generic events* (e.g., user-defined business or compliance-related events). They only support the definition of thresholds for parameters or SLAs to be monitored. Also, the ability to *compare* monitored business process executions or, more in general, business patterns with expected execution behaviors is not supported.

According to our expertise no *data mining approaches* have been specifically proposed to understand the root cause of the compliance violations. However, few related approaches for the mining of business processes are in place (Rozinat & Aalst, 2009), (Grigori et al., 2004), (Seol et al., 2007), (Grigori et al., 2001), (Apte et al., 2001), and (Bibelnieks & Campbell, 2000). Similar to our solution, they adopted log files and a consolidated warehouse containing business and process historical data, from where data subsets are extracted and used as input to mining algorithms in order to predict or understand the origin of undesired business process execution behaviors.

It is important to notice that we do not provide any new compliance checking technique; we rather focus on how to make the most of existing approaches by putting on top of them a visualization logic that is validated by auditors themselves, an aspect that is at least as important as checking compliance. As this paper has its roots in two EU FP7 research projects, i.e., Compas and Master, for the assessment of compliance and the identification of individual violations we rely on the techniques proposed there: *Compas* (www.compas-ict.eu) strongly focuses on model-driven development of compliant processes and proposes a compliance checking approach that is based on (1) compliance requirements expressed in logical rules or process fragments and (2) complex event processing (CEP) and business protocol monitoring to detect non-compliance with requirements. *Master* (www.master-fp7.eu), instead, specifically focuses on the security domain and proposes a two-layered approach to compliance assessment: first, it supports the CEP-based monitoring of running processes and the enforcement of individual rules; then, offline, it checks compliance of executed processes by assessing their conformance to a so-called ideal process model. Both approaches have in common the use of an instrumented service orchestration engine for the execution of business processes and the generation/logging of suitable execution events, starting from a signaling policy that specifies which events are necessary for compliance assessment.

Our work mainly focuses on the case of compliance and provides a conceptual and data model for both compliance and dashboards, i.e., we present the relevant concepts regarding compliance and visualization and show the interplay of these two aspects. The purpose is that of providing compliance dashboard designers with a holistic and comprehensive view of the business and compliance aspects that characterized a good CGD, as well as root cause analysis techniques to discover the reason of non-compliance behaviors.

CONCLUSION AND FUTURE RESEARCH DIRECTIONS

In this chapter we have discussed a relevant aspect in modern business software systems, i.e., compliance governance. Increasingly, both industry and academia are investing money and efforts into the development of compliance governance solutions. Yet, we believe compliance governance dashboards in particular, probably the most effective means for visualizing and reporting on compliance, have mostly been neglected so far. It is important to implement sophisticated solutions to check compliance, but it is at least as important (if not even more) to effectively convey the results of the compliance checks to a variety of different actors, ranging from IT specialists to senior managers.

Our contribution is a conceptualization of the issues involved in the design of compliance governance dashboards in service- and process-centric systems, the definition of a navigation structure that naturally supports drill-down and roll-up features at adequate levels of detail and complexity, a decision tree tool to discover the root cause of non-compliance behaviors, and a set of concrete examples that demonstrate the concepts at work. Our aim was to devise a solution with in mind the real needs of auditors (internal and external ones) and – more importantly – with the help of people who are indeed involved every day in the auditing of companies.

As a continuation of this work, we are planning to perform extensive usage studies in the context of the projects mentioned earlier. First, such studies will allow us to assess the acceptance of the proposed CGD by auditors in their everyday work. Second, the studies will allow us to understand which support for actions for mitigating compliance problems or violations directly through the dashboard is desirable.

REFERENCES

Apte, C., Bibelnieks, E., Natarajan, R., Pednault, E., Tipu, F., Campbell, D., & Nelson, B. (2001). Segmentation-based modeling for advanced targeted marketing. In the 7th ACM SIGKDD International Conference on Knowledge Discovery and Data Mining (pp. 408-413). New York, NY: ACM.

Awad, A., & Weske, M. (2009). Visualization of compliance violation in business process models. In *5th International Workshop on Business Process Intelligence BPI 09, vol. 43* (pp. 182-193).

Bellamy, R., Erickson, T., Fuller, B., Kellogg, W., Rosenbaum, R., Thomas, J., & Vetting Wolf, T. (2007). Seeing is believing: Designing visualizations for managing risk and compliance. *IBM Systems Journal, 46*(2), 205–218. doi:10.1147/sj.462.0205

Bibelnieks, E., & Campbell, D. (2000). Mail stream streamlining. *Catalog Age, 17*(12), 118–120.

Brunel, J., Cuppens, F., Cuppens-Boulahia, N., Sans, T., & Bodeveix, J. (2007). Security policy com-pliance with violation management. In *2007 ACM Workshop on Formal Methods in Security Engineering* (pp. 31-40).

Cannon, J., & Byers, M. (2006). Compliance deconstructed. *ACM Queue; Tomorrow's Computing Today, 4*(7), 30–37. doi:10.1145/1160434.1160449

Ceri, S., Fraternali, P., Bongio, A., Brambilla, M., Comai, S., & Matera, M. (Eds.). (2002). *Designing data-intensive Web applications*. USA: Morgan Kaufmann Publishers Inc.

Chowdhary, P., Palpanas, T., Pinel, F., Chen, S.-K., & Wu, F. Y. (2006). Model-driven dashboards for business performance reporting. In the *10th IEEE International Enterprise Distributed Object Computing Conference*, (pp. 374-386).

Chung, P., Cheung, L., & Machin, C. (2008). Compliance flow - Managing the compliance of dynamic and complex processes. *Knowledge-Based Systems, 21*(4), 332–354. doi:10.1016/j.knosys.2007.11.002

Daniel, F., D'Andrea, V., Strauch, S., Schumm, D., Leymann, F., & Mulo, E. … Hacid, M. (2009). Business compliance governance in service-oriented architectures. In *the 2009 International Conference on Advanced Information Networking and Applications* (pp. 113-120). Washington, DC: IEEE Computer Society.

Evans, G., & Benton, S. (2007). The BT risk cockpit – A visual approach to ORM. *BT Technology Journal, 25*(1), 88–100. doi:10.1007/s10550-007-0012-x

Few, S. (Ed.). (2006). *Information dashboard design: The effective visual communication of data*. Cambride, MA: O'Reilly Media, Inc.

Giblin, C., Müller, S., & Pfitzmann, B. (2006). From regulatory policies to event monitoring rules: Towards model-driven compliance automation. IBM Research Report RZ 3662, Zurich.

Grigori, D., Casati, F., Castellanos, M., Dayal, U., Sayal, M., & Shan, M. (2004). Business process intelligence. *Computers in Industry Journal, 53*(3), 321–343. doi:10.1016/j.compind.2003.10.007

Grigori, D., Casati, F., Dayal, U., & Shan, M. (2001). Improving business process quality through exception understanding, prediction, and prevention. In the *27th International Conference on Very Large Data Bases* (pp. 159-168). San Francisco, CA: Morgan Kaufmann Publishers Inc.

Hagerty, J., Hackbush, J., Gaughan, D., & Jacobson, S. (2008). *The governance, risk management, and compliance spending report, 2008-2009: Inside the $32B GRC market*. AMR Research.

Hall, M., Frank, E., Holmes, G., Pfahringer, B., Reutemann, P., & Witten, I. (2009). The WEKA data mining software: An update. *SIGKDD Explorations, 11*(1). doi:10.1145/1656274.1656278

Imrey, L. (2006). CIO dashboards: Flying by instrumentation. *Journal of Information Technology Management, 19*(4), 31–35.

Liu, Y., Müller, S., & Xu, K. (2007). A static compliance-checking framework for business process models. *IBM Systems Journal, 46*(2), 335–361. doi:10.1147/sj.462.0335

Lu, R., Sadiq, S., & Governatori, G. (2007). Compliance aware business process design. In *Lecture Notes in Computer Science: Business Process Management Workshops* (pp. 120–131). Berlin, Germany: Springer.

Mulo, E., Zdun, U., & Dustdar, S. (2009). Monitoring Web service event trails for business compliance. In the *IEEE International Conference on Service-Oriented Computing and Applications*. Washington, DC: IEEE Computer Society Press.

Namiri, K., & Stojanovic, N. (2007). *A semantic-based approach for compliance management of internal controls in business processes*. Paper presented at 19th International Conference on Advanced Information Systems Engineering, Trondheim, Norway.

Read, A., Tarrel, A., & Fruhling, A. (2009). Exploring user preference for the dashboard menu design. In *42nd Hawaii International Conference on System Sciences*, (pp. 1-10).

Rodríguez, C., Daniel, F., Casati, F., & Cappiello, C. (2009). Toward uncertain business intelligence: The case of key indicators. *IEEE Internet Computing, 14*(4).

Rodríguez, C., Silveira, P., Daniel, F., & Casati, F. (2010). *Analyzing compliance of service-based business processes for root-cause analysis and prediction*. In the 1st Workshop on Engineering SOA and the Web (ESW'10), Vienne, Austria.

Rozinat, A., & van der Aalst, W. (2009). *Decision mining in business processes*. BETA Working Paper Series, WP 164, Eindhoven University of Technology, Eindhoven.

Saqid, S., Governatori, G., & Naimiri, K. (2007). Modeling control objectives for business process-compliance. In G., Alonso, Dadam, P., & Rosemann, P. (Ed.), *BPM 2007, vol. 4714* (pp.149-164). Heidelberg, Germany: Springer.

Seol, H., Choi, J., Park, G., & Park, Y. (2007). A framework for benchmarking service process using data envelopment analysis and decision tree. *Expert Systems with Applications, 32*(2), 432–440. doi:10.1016/j.eswa.2005.12.012

Silveira, P., Rodríguez, C., Casati, F., Daniel, F., D'Andrea, V., Worledge, C., & Taheri, Z. (2009). *On the design of compliance governance dashboards for effective compliance and audit management*. In The 3rd Workshop on Non-Functional Properties and SLA Management in Service-Oriented Computing. Stockholm, Sweden: Springer.

Sloane, E., Rosow, E., Adam, J., & Shine, D. (2006). JEDI - An executive dashboard and decision support system for lean global military medical resource and logistics management. In *Annual International Conference of the IEEE Engineering in Medicine and Biology Society* (pp. 5440-5443). United States: Conf Proc IEEE Eng Med Biol Soc.

Trent, H. (2008). *Products for managing governance, risk, and compliance: Market fluff or relevant stuff?* In-Depth Research Report, Burton Group.

Trinh, T., Do, T., Truong, N., & Nguyen, V. (2009, October). *Checking the compliance of timing constraints in software applications*. 1st International Conference on Knowledge and Systems Engineering, Hanoi, Vietnam.

Witten, I., & Frank, E. (2005). *Data mining: Practical machine learning tools and techniques.* 2nd ed. Morgan Kaufmann. ISBN-0120884070

KEY TERMS AND DEFINITIONS

Compliance: A term generally used to refer to the conformance to a set of laws, regulations, policies, or best practices.

Compliance Governance Dashboards: User friendly GUI-based tool for the visualization of the compliance status of business process.

Compliance Root-Cause Analysis: Collection of techniques for discovering and understanding the reasons of non-compliance behaviors in business process executions.

Key Compliance Indicator: A quantitative summarization referring to the achievement of the stated compliance objectives (e.g., the number of unauthorized accesses to our payroll data).

SOA: An architectural paradigm for the development of distributed applications where software functionalities are encapsulated as services using well-established communication protocols.

ENDNOTES

[1] Compliance-driven Models, Languages, and Architectures for Services (http://www.compas-ict.eu/)
[2] Managing Assurance Security and Trust for sERvices (http://www.master-fp7.eu/)

Section 5
Future Directions

Chapter 23
An Outlook on the Future of Services and Non–Functional Properties Management:
A Web Centric Perspective

Carlos Pedrinaci
The Open University, UK

Dong Liu
The Open University, UK

Guillermo Álvaro
Intelligent Software Components, Spain

Stefan Dietze
The Open University, UK

John Domingue
The Open University, UK

ABSTRACT

Impelled by the hype and interest surrounding the Web, Microsoft and IBM among others seized the opportunity to propose the use of Web Services as a means to support the creation of complex distributed applications over the Internet. The fundamental advantage of this technology lies in the support it brings to developing highly complex distributed systems maximising the reuse of loosely coupled components. Web Services were supposed to be a new technology better supporting traditional Remote Procedure Calls over the Web, which would ultimately lead to the creation of a largely automated Web-based eServices economy, i.e., an economy based on services largely delivered electronically.

DOI: 10.4018/978-1-61350-432-1.ch023

Over the years a large number of technologies have been devised in order to describe service interfaces, e.g., WSDL (Booth & Liu, 2007), combine services in a process-oriented way, e.g., WS-BPEL (OASIS Web Services Business Process Execution Language (WSBPEL) TC, 2007), provide support for transactions, e.g., WS-Transaction, and cover non-functional properties (NFP) of services such as security aspects and the like, see for instance WS-Security and WS-Policy to name just a few (Erl, 2007). There is in an overwhelming stack of technologies and specifications dubbed WS-*, covering most aspects researchers have faced thus far. There remain nonetheless a number of outstanding issues (Papazoglou, Traverso, Dustdar, & Leymann, 2007) some of which are of a general technical nature, and some, indeed, are specifically related to NFPs. The latter will be dealt with in more detail in the next section.

ON THE EVOLUTION AND RECENT TRENDS AROUND SERVICES

Despite the initial expectations, in reality, however, Web Services have hardly been adopted beyond the boundaries of enterprises (Davies, et al., 2009). Today, Seekda.com provides one of the largest indexes of publicly available Web Services which currently accounts for 28,500 with their corresponding documentation. The number of Web Services publicly available contrasts significantly with the billions of Web pages available, and interestingly is not significantly bigger than the 4,000 Web Services estimated to be deployed internally within Verizon (Stollberg, Hepp, & Hoffmann, 2007). Other academic efforts in crawling and indexing Web Services on the Web have found far lower numbers of services (Al-Masri & Mahmoud, 2008).

A number of technical limitations have been argued to be at the core of this lack of uptake (Pilioura & Tsalgatidou, 2009), some of which have been addressed by additional specifications, like the WS-* stack, as well as by the Semantic Web Services community (Erl, 2007) (Pedrinaci, Domingue, & Sheth, Semantic Web Services, 2011). However, recent trends driven by the Web 2.0 phenomenon have highlighted that socio-economic aspects have been as much an impediment as technological drawbacks. In fact, the major revolution behind Web 2.0 is not on the use of particular technologies such as AJAX as initially believed, but rather on realising that, on

the Web, value largely resides on the data about and the communication between people and this value is subject to the network effect (Hendler & Golbeck, 2008). On the Web, Web Services never reached the critical mass that would justify the additional efforts and investment.

Stirred by the Web 2.0 phenomenon, the world around services on the Web, thus far limited to "classical" Web Services based on SOAP and WSDL, has significantly evolved with the proliferation of Web APIs, also called RESTful services (Richardson & Ruby, 2007; Schreiber, et al., 1999) when they conform to the REST architectural style (Fielding, 2000). This more recent breed of services is characterised by the simplicity of the technology stack they build upon, i.e., URIs, HTTP, XML and JSON, and their natural suitability for the Web. Nowadays, an increasingly large quantity of Web sites offer (controlled) access to part of the data they hold through simple Web APIs, see for instance Flickr[1], Last.fm[2], and Facebook[3]. This trend towards opening access to previously closed data silos has generated a new wave of Web applications, called mashups, which obtain data from diverse Web sites and combine it to create novel solutions (Benslimane, Dustdar, & Sheth, 2008).

At the time of this writing, ProgrammableWeb. com lists about 3,250 Web APIs, and 5,800 mashups and this number has been increasing steadily during the last years. Those APIs and mashups listed are in most cases used on a daily basis by a growing number of applications and mobile devices which exploit the data and functionality provided by enterprises on a world-wide basis over the Internet, precisely what was initially hoped and predicted for Web services. Talking about services thus nowadays necessarily needs to contemplate this new increasingly popular type of services whose development is, interestingly, not guided by standards, patterns, or guidelines. It is more an art than a science whereby Web APIs are more often than not solely described in HTML as part of a webpage rather than using an interface description language that could better support software development.

In the remainder of this chapter we analyse the main outstanding issues concerning non-functional properties for services in the light of the state of the art and the main trends we have just identified.

Outstanding Issues

Thus far the book has covered in detail a considerable number of technologies and approaches devoted to capturing, managing, and exploiting the non-functional properties of services to enhance service-oriented systems. A fundamental aspect of non-functional properties the reader has probably distilled after reading this book is the large-scope and diversity that characterizes them (see *chapter 1*, *chapter 4*, or *chapter 13*) (Al-Masri & Mahmoud, 2009). NFPs cover an extremely wide range of aspects which is virtually unbound since, depending on the domain, the set and understanding of the relevant properties can vary significantly. For instance, in some cases a very fast response time may be essential whereas in other cases the accuracy of the results obtained clearly prevails over the response time. This diversity (Palpanas, Vlachos, Keogh, & Gunopulos, 2008) (Al-Masri & Mahmoud, Investigating Web Services on the World Wide Web, 2008) is augmented even further by the different levels of granularity that one can adopt while observing and assessing services which may span from the low-level operation used

to the actual real-world service contracted by the end customer.

From a general perspective and regardless of the domain the nature of different properties also varies. Some researchers divide these properties into those that are of an objective nature, e.g., response time, and those of a subjective nature, e.g., trust (Al-Masri & Mahmoud, 2009). For those NFPs which actor is carrying out the assessment is essential and, indeed, the same property may present different, possibly contradicting, values. Similarly, from an orthogonal perspective, NFPs can be of a quantitative nature, e.g., throughput, or of qualitative nature, e.g., user rating.

Indeed, the diversity of their nature calls for different means for calculating or obtaining them, for tracking them over time, and for exploiting or combining them at runtime. In particular this diversity presents us with a number of outstanding difficulties one needs to address:

- *Efficient management of large quantities of data:* The existence of such a wide range of properties that may potentially be relevant for managing services leads to the need for managing a possibly large quantity of data. Additionally, a number of these properties vary over time (e.g., response time) and it is often necessary to track a certain period of time to derive a more reliable measure for these NFPs. Managing NFPs thus requires applying state of the art techniques for managing large quantities of data notably those able to track the evolution of properties over time. The infrastructure should indeed provide efficient support for both storing and retrieving NFPs at runtime so as to allow taking appropriate actions at runtime, maximizing the precision and quantity of data handled within resource constrained settings, etc.
- *Advanced data integration techniques:* Given the diversity characterizing NFPs we previously highlighted, one is likely

to face a number of typical data integration issues. For instance, different properties may be represented using different formats which may need to be harmonized and integrated. Similarly, data concerning diverse NFPs may be provided by different actors. It is thus crucial to have in place appropriate mechanisms able to track the provenance of data in order for systems to be able to select the data provided by concrete actors given the task at hand. Indeed, many actors may have different preferences with respect to which properties are more crucial, they may have different assessments for certain properties, and data providers may be more or less trusted. Additionally, and closely related to the previous issues, integration at large scale of heterogeneous data provided by potentially numerous actors often may trigger the need for appropriate managing the identity of the elements tracked within the NFP management framework. Note in this respect that typically each of the elements (e.g., services, users, properties) will presumably be handled differently internally by each of the actors and systems involved and it is fundamental to be able to refer to this body of data in a global manner avoid identity clashes, etc. Among the elements requiring homogenizing one can cite for instance, the identity of the different actors (e.g., service providers, users, etc), that of the services, and the NFPs themselves.

- *Efficient and time sensitive processing of NFPs:* Closely related to the aforementioned aspects is the actual processing and derivation of NFPs in a swift and efficient manner which presents a number of challenges. In particular, taking into account the heterogeneity, dynamicity, and time sensitivity of some of the NFPs tracked, NFPs management frameworks need to be able to combine and process large amounts of data in near real-time so that the service-oriented infrastructure can adapt quickly, for example, to the reduced performance of a concrete service. Swiftly filtering the data or prioritizing the computation for achieving a good performance while carrying out these activities turns out to be particularly relevant. Furthermore, intelligent frameworks may also need to combine swift and temporally localized computations with global mining activities. This would enable, for instance, detecting that the degraded behavior of some services is actually an indication of problems in the infrastructure of a concrete provider and thus other services are likely to present the same issues.

- *Capturing declaratively the means for computing NFPs:* The processing of data requires not only specifying the static domain knowledge (Schreiber, et al., 1999), e.g., elements such as the *response time*, *latency*, and *QoS*, but also the dynamic knowledge (Schreiber, et al., 1999) that indicates how they should actually be computed. Commonly the static domain knowledge is captured and transmitted in a more or less explicit manner. All the frameworks and systems define explicitly a set of properties they can deal with and in many cases these properties are defined in a more or less formal and standardized manner via ontologies or through agreed specifications. Having an agreed means for capturing this is certainly a fundamental requirement. However, the actual knowledge for computing these NFPs, consider in particular composite properties, is most often than not hardwired within the software taking care of it. Although certainly a viable option, this way of doing it abstracts aspects of a particular importance regarding the properties, which are, in the case of subjective properties, essential.

Moreover, should the means for computing require adaptation or the NFPs handled change, the NFP management framework would require to be changed. Similarly, should some data not be readily available the framework will hardly have any means for approximating the computation of simply using a different formula. These issues may be avoided within closed settings like enterprises but they are more of an issue in open environments like the Web where many actors are involved and things change constantly.

- *Systems need to embrace RESTful services and Web APIs:* As we previously introduced the world of services is currently under a substantial technical evolution since the RESTful services and Web APIs started gaining adoption. The use of these services is growing both within and outside enterprises and it looks like, despite the relative lack of standardization in this area, it will continue so. Although this is by no means an issue per se NFPs and related software have thus far focused mostly on "classical" Web services where the WS-* stack can be used. RESTful services and Web APIs on the contrary do hardly use any IDL like WSDL and thus attaching properties to them or even issues like deciding what is the service and how to identify it (e.g., is it http://www.facebook.com? is its http://developers.facebook.com/docs/reference/api/ ? should it just be given an arbitrary name?) become an issue. Additionally, methods for checking compliance with respect to certain preferences over NFPs may need to be adapted, e.g. is it enough to use HTTPS instead of the formerly established WS-Security specification?

The issues presented in this section are but a selection of some of the challenges we believe will be most relevant in the forthcoming years.

We have in particular focused on those that are more likely to arise in the open Web for we believe that (1) in the future the tendency would be towards building systems which are increasingly integrated with the Web and may thus involve a large number of actors and systems over which we may have little or no control whatsoever; and (2) solving problems for this scenario should also lead to solutions in more controlled settings. In the following section we shall cover the issues raise and provide an outlook on how one could tackle these and the main fields and technologies that we believe could be at the basis of future NFP management frameworks.

Outlook

In the light of the aforementioned challenges, we provide in this section a number of pointers to technologies and approaches that we believe are particularly relevant for tackling them. The outlook shall first focus on data management and integration and then on data processing concerns.

Data Management and Integration

A number of challenges highlighted previously are related to data management issues which have been and continue being subject of research in the area of Databases. Any advances in this area in general is thus likely to have a positive impact in the management of NFPs any other activity requiring the management of data for that matter. We shall thus not focus in detail in this topic for its general nature. The interested reader is referred to (Lith & Mattsson, 2010) for an overview of current advances and research directions in the area. Tightly bound to research on databases and certainly closer to the management of NFPs is the work on Data Warehousing (Sen & Sinha, 2005). Therein large efforts have been devoted to the construction of powerful Extract-Transform-Load solutions that would enable gathering diverse data spread across the IT infrastructure, consolidating it into a global database and eventually generating different views that could be sliced and diced in order to better analyse the data and support decision making processes. An interesting challenge in this respect concerns data summarization which is a fundamental challenge in highly dynamic environments (Palpanas, Vlachos, Keogh, & Gunopulos, 2008), (Della Valle, Ceri, van Harmelen, & Fensel, 2009).

Another effort with a strong emphasis towards better supporting the integration, management and processing of heterogeneous and distributed data focused in this case on Web-scale settings is the Semantic Web (Berners-Lee, Hendler, & Lassila, 2001). The Semantic Web is an extension of the current human-readable Web, adding formal knowledge representation so that intelligent software can reason with the information in an automatic and flexible way. Semantic Web research has therefore largely focused on defining languages and tools for representing knowledge in a way that can be shared, reused, combined, and processed over the Web. This research has led to a plethora of standards such as RDF(S) (McBride, 2004), OWL (Antoniou & van Harmelen, 2004), as well as corresponding tools such as ontology editors (Noy, Sintek, Decker, Crubezy, Fergerson, & Musen, 2001), RDF(S) storage and querying systems (Broekstra, Kampman, & Van Harmelen, 2002) and reasoners (Haarslev & Möller, 2003), to name a few. Despite the advances in this area, a good deal of these technologies have thus far required complex knowledge engineering efforts and relatively heavy-weight processing technologies which face certain limitations specially when dealing with large amounts of dynamic data as is often the case for NFPs. Circumventing these issues is certainly a crucial step for the adoption of semantic technologies within this particular area and in general for a wider adoption by software vendors.

The Web of Data is a relatively recent effort derived from research on the Semantic Web, whose main objective is to generate a Web exposing and interlinking data previously enclosed within silos. The Web of Data is based upon four simple principles, known as the Linked Data principles, which essentially dictate that every piece of data should be given an HTTP URI which, when looked up, should offer useful information using standards like RDF and SPARQL (Bizer, Heath, & Berners-Lee, 2009). Additionally, data should be linked to other relevant resources therefore allowing humans and computers to discover additional information. The Web of Data, initially mostly an academic endeavour, is gradually capturing the attention of companies and institutions some of which have already taken steps towards making use of these technologies. Examples of this latest trend are for instance, the acquisition of Metaweb[4] by Google, the use of Semantic Web technologies in public services provided by the BBC[5], and the release of governmental data following Linked Data principles by countries like the United Kingdom or the United States of America.

The recent evolution seems to indicate that Linked Data is currently establishing itself as the de-facto standard for data integration on a Web scale. Although certainly in harmony with Semantic Web research, work on Linked Data has focused on applying lighter technologies, e.g., RDF(S) and SPARQL, on devising simple, yet extensible and integrated vocabularies, and on establishing the fundamental means for exposing and interlinking data. Effectively these technologies have simplified the integration of heterogeneous data sources to a certain extent, providing common languages for data representation and querying, as well as by borrowing Web standards for uniquely and globally identifying entities and transporting data. These very aspects make these technologies particularly appealing for capturing and integrating NFPs which, as we introduced earlier, are likely to be highly heterogeneous, provided by diverse actors, and yet need to be effectively integrated on global basis.

Driven by the challenges highlighted earlier and the presumed benefits Linked Data technologies could bring to service-oriented systems, we have developed a number of technologies which exemplify their application as well as they provide a proof of concept of some of the main benefits that can be obtained. Notably we have started generating a Web of Data about services providing both functional and non-functional service descriptions, and we have developed added-value infrastructural services on top. At the core of this effort lies iServe, a public platform that unifies service publication and discovery on the Web through the use of Linked Data. iServe, previously introduced in (Pedrinaci, Liu, Maleshkova, Lambert, Kopecky, & Domingue, 2010), is what we refer to as a service warehouse for it provides the typical features of service registries and additional functionality that exploits both internal (e.g., functional descriptions and usage data) and distributed Linked Data as well as other sources of information for supporting advanced discovery or even recommending refined service descriptions.

In particular we currently have at our disposal a Functional Classifications Recommender and a Services Recommender, which apart from extending the traditional notion of registry to include annotation recommendation and social networking analysis, also help us validate further the infrastructure devised and some of the advantages brought by the use of Linked Data principles to capture data about services. Service Recommendation, the functionality most relevant for this book, is provided by integrating two external services: Linked User Feedback (LUF)[6], and a Recommender System (Dell'Aglio & Celino, 2010). LUF is a system based on Linked Data principles and supports any user in storing comments, ratings and tags about any kind of RDF resource. Thus, one can simply rate, comment or tag any service published within iServe providing in this way valuable (subjective) non-functional properties about services in a distributed manner. Thanks to the use of Linked Data principles it is straightforward for iServe, or any other system for that matter, to retrieve data from LUF and correlate it with

iServe's data in order to better manage services. In fact, the Recommender System retrieves all the existing ratings for services, service descriptions and log information concerning previous users' interactions in order to profile both services and users providing in this way both collaborative filtering and content-based recommendations.

Another system that has been devised following a similar vision is SmartLink (Dietze, Yu, Pedrinaci, Liu, & Domingue, 2011). SmartLink provides two functionalities (1) an extension to the data captured within iServe covering some additional non-functional properties (*SmartLink-NfP*) and (2) an editing and browsing environment for Linked Data about services residing in different stores such as iServe and SmartLink-NfP. SmartLink-NfP thus provides its own Linked Data repository using a dedicated schema[7] covering for instance details such as the contact person, the developer name, the Quality of Service (QoS), the development status, and the service license. A very important feature of this approach to combining data lies in the fact that anybody can provide their statements thus catering both for the plurality and diversity needed in particular for NFPs but also paving the way for a continuous extension and enrichment of the data available. Figure 1 shows how these systems are incrementally producing a Web of Data about services integrating functional and non-functional aspects coming from heterogeneous sources.

In the presence of distributed third-party provided information, provenance becomes essential and indeed the Linked Data community in general has been devoted efforts to capturing and processing the provenance of information. The approach we have followed integrates some of this research results which we believe are relevant in general for the management of NFPs in distributed multi-party settings. Notably, iServe tracks both the provenance of service descriptions as well as the use and interest demonstrated by users regarding services in terms of the provenance vocabulary (Hartig & Zhao, 2010), thus allowing

Figure 1. Towards a Web of data about services

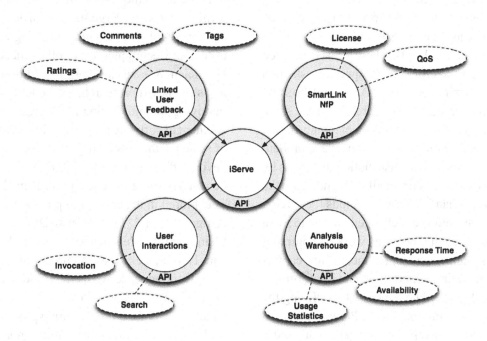

the infrastructure to use this information to assess its trustworthiness, its potential accuracy or simply to use the correct subjective statements (see the previous example on service ratings).

Data Processing

The remaining challenges highlighted earlier can basically be classified into data processing challenges. The first challenge we contemplate with respect to processing data concerning non-functional properties concerns the outstanding diversity of properties to take into account and likelihood for these properties to be extended with new ones or be treated differently by different actors. To cater for this we stressed previously that it is not sufficient to just capture and provide shared models for the static knowledge (i.e., the actual properties contemplated). It is also fundamental to formally capture and share the dynamic knowledge necessary for computing the properties, e.g., the actual formulas used for computing the properties, in a way that would allow computers

to automatically carry out the computation on the non-functional property on demand even in the presence of new previously unknown properties.

Capturing the dynamic knowledge for computing NFPs in a declarative manner would provide an additional and, we believe, fundamental level of genericity to NFP management frameworks. This would for instance allow frameworks to deal with new properties defined by third parties (including even the user) and to adapt the computation of existing ones without having to change the underlying software. Additionally, these mechanisms combined with complementary background knowledge concerning the properties, the methods for computing them, and their relationships could enable the development of smart techniques able to adapt the computation mechanisms under different performance requirements and infrastructure load, or to derive properties through other means while dealing with inaccurate or missing data.

Although we believe these techniques are relatively new in the area of NFPs, they have been applied quite successfully in other areas.

First, earlier research in Knowledge Engineering devoted significant efforts to conceptualizing what is referred to as Problem-Solving Methods (PSM) (Schreiber, et al., 1999). These PSMs captured concrete methods for solving specific tasks in a domain-independent manner. As a result the same components could be used for solving the same task in different domains (e.g., a planning engine could be applied to plan software development processes as well as the distribution of parcels by a logistics teams). Additionally, depending on the actual case at hand different methods for solving the same task could be exchanged in order to solve the given problem. Secondly, work on computer algebra systems developed means for capturing and resolving generic mathematic formulae which could indeed be the basis for defining the formulae for computing NFPs. Perhaps the main work on capturing representing generically these formulae on the Web is MathML (Carlisle, Ion, & and Miner, 2010) although it does not seem to integrate easily with external specifications as one would provide for NFPs. On earlier research we approached this topic in the context of Business Process Analysis (Pedrinaci & Domingue, Ontology-based Metrics Computation for Business Process Analysis, 2009). Although the technical solution remains an academic proof of concept the principles could indeed be applied for a more thorough and efficient solution.

In addition to the genericity of the infrastructure for managing and computing NFPs, we previously highlighted that an essential feature for NFP frameworks concerns the rapid reaction in the light or large quantities of dynamic data. These are some of the main challenges tackled by research on monitoring systems, e.g., Business Process Monitoring (Mühlen, 2004), but also on Complex Event Processing (Luckham, 2001) (Noy, Sintek, Decker, Crubezy, Fergerson, & Musen, 2001). Therein research efforts are being devoted to improving exiting rule engines with complex event detection, e.g., RETE (Schmidt, Stühmer, & Stojanovic, 2008), to implementing intelligent techniques for discerning relevant information from the large amounts of data received and for combining semantic reasoning with event processing techniques, etc (Della Valle, Ceri, van Harmelen, & Fensel, 2009). In addition to these areas of specific research, we believe that work involving the monitoring and longer term management of software properties for the adaptation of systems, thus including NFP research, should devote efforts to better exploiting the synergies between runtime and batch processing. Doing so, as explored in the context of process monitoring (Grigori, Casati, Castellanos, Dayal, Sayal, & Shan, 2004), (Pedrinaci, Lambert, Wetzstein, van~Lessen, Cekov, & Dimitrov, 2008), (Pedrinaci, Domingue, & Alves de Medeiros, A Core Ontology for Business Process Analysis, 2008) paves the way for both exploiting processing carried out at runtime while monitoring systems to enrich background models about these systems being managed, and conversely it allows applying heuristics derived during some batch processing activities for adapting systems at runtime.

CONCLUSION

In this final chapter we have briefly gone through the state of the art on service-orientation in general, and NFP in particular highlighting the aspects that we believe present some of the main outstanding challenges in the area. This analysis is indeed biased by the understanding of the authors that the future of service-oriented systems will necessarily be closely tied to that of the Web, and by our belief that solutions able to support service-oriented systems on a Web-scale would also via good options for more reduced settings like enterprise environments.

The main challenges highlighted concern the management and processing of distributed, heterogeneous, multi-party provided, and highly dynamic information. We have then provided a quick outlook on what we believe are nowadays among the most relevant research and technologies in this respect. By doing so we have aimed, on the one hand, to provide pointers for the interested researcher to dig further into existing research, and on the other hand, to briefly introduce our vision for NFP for service-oriented systems. Service-oriented systems and NFPs management present both a large number of challenges which shall indeed lead to continued exciting research in the forthcoming years. We hope this book will be a brick towards a bright future.

REFERENCES

Al-Masri, E., & Mahmoud, Q. (2008). Investigating Web services on the World Wide Web. *17th International World Wide Web Conference*, (pp. 795-804).

Al-Masri, E., & Mahmoud, Q. (2009). Web service discovery and client goals. *Computer, 42*(1), 104–107. doi:10.1109/MC.2009.31

Antoniou, G., & van Harmelen, F. (2004). Web ontology language: OWL. In S. Staab, & R. Studer, *Handbook on ontologies* (pp. 67-92). Springer-Verlag.

Benslimane, D., Dustdar, S., & Sheth, A. (2008). Services mashups: The new generation of Web applications. *IEEE Internet Computing, 12*(5), 13–15. doi:10.1109/MIC.2008.110

Berners-Lee, T., Hendler, J., & Lassila, O. (2001). The Semantic Web. *Scientific American, 5,* 34–43. doi:10.1038/scientificamerican0501-34

Bizer, C., Heath, T., & Berners-Lee, T. (2009). Linked data - The story so far. [IJSWIS]. *International Journal on Semantic Web and Information Systems, 5*(3). doi:10.4018/jswis.2009081901

Booth, D., & Liu, C. K. (2007, June 26). *Web services description language (WSDL) version 2.0 part 0: Primer.* Retrieved March 20, 2011, from http://www.w3.org/TR/2007/REC-wsdl20-primer-20070626/

Broekstra, J., Kampman, A., & Van Harmelen, F. (2002). Sesame: A generic architecture for storing and querying RDF and RDF schema. *International Semantic Web Conference - ISWC* (pp. 54-68). Springer.

Carlisle, D., Ion, P., & Miner, R. (2010, October 21). *Mathematical markup language (mathml) version 3.0.* Retrieved May 17, 2011, from http://www.w3.org/TR/MathML3/

Davies, J., Domingue, J., Pedrinaci, C., Fensel, D., Gonzalez-Cabero, R., & Potter, M. (2009). Towards the open service Web. *BT Technology Journal, 26*(2).

Dell 'Aglio. D., & Celino, I. A. (2010). Anatomy of a semantic web-enabled knowledge-based recommender system. *Proceedings of the 4th International Workshop Semantic Matchmaking and Resource Retrieval in the Semantic Web.*

Della Valle, E., Ceri, S., van Harmelen, F., & Fensel, D. (2009). It's a streaming world! Reasoning upon rapidly changing information. *IEEE Intelligent Systems, 24*(6), 83–89. doi:10.1109/MIS.2009.125

Dietze, S., Yu, H. Q., Pedrinaci, C., Liu, D., & Domingue, J. (2011). SmartLink: A Web-based editor and search environment for linked services. *Demo at 8th Extended Semantic Web Conference, Heraklion, Greece.*

Erl, T. (2007). *SOA principles of service design.* Prentice Hall.

Fielding, R. T. (2000). *Architectural styles and the design of network-based software architectures. Irvine, CA.* Irvine: University of California.

Grigori, D., Casati, F., Castellanos, M., Dayal, U., Sayal, M., & Shan, M.-C. (2004). Business process intelligence. *Computers in Industry, 53*(3), 321–343. doi:10.1016/j.compind.2003.10.007

Haarslev, V., & Möller, R. (2003). Racer: A core inference engine for the Semantic Web. *Second International Semantic Web Conference ISWC*. Springer.

Hartig, O., & Zhao, J. (2010). Publishing and consuming provenance metadata on the Web of linked data. *Proceedings of the 3rd International Provenance and Annotation Workshop (IPAW)*.

Hendler, J., & Golbeck, J. (2008, january). Metcalfe's law, Web 2.0, and the Semantic Web. *Web Semantics: Science, Services and Agents on the World Wide Web*.

Lith, A., & Mattsson, J. (2010). *Investigating storage solutions for large data*. Chalmers University of Technology, Department of Computer Science and Engineering. Chalmers University of Technology.

Luckham, D. C. (2001). *The power of events: An introduction to complex event processing in distributed enterprise systems*. Addison-Wesley Longman Publishing Co., Inc.

Maleshkova, M., Pedrinaci, C., & Domingue, J. (2010). *Investigating Web APIs on the World Wide Web*. European Conference on Web Services (ECOWS). Springer.

McBride, B. (2004). The resource description framework (RDF) and its vocabulary description language RDFS. In Staab, S. A. (Ed.), *Handbook on ontologies* (pp. 51–66). Springer-Verlag.

Mühlen, M. Z. (2004). Workflow-based process controlling. In *Foundation, design, and implementation of workflow-driven process Information Systems (Vol. 6)*. Logos.

Noy, N. F., Sintek, M., Decker, S., Crubezy, M., Fergerson, R. W., & Musen, M. A. (2001). Creating Semantic Web contents with Protege-2000. *IEEE Intelligent Systems, 16*(2), 60–71. doi:10.1109/5254.920601

OASIS Web Services Business Process Execution Language (WSBPEL) TC. (2007, January 31). *Web Services business process execution language version 2.0 committee specification*. Retrieved April 26, 2007, from http://docs.oasis-open.org/wsbpel/2.0/CS01/wsbpel-v2.0-CS01.pdf

Palpanas, T., Vlachos, M., Keogh, E., & Gunopulos, D. (2008). Streaming time series summarization using user-defined amnesic functions. *Transactions on Knowledge and Data Engineering, 20*(7), 992–1006. doi:10.1109/TKDE.2007.190737

Papazoglou, M. P., Traverso, P., Dustdar, S., & Leymann, F. (2007). Service-oriented computing: State of the art and research challenges. *Computer, 40*(11), 38–45. doi:10.1109/MC.2007.400

Pedrinaci, C., & Domingue, J. (2009). *Ontology-based metrics computation for business process analysis*. Workshop: 4th International Workshop on Semantic Business Process Management (SBPM2009) at The 6th European Semantic Web Conference (ESWC2009). CEUR.

Pedrinaci, C., Domingue, J., & Alves de Medeiros, A. K. (2008). A core ontology for business process analysis. 5th European Semantic Web Conference. Springer.

Pedrinaci, C., Domingue, J., & Sheth, A. (2011). Semantic Web services. In Domingue, J., Fensel, D., & Hendler, J. (Eds.), *Handbook on Semantic Web technologies*. Springer. doi:10.1007/978-3-540-92913-0_22

Pedrinaci, C., Lambert, D., & Wetzstein, B. van~Lessen, T., Cekov, L., & Dimitrov, M. (2008). *SENTINEL: A semantic business process monitoring tool*. Ontology-supported Business Intelligence (OBI2008) at 7th International Semantic Web Conference (ISWC2008). CEUR.

Pedrinaci, C., Liu, D., Maleshkova, M., Lambert, D., Kopecky, J., & Domingue, J. (2010). iServe: A linked services publishing platform. *Proceedings of Ontology Repositories and Editors for the Semantic Web at 7th ESWC.* CEUR.

Pilioura, T., & Tsalgatidou, A. (2009). Unified publication and discovery of Semantic Web services. *ACM Trans. Web, 3*(3), 1–44. doi:10.1145/1541822.1541826

Richardson, L., & Ruby, S. (2007). *RESTful Web services.* O'Reilly Media, Inc.

Schmidt, K.-U., Stühmer, R., & Stojanovic, L. (2008). Blending complex event processing with the RETE algorithm. *iCEP2008: 1st International workshop on Complex Event Processing for the Future Internet colocated with the Future Internet Symposium (FIS2008)*, (p. 412). CEUR.

Schreiber, G., Akkermans, H., Anjewierden, A., de Hoog, R., Shadbolt, N., & de Velde, W. V. (1999). *Knowledge engineering and management: The CommonKADS methodology.* MIT Press.

Sen, A., & Sinha, A. P. (2005). A comparison of data warehousing methodologies. *Communications of the ACM, 48*(3), 79–84. doi:10.1145/1047671.1047673

Stollberg, M., Hepp, M., & Hoffmann, J. (2007). A caching mechanism for Semantic Web service discovery. *6th International and 2nd Asian Semantic Web Conference (ISWC2007+ASWC2007)* (pp. 477-490). Springer.

KEY TERMS AND DEFINITIONS

Linked Data: A method of publishing structured data so that it can be interlinked and consequently become more useful.

Linked Data Principles: Four principles that Linked Data should adhere to (URIs should identify things, URIs should be usable by people and user agents, the URI should lead to useful information and links to other, related URIs should be included.

RESTful Services: Web services that focus on how states of resources are addressed and transferred.

Web APIs: Well defined sets of HTTP request messages with definition of the structure of the respective response messages.

ENDNOTES

[1] http://www.flickr.com/services/api/
[2] http://www.last.fm/api
[3] http://developers.facebook.com/docs/
[4] http://www.freebase.com/
[5] http://bbc.in/codPLr
[6] See http://soa4all.isoco.net/luf/
[7] http://purl.org/smartlink/service-nfp

About the Contributors

Stephan Reiff-Marganiec is a Senior Lecturer in the Department of Computer Science at the University of Leicester, which he joined in 2003 as a lecturer. He worked in the computer industry in Germany and Luxembourg for several years. From 1998 to 2001 he was as a Research Assistant at the University of Glasgow, while at the same time reading for a PhD in Computing Science. The work performed at Glasgow investigated hybrid approaches to the feature interaction problem. From 2001 to 2003 Stephan was as a Research Fellow at the University of Stirling, investigating policies, emerging features and associated conflict resolution techniques. Stephan was responsible for organising the British Colloquium for Theoretical Computer Science in 2001 and again in 2004 and since 2004 has been Treasurer of BCTCS. He was also co-Chair of the 8th and 10th International Conference on Feature Interactions in Telecommunications and Software Systems, he was co-Chair of the second, third and fourth Young Researchers Workshop in Service Oriented Computing (YR-SOC 2007, 2008 and 2009) and is senior member of the steering committee for YR-SOC. Stephan was principal investigator of the project "Ad-Hoc Web Applications" funded by the Nuffield foundation and leader of workpackages and tasks in the EU funded projects Leg2Net, Sensoria, and inContext focusing on automatic service adaption, context aware service selection, workflows, and rule based service composition. Stephan has published in excess of 40 papers in international conferences and journals and has been a member of a large number of programme committees.

Marcel Tilly has received a Master's degree in physics at the Technical University of Dortmund. Since then he has worked for more than 10 years in the area of software development and engineering. During this time he worked in a variety of roles within the technical architecture teams of several projects on the development of large distributed software systems. His work was primarily focused on model-driven development and service-oriented architecture. In 2006 he joined the European Microsoft Innovation Center in Aachen as a Program Manager. In this role he is mainly focused on service-oriented computing, service compositions, and event-stream processing. He was co-chairing the workshops (NFPSLA-SOC and NFPSLAM) about non-functional properties and service level agreements for service-oriented computing. He is co-author of a German book about web development and speaker at several conferences.

* * *

João Abreu currently manages a R&D quality and process improvement program at Altitude Software. Previously, he has done research in formal design and verification of software systems and obtained a PhD in Computer Science from the University of Leicester, UK.

Assia Ait-Ali-Slimane is currently a PhD student at the Computer Science Research Center (Centre de Recherche en Informatique) of the University of Paris 1 Panthéon-Sorbonne, Paris, France. From September 2008 until August 2010, she occupied a Research Assistant position at University of Paris 1 Panthéon-Sorbonne. Previously, she received her MS degree in Computer Sciences from the University of Paris 8, Paris, France, and her BS degree in Computer Sciences from the National School of Computer Science (Ecole Nationale Supérieure d'Informatique), in Algiers, Algeria. Her research interests include service engineering, quality of service, and requirement engineering.

Guillermo Álvaro Rey is a Researcher at iSOCO in Madrid, Spain. He holds a degree in Telecommunications Engineering from the Technical University of Madrid (UPM), and he also obtained an M.Sc. by Research in the Distributed Systems Group of Trinity College Dublin (TCD). In 2008, after three years of work in a project at the Research and Development division of Telefónica (Telefónica I+D), he joined iSOCO to work in areas such as Semantic Web Services and Web 2.0.

Yolande Berbers obtained her MSc degree in Computer Science from the K. U. Leuven in 1982. In 1987, she received a PhD degree in Computer Science with a thesis in the area of distributed operating systems at the same university. Since 1990 she has been an Associate Professor in the department of computer science. She spent 5 months during 1985 and 1986 at the INRIA, France. She teaches advanced courses on software for real-time and embedded systems, and on computer architecture. Her research interests include software engineering for embedded software, ubiquitous computing, service architectures, middleware, real-time systems, component-oriented software development, distributed systems, environments for distributed and parallel applications, and mobile agents. She is co-founder of EuroSys, a European Association for the advancement of systems research in Europe, linked with ACM SIGOPS. She has more than 50 scientific publications in the last five years.

Aliaksandr Birukou is currently a PostDoc at the Department of Information Engineering and Computer Science (DISI) at the University of Trento, Italy. He received his PhD in Information and Communication Technologies from the University of Trento, Italy in 2009 and an MS degree with distinction in Applied Mathematics and Computer Science from the Belarusian State University, Minsk, Belarus in 2002. His current research interests include dissemination of novel scientific and teaching media formats, diversity-, culture-, and community-aware recommendation systems, science 2.0 (improving the way science works), recommendation systems, patterns, and service-oriented computing. He has background in data mining, multi-agent systems, compliance management, queuing systems, banking and experience in managing research and industrial projects. He is in PC and Focus Group Chair for EuroPLoP 2011, served as a PC member for several international workshops, and reviewed papers for several journals (DKE, IJAOSE, IEEE TKDE, IP&P) and a number of conferences (including AAMAS, CAISE, ICCBR, ICSOC).

Laura Bocchi is a Research Associate in the Department of Computer Science at the University of Leicester. She received a PhD in Computer Science at the University of Bologna with a thesis on formal models for service composition and coordination. Her research interests are in software engineering of service-oriented systems, transactions in service oriented architectures, formal methods and concurrency.

Franz Brosch studied Computer Science at the Karlsruhe Institute of Technology (KIT) in Germany. After a period of four years working as a Software Engineer in industry, he started a PhD at the KIT in February 2008. His research interests are software reliability, component-based software architectures, and model-driven software development.

Dave Bustard joined the University of Ulster, Coleraine, as a Professor of Computing Science in 1990. Before that he was at Queen's University (1974-90) and worked briefly in industry at Ferranti Digital Systems (1972-74) in Berkshire. He has also been a Visiting Scientist at the Software Engineering Institute, Pittsburgh (1990) and at BT Research Labs in Ipswich (1989). At Ulster, he is Head of the School of Computing and Information Engineering (since 1998), and previously was Head of the Informatics Research Graduate School (1996-98). His research interests are in software engineering, especially in requirements engineering, agile software development, autonomic computing, and applications of soft systems methodology. Much of his work has been in collaboration with industry, including projects with BT, Nortel, AVX, KTL, and the Northern Ireland Civil Service.

Yudith Cardinale is a Full Professor in Computer Science Department at Universidad Simón Bolívar (USB) since 1996. She graduated with honors in Computer Engineering in 1990 at Universidad Centro-Occidental Lisandro Alvarado, Venezuela. She received her MSc Degree and PhD in Computer Science from USB, Venezuela, in 1993 and 2004 respectively. Her research interests include parallel processing, distributed object processing, operating systems, high performance on grid and cloud platforms, and web services composition, including web and grid semantic. She is the Director of the Parallel and Distributed Systems Group (GRyDs) at USB and coordinates several research projects. She has written a range of publications in areas such as parallel computing, grid computing, parallel checkpointing, collaborative frameworks, and Semantic Web.

Regina Helena Carlucci Santana received her PhD degree in Electronics and Computer Science in 1989 from Southampton University, UK, the MSc degree in Computer Science in 1985 from the Institute of Mathematics and Computer Science, University of São Paulo, Brazil, the Engineer degree in Electronics from the School of Engineering of São Carlos, University of Sao Paulo in 1980. She has experience in computer science with emphasis in computer systems architecture, acting on the following themes: service oriented architectures, web services, performance evaluation, distributed systems and simulation. She is an Associate Professor working at the Department of Computer Systems of the Institute of Mathematics and Computer Science, University of Sao Paulo. She is member of the Brazilian Computer Society.

Fabio Casati is Professor of Computer Science at the University of Trento. He got his PhD from the Politecnico di Milano and then worked for over 7 years in Hewlett-Packard USA, where he was technical lead for the research program on business process intelligence. Fabio has also contributed (as software and data architect) to the development of several HP solutions in the area of web services and process management. In Trento, he is currently leading or participating to six FP7 projects, is active in many industry-funded projects, both local and international, and has over 30 patents. His research passions are now in social informatics.

Ajay Chakravarthy has expertise in knowledge management using Semantic Web technologies (ontology modelling, RDF, semantic search, semantic annotation, semantic web services). He holds an MSc degree in Advanced Computer Science from the University of Sheffield and also a PhD in Computer Science (knowledge acquisition through the use of semantic web technologies) from the University of Sheffield. Ajay has been the lead researcher in many innovative semantic web applications during his PhD studies in Sheffield. A knowledge management start-up company K-Now was established as a direct outcome of his PhD research. He has published over 20 papers in peer reviewed conferences, journals, and workshops and is on the program committee and peer review panel for International Conference on Internet and Web Applications and Services (ICIW 2010). Ajay joined The University of Southampton, IT Innovation Centre in August 2008 and works on ontology modelling and user interface design and architectures for the SERSCIS and ANSWER and ICON projects.

Marco Comerio is a Research Fellow at Università degli Studi di Milano Bicocca. He received his laurea degree in Computer Science in 2006 and his PhD in 2010 at the same university. From 2006 to 2009, he participated in the European IST project n. 27347 SEEMP (Single European Employment Market-Place) and in the Italian FIRB project RBNE05XYPW NeP4B (Networked Peers for Business). His current research activity is mainly in the field of Service Oriented Computing. The main results of his research activity are: (1) the definition of a meta-model to semantically describe non-functional properties (NFPs); (2) the definition of techniques to allow the management of heterogeneous service contracts along the Web service selection and composition activities; (3) the definition of an approach to NFP-based hybrid multidimensional ranking of Semantic Web Services; (4) the implementation of the approach in a WSMO-compliant ranker. He has published his research results in about 20 papers in international conferences and journals.

Agostino Cortesi is full Professor of Software Engineering at Università Ca' Foscari Venezia. He holds a Laurea degree in Mathematics and a Ph.D. in Applied Mathematics and Computer Science from the University of Padova. His research interests cover the following fields: programming languages, static analysis techniques, security, and e-government systems. He published more than 80 papers in high level international journals and proceedings of international conferences.

Vincenzo D'Andrea is an Associate Professor at the University of Trento, Italy, where he teaches Information Systems. He holds a joint appointment with the Department of Information Science and Engineering and with the School of Sociology. He leads Trento research unit in the EU founded project COMPAS, Compliance-driven Models, Languages, and Architectures for Services. His research interests include service-oriented computing, participatory design, free and open source licensing, and sociotechnical systems. He received his PhD in Information Technology from the University of Parma. He's a member of the IEEE Computer Society and the ACM.

Florian Daniel is a Postdoctoral Researcher at the University of Trento, Italy. He has a PhD in Information Technology from Politecnico di Milano, Italy. His main research interests are mashups and web/service engineering, and compliance, quality, and privacy in business intelligence applications. He is co-author of the book "Engineering Web Applications" (Springer, 2009) and has published more than 60 scientific papers in international conferences and journals.

Stephen Dawson joined SAP Research Belfast as a researcher in 2006. He is currently a member of the technology infrastructure research practice within SAP, where he is responsible for managing a joint research initiative with Intel. His research interests are primarily in the area of modelling non-functional requirements for service-oriented architectures. Stephen graduated with a degree in Electronic and Software Engineering from Queen's University Belfast. Following this he then continued within the University to complete his PhD. Stephen is also active as both a working group and technical committee member for the Innovation Value Institute (IVI).

Flavio De Paoli is an Associate Professor at the University of Milano Bicocca. His research activity includes software engineering, software architecture, cooperative distributed systems, Semantic Web services, and knowledge management. His main current interests deals with the definition of service-based models and architecture for the development of collaborative Web applications to support communities of practices; semantic profiling and ontology definition; semantic browsing; non-functional quality definition for web service design, description, and selection. He is currently involved in several projects, among others (2006-08) IST project 27347 "SEEMP - Single European Employment Market-Place"; (2006-08) IST project 518513 "NEUROWEB - Integration and sharing of information and knowledge in neurology and neurosciences." He is author of three books and several papers on international journals and conference proceedings.

Stefan Dietze is a Senior Researcher at the L3S Research Centre, Germany and was previously a Research Fellow at the Knowledge Media Institute of The Open University. He holds a PhD (Dr. rer. nat.) in Applied Computer Science from Potsdam University. His main research interests are in knowledge-based systems, Semantic Web and linked data technologies and their application to various domains, in particular technology-enhanced learning (TEL). He has been involved in leading roles in numerous EU research projects, such as LUISA, NoTube or mEducator, and has published over 60 papers throughout major conferences, journals, and workshops in the area of Semantic Web, SOA, and TEL. Also, Stefan is reviewer and organising/programme committee member for a large number of scientific events and publications.

John Domingue is the Deputy Director of the Knowledge Media Institute at The Open University and the President of STI International, a semantics focused networking organization with over 50 members. He has published over 180 refereed articles in the areas of artificial intelligence and the Web, and his current work is focused on how semantic technology can automate the management, development, and use of Web services. Currently he serves as the Scientific Director of SOA4All, a 13MM Euro project which aims at creating a Web of billions of services. Previously, Prof. Domingue has served as the Scientific Director for two other large European projects: DIP, which focused on Semantic Web Services (SWS), and SUPER, which integrated SWS, workflow engines, and business process management. He current serves as Chair of the Steering Committee for the European Semantic Web Conference Series, Chair of the OASIS Semantic Execution Environment Technical Committee, and Co-Chair of the Conceptual Models of Services Working Group within STI. Within the Future Internet arena he serves as a member of the Future Internet Assembly Steering Committee. The Future Internet Assembly is a collaboration amongst over 150 European projects with a combined budget approaching 1 billion Euros aiming to develop a next-generation Internet. Prof. Domingue is also serves on the editorial boards for the *Journal of Web Semantics* and the *Applied Ontology Journal.*

Schahram Dustdar is Full Professor of Computer Science heading the Distributed Systems Group, TU Vienna. From 2004-2010 he was an Honorary Professor of Information Systems at the Department of Computing Science at the University of Groningen (RuG), The Netherlands. Since 2009 he is an ACM Distinguished Scientist. He is Editor-in-Chief of Computing (Springer) and an editorial board member of IEEE Internet Computing. From 1999 - 2007 he worked as the co-founder and chief scientist of Caramba Labs Software AG (CarambaLabs.com) in Vienna (acquired by Engineering NetWorld AG), a venture capital co-funded software company focused on software for collaborative processes in teams. Caramba Labs was nominated for several (international and national) awards: World Technology Award in the category of Software (2001); Top-Startup companies in Austria (Cap Gemini Ernst & Young) (2002). More information about his research can be found at http://www.infosys.tuwien.ac.at/Staff/sd.

Joyce El Haddad received her PhD thesis in Computer Science in 2004 from Université Paris-Dauphine where she is currently working as an Assistant Professor. She is member of the LAMSADE Lab and a member of the PERSO Project funded by the French National Agency for Research 2007-2010. Her research interests are focused on distributed algorithms, fault-tolerance, and services composition for pervasive systems.

Julio Cezar Estrella received his PhD degree in Computer Science in 2010, the MSc degree in Computer Science in 2006, both at the Institute of Mathematics and Computer Science, University of São Paulo, and the BSc in Computer Science at the State University of Sao Paulo - Julio de Mesquita Filho in 2002. He has experience in computer science with emphasis in computer systems architecture, acting on the following themes: service oriented architectures, web services, performance evaluation, distributed systems, computer networks and computer security. He is an Assistant Professor working at the Department of Computer Systems at Institute of Mathematics and Computer Science of University of Sao Paulo. He is member of the Brazilian Computer Society, IEEE, and ACM.

Dieter Fensel holds a Professorship at the University of Innsbruck and is the Director of STI Innsbruck, a research institute with approx. 40 employees. He has over 250 publications in the form of scientific books and journals, conferences, and workshop contributions. He has co-organized over 200 conferences and workshops. He has supervised over 40 Master and PhD theses and is a recipient of the Carl-Adam-Petri-Award of the Faculty of Economic Sciences from the University of Karlsruhe. His current research interests focus on the development and application of semantics to all areas of Computer Science. Dieter Fensel is founding president of the Semantic Technology Institute (STI) International, whose major aim is to establish semantics as a core pillar of modern Computer Science. He has been the Scientific Director and Coordinator of over more than 70 ICT and IST funded project.

José Luiz Fiadeiro is a Professor of Software Science and Engineering in the Department of Computer Science at the University of Leicester. His research interests are in the formal aspects of software-system modelling and analysis in the context of global ubiquitous computing. Fiadeiro received a PhD in mathematics from the Technical University of Lisbon, Portugal. He is a Fellow of the British Computer Society.

G.R. Gangadharan works as a Researcher at IBM Research, Bangalore, India. His research interests are mainly in the interface between technological and business perspectives. His research expertise includes service-oriented computing, free and open source software, intellectual property rights, business models for software and services, and green information systems. He has a PhD in Information and Communications Technology (with Doctor Europaeus) (2008) from the University of Trento, Trento, Italy. He holds an M.S. in Information Technology (2004) from Scuola Superiore Sant'Anna, Pisa, Italy, and an M.Sc. in Computer Science (1999) from Manonmaniam Sundaranar University, Tirunelveli, India. He is a member of IEEE.

Wasif Gilani is a Senior Researcher at SAP UK working in the domain of Business Process Management and Business Intelligence. Wasif has been leading several European as well as SAP internal technology transfer projects related to Enterprise Intelligence (Business-Process Centric Decision Support based on simulation, analytics for performance, optimisation, etc.). He is further leading research and transfer projects related to the topic of event-driven business process management and business continuity management within SAP. Wasif has received his Master's and PhD degree in Computer Science from Friedrich Alexander University Erlangen Germany.

Stephen Gilmore is a Reader in the School of Informatics at the University of Edinburgh. His research interests lie in the quantitative modelling of software systems using stochastically-timed process algebras, and the design of modelling tools to support this process. He received his PhD in Computer Science from the Queen's University of Belfast. He is a member of the Laboratory for Foundations of Computer Science at Edinburgh.

Sergio Garcia Gomez is a Technology Specialist at Telefónica I+D within the business framework initiative (eMarketplace) in the service layer architecture area. He has participated in several European projects (AlbatrOSS, MEDSI) and in Telefonica's internal OSS developments, and currently, he participates in SLA@SOI project and leads the marketplace workpackage of FP7 project 4CaaSt. He received his degree in Telecommunication Engineering and a Master in Project Management from the University of Valladolid. His main interests are the services science and Semantic Web technologies.

Martin Hall-May holds an MEng (University of Bristol) and PhD (University of York) in Computer Science. He is currently a Senior Research Engineer at the University of Southampton IT Innovation Centre, where he leads research and integration activities in the EC FP7 SERSCIS project. His current research interests include the dependability of service oriented architectures and automated system management. Prior to joining IT Innovation, Martin carried out research into large-scale system safety and the implications of deploying autonomous vehicles in safety-critical applications.

Mohamed Hamdy got his PhD 2010 from at University of Jena, Germany. Between 2006 and 2010 he joins the Heinz-Nixdorf Endowed Chair for Practical Computer Science at the same University. Now, he is a Teacher at Ain Shams University in Cairo, Egypt. His research is focused on services. In particular, service execution and planning for wireless networks.

Peer Hasselmeyer has many years of experience in the field of service-oriented architectures and distributed computing. He received a MS degree in Computer Science from the University of Colorado at Boulder, USA, and a PhD from the Darmstadt University of Technology, Germany. He is currently working as a Senior Researcher at NEC Laboratories Europe in Heidelberg, Germany. His main research interests are service-oriented architectures, cloud computing, and data center and service management. Peer published numerous research papers in international conferences and magazines.

Manuele Kirsch-Pinheiro has, since September 2008, been Associate Professor in the Computer Science Research Center (Centre de Recherche en Informatique) of the University of Paris 1 Panthéon-Sorbonne. Previously, she occupied a post-doctoral position on the Katholieke Universiteit Leuven's Department of Computer Science. She received her PhD in computer science from the "Université Joseph Fourier – Grenoble I" (2006), and her Master's degree from the "Universidade Federal do Rio Grande do Sul", Porto Alegre, Brazil. Her research interests include ubiquitous computing, context-aware computing, adaptation (personalization), cooperative work (CSCW), group awareness, and information systems.

Benjamin Klatt is a Research Scientist at the FZI Research Center for Information Technology. He completed an apprenticeship in computer science as well as a diploma in computer science at the Karlsruhe Institute of Technology (KIT). Beyond that, he worked as a consultant for enterprise software solutions for meanwhile 10 years. In January 2011 he started a PhD at the KIT with a focus on software quality, architecture landscapes, and model driven software development.

Birgitta König-Ries holds the Heinz-Nixdorf Endowed Chair for Practical Computer Science at the University of Jena, Germany. Prior to this, she has worked with the Technical University of Munich, Florida International University, the University of Louisiana at Lafayette, and the University of Karlsruhe. Birgitta holds both a diploma and a PhD from the latter. Her research is focused on the transparent integration of both information and functionality. In particular, her group is working on Semantic Web services, portal technology, and mobile applications.

Bastian Koller is working since 2004 in the area of Grid and Cloud Computing with a special focus on the management and description of service level agreements. He received his diploma degree in Computer Science from the University of Wuerzburg, Germany in 2003 and is just finishing his PhD thesis on "Enhanced SLA Management in the High Performance Computing Domain". From 2006 to 2010 he acted as Technical Manager of the IST project BREIN, which dealt with the integration of Semantics and Multi-Agents into the Grid. Since 2007 he has his own research group "Service Management and Business Processes," which is strongly focused on the SLA topic. Bastian is involved in many research activities, within HLRS projects (national, international, internal) as well as in standardisation bodies such as the Open Grid Forum.

Samuel Kounev is Head of the Descartes Research Group at Karlsruhe Institute of Technology (KIT), which is funded by the German Research Foundation (DFG) within the Emmy-Noether Programme. He received a MSc degree in mathematics and computer science from the University of Sofia and a PhD degree in computer science from Darmstadt University of Technology (2005). His research is focused on novel methods for autonomic management of system quality-of-service (availability, performance and reliability) and resource efficiency throughout the system life-cycle. He is a member of the ACM, IEEE, and the GI e.V.

Kyriakos Kritikos received his BSc, MSc, and PhD degrees in Computer Science from the University of Crete. From 2000 to 2008, he was a Researcher at the Information Systems Laboratory of the Institute of Computer Science, FORTH in Greece. Then, he worked as an ERCIM Post-Doc Researcher at the HIIS laboratory of the ISTI institute of CNR and as a researcher at the Information Systems Group of the Department of Electronics and Information of the Technical University (Politecnico) of Milan in Italy. Currently, he is an ERCIM Post-Doc Researcher at CRP Henri Tudor in Luxembourg. His research interests include: business service modeling and analysis, quality-based service description, discovery, composition, negotiation, and adaptation, design of interactive service-based applications, ontology modeling and reasoning, constraint and mathematical programming, and information retrieval.

Lea Kutvonen, Adjunct Professor, leads the Collaborative and Interoperable Computing (CINCO) group at the Department of Computer Science at the University of Helsinki, Finland. The CINCO group conducts research with interest to federated management of B2B collaboration lifecycle and interoperability. The themes emerging from the area include architecture issues, e-contracting, non-functional features such as trust management, and coordination and composition of Web Services.

Thomas Leonard has a PhD in Computer Science from the University of Southampton. He works on secure B2B service-oriented infrastructures. His research is now focusing on federated security mechanisms and dynamic access control.

Dong Liu received his PhD degree in Computer Science from Beijing University of Posts and Telecommunications. His thesis was on context-aware computing technology and its application in semantic Web services. In 2008, he joined the Knowledge Media Institute of The Open University, UK, and participated in several EU research projects, i.e. SUPER, SOA4All, and NoTube. His research interests include Web services and semantic technology.

Francesco Logozzo is a Researcher in the PLA group at Microsoft Research since October 2006. He was a Postdoctoral Researcher in the abstract interpretation team at the Ecole Normale Superieure in Paris. He has done his PhD under the supervision of Dr. Radhia Cousot. The title of the thesis is Modular static analysis of object-oriented languages. He is a former student of Scuola Normale Superiore of Pisa (Italy).

Davide Lorenzoli is Research Assistant at City University London. He works on problematic related to monitoring and prediction of QoS property violations. Currently, within the European Integrated Project SLA@SOI, his research focuses on dynamic monitoring systems and run-time prediction of SLA violations. Davide received his Doctoral degree in Computer Science from the University of Milano Bicocca where he worked on the topic of self-healing systems. His research interests are monitoring and prediction of QoS property violation, software testing, and verification. He is also interested in test driven development and software designing.

Maude Manouvrier received her PhD thesis in Computer Science in 2000 from Université Paris-Dauphine where she is currently working as an Assistant Professor. She is member of the LAMSADE Lab. Her research interests are focused on spatio-temporal and multimedia databases, access methods and indexing structures, content-based image retrieval, and web services for transactional composition.

Sarita Mazzini Bruschi received her PhD degree in Computer Science in 2002, the MSc degree in Computer Science in 1998, both at the Institute of Mathematics and Computer Science, University of São Paulo, and the BSc in Computer Science at the State University of Sao Paulo - Julio de Mesquita Filho in 1994. He has experience in computer science with emphasis in computer systems architecture, acting on the following themes: service oriented architectures, web services, performance evaluation, simulation, and distributed simulation. She is an Assistant Professor working at the Department of Computer Systems at Institute of Mathematics and Computer Science of University of Sao Paulo. She is member of the Brazilian Computer Society and ACM.

Sally McClean is Professor of Mathematics at the University of Ulster. Her main research interests are in statistical modelling and optimisation, particularly for healthcare planning, and also computer science, specifically database technology and telecommunications. She has published and edited six books and has published over 200 research papers. She was recently co-investigator on the EPSRC funded RIGHT project and is currently co-investigator on the EPSRC funded MATCH project, both concerned with Healthcare Modelling. In addition she is co-investigator on the EPSRC funded SUAAVE and IU-ATC projects, with a focus on optimising and controlling the behaviour of Unmanned Autonomous Vehicles and computer networks, respectively. She is also grant-holder on an Alzheimer's Society funded project on Smart Homes and on an ESRC funded project on Design for Ageing Well.

Adrian Moore has been a member of academic staff at the University of Ulster since 1990, taking up the post immediately after completing a D.Phil in Computer Graphics at the university. At Ulster, he is the School Coordinator for Internet and E-Learning activities, and represents the university on Coleraine Borough Council's broadband working group. Adrian has taught in a wide number of subject areas of computer science, especially in Web applications development, multimedia, and computer graphics, and has completed a textbook on Multimedia Web Development, published by Palgrave Macmillan. He has written and delivered a number of professional development courses for local industry, including Web development and C programming. Adrian has also undertaken a number of external consultancy projects and is the Technical Director of Consultus International Limited, a Northern Ireland e-consultancy company.

Michael Papazoglou is Scientific Director of the European Research Institute in Service Science (ERISS) and of the EC's Network of Excellence, S-Cube. He is also an honorary Professor at the University of Trento in Italy, and Professorial Fellow at the Universities Lyon (France), New South Wales (Australia) and Rey Juan Carlos, Madrid (Spain). He has acted as an Adviser to the EC in matters relating to the Internet of Services and as a reviewer of national research programs for numerous countries around the world. His research interests lie in the areas of service oriented computing, web services, large scale data sharing, business and manufacturing processes, and distributed computing systems, where he has published 22 books (including monographs and conference proceedings), and well over 200 journal and conference papers with an H-index factor of 37.

Gerard Parr holds the Full Chair in Telecommunications Engineering in the Faculty of Computing & Engineering at the University of Ulster at Coleraine in Northern Ireland. He holds a PhD in Self Stabilizing Protocols, aspects of which he developed whilst a Visiting Scientist at the DARPA-funded

Information Sciences institute in Los Angeles. Areas of research within the group include self-stabilizing protocols, interplanetary network protocols, real-time network management systems, CNNs and intelligent mobile agents in xDSL and SNMP, real-time data analytics for NMS, energy aware infrastructure, resource management protocols, applications performance management in virtualised environments, bandwidth provision over SONET/SDH in the presence of chaotic impulses and fuzzy inference systems for multicriteria handoff in tactical communications. He is the UK PI of the EPSRC-DST India-UK Centre of Excellence in Next Generation Networks of which BT is the lead industrial partner and also a PI in the EPSRC funded Project Sensing, Unmanned, Autonomous Aerial Vehicles- SUAAVE. For further information see http://www.suaave.org.

Carlos Pedrinaci is a research fellow of the Knowledge Media Institute at the Open University. He holds an MSc in Computer Science and a PhD in Artificial Intelligence from the University of the Basque Country (Spain). His research interests include Semantic Web services, knowledge-based systems, knowledge engineering, and business process analysis. Carlos has worked in several EU research projects in the area of services such as OBELIX, DIP, SOA4All, where he serves as leader of the Fundamental and Integration Activity, and VPH Share. He has been involved in the standardization of Semantic Web Services technologies notably as member of the W3C SAWSDL Working Group. Carlos has published over 60 papers in major conferences and international journals. Dr. Pedrinaci has co-organized a number of conferences, workshops, and summer schools such as ESWC 2010, Beyond SAWSDL, and the Service and Software Architectures, Infrastructures and Engineering (SSAIE).

Pierluigi Plebani is Assistant Professor at the Dipartimento di Elettronica ed Informazione of Politecnico di Milano. He received the Master's degree in Computer Science Engineering and the PhD degree in Information Engineering from Politecnico di Milano, Italy, in 2000 and 2005, respectively. He currently belongs to the Information Systems group and his research interests concern Web service retrieval methods driven by both functional and quality aspects, and the design of adaptive information systems. Recently, his work had been applied to Green IT solutions and Emergency Management Information Systems.

Dimitrios Plexousakis is a Professor of the Department of Computer Science, University of Crete and a Researcher at the Information Systems Laboratory of the Institute of Computer Science, FORTH in Greece. He received his BSc degree in Computer Science from the University of Crete and M.Sc. and PhD degrees in Computer Science from the University of Toronto. His research interests span the following areas: knowledge representation and knowledge base design; formal knowledge representation models and query languages for the Semantic Web; formal reasoning systems with focus on dynamic action theories and belief revision; business process and e-service modeling, discovery, and composition. He is a member of ACM and IEEE.

Filippo Ramoni is an Adjunct Research Assistant at the Dipartimento di Elettronica ed Informazione of Politecnico di Milano, Italy. He received a Laurea Degree in Informatics Engineering from Politecnico di Milano in 2006 with a thesis on user-driven quality policies for web service applications. His research interests are on web services selection, based on quality of services, and testing methodologies applied to composed web services. He has published some papers at International Conferences and Journals on web service platforms development and testing. Recently he is also involved in research on risk management Information Systems.

Christoph Rathfelder is Research Scientist at the FZI Research Center for Information Technology in Karlsruhe, Germany. He is working on architecture level performance predictions with focus on service oriented and event-based systems. In addition to his work in the European Project SLA@SOI, he was member of the strategic research group for service oriented applications within the FZI. Christoph studied Computer Science at the University of Karlsruhe with focus on management in service oriented systems. He is now PhD student at the Karlsruhe Institute of Technology and member of the Chair of Design and Quality and the Descartes Research Group.

Carlos Rodríguez is a PhD student at the University of Trento, Italy. He is involved in the European research project MASTER (Managing Assurance, Security and Trust for Services) where he works on compliance assessment by analyzing and mining execution data obtained from business processes. He has recently joined another European project, OMELETTE (Open Mashup Enterprise service platform for LinkEd data in The TElco domain), were he is working on community-based composition advices for Mashup development. His current research interests include Web mashups, uncertain data management and data mining, with special focus on analysis of business execution data and process discovery.

Thomas Roeblitz is a post-doc at Technical University of Dortmund. His main research interests are resource management and scheduling in large distributed systems such as Grids, Clouds, and P2P. He is also researching virtual data infrastructures and emerging highly-parallel programming models such as MapReduce and GPU programming. At the Computer Science Department, he gives courses and lab work in parallel computer systems, service computing, Cloud computing, and applied scientific computing. Thomas received his doctoral degree in Computer Science from Humboldt-University Berlin. During his PhD he worked at Zuse Institute Berlin conducting research on scheduling co-reservations of resources in Grids, distributed data management, and steering of remote instruments.

Marta Rukoz received a PhD in Computer Science of the UPMC University (France) in 1989. She is currently working as Professor at the Université Nanterre. She has been working as Assistant Professor (1981-1992), as Professor (1992-2005), and as Coordinator of the CCPD (1990-1999) at the University Central of Venezuela. She has been working as an invited Professor at the University of Central Florida (USA), the IUT of Villetaneuse (France), and UPMC and Paris-Dauphine Universities. Her research interests are focused on spatio-temporal and multimedia databases, access methods and indexing structures, content-based image retrieval and Web Services for transactional composition.

Toni Ruokolainen holds a Ph.Lic. in Computer Science and he is currently a PhD candidate in the CINCO group at the University of Helsinki. His research interests include service ecosystems, service-oriented software engineering, model-driven engineering, and corresponding knowledge management facilities in the context of service-oriented middleware platforms.

Marcos José Santana received his PhD degree in Electronics and Computer Science in 1989 from Southampton University, UK, the MSc degree in Computer Science in 1985 from the Institute of Mathematics and Computer Science, University of São Paulo, Brazil, the Engineer degree in Electronics from the School of Engineering of São Carlos, University of Sao Paulo in 1980. He has experience in computer science with emphasis in computer systems architecture, acting on the following themes: service oriented architectures, web services, performance evaluation, distributed systems, and simulation. He is an Associate Professor working at the Department of Computer Systems at the Institute of Mathematics and Computer Science, University of Sao Paulo. He is member of the Brazilian Computer Society.

Bryan Scotney received a BSc in Mathematics from the University of Durham, UK in 1980, and a PhD in Mathematics from the University of Reading, UK in 1985. He is Professor of Informatics and currently Director of the Computer Science Research Institute at the University of Ulster. He has over 150 publications in total, spanning statistical databases, image processing, and mathematical computation. He has published widely in the area of knowledge discovery and data mining, focusing on solving the problems of integration of heterogeneous data from distributed sources, particularly where the information available is imprecise and / or uncertain. Much of this work has been supported by funding from four EU FP5 projects (with McClean) to address issues of harmonisation of Official Statistics. Most recently, he is Co-Investigator on EPSRC award EP/F030118/1. His early research interest in computational mathematics is now focused onto the area of digital image processing; this work is concerned mainly with methodological development, but also has application to machine vision and medical imaging. He is currently President of the Irish Pattern Recognition and Classification Society.

Patrícia Silveira is a PhD student in the Information and Communication Technology Doctoral School, University of Trento, Italy. She is involved in the European research project, COMPAS (Compliance-driven Models, Languages, and Architectures for Services), in which she works designing and developing a data warehousing environment and graphical components to analyze the compliance performance of business processes. Additionally, she is also interested in patterns and models to represent lifestyles and their correlation with non-communicable diseases.

Ernest Sithole received a B. Eng. (Hons) (1999) from NUST Zimbabwe, an MS.c. (2003) from the University of Surrey, and a PhD (2007) from the University of Ulster, Northern Ireland. He is a Postdoctoral Researcher in the School of Computing and Information Engineering at the University of Ulster Coleraine. His main research interests are primarily in performance modelling and evaluation of IT systems, particularly for emerging computing solutions based on SOA, Grid, Virtualization, and Cloud computing technologies. Previously, Ernest has worked on the design, configuration, and deployment and monitoring of real-time, enterprise-wide services across Data Grid fabrics given the knowledge of prevailing network conditions. More recently, he has been involved in the PERSERVE research project, whose research aims have focussed on strategies for developing a range of performance and resource models of Enterprise Service Oriented Architectures (SOAs) towards achieving scalable deployments, accurate performance prediction, and providing firm QoS guarantees and performance optimisations.

Monika Solanki is a Teaching Fellow in the Department of Computer Science at the University of Leicester. Her research interests are in the runtime monitoring and offline verification of semantically described service oriented systems. She received a PhD in Computer science from De Montfort University Leicester.

Paul Sorenson is Professor Emeritus of Computing Science at the University of Alberta. He previously held several academic positions at the University of Saskatchewan (Professor & Head) and the

University of Alberta (Professor, Chair of Computing Science, Assoc. VP (Research) and Vice-Provost (Information Technology)). He teaches courses and has research interests in software engineering and the management and delivery of software service systems. He co-authored books in data structures and compiler design, and he co-founded two start-up companies: Avra Software Lab and Onware Systems. He is co-author on more than one hundred journal and conference papers and has served on the Boards of a large number of research institutes and centres.

Carine Souveyet got her PhD Degree in Computer Sciences at the University of Paris Jussieu in 1991 and her HDR Degree at the University of Paris 1 Panthéon Sorbonne in 2006. She is Professor in Computer Sciences at the University of Paris 1 since 2008 and research member of the Centre de Recherche en Informatique (CRI) since 1991.

Abhishek Srivastava is a PhD student in the Department of Computing Science, University of Alberta, Edmonton, Canada working under the supervision of Dr. Paul Sorenson. The area of his research thesis is the development of a dynamic service composition model that utilizes the non-functional attributes of service elements to make selections. Prior to this, he was serving as a Lecturer in the Department of Computer Science and Engineering, Birla Institute of Technology, Ranchi, India for a little over four years. He completed his Master of Engineering degree in Software Engineering from the Birla Institute of Technology, Ranchi, India and his Bachelor of Engineering degree in Electrical Engineering from the Nagpur University, India.

Bryan Stephenson received a BS in Computer Science from Iowa State University in Ames, Iowa, USA. He has worked at HP since 1988 and at HP Labs since 2004. He was the technical lead for the team which incubated and created HP's Flexible Computing Services business. His research interests include information security. Bryan holds five US patents with fifteen US patents and five related foreign patents in application.

Mike Surridge is Research Director at IT Innovation, an applied research centre in electronics and computer science at the University of Southampton. IT Innovation is dedicated to working with business and industry to stimulate the adoption of novel IT, through research and development of proof of concept and pilot systems, analysing business models and processes for the use of such systems, and providing consultancy on technology roadmaps and due diligence. Mike has over 20 years experience in applied IT research. Since the mid-1990s he has focused on Grid and Service Oriented Architectures (SOAs) including cloud computing, with a specific interest in dynamic security, system adaptation, and quality of service. He coordinated the FP5 GRIA project which created a Grid middleware specifically for business services, was Principal Investigator of the UK Semantic Firewall project, and is now Coordinator of the FP7 ICT-SEC SERSCIS project on dynamic SOA for critical infrastructure protection. He was a co-founder of the UK e-Science Security Task Force, and he is currently chair of the EC Internet of Services Trust and Security Working Group, and a co-chair of the NESSI Trust, Security and Dependability working group.

Zouhair Taheri works as an IT advisor and auditor at PwC in Rotterdam, The Netherlands. He has over 4 years of experience with analysing, auditing, and consulting on systems and processes at companies operating in various industries. His main focus is the Transportation & Logistics sector. He has been involved in the last three years in the COMPAS project, where he brings in knowledge and experience in the field of auditing, compliance in combination with Service-Oriented Architectures. Zouhair wrote his Master's thesis on this subject for his Master's degree at the Tilburg University in The Netherlands.

Wolfgang Theilmann is Senior Researcher within SAP Research. He is responsible for the research cluster Business Grids where he works on topics such as Grid computing, virtualization, system modelling, and performance prediction. Wolfgang participated and led various national and international research projects in the areas of Business Grids and Knowledge Management. Currently, Wolfgang leads the European Integrated Project SLA@SOI which aims at exploring the systematic management of service level agreements in service-oriented infrastructures. Wolfgang received his doctoral degree in Computer Science from the University of Stuttgart where he worked on the topic of Internet information retrieval. Before, he studied computer science at the University of Karlsruhe with specializations in cognitive systems.

Ioan Toma works as a Researcher at STI Innsbruck, Austria. His current research areas include Semantic Web Services and Semantic Web, with focus on modeling and ranking of services based on non-functional properties. Before joining STI Innsbruck, he obtained his graduated engineer of computer science (Dipl. Eng.) and M.S. titles from Technical University of Cluj-Napoca. Ioan has been involved in several research projects at European and Austrian level (i.e., SEALS, ENVISION, LARCK, SOA4All, ServiceWeb3.0, ASG, DIP, Grisino). He published more than 50 articles as book chapters, conferences, workshops, and journals articles. Ioan Toma co-organized multiple workshops, including Non-Functional Properties and Service Level Agreements in Service Oriented Computing workshop and was a member of several conference and workshop program committees.

Hong-Linh Truong currently is a Senior Research Scientist at Distributed Systems Group, Institute of Information Systems, Vienna University of Technology (TU Vienna). He received an engineer degree from the Ho Chi Minh City University of Technology, Vietnam, in 1998, and a PhD degree from Vienna University of Technology, Austria, in 2005, both in computer science and engineering. His research interests focus on understanding of performance, context, and data quality metrics associated with distributed and parallel applications and systems through monitoring and analysis, and on utilizing these metrics for the adaptation and optimization of these applications and systems. His research has been applied to performance/context-aware monitoring and analysis techniques and tools, Grid, cloud and service-oriented systems, collaborative and workflow systems, context-aware Web services and smart environments, and adaptive processes. He is a member of ACM, the IEEE and the IEEE Computer Society.

Vishnu Vankayala is a Vice President, General Business at Lapilluz Software Solutions, India. He is holding distinction in Master's of Advanced Software Engineering from University of Leicester. Vishnu is actively involved in implementing hi-tech data-analytic solutions for various sectors like education, banking and finance, and retail. He is providing consultation for various universities in India.

Yves Vanrompay is a PhD student in the DistriNet research group of the Katholieke Universiteit Leuven's Department of Computer Science. He received his MSc degree in Informatics in 2003, and his

MSc in Artificial Intelligence in 2004 from the Katholieke Universiteit Leuven. His research interests include context-aware systems, self-adaptation, context reasoning and prediction. He has been involved in the EU FP6 MUSIC project. The focus of MUSIC is on the development of a middleware, a methodology and tools to support context-aware adaptive applications for mobile devices in dynamic environments.

Philipp Wieder is active in the field of distributed systems for many years, primarily in the areas of scheduling and resource management, service-level management, infrastructure design, and standardisation. He received his Diploma in Electrical Engineering from the RWTH in Aachen, Germany. Currently, he is a Senior Researcher at the Service Computing Group of the TU Dortmund University, leading the SLA4D-Grid project. His experience includes leadership and contribution to numerous international projects, publication of research papers, organisation of scientific events, and contribution to standards.

Ulrich Winkler is a Research Associate at SAP Research and a PhD Student at Queen's University Belfast. Currently Ulrich is involved in the European research project SLA@SOI where he drives research work around the areas of business continuity planning and management with a particular focus on business processes, IT landscapes optimisation, and automated SLA translations. Ulrich received his Master's in Computer Science from Technical University Dresden, Germany.

Claire Worledge worked as a Manager at Deloitte Consulting, France. She has over 10 years of experience with implementation of Enterprise Resource Planning systems (ERP) for Finance departments and understanding of Governance/Internal Control (e.g., COSO, COBiT, ISO standards, and (International Standards on Auditing). She has strong knowledge of regulatory requirements like Sarbanes-Oxley law (SOX) and tax regulation. Claire wrote her Master's thesis on security in the Royal Holloway, University of London.

Hong Qing Yu is a Research Associate in Knowledge Media Institute and a member of the Semantic Media Group at The Open University. His research area includes next generation service oriented architecture, Semantic Web, context-aware system, e-learning, and multi-media technologies. He holds a PhD in Computer Science from University of Leicester. He is currently working on three EU funded research projects namely NoTube (Networks and Ontologies for the Transformation and Unification of Broadcasting and the Internet), mEducator (Multi-type Content Repurposing and Sharing in Medical Education), and SOA4ALL (Service Oriented Architectures for All). He has previously worked as Research Associate at University of Leicester on two other EU projects: SENSORIA (Software Engineering for Services-Oriented Overlay Computer) and inContext (Interaction and Context Based Technologies for Collaborative Teams).

Gabriele Zacco is Technology Manager at Fondazione Bruno Kessler. He is responsible for developing software prototypes and applications within the laboratory of the Service Oriented Applications research group. Gabriele has participated in various national and international technology transfer and research projects. Currently, he is the integration manager of the European Integrated Project SLA@SOI. Gabriele received his Master's degree in Computer Science from the University of Milan where he worked on relational databases and description logics. His main interests are currently focused on software engineering and systems integration.

Index

A

B

C